Why You Need This New Edition

❶ The 5th edition of *Ethnic Families in America: Patterns and Variations* is a cutting-edge revision that examines the history and progression of contemporary ethnic families in America.

❷ Each chapter has been thoroughly revised and updated by well known and highly respected scholars in the field of family studies.

❸ Covers the most recent issues in ethnicity in America and immigration debates, such as the recent changes in immigration laws in Arizona.

❹ New chapters on the Dominican, Filipino, and Muslim families affirm the continuing change in the ethnic makeup and cultural diversity of the United States.

❺ Includes discussion of the growth of ethnic pride and ethnic self-determination.

❻ Includes discussion of the American practice of sheltering refugees from war-torn countries.

D1216108

PEARSON

Fifth Edition

Ethnic Families in America

PATTERNS AND VARIATIONS

Roosevelt Wright
University of Oklahoma, Norman, Oklahoma

Charles H. Mindel
University of Texas, Arlington

Thanh Van Tran
Boston College

Robert W. Habenstein
University of Missouri, Columbia

Pearson

Boston   Columbus   Indianapolis   New York   San Francisco   Upper Saddle River
Amsterdam   Cape Town   Dubai   London   Madrid   Milan   Munich   Paris   Montreal   Toronto
Delhi   Mexico City   Sao Paulo   Sydney   Hong Kong   Seoul   Singapore   Taipei   Tokyo

To my loving wife and best friend, Elaine, my three daughters (Kimberly, DeShawn, and Monet) and their husbands (Jon, Aaron, and Damon) and my eight grandchildren (Isaac, Isaiah, Ocean, Rain, Pier, Asia, India and London).
—RW

To my wife Gloria, my loving, lifetime companion.
—CHM

To Dai-Chi Tran, Minh-Y and Uyen-Sa Nguyen for their love and support.
—TVT

To the memory of Jane Habenstein.
—RWH

Publisher: Karen Hanson
Editorial Assistant: Christine Dore
Executive Marketing Manager: Kelly May
Marketing Assistant: Janeli Bitor
Production Manager: Fran Russello

Cover Administrator: Jayne Conte
Cover Designer: Suzanne Duda
Cover Image Credit: Fotolia: © deanm 1974
Editorial Production and Composition Service:
Sandeep Rawat/Aptara®, Inc.

Credits and acknowledgments for materials borrowed from other sources and reproduced, with permission, in this textbook appear on the appropriate page within text.

Every effort has been made to provide accurate and current Internet information in this book. However, the Internet and information posted on it are constantly changing, so it is inevitable that some of the Internet addresses listed in this textbook will change.

Many of the designations by manufacturers and seller to distinguish their products are claimed as trademarks. Where those designations appear in this book, and the publisher was aware of a trademark claim, the designations have been printed in initial caps or all caps.

Library of Congress Cataloging-in-Publication Data
Ethnic families in America: patterns and variations /
Roosevelt Wright . . . et al.—5th ed.
    p. cm.
   Includes index.
   ISBN-13: 978-0-13-091839-0
   ISBN-10: 0-13-091839-3
   1. Ethnology—United States.   2. Families—United States.   3. Minorities—United States.   4. United States—
Social conditions—1980-   I. Wright, Roosevelt.
   E184.A1E78 2012
   305.800973—dc23
                                 2011018723

10 9 8 7 6 5 4 3 2 1—V013—15 14 13 12 11

ISBN 10:   0-13-091839-3
ISBN 13: 978-0-13-091839-0

CONTENTS

PART 3 Hispanic/Latino Ethnic Families

PART 4   Asian American Ethnic Families

PART 6   Socio-religious Ethnic Families

PREFACE

This is the fifth edition of *Ethnic Families in America*. At the time of the publication of the first edition early in the 1970s, the prevailing view of ethnicity seemed to be that the United States was an assemblage of mostly European ethnic groups who had been forged into a new amalgamation by means of a great "melting pot." Assimilation as a cultural value—the view that immigrants to the United States should somehow give up their strange cultural ways, beliefs, and languages and adopt the "American" way—was dominant. The idea that separate ethnic group identification in the United States was valuable in its own right was only beginning to be appreciated. Competing notions of ethnic pride and ethnic self-determination, which challenged the value of assimilation, were in their infancy.

These changing views were probably the result of a confluence of historical events. The great civil rights struggles of the 1960s had not only mobilized great numbers of the African American population but also spawned other liberation struggles as well. The war in Vietnam had, among its many consequences, a profound splintering effect on group consensus in the United States. That conflict had strong ethnic and class overtones, centering around a war with Asians fought disproportionately by poor Black Americans; that war produced great tears in the American civil fabric that have lasted even to this day.

An equally momentous historical event centered around changes in the immigration laws. The United States had been largely closed to new immigration after 1924, when a discriminatory law effectively barred immigrants from eastern and southern Europe and Asia. Beginning with the Immigration and Nationality Act of 1965, and later with the opening of the immigration doors to Cuban, Vietnamese, Soviet, and Salvadoran refugees, among others, as well as swelling numbers of immigrants who arrived and stayed on illegally, the nature of ethnicity in the United States changed profoundly. As a result of this transformation and evolution of the role of ethnicity in American life, it was felt that a new edition of *Ethnic Families in America* was appropriate. The original authors of the chapters in the fourth edition were contacted and asked to revise and update their chapters. When they could not or would not revise their chapter or when they could not be reached, new authors were sought. In several cases, chapters were updated by the editors. New chapters on Dominican, Filipino, and Muslim families were added as another affirmation of the continuing change in the ethnic makeup and diversity of the United States of America.

Currently the ambience in the United States, as reflected in recent changes in the immigration laws (i.e., in Arizona) is one of anti-immigration, a systemic pattern that has, presumably, afflicted this country almost from its inception. As editors of this book, we can only hope that as the story of ethnicity in America continues, we will be here to record the changes.

We thank all the authors who contributed to this new addition, especially those who diligently tried to meet the tight deadlines and requests for changes that we sought. We would like to especially thank one of our co-editors, emeritus Professor Robert W. (Hobby) Habenstein, for the insightful contribution that he makes to the book in Chapter 2. Portions of that chapter are taken from his previously published scholarly work entitled "The Ethnic Immigrant Family" in S. Queen, R. Habenstein, and J. Quadagno (1984), *The Family* in *Various Cultures*, New York, Harper & Row. In short, Hobby's chapter is beautifully written and provides a scholarly synthesis of the history of immigrant families in the United States.

Roosevelt Wright
Charles H. Mindel
Thanh Van Tran
Robert W. Habenstein

SUPPLEMENTARY MATERIALS

Instructor's Manual and Test Bank (ISBN 0205022324) The Instructor's Manual and Test Bank has been prepared to assist instructors in their efforts to prepare lectures and evaluate student learning. For each chapter of the text, the Instructor's Manual offers different types of resources, including detailed chapter summaries and outlines, learning objectives, discussion questions, classroom activities and much more. Also included in this manual is a test bank offering multiple-choice, true/false, fill-in-the-blank, and/or essay questions for each chapter.

MyTest (ISBN 0205022618) The Test Bank is also available online through Pearson's computerized testing system, MyTest. MyTest allows instructors to create their own personalized exams, to edit any of the existing test questions, and to add new questions. Other special features of this program include random generation of test questions, creation of alternative versions of the same test, scrambling question sequence, and test preview before printing. Search and sort features allow you to locate questions quickly and to arrange them in whatever order you prefer.

PowerPoint Presentation (ISBN 0205022626) Lecture PowerPoints are available for this text. The Lecture PowerPoint slides outline each chapter to help instructors convey sociological principles in a visual and exciting way.

All supplementary materials are available online to adopters at www.pearsonhighered.com

MYSEARCHLAB

MySearchLab provides a host of tools for students to master a writing or research project, It provides online access to reliable content for internet research projects, including thousands of full articles from the EBSCO ContentSelect database, a complete online handbook for grammar and usage support, a tutorial on understanding and avoiding plagiarism, and AutoCite, which helps students correctly cite sources.

CONTRIBUTORS

Carl L. Bankston III, Ph.D.
Professor and Chair, Department of Sociology, Co-Director Asian Studies Program,
Tulane University, New Orleans, Louisiana

Danielle Battisti, Ph.D.
Visiting Assistant Professor, Department of History, Kalamazoo College, Kalamazoo, Michigan

Rosina M. Beccera, Ph.D.
Professor and Vice Provost, Department of Social Welfare and Department of Chicano Studies,
University of California at Los Angeles, Los Angeles, California

David C. Dollahite, Ph.D.
Professor of Family Life, Brigham Young University, Provo, Utah

Mary Patrice Erdmans, Ph.D.
Professor, Department of Sociology, Central Connecticut State University, Hartford, Connecticut

Patricia J. Fanning, Ph.D.
Professor and Chairperson, Department of Sociology, Bridgewater State College,
Bridgewater, Massachusetts

Ramona Hernández, Ph.D.
Professor of Sociology, Director, CUNY Dominican Studies Institute,
The City College of New York, New York, New York

Robert John, Ph.D.
Professor, Department of Health Promotion, College of Public Health, University of Oklahoma
Health Sciences Center, Oklahoma City, Oklahoma

Anna Karpathakis, Ph.D.
Associate Professor, Department of Behavioral Science and Human Service,
Kingsborough Community College of CUNY, Flushing, New York

Donald B. Kraybill, Ph.D.
Senior Fellow, Young Center for Anabaptist and Pietist Studies, Elizabethtown College,
Elizabethtown, Pennsylvania

Pyong Gap Min, Ph.D.
Professor, Department of Sociology, Queens College and Graduate Center,
City University of New York, Flushing, New York

Charles H. Mindel, Ph.D.
Professor Emeritus of Social Work, University of Texas at Arlington, Arlington, Texas

Lirio K. Negroni, Ph.D.
Associate Professor and Chair Casework Concentration, School of Social Work,
University of Connecticut, West Hartford, Connecticut

Dwain Pellebon, Ph.D.
Associate Professor of Social Work, Anne and Henry Zarrow School of Social Work,
University of Oklahoma, Norman, Oklahoma

Arthur Sakamoto, Ph.D.
Professor, Department of Sociology, University of Texas, Austin, Texas

Uma A. Segal, Ph.D.
Professor of Social Work, School of Social Work, College of Arts and Sciences,
University of Missouri–St. Louis, St. Louis, Missouri

Zulema E. Suarez, Ph.D.
Adjunct Faculty, Capella University, Minneapolis, Minnesota

Thanh Van Tran, Ph.D.
Professor of Social Work, Graduate School of Social Work, Boston College, Chestnut Hill,
Massachusetts

Bahira Sherif-Trask, Ph.D.
Professor and Associate Chair, Department of Human Development and Family Studies,
University of Delaware, Newark, Delaware

Morrrison G. Wong, Ph.D.
Professor and Chair, Department of Sociology, AddRan College of Liberal Arts,
Texas Christian University, Fort Worth, Texas

ChangHwan Kim, Ph.D.
Assistant Professor of Sociology, Department of Sociology, University of Kansas,
Lawrence, KS 66045

Isao Takei, ABD
PhD Candidate, Department of Sociology, University of Texas, Austin, TX 78712

Phu Tai Phan, MSW, Ph.D.
Associate Professor of Social Work, Dept. of Social Work, California State University East Bay,
Hayward, CA.

Roosevelt Wright, Ph.D.
Professor of Social Work, Anne and Henry Zarrow School of Social Work, University of Oklahoma,
Norman, OK 73019

Jeanette R. Davidson, Ph.D.
Associate Professor of Social Work, Director, African and African-American Studies Program,
University of Oklahoma, Norman, OK 73019

Rose M. Perez, Ph.D.
Assistant Professor of Social Work, Graduate School of Social Service, Fordham University, New
York, NY 10023.

Chigon Kim, Ph.D.
Associate Professor, Department of Sociology and Anthropology, Wright State University,
Dayton, OH 45435

Gertrude Enders Huntington, Ph.D.
Professor (Retired), University of Michigan, Ann Arbor, MI 48128

Robert W. Habenstein. Ph.D.
Professor Emeritus of Sociology, University of Missouri at Columbia, Columbia, Missouri

Bernard Farber, Ph.D.
Professor Emeritus of Sociology, Arizona State University, Tempe, Arizona

Bernard Lazerwitz, Ph.D.
Professor Emeritus of Sociology, Bar-Ilan University, Ramat Gan, Israel

1

■■■

Diversity Among American Ethnic Minorities

Roosevelt Wright
Charles H. Mindel
Jeanette R. Davidson

INTRODUCTION

In this, the fifth edition of *Ethnic Families in America*, the opportunity again presents itself to take a brief retrospective view of changes in America's ethnic families and explore the continuing role of ethnicity and the ethnic factor in modern-day American life. In the early 1970s when the first edition of this book was published, the now-common notion of *multicultural diversity* had not yet been conceptualized in its current form, nor was it widely discussed, as it is now, as a strength for individuals and families as well as for other systems, including groups, organizations, and communities (Kirst-Ashman & Hull Jr., 2009). To a large extent, the emerging recognition of the importance of ethnic group identification (the ethnic factor) in the United States was only beginning to be appreciated in mainstream academia as evidenced by the growth of formal curricular programs in ethnic studies in predominantly white universities/colleges (Davidson, 2010). Also during the late 1960s and early 1970s the politics of race and ethnicity took on a much different form: The civil rights struggles of black Americans were still a vibrant memory; affirmative action was an emerging idea, and its social and political repercussions were not yet apparent; and the political machinery of the country (especially in large urban metropolitan areas) remained largely under the control of representatives of conventional white European ethnic groups.

The Role of Immigration and Ethnic Diversity

In the introduction to the first edition of this book, it was stated that "most of the large-scale immigration to America has ceased." However, by the time the editors wrote the fourth edition of this book in 1998, they knew that this statement was no longer accurate; they had not anticipated the ubiquitous societal consequences resulting, in part, from the changes in the Immigration and Nationality Act of 1965, nor did they anticipate the social and political impact of the rise in undocumented residents in the United States. Furthermore, the world had by then witnessed numerous tragic human events: genocide in Cambodia and other so-called "third world" countries, widespread starvation in Ethiopia and other countries, ethnic warfare between Hutus and Tutsis, and blood feuds (referred to as ethnic cleansing) between the Bosnians and the Serbs. In addition, the breakup of the Soviet Union empire and the end of the Cold War had occurred. One significant ramification of these global events was the creation of numerous refugee populations and global relocations of sizable ethnic groups.

The impact of the post-1960s waves of immigration with their increasing numbers of non-European immigrants, shifting national and ethnic origins, and sometimes undocumented (oftentimes known as "illegal alien") status was, not surprisingly, unsettling for many individuals in traditional white American ethnic groups. This sea of new ethnic faces was often perceived as containing the seeds of new and serious social problems for American society and an acceleration of its social and structural breakdown. Talk show commentators and others expressed fears that the United States had lost control of its borders, its language, its "American" core values, and, increasingly, its ability to afford the cost of caring for the new ethnic immigrant groups. None of us could have anticipated the historic events that have occurred since 1998, along with the repercussions for all families in the United States and for some ethnic families in particular.

The attack in the United States by al-Qaeda terrorists on September 11, 2001; America's subsequent involvement in wars in Iraq and Afghanistan and its war on terrorism; and the growth of antipathy toward Muslim, Islam, and Arab people have also affected the country significantly. Not unrelated has been the recent severe economic downturn for the middle-class in the United States, with unprecedented hardships for individuals and families in the areas of housing, insurance and banking, unemployment, and health care. Likewise, the steep increase in poverty rates for large numbers of individuals and families and the widening gap between the "haves" and the "have-nots" have taken serious tolls on the quality of life for individuals and families. Since the last edition of this book, the economic welfare of the American people has gone from times of relative growth and prosperity during the William (Bill) Clinton presidency to desperate setbacks in the economy during the George W. Bush years in the White House. As of this writing, President Barack Obama is vowing to get the country back to increased economic productivity and stability, all within the larger context of unprecedented international globalization and international economic change.

Following a pattern long established in history, poor economic conditions have had a deleterious impact on perceptions about new immigrants and ethnic groups of color, with contemporary fears manifesting in discussions about the "browning" of America, frequent demands for English to be the only recognized language, and protests about proposed pathways to citizenship. On a daily basis, cable television hosts and radio talk show hosts entertain debates, even hysteria, that demonstrate a country divided over matters of immigration with considerable scapegoating of people considered to be "different" (see, for example, Ratigan, 2010).

In Arizona, the passage of Senate Bill 1070, under the watch of Governor Jan Brewer, makes it a misdemeanor crime to be a non-U.S. citizen in Arizona without carrying required documents; bars state and local officials and agencies from restricting enforcement of federal immigration laws; and punishes those transporting, sheltering, and hiring undocumented persons. Senate Bill 1070 is criticized for encouraging racial/ethnic profiling and has resulted in local public disagreements and demonstrations, national discussions about states' rights versus federal rights related to immigration, boycotting of Arizona by other states' business groups, and a legal response by the Obama administration challenging the law's constitutionality and compliance with civil rights law. Other states are poised to follow Arizona's lead in this matter.

All of this may be couched within the current context of fierce ideological bickering and partisanship, locally and nationally, about virtually all aspects of politics. Some politicians have been accused of pandering to members of the populace espousing ethnically (racially) bigoted ideas, particularly about Arab/Muslim persons and immigrants from Mexico or of initiating these ideas for political gain. Such discussions have likely been exacerbated by the exponential growth of cable television channels and other new media (online news, blogging, tweeting, etc.) with round-the-clock coverage of stories, claims, and counter claims, the impact of which should not be underestimated. These forms of media and the ways they influence society have changed the political landscape and have at times put immigrant individuals and families under scrutiny.

The current concerns about the effects of immigration on American values, the economy, and the American way of life are not new. The mainstream American public has worried about the effects of immigration almost from the beginning of the settlement of this country by Europeans (surely, the Native American peoples also worried about the influx of these foreigners). From the beginning of the European settlement of this land, the issues concerning immigration have remained remarkably unchanged. Longer-established immigrants have almost always been bothered by the cultural distinctiveness or "difference" of the newcomers. Sometimes this difference manifested itself in language, other times in religion, or skin color, or unfamiliar family practices. Frequently, concerns have been expressed about the economic impoverishment of the newcomers and the fears about them "taking away" jobs from those already in the country or impacting their wages (even if neither claim is true). These concerns are also voiced as a fear that the newcomers will become a welfare burden placing undue pressures on the state to provide care and assistance. Thus, current concerns about the effects of large-scale immigration have extensive roots in America's past.

Protests and outcries about immigrants with different cultural practices, largely language and religious differences, occurred during the initial periods of immigration into the United States (the colonial period through 1860) and were largely directed against German and Irish immigrants. Even then, governments and citizens were not passive in their opposition. Many policies designed to curtail immigration, such as head taxes on ship captains, were enacted by colonials (Jensen, 1989).

The second great wave of immigration, beginning around 1860 and continuing until about 1920, saw over 28 million people enter the United States. Most immigrants were culturally different from the existing population, had darker complexions, were not Protestant but usually Catholic or Jewish, and came from southern and eastern Europe rather than northern and western Europe. Significant numbers of Asians, largely Chinese and Japanese, came as well at this time. Although these great masses of people were absorbed into the growing industrial machine that demanded ever more workers, great concerns were voiced about the ability of the country to deal with poverty and the kinds of people being admitted. Rita Simon (1985:84) quotes comments from *The Yale Review* during this period, which sound like some of the commentary heard today and illustrate the attitudes often held by individuals from older ethnic groups:

> Ignorant, unskilled, inert, accustomed to the beastliest conditions, with little social aspirations, with none of the desire for air and light and room, for decent dress and home comfort, which our native people possess and which our earlier immigrants so speedily acquired, the presence of hundreds of thousands of these laborers constitutes a menace to the rate of wages and the American standard of living. . . . Taking whatever they can get in the way of wages, living like swine, crowded into filthy tenement houses, piecing over garbage barrels, the arrival on these shores of such masses of degraded peasantry bring the greatest danger that American labor has ever known.

Comments on the social character of the new immigrants were also often heard in the popular media (as quoted in Simon, 1985:85):

> The character of our immigration has also changed—instead of the best class of people, we are now getting the refuse of Europe—outcasts from Italy, brutalized Poles and Hungarians, the offscourings of the world (*Philadelphia Enquirer,* Nov. 29, 1890).
>
> The swelling tide of immigrants from Southern Europe and the Orient who can neither read or write their own language and not even speak ours, who bring with them only money enough to stave off starvation but a few days, is a startling national menace that cannot be disregarded with safety (*New York Herald,* Nov. 10, 1900).

These remarks reflect a deep strain of virulent racism in this country, in addition to the horrific racism suffered by African slaves and their descendants. Chinese and Japanese immigrants suffered great indignities and violence. The Chinese Exclusion Act of 1882 effectively halted Chinese immigration, and the Native American population was either slaughtered or forcibly removed to reservations during this period. Although the impetus behind these moves was couched in economic terms, the passage of the Immigration and Nationality Acts of 1921 and 1924 were essentially cultural and racial in nature. Grounded in notions of "Nordic" supremacy, they effectively cut off immigration from all but northwestern European countries until 1965 (Jensen, 1989).

The effects of World War II on emigration cannot be underestimated. After the war, there was a stronger move toward changing the rules of immigration. When the Immigration and Nationality Act was ultimately amended in 1965, some of the more egregious biases were eliminated, quotas were then distributed more evenly across countries, and first preference was given to persons wishing to be reunited with their families (although this preference was not accorded to Mexicans until 1976). In addition, exceptions were made for refugees from Cuba (over 600,000 between 1960 and 1990), Vietnam and other Southeast Asian countries after the Vietnam War (over 600,000 from 1975 to 1990), and Soviet Jews (approximately 150,000) (U.S. Immigration and Naturalization Service, 1996). There were also an additional 150,000 refugees from such other countries as Poland, Romania, Iran, Afghanistan, and Ethiopia from 1981 through 1990 (U.S. Immigration and Naturalization Service, 1996). The Immigration Reform and Control Act of 1986 added restrictions on immigration while also allowing a one-time amnesty for undocumented immigrants.

More recently, an analysis by the Center for Immigration Studies of the Current Population Survey (CPS) indicates that in 2002, 33.1 million immigrants (legal residents and undocumented residents) resided in the United States and that by the end of the decade, if trends continued, the immigrant share of the total population would surpass the high of 14.8 percent reached in 1890 (Camarota, 2002). The countries of origin for 70 percent of recent immigrants include Mexico, Central and South America, the Caribbean, and East Asia, with 15.9 percent from Sub-Saharan Africa and Europe (Camarota, 2002). States with the largest immigrant populations include California, New York, Florida, Texas, and New Jersey. States with substantial growth in foreign-born populations include Arizona, Colorado, North Carolina, and Nevada (Camarota, 2002).

The economic impact of immigration has been varied. Julian Simon (1995), reviewing a number of economic studies, found that:

> A spate of respected recent studies, using a variety of methods, agrees that "there is no empirical evidence documenting that the displacement effect [of natives from jobs] is numerically important" (Borjas, 1990:9). The explanation is that new entrants not only take jobs, they make jobs. The jobs they create with their purchasing power, and with the new business which they start, are at least as numerous as the jobs which immigrants fill.

Special note, of course, must be made with regard to ethnic populations whose collective and personal stories are not about immigration. Indigenous people, generally referred to as American Indians or Native Americans, suffered greatly as European settlers overtook their land through genocide, colonization, and forced relocation. To this day their oppression is institutionalized and ongoing. African Americans, whose ancestors were brutally stolen from their continent, forced into enslavement in the United States, and then subjected to the cruel enforcement of Jim Crow laws, even now having to bear the brunt of institutional inequities throughout U.S. society. Ethnic families from these groups have faced racism in the extreme. Their very survival is testament to the resilience of their families, their cultural inheritance, and their strengths.

At no time in history has the United States been so ethnically diverse. Today, ethnic diversity is perhaps more readily understood to be important in the way people live their lives and raise their families. New immigrant groups use their ethnic institutions, where possible, to aid them in their struggle to survive in a difficult global economy, where any advantage they can muster helps. Often they maintain their traditions as they adjust and cope in a foreign land. Residents of some earlier established ethnic groups use their ethnicity as something to be recalled and celebrated, at festive occasions such as weddings, confirmations, and bar mitzvahs, or at more solemn events such as funerals. For some ethnic families, assimilation is not the preferred paradigm and so they attempt to continue ethnic traditions and values in meaningful ways in their lives. With all ethnic populations, it is now more clearly acknowledged that considerable within-group diversity exists, based on factors such as geographic location, socioeconomic status, date of entry to the United States, and so forth. It should be noted, too, that many people today in the United States proudly claim, and integrate into their identity, dual or multiple ethnic heritage. Overall, ethnicity remains important, providing sources of identity, values, and unity, in all their complexity.

In light of these circumstances, the editors of this book feel that this fifth edition of *Ethnic Families in America* retains its original purpose and roles. As in previous editions, the editors seek to examine a wide variety of American ethnic groups, probing the historical circumstances that subjugated them, forcibly removed them from their homelands, or impelled them to come to the United States. The primary aim of this edition is to focus on the structure and functioning of diverse ethnic family life to determine or at least raise clues about how and why, and to what extent, different ethnic families have been able or unable to maintain an ethnic identification over the generations. Finally, the editors look ahead to speculate on what the future has in store for these ethnic groups and their constitutive families.

THE CONTINUING IMPORTANCE OF ETHNICITY

What does it mean to be ethnic? Certainly, ethnicity can be divisive and destructive, and ethnic ties can evoke some of the worst in humankind. As Greeley (1974:10) states:

> In fact, the conflicts that have occupied most men over the past two or three decades, those that have led to the most appalling outpourings of blood, have had precious little to do with ideological division. Most of us are unwilling to battle to the death over ideology, but practically all of us, it seems, are ready to kill each other over noticeable differences of color, language, religious faith, height, food habits, and facial configurations.

Greeley further points out that

> Thousands have died in seemingly endless battles between two very Semitic people, the Jews and the Arabs. The English and French glare hostilely at each other in Quebec; Christians and

Moslems have renewed their ancient conflicts on the island of Mindanao; Turks and Greeks nervously grip their guns on Cyprus; and Celts and Saxons in Ulster have begun to imprison and kill one another with all the cumulative passion of a thousand years' hostility.

Historically, many conflicts seem to share a concern in some sense with very basic differences among groups of people, particularly cultural differences. There are concerns reflected in these conflicts that apparently are important to people—matters for which they are willing to fight to the death to defend. Clifford Geertz (1963:109) referred to these ties that people are willing to die for as "primordial attachments":

> By a primordial attachment is meant one that stems from the "givens"—or more precisely, as culture is inevitably involved in such matters, the "assured givers"— of social existence: immediate contiguity and kin connection mainly, but beyond them, the givenness that stems from being born into a particular religious community, speaking a particular language or even a dialect of language and following particular social patterns. These congruities of blood, speech, custom and so on, are seen to have an ineffable, at times overpowering, coerciveness in and of themselves. One is bound to one's kinsman, one's neighbor, one's fellow believer, *ipso facto,* as a result not merely of one's personal affection, practical necessity, common interest, or incurred obligation, but at least in great part by the virtue of some unaccountable absolute import attributed to the very tie itself. The general strength of such primordial bonds, and the types of them that are important, differ from person to person, from society to society, and from time to time. But for virtually every person, in every society, at almost all times, some attachments seem to flow [more] from a sense of natural—some would say spiritual—affinity than from social interaction.

These attachments, these feelings of belonging to a certain group of people for whatever reason are a basic feature of the human condition. They are called *ethnic ties*, and the group of people that one is tied to is an ethnic group. In this general sense, an *ethnic group* consists of those who share a unique social and cultural heritage that is passed from generation to generation.

Gordon (1964), in slightly different terms, sees those who share a feeling of "peoplehood" as an ethnic group but believes the sense of peoplehood that characterized most social life in past centuries has become fragmented and shattered. This, he suggests, has occurred for a variety of reasons including, in the last few centuries, massive population increases, the development of large cities, the formation of social classes, and the grouping of peoples into progressively larger political units. However, as many other writers have noted, individuals have shown a continuing need to merge their individual identity with some ancestral group—with "their own kind of people." Gordon proposes that the fragmentation of social life has left competing models for this sense of peoplehood; people are forced to choose among these models or somehow to integrate them completely. In America, the core categories of ethnic identity from which individuals are able to form a sense of peoplehood are race, religion, national origin, or some combination of these (Gordon, 1964). It is these categories, emphasizing substantively cultural symbols of consciousness of time, that are used to define the groups included in this book.

Ethnicity in America

Since the 1970s, we have seen a growing public articulation of the value of cultural diversity, ethnic pluralism, and ethnic differences in the United States. As already indicated, this level of appreciation was not always the case, and some have argued that the reason that a scholarly examination of ethnic differences was often lacking has much to do with the dominant assimilationist model of mainstream American society at the time. According to the assimilationist model, ethnic difference, though perhaps useful in the past to preserve the familiar or *Gemeinschaft* character of the Old Country, was no longer seen as useful in a so-called more "rational" and class-oriented society. In addition, the divisive aspects of ethnicity were emphasized and seen as barriers to peaceful coexistence within the American social fabric. Seen through the assimilationist lens, the integrative aspects of ethnic ties and culture were not recognized in the mainstream, and individuals with rich ethnic heritages were encouraged, coerced, and in other ways pushed toward giving up their heritage and becoming "Americanized."

Stereotypes of the negative aspects and consequences of ethnic culture abound: Italians are *mafioso*; Polish are ignorant; Muslims and Arabs are terrorists; and any number of different ethnic groups are lazy and will not work. Such stereotypes have long been part of the general American culture. The bias of the assimilationist approach was (and still is) that as soon as these people give up their inferior beliefs and ties, as soon as they leave this life—this narrow, dull, provincial life—the better off they will be.

The fact that "Americanization" is now seen by many as overly simplistic, oppressive, and ethnocentric reflects a major shift in attitude—a shift that has not come easily. This shift reflects a growing awareness by those in the mainstream about the value of distinctive ethnic culture. Persons from different ethnic groups are now more empowered in asserting their ethnic heritage and are more likely to be affirmed for so doing. This reflects the larger changes and upheavals that American society experienced during the 1960s and 1970s, especially the various liberation movements that emerged during this period, most notably the black civil rights movement. These movements in their turn helped underscore the ethnic consciousness of the so-called white or "unmeltable" ethnics, as Novak (1973) has referred to them, inspiring interest in cultural diversity and a new sensitivity toward others and their differences. We have seen increases in the personal, conscious self-appropriation of cultural history and a willingness to share in the social and political needs and struggles of one group. The reemergence of publicly espoused ethnic feelings and interests has not necessarily meant a return to Old World culture; it does not, as Novak (1973) points out, represent an attempt to hold back the clock. It represents rather a defense of ties that are important to large numbers of individuals in this country.

The reason these interests are regarded as important to defend and—as we have seen in various locales—sometimes to fight for is that they are not a mere nostalgic defense of some useless cultural artifact but, rather, very important to individuals in their daily lives. There are (and were) many reasons for maintaining ethnic communal ties. Some ties are primarily useful when members of ethnic groups are new immigrants; others continue to be important for a lifetime. The utility of ethnic ties and ethnic groups is in large part the reason for their continued existence.

The melting pot, of course, was never a reality for many Americans, and many families were forced to maintain ethnic communal ties as a matter of self-defense. In their work on ethnicity and their analysis of the evolution and persistence of ethnicity, Glazer and Moynihan (1970) argued that "the adoption of a totally new ethnic identity, by dropping whatever one is to become simply American, is inhibited by strong elements in the social structure of the United States." These inhibitions range from brutal discrimination and prejudice to the "unavailability of simple 'American' identity" (Glazer and Moynihan, 1970:xxxiii). Most positively seen, ethnic communities provide individuals with congenial associates, help organize experience by personalizing an increasingly impersonal world, and provide opportunities for social mobility and success within an ethnic context (Greeley, 1969).

Ethnic Family Life

The maintenance of ethnic identification and solidarity rests, to an extent, on the ability of the family to socialize its members into the ethnic culture and thus to channel and control, perhaps program, future behavior. Consequently, the distinctive family life that developed as a result of historical and contemporary social processes becomes the focal concern of this work. Contributors were asked to examine the relationships and characteristics distinctive of ethnic family life, to look to the past for an explanation of historical or genetic significance, to describe the key characteristics of the ethnic family today, and to analyze the changes that have occurred in the family and speculate about what lies ahead.

It bears repeating that the historical experience of the ethnic group—both the time when the group arrived on these shores and the conditions under which the members of the group were forced to live—is a vitally important factor in the explanation of the persistence of the ethnic family and the ethnic group in the United States. For this reason, each chapter contains an important discussion of the historical background of the ethnic group under consideration. Besides describing the Old Country settings, each contributor has summarized the major characteristics of the family as it previously existed or first appeared in America to show subsequent changes and adaptations more clearly.

One of the most significant ways an ethnic culture is expressed is through those events that we identify as family activities. The family historically has been a conservative institution, and those cultural elements concerning family life, if not affected by outside influences, will tend to replace themselves generation after generation (Farber, 1964). Experiences within the family are intense, heavily emotion laden, and apt to evoke pleasurable or painful memories for most individuals. For example, it is no accident that for many of the ethnic groups discussed here, eating—particularly eating ethnic food—remains a significant part of the ethnic identity. Such are the activities that occur in a family context; if traditional ethnic values are to be found anywhere, they will be found in the family. In addition to developing historical context, each contributor discusses four major areas of ethnic family life in which ethnic culture might be generated, be sustained, or have an impact. First are demographic characteristics: How is the ethnic culture specifically expressed in fertility, marriage, and divorce rates? How does the group cope with intermarriage? Intermarriage is a cultural matter that can be viewed as an indicator of assimilation for the ethnic group and ranges in incidence from very low among African Americans and Amish to relatively high among Japanese Americans. Second is the question of family structure, which involves the distribution of status, authority, and responsibility within the nuclear family and the network of kin relationships linking members of the extended family. Most discussions of ethnic family life have focused on this area because many ethnic groups have been characterized as patriarchal, as matriarchal, or as having very close-knit extended family relationships. It is in this context that we hear comments about "black matriarchy" or the "Jewish mother." How much is cultural myth or ideology? How much is fact? How much has been the effect of the American experience?

Along with the cultural patterns that define family roles and statuses, rights, and obligations, are found issues of value transmission: attributes of an ethnic culture that are mediated through the family. These are cultural values that concern such issues as achievement, lifestyle, and educational or occupational aspirations. Although many historical, economic, and other factors, such as discrimination and prejudice, have limited the mobility of individuals in many ethnic groups, the possession of a cultural reservoir of motivations and skill has worked to the distinct advantage of many. The cultural tradition of the Jews, for example, with its emphasis on literacy and education, has helped them immeasurably from a socioeconomic standpoint. Finally, in discussing ethnic family life, it is important to examine the family at different stages of the family life cycle. In this collection of essays, contributors analyze those aspects of childbearing, adolescence, mate selection, and the place of the elderly in which ethnic culture has had significant influence. The culture of many groups usually specifies what the most desirable end product of the socialization process should be. Regardless of the end product, the family as the major force of socialization, especially in the critical early years, is the most responsible ethnic institution for making it happen.

ETHNIC DIVERSITY AS THE CRITERION OF SELECTION

Although many more ethnic groups qualify, the twenty ethnic families presented in this book were chosen to represent a rather wide spectrum of distinguishable groups, ranging from fewer than 244,000 Amish to approximately 36.5 million African Americans, whose ethnicity continues to be expressed through identifiable institutions and, significantly, the family. Nevertheless, large numbers of Americans who find it possible to trace descent to foreign nations and cultures such as Germany, Great Britain, and Canada retain little, if any, of the Old World cultural identity. Because their family life is largely indistinguishable from that of others of similar socioeconomic classes (except in certain isolated enclaves), for this reason these groups have been excluded from this work.

As in the previous editions of this book, the editors have chosen to group ethnic families into five substantive categories: (1) European ethnic minorities, (2) Hispanic ethnic minorities, (3) Asian ethnic minorities, (4) historically subjugated ethnic minorities, and (5) socioreligious ethnic minorities. These categories help sort out the groups according to several dimensions, but they should in no way be taken as definitive, exclusive, or the only useful classification. The most important criterion in the minds of the editors is that the categories appear to capture a particularly important contingency or group experience that has a continuing influence on its collective fate. In almost all cases, the chapter on a particular ethnic group is written by a person who identifies him- or herself as a member of that group. In the following paragraphs, we briefly discuss the scheme that we have chosen.

1. European Ethnic Families

The four ethnic families in this category are the Irish American, Greek American, Italian American, and Polish American immigrants who arrived in the United States during a period extending roughly from the early 1880s until the outbreak of World War I. In this relatively short time, almost 25 million European immigrants entered the United States, an influx that resulted from great upheavals rent by industrialization and war. This is the period we most often think of when we visualize immigrant life, and it is from this wave of European immigration that most of today's non-Protestant white ethnics are descended.

2. Hispanic Ethnic Families

The four ethnic families in this category are the Mexican American, Cuban American, Puerto Rican American, and Dominican American. Hispanic ethnic groups have entered the United States in a variety of ways. Although Mexicans have come to this country in the nineteenth and twentieth centuries as voluntary immigrants, they also are by far the source of the largest number of recent immigrants into the United States. Puerto Ricans, too, are a group not clearly part of either voluntary immigration or conquest. Puerto Rico became a territory of the United States in

1898 following the Spanish American War, and in 1917 the inhabitants of the island were granted American citizenship. The greatest influx of Puerto Ricans to the United States was during the 1950s, when nearly 20 percent of the island's population moved to the mainland.

The movement of Cubans to the United States since 1960 has come in a series of waves. Initially impelled mainly by political motives, later waves are increasingly the result of economic reason as well. Although a relatively large contingent of Dominicans migrated to the United States during the nineteenth century, the largest wave came to this country after the passage of immigration reform in 1965. The challenges that all of these ethnic groups have faced include economic integration and social assimilation into American society.

3. Asian Ethnic Families

The six ethnic families in this category are the Korean American, Vietnamese American, Chinese American, Japanese American, Asian Indian American, and Filipino American. Chinese and Japanese American ethnic families have been in this country in substantial numbers for seventy-five to a hundred years. Korean, Asian Indian, Vietnamese, and Filipino ethnic families, however, represent a sizable number of recent and continuing immigrants. Important questions for the study of all these ethnic groups relate both to the effects of time and generation on the cultural heritage and, more particularly, to how they directly affect family life. The extent to which assimilation and acculturation has had an impact on ethnic identity and lifestyle remains one of the key challenges encountered by these immigrant groups. Other challenges include adjusting to a modern business cycle and war-plagued industrialized society and to constant infusion of new representatives from their respective countries of origin.

4. Historically Subjugated Ethnic Families

African American and Native American ethnic families are placed together because their identity and experience in this country have been strongly influenced by their race and their brutal treatment by white Europeans. These ethnic groups either preceded the arrival of the European Americans or arrived later and were immediately or later placed in extreme forms of bondage. Enslaved to the land, alienated from it, or bound in a latter-day peonage, African Americans and Native Americans have endured the harshest of treatment. In both of these ethnic groups, the role of the family—whether truncated or extended—becomes crucial for ethnic survival.

5. Socioreligious Ethnic Minorities

The four ethnic families in this category are Jewish American, Amish American, Muslim American, and Mormon American. These families are placed together because their identity and experience have been largely a result of, or strongly influenced by, their religion. All sought in America a place to live the kind of social existence in which religion could continue to be vitally conjoined with all aspects of their family life and livelihood.

References

Camarota, S. A. 2002, November. *Immigration in the United States—2002: A Snapshot of America's Foreign-Born Population*. Washington, DC: Center for Immigration Studies.

Borjas, G. J. 1990. *Friends or Strangers: The Impact of Immigrants on the U.S. Economy*. New York: Basic Books.

Davidson, J. R. (Ed.). 2010. *African American Studies.* Edinburgh, Scotland: Edinburgh University Press.

Farber, B. 1964. *Family Organization and Interaction.* San Francisco: Chandler.

Geertz, C. 1963. *The Integrative Revolution: Primordial Sentiments and Civil Politics in the New States.* In Clifford Geertz (Ed.), *Old Societies and New States* (pp. 105–157). Glencoe, IL: Free Press.

Glazer, N., and D. P. Moynihan. 1970. *Beyond the Melting Pot* (2nd ed.). Cambridge, MA: MIT Press.

Gordon, M. 1964. *Assimilation in American Life.* New York: Oxford University Press.

Greeley, A. M. 1969. *Why Can't They Be Like Us?* New York: Institute of Human Relations Press.

———. 1974. *Ethnicity in the United States: A Preliminary Reconnaissance.* New York: John Wiley.

Jensen, L. 1989. *The New Immigration: Implications for Poverty and Public Assistance Utilization.* New York: Greenwood Press.

Kirst-Ashman, K. K., and G. H. Hull, Jr. 2009. *Generalist Practice with Organizations and Communities.* Belmont, CA: Brooks/Cole.

Novak, M. 1973. "Probing the New Ethnicity." In J. Ryan (Ed.), *White Ethnics: Their Live in Working-Class America* (pp. 158–167). Englewood Cliffs, NJ: Prentice Hall.

Simon, J. 1995. *Immigration: The Demographic and Economic Facts.* New York: Cato Institute.

Simon, R. 1985. *Public Opinion and the Immigrant: Print Media Coverage, 1880–1980.* Lexington, MA: Lexington Press.

Ratigan, D. 2010, September 9. *The Dylan Ratigan Show.* MSNBC.

U.S. Immigration and Naturalization Service. 1996. *Immigration to the United States.* Washington, DC: U.S. Government Printing Office.

2

■■■

A "Then and Now" Overview of the Immigrant Family in America

Charles H. Mindel
Robert W. Habenstein

INTRODUCTION

Rather than beginning this chapter on immigration in the nineteenth century, as in earlier editions, we move back a century to broaden the sociohistorical context of this analysis and to mention some of the economic, technological, and demographic developments of earlier times. Later in this chapter we analyze the nineteenth- and early twentieth-century immigrant ethnic family as a transplanted, adaptive, primary social unit engaged in the business of conserving and rebuilding ethnic culture. Finally, we review the remainder of the twentieth century, with its remarkable influx of immigrants from Third World and established countries after 1965. The focus is on the impact and consequence of this phenomenon mainly for the immigrants' families but, also, to a lesser extent, on their often strange and unyielding host society.

THE MERCANTILIST SCENARIO

After nearly a thousand years of manorial-centered feudalism—with its slow economic growth and a population held stable mostly by wars, famines, epidemics, and a low level of agricultural technology—a new era in the form of a maritime-centered mercantilism promised a more vibrant and richer society to Western Europeans.

For centuries during the late Middle Ages, the city-states that existed along the Mediterranean coast, around the Iberian Peninsula, and north to Scandinavia were known not only for shipping trade but for their banking houses, financiers, and underwriters (known then as undertakers). Out of this new financial environment came a range of market instruments and accounting innovations—not the least of which was double-entry bookkeeping (Braudel, 1982). The transition from city- to nation-states, carried upward by a newfound nationalist fever, advanced the mercantilist idea beyond simple control of maritime commerce and the creation of exporting seaports abroad. The expansionist urge led to exploration and colonization as a primary method of increasing wealth for the mother country. At the same time, revenues could be increased by subjecting land trade to duties, customs, and devices for collecting money from itinerant merchants, peddlers, and even those exporting from one part of a nation to another (Braudel, 1982). The idea of continuously funneling money into a centralized nation-state took on an extreme character when gold and silver became the preferred plunder or medium of exchange. Nationalism took on a take-charge ideology that led to the building of navies, including battleships, to control and protect the nation's ocean commerce.

The Great Transformation

Maritime-centered mercantilism reached its apogee in the eighteenth century. But even in its expanded form, mercantilism could not restrain a growing industry-based society. By the beginning of the nineteenth century, mill towns in England and America had sprung up along rivers or near exploitable fossil-fuel deposits. Industrialization soon spread over great segments of western Europe. By mid-century, engineers supported by civil authorities and men of commerce and capital enterprise advanced a large-scale technology that soon revolutionized not only industry but also transportation, communication, and agriculture.

The great transformation of the time, then, involved the rapid change of a mercantile-oriented, town-centered, small-scale, agriculturally undergirded society into one featuring large-scale capital enterprises, advanced technology, extensive marketing systems, and a large proletarianized labor force. People of the soil—peasants, small landowners, and rural villagers—found their commons enclosed, rents increased, and land increasingly expensive. In the wake of expanded mechanized agricultural production, the small-scale producers and the farm laborers were driven off the lands that they had rented or owned and cultivated for generations. Likewise, artisans organized in guilds lost control of the quality, quantity, and marketing outlets of their goods to merchants, who were themselves organized into leagues and early forms of trade associations.

The ironic result of these developments was that at the very time production of foodstuffs and other agricultural products was increasing along with life expectancy, millions of small farmers, peasants, small producers, and independent artisans were suffering economic dislocation and loss of place in traditional community life (Braudel, 1982; Knapp, 1976). Writes historian Paul Kennedy (1994:4):

> The major cities, swelled by the drift of population, grew fast. On the eve of the French Revolution (1793), Paris had a total of between 600,000 and 700,000 people including up to 100,000 vagrant—combustible material for a social explosion. London's total was even larger, its 570,000 inhabitants of 1750 having become 900,000 by 1801, including a mass of bustling street hawkers, pickpockets, urchins, and felons so well captured in contemporary prints. With more and more "have-nots," was it any wonder that the authorities were fearful and tightened up restrictions on public assemblies, pamphleteering, "combinations" of workers, and other potentially subversive activities?

Throughout the nineteenth century, the great industrial and commercial revolutions, kept dynamic by rapidly changing and improving technology, not only uprooted masses of people but also reaggregated them in areas where an expanding, vigorous labor force was necessary to keep the mills, factories, mines, and seaports of an expanding capitalism operating at appropriate capacities. Major political and religious institutions, never too stable in Western society, became increasingly incapable of providing protection for, guidance of, and control over the great numbers of people who had come to occupy and identify with particular geographic regions. Likewise, the vagaries of local, national, and international economies (and of nature itself) introduced crises of magnitude often great enough in themselves to effect large-scale social change.

"Push" Factors

The social and historical forces described here have been characterized as *push factors*. Some of these push factors operated in limited geographical contexts, such as the Irish potato blight of 1847, the religious persecution of Germans in Prussia, the failed German revolution of 1848, and internecine strife among ethnic peoples inside thinly laced-together empires. More widespread disjunctions and large-scale crises might involve regional economic depressions, wars among great nations, crop failures, plagues, and epidemics. But behind all the push factors stood the long-term transformation of land and commercial enterprise in the direction of larger units of production owned and operated by fewer persons. As Europe was shifting from labor-intensive to capital-intensive enterprise, the United States seemed ready to absorb the surplus labor, energies, hopes, and aspirations of Europe's dislocated, migration-prone peoples.

"Pull" Factors

America, Lord Acton had proclaimed in an 1866 address to the Literary and Scientific Institution of Bridgnorth, not far from his Shopshire estate, had become a "distant magnet" whose force had extended across Europe (Taylor, 1971:xi–xii). Perhaps there was a generalized nineteenth-century concept or stereotype of the United States as a land of opportunity where all dreams might be fulfilled. But it is more appropriate to think of the multitudinous Europeans who had to decide whether to move or to stay as constituting an emigration *public*, a loose group of persons who, in the end, made individual decisions—for many of them the most important decision of their lives. Slaves, of course, had no options and were shipped callously to the Americas in increasing numbers from the early seventeenth into the early eighteenth century. Convicts were exiled from England to Australia, as they were for a brief time to the American colonies. Almost all emigrants, however, went to America out of choice. Dreams were possible, but hope was omnipresent.

The "one big magnet" notion had an important counterpart in the groups, agencies, companies, kin, and native-born Americans already well situated in the United States who exerted their own "magnetic" force in the hope of dislodging and attracting emigrants from their Old World communities. The word was spread across Europe by thousands of publicity agents who worked for passenger ship lines, railways, canal authorities, land developers, towns, and large-scale business enterprises. Their evocative speeches and hortatory literature were reinforced by the rhetoric of journalistic publications, guides, handbooks, pamphlets, and lecturers—all extolling the virtues of and opportunities in America. Many immigrants who had settled into American cities, towns, and farms wrote to European kin as true believers, assuring them that the riches of the new land were available for the taking (Taylor, 1971).

IMMIGRATION WAVES

From the mid-nineteenth century until shortly after World War I, between 30 and 35 million emigrants left Europe for American shores. They came in large waves, from different countries, and at different times—first in cargo-carrying sailing ships, then in passenger sailing ships, and finally in steamships, which hauled hundreds of thousands of people each year in the last three decades of the nineteenth century. The ships also hauled great numbers back again, perhaps as many as one-third of the former immigrants, who either had failed to find fortune in the New World or had accumulated enough wealth to ensure a comfortable, enviable life in the community once left behind (Saloutos, 1964).

Historians and scholars refer to the period from 1830 to 1882 as that of the "old" immigration and the period from 1882 to 1930, when federal control replaced that of the states, as that of the "new" immigration. The 10 million immigrants who arrived in the "old" period were predominantly Irish, German, Scandinavian, English, Scottish, and Scots-Irish (Feldstein and Costello, 1974). They came during the preindustrial years, when there were millions of acres to be settled and canals, bridges, and railroads to be built, and when urban work complements were still in their formative years. There was both dispersion and concentration of the "old" immigrants, by ethnic group and often by religious affiliations. Scots-Irish Protestants arrived early in the century and became some of Pennsylvania's most successful farmers. Irish Catholics—suffering famine, plague, and loss of their small farms in the old country because of absentee landlords' desire for large-scale agriculture units—settled in the larger cities in the Northeast, staying put even though they faced poverty, low wages, and the prejudice of native-born American citizens. The English dispersed almost everywhere, but most shelved their plans for independent living on small farms and ended up in the larger towns and cities. Germans in great numbers went everywhere in the Northeastern, Middle Atlantic, and Midwestern states; some were content to gather into ethnic communities in cities, and others settled on fertile lands and became successful, often prosperous, farmers. Scandinavians, bridging the "old" and "new" periods, concentrated their settlements mainly in the Midwestern states and, like the Germans, became serious and successful farmers but also contributed artisans, professionals, and intellectuals to such rapidly growing cities as Cleveland, Chicago, and Minneapolis.

The "new" immigration followed the great wave of Irish and German immigration of the 1850s. It crested in the 1880s and again, each time higher, in the decades immediately preceding the outbreak of World War I, when immigrants were entering the United States at the rate of 1 million a year (Jones, 1976). Beginning in the early 1880s, the center of gravity of emigration moved steadily southward and eastward. By the end of the century, the bulk of America's immigrants consisted of Slavs, Italians, Greeks, and Eastern European Jews.[1] By 1914, the "new" immigrants constituted over 80 percent of all total immigration. According to Maldwyn Jones (1976:50), a historian of immigration:

> These "new" immigrants came from the most backward and reactionary regions of Europe. The cultural differences between them and the Americans were infinitely greater than had been the case with the "old" immigration. Hence, the "new" immigrants would be more difficult to assimilate. . . .
>
> In any case, it was becoming apparent that the immediate effect of immigration was to fragment, rather than to unite American society. Although the concept of class was alien to American thinking, a great gulf was developing between the native born and middle classes

---

[1]From before the turn of the century until the 1920s, scholars, popular writers, historians of immigration, and social scientists tended to view the mass immigration of millions of southern and eastern Europeans with varying degrees of alarm. The "threat" point of view is somewhat luridly presented by journalist Kenneth L. Roberts (1920); a sympathetic treatment is found in the important sociological novel by Upton Sinclair (1905), *The Jungle.* Written before or after World War I, the arguments presented by Roberts and Sinclair are still alive in the writings of current disputants; see, for example, Sanford J. Ungar (1995), Peter Brimelow (1996), and Roy Beck (1996). A collection of contemporary points of view is found in *Arguing Immigration,* edited by Nicolaus Mills (1994). For an absorbing novel, the first part of a trilogy starting in 1888, see Howard Fast's (1977) *The Immigrants.*

and the predominantly foreign working class. Under the impact of immigration the United States became in effect two nations, differentiated by language and religion, by residence and occupation. The two nations had no more contact with one another than they had when separated by 3000 miles of ocean.

The reaction to the "new" or late-arriving immigration was threefold. In the industrial realm, these migrants, most of whom were between the ages of fifteen and thirty-five, were exploited by industrialists and their managers, who sought to pay them low wages, and they were resented by established labor as a threat to its hard-earned wage and living standards. In the social realm there were ostracism and prejudice, not all completely unfounded because many of the "new" immigrants had no intention of staying permanently and worked for little, lived on little, showed little or no interest in the problems of the wider society, and sought to accumulate as much wealth as possible and return to their homelands as soon as possible (Park and Miller, 1921).[2]

Roy Beck (1996:37), a current critic of open-door immigration policy, writes:

> Most of our ancestors who came during the Great Wave (1880–1924) placed an enormous burden on the country. Large numbers didn't learn the language and culture quickly; they were clannish and lived in ethnic enclaves, they remained poor, and their arrival was in numbers that were devastating to many communities. For many of the immigrants themselves, life was a struggle for even a tenuous hold on the American dream.

This perception of immigrants as essentially burdensome to the host society was central to the clamor of anti-immigrationists after World War I, and federal immigration laws were passed in 1921 and 1924 that severely restricted immigration in general and, through a nation-quota system, discriminated against the people of southern and eastern Europe (Jones, 1976).[3]

CHARACTERISTIC FEATURES OF WESTERN EUROPEAN IMMIGRANT FAMILIES

Possessions: The Baggage of Life

Emigrants leaving their homelands faced the difficult and often heartrending problem of which material possessions to take and which to leave. The problem was complicated by marital status and family size. Single persons could travel light more easily; those married and with children had to sacrifice things of symbolic value to practical, basic necessities such as cookware, bedding (nearly always down-filled ticks and pillows), clothing, and tools (important to the immigrant artisan). A few cherished mementos—pictures, Bibles, and missals—could be tucked in the baggage somewhere, but most bulkier household possessions had to be left behind, along with farm equipment, livestock, pets, machinery, and other paraphernalia too large to be transported as passenger luggage. Families whose growth and sense of an immediate, "close" environment had included the accumulation of material objects—some symbolic, others pragmatic, but all incorporated into their lives and work—were subject to the trauma of separation from a significant part of their real world. Memories of this world, romanticized in

---

[2]Park and Miller developed a sixfold typology of immigrants: settler, colonist, political idealist, allrightnick, *caffone*, and intellectual. In their terms, the *caffone*—the "pure opportunist wanting only to make money and go back"—became the stereotype applied, with only partial justification, to all immigrants who eventually returned to their homelands.

[3]A labor-supported Chinese Exclusion Act was passed in 1882, and in 1885 an Alien Contract Law was passed prohibiting indentured servants' contracts.

musings and life reviews, contributed to a diffuse nostalgia, often tinged with melancholy (Feldstein and Costello, 1974).

Transitory Existence

Immigrants, by definition, are people who purposely move to new geographical settings. Most European immigrants became migratory and moved a number of times, with several transportation breaks between the initial move and arrival at the final destination. Many had a specific goal in mind—Buffalo, St. Louis, or Pittsburgh. They hoped to find a place to settle with or near close relatives in a colony, a settlement, or an area of concentration of their country-people (Park and Miller, 1921). Some announced a destination but never got there; others, having reached the proclaimed destination, did not stay—because of disappointment or inability to find an ensured means of survival or because other cities or towns seemed to hold out more promise.

The transitory nature of much immigrant life was, of course, countered by the large numbers who settled down and tenaciously hung on to their dwellings, strongly motivated to acquire land and homes of their own even if it meant living in the basement and renting out the top two floors and attic! The tendency to become place centered was reinforced by and to some extent led to the growth of ethnic enclaves into which a person or a family and extended kin might embed themselves, supporting and receiving support from immigrant organizations (Habenstein and Mindel, 1981).

The Family as a Buffer, Filter, and Sorting Mechanism

Insecurity, hopes, fears, misgivings—a panoply of conflicting emotions—heaped themselves on the immigrants' heads. The phrase "ordeal of assimilation" (Feldstein and Costello, 1974) appropriately describes the process by which immigrants as supplicants were required to or at least expected to organize their lives. Even so, there was no guarantee of a full, happy, prosperous life even for the assimilated, who were well aware of the "busts" as well as the "booms" in the American economy. In these periods, ethnic immigrant families operated as buffering, filtering, and sorting social mechanisms. All prescriptions and proscriptions of the host society were carefully judged against traditional standards, and all possible meanings and consequences were pondered at length. The new might or might not be suspect, but it was seldom ignored or left unexamined by members of the immigrant family—often including close relatives who temporarily or permanently might make up a partially extended family.

Generational Frictions

The large multigeneration family was found less among first-generation and more among second-generation immigrant families. Yet as a social unity, it remained an ideal, even if it often was difficult to achieve. As the aging generations became grandparents and great-grandparents, relationships between rapidly Americanizing children and the elderly and very elderly—whose minds were embedded in the amber of their native language and culture—often became difficult and frustrating. In somewhat varying degrees, depending to a great extent on the language and cultural leap required to become a properly assimilated immigrant or a descendent of such, all immigrant families experienced the anxieties and strains of what has come to be called the "generation gap" (Ross, 1914). When the family and close relatives seemed unable to appreciate and deal properly with children's problems or to give useful advice, alternative sources—schoolteachers, street friends, classmates—were consulted. Some vague sense of family weakness revealed in the family's inability to cope with each member's problems was characteristic of almost all immigrant families.

FAMILY LIFE CYCLE

The Marriage Institution

Marriage has always been a serious and important event among immigrants, both "old" and "new." Its significance rested in the economic impact on ongoing households and in the social, economic, and interpersonal consequences for the married couple. The productive energies of the unmarried family members were an important contribution to the household. Marriage of a son or a daughter usually led to a significant reduction in the income of established households (Tender, 1981). The gain to society through the addition of legitimately procreating couples was often accomplished at the expense of the economic viability of the newlyweds' parental households. Thus for immigrant families, most of whom were near the poverty line, the marriage of a young adult member was a serious matter. Marriages were not to be entered into lightly. Young people were under heavy social obligation to marry for life and to establish independent households of their own, and mostly by their own efforts.

Marriage had its exactions, but it also had obvious compensations. Whatever the "new freedom" in America might dictate or permit in terms of relations between the sexes, young immigrants still considered marriage to be the overriding legitimating mechanism for a couple to remove the bars to intimacy and companionship. Marriage was not yet equalitarian, but if marriages traditionally had been a family, kin, and community affair, the freedom of a marrying couple to develop an interpersonal unity, even if not always taken advantage of, was at least acknowledged by the traditional groups.

Mate Selection

The choice of a mate was both an important and a difficult matter. *Endogamy,* marriage within a specific group, was preferred in all ethnic groups and prescribed in immigrant families (Habenstein and Mindel, 1981). Given the same ethnic group and religious preference, wives might marry up, becoming the wife of a man of a slightly higher socioeconomic class—a "good catch." Men might look for an attractive younger woman with domestic skills and possibly a small, self-accumulated dowry to help get the marriage off to a good start.

Difficulties arose because of a sex ratio highly favoring males.[4] In some ethnic groups (the Greeks are a good example), opportunities for men to meet and marry eligible women were severely limited because of the scarcity of women. The bachelor ethnic immigrant was a familiar and socially acceptable member of the community. He often lived in a lodging house or perhaps with married friends, unless he returned to his European community. Substantial economic success might, of course, turn the picture around; highly age-discrepant marriages were not uncommon, particularly when the husband-to-be had acquired wealth.

Parental influence on marital choice could be direct and substantial but not necessarily decisive. Daughters increasingly sought to enlarge the scope of their freedom of choice of mates. Parents, relatives, friends, and clergymen nevertheless felt obliged to give friendly, sometimes

---

[4]Duncan (1933) estimates that out of total immigration to about 1930, 65 percent of immigrants were males and 80 percent were between fourteen and forty-five years old.

strong counsel. Arranged marriages through professional matchmakers accounted for a very small percentage of the mate selections made, mostly in Russian and Polish-Jewish ethnic groups. Engagements preceded weddings; marriage ceremonies were important and often elaborate affairs. Civil marriages occasionally took place, but the norm was a church wedding—the larger, the better—with spirited receptions, bands, dancing, presents, speeches, and photographs. The community, in effect, laid hands on the principals. Sanctified by the church and sanctioned by the community, the marriage was supposed to last forever—as it usually did.

Children and Childhood

Once married, young immigrants immediately set about bringing children into the world. A good—that is, steady—job, an industrious and provident wife, and a large number of children were the cornerstones of immigrant adult existence. Families were expected to grow large (six to eight children were not too many), since children were not only nice to have but also were potential economic assets to the household. Newly married wives might continue to work for a short while, but when they settled down to the long and full-time job of being a mother, they almost never worked outside the home (see, for example, McLaughlin, 1978).[5]

The care of children was primarily the mother's responsibility. Grandmothers who lived with married daughters or sons were helpful and were occasionally used as surrogate mothers if the mother worked away from home. Mothers' sisters who lived near might develop close ties with nieces and nephews. Mothers, grandmothers, and aunts, then, made up one significant sector of the extended or partially extended kinship systems in which the nuclear unit of wife, husband, and children was embedded. Uncles, particularly to male children, and father's best friends, often indistinguishable in the children's minds from "real" relatives, were also important; the latter often became godfathers, who were pledged to take an interest in fictive kin a generation below them (Habenstein and Mindel, 1981).

Childhood was a hit-or-miss proposition. For immigrants, there was little self-conscious domesticity (Ryan, 1982), little concern about the rights of the child, and much concern that the child grow up rapidly to become a sturdy participant in the labor force. Small children were family reared, with parents playing the dominant role in the socialization process but with siblings and close relatives very much involved. Chronic tensions between parents and offspring developed when the children started to attend school. The Old World language, almost always spoken in the first-generation immigrant family, suddenly became extraneous and burdensome to the child in the classroom—where teachers could be unsympathetic to young pupils trying to learn English as a second language—and marked him or her as "Polack," "Mick," "Wop," or "Dago" among other children. What was learned at home might have little meaning compared with or might be at odds with what was learned in the classroom. The embarrassment of poverty and the impoverishment of language brought out resentment not only between children and parents but also between children and the culture and institutions that gave meaning and direction to the lives of the older generations.

Coming of Age

Children of both sexes were expected to become responsible young adults by the time they were fourteen years old, at which age they had completed grade school and were, in most states, eligible for a work permit. Long before this, children had had work experience of some sort—part

---

[5]Note, however, that many immigrant wives did cottage industry work at home.

time, in the summer, after school, in or outside of the home. The emphasis on work was matched by an unyielding familism; the goals and needs of the family, nearly always defined by the father, were first and foremost in the minds of all family members. Children spoke of "my family" rather than of "my parents." The dominance of the authoritarian father was buffered and tempered by the mother, who played a mediating and protective role in respect to her children. Thus the mother–child relationship was intensely close and emotional; for children, the most horrible event imaginable would be the loss of the mother.

Formal education was legally required and regarded as a necessity for children, but it was not expected to unduly delay the maturing child from entering the workforce. Boys might reluctantly be permitted to continue attending school past the age of fourteen if it seemed that further education might enhance their vocational prospects. For daughters of immigrant parents, opportunities for education beyond the eighth grade were slim. Doubtful parents might accede to some type of business-school training, but girls usually were pitched into the workforce as soon as their parents could get them there, legally or not.

As they came of age and entered the workforce, or perhaps vice versa, immigrants' daughters developed even stronger bonds with their mothers. It was a matter of great pride for the young daughter to give her wages to her mother. Until she was ready for marriage, the working daughter did not pay "board"—a stipulated weekly amount that represented only a portion of her wages (Tender, 1981). Mothers gave back a relatively small amount of the daughters' wages for carfare, other necessary expenses, and clothing. Sons, however, from the time they began working, were permitted to pay board and were expected to save most of their wages with an eye toward having a reasonable amount of money with which to get married.

Marriage of sons or of daughters, we have already noted, led to loss of family income and thus was a family contingency as well as an individual matter. But if the family was large, as it usually was, the departures of the eldest children through marriage were offset by the entry into the workforce of the younger sons and daughters. Perfect synchronization might not be effected, but continual replacement with junior breadwinners could take place in the very large families for fifteen or more years. The blurring between adolescence and manhood or womanhood stemmed directly from the immigrants' universal practice of putting their children to work as early as possible, keeping them in the household as long as possible, and exacting from them as much income as possible. Adolescence in families of this sort could hardly be called a "dalliance" period. What dallying might have occurred was done on Saturday nights, in ethnic-group dance halls, clubs, community centers, and possibly settlement houses.

Adulthood

Adult status for males was achieved by combining efforts to succeed vocationally, taking seriously one's marital responsibilities, and showing concern for parents, relatives, and the "family name." Having sons was somewhat more important—since sons would perpetuate the family name—than was having daughters, although it was generally accepted that the mix of sexes was to be preferred.

As children matured and entered the workforce, the husband accepted the responsibility or challenge for raising the living standard of the family. Having lived for a decade or more in tenements, basement apartments, or occasionally duplexes—sometimes with a household that was much larger than the nuclear family—the family bought or built its own home. Since they had emigrated from countries where social-class division was a crystallized, integral part of social organization, established immigrants in the United States strove to better their lot. The husband was the moving force, making decisions unilaterally if he cared to, but often with the help or encouragement of the wife and other household members. Ownership of one of the nicest houses on the block brought the highest meaning and self-satisfaction to immigrants, for whom such an acquisition would have been impossible in their homelands.

Wifehood for the immigrant generation was a transient and never clearly developed female role. Motherhood, however, in modern parlance, "went on forever." Specifically, being a mother involved nurturing and monitoring children's health and well-being, breast-feeding babies, keeping tabs on children, managing domestic affairs, and at least maintaining household discipline until the father came home from work. Mothers also paid attention to and helped keep alive kinship networks, acting as "kin keeper" for the family and spending what little discretionary time was available in visiting close kin in neighborhood and community.

It is difficult, in describing the immigrant family, to overestimate the importance of the immigrant mother, particularly the energy she expended in carrying out her multidimensional role. Daughters had learned the responsibilities and hazards of motherhood long before they left adolescence. Some rejected the prospect of becoming a working-class wife, burdened with children and with crushing domestic responsibilities, and sought careers. Spinster aunts were no novelty among first-, second-, and third-generation immigrants and descendants. The majority of women had no careers, finding their work tedious and unrewarding. Marriage and motherhood offered a dubious alternative to a life of industrial or shop work, but most women finally chose it.

Sexual Relations

Immigrant men found in America a land where sexual mores were less restrictive and channeled than in the Old World communities. Single men traditionally sought sexual partners among women who were not to be seriously considered as future marriage mates. Once married, men expected their sexual needs to be satisfied by a dutiful and accommodating wife. Ambivalently, the wife might be seen as a replica of the sainted mother or as someone with a suspicious but appealing sexuality. Immigrant husbands found it difficult to assimilate both images, but they did not hesitate to apply a double standard. Wives' sexual needs were considered secondary, at best; in many immigrant communities, they were not considered at all. That part of Victorianism which cautioned that sexual activity was a form of depletion of one's vitality apparently left immigrant men unfazed, except that some believed that it might apply to masturbation (Barker-Benfield, 1976).

Men were not above reproach if it was true or suspected that they might be lacking in manliness. The problem was easily resolved by fathering children, especially sons. If he had no children, the husband had an excuse—his wife obviously was barren!

Old Age

Many immigrant men, particularly the several million who came to the United States between 1880 and 1900, went through all the later stages of the life cycle, starting out in young adulthood and living the next thirty or more years as husbands, fathers, and grandfathers. For women, it was a similar story, although some only later joined husbands who had preceded them to their new country. By 1920, the immigrants of the 1880s were either grandparents, returned emigrants, or dead.

Whatever economic security could be achieved by adults as they aged had to be gained through their own efforts and through the efforts of growing and grown family members. A federally operated Social Security system was several generations away; industrial pensions, when they existed, were woefully small; and investment in stocks and bonds was impossible for the majority of immigrants, who found it difficult to stay above the poverty line.

To achieve an income base sufficient to maintain a comfortable, if scaled-down, old age, adults had to save or invest wisely every possible penny. In the trade-off between putting money into children's health and education or into savings, real estate, or other modes of income-earning investments, the children's needs usually came out a bad second. It should be remembered that despite the prevailing ideology of America as a land of opportunity and riches, poverty was omnipresent. Immigrants first had to rise above poverty and start families before beginning to build, albeit slowly, their own type of retirement "package." As already mentioned, the goal of achieving a higher standard of living could best be accomplished by the utilization of each family member's resources and energies to bring money into the household. The standard retirement "package" then consisted primarily of a paid-for house—possibly with rooms rented and rooms full of dated but paid-for furniture—a savings account, and paid-up industrial (burial) insurance. A pension derived from a life of work would complete the package, but it was not always available. Old immigrant workers who had toiled long and hard were less likely to be pensioned off and more likely to be permanently laid off or simply fired.

Older people preferred to live on their own, but many found the desired, often realized retirement "package" impossible to assemble. Living with adult children, however, carried little onus. For most adult children of immigrants, concern and care for aging parents were indubitable signs of maturity, and status was accorded those who were most active in parental and grandparental care. Parents who lived with grown children assumed the usual roles of persons of wisdom and experience who could be helpful, of storytellers and purveyors of cultural heritage, and of performers of practical and necessary small chores about the house. When not too busy with household duties, the elderly had ready access to numerous local immigrant institutions, stores, markets, taverns, clubs, and community centers, and some visited the local library.

Still, the road to old age was rocky and strewn with a variety of obstacles. Most elderly people had exhausted their energies in long hours of shop and mill work. Poor health was endemic among the old, and life expectancy was short (fifty years in 1900). Most could not amass the assets necessary to live an independent, comfortable old age, and those who did might not be well enough in their old age to enjoy it.

FAMILY CONTROLS, FUNCTIONS, AND DYSFUNCTIONS

Most, but by no means all, of those Europeans who emigrated to the United States through the nineteenth century and into the twentieth left behind rural societies in which local folkways and mores provided the boundaries for and set the controls over everyday life. External authorities added another dimension of social control, but the villages and towns usually developed local institutions that provided the rules of the everyday game of life for the inhabitants. Folk beliefs—partly mystical and incomprehensible, partly pragmatic and cautionary—gave meaning and instruction to those of a peasant background (Campisi, 1948; Habenstein and Mindel, 1981; Park and Miller, 1921; Ross, 1914). Life was restrictive but more or less predictable. The pace was slow, and change was strongly resisted.

In American society, immigrants found that external authorities could and did affect their families and their institutions and could modify these social instrumentalities in sometimes alarming ways. School, health and sanitation, police, and taxing authorities are good examples. Against them, the distrustful immigrants could offer noncompliance and avoidance, rejection, and indifference. The history of the Great Emigration is not only a history of movement of people from one land to another; it is also a history of efforts, group and individual, to maintain the integrative mechanisms and forces of one kind of society and lifestyle against the influences and controls of a much larger host society.

If the United States were to become a melting pot, the immigrant family, metaphorically speaking, was not to be its cauldron. Rather, the family provided in varying degrees a safe haven from quick assimilation, ethnic bashing, and the Americanization for which in the early part of the twentieth century there was such a clamor. The immigrant family did not foster change; it resisted change—especially when its social space and traditional internal roles were threatened. But it did not, by the same token, declare war on change. To a judicious degree, public education was accepted, ambition and social mobility were encouraged, family members were helped to better themselves, and the American culture brought into immigrant families through the mass media was sifted and sometimes accepted. Fashions, fads, large-scale social and political movements, labor unions, child-labor laws, pensions, and medical insurance came to concern and affect immigrant families. The door to progressive thinking was never completely barred, even though the immigrant family was not a change-producing and change-oriented institution.

The test of this openness was in the experiences of immigrants who after some or many years in America, in immigrant families and communities, returned to their homelands and found the often-romanticized folk society to be small scale, "small time," restrictive, dull, and vaguely oppressive. The immigrant family in America might not have been a dynamic institution, but it possessed a protean ongoingness (Habenstein and Mindel, 1981) that must demand the social historian's respect.

THE "GREAT LULL": 1925–1965

Following World War I, in which America was a late but important participant, the country was faced with the pleasant prospect of becoming the world's greatest nation. There was no longer a fear of the German Hun, but America soon became less concerned about prosperity and more apprehensive about the conduct of its citizens and the emergence of a threat much larger than that posed by Kaiser Wilhelm and the often-warring Germans.

"Conduct" problems swirled around the refusal of most Americans to take seriously the Volstead Act, prohibiting the sale and drinking of alcoholic beverages, and the turn of the feminist movement, which had succeeded in bringing about women's suffrage, toward a new independence expressed in the appearance of the flapper, a new free-spirited female who challenged the traditional role of woman as mother, housewife, and dutiful helpmate to a dominant husband.

However deeply these social phenomena were to jolt the expectable placidity of the twenties and beyond, they were of considerably less importance to a populace that had turned conservative than was a stereotypical response to the specter of *bolshevism*, the leaders and followers of the Russian Revolution, who created a huge and threatening socialist nation in 1917.

The blame for this catastrophe, in the minds of most Americans—and certainly most politicians—lay squarely on the Jewish intellectual. Reversing an earlier tolerance, if not exactly a welcome, toward Jewish immigrants, this attitude was new and bordered on the hysterical. Writes Ben-Ami Shillony (1993:82) about Jews of the late nineteenth century:

> When integration into European society failed, the only recourse for them was to leave Europe and start a new life elsewhere. Most of the emigrants went to the United States, the land of opportunity, where they could be admitted without restriction, and where they found a democratic society nearly free of anti-Semitism. Between the Russian pogroms in 1881 and the outbreak of World War I in 1914 more than two million Jews, or about one-fifth of the

worldwide Jewish population, emigrated to the United States. No other people, except the Irish, has transferred such a large part of its population to America.

But even before World War I was over, Americans were being bombarded with anti-Jewish propaganda that often depicted the "Jew-Bolshevik" as a bewhiskered bomb thrower. Again Shillony (1993:83–84):

> The high percentage of Jews who took part in the Russian revolution and who belonged to European communist parties raised fear that Jewish immigrants from Eastern Europe might introduce the communist "bug" into America, The fear was enhanced by the fact that Jews figured prominently in American trade unions and left-wing organizations of the time. The resulting panic led to the U.S. Immigration Law of 1924, which limited each country's annual immigration quota to 2 percent of the number of its nationals in the United States in 1890. The law, aimed at preserving the Nordic character of American society, gave preference to immigrants from Northern and Western Europe over those from Eastern and Southern Europe. As a result, the annual number of Jewish immigrants dropped from one hundred thousand to only ten thousand.

On the other side of America, immigration from Japan and China was totally cut off by a Congress that, spooked by the specter of the "yellow peril," did not grant these countries even the 2 percent quota it granted European countries. To put the matter of the reasons for the great clampdown on immigration in 1924 more adequately: Jews were to be kept out for their intelligence and political acumen; Japanese and Chinese for their diligence and ambition; and eastern and southern Europeans for their poverty, ignorance, and clannishness. The argument that the 1924 immigration law and those preceding it back to the early nineteenth century were necessary to keep America from being overrun by the "hard to Americanize" or to safeguard the well-being of Americans in an established labor force being diluted by immigrants of a peasant or "coolie" mentality does not stand up to a careful examination of historical fact. A last point to remember: It was not immigrants who plunged America into its worst-ever economic depression, but rather an instrument of the well-to-do: the New York Stock Market and the untrammeled greed of its wildly behaving investors.

MOVEMENT AND FAMILIES: 1920–1965

Before World War I was over, several forms of internal migration were discernible. Those who found themselves in cities but were oriented to farming and rural life would push west, finding, in the latter half of the nineteenth century, rail transportation available and comparatively cheap. Much earlier, wagon trains had moved people to and across the Great Plains, but the railroads could do it better and, of course, much faster. The federal government assisted greatly with the Homestead Act of 1862 and with various mining claims arrangements.

For the urban oriented, all larger cities by the end of World War I would have had grown within them nuclei of ethnic and racial groups containing, importantly for our concerns, three major social institutions: families, neighborhoods, and communities. Immigrants may have had it in their minds that they were coming to a country, but they first found their bearings in all three of these institutions. In many cases, the signal event would be a reunification with other primary relations; often this blood tie would be the basis for being allowed into the country.

Many familiars would be found within the neighborhood of an immigrant's choice: butcher shop, bakery, grocery store, dry goods store, and, of course, tavern. Other medical/dental and legal services and service providers, if they were not in the immigrant neighborhood itself, would almost surely be found in the community, which would also likely contain an immigrant-serving bank and, for parties, reunions, marriages, and other social gatherings, the community center, often on the second floor of one of the larger buildings in the area.

The localistic life led in ethnic communities suited many occupants, from the newly arrived to those well settled. But caught up in the ecological metabolism of the larger cities with their shifting, mostly centrifugal population movements, communities would move, one succeeding another, leaving behind a community name and often a few difficult-to-move institutions, banks, and funeral homes. A frequent relic was a small park dotted with statues of war and civic heroes not likely to be known by the new ethnics, racial groups, or (if downtown—and much later) white-collar workers caught up in the gentrification movement. Those who moved might find their ethnicity somewhat tattered by the trauma of loss of place in the new country as much as the old.

Working-Class Dormitories

One much overlooked but important pattern of ethnic residential change, well underway by World War I, was the "working-class dormitory" movement that took blue collar workers and their families beyond city limits to open areas and small villages, where the mix of ethnics could be almost random. This type of interior immigration substituted a new and different form of settlement to places "in the sticks"—five, ten, or perhaps as many as fifteen miles beyond the limits of the mother city, in which could still be found the old homes and inhabitants left behind in the ethnic nuclei.

Working-class dormitory suburbs could be distinguished physically by rows of low-cost, often jerry-built homes lining the streets that usually began at a 90-degree angle to a main highway, which itself might begin in the nearby city and continue on a straight line toward the state border. Often these major service highways were accompanied by an interurban streetcar line. With streetcars, busses, and private cars, the growing workers suburbs were well served in their transportation needs. Systems of transfers blossomed. The various forms of physical separation between the old and the new are mostly obvious; the difference sociologists notice are changes in place, including workplace commutation, greatly lengthened and time consuming; change of home styles, neighborhood, community; and what has been noted above as "familiars," many of which are subjective, hardly noticed or taken for granted, such as a vine-covered fence marking property ownership. Songs decrying the loss of homesteads are, of course, common in all languages. But new attachments to home, neighborhood, friends, and local institutions are eventually rebuilt "in the sticks." The relevant question for sociologists is the extent to which all these changes through the decades have affected ethnicity, the repairability of old social bonds, and the construction of new.

A Case of Social and Geographical Mobility

The following case example of ethnic descent, marriage, and occupation is drawn from the history and genealogy of one of the authors. It is meant to exemplify the rapid mixing of ethnicity and occupational mobility in an urban/suburban context.

> Gustav and Anne, immigrants, arrived in Cleveland, Ohio, in 1880 and moved into the city's major German settlement. Gus was a skilled craftsman, a cooper. His wife was, all her life, a housewife.
>
> The couple had three children. Two sons went through grade school, as did the daughter. All three married Germans from the area. The sons became skilled workers in a steel wire mill. The daughter's husband also worked there, and the daughter became a housewife, as did the marrying-in wives.
>
> The two sons and daughter of Gustav and Anne had a total of three spouses, and later ten children, all of whom were German on both sides of the family. As the second-generation descendants married and started families, two moved to rural suburbs and one farther east from the German settlement, almost to a suburb.

Of the ten children in the third generation, three were female, two of whom became skilled in service and business; the third earned a college degree and became a professional. Three males became skilled workmen and went through high school, and four became professionals. The husbands of the three females became skilled service or businessmen. The wives of the seven males all had work careers, mainly in skilled services or business. Two became professionals.

In the fourth generation, all sixteen descendants and spouses have had advanced careers based mostly on college and graduate school training. Since the third generation, no females became "housewives only." One descendant became a skilled craftsperson, one worked in sales, six were or are in skilled service and business, and the other eight were or are professionals. Gus and Anne would have been proud!

But their pride may have been tempered by the fact that although their sons and daughters married Germans, none of the third generation "marrying in" were Germans. Rather, the spouses from the outside were Polish, Italian, Irish, English-American, and one half-German. Gus and Anne would have been more than satisfied by the fact that all those descendants became professionals and/or skilled service and businesspersons, even if the trade of cooper got lost among the generations.

Eventually the "sticks" became suburbs that are all now incorporated and sit cheek by jowl with no open land in between. Currently a few light rail lines connect some suburbs, bus service is patchy, and most suburbanites, who take their ethnicity lightly, are multiple car owners and build their own environments around lawns and electronic technologies. Much like the "old" and "new" European immigrations, internal movements within the United States, particularly in the period between the two world wars, have also had an "old" and "new" character. Suburbanization in contemporary times has little to do with the "sticks."

ETHNIC IMMIGRATION SINCE 1965

Social scientists writing about periods of change in American immigrant history will likely not use the break-off period of the year 2000 but instead may well start at 1965, when Congress passed the Hart-Cellar Amendments to the Immigration and Nationality Acts of 1920 and 1924. This radical legislation abolished the national origin system and all restrictions against Asian and Pacific people. An unrealistic quota of 120,000 persons a year from the Western Hemisphere was established, and preference was given to those with occupational skills judged to be needed in this country (Chilman, 1993; La Porte, 1977). The nation had already experienced a ten-year surge and ordinarily would have been ready for a lull. Not only was the quota immediately breached, but the tradition of surges and lulls ended abruptly, and by 1989 the annual figure had climbed to 507,000 (Beck, 1996:40–41). After another seven years—and counting legal immigrants, including students on visas (many overstaying), and a realistic estimate of illegal immigrants—the total for 1996 was at least a million![6]

---

[6]In February 1997, an estimated 11 million legal immigrants were residing in the United States, most of whom were working or were in families in which the head of the household works. Most of these wanted to and were trying to become citizens; they faced, however, a five-year residence requirement and an examination in English. Many would remain legal noncitizens. A federal law passed in 1996 makes legal immigrants who are not citizens, including those working and paying taxes, largely ineligible for food stamps, cash welfare, Medicaid, and disability. Of the 11 million legal immigrants (about 4 percent of the country's population), about 1.4 million receive some form of welfare aid. Their ineligibility for federal benefits will shift responsibility for providing aid to the states (*Arizona Daily Star*, February 9, 1997). According to the first official estimate from the Immigration and Naturalization Service in four years, added to the legal immigrant population are 5 million immigrants living illegally in the United States. About 40 percent live in California, which together with Texas, New York, Florida, Illinois, New Jersey, and Arizona account for 83 percent of the illegal immigrants. More than half are of Mexican origin. El Salvador, Guatemala, Canada, and Haiti were the other major countries of origin (*Arizona Daily Star*, February 8, 1997). These figures double those of 1993, helping to shore up the argument that the problem of undocumented immigrants in America has dangerously worsened.

Granting the fact that the rate of immigrant growth, as a percentage of the total population of the United States, remains no worse than during previous surges, some view this gross number with alarm, pointing to specific impact areas such as Miami, Manhattan, Anaheim, San Diego, San Francisco, Minneapolis-St. Paul, and large agricultural areas where extra migratory workers by the thousands can drive down wages and displace established laborers. Organized labor groups have always felt trepidation about what seems to them the hardest of hard-to-organize newcomers. Other interest groups work in the opposite direction, and one critical example might be the relatively recent boost of Irish immigrant quotas, described by Beck (1996:41):

> In 1990, after years of protests from citizens that the immigration numbers were too high, Congress approved what might be called the "Irish-Booster Wave." Congress approved the huge boost incongruously just before the nation sank into an economic recession.

What seems more inglorious than incongruous was the fact that the Irish-American members of Congress seeking legislation to greatly increase Irish admissions found it necessary "to accept all manner of promises that helped other special interest groups, and ballooned the total immigration numbers by 30 to 40 percent" (Beck, 1996:41).

What is most evident here are that the ties between the life chances of the immigrant, the direction of his or her ethnic group, and the ebb and flow of interest group involvement are virtually inextricable. And, as we continue into the early years of the new century, the prospects for meaningful and workable change do not seem all that bright. Some are not that concerned. Sanford J. Ungar writes (1995:20):

> Since World War II, a much broader range of people have come to live in the United States than ever before. The laws have changed, and the doors have opened wider once more—at least temporarily. But now the people seeking economic or political refuge and human fulfillment has [sic] grown dramatically, many of these immigrants look different[,] sound different, and may dress and eat differently from what we have come to regard as typically "American." At first, some immigrant groups may seem far more difficult to assimilate into America's daily routine than most of us think our own ancestors must have been. . . . Despite whatever American customs they begin to observe, once these newcomers reach critical mass, they may try to hold on to and cherish their cultural distinctiveness and separateness as long as possible. They may choose to remain quietly apart from the crowd, to resist being smothered by the materialism and high-tech consumerism they see on television and their children bring home from school. Often this means that they continue to speak the language they brought with them and make a special effort to pass it on to their children and grandchildren.

Yet Ungar goes on to say that with the dream of economic success and financial independence and of being citizens, living without fear in a democratic country, immigrants soon began to see themselves as Americans, an intangible but self-fulfilling feeling. He continues: "The great ethnic, racial, and linguistic diversity among the new immigrants is probably the main factor causing the old sacred melting-pot image of America finally to give way to something more realistic, like a mosaic or a salad bowl" (1995:20).

Ungar's term to define the ethnic environment of new America is "benign multiculturalism" (1995:21). Obviously, before we can use this concept intelligently, we must have more than a passing awareness of the multiplicity of cultures, particularly the new ones that are contributing to expansion of traditional American society.

Asians, Indians, and Pacific Islanders

Who are the new immigrants, and what in general can be said about them—particularly the cultures embraced, evaluated, and changed in the interminable process of family interaction and fusion of kith and kin? We can think of at least a dozen Asian countries whose names, if not people, are familiar: Bangladesh, Cambodia, China, India, Japan, Korea, Laos, Pakistan, Philippines, Taiwan, Thailand; Burma, of course, could be added, along with Malaysia, the Hmong people (without a country), and a generous number of Pacific Island countries.

People from these countries are settling, sojourning, and studying in the United States. They include mostly legal immigrants, many political refugees, and not a small number who have paid thousands of dollars to be smuggled into the country. More than half have a good education and would like to improve it. Some find employment hard to come by and will work harder for less, to the dismay of long-settled Americans. They will live several families to a room and eat sparingly to save the money needed to open a small shop. While they have a record of success in climbing the economic ladder, some who come as refugees are in effect supplicants, with as many as one out of seven living at or below the poverty line. Wherever they are, the newcomers are likely to be in groups and among relatives. They will inevitably speak their native language at home (Asian Indians are an exception), and even a third or so will admit to speaking English poorly. Although virtually no first generation would or could speak English as immigrants, those in the third generation today are almost totally absorbed into, and making exceptional contributions to, the culture and prospects of America.

Circular Migration: The Hispanic Example

In his comprehensive *Migrations and Cultures: A World View,* Thomas Sowell (1996) brings together economics and social history in describing large-scale, repetitive movements of people who live in one place but migrate to and work in other countries. Some may remain and form settlements, but the majority have a circular work history. They are not refugees, they have almost a certain anchorage when they migrate, and they have a home, a place to which they are almost certain to return. Understanding migratory worker patterns puts a new face on current immigration as a social problem.

From Asia and the Pacific islands the movements to America took place in the past half-century and were undertaken with the intent to stay. Hispanics in America, some of whose ancestors might have been living here for centuries, include those who have come to stay, some who cross and recross the border repeatedly, and an interesting and large segment whose peregrinations are routinely circular. Those in this last group live in their homes in Mexican towns and villages but spend many if not most of the spring, summer, and fall months moving from the rich agricultural valleys along the Rio Grande to states bordering Canada, working in fields and orchards. Writes Mark Potok (1996) in *USA TODAY*:

> The vast majority of Mexicans crossing the border into [the] United States are migrants, not immigrants who intend to stay permanently. Like immigrants, many of the migrants cross the border illegally. But they come here to help harvest crops, and they maintain permanent residences in Mexico and return there when they can.

Migratory workers have a "limbo" status. Without migratory work, which pays Mexican laborers seven to ten times as much as they make in their home country, the costs of fruit and vegetables would soar in the United States. Thus they are necessary to big business agriculture, but they no longer have "guest worker" status as they had during World War II and, as noted, they have permanent homes in Mexico. All in all, of those crossing the border illegally about 70 percent will return in two years.

In the rest of the country many non-Hispanic agricultural laborers live in labor camps, using these for a base of departure as they move in and out of places of work. They may be lucky just to have a home base; but when they do, most still live in rural poverty. Florida provides a good example of the sheltering of labor camp migratory workers; for circular migrants, Texas or California. The circular work of Hispanics may or may not be better for families left behind than for those who go along and do harvesting alongside husbands and parents. The latter choice offers more money per family, life together, and a little more independence from work bosses who "look after" the migrants' needs, housing, food, and the rest. For children, however, the constant movement from school district to school district is not a good way to get an education, but at least one way to live in a bilingual world.

CONCLUSION

The concept of America as a Christian, ethnically European nation with certain core cultural values now being threatened by those coming from other cultures is erroneous, says Francis Fukuyama. "In contrast to other West European democracies, or Japan, the American national identity has never been linked directly to ethnicity or religion" (1993:154). Rather, there is a common American culture whose elements are visible today, including belief in the Constitution and the individualist–egalitarianism principles underlying it.

The notion that immigrants' family values are discordant and erosive does not stand up to examination. The social pathologies of American center cities and the concurrent collapse of family structure are not a foreign import. As Fukuyama points out, third world family values have remained relatively strong and remain so wherever immigrant ethnic groups are together. It is not the family values that are collapsing in third world countries but the local economies that are being swept aside by invasive large-scale, internationally based capitalistic enterprises (Greider, 1997).

Given rising birth rates and internal migration to new foreign-owned or controlled factories, a surplus of labor and the introduction of cost-cutting measures almost inevitably follow. Employment in third world countries may, ironically, lead to unemployment, and cost cutting to overproduction. The excess of labor, particularly low-skilled labor, is a major cause of migration, uninformed and undirected (Greider, 1997:44–52). Unskilled migrants are the new *lumpenproletariat*.

But the labor-seeking emigrants do not leave behind family values any more than language and other aspects of their culture. Emigration nearly always involves some separation of kin, but it does not mean family ties are ipso facto lost forever. For Asians in particular, work is seen as enterprise, even if to indigenous workers it can only be defined as toil. It would be difficult to define the enterprise of emigrants that has as its goal the growth and rising fortune of an extended family as somehow a dilution of American family values. Rather, networks of communication arise, permitting families and relatives to keep in touch, and great efforts will be expended to bring them together. Informal networks are boosted by formal agencies and federal offices. As the body of immigration law swells, so do the number of immigration lawyers. Things may move slowly, particularly for emigrants seeking refugee status, with hearing officers overwhelmed by applicants. Under these circumstances, it is hard to fault emigrants for their ethnic cohesion, or family members and extended kin for their solidarity.

When center cities overflow with an incredible number of emigrants, who willy-nilly find themselves displacing each other person by person, ethnic group by ethnic group, in hotel service, parking houses, or chicken processing, it is not difficult to understand the rising antagonism among the new groups. It is at this time that both third world and indigenous groups, particularly the young, begin to question traditional American values.

References

Barker-Benfield, G. 1976. *The Horrors of the Half-Known Life.* New York: Harper & Row.

Beck, R. 1996. *The Case Against Immigration: The Moral, Economic, Social, and Environmental Reasons for Reducing U.S. Immigration Back to Traditional Levels.* New York, London: W. W. Norton.

Braudel, F. 1982. *The Wheels of Commerce, Vol. 4: Civilization and Capitalism.* New York: Harper & Row.

Brimelow, P. 1996. *Alien Nation: Common Sense About America's Immigration Disaster.* New York: Harper Perennial.

Campisi, P. 1948. "Ethnic Family Patterns: The Italian Family in the United States." *American Journal of Sociology 53,* 443–449.

Chilman, C. 1993. "Hispanic Families in the United States." In H. P. McAdoo (Ed.), *Family Ethnicity: Strength in Diversity* (pp. 141–163). Newbury Park, CA: Sage.

Duncan, H. 1933. *Immigration and Assimilation.* Lexington, MA: D. C. Heath.

Fast, H. 1977. *The Immigrants.* Boston: Houghton Mifflin.

Feldstein, S., and L. Costello (Eds.). 1974. *The Ordeal of Assimilation.* Garden City, NJ: Doubleday Anchor Books.

Fukuyama, F. 1994. "Immigrants and Family Values." In N. Mills (Ed.), *Arguing Immigration* (pp. 151–168). New York: Simon & Schuster.

Habenstein, R., and C. Mindel. 1981. "The American Ethnic Family: Protean and Adaptive." In C. Mindel and R. Habenstein (Eds.), *Ethnic Families in America: Patterns and Variations* (2nd ed., pp. 417–432). New York and Oxford, England: Elsevier.

Jones, M. 1976. *Destination America.* New York: Holt, Rinehart and Winston.

Kennedy, P. 1994. *Preparing for the Twenty-First Century.* New York: Vantage Books. (See the excellently chosen comprehensive bibliography, including institutional works, government publications, and authored works.)

Knapp, V. 1976. *Europe in the Era of Social Transformation: 1700–Present.* Englewood Cliffs, NJ: Prentice Hall.

La Porte, B. 1977. "Visibility of the New Immigrants." *Society 14*(6), 18–22.

McAdoo, H. (Ed.) 1993. *Family Ethnicity: Strength in Diversity.* Newbury Park, CA: Sage.

McLaughlin, V. 1978. "Patterns of Work and Family Organization: Buffalo's Italians." *Journal of Interdisciplinary History 2* (1971), 299–314. Reprinted in M. Gordon (Ed.), *The American Family in Social-Historical Perspective* (pp. 347–372). New York: St. Martin's Press.

Mills, N. (Ed.) 1994. *Arguing Immigration: The Debate Over the Face of America.* New York: Simon & Schuster (Touchstone Books).

Park, R., and H. Miller. 1921. *Old World Traits Transplanted.* New York: Harper & Row.

Roberts, K. 1920. *Why Europe Leaves Home: A True Account of the Reasons Which Cause Central Europeans to Overrun America.* New York: Bobbs-Merrill.

Ross, E. 1914. *The Old World and the New.* Englewood Cliffs, NJ: Prentice Hall.

Ryan, M. 1982. *The Empire of the Mother.* New York: Haworth Press.

Saloutos, T. 1964. "Exodus USA." In O. Ander (Ed.), *In the Trek of the Immigrants: Essays Presented to Carl Wittke* (pp. 197–215). Rock Island, IL: Augustana College Library.

Shillony, Ben-Ami. 1991. *The Jews and the Japanese.* Rutland, VT: Charles T. Tuttle.

Sinclair, U. 1905. *The Jungle.* [Reprinted 1960.] New York: New American Library.

Sowell, T. 1996. *Migrations and Culture: A World View.* New York: Basic Books.

Taylor, P. 1971. *The Distant Magnet: European Emigration to the USA.* New York: Harper & Row.

Tender, L. 1981. "The Working-Class Daughter, 1900–1930." In M. Albin and D. Cavallo (Eds.), *Family Life in America, 1600–2000* (pp. 184–202). St. James, NY: Revisionary Press.

Ungar, S. 1995. *Fresh Blood: The New American Immigrants.* New York: Simon & Schuster.

3

■ ■ ■

The Irish American Family

Patricia J. Fanning

INTRODUCTION

The Irish have been immigrating to America for over two hundred years. As of 2008 over 36.3 million residents of the United States claim Irish ancestry, second in number only to those of German ancestry. In addition, those with Irish ancestry have spread themselves across the nation with Irish being among the top-five ancestries in every state except Hawaii and New Mexico (U.S. Census, 2011). The length of time the Irish have been arriving and the sheer number identifying themselves as Irish Americans make it difficult to generalize about commonalities and characteristics. The assimilation of the Irish into American culture and lifestyle has been extensive. This chapter aims to explore the history of the Irish immigration and identify at least a few significant aspects of the Irish experience in America.

HISTORICAL BACKGROUND

Immigration

The influx of Irish immigrants to America began in the eighteenth century when some Ulster Presbyterian settlers lost their leases due to a combination of rising rents and crop failures and made their way across the Atlantic. For the remainder of that century, this Ulster migration continued at the steady rate of three to five thousand per year. Still, as historian Kerby Miller observes, even then, "if one considers the regional, socioeconomic, cultural, and doctrinal differences that prevailed in eighteenth century Presbyterian Ulster itself, then the possible variations and permutations among the American immigrants are practically endless" (Miller, 2000:76; Connolly, 2004). Emigration from other parts of Ireland rose following a serious potato crop failure in 1740–1741, and by the end of the century immigrants were arriving in America from nearly every county in Ireland (O'Day, 2000:98). These eighteenth-century immigrants, mostly men, included not only small farmers and tradesmen but also indentured servants and convict transportees.

After 1815, emigration from Ireland continued at a steady rate, topping a total of 400,000 by 1845. These immigrants who were tradesmen, fishermen, shopkeepers, domestic servants, and small farmers also originated from nearly every county in Ireland. Once in the United States, these early immigrants were slow to set down roots and become part of the American fabric. The seeming reluctance to become citizens—the average Irish immigrant still resided in the United States for close to ten years before becoming naturalized—may be the result of the itinerancy of their lives; most worked at the often temporary employment of mills, labored in the transient road and canal construction camps, or took up the seafaring life of sailors or mariners (O'Day, 2000:99). Despite these realities, this early migration enabled the formation of a somewhat extensive network of Irish American citizens, particularly in New England, by the 1830s. As if a harbinger of things to come, by the mid-1830s an increasing number of immigrants were also women, Irish speaking, and poor (Adams, 1932; Fanning, 1997; Handlin, 1979; Horgan, 1998; Miller, 1985; Miller, 2000; O'Day, 2000; Shannon, 1963).

It was, of course, the Great Hunger of the late 1840s that changed everything and brought to America "the unexpected and unplanned mass diasporas of the Famine years" for which no one was prepared (O'Day, 2000:110). Beginning with the ruination of the potato crop over one-third of Ireland in 1845, crop failures continued each year through the final universal blight of 1848 in which virtually the entire potato harvest was lost. The Great Famine that followed, the result of natural, cultural, and political forces, drove close to 1.5 million primarily poverty-stricken Catholic Irish to America between the years 1846 and 1855. For the remainder of the nineteenth century, the incredible migration continued at the rate of over 500,000 people every decade (Byron, 1999; Fanning, 1997; Horgan, 1998; Kenny, 2000; Schrier, 1958). What is more, it was a migration not only of the poor but also of the young. During the third quarter of the nineteenth century, over 60 percent of emigrants were between the ages of fifteen and thirty-five; for the rest of the century, the proportion in that age bracket was never less than 80 percent (Horgan, 1998; Schrier, 1958). In addition, between 1846 and 1875 nearly half the people fleeing Ireland were women, a pattern very different from other ethnic migrations (Diner, 1983; Horgan, 1998; Nolan, 1989).

The historical patterns of family life and their disruption by the Great Famine are important to an understanding of the distinct characteristics of the nineteenth-century Irish immigrant. Historically, the family system in Ireland was patrilineal, tracing its descent through the father. It was also bilateral, with marriage uniting two families instead of absorbing one into the other. Legally, throughout most of the eighteenth century, British-imposed penal laws mandated that land, whether owned, or more likely rented, had to be divided among all sons equally. This prevented the accumulated acquisition of large tracts of land by Catholics. When these laws were rescinded, the Irish farmer reverted to a stem-family system in which one son inherited the land or, if there were no sons, one of the daughters. This allowed for the evolution of a patriarchal system in which the father was the unquestioned head of the family and his sons remained "boys" until the father retired or died. At that point, his designated heir would become head of the family (Arensberg and Kimball, 1968; Greeley, 1972; Horgan, 1998; Kenny, 2000).

This practice resulted in enforced celibacy and delayed marriage of the designated heir; the migration of unmarried, non-inheriting siblings; and familism, which placed the family's welfare above any one individual (Schrier, 1958). Familism, in turn, fostered a strong sense of sibling loyalty, characterized by emigrant siblings sending money home to help support the family members they had left behind. There was not necessarily an emotional closeness among siblings but, rather, a loyalty and responsibility to the family as a whole.

Since Arensberg and Kimball in *Family and Community in Ireland* (1968) make no mention of the Irish matriarch, instead focusing on the domination of the rural father, sociologist Andrew

Greeley (1972) postulates that the power of the Irish mother emerged in urban areas. If a family shifted to an urban environment in Ireland, and later to the United States, the wife was frequently more employable than her husband. This fact diminished the husband's role as provider and leader and increased the importance and power of the Irish mother. Greeley (1972) also cites the research of Herbert Gutman who contended that the number of absent fathers was higher among Irish immigrants than for other ethnic groups. Thus, the mother-supported, matriarchal family system was more likely to exist among the Irish in America.

In addition, the subordinate status of women within the patriarchal system, combined with the family's inability to provide for more than one dowry, resulted in single women who were more autonomous than their counterparts among other ethnic groups (Diner, 1983). This made it possible for unmarried female children to leave home, find employment, or emigrate independently.

The result of this continual population loss beginning in the 1840s was devastating to Ireland. Prior to 1845, the population of Ireland had been nearly 9 million. By the time the first immigration restriction laws were enacted in the United States in 1921, more than 4.6 million had come to America, leaving Ireland with an unprecedented net decrease in population, a pattern that was not reversed until the mid-twentieth century (Sarbaugh, 1991).

In the 1920s, the United States enacted immigration restriction legislation that set quotas on the number of immigrants allowed from individual countries and required that visas be obtained from the American consulate in the originating country. After these restrictions were enacted in the 1920s, Irish immigration to the United States declined steadily. The Great Depression of the 1930s and the Second World War in the following decade further discouraged immigration. Still, in Ireland, the patterns of late inheritance and delayed marriage that began in the nineteenth century continued. Industrialization also stagnated, and new agricultural techniques tended to be the kind of labor-saving devices that reduced the need for manual labor as well. These two aspects of Irish life thereby continued to encourage emigration—but primarily to Britain (Kenny, 2000). A steady but small number of immigrants continued to come to America in the next few decades via a chain migration fostered by family members who had arrived earlier.

The 1970s brought social, legislative, religious, and cultural changes to Ireland. An unprecedented return migration to Ireland took place, attracted by improved academic opportunities, a rising standard of living, and a nascent Irish tourist industry (Almeida, 2001; Kenny, 2000). During the 1980s, however, a new influx of Irish immigrants arrived in America, forced out of their homeland by a debt-ridden economy, high unemployment, and oppressive taxation. The "New Irish," as they were dubbed, were a diverse group, stratified by class, education, and legal status. Although accurate statistics on the population were hard to come by, some studies claim as many as 250,000 Irish immigrants, both legal and illegal, made the journey to America during that decade, and anecdotal evidence backed up those numbers (Almeida, 2001; Sarbaugh, 1991). Those with a higher level of education were more likely to have green cards, thus allowing them to arrive through legal channels (Almeida, 2001).

The Irish economy recovery of the 1990s—the "Celtic Tiger"—coupled with progress on solutions to the Troubles and the contentious political front, resulted in another, larger return migration, but Ireland's membership in the European Union and the worldwide economic uncertainly of recent years, have brought new, even more complicated economic, political, and cultural travails to Ireland's shores. As in the 1980s, many of the Irish who now immigrate to the United States may well be illegal, but their numbers are relatively small. In addition, new schisms have arisen within the Irish in America. As Linda Dowling Almeida points out, "Many of the Irish, now coming as they do from a modern, cosmopolitan society, find it difficult to assimilate into an established Irish American community whose perceptions of Ireland, Irish people, and emigration to America is grounded in a pre-modern society" (2001:82).

Historically, the experience of the Irish, particularly in the urban Northeast—including ghettoes, widespread discrimination, conflict, and delayed upward social mobility—has been well documented. However, Irish immigrants and Irish Americans who populated other regions in the United States encountered a different experience. As Greeley notes, "There were more opportunities in the Midwestern cities than the East Coast cities for the Irish, and perhaps also more Irishmen who were more likely to seize the opportunities" (1981:117). And their advancement into the middle class was accelerated as well: Nativism was not so deeply entrenched, and the economy was more dynamic in the Midwest (McCaffrey, 2000). As a result, the Midwest Irish gained an educational advantage over their Eastern counterparts by the early decades of the twentieth century (Greeley, 1981).

Similarly, the Irish who settled in California and Montana seemed to thrive on the frontier and rapidly became successful in all walks of life (Dezell, 2000; Emmons, 1990; Greeley, 1981). (Butte had a higher percentage of residents of Irish descent in 1900 than did Boston, New York, Philadelphia, Chicago, or San Francisco.) As far as the South was concerned, the Irish arrived in the 1700s and quickly became a distinct minority. Once again, their experiences differed depending on their Protestant (Charleston, SC) or Catholic (Savannah, GA) roots and social networks. Savannah, Georgia, for example, has been celebrating St. Patrick's Day since 1824 (Dezell, 2000; Gleeson, 2001; Gleeson & Buttimer, 2005; Miller, 1985).

In any event, today more than 40 million Americans claim Irish descent. Many of these are third- and fourth-generation Irish Americans, and they are spread across the country. They know little about their ethnic roots except what they learn through the hazy lens of Hollywood, memoir, and folklore.

Irish American Family Characteristics

Because of the size, scope, length, and diversity of the Irish immigration, any attempt to generalize about the behavior and attitudes of the Irish in America as a whole is nearly impossible. Yet those analyses that do exist capture an ethnic group filled with contradictions (Dezell, 2000; Greeley, 1972; Horgan, 1998; Kenny, 2000; McGoldrick, 1996).

Traditionally, the American Irish family has been depicted as more authoritarian and less affectionate than other ethnic groups, with the mother playing a subsidiary and somewhat subservient role to the male head of the household (Greeley, 1981). Yet even within this perspective, in most Irish American families the mother is a very important figure, providing stability, strength, and service to her children and spouse. She is often seen as the pragmatic, morally superior partner, who tolerates the childlike delusions of her husband. She is a religious, loving, and loyal mother. The father, on the other hand, often remains a shadowy, indistinct figure. Sometimes literally absent, at work or elsewhere, even when he is at home he seems to be one step removed from the center of family activity. A silent presence, he leaves the majority of the discipline and planning to the mother (Dezell, 2000; Greeley, 1972; Horgan, 1998; McGoldrick, 1996). In old age, these roles change very little. The mother remains the center of the family network and glides effortlessly into the role of matriarch over a burgeoning number of grandchildren. The father, if still present, remains somewhat solitary but is seen as gentle, mild mannered, and good humored and is known for his reminiscing and storytelling. In James T. Farrell's (1940, 1953) O'Neill-O'Flaherty pentalogy, Tom O'Flaherty provides an example of this elusive, aged, fanciful Irish man. The mother–son bond is particularly intense, with the Irish mother doting on her sons and expecting her daughters to do the same (Greeley, 1972; McGoldrick, 1996). Yet the Irish matriarch transmits to her daughters the will, courage, and spirit to strike out on their own.

As noted earlier, in contrast to other ethnic groups the rate of emigration of single women from Ireland was quite high in the nineteenth century. During some periods, it was even higher than that of men (Diner, 1983; Kennedy, 1973; McGoldrick, 1996; Nolan, 1989). This independence and self-sufficiency were carried over to America where delayed marriage and singlehood continued to be common. A large proportion of Irish American women seemingly were unwilling to give up their economic and emotional self-reliance for marriage and partnership (Diner, 1983; Greeley, 1972; Kenny, 2000; McGoldrick, 1996; Nolan, 1989). As McGoldrick (1996:557–558) comments, "Irish women have generally had little expectation of or interest in being taken care of by a man. Their hopes have been articulated much less in romantic terms than in aspirations for self-sufficiency." Family life seems to support these goals, with Irish families often encouraging the education of daughters as well as sons (Greeley, 1972; Nolan, 1989; Nolan, 2004), although daughters "knew that the resources of the family would go first to their brothers" (Horgan, 1998:55). And, as a further acknowledgement of their importance within the Irish family, the unmarried daughter, sibling, or aunt makes significant contributions as a role model to young girls, nucleus of the extended family, and caregiver to aging parents (Connolly, 2004; Horgan, 1998; Kane, 1968; Kenny, 2000; McGoldrick, 1996).

The American Irish woman's tendency to stand alone is also reflective of a culture that is less focused on romance than that of the United States in general. For quite some time Ireland had the highest age at marriage and the lowest marriage rate of any nation in the world (Kennedy, 1973). Charlotte Ikels (1988:102) notes, "Historically, singlehood has been, and to a lesser extent remains, an honorable estate in Ireland." In addition, the Irish place less emphasis on romance as the foundation for marriage (Connolly, 2004; McGoldrick, 1996; Miller, 1985). This unsentimental attitude has been traced into the second generation of Irish in America (Heer, 1961), although in other respects there was considerable assimilation by that time (Greeley, 1972; Horgan, 1998).

Once married, the American Irish are superficially talkative, hospitable, and good humored, but they do not encourage intimacy. Reticent about their emotions, they tend to avoid effusive demonstrations of tenderness, often relying on humor, teasing, and ridicule to express affection (Barrabee and von Mering, 1953; Dezell, 2000; Greeley, 1972; Spiegel, 1971). Family ties are seemingly weak, with relationships between husband and wife, parents and children, and among siblings loose and apparently indifferent (Greeley, 1972; Zborowski, 1969). Withdrawal and distancing from intense interactions are seen as solutions to interpersonal problems (McGoldrick, 1996). Couples, children, and siblings drift away from one another, usually without causing trauma or distress, in what Mark Zborowski (1969:227) has called "the centrifugal tendency of the Irish family."

Here is yet another paradox. There is evidence to support the contention that sibling loyalty is extraordinarily high among the Irish American populations (Greeley, 1972; Harris, 1989), as it was in Ireland itself; however, that loyalty appears to be more dutiful than emotional. As Greeley (1972:115) points out, "In many second- and third-generation Irish American families, it seems clear that the siblings are not friends . . . that is to say, often they do not have common interests, [and] they are not especially eager to spend time with one another." Yet, their sense of obligatory familism requires that they show up on holidays, special occasions, and in times of trouble and conflict (Greeley, 1972; Horgan, 1998). This behavior is a significant characteristic of extended family relationships as well, with cousins, aunts, and uncles seeing one another only on holidays or, most notably, at wakes and weddings (Greeley, 1972; Kane, 1968; McGoldrick, 1996). As McGoldrick (1996:559) explains it, "The Irish have a tremendous respect for personal boundaries, are enormously sensitive to each other's right to privacy, and will make strong efforts not to impose or intrude on one another."

It is not merely a sense of privacy but also pride that causes this reluctance. Horgan (1998:56) recollects that "household members were ambivalent about giving and seeking help, however, for household self-sufficiency was a matter of great pride." Similarly, McGoldrick (1996:558) asserts that "Family members tend not to rely on one another as a source of support, and when they have a problem, they may even see it as an added burden and embarrassment for the family to find out." Elaine McGivern (1979) in her examination of ethnic Irish in metropolitan Pittsburgh agrees that Irish American families are reluctant to seek assistance. "The reason is a matter of preserving the family's pride. What was indicated by some in the interviews was that it was very important for the family not to be made to feel that they were accepting a form of charity." McGivern's interviewees acknowledged that "it's easier to give aid than to receive it" (1979:111). Thus partners, parents, siblings, and children seem to derive and expect little emotional support from one another. Although this attitude may develop feelings of independence and self-reliance, it may also result in isolation and loneliness (Dezell, 2000; McGivern, 1979; McGoldrick, 1996; Zborowski, 1969).

CHANGES AND ADAPTATIONS

The Catholic Church

The history of the Catholic Church in Ireland is long, complicated, and varied with married priests and bishops, lax church regulations, and a pagan folklore all leaving their mark. The Irish Catholicism that was known to the early immigrants was largely a counter-Reformation phenomenon. During the Cromwell years, priests were hunted, kept on the move, and took great risks to hold religious services at night and in secret (Greeley, 1972; Kenny, 2000). As Greeley points out, with the restoration of Charles II, priests were "the only successful resisters of the Cromwellian tyranny, [and] were the acknowledged leaders of their hungry, miserable, persecuted people" (1972:81–82). There was a bond forged between clergy and parishioners at that time that was, some argue, further codified after the Famine when a devastated people tried to building a new identity: "The Irish came to the United States with a stubborn, dogged, counter-Reformation form of Irish-Catholicism, about the only explicit cultural form left them by their tragic history" (Larkin in Greeley, 1972:81–84).

Particularly in urban enclaves where the Irish were greeted with disdain by the native-born populations, the parish was the central unifying force of the neighborhood. As Ellen Skerrett notes, "the parish was far and away the most important institution in the lives of Irish immigrants and their children and grandchildren throughout the nineteenth century and well into the twentieth" (1997:21). The parish became a community of families and it provided its members with education, recreation, entertainment, social support, friendship, and spouses (Almeida, 2001; Greeley, 1972; Horgan, 1998; Kenny, 2000; O'Connor, 1995; Skerrett, 1997). In urban areas in particular, the unique proximity within a small geographical area of home, church, school, and even work helped create this distinctive community. Because of this, the parish was used as a setting by many Irish American writers, including James T. Farrell, Finley Peter Dunne, Edwin O'Connor, Maureen Howard, Elizabeth Cullinane, William Kennedy, and Alice McDermott.

The parish also provided a means of advancement for Irish and Irish American men and women. Scores of young men were encouraged to enter the priesthood while women found that a religious order was an effective means for single women to gain an education and acquire a position where their talents could be utilized. Through their combined devotion and diligence, institutional networks including church, school, hospital, orphanage, and settlement house were established. While Jane Addams garnered praise for her work among Chicago's immigrants in the 1890s, for example, her Hull-House was itself dwarfed by the massive Holy Family Church (1860) and St. Ignatius College (1870) only a few blocks away. Each of these institutions fostered the education and advancement of thousands and provided assistance to the poor, sick, and elderly of the neighborhood (Skerrett, 2000). Irish and Irish Americans were at the forefront of these institutions. From their arrival in America, the Irish created institutions that paralleled those of the dominant community; the parish became the epicenter of many of these endeavors.

Throughout the first half of the twentieth century, the Irish dominated the Catholic Church in America. Most estimates agree that approximately 12 million Catholics were in the United States by 1900, 15 million by 1915, and close to 40 million by the 1950s—the majority Irish or Irish American (Kenny, 2000). And although generations of Irish Americans had become assimilated into the cultural mainstream of America, an anti-Catholic (mainly anti-Irish) bias still existed (Dezell, 2000; Greeley, 1972; Kenny, 2000; O'Connor, 1995). As Kenny notes, "It has been remarked justly that anti-Catholicism was the one intellectually respectable form of bigotry in the U.S. in the first half of the twentieth century" (2000:209). Through its network of institutions—most notably colleges, hospitals, and social service facilities—the Church continued to resist these remnants of prejudice.

In the 1960s and 1970s, the cultural landscape changed. It was a complex mixture of events and trends. First came an Irish American exodus from the urban enclaves into the suburbs. This shift in population was fueled primarily by upwardly mobile middle-class Irish Americans who, like their counterparts in many ethnic groups, followed the post–World War II corporate migration out of the inner city and chased the American Dream into the suburbs. In some cities, however, the influx of blacks and new immigrant groups into the urban neighborhoods contributed to what became known as the "white flight" (Kenny, 2000; O'Connor, 1995). For a time, the Catholic Church underwent a dramatic expansion in the suburbs, which resulted in a noteworthy church and school building boom. But the culture and sensibilities of the parishioners had changed. These churchgoers were more educated, decidedly middle class, and assimilated into American consumerism. In addition, they no longer felt the need to maintain insular institutions to protect them from the disdain of natives.

Then, the Second Vatican Council (1962–1965) enacted profound changes to the liturgy and day-to-day church life. The Mass was demystified—altars were turned to face the congregation, Latin was no longer spoken, people were expected to greet one another in a sign of peace, and Saturday Mass was introduced. And old habits were dismissed—for example, eating meat on Fridays was allowed, and confession became optional. The relaxation of the dogmatic, unquestioned authority of the Church resulted in a laity that splintered. People began to follow their own conscience on issues ranging from contraception to church attendance; tradition-bound priests and nuns dropped out or retired; liberals did away with their religious dress, became activists, and encouraged dissent. More and more, Catholics began to choose which aspects of the Church they wanted to follow; they became known as "Cafeteria-Catholics"(Dezell, 2000; Greeley, 1972; Greeley, 1999; Kenny, 2000). As Alan Wolfe, head of the Center for the Study of Religion and Society at Boston College, notes, "American Catholicism is a religion by itself. It sees the Vatican in an advisory capacity if anything, and most Catholics simply lead their lives and make their own moral decisions. Their Catholicism is very important to them, but they don't accept the church's teachings" (Dezell, 2000:178).

Third, the women's movement resulted in more pressure on the Church. Talented, intelligent women could obtain an education and enter other fields; they no longer relied on the Church or religious orders to provide intellectual challenges and managerial positions. Still, many stayed. As Dezell points out, "The majority of those who both manage and do the hands-on, day-to-day, nitty-gritty work of teaching and caretaking are Catholic sisters and laywomen, a disproportionate number of them of Irish descent. By the turn of the twenty-first century, 80% of jobs in Catholic parishes are held by women and women hold approximately half the diocesan, administrative, and professional positions in the U.S. Catholic Church" (2000:177). Their numbers continues to foster debate, particularly in the United States, about women's eligibility to join the priesthood (Dezell, 2000; Greeley, 1999; Kenny, 2000).

In addition, many of those who remained devoted to the Church's teachings were further rocked by the sexual abuse scandals that began to surface in the mid-1980s, gained momentum and headlines in the 1990s, and continue to haunt the Church and its hierarchy to this day.

American Irish Catholics disagree broadly today about gender, authority, and sexuality. Irish Americans' influence on and participation in the contemporary Catholic Church in the United States is an ever-evolving story.

Health and Illness

Health is of utmost importance to the Irish, and their views toward health and illness are predictable within the structure of the American Irish family. The profile of an Irish American patient that emerges from the sociological and medical data is of a stoic, passive person who presents with specific symptoms and/or dysfunction. With regard to psychosis and psychopathology, the Irish tolerate mental deviance, including delusions, hallucination, fantasy, and dreaming, far more readily than they tolerate emotional expressiveness, such as screaming, crying, and hostile action (McGoldrick, 1996; Opler and Singer, 1956; Ortiz, Simmons, and Hinton, 1999; Scheper-Hughes, 1987; Singer and Opler, 1956; Wylan and Mintz, 1976). Researchers also note that the Irish patient is a compliant but skeptical patient (Greeley, 1972; Lipton and Marbach, 1984; Suchman, 1964; Zborowski, 1969; Zola, 1966; Zola, 1973) who minimizes pain and accepts it without complaint.

According to Zola some patients even go so far as to qualify or deny the existence of pain altogether using phrases such as "It was more a throbbing than a pain" or "It's a pressure not really a pain" (1966:625). Researchers have also found that the Irish and Irish Americans also attempt to endure pain without doing anything to relieve it (Zborowski, 1969; Zola, 1966). Zborowski's (1969:193–194) Irish informants described two techniques for withstanding pain: relaxing and fighting. "Relaxing" consists of sitting quietly and moving only when the pain becomes unbearable. "Fighting pain" is more active and requires the patient to "Just grit your teeth and hang on." Both techniques are best employed when the patient is alone, hence the desire on the part of the Irish patient to withdraw when in pain. Although he ordinarily enjoys company, and Zborowski notes that the Irish patient "is not ashamed of being seen in pain," he would prefer "to suffer by himself" (1969:196). The researcher also comments on the use of the word *suffering* when speaking about pain. The word was used by almost every Irish American informant, thus leading Zborowski to contend that, for the Irish, the experience of pain is "an extremely complex process" and "the stoic behavior acquires a deeper and more dramatic character, for which the only adequate word is suffering—a word that implies time and anguish" (1969:196).

As a group, Irish Americans fear physical disability and internal disease, especially as they relate to their ability to work (Zborowski, 1969). It is this capacity to perform physical labor that indicates to them whether they are in good health or not (Cohler and Lieberman, 1979; McGoldrick, 1996). Thus, as they age, their self-esteem remains tied more to physical activity and ability and, in essence, self-sufficiency than it is in other ethnic groups. A poignant example of these patterns can be found in the O'Neill-O'Flaherty pentalogy of James T. Farrell. When Jim O'Neill suffers a stroke he returns to work, dragging his right foot and wearing glasses: "He would rather be dead than helpless. Well, thank God, he wasn't helpless. Even if he was impaired, he was still doing a full-time man's job, and doing it well" (1940:259). The ultimate blow to the man comes when his son Bill begins to support the family and Jim realizes "[h]is very presence was unnecessary . . . rob a man of his strength and his independence, and he might as well be dead" (1940:522).

When illness or disability strikes, the Irish are therefore more likely to see sickness as a private matter, something to be kept to themselves. Often, as noted earlier, the patient's family ties are weak; relationships between husband and wife, parents and children, and among siblings are loose, and the patient often apparently indifferent to them. Thus, partners, parents, siblings, and children derive and expect little emotional support from one another. Consequently they delay seeking treatment, even when it is obvious they need it, and they have difficulty communicating with one another about their ailments (Fitzpatrick and Barry, 1990; McGoldrick, 1996; Ortiz, Simmons, and Hinton, 1999; Zborowski, 1969; Zola, 1966, 1973).

Irving Zola (1966:627) attributes these attitudes to the restrictive life of the Irish: "Life was black and long-suffering, and the less said the better." He sees their understatement, restraint, and resignation as the defense mechanism "singularly most appropriate for their psychological and physical survival." Zola links these behaviors to the unique religious perspective of the Irish, a perspective dominated by sin, guilt, and fear of punishment and concludes, "Thus, when unexpected or unpleasant events take place, there is a search for what they did or must have done wrong" (1996:627–628). Farrell's characters once again demonstrate these beliefs. When Tom O'Flaherty begins to feel the pain that is eventually diagnosed as stomach cancer, he wracks his memory: "Was God punishing him for his sins? But there was never a sin, no, nary a sin he ever committed that he could think of that he hadn't confessed and been given absolution for" (1953:236).

Zola (1966) also sees the most common locations of medical complaints among the Irish—the eyes, ears, and throat—as symbolic. He sees these symptomatic locations as a physical manifestation of the patients' guilt over "what they should not have seen; what they should not have heard; and what they should not have said." When illness strikes, then, there is a tendency to believe it is punishment from God and must be accepted and endured alone, without complaint. The sense of suffering likewise has religious undertones. Zborowski (1969:235) despairs of his Irish patients, who, although worried and afraid of pain and illness, are "unable to share his emotions, anxieties, and fears with a close person who would understand them and offer some comfort and support."

Care of the Elderly

From the time the Irish began to arrive in America, they created cultural, political, social, and medical institutions that in many instances paralleled the institutions of the dominant community. Within that structure, formal caregiving and institutional arrangements to care for the elderly have always been acceptable. The research of Alfred Kutzik (1979) demonstrates that since Colonial times the aged members of ethnic mutual aid societies received benefits along with widows, orphans, and the sick. Initially, Irish Americans tried to take care of their own elderly in this fashion. Through fraternal or religious emigrant aid societies, the Irish offered financial assistance to the functionally independent aged. Another common practice was to board an elderly parent in a private third-party home for a fixed fee. This rather formal arrangement is consistent with the recognized Irish tendencies toward emotional and physical distance. As Seamus Metress (1985:19) points out, "Treatment rendered on a contract basis by a third party could be less stressful to the family, as well as the elderly parent, whose status and self-image might be transformed as a result of their dependent state."

Issues of privacy, emotional reticence, and the perception of independence are thus successfully avoided. It is far easier for the Irish to give and receive aid through a third-party than it is to articulate a direct expression of need and a reciprocal acknowledgement of love and support. Even recent data demonstrate that third- or fourth-generation Irish Americans consistently are reluctant to support the idea of older people living with their grown children (Fanning, 2000; Levkoff, Levy, and Weitzman, 1999; Vosburgh and Juliani, 1990).

As the nineteenth century progressed and Irish immigration increased, there were calls for immigrant groups to care for themselves: Poverty and aging, which previously had not been stigmatized conditions, now were labeled as symptomatic of intemperance and unworthiness. However, as noted previously, the Irish immigrants, although poor, were overwhelmingly young. Consequently, for a time at least, relatively few Irish immigrants were elderly, and even fewer lived long enough to become aged (Handlin, 1979; Kenny, 2000; Kutzik, 1979; Shannon, 1963; Woodham-Smith, 1963). Still, as Kutzik (1979:48–49) points out, it is likely that a high percentage of the Irish aged were provided for in community poorhouses around the United States. In addition, Irish political machines in many United States cities developed their own system of public welfare, offering food, housing, and fuel assistance to the poor and aged without the risk of humiliation (Metress, 1985).

In both these options, it is the self-esteem and perception of independence that are significant to the Irish aged. They had generally migrated from rural Ireland where the older generation maintained control of the family and its resources until death or voluntary retirement. This afforded the aged a certain status: "Irish culture is well-known for both its emphasis on familism and for the honor, power and privilege that it afforded to its elderly" (Dickerson-Putnam, 1997:366). In America, however, all that changed. The older generation, as well as the younger, often arrived destitute; they had no control over the family's assets and suffered a disturbing further decline in status when they could no longer perform physical labor. Seeking refuge in a poorhouse or other aid from the political system was preferential to becoming a burden to family or extended family in old age (Metress, 1985).

By the late nineteenth century, a third alternative for care had emerged as the American Catholic Church strengthened and became more involved in assistance to the needy of all ages, operating its own asylums, orphanages, hospitals, and homes for the aged. Although care of the aged continued to be secured chiefly by a combination of ethnic organizations, the public poorhouse, assistance programs of big city machines, and families, institutions designed especially for the aged opened for operation. Although most of these formal homes for the aged were affiliated with the Catholic Church and were technically not ethnic, they were overwhelmingly staffed by Irish nuns and administrators were chiefly Irish priests. In essence, at the outset, they were primarily homes providing care for the Irish by the Irish (Kutzik, 1979; Metress, 1985).

Eventually, individual local parishes also saw to the needs of their aged parishioners, especially those without family support. The parish hierarchy provided financial allowances that enabled the elderly to remain independent. In addition, pastors made referrals to Catholic hospitals when illness struck or to Catholic homes for the aged when the need arose (Horgan, 1998; Kutzik, 1979; Metress, 1985). For the aged with families, Horgan recalls that "All cared for elderly parents but in different ways, depended on their resources—paying bills, shopping, visiting, and having the parents live in their homes" (1998:55). Certainly this is the paradigm most often seen in Irish American literature, with the novels of James T. Farrell providing notable examples of Irish families keeping their aged parents and relatives at home (Loughman, 1985).

In the early twentieth century, as Judith Witt notes, "a noticeable shift in responsibility for the growing aged population from the family to the community" (1994:68) took place in the United States. In response to the growing elderly population and emerging cultural beliefs in personal growth and individualism, placing aging parents or relatives in nursing homes became more acceptable. Subsequently, the Great Depression and the Social Security Act of 1935 transformed the delivery of formal public assistance to the aged. Mutual aid societies and ethnic charities, including homes for the aged, disappeared when new government programs took over their functions (Kutzik, 1979; Metress, 1985). The government's willingness to take responsibility for the aged coalesced with the family's newfound individualism. The result was lower expectations of kin support. By the mid-twentieth century, families of all types were relying more on government and institutional supports to care for the aged (Ortiz, Simmons, and Hinton, 1999; Sokolovsky, 1997; Witt, 1994).

While appealing to the Irish, who already had a history of third-party and nonfamilial assistance, this shift led to another dilemma. Studies of the interactions between the aged and their kin, especially when the health of the elderly weakens, confirm the awkwardness of role reversals between the generations and the reluctance on the part of children to acknowledge the growing dependency of a parent (Gordon, Vaughan, and Whelan, 1981; Hill, 1970; Kutzik, 1979; Metress, 1985; Ortiz, Simmons, and Hinton, 1999). There is also evidence that, in some instances, this reluctance can lead to avoidance (Hill, 1970) or resentment. Mary Gordon, for example, depicts the resentful Irish American caregiver in her novel *Final Payments* (1978). The ambivalence such a caregiver creates within the Irish American family is particularly acute. Certain aspects of the American Irish family—loose attachments, lack of emotional support, and self-sufficiency for young and old—are compromised by the ever-present guilt over familial obligations. In families in which physical prowess and self-sufficiency are highly valued, the increasing dependency and frailty of a parent are difficult to confront. Moreover, since intimate interactions are to be avoided, the illness and even impending death of a parent are extraordinarily difficult to manage (Ortiz, Simmons, and Hinton, 1999).

Older Irish American men and women are reluctant to become a dependent part of a relative's household. They have indicated an increased concern with achievement, physical health, and self-reliance as they age (Cohler and Lieberman, 1979). They continue to consider independence and living alone the most desirable of alternatives. Again and again respondents in a recent study report self-sufficiency and independence as their primary goals. They consider housing for the elderly and assisted living facilities as preferable to living with the family of an adult child. It is vital for them to maintain their independence for as long as possible. When the elderly become too frail or too ill to be alone, however, Irish Americans are ambivalent about the delivery of care (Fanning, 2000). Horgan found that there is no blueprint for satisfaction: "Some middle-aged children prefer expanding families to include older adults, others prefer care within a long-term care residence managed by Catholic orders, and still others prefer use of public or private long-term care settings" (1998:63).

It is difficult to generalize about a group as large and diverse as the Irish in America today, yet it seems that in times of need, Irish Americans believe it is primarily the family's responsibility to care for the aged (Fanning, 2000; Horgan, 1998; Larragy, 1993; Levkoff, Levy, and Weitzman, 1999; Ortiz, Simmons, and Hinton, 1999). Gender, marital status, and proximity are all predictors of an individual's likelihood of becoming a caregiver (Fanning, 2000; Ikels, 1983).

American Irish daughters are more likely to live near their parents and provide physical care to them. Thus, the Irish aged look first to their own daughters to take on the primary caregiving role and to their sons for more financial and instrumental assistance (Fanning, 2000; Horgan, 1998). One study (Ortiz, Simmons, and Hinton, 1999) also found that many caregivers included nostalgic images of Ireland in their caregiver narratives. "This romanticized imagery has empowered some caregivers, notably women, who draw on idealized notions of Irish matriarchal traditions and resilience in the face of hardship." There is also evidence of marital status affecting the caretaker selection process. An unmarried child is seen by both parents and siblings as the person most likely to assume the caregiving role (Fanning, 2000; Ikels, 1983). Geographical distance is another important factor in the selection of a caretaker for the American Irish.

Studies have demonstrated that "the frequency of primary kin contacts is to a large extent determined by proximity" (Gordon, Vaughan, and Whelan, 1981:504). Even when variables such as affection, financial capabilities, and occupational commitments are examined, location is seen as a salient factor in determining the caregiving function. As Charlotte Ikels summarizes, "Leaving town is one of the most acceptable ways of avoiding a caretaking future. . . . Proximity exerts tremendous influence on these decisions. If there is only one child in the area at the time of the crisis, that child has no choice but to step forward. . . . When several children of the appropriate sex are more or less equally proximate, other practical considerations arise" (1983:494–495). Those who are married, and especially those with children, have competing obligations that are seen as lessening their ability to provide continual care.

Some evidence suggests that the Irish expect long-term assistance to be provided by family members, with a division of the caregiver roles. One study found that "While a few of the Irish-American caregivers reported family conflicts which arose around caregiving, most either explicitly mentioned sharing the responsibility of decision making with other family members or used the pronoun 'we' when discussing decision making" (Levkoff, Levy, and Weitzman, 1999). Still, there is some ambivalence, and a sizable number believe that institutional resources should alleviate the financial, emotional, and physical burdens of elder care. The American Irish are aware of available formal resources, and they are likely to utilize social services, including hospice, visiting nurses, and support groups (Cleary and Demone, 1988; McGoldrick, 1996). McGoldrick finds that although the Irish are "the least likely to report problems, they are the most likely to seek help for problems they do acknowledge, especially if there is a formal, nonfamilial solution available" (1996:548). This expectation and use of institutional support are consistent with Irish Americans' historical pattern of utilizing third-party providers, homes for the aged, and formal resources in the care of the elderly.

The childless, never-married, or widowed aged within the Irish American family look to their brothers and sisters as an important source of support. This attitude is reflective of the importance placed on obligations and loyalty among siblings, both in Ireland and in America. Unmarried or widowed siblings often live together, providing support to one another as they age. These arrangements are found most often in sister–sister relationships, less frequently as sister–brother households. Brother–brother households are the least likely to occur (Ikels, 1983; Ikels, 1988; Horgan, 1998). Ikels' (1983; 1988) research has also revealed the informal reciprocity of caregiving within the Irish family. In exchange for helping an aged parent, the caregiver is provided care by siblings, nieces, or nephews in tacit acknowledgement of familism and sibling loyalty. For those without family, social supports are more difficult to obtain, especially with the gradual loss of informal social networks through retirement and the death of friends. Need can also be exacerbated by the Irish Americans' characteristic reticence and reluctance to share problems with others.

CONCLUSION

The centuries and generations have brought huge numbers and diversity to the Irish in America. As such, it is difficult, if not impossible, to condense the characteristics of the Irish American family or the changes and adaptations they have gone through into a few brief pages. Although individual experiences have varied greatly, hard work and education are still valued; familism, especially sibling loyalty remains strong; extended families still gather at weddings and wakes; and Catholicism remains a significant, if evolving, influence. The Irish still cling to their independence and retain self-sufficiency as long as possible. Yet assimilation has played its part. As Irish Americans became more American than Irish, in many instances they were left with a more symbolic than actual ethnicity (Gans, 1985). Today being Irish may satisfy an emotional desire rather than fulfill an actual purpose. The communal need to band together to survive or to confront prejudice has disappeared. The yearning for an imagined homeland has devolved into a less urgent fondness for an ethnic identity that perhaps holds no real relevance to lifestyle, family structure, or behavior.

References

Adams, W. F. 1932. *Ireland and Irish Emigration to the New World from 1815 to the Famine.* New Haven: Yale University Press.

Almeida, L. D. 2001. *Irish Immigrants in New York City: 1945–1995.* Bloomington: Indiana University Press.

Arensberg, C. M., and S. T. Kimball. 1968. *Family and Community in Ireland.* Cambridge, MA: Harvard University Press.

Barrabee, P., and O. von Mering. 1953. "Ethnic Variations in Mental Stress in Families with Psychotic Children." *Social Problems 1,* 48–53.

Byron, R. 1999. *Irish America.* Oxford, England: Clarendon Press.

Cleary, P. D., and H. W. Demone, Jr. 1988, December. "Health and Social Service Needs in a Northeastern Metropolitan Area: Ethnic Group Differences." *Journal of Sociology and Social Welfare 15*(4), 63–76.

Cohler, B. J., and M. A. Lieberman. 1979. "Personality Change Across the Second Half of Life: Findings from a Study of Irish, Italian, and Polish-American Men and Women." In D. E. Gelfand and A. J. Kutzik (Eds.), *Ethnicity and Aging: Theory, Research, and Policy* (pp. 227–245). New York: Springer Publishing Company.

Connolly, M. C. (Ed.). 2004. *They Change Their Sky: The Irish in Maine.* Orono: The University of Maine Press.

Dezell, M. 2000. *Irish America Coming into Clover: The Evolution of a People and a Culture.* New York: Doubleday.

Dickerson-Putnam, J. 1997. "History, Community Context and the Perception of Old Age in a Rural Irish Town." In J. Sokolovsky (Ed.), *The Cultural Context of Aging: Worldwide Perspectives* (pp. 364–373). Westport, CT: Bergin and Garvey.

Diner, H. R. 1983. *Erin's Daughters in America: Irish Immigrant Women in the Nineteenth Century.* Baltimore, MD: Johns Hopkins University Press.

Emmons, D. M. 1990. *The Butte Irish: Class and Ethnicity in an American Mining Town, 1875–1925.* Chicago: University of Illinois Press.

Fanning, C. 1997. *The Exiles of Erin: Nineteenth Century Irish-American Fiction.* Chester Springs, PA: Dufour Editions.

Fanning, P. 2000. Unpublished survey of Irish American attitudes toward eldercare.

Farrell, J. T. 1940. *Father and Son.* New York: Vanguard Press.

———. 1953. *The Face of Time.* New York: Vanguard Press.

Fitzpatrick, C., and C. Barry. 1990. "Cultural Differences in Family Communication About Duchenne Muscular Dystrophy." *Developmental Medicine and Child Neurology 32*(11), 967–973.

Gans, H. J. 1985. "Symbolic Ethnicity: The Future of Ethnic Groups and Cultures in America." In N. R. Yetman (Ed.), *Majority and Minority* (pp. 429–442). Boston: Allyn & Bacon.

Gleeson, D. T. 2001. *The Irish in the South: 1815–1877.* Chapel Hill: University of North Carolina Press.

Gleeson, D. T., and B. J. Buttimer. 2005. "'We Are Irish Everywhere': Irish Immigrant Networks in

Charleston, South Carolina, and Savannah, Georgia." *Immigrants & Minorities 23*(2–3), 183–205.

Gordon, M. 1978. *Final Payments.* New York: Random House.

Gordon, M., R. Vaughan, and B. Whelan. 1981, Autumn. "The Irish Elderly Who Live Alone: Patterns of Contact and Aid." *Journal of Comparative Family Studies 12*(4), 493–508.

Greeley, A. M. 1972. *That Most Distressful Nation: The Taming of the American Irish.* Chicago: Quadrangle Books.

———. 1981. *The Irish Americans.* New York: Harper & Row.

———. 1999. *Furthermore! Memories of a Parish Priest.* New York: Forge.

Handlin, O. 1979. *Boston's Immigrants: A Study in Acculturation.* Cambridge, MA: Harvard University Press.

Harris, R. A., and D. M. Jacobs (Eds.). 1989. *The Search for Missing Friends: Irish Immigrant Advertisements Placed in the Boston Pilot, Volume I: 1831–1850.* Boston: New England Genealogical Society.

Heer, D. M. 1961. "The Marital Status of Second-Generation Americans." *American Sociological Review 26*(2), 233–241.

Hill, R. 1970. *Family Development in Three Generations.* Cambridge, MA: Schenkman Publishing Company.

Horgan, E. S. 1998. "The Irish-American Family." In C. H. Mindel, R. W. Habenstein, and R. Wright, Jr. (Eds.), *Ethnic Families in America: Patterns and Variations* (pp. 39–67). Upper Saddle River, NJ: Prentice Hall.

Ikels, Charlotte. 1983. "The Process of Caretaker Selection." *Research on Aging 5*(4), 491–509.

———. 1988. "Delayed Reciprocity and the Support Networks of the Childless Elderly." *Journal of Comparative Family Studies 19*(1), 99–112.

Kane, E. 1968. "Man and Kin in Donegal: A Study of Kinship Functions in a Rural Irish and an Irish-American Community." *Ethnology 7*(3), 245–258.

Kennedy, R. E., Jr. 1973. *The Irish: Emigration, Marriage, and Fertility.* Berkeley: University of California Press.

Kenny, K. 2000. *The American Irish: A History.* New York: Pearson Education.

Kutzik, A. J. 1979. "American Social Provision for the Aged: An Historical Perspective." In D. E. Gelfand and A. J. Kutzik (Eds.), *Ethnicity and Aging: Theory, Research, and Policy* (pp. 32–65). New York: Springer Publishing Company.

Larragy, J. 1993, September. "Views and Perceptions of Older Irish People." *Social Policy and Administration 27*(3), 235–247.

Levkoff, S., B. Levy, and P. F. Weitzman. 1999. "The Role of Religion and Ethnicity in the Help Seeking of Family Caregivers of Elders with Alzheimer's Disease and Related Disorders." *Journal of Cross-Cultural Gerontology 14,* 335–356.

Lipton, J. A., and J. J. Marbach. 1984. "Ethnicity and the Pain Experience." *Social Science and Medicine 19*(12), 1279–1298.

Loughman, C. 1985, Fall. "'Old Now, and Good to Her': J. T. Farrell's Last Novels," *Eire Ireland: A Journal of Irish Studies 20*(3), 43–55.

McCaffrey, L. J. 2000. "Diaspora Comparisons and Irish-American Uniqueness." In Charles Fanning (Ed.), *New Perspectives on the Irish Diaspora* (pp. 15–27). Carbondale: Southern Illinois University Press.

McGivern, E. P. 1979. "Ethnic Identity and Its Relation to Group Norms: Irish Americans in Metropolitan Pittsburgh." Unpublished dissertation, University of Pittsburgh.

McGoldrick, M. 1996. "Irish Families." In M. McGoldrick, J. Giordano, and J. K. Pearce (Eds.), *Ethnicity and Family Therapy* (pp. 544–566). New York: Guilford Press.

Metress, S. P. 1985, March. "The History of Irish-American Care of the Aged." *Social Science Review 59*(1), 18–31.

Miller, K. A. 1985. *Emigrants and Exiles: Ireland and the Irish Exodus to North America.* New York: Oxford University Press.

———. 2000. "'Scotch-Irish' Myths and 'Irish' Identities in Eighteenth- and Nineteenth-Century America." In Charles Fanning (Ed.), *New Perspectives on the Irish Diaspora* (pp. 75–92). Carbondale: Southern Illinois University Press.

Nolan, J. A. 1989. *Ourselves Alone: Female Emigration from Ireland: 1885–1920.* Lexington: University Press of Kentucky.

———. 2004. *Servants of the Poor: Teachers and Mobility in Ireland and Irish America.* Notre Dame, IN: University of Notre Dame Press.

O'Connor, T. H. 1995. *The Boston Irish: A Political History.* Boston: Back Bay Books.

O'Day, E. J. 2000. "The 'Second Colonization of New England' Revisited: Irish Immigration Before the Famine." In Charles Fanning (Ed.), *New Perspectives on the Irish Diaspora* (pp. 93–114). Carbondale: Southern Illinois University Press.

Opler, M. K., and J. L. Singer. 1956. "Ethnic Differences in Behavior and Psychopathology: Italian and Irish," *International Journal of Social Psychiatry 2,* 11–23.

Ortiz, A., J. Simmons, and W. L. Hinton. 1999. "Locations of Remorse and Homelands of Resilience: Notes on Grief and Sense of Loss of Place of Latino and Irish-American Caregivers of Demented Elders," *Culture, Medicine and Psychiatry 23,* 477–500.

Sarbaugh, T. J. 1991. "Irish America at the Crossroads." *Migration World 19*(3), 5–8.

Scheper-Hughes, N. 1987. "'Mental' in 'Southie': Individual, Family, and Community Responses to Psychosis in South Boston." *Culture, Medicine and Psychiatry, 11*(1), 53–78.

Schrier, A. 1958. *Ireland and the American Emigration: 1850–1900.* Minneapolis: University of Minnesota Press.

Shannon, W. V. 1963. *The American Irish.* New York: Macmillan.

Singer, J. L., and M. K. Opler. 1956. "Contrasting Patterns of Fantasy and Motility in Irish and Italian Schizophrenics." *Journal of Abnormal Social Psychology 53,* 42–47.

Skerrett, E. (Ed.). 1997. *At the Crossroads: Old Saint Patrick's and the Chicago Irish.* Chicago: Loyola Press.

Skerrett, E. 2000. "The Irish of Chicago's Hull-House Neighborhood." In Charles Fanning (Ed.), *New Perspectives on the Irish Diaspora* (pp. 189–222). Carbondale: Southern Illinois University Press.

Sokolovsky, J. 1997. "Bringing Culture Back Home: Aging, Ethnicity and Family Support." In J. Sokolovsky (Ed.), *The Cultural Context of Aging: Worldwide Perspectives* (pp. 264–275). Westport, CT: Bergin and Garvey.

Spiegel, J. 1971. "Cultural Strain, Family Role Patterns, and Intrapsychic Conflict." In J. G. Howells (Ed.), *Theory and Practice of Family Psychiatry* (pp. xx–xx). New York: Brunner/Mazel.

Suchman, E. A. 1964. "Sociomedical Variations Among Ethnic Groups." *American Journal of Sociology 70,* 319–331.

U.S. Census Bureau. 2011. "Statistical Abstract of the United States: 2011, Table 52: Population by Selected Ancestry Group and Region: 2008," p. 50. www.census.gov/prod/2011pubs/11statab/pop.pdf (accessed April 2, 2011).

Vosburgh, M. G., and R. N. Juliani. 1990, Summer. "Contrasts in Ethnic Family Patterns: The Irish and the Italians." *Journal of Comparative Family Studies 21*(2), 269–286.

Witt, J. B. 1994. "The Gendered Division of Labor in Parental Caretaking: Biology or Socialization?" *Journal of Women and Aging 6*(12), 65–89.

Woodham-Smith, C. 1963. *The Great Hunger.* New York: Harper & Row.

Wylan, L., and N. L. Mintz. 1976. "Ethnic Differences in Family Attitudes Towards Psychotic Manifestations, with Implications for Treatment Programs." *International Journal of Social Psychiatry 2*(2), 86–95.

Zborowski, M. 1969. *People in Pain.* San Francisco: Jossey-Bass, Inc.

Zola, I. K. 1966. "Culture and Symptoms: An Analysis of Patients' Presenting Complaints." *American Sociological Review 31,* 615–630.

———. 1973. "Pathways to the Doctor: From Person to Patient." *Social Science and Medicine 7*(9), 677–689.

4

■■■

The Greek American Family

Anna Karpathakis

INTRODUCTION

When I told a friend that I was working on a chapter on the Greek American family, she said, "Don't forget. Men may be the heads of the family, but women are the necks that move the heads." We spent the next hour recounting different scenes in the movie *My Big Fat Greek Wedding*. We loved the movie. We were laughing hard and loud. It smacked us straight in the face with all the myths and stereotypes regarding Greek American men, women, and families. The most common of these myths is that the Greek American family is one patriarchal and homogeneous institution. Wives and mothers are imaged as primarily stay-at-home moms, ruling over the nest with the eyes of an eagle during the hours the fathers are out of the home and at work. The idea of the Greek American family as a nuclear unit led by the father, but daily surrounded by extended kin who often live within walking distance, is one of the steadfast images in our minds. These myths are in many ways a congratulatory statement addressed to an ethnic group that has, like other immigrant groups, surpassed the initial entry and eventual integration into American society and successfully entered the American middle classes. And yet, this is not the whole story.

Studies of Greek American families have given us a wealth of information and analysis on gender relations through the prism of assimilation (see, for example, Callinicos, 1990; Kourvetaris, 1976; Scourby, 1980, 1984). Triandis's (1988, 1993, 1995) conceptualizations of Greek and Greek American cultures and families as "allocentric" (as opposed to "egocentric") provide the social psychological explanations for the sociological findings of the key role that the family plays in immigrant upward mobility (see, for example, Karpathakis, 1993; Karpathakis and Harris, 2009; Tavuchis, 1972; Vlachos, 1968). Studies on gender relations within the family seem to be of two schools. One school sees a patriarchal institution that lessens in its oppressive hold over its members only through assimilation (see, for example, Callinicos, 1990; Scourby, 1984). The other perspective sees patriarchy as multidimensional and simply changing in its nuances through assimilation (see, for example, Karpathakis, 2002; Karpathakis and Harris, 2009; Laliotou, 2004; Papanikolas, 2002) so that it in effect is not clear that assimilation brings with it the kind of freedom from patriarchy that earlier researchers and feminists envisioned; in this perspective, we are reminded that we rather need to be more aware of the conflation of upward mobility and increasing gender equalities and that patriarchy takes different forms in different societies and cultures.

There is no one single Greek American family. Rather, a wide range is seen in the demographics of these families. Three variables are critical in understanding these diverse demographics: region of the country persons of Greek ancestry settled/live in, gender, and ethnicity. Regional variation is also found in all of the family-related variables examined (e.g., structure of household/family, income, poverty, and divorce/separation rates). Although this chapter does not address or conceptualize the possible explanations for these variables, we can nevertheless reflect on them. Regional variation is most likely important because it is an indicator of three additional variables. First, region of settlement and time of arrival of immigrants (i.e., immigrant cohort as an indicator of assimilation) are related. Earlier immigrants were more likely to settle in different parts of the country as the men were mobile in search of work; as such, for example, we now see that Greek Americans living in the West and the South are more likely to be second- (i.e., grandchildren of immigrants) and later-generation American born while those in the Northeast and Midwest are more mixed cohortwise. Second, depending on the region of the country, the local labor markets and other institutions impact occupational opportunities but also provide stressors and/or opportunities for families, thereby affecting family structure. Third is the issue of size of the immigrant/ethnic communities. Presumably, the larger the ethnic community the greater the support networks to protect and buffer the family from external and internal pressures. The South and West, for example, are the regions with the fewest number of Greek Americans and fewest ethnic communities, organizations, and parishes. Greek Americans in the South (outside of a few cities/areas) and West are less likely than those in the Northeast and Midwest to be living in ethnic neighborhoods or near parishes; they tend to be residentially dispersed over great distances so that forming and maintaining formal community structures with numerous support networks is the most difficult for these Greek Americans compared to those living in other regions. The assumption here is that community support systems act as buffers reducing stressors on the family.

This is in effect borne out by the data in the 2000 U.S. Census as we see that ethnicity does provide a buffer for families against divorce, poverty, and children growing up in single-parent households, or both. Greek American families, regardless of structure, appear to enjoy higher median income and lower poverty rates than their similarly structured counterparts in the larger population. Having said this, however, it is also true that one-third of Greek American female-headed households still live in poverty. In short, Greek American families tend to score higher on the "positive" variables of, for example, median income and lower on the "negative" variables of, for example, poverty and divorce, but these "negative" variables or problems also exist within Greek American families, albeit in lower percentages.

This chapter is ambitious. First, we present an overview of Greek American families obtained through the 2000 U.S. Census and examine the demographics, including how the families are situated within the country's social class structures. Although general trends and patterns are apparent, it is nevertheless difficult to write of one Greek American family because Greek Americans are a diverse group in terms of class and time of immigration, and thereby ethnic cohort and region of settlement. The second part of the chapter tackles some of the cultural myths regarding Greek American families, using interviews of both Greek and American born men and women; these interviews were carried out between 1996 and 2008 in different parts of the country.

DEMOGRAPHICS

According to the U.S. Census 2000 (U.S. Census Bureau, 2000), 1,153,295 individuals identified as being of Greek ancestry. The majority of these Greek Americans live in the Northeast, the region where the majority of the post-1965 immigrants settled near family. Greek Americans, however, are found in all fifty states.

Two of the myths regarding Greek Americans are that they marry young and live in large families. Data from the census dispel these myths and show in fact that Greek Americans are less likely than the overall population to live in families. The exception to this pattern is in the Northeast, the area where the majority of post-1965 immigrants settled. At the same time, however, Greek Americans are more likely to be living in households with others and less likely to be living alone compared to the overall population. (See Table 4.1.)

The census shows that Greek American families are slightly smaller in size than the families in the overall population in the South and West, and on the national average. The Northeast and Midwest are exceptions to this. (See Table 4.2.)

Table 4.3 shows that on the national level Greek American men and women were less likely to be married, less likely to be separated and/or divorced, and more likely to never have married at the time of the census; this last fact is perhaps due to Greek Americans marrying at a later age than persons in the overall population. Having said this, it is also important to note the variations

TABLE 4.1   Population in Families and Households, National and Regional, U.S. and Greek American Populations

	National	Northeast	Midwest	South	West
Families					
General population	226,741,608	42,745,385	51,773,202	81,396,490	50,826,531
	80.6%	79.8%	80.4%	81.2%	80.4%
Greek American	912,926	335,986	205,150	201,879	169,911
	79.2%	81.3%	78.4%	79%	76.3%
Households					
General population	273,637,396	51,925,044	62,598,853	97,397,987	61,715,512
	97.2%	96.9%	97.2%	97.2%	97.7%
Greek American	1,135,526	406,679	257,438	251,556	219,853
	98.5%	98.4%	98.4%	98.5%	98.8%

Source: U.S. Census Bureau, 2000.

TABLE 4.2   Average Family Size, U.S. and Greek American Populations

	National	Northeast	Midwest	South	West
Average Family Size					
Overall Population	3.14	3.14	3.09	3.08	3.29
Greek American	3.08	3.15	3.12	3.0	3.0

Source: U.S. Census Bureau, 2000.

TABLE 4.3   Marital Status by Gender, Population, and Greek Ancestry (%)

	United States		Northeast		Midwest		South		West	
	Men	Women	Men	Women	Men	Women	Men	Women	Men	Women
General population										
Married	56.7	52.1	55.8	49.8	57.4	53.2	57.8	52.6	55.3	52.4
Never Married	30.3	24.1	32.2	26.7	29.9	23.9	28.4	22.5	31.9	24.8
Separated	1.8	2.5	2.1	2.8	1.3	1.6	2.1	2.8	1.7	2.4
Widowed	2.5	10.5	2.9	11.5	2.5	10.7	2.6	10.9	2.2	8.8
Divorced	8.6	10.8	7.0	9.2	8.9	10.6	9.2	11.2	8.9	11.6
Greek American										
Married	56.3	51.9	56.8	52.1	56.6	52.3	57.5	53.5	53.7	49.5
Never Married	32.9	27.6	34.0	28.7	33.6	28.1	30.3	25.1	33.2	27.7
Separated	1.2	1.6	1.2	1.8	0.7	1.0	1.5	1.6	1.1	1.7
Widowed	1.9	9.0	2.0	9.7	1.7	9.2	1.8	8.8	1.8	8.0
Divorced	7.7	9.9	5.9	7.8	7.3	9.4	8.9	10.9	10.2	13.2

Source: U.S. Census Bureau, 2000.

by gender and region of the country. In the West, for example, Greek American men and women have higher rates of being divorced than those in the overall population.

HOUSEHOLD AND FAMILY STRUCTURES

In Table 4.4, we see that compared to the overall population Greek American families are more likely to be married, more likely to have a male head of household, and less likely to have a female head of household. Once again, the West shows a more complex picture of Greek American family demographics.

In Table 4.5, we see that Greek American married-couple families are slightly less likely than families in the overall population to have children under the age of 18. This information confirms what we saw in Table 4.2—namely, that Greek American families tend to be smaller than families in the overall population. Similarly, the percentage of Greek American families with children under the age of 18, headed by a woman with no husband present, is lower compared to the overall population.

FAMILIES AND WORK

Overall, in 1999 Greek American husbands and householders had higher rates of employment than husbands and householders in the overall population. National statistics show that Greek American married women were more likely than married women in the overall population to have been employed in 1999. On the regional level, however, Greek American married women in the Northeast and Midwest were less likely to have worked in 1999, and those in the South and West were more likely to have worked when compared to married women in the overall population. (See Table 4.6.)

TABLE 4.4 Married Couple and Female Householder with No Husband Present as Percentage of All Family Types

	National		Northeast		Midwest		South		West	
	Overall Population	Greek American	Overall Population	Greek American	Overall Population	Greek American	Overall Population	Greek American	Overall Population	Greek American
Married couple family	52.5	54.8	50.8	56.8	53.2	55.8	52.8	54.4	52.9	50.6
Male householder	51.2	52.6	48.3	53.8	52.3	54.8	51.6	52.1	52.0	48.5
Female householder, no husband present	11.8	8.3	12.4	8.2	10.8	8.4	12.7	7.5	11.1	9.3

Source: U.S. Census Bureau, 2000.

TABLE 4.5 Householder and Children Under 18 (%)

	National		Northeast		Midwest		South		West	
	Overall Population	Greek American	Overall Population	Greek American	Overall Population	Greek American	Overall Population	Greek American	Overall Population	Greek American
Married-couple families with own children under 18	46.3	46.0	47.7	46.4	45.7	47.4	45.1	45.9	49.3	46.0
Female-headed families with own children under 18	68.6	52.9	55.5	44.7	61.1	54.2	58.9	57.8	60.2	59.4

Source: U.S. Census Bureau, 2000.

TABLE 4.6 Employment and Work Status of Married Couple Families and Family Householder, 1999 (%)

	National		Northeast		Midwest		South		West	
	Overall Population	Greek American	Overall Population	Greek American	Overall Population	Greek American	Overall Population	Greek American	Overall Population	Greek American
Married-Couple Families										
Husband employed	73.2	75.6	73.1	73.8	74.9	76.8	72.6	76.7	72.6	76.2
Wife employed	49.8	50.2	50.3	48.3	53.9	51.8	42.3	51.3	47.5	50.5
Husband unemployed	1.9	1.5	2.0	1.5	1.8	1.5	1.7	1.3	2.3	1.6

Source: U.S. Census Bureau, 2000.

Table 4.7 shows, based on national statistics, that Greek American women (with children) in the labor force are comparable to women in the overall population. There are, however, regional variations. Greek American women with children under six years of age in the Northeast, Midwest, and South have slightly lower rates of labor force participation while those in the West have significantly higher rates compared to their counterparts in the overall population. Greek American female householders, however, were more likely to have worked than female householders in the overall population.

Table 4.8 shows that Greek American children under the age of six are slightly less likely to have both parents in the labor force compared to their counterparts in the overall population, again with the exception in the West. Compared to the overall population, Greek American children between the ages of six and seventeen living with both parents are more likely to have both parents in the labor force. Regional variation is also seen here. With the exception of those living in the West, the percentage of Greek American children living with one parent who is in the labor force is less compared to the percentage for the overall population.

Table 4.9 quantifies children's relationship to the householder. Greek American children are more likely than children in the overall population to be living in a household lead by a parent, more likely to be living with both parents, less likely to be living with the mother with no husband or father present, and less likely to be living in the household of a grandparent, other relatives, or non-relatives. Once again, we see regional variations on this variable.

THE ELDERLY

One of the myths of Greek American families is that the elderly grandparents live with extended family members. Table 4.10 focuses on the household structure of individuals sixty-five years of age and older. Once again, we see patterns that slightly distinguish Greek Americans from the overall population. Greek Americans over the age of sixty-five are more likely to be family householders than non-family householders compared to the same age cohort in the overall population. Greek American males in the Northeast and the Midwest are slightly less likely to be living alone, and those in the South and the West are more likely to be living alone compared to their counterparts in the overall population. Greek American women age sixty-five and older are in all regions less likely to be living alone compared to the same age cohort of women in the overall population. Also, Greek American women age sixty-five and older in the Northeast and Midwest are more likely to be living with relatives compared to their counterparts in the South and West who are less likely to be living with relatives compared to both the overall and regional percentages. As such, the picture that emerges is complex.

SOCIAL CLASS

We look in this section at the three variables sociologists use to measure social class—education, occupation, and income—to determine an approximate location of Greek American families on the continuum of social class. Just as the data on demographics show a complex picture of Greek American families, so do the data on social class.

Table 4.11 shows that Greek American women outperform women and men in the overall population (although not Greek American men) in terms of education. The rates do, however, vary regionally, which is a reflection of the demands of regional/local labor markets.

TABLE 4.7 Women with Children in the Labor Force, 1999 (%)

	National		Northeast		Midwest		South		West	
	Overall Population	Greek American	Overall Population	Greek American	Overall Population	Greek American	Overall Population	Greek American	Overall Population	Greek American
With own children under 6 years old	61.9	61.7	61.3	60.3	66.6	63.1	62.1	60.5	57.5	63.9
With own children 6–17 years old	75.0	75.0	75.0	73.7	79.3	75.7	73.9	75.7	72.2	75.6
Female Householder Worked full time year-round	41.6	44.3	39.3	40.9	44.4	46.2	42.1	48.0	39.9	44.1

Source: U.S. Census Bureau, 2000.

TABLE 4.8 Children by Employment Status of Parents, 1999 (%)

	National		Northeast		Midwest		South		West	
	Overall Population	Greek American	Overall Population	Greek American	Overall Population	Greek American	Overall Population	Greek American	Overall Population	Greek American
Children under age 6										
Both parents in labor force	58.6	58.1	57.9	56.2	63.3	58.4	58.8	58.7	54.2	60.3
Living with 1 parent in labor force	20.1	11.5	18.6	9.8	20.3	11.5	21.8	12.2	18.6	13.7
Children ages 6–17										
Both parents in labor force	67.4	68.0	67.4	66.6	72.4	70.3	66.9	67.3	63.3	68.3
Living with 1 parent in labor force	22.0	16.5	21.4	14.3	21.2	16.3	23.6	16.4	20.9	20.9

Source: U.S. Census Bureau, 2000.

TABLE 4.9 Children Under Age 18, Relationship to Householder (%)

	National		Northeast		Midwest		South		West	
	Overall Population	Greek American	Overall Population	Greek American	Overall Population	Greek American	Overall Population	Greek American	Overall Population	Greek American
Householder or spouse	0.1	0.1	0.1	0.0	0.1	0.0	0.1	0.1	0.1	0.0
Child of householder	89.9	95.3	91.0	95.8	91.9	95.2	88.7	95.6	88.9	94.3
Child of married-couple family	67.1	79.9	67.9	81.9	69.8	80.3	64.6	80.1	67.7	75.1
Child of female householder, no husband present	18.0	12.1	18.7	10.8	17.4	11.9	19.5	12.2	15.7	14.7
Grandchild	6.1	3.1	5.5	2.9	4.8	3.5	7.3	2.9	6.0	3.4
Other relatives	2.2	0.7	1.8	2.6	1.5	0.6	2.3	0.6	2.9	1.2
Non-relatives	1.8	0.8	1.6	0.7	1.8	0.7	1.6	0.80.0	2.1	1.1

Source: U.S. Census Bureau, 2000.

TABLE 4.10 Household Population 65 Years of Age and Older (%)

	National		Northeast		Midwest		South		West	
	Overall Population	Greek American	Overall Population	Greek American	Overall Population	Greek American	Overall Population	Greek American	Overall Population	Greek American
Family householder	36.4	40.2	35.0	39.7	36.3	40.7	37.4	40.8	36.1	39.9
Non-family householder	31.1	27.2	32.4	26.1	33.0	27.3	30.4	27.9	28.8	28.8
Male living alone	7.2	7.1	7.6	6.6	7.4	6.4	7.0	7.2	7.2	8.5
Female living alone	22.6	19.1	23.6	18.6	24.6	20.1	22.0	19.2	19.9	18.5
Living with spouse	23.7	23.3	22.5	23.1	24.5	23.0	23.8	23.4	23.9	23.7
Living with relatives	7.3	8.2	8.5	9.9	5.1	8.3	7.0	6.7	9.0	5.8
Living with non-relatives	1.5	1.2	1.5	1.1	1.2	0.7	1.4	1.2	2.1	1.8

Source: U.S. Census Bureau, 2000.

TABLE 4.11 Individuals with Bachelor's Degree and Higher, by Region, Gender, and Greek Ancestry, Compared to Overall Population (%)

	United States		Northeast		Midwest		West		South	
	Overall Population	Greek American	Overall Population	Greek American	Overall Population	Greek American	Overall Population	Greek American	Overall Population	Greek American
Bachelor's Degree	15.5	21.3	16.4	20.0	15	20.5	17.0	23.1	14.5	22.6
Men	16.1	22.1	17.2	20.8	15.4	21	17.5	24.4	15.1	23
Women	15.0	20.6	15.8	19.3	14.5	20.1	16.6	21.9	14.0	22
Master's Degree Plus	8.9	13.9	10.9	14.2	7.9	13	9.3	13.9	8.0	14.3
Men	10.0	15.9	12.1	15.2	9.0	15.1	10.7	16.1	9.0	17.9
Women	7.8	12	9.8	13.1	7.0	10.8	7.8	11.8	7.1	11.4

Source: U.S. Census Bureau, 2000.

The higher rates of education among Greek Americans are most likely related to the higher median income the group enjoys, compared to the overall population.

In Table 4.12 we see that Greek American households are less likely to receive public assistance income, and that Greek American families of all types enjoy higher median income than families in the overall population. Similarly, Greek American families with a female householder with no husband present have a higher median income than similar families in the overall population; thus, ethnicity does play a role in the families' median income. The regional variation in median income is reflective of regional labor markets and, in this case, shows that family householders of Greek ancestry are integrated in the labor market in an advantaged position in all four regions of the country.

Occupationally, Greek American men and women are more likely to work as managers and professionals in professional, scientific, and technical positions than the overall population; indeed, higher percentages of women of Greek ancestry are found in these occupations than are the men in the overall population. Greek American women are also more likely to be self-employed than men and women in the overall population. (See Table 4.13.)

The data on education, income, and occupation show Greek Americans, and thereby their families, to have integrated themselves into the middle ranks of American mainstream institutions.

Poverty rates are significantly lower among Greek American families (see Table 4.14). Although we see that ethnicity may act as a buffer to protect families against poverty, it does not do so completely, since female-headed Greek American families are more likely to be living in poverty than Greek American married-couple families; at the same time, however, female-headed Greek American families are less likely to be poor than similarly structured families in the overall population. Having said this, however, it is important to note that more than one-third of Greek American female-headed families with children under age five are living in poverty.

SECTION SUMMARY

Greek American families tend to be smaller than families in the overall population, are more likely to be married-couple families, are less likely to experience disruption resulting from separation or divorce, and are less likely to be headed by women with no husband present (i.e., "single moms"). Greek American men and women have higher rates of education, were more likely to have worked in 1999 (the year measured in the 2000 Census), and as a result are more likely to enjoy a higher median income and lower poverty rates—this last even among the female-headed households, although the rates for this group are still high. Despite the fact that these statistics do vary regionally, ethnicity does provide a buffer for family disruption with the exception of the West, where the majority of Greek Americans are American-born second and later generations (i.e., grandchildren and great-grandchildren of immigrants). Gender, ethnicity, and region of the country interact to structure Greek American family experiences. The census numbers show that Greek American families are integrated into the regional institutions in advantaged positions, that ethnicity does have a mitigating or buffering effect, and that ethnicity does not override gender, which is perhaps the stronger variable of the two, depending on the issue.

The data from the 2000 Census bring into question some of the myths of Greek American families. The argument here is not that the Greek American family is not patriarchal; on the contrary, patriarchy is alive and well. The argument is rather that patriarchy does not take one quantifiable form cross-culturally; despite its cross-cultural similarities, it does vary on a number of points and axes.

TABLE 4.12 Income for Families, in Dollars, 1999 (%)

	National		Northeast		Midwest		South		West	
	Overall Population	Greek American	Overall Population	Greek American	Overall Population	Greek American	Overall Population	Greek American	Overall Population	Greek American
Households with public assistance income	3.4%	1.8%	3.8%	1.9%	3.1%	1.7%	3.0%	1.3%	4.2%	2.4%
Median income										
Families	50,046	63,240	54,820	64,707	51,471	62,572	45,664	61,613	51,426	63,803
Married couple families	57,345	69,590	63,834	70,413	58,170	68,390	53,091	67,392	59,099	71,958
With children under age 18	59,461	74,823	66,656	75,753	61,254	71,965	54,716	73,479	58,573	77,898
Female householder with children under age 18	20,284	26,932	20,772	26,934	21,005	25,719	18,849	26,354	21,735	28,642

Source: U.S. Census Bureau, 2000.

TABLE 4.13 Occupations, Self-Employed by Ancestry, Gender, and Region (%)

	U.S.		Northeast		Midwest		West		South	
	Overall Population	Greek American	Overall Population	Greek American	Overall Population	Greek American	Overall Population	Greek American	Overall Population	Greek American
Managers, Professional	33.6	42.9	36.5	43.1	32.1	39.8	34.8	44.1	32.4	44.8
Men	31.4	42.5	34.3	42.0	30.2	39.6	33.2	44.1	29.6	44.6
Women	36.2	43.4	38.9	44.3	34.2	40.0	36.8	44.0	35.6	45.0
Self-Employed	6.6	8.0	6.1	8.1	6.1	6.0	8.0	10.6	6.4	7.4
Men	5.3	11.4	5.1	13.6	4.8	11.1	6.2	7.9	5.2	11.1
Women	7.0	9.1	5.7	9.4	7.0	9.7	7.6	7.8	7.3	9.3
Professional, Scientific, and Technical	5.9	8.3	6.8	8.3	4.9	7.3	6.7	8.7	5.5	8.9
Men	6.0	8.6	7.0	8.4	5.0	8.1	6.8	9.0	5.5	9.2
Women	5.7	7.9	6.5	8.2	4.9	6.4	6.6	8.4	5.4	8.6

Source: U.S. Census Bureau, 2000.

TABLE 4.14 Families Living Below the Poverty Level (%)

	National		Northeast		Midwest		South		West	
	Overall Population	Greek American	Overall Population	Greek American	Overall Population	Greek American	Overall Population	Greek American	Overall Population	Greek American
All Families	9.2	4.9	8.4	5.3	7.2	4.2	10.6	4.6	9.5	5.2
With children under 18	13.6	6.5	12.8	6.9	10.9	5.8	15.4	6.0	13.9	7.4
With children under age 5	17.0	7.5	15.6	8.0	14.3	6.8	18.9	7.2	17.6	8.1
Married-Couple Families	4.9	3.0	4.1	3.7	3.4	2.2	5.8	2.9	5.8	2.9
With children under age 18	6.6	3.2	5.3	3.9	4.3	2.3	7.6	3.1	8.3	3.1
With children under age 5	8.5	3.6	6.7	4.2	5.8	2.6	9.6	3.6	11.0	3.6
Female-Headed Families, No Husband Present	26.5	16.2	25.2	15.3	24.2	16.3	29.3	16.2	24.9	17.7
With children under age 18	34.3	23.7	34.4	25.7	31.7	24.3	36.8	20.7	32.1	23.6
With children under age 5	46.4	36.5	46.4	40.0	45.0	36.9	48.3	33.1	44.2	34.8

Source: U.S. Census Bureau, 2000.

TACKLING CULTURE

Sociologists often find cultural explanations difficult to construct and accept as valid explanatory models of social reality. However, given that most of us try to create a viable framework through which to understand events and phenomena around us through cultural lenses, this next section will "tackle" cultural issues regarding Greek American families.

Greek immigrants arrived in the United States in three cohorts. The first arrived at the end of the nineteenth and beginning of the twentieth centuries, the second immediately after World War II, and the third and final cohort in the post-1965 period with the passage of the Immigration and Nationality Act of 1965 (Hart-Celler Act). The first wave of immigrants consisted overwhelmingly of sojourning men, and by 1930 one-third of these early immigrants returned to Greece. However, the women began arriving, many as "picture brides," and a community was thereby created. The early immigrant men moved and settled in various parts of the country as they followed work on the railroads and in mining, many settling in the South and West. Immigrants arriving in the post-war period and later settled overwhelmingly in the Midwest and Northeast, near family and compatriots. Currently, approximately 2,000 new immigrants are arriving from Greece annually, and they settle near family, mostly in the Midwest and Northeast. The largest Greek American immigrant and ethnic communities are in the Northeast and Midwest; these regions also have the most parishes and immigrant and ethnic organizations. Immigrants and the American born of Greek descent in these regions thereby have greater opportunities to live out and re-create their ethnic identities, create relations with fellow ethnics, and maintain relations with family and friends in Greece, while those in the West and South lack these structural opportunities.

Even though the West is geographically a huge area, it is the area with the fewest persons of Greek ancestry, fewest Greek Orthodox parishes, greatest concentration of grandchildren and great grandchildren of immigrants, fewest secular community (such as cultural or hometown) organizations, and fewest clusters of Greek Americans in particular cities or towns (i.e., greater residential dispersion over greater distances, which is reflective of the original immigrants' moves in search of work). This is the region of the country that is home to the fewest Greek Americans who speak an Indo-European language other than English (presumably Greek) as well as home to those with the greater likelihood of speaking Spanish, an Asian language, or both; if language in the home can be used as a rough indicator of intermarriage, then we see that the rates of intermarriage for Greek Americans are higher in the West. Given the lack of numbers of Greek Americans living in this region, it is only to be expected that this is the region of the country with the higher rates of intermarriage; indeed, reaching as high as 80 percent among the fourth generation (Konstantellos, 1999). Many of those who identify Greek among their ancestries in the census are more likely to experience this as a symbolic ethnicity than those who live in the Northeast. Given the demographics of this region, it is difficult to talk about a distinctive Greek American family culture among third- and fourth-generation American-born individuals—they are far removed from the family's immigrant roots, and most live in families of mixed cultural backgrounds.

One grandson of immigrants describes his experiences growing up in a small western town and reflects on living in a family of mixed ancestry as follows:[1]

> "We were the only Greek American family in the town. My grandfather settled there and my parents stayed. My mother is not of Greek descent, her grandparents were Russian. We used to

---

[1] The author carried out the following interviews, beginning in 1996. The early interviews were done in person, and later interviews were carried out primarily via e-mail and telephone. Excerpts are reprinted here with the signed informed consent of the interviewees.

go to the Russian Orthodox Church until my father died and my mother . . ., out of loyalty to my father[,] started driving us 40 miles away to go to a Greek Church. . . . My wife was the only Latina in town. . . . [We] met in fourth grade when her family moved to the town. . . . My older sister married a tall German man, her kids don't even know about her Greek roots, they have a German last name and go to a Catholic church. . . . [M]y other sister's husband is mixed but mostly British and her kids go to a Methodist church. . . . Both my sisters are now divorced and raising their kids on their own. . . . My brother married a fourth generation Chinese American woman. . . . He changed his name and his wife doesn't like it. . . . It's a very English sounding name . . . (laughs). . . . [S]he respects family like my wife. . . . Both my sister-in-law and wife converted. We didn't ask them, it was done with the mother-in-law. My mother (laughs). We celebrate both holidays but only because my wife has read more about Greek culture than me and insists on celebrating Greek holidays. Easter is her favorite . . . she does the whole week of preparations . . . the red eggs, the koulourakia (Greek Easter cookies), the whole spread. . . . She bought books but mostly she learned from my mother and the Church. Once a month she and my sister in law will drive over fifty miles to take the kids to the Greek Church. . . . My nephews and sons want to go to Greece to the Ionian Village Camp that the Church sponsors. . . . My sisters' kids have never been to Greek Church. . . . One asked me, '[U]ncle, why do you have such a funny last name?'. . . . The father doesn't want them to know about their grandparents. . . . My sisters made bad choices. I met a lot of Greek Americans in the Church who married non Greeks and they are still married, the husbands and wives respect each other. Most of the families in the Church are mixed. . . . [My wife is] raising our children to know both Greek and Mexican history and culture . . . if it was up to me, I would have changed my name long ago, this stuff is meaningless. My mother, a Russian American did not allow my father to change his Greek name, my wife, a Mexican American does not allow me to change the name. . . . My wife knows more Greek than me. We go to Mexico a few times a year, it's just a few hours driving and she wants us to go to Greece to my grandparents' village. . . . She's learning Greek, she now reads novels. . . . Not my sister-in-law . . . but we're all gonna go to the village . . . yeah, this coming summer. . . . The kids will join us after camp finishes. . . . My cousin who grew up the next town over had travelled to Greece and met his wife there. . . . Their kids know Greek, one married a Greek man just last month . . . they met at the university." (anonymous interview, May 2, 2001)

Greek American families in the West tend to be mixed culturally and generationally. The interviews pointed to a number of interesting patterns that need to be tested in a statistical study. Greek Americans who maintained relations with other Greek Americans and with the Church, and those who married other ethnics, tended to be less likely to be divorced than those marrying "whites" and maintained marginal or no relations with ethnic community institutions. In addition, the day-to-day experience of the families in the West were such that maintaining Greek cultural traditions in the home required thought, planning, and considerable expense compared to, for example, families in the Northeast, who were more likely to be living nearby fellow ethnics and a Greek Orthodox Church.

Despite these families' privileged position on the class structure, individuals still expressed and discussed, to use the words of one interviewee, the "unease of being an ethnic family in a sea of whiteness." Culture, as symbolized in a "strange" and "long" ethnic last name, distinguished them from others in their communities. As one woman said, "I really think that we in the West and in general those in small towns with no other Greeks around change our names more than anybody else. We still do it. If you come across a Mann or Mannes in the West, you gotta ask them if they were Mathopoulos or Manoilidis or something. Michaels for Michalopoulos and on and on. And my favorite is Johnson . . . for Giannopoulos. Son of John. . . . And the children and grandchildren forget because it's just easier to forget than to remember, forgetting also that in the long run you're better off having a community to fall back on."

When interviewed, Americans born of Greek descent who grew up in a working-class family in immigrant or ethnic communities of the Northeast and Midwest, on one hand, but achieved a college education and are now solidly in the middle class, talk with nostalgia about "a house full of people all the time. Relatives, neighbors, friends, women from our parents' village. It feels like someone was over every single day. Just passing by and ringing the bell to have coffee, sit and chat, somebody was there always. . . . We used to call these women 'thia' ('aunt'). Of course we weren't related to them but we didn't know back then. Everybody was a 'thia' or a 'thio' ('uncle')."

Because Greece is regionally diverse in terms of gender relations in the family, Greek immigrant men and women arrived in the United States with a diversity of cultural expectations regarding gender relations in the family. For all, however, one expectation was and remains absolute—that is, the woman's primary responsibility is to her family's well-being, and she is to act on this responsibility however necessary. Greek patriarchy, which posits the family as the woman's primary sphere of action/s, in a sense, creates a strong and dynamic woman, both inside and outside the home and family, rather than a woman who gives up authority and responsibility to the man.

The mother is a central actor in the Greek immigrant and Greek American family (Kourvetaris, 1976). She is responsible for the family's daily affairs as well as long-term planning. Historically Greek women worked outside the home, primarily on the farms; Greece was an agriculturally based society well into the last quarter of the twentieth century, and the women worked on the farms alongside the men. It was only in the urban areas among the middle and upper classes that women had the luxury of not working; this was seen as a luxury because the work that the women engaged in was physically demanding. The public versus private dichotomy in Greece took a different form than it did in the industrialized societies of the twentieth century. In the rural areas (i.e., the places from where the majority of immigrants arrived), Greek women were often the "superwomen" that American women of the late twentieth century came to herald as an indicator of their liberation. Greek women, including the women who arrived as immigrants, were accustomed to working outside the home alongside men and active in the local markets buying and selling their goods and negotiating with middlemen and customers on prices. These activities were an integral element of the woman's responsibilities to her family as was the domestic work needed on a daily basis. (Again, this is not to say that sexism was not or is not alive and well in these communities; it simply took a different form than it did in the United States).

Upon their arrival in the United States, Greek immigrants faced a gender-segregated industrial economy, and the immigrants' creation and use of their networks reflected this gender segregation, but only partially. While the men frequented the coffeehouses for sociability and support (e.g., in finding work), the women created extensive networks of acquaintances and support among themselves. It was and still is the women who cross the gender-bounded networks in search of resources for family members and friends. Men limit themselves to being informed only about men's work-related resources and information, while the women are well informed about job resources for both genders and cross gender-bounded networks to seek out those resources. While the women are less likely to cross gender-bounded networks to request work information for married women, they become quite aggressive in crossing the gender boundaries to request work information for women who (through separation, divorce, or death of the husband/father) have become the main breadwinners of their families. The idea is that with no husband present, the mother is now the head of the family and must provide "like a man," so she needs work that "pays good wages" (Karpathakis and Harris, 2009). The men do respond to these requests by providing information. This could be partly responsible for the data we see in the census that Greek

American female-headed families have higher median income than their counterparts in the overall population.

It is not clear whether Greek Americans value education more than other ethnic groups. The importance of education was especially clear among the post-65 immigrants who arrived in the United States at a time when the economy was changing from a manufacturing to a service-based economy and the better-paying jobs required a college education. In addition to this, the majority of Greek immigrants had settled in urban areas with public university systems, making a college education a realistic goal for their children. Interviews with both Greek- and American-born women of Greek descent growing up in the post-1960s period reveal those parents assumed that both sons and daughters would receive a college education. The ideology that emerges from these interviews is that a college education and the ability to have an occupation that earns "descent money" is perceived as outside the realm of the gender relations but within the framework of one's responsibility to their family of procreation.

As one fifty-two-year-old financial analyst said,

> "How else would we get a job? . . . We never discussed why, it was assumed that my sister and I would go to college. . . . My father a feminist? By American standards he was very sexist. He wanted his dinner set at the table by his wife, he had all three women in the house on our tippy toes (laughs). But a college education, that's a different story. A woman must be prepared to support her family under any circumstances. She has responsibilities just like the man. A woman is not for looking pretty, according to my father. He would say, '[Y]ou want a pretty woman in your house? Go get yourself a statue to decorate. But you can't marry a statue. You need a real woman as a wife. . . .' My brother dated an American girl, a very pretty girl, no fire in her, but very very pretty and my father made her six month relationship with my brother miserable. He kept asking her what she wanted to do with her life besides get married, have kids and go shopping. . . . How would she take care of her family? He kept saying she wasn't *noikokyra* (housemistress) material. In his thick accent he was yelling at my brother, '[Y]ou have to marry a woman who will have the heart and arms and mind to raise your children and support them if something happens to you.' Anyway, she finally broke up with my brother because of my father. (Shakes her head laughing). . . . He married an Irish German no nonsense woman, an accountant and my father loves her. . . . he knows that for her the most important thing is her husband and children and that's why I think my father respects her so much. . . . She gave up a really good paying job when she had the twins but my father actually helped her get part time work from home while the kids are in school. . . . Oh no, it has nothing to do with feminism. Americans see it as feminism. My father sees it as a reality, a must." (anonymous interview, January 18, 2006)

Women born prior to this period, however, do posit a college education within the nexus of gender relations and ideologies. Callinicos (1990) and Scourby (1984), for example, discuss how Greek American women growing up in the decades of the 1930s to 1950s wanted to achieve a college education but were instead faced with parental and social expectations of marriage and family. Neither Callinicos nor Scourby, however, connect these ideologies to the social ideological frameworks created by a gender-segregated industrial economy and, instead, see the roots of this patriarchy as strictly within the Greek American family. It is important to keep in mind that during the manufacturing period, up until the late 1960s, a college education was rare for working-class men and women, and until the 1960s and 1970s the majority of Greek Americans were still working class in the manufacturing sectors. As such, it is quite possible that the ideologies relating gender with education were created in tandem with the labor markets and their requirements. As one sixty-nine-year-old second-generation American-born woman said,

"[W]omen didn't go to college back then. Men didn't go either for that matter. . . . This is the 1950s and women didn't work. It wasn't just the Greek Americans. Only the immigrant women worked because they had to. But we were expected to be housewives. My grandmother worked on the farms when she was a little girl before she came here and she worked till she was sixty two. My mother . . . she was born here . . . did not work a day in her life. My father had a coffee shop and she didn't have to work. . . . My daughter has a Master's degree in social work, my other daughter is a teacher. My grandson is a doctor and my granddaughter is in medical school. But my generation didn't go to college. The men found a job and the women got married and stayed home. . . . My father . . .he was born there . . . especially valued education. When my daughter was born in 1954 I remember my father telling me, 'I made the mistake of not sending you and your sisters to college.' He opened savings accounts for college for both mine and my sister's kids. . . . Five dollars a week for each of them. . . . We just didn't go to college. There was no need. I found a job after high school, my husband got a good job in the steel mills ten minutes from home after high school. He was making very good money. Men in union jobs got good money back then. Women didn't have to work, we could stay home with our kids." (anonymous interview, January 1999)

Greek American women, like all American women, growing up in the pre- and post-1960s periods had very different experiences regarding gender ideologies and roles. Greek American women, growing up either pre- or post-1965, were raised with the cultural command that their primary responsibility is to their families and that they were and are to meet these responsibilities however and whenever necessary. This simple proposition does not limit the woman to any one particular role or sphere; rather, the expectation is flexible and accommodative of different life stages and circumstances. As the census data show and contrary to myths, Greek immigrant and Greek American married women have high rates of labor force participation, but clearly in different family cycle stages.

Greek immigrant working-class women, as one American-born daughter expressed during the interview, "run the show. My mother wrote the script, produced and directed the show. She even designed and sewed the costumes. It was the same for my aunts and all their friends." The show is, of course, for this Greek American artist, the family life and the home. Again, "my father would come home, leave his pay check on the table and my mother took over . . . no, her paycheck was never laid on the table (laughs), she didn't have to I guess since she kept everything and managed everything."

The Greek immigrant woman is the *noikokyra* (housemistress). She works, she manages the finances, she runs the household while raising the kids, she is the "superwoman." She is responsible for her family's well-being and is a central stage actor in her family's upward mobility. She creates extensive support networks and taps into these for class-related and other resources.

Upward mobility, however, brings changes to the gender division of labor in the home as well as the gender-based relations between the spouses. As the family achieves upward mobility through the development of a small business, the woman quits her job and becomes a full-time housewife. This is the American Dream, the hallmark of a middle-class lifestyle.

The small family business brings financial ease and comfort; this means that the working-class woman can now exit the labor force and leave behind her a position of low wages, low prestige, and low authority. She gladly takes on this new role and redefines the concept of a *noikokyra* to a middle-class concept of a full-time homemaker. This is part of the American dream that the working-class women strive to achieve for themselves (although not for their daughters, for whom they desire a college education). Indeed, for immigrant women, having the capacity to stay at home as full-time homemakers is an integral element and indicator of having achieved the American Dream.

Along with the financial ease that the small business brings comes the search for social prestige and status. Modeling on American ideologies and images garnered through the mass media, the immigrant women begin a journey toward becoming a "lady" who is taken care of and protected by the gentleman. The women begin socializing themselves and the men into new roles and behaviors, behaviors as insignificant as holding the door open for the "lady," helping the "lady" with her overcoat, or moving the chair for her as she sits down. The men see their wives changing in their behaviors, dress, and consumption styles as well as their expectations of them, and it is not clear that they are always in approval. One woman recounts her husband's outburst: "You did not marry a British gentleman. You married a Greek from a village." Again, "No fairy will transform this roguish Greek villager into a northern European gentleman. I will not open the door for you as long as you are strong and healthy and you do not need help opening the door."

The new material comfort, financial ease, and higher discretionary income (i.e., the ability to purchase such luxury goods as clothing, cars, and vacations), as well as the new relations between spouses, are often interpreted as greater gender equality between the husband and wife. When the family purchases the small family business and the wife chooses not to be actively involved in it, along with the business finances the husband also assumes the responsibility of managing the family's daily and long-term finances. The end product of this process is that the function of managing the family's finances is removed from the woman's to the man's purview and authority. In short, upward mobility through the purchase of a small business results in the woman's loss of control over the family's finances. Rather than receiving the husband's paycheck weekly, the woman now receives a generous allowance for personal and household expenses. Since this allowance is greater than the paycheck, this money and new situation are interpreted as "having achieved the American Dream." To the extent that one of the myths of this American Dream is greater gender equality (compared to other cultures), there is the idea that since these women now are living the American Dream they are also living in "better" and "less sexist" relations with their husbands.

Greek- and American-born women combine elements of the two different cultural traditions, as they perceive them, to explain and make sense of their experiences. Although the women do try to sort through and distinguish which are the Greek and which are the American cultural elements that are part of their lives, it is still not clear that the ideals can in effect be so easily dichotomized.

One American-born woman whose immigrant father died at a young age began working full time after high school. She worked in a number of jobs, from food server to receptionist, and finally worked alongside her immigrant husband for five years when they bought a small coffee shop. As she said,

> "I was already in my thirties, I started working at fifteen. When my first son came I was thirty-four. He was a gift. I told my husband I wanted to stay home . . . he said '[I]t's your choice, you're the mother' (laughs). . . . Then my daughter came within two years. Suddenly I had it all. Two children, a wonderful and loving husband, a beautiful home, a brand new mini-van, no more arguments with my mother getting on my case because I had time to do everything. . . . My mother is Greek. The old school. The woman has to do everything in the home, she is the *noikokyra*. Look, this woman lost her husband when she was not even thirty, raised three kids on her own, she was never a weak woman to begin with, she was running the household from the day she got married while working. . . . I'm luckier than my mother was. I was home with my kids and living comfortably. I didn't have to work twelve hours a day worrying where my kids are and what they're doing. My mother told me, '[Y]ou don't have

to work anymore, you can stay home with your kids.' I don't know, this is what the American dream is all about . . . no more work for me. . . . My mother is living with my sister-in-law and takes care of the kids so she can work since my brother passed away five years ago. . . . My husband, my children, and my home. Maybe later when the children are older I'll go back to the restaurant and try out my new recipes but not now. The little one still needs her mommy at home."

References

Callinicos, C. 1990. *American Aphrodite: Becoming Female in Greek America.* New York: Pella Publishing.

Karpathakis, A. 1993. "Sojourners and Settlers: Greek Immigrants in Astoria, NY." Unpublished Ph.D. dissertation, Columbia University, New York.

———. 2002. "From Noikokyra to Lady: Greek Immigrant Women, Assimilation and Race: In E. Tastsoglou and L. Maratou-Alipranti (Eds.), The Greek Review of Social Research (Special Issue), *110,* 5–22.

Karpathakis A., and H. Harris. 2009. "Women Networking for Families: Class, Gender and Ethnicity in Job Searches Among Greek Immigrants in New York." In Evangelia Tastsoglou (Ed.). *Women, Gender and Diasporic Lives: Labor, Community, and Identity in Greek Migrations.* Langham, MD: Lexington Books.

Konstantellos. 1999. "Church and Family in Greek Orthodox Society from the Byzantine Era to the Present-Day United States: Problems and Issues." In S. Tsemberis, A. Karpathakis, and H. Psomiades (Eds.), *Greek American Families: Traditions and Transformations.* New York: Pella Publishing.

Kourvetaris, G. 1976. "The Greek American Family." In C. H. Mindel and R. W. Habenstein (Eds.), *Ethnic Families in America* (pp. 168–191). New York: Elsevier.

Laliotou, I. 2004. *Transnational Subjects: Acts of Migration and Cultures of Transnationalism Between Greece and America.* Chicago and London: University of Chicago Press.

Papanikolas, H. 2002. *An Amulet of Greek Earth: Generations of Immigrant Folk Culture.* Athens, OH: Swallow Press/Ohio University Press.

Scourby, A. 1980. "Three Generations of Greek Americans: A Study in Ethnicity." *International Migration Review 14*(1), 43–65.

———. 1984. *The Greek Americans.* Boston: Twayne Publishers.

Tavuchis, N. 1972. *Family and Mobility Among Second Generation Greek-Americans.* Athens, Greece: National Centre of Social Research.

Triandis, H. C. 1988. "Collectivism Versus Individualism: A Reconceptualization of a Basic Concept in Cross-Cultural Social Psychology." In G. K. Verma and C. Bagley (Eds.), *Cross-Cultural Studies of Personality, Attitudes and Cognition* (pp. 60–95). London: Macmillan.

———. 1993. "Collectivism and Individualism as Cultural Syndromes." *Cross-Cultural Research 27,* 155–180.

———. 1995. *Individualism and Collectivism.* Boulder, CO: Westview Press.

U.S. Census Bureau. 2000. United States Census 2000. www.census.gov/main/www/cen2000.html (accessed April 1, 2011).

Vlachos E. C. 1968. *The Assimilation of Greeks in the United States.* Athens, Greece: National Centre of Social Research.

5

■■■

The Italian American Family

Danielle Battisti

INTRODUCTION

This chapter provides an overview of Italian ethnic families in the United States from the period of mass Italian migration to the United States, beginning in the 1880s, to the present day. It will explore a variety of topics that have influenced the development of Italian American families, and Italian American individual and group identity as well.

However, a discussion of Italian American families must begin with the term itself. The term *Italian American* connotes assimilation while maintaining the persistence of an ethnic identity in some form. The term correctly asserts a trajectory of assimilation into life in the United States, yet it also suggests that transnational ties and identifications have continued to shape Italian American individual and group identities as well. Second, like other ethnic identities, groups, or forms of organization, the ethnic *family* is not a static or unchanging subject (Neils Conzen, 1992). At the turn of the century, Italian American families were drastically different in their composition, social organization, interactions, and identifications from Italian American families throughout much of the twentieth century. Moreover, the structure and role of ethnic families in individual lives may have been different for the immigrant generation than for American-born children and grandchildren of immigrants. Therefore, historians must assess the degree to which, and the ways in which, ethnic identities remained salient in individual, family, and community lives at any given time in the immigrant and ethnic experience. These are only a few conceptual issues to keep in mind while examining the history and development of Italian American families.

ITALIAN IMMIGRATION AND FAMILY LIFE

The establishment of Italian ethnic families in the United States must be understood in the context of the migration decisions, patterns, and practices that shaped their early existence. From the start of Italian mass migration to the United States in the late nineteenth century, continuing through the post–World War II period, the decision to migrate has most often been the result of family strategies aimed at maintaining household economies in the face of economic, social, and political changes. Like other migrant families, many Italians chose seasonal, semi-permanent, or permanent migration as a strategy for economic gain, social stability or advancement, and family maintenance in their homelands. Most often, resettlement in a far-away land was not the primary goal for many migrants. Historians have estimated that anywhere from one-third to one-half of all Italian immigrants to the United States from 1880 through the 1920s returned to Italy at some point in their lives (Bodnar, 1985; Cinel, 1991; Reeder, 2003:134; Wyman, 1993:10–11).

Furthermore, familial ties have also shaped the Italian immigration and resettlement process in another way. Italian immigration to the United States and elsewhere was shaped by the establishment of familial or village-based chain migration networks that sustained and shaped Italian immigration and resettlement patterns. Therefore, the maintenance of family life has been an essential component of the migration process itself. In his noteworthy study of Italian immigration to the United States and Argentina in the late nineteenth and early twentieth centuries, historian Samuel Baily has demonstrated the centrality of the family in Italian chain migrations to both countries. Baily (1999) reports that in 1908 and 1909 the U.S. Immigration Commission found that 98.7 percent of recently arrived southern Italians and 92.6 percent of northern Italians joined their relatives or friends already in the United States (1999:40). According to Baily, family and village-based networks made immigration and resettlement possible for Italians abroad. These networks helped determine how and why individuals migrated, where they chose to go, and how they resettled after their arrival. Moreover, family members and *paesani* not only spread information about the migration process and conditions abroad but also helped migrants find jobs, homes, and social connections after they had resettled in the United States and elsewhere (Baily, 1999; Yans-McLaughlin, 2005:39–47).

Mass Italian immigration to the United States began in the late nineteenth century and continued throughout the early twentieth century. The height of Italian immigration to the United States took place from 1870 to 1920 when roughly four million Italians entered American ports. However, this figure is slightly misleading. Many of these migrants were "birds of passage," who made multiple and seasonal migrations for economic opportunities. Others permanently returned to Italy after a period of residence in the United States. However, even with these seasonal and return migrations, a great number of Italians chose to stay in the United States. Approximately two million Italian immigrants permanently resettled in the United States from 1870 through the 1920s. They, and their children, helped make Italians one of the largest ethnic groups in the United States in the early twentieth century (Baily, 1999; Choate, 2008; Cinel, 1991; Wyman, 1993).

Many factors both pushed and pulled Italian migrants to the United States around the turn of the century. Italian immigrants in this period were part of a larger wave of European peasant and laborer migrations to the Americas in the late nineteenth and early twentieth centuries. Individuals and families chose migration as a strategy to cope with economic, social, and political changes resulting from rapid population growth, the development of industrial capitalism, and the advance of commercial agriculture in Europe. In Italy, national unification from 1866 to 1871 and unpopular policies imposed by the newly unified state, particularly regarding land tenure in the Italian South, also spurred emigration. These conditions prompted rural southern Italian peasant or agricultural families in particular, who were often the hardest hit by the forces of modernization, to look for work abroad. Italians and other groups of migrants were drawn to the burgeoning U.S. industrial economy and the abundant economic opportunities for laborers relative to those in their homeland. Throughout this period, the United States' open door policy toward European migrants allowed virtually unfettered Italian immigration to take place. Likewise, the Italian state failed to create barriers for emigrants; indeed it encouraged Italian emigration in a variety of ways. Moreover, new technology and services such as railroads, steamships, telegraph communication, international banking systems, quicker and more reliable postal systems, and shipping and labor agents all made international migrations more feasible for Italians and other European immigrant groups than ever before (Baily, 1999; Choate, 2008).

Italian immigration to the United States slowed to a trickle during the 1920s and remained low through the 1940s. In the 1920s, the relatively unrestricted access to the United States that Italians had once enjoyed ended as American lawmakers responded to increasing American nativism, racial anxieties, fears of immigrant radicalism, and anti-Catholicism. With the establishment of the National Origins System in 1924, Congress passed major restrictions to halt the immigration of Southern and Eastern European, Asian, and other "undesirable" immigrant groups. Moreover, policy shifts in Italy also slowed Italian immigration to the Americas. After 1927, Benito Mussolini's government began to discourage Italian migration abroad in an attempt to buttress Italian nationalism and recent territorial acquisitions by redirecting Italian migrants to colonial possessions in North Africa and elsewhere. Finally, the global impact of the Great Depression, as well as the outbreak of World War II, both contributed to the dramatic decrease in European immigration to the United States in the 1930s and 1940s (Choate, 2008; Cinel, 1991; Higham, 1955; Wyman, 1993).

After World War II Italian immigration to the United States resumed, albeit at lower rates than previous waves of immigration. From 1945 to 1980, roughly 600,000 Italians immigrated to the United States. Those migrants were part of a larger cohort of millions of Italian emigrants after World War II who, in the decades after the war, resettled in Europe, Oceania, Canada, South America, and the United States. The invasion, bombing, and occupation of Italy during World War II had damaged or destroyed industries, farms, homes, and basic infrastructures throughout the country but especially in the already relatively underdeveloped South, or *Mezzogiorno*. Wartime damage and the loss of Italian colonial possessions after the war helped to create a significant Displaced Persons and refugee population within the country. All these factors threatened political stability and economic recovery in Italy at the end of the war. For those reasons many Italians again turned to emigration to improve their lots. The Italian government, led by the Christian Democratic Party, estimated that the country suffered from a "surplus population" of two million people in 1952. It actively encouraged and supported emigration abroad in an attempt to avoid social unrest and to achieve economic and political stability throughout the postwar period (Gabaccia, 2000; Kraly, 1990).

As in previous migration waves, family unification continued to play a significant role in postwar Italian immigration to the United States. Throughout the 1950s and 1960s, Italian Americans with relatives in Italy who desired to immigrate to the United States, but who faced long waiting periods for immigrant visas under the restrictive quota limitations of the National Origins System, labored on behalf of their kinfolk. Italian Americans helped their Italian family members take advantage of nonquota refugee relief visas, lobbied for the extension of Italian immigration opportunities, and joined in a broader campaign to overturn the National Origins System. In 1965, the National Origins System was repealed and replaced with a policy that favored family unification as a mechanism for regulating American immigration. The activism and support of Italian Americans and other ethnic groups were significant in bringing about such a change in policy. As a result of the new immigration policy based on family unification, tens of thousands of Italians immigrated to the United States each year through the 1980s and joined their family members already in the country. However, immigration from Italy to the United States has again slowed in recent years (Battisti, 2010; Kraly, 1990).

THE FAMILY AND HOUSEHOLD WITHIN ITALY AND THE UNITED STATES

As previously argued, the immigrant and ethnic family in the United States was inherently shaped or influenced by the migration process itself. As such, family organization patterns could take a variety of forms. Italian American families could be nuclear or extended; they could span national boundaries or be contained within them; they could be mobile and migratory or permanently resettled. And although the institution of the family transmitted traditions and culture, it also changed over time and over generations. Italian immigrant and ethnic families are perhaps best described by one historian as "enduring but flexible institutions" (Baily, 1999).

At the turn of the century, more often than not, the Italian immigrant family must be viewed within a transnational context. Transnationalism connotes migration experiences that frequently link a migrant's movements and mentalities beyond or between borders in terms of economic, social, and cultural connections. Transnationalism does not place the migrant within one national narrative or society but, rather, identifies how he or she is a product of, and participant in, several societies even within a distinct national context. This is a point that, until recently, has been often overlooked when considering the immigrant and ethnic experience in the United States (Levitt and Waters, 2002; Schiller, Basch, and Blanc, 1992:12).

A transnational context is particularly important for understanding Italian immigrant families in which young single men or married male heads of households seasonally or semipermanently migrated without their families for short-term economic gain. Although Italians certainly immigrated to the United States as family units in the late nineteenth and early twentieth centuries, more often than not male workers preceded their family members abroad. Among those men, many ultimately chose to remain in the United States and later sent for their wives, children, and other relatives. However, the fact that so many Italian men lived transitory lives and maintained families across national boarders contributed to the transnational character of the typical Italian immigrant family in this period (Baily, 1999; Reeder, 2003).

The transnational family lives of many turn-of-the-century Italian immigrants are expertly demonstrated in the works of Linda Reeder (2003) and other historians (see, for example, Baily, 1993; Gabaccia and Iachovetta, 2002; Peck, 2000). According to Reeder (2003), three-quarters of all Sicilian migrants to the United States from 1880 to 1914 were male, suggesting the high rate of transnational households for the group during that period. In her study of Italian households in Sutera, Sicily, Reeder has shown how the women who stayed behind while their husbands, sons, and other male relatives migrated abroad were active participants in both the migration process and in maintaining their families. She aptly calls these women "household managers and kinship keepers" (Reeder, 2003). Italian women remaining in Italy shared in decisions about family migrations and helped raise money for the voyages of their male family members. In addition, they managed remittances sent home and often used their family's newly acquired resources to purchase land, household goods, or whatever else was needed to facilitate their family's upward mobility, including an education for their children. In these and other ways we see both how Italian households spanned the Atlantic and how they were shaped by both migrants and those family members who stayed behind (Reeder, 2003).

Maintaining transnational families could certainly put a strain on familial relationships. The physical and emotional distance between husbands and wives, and parents and children, could weaken bonds among family members. But just as often, transnational relationships became a source of strength and family maintenance. A family's economic success, facilitated by taking advantage of opportunities in an international labor market, could allow parents to maintain authority over their sons and daughters. By seeking out the best economic opportunities, struggling rural peasant families, particularly those from the impoverished and underdeveloped *Mezzogiorno*, could provide sons and daughters with material comforts, inheritances, dowries, and educations that they otherwise would have been unable to provide (Peck, 2000; Reeder, 2003).

THE ITALIAN AMERICAN FAMILY WITHIN THE ETHNIC COMMUNITY

While many Italian migrants maintained transnational families, for at least a period of their lives, other immigrants located the center of their family life in their new or adopted country. This pattern became increasingly common for Italian immigrants in the early twentieth century as sojourners decided to resettle in the United States and then sent for their families, or alternatively as they established families with other immigrants or American-born men and women who became their spouses in the United States. This trend was hastened with the increasing restrictions limiting Italian immigration in the 1920s. New laws regulating immigration made Italian return and reentry to the United States increasingly difficult, thereby indirectly promoting permanent resettlement in the country.

Just as family members and *paesani* migrated one after the other to the United States, they often settled together in family- and village-based neighborhoods, thereby creating ethnic enclaves and immigrant communities in American cities throughout the late nineteenth and first half of the twentieth centuries. Although Italian American communities formed in towns and cities throughout the United States, the largest, most enduring, and most notable of these communities include Italian settlements in the greater New York City area, Philadelphia, Boston, and Chicago (Alba, 1985).

In their studies of Italian American settlements Samuel Baily (1999:121–171, quote 159) and Donna Gabaccia (1984) found that late nineteenth- and early twentieth-century Italian immigrants based their resettlement decisions on several factors. First, as the result of kinship- and village-based migration and resettlement patterns, Italian immigrants settled close to their family members and fellow villagers. Therefore many early Italian American communities not only reflected the ethnic character of the settlement but a regional character as well. Calabrians settled with other Calabrians, Sicilians with other Sicilians, and so on. Not only did immigrants live side by side with their relatives or fellow villagers, but it was not uncommon for recently arrived immigrants to live in their relatives' homes. While getting a job and learning the lay of the land, many immigrants stayed temporarily with relatives who had already immigrated. Then after a period of residence with their relatives, the new immigrant would find more permanent accommodations, often nearby. Thus, Italian American neighborhoods cannot only be understood as ethnic enclaves; in many ways they were sites that reflected a complicated web of familial connections as well (Baily, 1999; Gabaccia, 1984).

Italian American communities were also shaped by economic and labor patterns. In an age before accessible and affordable mass transportation, immigrants often chose to settle close to their work spaces. The combination of these resettlement decisions had a significant impact on the formation and maintenance of Italian American communities in the United States. Living and working in close proximity to one another helped foster and sustain Italian cultural interactions and language maintenance among immigrants and their children at work, at home, and in shared neighborhood social spaces including churches, schools, clubs, mutual aid societies, and commercial sites. For these reasons, Baily has called the Italian American neighborhood, "the most important sphere of social and economic activity beyond the family" (Baily, 1999:121–171; Cohen, 1992:37–86).

Although men and women certainly interacted in a variety of ways and in a variety of settings within Italian American neighborhoods, Italian men and women often occupied distinct social spheres as well. Women most often socialized with their female relatives and neighbors primarily in their homes, at work, and in neighborhood shops and public spaces while they were going about their daily activities. Italian American men, however, had more time for socialization with other men in a recreational setting. Certainly workplaces were sites of male camaraderie, but after hours Italian American men were less tied to their homes than women. They joined social clubs and left their homes for activities such as card games and bocce ball matches. But Italian American men also brought friends and relatives into their homes for meals, games, and political discussions, all of which facilitated interactions among Italian American men and women as well (Cohen, 1992; Guglielmo, 2010).

The formation of spaces where Italian immigrants and their children lived, worked, and socialized together created conditions that made endogamous Italian marriages common in the late nineteenth and early twentieth centuries. Despite increased parental anxiety about the enlarged pool of unfamiliar partners available to their sons and daughters, young Italian American men and women tended to meet their future mates at affairs sponsored by ethnic associations, at family gatherings, or in their neighborhoods. Under these circumstances Italian immigrants and the American-born children of Italian immigrants continued to transmit Italian or Italian American cultural traditions and identities to their children throughout much of the twentieth century. By the World War II era, while in-group marriages remained common for Italian ethnics, a variety of factors would lead to decreases in rates of endogamous marriage among Italian Americans and therefore have an effect on the transmission of Italian American cultural identity in the late twentieth century (Baily, 1999:150–153; Cohen, 1992:74, 187–189).

But it was not only the structural conditions of Italian American communities that helped facilitate in-group marriages and Italian American family identities. In his study of Italian Harlem, Robert Orsi has argued that Italian Americans in that community considered the family a central cultural marker in their individual and collective lives. Men and women understood themselves, and were understood by others, in their ethnic community in terms of their familial relationships and the links among their families and other members of the community. Moreover, Italian Americans in Harlem also created familial links with those not biologically related to them. Orsi (1985) argues that lines between the home, the apartment complex, and the larger neighborhood were not clearly defined; and that the scope of the "blood" family was enlarged by the adoption of special relationships with *comari* and *compari*. It was these cultural values centered around the ethnic family that helped promote in-group marriages and the maintenance of Italian or Italian American familial identities as well (1985:75–106).

ITALIAN AMERICAN FAMILIES AND GENDER ROLES

The vast majority of Italians who immigrated to the United States around the turn of the century had been rural peasant farmers in Italy. Therefore, throughout the early twentieth century, Italian immigrant and ethnic families in the United States were overwhelmingly working class in character. In her study of Italian immigrant and Italian American families in New York City in the first half of the twentieth century, Miriam Cohen (1992) found that ethnic Italians generally came from relatively large families headed by men with a low earning capacity. Approximately half of the male heads of household in her study were unskilled laborers who were often engaged in temporary or seasonal work throughout much of the twentieth century. Under these circumstances, the practical concerns of these working-class people often dictated that all family members pool their resources and contribute financially to the household income. Therefore, despite patriarchal cultural ideals that placed women within the household, Italian immigrant and Italian American wives and daughters often joined their husbands, sons, fathers, and brothers in the workforce (Cohen, 1992:1–14, 41–44, 88–93; for peasant origins of Italian immigrant families and patriarchal cultural norms, see Ewen, 1985:33–35).

Adult sons were certainly expected to work, and Cohen (1992:41–53, 90–91) found that an overwhelming majority of them did so. But perhaps more unexpectedly given common preconceptions about the role of women in ethnic Italian households, Italian women went to work outside of the home as well. Certainly home work, including taking in boarders and engaging in piecework from the home to be returned to manufacturing industries, were ways Italian women contributed to their family's income. However, industries in New York City offered ample opportunities for female employment outside of the home as well. New York City was the center of the country's garment industry throughout the early twentieth century, as well as the site of other manufacturing industries that regularly employed women. Italian American adult women and young girls regularly found work in New York's garment industry—either in factories, small shops, or within the home. The fashion industry, which included garment, millinery, and artificial flower production, employed 80 percent of all Italian female workers in New York City in 1905. Further attesting to the importance of daughters' contributions to their family's household income, Cohen (1992) reports that 46 percent of all single Italian-born women over the age of sixteen in 1905 were wage earners. That statistic was double the rate of their American-born counterparts. In 1925, among second-generation Italian American young women, the figure rose to 61 percent (Cohen, 1992; for more about Italian American women in garment work, see Ewen, 1985).

Despite the fact that so many Italian immigrant and ethnic women worked outside of the home, Cohen (1992) and other historians have found that the experience was not necessarily an Americanizing one. Cohen has argued that familial, residential, and labor patterns tended to overlap and reinforce one another. These women lived together, traveled to work together, and worked in overwhelmingly ethnic shops, where they generally spoke Italian. Such factors helped to maintain an ethnic identity in their individual, family, and community lives (1992:64–68).

Both sons and daughters in ethnic Italian working-class families contributed to their household's economy, but there were qualitative and quantitative differences in their contributions. Family strategies for economic success did not benefit all members alike. Italian immigrant and ethnic women were often expected to make extra sacrifices for their families. Italian sons normally turned over about half of their wages to their family to cover room and board expenses. They were allowed to keep their remaining wages for personal use or savings. Daughters, however, were generally expected to turn over most of their pay to their family, keeping only a small portion for purchasing clothes. Daughters were also expected to do household chores as well and therefore had less free time than their brothers. Sometimes, Italian daughters in working-class households worked even more than their brothers so that their brothers might stay in school or obtain skilled training of some kind (Cohen, 1992:83–84, 98–99).

Yet even while working outside of the home was not uncommon for working-class Italian women, the lives of Italian immigrant and ethnic women were fundamentally shaped by their roles within the home. During their childbearing and childrearing years, Italian American women usually remained within the home. In the early twentieth century the average Italian immigrant woman bore five to six children during her lifetime. The responsibilities of motherhood in these cases kept many Italian women within the home regardless of their family's financial needs. For these reasons, it was wives and mothers, more so than their daughters, that engaged in home piecework to supplement their family's income. Such work could be done while juggling the responsibilities of child care and homemaking. This is not to say that men in Italian American families never helped with household chores or child care. However, for Italian immigrants and ethnic Italians around the turn of the century, preserving gender differences and, at the very least, the outward appearance of proper male and female behavior was a matter of honor and culturally valued. For these groups, the breakdown of culturally proscribed gender roles was a sign of economic failure and social turmoil (Cohen, 1992:88–113).

Along with earning income for their families and taking care of the home and children, women were also the primary managers of money and household consumption in Italian American families. In both Italy and the United States, family members turned over their income to their wives and mothers to manage. While saving as much as possible, women were responsible for spending the family's income on household goods and exercised a great deal of influence in determining how it would be allocated. Therefore, while early Italian American families operated within patriarchal cultural ideals, Italian American women wielded a great deal of authority within them (Cohen, 1992: Ewen, 1985).

THE ITALIAN AMERICAN FAMILY AND THE CATHOLIC CHURCH IN AMERICA

Italian American individuals and families have often found cultural expression in their religious identity and practices. The Catholic Church—as both an institution and a cultural construct—has deeply influenced, and been influenced by, Italian American familial identities in a variety of ways. First, the construction of an Italian American ethnic identity for many individuals has been linked to and influenced by Italian and Italian American Catholicism. Italian American Catholicism has been less characterized by regular attendance at Mass and more associated with popular folk Catholicism in both Italy and the United States. Along with more traditional forms of worship, public celebrations or *festas*, the veneration of the Virgin Mary, and the honoring of one's hometown patron saint have become important aspects of Italian American Catholicism and Italian American ethnicity as well (Orsi, 1985:1–106, 168–171).

Practicing popular and traditional forms of Catholic worship, however, have not only become a marker of Italian ethnicity for many Italian Americans but the Catholic Church has also provided a social space in which Italian American families and members of the community have come together and reaffirm their relationships with one another. In taking part in rituals such as baptisms, holy communions, marriages, funerals, and even public *festas,* Italian Americans were demarcating their membership in the family unit at various points in their life cycle. Moreover, in commemorating these religious occasions, Italian Americans were taking part in important social activities. Religious ceremonies and celebrations gathered family members to take part in, to witness, and to collectively celebrate such events. Italian American women were often significant in fostering the connections between religion and family life in this way. In planning and preparing for christenings, weddings, holidays, and other celebrations, Italian American women linked religious practices with their familial and ethnic identities (Cohen, 1992:107–108; Orsi, 1985:100–101, 177–178).

Symbolic representations of the family were also important to many practicing Italian American Catholics. Religious symbols underscored the importance of the family for many Italian American Catholics. The Madonna, often depicted holding the infant Christ in her arms, and Saint Ann, Mary's mother, were common symbols of motherhood revered by Italian American women. The Trinity was often conceptualized as the Holy Family. These, and other figures in the Catholic tradition, demonstrated the central role that the family played in infusing Catholicism with meaning for many Italian Americans (Orsi:1985: 86).

CONTEMPORARY ITALIAN AMERICAN FAMILIES

Italian Americans continue to cluster in certain areas of the United States—with about 70 percent living in the Northeast and making up approximately one-sixth of New York City's population throughout much of the twentieth century (Alba, 1985:115–117; Gallo, 1974). But, with notable exceptions, Italian American ethnic neighborhoods have all but disappeared in the postwar period. The most famous Italian enclave, New York City's "Little Italy," is now occupied mostly by Chinese immigrants and Chinese Americans and has been reduced to a tourist destination that people visit to imagine a nostalgic past. Some Italian American communities do still exist. Jordan Stanger-Ross's (2009) recent study of the persistence of Italian American neighborhoods in Philadelphia after World War II has shown that Italian American communities, and construction of Italian American ethnicity that is related to public life and place, continue to exist. However, such examples are distinctly in the minority.

Declining rates of new Italian immigration and changes within White ethnic communities have profoundly affected Italian Americans. By the mid-twentieth century, White ethnic communities in the United States were experiencing significant changes in their composition and relationships with other Americans. White ethnics had become increasingly incorporated into the American mainstream through their participation in American labor unions and national political parties in the early twentieth century. They were also increasingly influenced by mass cultural forms even before World War II (Cohen, 1990; Ewen, 1985:228–234). Moreover, during World War II many young men and women left ethnic neighborhoods for service in the army or jobs in wartime industries where they increasingly interacted with members of other ethnic groups for the first time. This trend continued after the war as White ethnic Americans left urban ethnic enclaves for college or for residence in ethnically mixed suburbs for perhaps the first time (Alba and Nee, 2003: 67–123; Cohen, 1992:187–189; Cohen, 2003; Fleegler, 2008:59–84; Gleason, 1981; Wall, 2008; for figures on Italian American postwar suburbanization, see Alba, 1985:86–89, 115–117).

Accompanying such geographic or residential mobility was the increasing social mobility of many Italian Americans in the postwar period. All of these factors helped contribute to the rising social status of Italian Americans after World War II. Many Italian Americans and other White ethnics were now able to achieve middle-class status. From 1947 to 1968, American economic growth allowed American families to achieve real income increases of about 50 percent. Many second- and third-generation Italian Americans not only benefited from such growth, but having been the beneficiaries of American public education and, more recently higher education, were increasingly able to enter into white-collar and professional work as well (Alba, 1985:81–84, 116–129).

Another important factor contributing to postwar changes for American ethnic groups, including Italian Americans, was their increasing cultural acceptance by older-stock White

Americans. Wartime and postwar unity campaigns promoted ethnic tolerance and cultural pluralism. Likewise, advances in anthropology, sociology, biology, and other fields produced a shift from biological to social explanations of racial, ethnic, and cultural differences among groups of people by mid-century. Members of distinct racial and ethnic groups were once believed to inherent distinct traits. Such ideas were dispelled by mid-century. These ideological shifts helped facilitate the social acceptance of once marginalized ethnic groups into the American mainstream (Barkan, 1992; Brattain, 2007:1386–1413; Fleegler, 2008:59–84; Roediger, 2005).

These and other factors account for the increasing rates of out-of-group marriages for Italian Americans. Sociologists who study White ethnic intermarriages have found that intermarriage rates increase for each generation in the United States, although they increased at lower rates for Italian Americans than for other White ethnic groups (Alba, 1976). Even so, Italian Americans have married outside of their ethnic group in increasingly large numbers throughout the twentieth century. The 1980 census indicated that 43.5 percent of self-identified Italian Americans come from families of mixed ancestry (Alba, 1985:111, 145–150). Using twentieth-century census data, sociologists Richard Alba and Victor Nee (2003) forecast that rates of White ethnic intermarriages will continue to occur at high levels but that a significant minority of White ethnics will continue to marry within their ethnic group.

However, even intermarriage does not completely negate some form of ethnic cultural persistence for all White ethnics, including self-identified Italian Americans. Ethnic identity continues to be important for many individuals and families despite increasing rates of intermarriage and the existence of second-, third-, and even fourth-generation American-born Italian Americans. Given the statistics about Italian American residential patterns and intermarriage, it should be no surprise that Italian American communities no longer provide the primary frame of reference for the socialization of the children of ethnic Americans. The transmission of ethnicity or an ethnic identity takes place less within an ethnic community or within public spaces than it does within the family and within private homes (Alba, 1990:185–206).

For contemporary White ethnic Americans, including self-described Italian Americans, one's ethnic identity is often "voluntary" and "symbolic" (Alba and Nee, 2003:67–123; Gans, 1996). In this view, member of the third or fourth generation of an ethnic group continue to perceive themselves as a member of an ethnic group, but their ethnic identity is no longer a determining factor in their everyday lives. For contemporary Italian Americans, and other White ethnics, ethnicity may consist of little more than ethnic ancestry, memories, and private ethnic attachments such as eating "authentic" ethnic foods or engaging in periodic ethnic celebrations. The expression of ethnicity can be suppressed at various times and expressed at others. Such popular contemporary expressions of Italian ethnicity are almost always private rather than public. They are born out of private experiences rather than public identities. Ethnic identities are therefore intricately linked with one's family organization and personal experiences (Alba and Nee, 2003:67–123). Evidence for the privatization of an Italian American ethnic identity is found in the frequency with which contemporary Italian Americans identify their ethnicity with their family life. In a survey of postwar working-class and middle-class Italian Americans, Andrew Greeley (1971) found that more so than any other ethnic group, Italian Americans were more likely to live near their close relatives and to visit with them frequently. Contemporary ethnicity is often manifested in the home, in family relationships, memories, celebrations, and in meals. In popular culture this phenomenon has found expression in a variety of examples. Michael Corleone's insistence that his actions are done to protect his family in *The Godfather* series; the Castorinis' toast, "*alla famiglia*," concluding the 1987 romantic comedy *Moonstruck;* and even the interrelated web of Italian American New Jersey housewives in the recent Bravo television series all showcase the centrality of the family to modern-day constructions of Italian American ethnicity (see also Jacobson, 2006).

These trends have prompted some scholars to wonder whether Italian Americans have entered "into the twilight of ethnicity" (Alba, 1985). They speculate whether ethnicity will continue to play a central role in individual, family, and broader group life for Italian Americans of the third and fourth generation and beyond. This is an important question, and it reflects the degree to which Italian Americans have become part of the American mainstream, and how much definitions of the "mainstream" have changed throughout the twentieth century. However, recent work suggests that ethnicity will continue to be a salient identity marker in the lives of Italian Americans and other White ethnic groups in the United States. Although ethnic identities are certainly fluid and will continue to change, scholars theorize that ethnicity will likely continue to play a significant influence in the private lives, and especially the family lives, of Italian Americans and other White ethnic groups (Alba and Nee, 2003:67–123).

References

Alba, R. 1976. "Social Assimilation Among American Catholic National Origin Groups." *American Sociological Review 41* (December), 1030–1046.

———. 1985. *Italian Americans: Into the Twilight of Ethnicity.* Englewood Cliffs, NJ: Prentice Hall.

———. 1990. *Ethnic Identity: The Transformation of White America.* New Haven: Yale University Press.

Alba, R., and V. Nee. 2003. *Remaking the American Mainstream: Assimilation and Contemporary Immigration.* Cambridge, MA: Harvard University Press.

Baily, S. 1999. *Immigrants in the Lands of Promise: Italians in Buenos Aires and New York City, 1870 to 1914.* Ithaca, NY: Cornell University Press.

Barkan, E. 1992. *The Retreat of Scientific Racism.* New York: Cambridge University Press.

Battisti, D. 2010. "Refugees, Relatives, and Reform: Italian Americans and Italian Immigration During the Cold War, 1945–1965." Ph.D. dissertation, State University of New York at Buffalo.

Bodnar, J. 1985. *The Transplanted: A History of Immigrants in Urban America.* Bloomington: Indiana University Press.

Brattain, M. 2007, December. "Race, Racism, and Anti-Racism," *American Historical Review 112* (December 2007), 1386–1413.

Choate, M. 2008. *Emigrant Nation: The Making of Italy Abroad.* Cambridge, MA: Harvard University Press.

Cinel, D. 1991. *The National Integration of Italian Return Migration, 1870–1930.* Cambridge, UK: Cambridge University Press.

Cohen, L. 1990. *Making a New Deal: Industrial Workers in Chicago, 1919–1939.* New York: Cambridge University Press.

———. 1992. *Workshop to Office: Two Generations of Italian Women in New York City, 1900–1950.* Ithaca, NY: Cornell University Press.

———. 2003. *A Consumer's Republic: The Politics of Mass Consumption in Postwar America.* New York: Knopf.

Ewen, W. 1985. *Immigrant Women in the Land of Dollars: Life and Culture on the Lower East Side, 1890–1925.* New York: Monthly Review Press.

Fleegler, R. L. 2008, Winter. "Forget All Differences Until the Forces of Freedom Are Triumphant": The World War II–Era Quest for Ethnic and Religious Tolerance. *Journal of American Ethnic History 27*(2), 59–84.

Gabaccia, D. 1984. *From Sicily to Elizabeth Street: Housing and Social Change Among Italian Immigrants, 1880–1930.* Albany: State University of New York Press.

———. Gabaccia, D. 2000. *Italy's Many Diasporas.* Seattle: University of Washington Press.

Gabaccia D., and F. Iachovetta (Eds.). 2002. *Women, Gender, and Transnational Lives: Italian Workers of the World.* Toronto: University of Toronto Press.

Gallo, P. 1974. *Ethnic Alienation: The Italian Americans.* Rutherford, NJ: Fairleigh Dickinson Press.

Gans, H. 1996. "Symbolic Ethnicity: The Future of Ethnic Groups and Cultures in America." In W. Sollors (Ed.), *Theories of Ethnicity: A Classical Reader* (pp. 425–459). New York: New York University Press.

Gleason, P. 1981. "Americans All: World War II and the Shaping of American Identity." *The Review of Politics 43*(4), 483–518.

Greeley, A. 1971. *Why Can't They Be Like Us? America's White Ethnic Groups.* New York: E. P. Dutton.

Guglielmo, J. 2010. *Living the Revolution: Italian Women's Resistance and Radicalism in New York City, 1880–1945.* Chapel Hill: University of North Carolina Press.

Higham, J. 1955. *Strangers in the Land: Patterns of American Nativism, 1860–1925.* New Brunswick, NJ: Rutgers University Press.

Jacobson, M. F. 2006. *Roots Too: White Ethnic Revival in Post–Civil Rights America.* Cambridge, MA: Harvard University Press.

Kraly, E. P. 1990. "U.S. Refugee Policies and Refugee Migration." In Tucker et al., *Immigrant and United States Foreign Policy* (pp. 88–95). Boulder, CO: Westview Press.

Levitt P., and M. C. Waters (Eds.). 2002. "Introduction." In *The Changing Face of Home: The Transnational Lives of the Second Generation.* New York: Russell Sage Foundation.

Neils Conzen, K., et al. 1992, Fall. "The Invention of Ethnicity: A Perspective from the U.S.A." *Journal of American Ethnic History 92*(12), 3–39.

Orsi, R. 1985. *The Madonna of 115th Street: Faith and Community in Italian Harlem, 1880–1950.* New Haven, CT: Yale University Press.

Peck, G. 2000. *Reinventing Free Labor: Padrones and Immigrant Workers in the North American West, 1880–1930.* New York: Cambridge University Press.

Reeder, L. 2003. *Widows in White: Migration and the Transformation of Rural Women, Sicily, 1880–1928.* Toronto: University of Toronto Press.

Roediger, D. 2005. *Working Toward Whiteness: How America's Immigrants Became White—The Strange Journey from Ellis Island to the Suburbs.* Cambridge, MA: Basic Books.

Schiller, N. G., L. Basch, and C. S. Blanc (Eds.). 1992. *Towards a Transnational Perspective on Migration, Race, Class, Ethnicity and Nationalism Reconsidered.* New York: Annals of New York.

Stanger-Ross, J. 2009. *Staying Italian: Urban Change and Ethnic Life in Postwar Toronto and Philadelphia.* Chicago: University of Chicago Press.

Wall, W. 2008. *Inventing the "American Way": The Politics of Consensus from the New Deal to the Civil Rights Movement.* New York: Oxford University Press.

Wyman, M. 1993. *Round-Trip to America: The Immigrants Return to Europe, 1880–1930.* Ithaca, NY: Cornell University Press.

Yans-McLaughlin, V. 2005. "New Wine in Old Bottles: Family, Community, and Immigration." In D. Gerber and A. Kraut (Eds.), *American Immigration and Ethnicity* (pp. 39–47). New York: Palgrave Macmillan.

6

■■■

The Polish American Family

Mary Patrice Erdmans

INTRODUCTION

Prior to World War I, an estimated 1.5 million Poles immigrated to the United States. Mostly a labor migration (as rural farm workers were dislocated by the transition from feudalism), the immigrants settled primarily in the Mid-Atlantic and Midwestern regions near industries where they found work—for example, the meat-packing industries in Chicago, the brickyards in Grand Rapids, Michigan, and the coal mines of Pennsylvania. The descendants of these early immigrants continued to work in manufacturing industries in cities such as Detroit, Pittsburgh, Cleveland, Buffalo, and Chicago—which has the largest Polish American community. By the end of the twentieth century, later-generation Polish Americans were moving into the middle class with postsecondary educations and professional occupations. In the 2000 census, roughly 9 million Americans identified themselves as having Polish ancestry.

This chapter describes one particular Polish American family composed of five sisters born between 1923 and 1936. Like many Polish American women of their generation, their identities were developed in the home and in the church. These five sisters—Caroline, Fran, Nadine, Angel, and Mari, referred to as the Grasinski Girls—are also my mother and my aunts. They grew up in Southwest Michigan, and I conducted life story interviews with them between 1998 and 2002.[1] Their discussions about what it means to be Polish American illustrate the salience of the family as a site for the reproduction of ethnicity. Ethnic identity changes over time and space so that the meaning of Polishness for the later generations differs from earlier generations. The ways that ethnicity influences the family is often hidden in the later generations as a result of assimilation, but it is nonetheless important as a means of connecting the generations and providing history to the family. Women play a primary role in the reconstruction and continuation of both ethnicity and the family.

---

[1]This chapter is an adaptation from Mary Patrice Erdmans, *The Grasinski Girls: The Choices They Had and the Choices They Made*, Athens: Ohio University Press, 2004.

THE GRASINSKI FAMILY: BLOODLINES AND TRADITIONS

At one point during the middle of this project, one of my aunts pulled me aside and confided, "You know, there's not much that's Polish about us except the name Grasinski, and that isn't really Polish, it's Russian." Other family members pointed out that our bloodlines are predominantly German. Johann Fifelski, rumored to have been born out of wedlock, would have been a Von Wagonner had his father the lord married his mother the peasant. Instead, the single mother's surname got passed down, and with it, Polishness. Or so the story is told. Johann's great-granddaughter and granddaughter-in-law wrote a detailed Fifelski history that never mentions this bloodline slippage. But my aunts and my own sisters have all heard this. The story that we come from aristocracy through illegitimacy is a rewarding fantasy of origin that helps us to accept our class position while at the same time reminding us that class and status do matter. In this case, status was linked to ethnicity because the lord was German and the peasant Polish.

Not only are we German, but we're supposedly Russian as well. Mari believes she is mostly Russian; Nadine acknowledges Russian bloodlines (she sells her crafts under the label "Vineyard Couture, made by Nadja," using a Russian spelling of her name); and Caroline, the most "practicing" Polish American of the sisters, laments:

> I'm not even sure they were Polish. That Gruszczynski, he could have been Russian, 'cause you see that name a lot on the Russian side, and could even have been Russian-Jewish or something a little bit in there, I mean. And then my dad is German too, because his mother was pure German, you know, Grandma Anna was pure German. And then on [the] Fifelski side, they say there was a lot of German and then Polish [laugh].

The older sisters support their claims to Russian ancestry (and perhaps even that they were Russian Jews) by noting that the priest wrote their father's name with a "y" ("Grushinsky") on his baptismal certificate (evidence of his Jewishness is found in a Catholic ceremony?), that their father spoke some Yiddish words (they remember the word *shiksa*), that their brother "looked Russian," and that their mother Helen told them that their Grandma and Grandpa Gruszczynski had Russian blood (yet in the same breath they tell me that their grandma Anna Tice Gruszczynski was "pure German").

The confusion in part relates to the political morass of history: because Poland was annexed in the 1790s by its more powerful neighbors Prussia, Russia, and Austria, the emigrants who left before Poland regained its independence in 1918 were not Polish nationals. The Grasinski sisters vaguely understand this. This ambiguity of borders allows them more freedom to construct their myth of origin, though they would never think of themselves as actively constructing their ethnicity. They confess to blood mixing and lineage confusion because they understand ethnicity as a descent identity—something that is passed down the generations, that is "given" to them.[2] Polishness is in the blood; they feel its primordial pulse in their toes tapping to the accordion and their fingertips moving over the shiny amber beads of the rosary. Mari finds her Polishness "in my face, my legs, and my mannerisms." Nadine says the Grasinski Girls may be more Russian and German, but they "still got that Polish blood."[3]

Their reputably thin Polish bloodline is more than offset by their thick Polish heritage. They were raised by ethnic Poles. Despite their modest abjuration of Polishness, all records

---

[2]See Werner Sollors' discussion of consent and descent identities in *Beyond Ethnicity* (1986).

[3]Mary Waters, in *Ethnic Options*, shows that later-generation European Americans often define themselves predominantly by one ethnicity even when they descend from various ancestries. Factors influencing choice of ancestry include generation, knowledge of the ancestry, signifiers like surnames or physical appearance, and social desirability of the ethnic group (1990: Chapter 3). See also Sollors (1986:232).

indicate the Fifelskis, Chylewskas, Zuławskis, and Gruszczynskis were Polish Roman Catholics. They came from the Prussian partition of Poland; and spoke Polish; their gravestones were written in Polish; and they moved to a Polish rural community in the United States, were part of a Polish Roman Catholic parish, and taught their children that they were Polish.

Leaving aside bloodlines, Fran makes a more sociological argument for why "we are not Polish!" The Grasinski Girls don't "do" Polish things, she says: they don't follow many Polish traditions, cook or eat much Polish food, speak Polish, belong to Polish organizations, or visit Poland. Compared to her friends who are actively Polish, she and her sisters fall short.

Do you keep Polish traditions? I ask Nadine. "Not that much. I guess Polish traditions to me would be having the *opłatki*, getting blessed food for Holy Saturday." Do you do those things? "No, not really. Sometimes." And she "loves Polish food," especially "the sauerkraut and *gołąbki* and some of the Polish things." And even though she edits the first draft insisting I include that she "enjoys cooking this way," she seldom does—in fact only on Christmas, and then not every year. Nadine finally concedes, "Aaah, not that many Polish customs." The Grasinski Girls are not unique. Most Polish American families of later generations do not "do" much that is Polish. It is hard to distinguish a third-generation Polish family from a third-generation Italian family except in terms of the religious icons on the walls and the aroma coming from the kitchen.

Nadine said, "I love being Polish, I love Polishness." Mari said, "It's not something I think about, but it's with me every day of my life." All the Grasinski Girls expressed a similar affection for being Polish. Although they may not "be" or "do" Polish in terms of bloodlines and behavior, Polishness still gives them something. So what does it give them? What does ethnicity mean to third- and fourth-generation women of European ancestry?[4] How does it shape their family?

KISS ME, I'M POLISH

In the early twentieth century, the Yankee Protestants and Dutch Calvinists were the industrial, political, and moral leaders of Grand Rapids, Michigan. Poles and other new immigrants (e.g., Lithuanians and Italians) occupied the lower class rungs.[5] The Poles were paid less than their Dutch co-workers, they were politically underrepresented, and they were morally criticized for their more unrestrained leisure activities (Bratt and Meehan, 1993; Kleiman, 1985; Lydens, 1976; Skendzel, 1999:5–10; Symanski, 1964). This all changed, however, by midcentury. With immigration sharply curtailed, the community was mostly second- and third-generation Americans of Polish descent. And that descent was often hidden, as in the case of the first Polish American mayor, Stanley (Dyszkiewicz) Davis, elected in 1953. Class mobility accompanied cultural assimilation, and the practices and homes of the professional middle class outgrew the Polish ethnic enclaves. Moreover, with the strong post–World War II economy and the presence of the automobile industry and its labor union, the United Automobile Workers, many Polish Americans occupied secure working-class positions.

---

[4]Three of their grandparents were born in Poland, but their maternal grandmother was born in the United States. Scholars have also found that most fourth-generation Polish Americans do not marry other Polish Americans, worship in a Polish American church, remember Polish American customs, visit Poland or know much about Poland, speak Polish, read Polish newspapers or magazines (in Polish or English), belong to Polish organizations, or vote for Polish American candidates (Obidinski, 1985; Sandberg, 1974). Other studies on third- and fourth-generation Polish Americans include Bukowczyk (1987: chapters 5–7), Silverman (2000), and Wrobel (1979).

[5]Methodists (Yankees and Germans) were also leaders in industry (as furniture executives and financiers), politics, and social organizations (e.g., the Rotary, the Kiwanis, and the Optimists). The Catholics were absent from the rosters of prominent politicians, industrial leaders, and even police chiefs (Bratt and Meehan, 1993, 32–33, 234–235).

The only discrimination the Grasinski Girls identified occurred more than forty years ago and was linked to their religious identity. In Grand Rapids, this identity is bundled with ethnic identity so that we speak of Polish Catholics and Dutch Calvinists. Fran recalls during the Depression years, "We had a hard time finding [a place to] rent because, uh, because we were Catholic. I mean, there were a lot of people against the Catholics at that time." Angel had the most explicit examples of discrimination. One of the reasons she was conscious of them was because she moved through Grand Rapids under the cover of her husband's Dutch surname. She could then see people treat her differently when they found out she wasn't Christian Reform or Dutch, and she made it clear she was not.

> We were discriminated against twice. The first place was when we got married. We wanted to rent a home from a lady, and it said, "Christian couple wanted." And we are Christian, we're Catholic. And everything was fine and dandy, she was going to rent it to us, and then Dad asked her where the nearest Catholic Church was. And just like that, she looked at us and said, "You're not Christian, you're Catholic. I would never rent to you." I said, "Okay." I guess I didn't want to live in a place where somebody didn't want me.

A second, similar instance occurred when they tried to buy a home in a predominantly Dutch suburb.

Forty years ago, ethnic identity was still a basis for ranking in Grand Rapids, but it was linked to religious identity. Even so, the discrimination they experienced was mild and infrequent; those were the only examples that any of the five sisters reported. By the time they married and bought houses in the suburbs, the Grasinski Girls were structurally and culturally assimilated, as were most third- and fourth-generation European Americans. This assimilation, along with the increased presence of Blacks and Latinos in the city, made race the more salient delineation of neighborhoods, friendships, and jobs.

Poles were subject to prejudice, discrimination, and racist beliefs of inferiority in the early part of the twentieth century, but by midcentury they had been racialized into the dominant white category.[6] As early as the 1960s, U.S. Census reports show that on measures of median school years completed and family income, Polish Americans were doing as well as other ethnic groups of European ancestry and better than non-White groups. Polish Americans were still more likely to be found in working-class positions, however, and their aggregate income levels were influenced more by the unionized high-wage blue-collar positions than a significant movement into the white-collar middle class. Although there has always been a Polish American middle class, the occupational mobility of Polish Americans was stunted until the 1970s, when the sons and daughters of the blue-collar aristocracy began graduating from college.[7] By the 1980s,

---

[6]The literature on the construction of whiteness in the United States documents how eastern and southern Europeans as well as the Catholic Irish, originally discriminated against on the basis of national origins, eventually lost their ethnic markers and became "white" (Ignatiev, 1995; Jacobson, 1995; Roediger, 1991, 1994).

[7]Chrobot (1973) and Lopata (1976b) demonstrate the overrepresentation of Polish Americans in the working class. In disagreement with them, Angela Pienkos argues that many Polish Americans were middle class (Taras, Pienkos, and Radzilowski, 1980). Sanders and Morawskas (1975) give the most complete description of the structural location of Polish Americans in the early 1970s. They conclude that Polish Americans were found most often in semi-skilled and skilled labor positions and were underrepresented (as compared to the national average) in professional and managerial positions (1975:28–36). The aggregate income levels for Polish Americans were high (among White ethnic groups they were second only to Russians), and they were even higher in industrial cities, especially in Detroit, where a large percentage were employed in the automobile industry. The salaries of these skilled laborers boosted the aggregate income level without raising the occupational class position. This was confirmed by lower levels of educational attainment. As a group, in the 1970s Polish Americans lagged behind the national average on years of education. Yet social mobility was evident, at this time, in the younger generation that already had educational levels surpassing the national average (pp. 36–49).

Polish Americans were as similar to other European descendants on indicators of income, occupation, and education as they were distinguishable from the descendants of African slaves and Latin American migrants (Alba, 1990, 1995; Erdmans, 2000; Lieberson and Waters, 1988; Pula, 1996:89–91).

Despite these indicators of parity, some scholars continue to argue that Polish Americans are a discriminated group, underrepresented in corporate, political, academic, and ecclesiastical hierarchies (Bukowczyk, 1987:107–110; Lopata, 1976a: 68–87; Sanders and Morawska, 1975; Napierkowski, 1983; Radzilowski, 1974; Taras, 1982:52).[8] And in fact there is evidence that Polish Americans are still negatively stereotyped as dumb, racist, and uncultured.[9] Anti-defamation groups continue to fight the stereotypes perpetuated in joke books, television sit-coms, advertisements, and documentaries (see Bukowczyk, 1987:107–110, 1996; Erdmans, 1998:224). Although there is some evidence that Polish Americans experience discrimination, this was not the case for the Grasinski Girls.

The Grasinski Girls did hear Polish jokes, which they brushed aside with self-confidence. Angel said, "Once in a while, somebody'd say a Polish joke, but you can make it Polish or Dutch; I don't get offended by that. Wherever I've worked, I've always managed to convince them that I was much smarter than they were." I laughed when she said this. "No! I'm not kidding you!" she responded. I found this somewhat incredible. Polish American anti-defamation organizations actively fight the Polish joke; scholars write about the problems of the Polish joke, and here a Polish American woman hears Polish jokes and it does not bother her because she believes she is smarter than the joke tellers. She sees no need to repeat Stanley Kowalski's defensive moan, "I am not a Polack. . . . I am a hundred percent American!" Angel's American status is not threatened by her Polish ancestry because, despite the lingering jokes, her family and most Polish Americans have become secure in their identity as Americans. Their acceptance as Americans gives them the confidence to more openly embrace their Polish heritage. Since the 1970s, the stigma of Polishness has given way to a "Kiss-me-I'm-Polish" attitude. Some of the factors accounting for this overt ethnic pride include the government-supported policy of multiculturalism, the identity movements of the 1960s, as well as the election of the Polish Pope in 1978 and the international attention on the Solidarity movement in Poland in the 1980s (Bukowczyk, 1987; Erdmans, 1998).[10]

The valuation of their ethnic heritage comes in part from their reference group, their co-ethnics. Except for Mari, all of the Grasinski Girls, while they were a "Grasinski," lived in Polish American communities where their ethnicity was valued. When they left the safe haven of the Polish neighborhoods they also left the mark of their stigma, their Polish names, behind. The two sisters who kept the Polish identifiers, Caroline Matecki and Nadine Grasinski, also remained

---

[8]In the second edition of her book (1994), Lopata continues to maintain that there is an underrepresentation of Polish Americans in the major institutions on America. Pula argues that while there have been "substantial economic and educational strides" among Polish Americans in the post–WWII era, placing them at parity or above the national averages on income and education, "full equality in hiring, promotion, and social acceptance remains to be achieved" (1996:92).

[9]Examining the portrayal of Polish Americans in literature, Napierkowski argues that one might conclude that Polishness is "a terrible heritage in which to be born" and that Polish life is debased, undemocratic, and impoverished (1983:43–44). Bukowczyk looking more specifically at the stereotypes of Polish women found contradictory images: crude and uncouth but also decent, wholesome, and virginal (2003:1–6). Stereotypes of Polish American men are also classed, as working-class men are often expected to be more brawny than brainy (Bukowczyk, 1987:113). Pula cites that 78 percent of Slavic characters on prime time television shows are portrayed as "muscular dimwits" or otherwise "socially dysfunctional" (1996:76). And yet Bukowczyk shows that, on closer examination, the portrayal of Polish characters in film is not all derogatory (2002).

[10]For a contradictory view, see the work by Jim Pula, who argues that Polish jokes and other negative stereotypes of inferiority promoted "poor self-image and rejection of heritage" among many Polish Americans (1996:92).

within Polish communities—Caroline in Hilliards and Nadine with the Polish Felician order of nuns. The others, as they moved into non-Polish neighborhoods, did so with non-Polish marriage surnames, which gave them the choice of whether and when to reveal their ethnic identity. For European Americans, the surname is a salient ethnic marker that becomes the lightning rod for prejudice and discrimination. Without their maiden Polish name (and by marrying men without Polish surnames) they decreased their chances of experiencing discrimination (see Bukowczyk, 2003:198).

For the Grasinski Girls, ethnicity is not an identity of social ranking. Ethnicity did not determine resources and opportunities. Instead, their most salient identity was their whiteness. While their whiteness was not articulated (they never talked about being White, but they did identify others as being Black or Hispanic), they also did not use their ethnic identity to hide their race—that is, they did not claim to be Americans of Polish descent as a substitution for being "White." Scholars such as Mary Waters have argued that European ethnicity persists into the latter generations because it helps Whites to hide the privileges of their whiteness and gain access to multicultural resources.[11] But the Grasinski Girls never pretended that their ethnicity was a structural identity. They never even hinted that being Polish was similar to being a racial minority. They do not claim the status of victims—that is, claiming that Polish Americans are an oppressed people, and therefore deserving of affirmative action preferences.

While vestiges of historical discrimination may produce disproportionate underrepresentation in government, education, and religious institutions; while negative labels may still accompany Polish names; and while working-class Polish Americans do not have the economic power and status of the professional middle class, Polish Americans are nonetheless white.[12] And in a racist society, that matters. In order to understand ethnicity in the third and fourth generations, we need to separate it from whiteness.

Whiteness is the identity, but ethnicity is the culture. Identity locates us in the social structure, determining who is above and below us. Thus, it is in the presence of the other (e.g., the Dutch or African Americans) that we see our relative position. In contrast, culture is a set of routines and values and as such it requires in-group members to teach these values and participate in the routines.[13] Identities are salient because they order resources, opportunities, and networks, as

---

[11]Mary Waters (1990) found that some European Americans equated their history of discrimination (and even present-day prejudice) with that of Mexican Americans and African Americans, claiming "we had it just as bad." Thomas Napierkowski, in an article about the defamation of the Polish character in literature, claims that "the situation of Polish Americans is probably even worse at present than that of blacks" (1983:6). It is on the basis of this fictitious parity that Whites both apply for and deny the resources meted out on the basis of historical and present-day discrimination. For example, Polish Americans actively fought against affirmative action in higher education by supporting the *Bakke v. California* case in 1976 (Erdmans, 1998:50). By invoking the history of discrimination toward Polish Americans, they can more easily dismiss the privileges of their white skin, and in doing so, Lillian Rubin states, use that ethnicity as "a cover for 'white'" (1994:195).

[12]John Bukowczyk shows correctly that whites are not all privileged equally, that class does matter. For many Polish Americans, "the advantages conferred by their "white" skin have been compromised by vestiges of their class backgrounds and by their unpronounceable names" (1996:37). Many working-class Polish Americans neighborhoods and labor sectors were devastated by the economic and urban transformations of the last forty years. The working class did not have the political or economic power to prevent newly constructed highways from slicing up their neighborhoods, to prevent realtors from ravaging house prices through block busting, or to prevent the automobile and steel industries from closing factories (Bukowczyk, 1987, chapter 5; Pacyga, 1996; Wrobel, 1979). The middle class is quick to blame the working class for being racist bigots, while their own neighborhoods, schools, and clubs remain predominantly white. Bukowczyk suggests that Polish Americans should claim their victimhood, their immigrant peasant, working-class roots, so that they may enter into dialogue with other minorities and distance themselves from the privileges of white middle-class Protestants, and claim innocence in the construction of racial ideology in America (1996:36–37).

[13]Joanne Nagel (1994) theoretically defines the difference between ethnic identity and culture.

well as determine privilege, define power relations, and proscribe positions of subordination and domination. But culture is meaningful because it patterns the routines of our lives, and it is those routines that challenge or reproduce the social structures. It is in culture that we find agency. So, what does Polish American culture look like in later generations at the end of the twentieth century? Where is Polishness situated in the family?

POLISHNESS AS A HYBRID IDENTITY

Suburbanization pulled many Polish Americans away from the ethnic neighborhoods in the cities; urban removal pushed out others. Declining property prices and wasted interiors lowered rents and brought in poorer populations, who, as in all other U.S. cities, have darker skin than the descendants of Europeans.[14] Banks contributed to the destruction by redlining the highway-ravaged, racially torn neighborhoods.[15]

This transformation of the Polish neighborhood is recapitulated in Polish American individuals. The Polish community no longer stands as a community apart from the city, and Polish American culture no longer uniquely defines the self. By the later generations, these Americans claim some Polish (or German and Russian) ancestry, but they are not Poles, nor even Polish Americans. Instead, they are Americans of Polish descent.[16]

Polishness for later-generation Americans of Polish descent is a consent identity—it is a choice. Like *kielbasa*, they can buy into their Polish heritage if they want. Bukowczyk writes of the third generation: "Homogenized–or, for the upwardly mobile, assimilated–they were Polish Americans only when they wanted to be" (Bukowczyk, 1987:144–145). And this homogenization was also partly a choice. The same assimilation processes affecting other white ethnic groups—intermarriage, suburbanization, mass consumer culture, and religious ties—took them away from co-ethnics and led them to forget and discontinue many of the cultural routines of Polishness (Bukowczyk, 1987:110). Although some of the attrition was forced, assimilation also represented a conscious desire, and ability, to join the dominant group.[17] They changed their surnames to avoid discrimination, but also so that their neighbors could more easily pronounce them.[18] Thus Grusczynski became Grasinski became Grayson (the name Joe Jr. used when performing as a country singer). And the Grasinski Girls married into Hrouda, Erdmans, and Hillary surnames.

---

[14]Between 1940 and 1950, the African American population in Grand Rapids grew from 2,600 to 6,813, and then more than doubled to 14,260 in the next decade, by 1970 African Americans were 14 percent of the city's population (Bratt and Meehan, 1993:157). The Latino population, mostly Mexicans who came to Michigan as seasonal farm workers and later Puerto Ricans migrating from Chicago, was at 10,588 in Kent County (where Grand Rapids is located) by 1970 (p. 206).

[15]This pattern has been repeated in Polonian neighborhoods across the United States. (Polonia is the name for the Polish community abroad.) Obidinski (1985) documents the process of decline and demoralization in Buffalo. Bukowczyk (1987) and Wrobel (1979) look at the decline in Detroit; Pacyga (1996) documents it in Chicago.

[16]Eduard Skendzel notes, "Today, Grand Rapid's citizens with Polish surnames are no longer 'Poles.' They are not even hyphenated 'Polish Americans.'" Instead, he says, that they are "Americans of Polish ancestry" (1983:11). See also Obidinski (1985).

[17]For Alba (1995), assimilation is an attainment of equality. He argues that assimilation represented a process of individuals choosing to change in order to take advantage of opportunities. Some Polish American scholars argue that Poles exhibited an eagerness to assimilate (Gladsky and Gladsky, 1997:2). More often, scholars describe assimilation as a reaction to discrimination, pointing out the anti-immigration movement and other xenophobic practices directed at the large wave of Catholic and Jewish immigration from eastern and southern Europe at the turn of this century, which led to self-negating practices such as abandoning native tongues, changing surnames, and moving away from ethnic neighborhoods (Bukowczyk, 1996:100; Lopata, 1976a; Pula 1980, 1996).

[18]Bukowczyk argues that Poles changed their names to avoid discrimination (1987:106). Waters (1990) also links surnames to discrimination.

Assimilation is linked to social mobility. Moving up the social ladder usually means moving away from the ethnic community (Bukowczyk, 1987:109–110; Sandberg, 1974). Yet members of the middle class do not necessarily lose their ethnicity when they move to the suburbs because they can keep ties to the community through participation in ethnic organizations, and keep an affinity to the culture through the reproduction of ethnic rituals.[19] But the Grasinski Girls without the Grasinski name did not belong to ethnic organizations, did not share their everyday routines with co-ethnics, and did not consciously practice many Polish rituals. So what does it mean when Mari says that her Polishness is "not something I think about, but it's something that's with me every single day of my life."

We assume, perhaps too quickly, that Polishness derives from Poland. Much of the discussion of ethnic culture is predicated on an assumption that something from the home country gets carried over to the United States with the immigrant group, and that culture gets transformed within the sociohistoric, class, and race culture of the new country. For example, the polka, traditionally working-class music, has changed over time as it was adapted to changes in class structures, musical tastes, and residential patterns. Today polka bands are performing in non-Polish venues and blending the strains together with the sounds of big band, rock, and country music (Greene, 1992; Savaglio, 1997; Silverman, 2000: chapter 11). Ethnicity is constructed and reconstructed over time so that what takes hold is a Polish American culture, which at most has only a shadow of a semblance to something from Poland.[20] In fact, the polka, although part of Polish American culture, originated in Czechoslovakia, and in Poland it is seen as something American.

The stuff of Polish American culture is family and religious based: foods (*kiełbasa, gołąbki, pierogi, pączki* and *chruściki*); dances (polka, *mazurka, oberek, krakowiak,* and *kujawiak*); religious rituals (advent, *roraty, Wigilia, opłatek, Pasterka,* the Christmas blessing of the house, the blessing of the Easter baskets, May processions to Mary and June processions for Corpus Christi); and religious icons (Our Lady of Czestochowa, the wreath of thorns around the Sacred Heart of Jesus).[21]

In addition, Polish American culture is reputed to include lavish flower gardens, stable marriages, robust men and women, modest small frame homes, and strong workers who are thrifty and resourceful. Polish American values include family solidarity, well-disciplined children, humble acceptance of social class, hard work, well-cared for lawns, and clean homes (Chrobot, 1973, 2001; Napolska, 1946).

Polishness may be a derivative of Poland, but the Grasinski Girls have no connection to Poland, neither political, nor social, nor intellectual. They carry no memories of Poland, have no understanding of Polish history, revere no Polish heroes. They know neither Sienkiewicz, nor Kosciuszko (though the older sisters tell me they recognize this name), nor Mickiewicz, Pilsudski, or Jaruzelski. However, the older sisters do know of the pianist Ignacy Paderewski, and they all know Karol Wojtyla as Pope John Paul.

[19]Galush (1990) shows how middle-class suburban residents maintain ethnicity through organizational participation, and Lopata (1976a) refers to the "superterritorial ethnic community" of national organizations. But this community can exist even outside an organizational network. Silverman (2000:4) refers to "Polonia without walls"—Polish Americans attached to Polonia through participation in rituals. Micaela di Leonardo (studying Italian Americans in Northern California) also rejects the notion that ethnicity resides only in a geographic ethnic community or even an organizational community (1984:25).

[20]For a mini-debate on the existence of a Polonian culture as distinct from American or Polish culture, see Taras (1982) and Symmons-Symonolewicz (1983).

[21]For a cataloguing of Polonian cultural traditions see Obidinski and Zand (1987), Silverman (2000), Taras (1982), Zand (1958). Although it is commonly understood that Polish Catholicism is Marion based, Jesus also figures prominently as the crucified Christ, which the Sacred Heart wrapped in thorns signifies (Bukowczyk, 1985:21).

Despite their minimal intellectual, affective, and political ties to Poland, they nonetheless posit Poland as the source of real Polishness, and in doing so they minimize their American-grown Polishness. For them, Poland creates genuine Polishness, the right way to be Polish, and they question their own ethnicity in this language of "realness"—we are not "that Polish," my friends are "more Polish" than me. In talking about the West Side of Grand Rapids, Caroline said that during the 1930s, the people who lived a few streets over from them, "came right from the old country, you know, like the *busias* with the scarves and stuff like that, but the people on that side, they were like, they were the real, you know, like the Polish people, Polish-Polish people." If that from Poland is real, then is that from America fake? One Christmas, Angel made *chruściki* [a pastry] for the first time and she said, "They are not like the ones from Little Warsaw (a Polish restaurant on the West Side of Grand Rapids now closed) but mine are the real *chruściki* like they make in Poland."

It is when they ground Polishness in Poland that they too feel "there is not much that is Polish" in them. Their own Polishness is diminished when they define its constructedness as some sort of bastardization, while that which originates from Poland is blue blood.

CAROLINE: I like my Polish ancestry, I mean I wish they would have kept Gruszczynski instead of Grasinski 'cause that has no meaning, that Grasinski, that's something they just made, you know, just made up. And the Gruszczynski, that's a good strong name. I feel really bad 'cause Grasinski, it doesn't belong to anybody. You know, and this is what you are, and that is a pretty good name, cause I've seen in books, that one book, the Russian one, his name was Gruszczynski, the captain of that boat.

Grasinski is a Polish American name. She is Polish American. But to her, the name is weakened by the fact that it was "made up." Angel agrees and wishes they would have kept "the real name." And yet Grasinski is a real name.

POLISHNESS HIDDEN IN THE FAMILY

Looking back toward Poland does not necessarily help later generations find the meaning of ethnic culture. After a century of American assimilation, Polishness for them is a shadow, a childhood faded, a language read but not understood. The Grasinski Girls can phonetically read Polish, sing Polish Christmas carols, and pronounce Polish names, but they have no understanding of what the words mean beyond a few rudimentary words like *Jezu* means Jesus.[22] As a result, their Polishness is hidden behind a cluster of pronounceable but incomprehensible consonants that beg for a vowel. They wish they knew Polish, but no one taught them, neither their parents nor the Felician nuns at St. Stanislaus.[23]

NADINE: At home it was the Polish church and school you attended, followed by a Polish convent. I taught at St. Stanislaus and St. Florians in Hamtramck and Detroit, big, huge huge wonderful churches and I remember sitting there and listening

---

[22]It is rare that language is passed down into the third and fourth generations. In the 1940s and 1950s, only 20 percent of the children of prominent Polish American leaders spoke Polish (Bukowczyk, 1987:108).

[23]Felician nuns staffed the grammar school at St. Stan's in Hilliards from 1937–1969 (Ziolkowski, 1984:69). The formal study of Polish language began to decline in the 1930s and was almost completely absent by the 1950s (Kuznicki, 1978a:11, 1978b:451, 454; Radzilowski, 1975:25–26; Ziolkowski, 1984:272).

to these Polish sermons and not knowing a word that they're saying.... I went to the convent, and everything was in Polish. When we went there all the signs were in Polish, and they would tell us, "Go do dishes" and we didn't understand. [laughs] So they changed the signs in a hurry. But in 1950 everything was Polish, the signs, everything.

ANGEL: We never knew what we were reading. [laughs] We just had Polish readers; I never knew what they were. But that stopped in about the third or fourth grade. I just remember something about Reba, R-e-b-a is fish[24] or something. [laughs] It's the only word I remember out of the whole Polish book.

Neither parent spoke to their daughters in Polish; they only used Polish when they didn't want the children to understand them. "She would talk to her sisters on the phone when she didn't want us to hear." Polishness was the secret language, a cryptic code of their ancestors, the haunting melody of the Polish song their aunts and uncles sang as they lowered the coffin of their grandmother into the ground—though they don't understand the words, they understand the feelings of sadness and connection evoked by the melody.

Their ethnicity, like their language, is present but not spoken, hidden not absent, private not public. It is housed in the words that they can sing but do not understand, it is in the daily prayers to the Sacred Heart of Jesus and the Blessed Virgin Mary, it is in the icons hanging on their wall that tell the symbolic history of Poland that they do not know, the dark-faced Madonna of Czestochowa with the two slash marks on her cheek, the grieving Mother of Jesus, and the twisted thorns around the Sacred Heart.[25] When their mother Helen was dying there were two icons in the room—Our Lady of Czestochowa and the Sacred Heart of Jesus. These are familiar icons. I ask them if they know why Our Lady has cuts on her cheek. What they know is that this is their mother's icon; they have seen it on the wall in every one of her houses and apartments. I explain the story of the Swedes invading and overrunning Poland in the seventeenth century and how the tide of the war changed and the Swedes were repulsed at Czestochowa. A miracle occurred when a Swedish soldier slashed the cheek of the Madonna and real blood flowed. I tell them the story one afternoon while we are sitting around the bed of my dying grandmother. They don't care that much. Their mother is dying. They turn to her, their mother, and the icons on the wall, the familiar Madonna and the bleeding Sacred Heart, comforting familiar pictures from Hilliards that have nothing to do with Swedes and swords.

They are not genuine Poles, they lament, because they don't speak Polish or belong to Polish organizations. But they are ephemeral Poles. Polishness is tucked away in their prayer cards and icons, in their laughter, cheekbones, skinny ankles and wide hips, in what gets passed down and what gets reworked. It is in them but overlooked, like so many private and small religious shrines and crosses in fields and backyards in rural central Wisconsin (see Kolinski, 1994). They remain unknown to us because we don't see them as part of our Polish heritage, part of the way that Poles shaped the landscape of America.

Some of their Polishness is hidden in the class-biased nature of defined ethnic artifacts. For example, Polish peasant fare, like potatoes and boiled beef, is not considered Polish.

---

[24]The correct spelling is *ryba*.

[25]These same symbols of Polishness are salient in the short stories of Anthony Bukoski (1999) about a Polish American town in rural Wisconsin. See also Bukowczyk (1985).

CAROLINE: My mom cooked good but she cooked very simple stuff, just like we do today, your meat and your potatoes and stuff like that and not any of the good Polish dishes you hear people talking about all the time. I know that she used to do pig's feet—clean 'em off, and then cook 'em and put 'em in a pot, and then you'd have them Sunday morning for breakfast. They'd turn that pot over upside down and the pig's feet were all in that gelatin setting. [laughter] They didn't eat stuff like you read in Polish cookbooks, like the real stuff, like they did in Poland. They didn't eat that kind of stuff. But I know they made brains [chuckles], must have been pig brains or cow brains or something, my dad would bring them and they would fry them up with egg or something like that.

Gelatin pig's feet were Polish fare for the peasants, as were potatoes. Ladislaus [the grandfather of the Grasinski Girls] is memorialized in the family history as a man who loved potatoes, heaping plates of steamed potatoes. But pig's feet and potatoes do not get counted as Polish food because they are not in the cookbooks. High-class culture gets constituted as authentic culture, and peasant culture gets discarded from the collective memory like the birth of an illegitimate child.[26]

Ethnicity is also hidden in women's work, the kinship work necessary to maintain relations between households (see di Leonardo, 1987). These interhousehold relations include intergenerational relations, and so kinship work involves "passing it down": keeping the family photo album, telling the stories, deciding who gets Helen's 1920s button-up shoes (Nadine) and her 1970s mod hot pink sunglasses (me) (see Krieger, 1996; Stone, 1988). This kinship work provides women with cultural power as they select what is kept, what is forgotten, and what is transformed.[27] But it is also work that is less obvious to those residing only in the public sphere, less known to people who don't do this type of work. Being an administrative secretary of a Polish organization will secure one a place in the public archives as someone involved in ethnic work, but telling the stories of life in Sercowo gets defined, if defined at all, as kinship maintenance (women's work) rather than ethnic work.

What did they pass down? Some may argue that they didn't keep much. Angel says she knows she's Polish because she laughs all the time. "Who else do you know that laughs, maybe the Italians, but we are always laughing. That's how you know we are Polish." And they kept a few religious pictures and phrases like *Jezu Kochana* (often uttered in frustration, it translates as "Jesus my love"). But we need to look harder. Ethnicity remains in phonetics without semantics, and religious icons that have been converted into family history.[28] And it is here, in the family, that we see their Polishness. Thomas Gladsky, referring to the short stories of Monika Krawczyk, states that the only things Polish about her characters are their names, but then he looks again and finds

---

[26]Silverman (2000) discusses the authenticity argument debated in Polonia (p. 174) and the split between high culture and low culture (chapter 15). Also see Radzilowski's defense of Wrobel's study where he argues that Polonian scholars do not want to admit to a working-class Polonian culture (Taras et al., 1980:45). The theoretical argument is discussed by Pierre Bourdieu (1984) who maintains that class culture is used to reproduce social rankings.

[27]Immigrant women were arbiters of ethnicity. They "had to think consciously about what it meant to be Polish and how to translate that into the rituals of daily life. They had to decide what to keep, and what to abandon, and how to celebrate holidays and rites of passage in an unfamiliar environment" (Radzilowski, 1996:71). Women were responsible for defining and redefining the meaning of Polishness in America (Majewski, 1997; see also di Leonardo, 1984). Pleck (2000) also shows how rituals are gendered routines enacted by women.

[28]See Rosenzweig and Thelen (1998), who have documented the common practice of personalizing history and understanding national history as a family narrative.

that "Polish ethnicity is in the prosperity and continuity of the family" in her stories (Gladsky, 1997:105). And, discussing a children's book written by Anne Pellowski, Koloski (1997) writes:

> The family is living an undeclared Polishness. The people do not work at being Polish; they do not much think about themselves in a Polish context.... Yet the opening pages of the first volume make clear that this is a distinct community of people bound together by an intense closeness of family, a fervent attachment to the Catholic church, and an unaffected acceptance of a body of folkways that identify them as Polish Americans. (p. 155)

In the same way, the Polishness of the Grasinski Girls is present in their familial relations and religious attachment. Their ethnicity is done in the family, through the family, and for the family.

Polish culture in their private sphere embraces a set of values and routines that help them perform their gender routines and reaffirm their gender ideals.[29] Polish women are valued for being hardy. Fran remembers her grandma Frances as the little woman pushing a large wheelbarrow. Caroline admirers her mother Helen as someone who hung a set of curtains when she was nine months pregnant and standing alone on top of a table. They also respect emotional hardiness, women who can manage the household when the husband is not present. Polish women also value cleanliness, and Polish homes are remembered as orderly and neat, and Polish women as good housekeepers (Chrobot, 1973, 2001; Gladsky and Gladsky, 1997; Napolska, 1946; Radzilowski, 1996, 1997; Wrobel, 1979). Talking about her mother, Fran said, "On Saturday she'd wash all the floors and the linoleum and everything, and they'd all get covered with newspaper so they wouldn't get dirty right away. It'd come off Sunday morning then. But maybe that was a Polish [laughter], something from the Polish neighborhoods."

In addition, Polishness supports the role of women as beautifiers. Through flowers and song and the rosary, Polish women engage the soul and humanize the world. Through rituals, lightness, tears, and laughter they transform the drudgery of the night into the lightness of the day. These gendered ethnic routines are acts of resistance against capitalism's instrumental rationality. Thaddeus Radzilowski writes of Polish American women, "Whatever light, beauty, love, and humanity appeared in the ugly landscapes of industrial America was in large measure their work" (1997:21). And as a subversion of the dominant order, Polishness celebrates their role as the matriarch of the family. Polishness in women is strength, intelligence, beauty, and responsibility. These traits become manifest in their care of the home, their children, and their husbands. Reproducing family reproduces ethnicity.

The private, gendered meanings of ethnicity are often missed by scholars who interview people like the Grasinski Girls whose ethnicity is suggestive and understated (see Waters, 1990). Their "undeclared Polishness" is also invisible to scholars who look for ethnicity in the public space of formal institutions (e.g., newspapers, organizational documents, phone books, government records, plat maps).[30] This documentation of public Polishness overlooks the ethnic work of kinship maintenance done in the private sphere. What is important is not the "cultural stuff" of ethnicity but the shared history of the family; and it is not ethnicity that creates a shared history but the shared history that creates ethnicity.

---

[29]Ethnic rituals "showcased gender ideals" (Pleck, 2000:15).

[30]Bukowczyk talks about formal organizations, institutions, and public spaces as expressions of ethnicity (1987:96). Most historians of Polonia, including Don Pienkos, John and Thaddeus Radzilowski, Dominic Pacyga, Stan Blejwas, and Bill Galush, also focus on public ethnicity. In contrast, novelists Leslie Pietrzyk, Suzanne Strempek Shea, and Anthony Bukoski and cultural studies scholars Karen Majewski and Thomas Gladsky provide more private sphere and emotional expressions of ethnicity.

Ethnicity for later-generation White working-class women is intermingled with religious routines. When I asked Angel what she did at home that was Polish she said, "probably the traditions." "What traditions?" Well, she pauses, "Easter and uh going to church." I scrunch my forehead, breathe through my nose in frustration, and shoot back, "Well, the Dutch Christian Reformers also go to church and celebrate Easter!" "It's different," she said. "Okay, how?"

> Well, all the Lenten services, going to church a lot. I mean, we would never think of not going to the Stations of the Cross, and going to mass, and going to confession once a month, I mean, if you needed it or not. And all, like, May devotions and Corpus Christi, and you know, during those days there was like lots of processions, and all that was so much part of your life. Christmas and Easter, probably those were like special times.

She also described the peripheral aspects of religion, such as the joy of eating chocolate on Easter morning after six weeks of Lenten fasting. Her Polishness is part of her life unconsciously today, when she resurrects the willpower to not eat chocolate with the pleasant memory of how sumptuous chocolate tastes on Easter morning.

When I asked Fran how she knew she was Polish, she also pointed to the routines of the church, "all them processions and everything like that," and the celebrations of the two main holidays, Christmas and Easter, at home.[31]

> We had our Polish food, your ham and your sausages and you get your coffee cakes from the Valley City Bakery, and then they'd take that down to the church, and your sausages, all your sausage, take that down to church and they'd bless it for us for Easter. And then I know that we would all dress up and everybody'd get up in the morning and run and kiss Dad and Mom, one right after the other we'd go give them their Easter morning kiss. And we had our Easter candy and stuff.

At another point she exclaimed, her eyes smiling, "And Polish songs! I mean, I sang in the choir. They had only one choir and I sang in the choir when I was ten and I was singing Polish songs. I was singing down here and my dad was up there, singing up above, we were in the same choir!" And when asked to talk about her Polishness, Nadine also mentioned Christmas when "the *kolędy* are played and *Bóg się Rodzy* always brings back my Daddy singing in the choir." Ethnicity is performed both at church and at home, both in the public processions and the morning kisses.

Co-ethnics share space as well as a history, and the later generations keep returning to the locality, to the rural and urban landscapes, to do ethnicity. They return for the funerals, sitting on metal chairs in a grade school auditorium, drinking weak coffee out of Styrofoam cups. An aged aunt brings the photo albums and they talk about this old uncle or that dead grandfather, and all the others who died before and those yet to die. Polishness in Anthony Bukoski's rural Wisconsin town is a barren landscape of closed churches, vacant buildings, faded signs, and diseased minds: "Overgrown fields now grew where the church stood. . . . It's come down to remembering people in a graveyard" (1999:179). In writing this book, the five sisters all wanted me to include their brother, "because he's a Grasinski, too," as well as their sister who died. Polishness is something that was here but has not fully left; it hangs around like a dusty red film on the bushes alongside the unpaved country roads. Polishness is cracked pictures and mangled names, younger generations who have moved away, and routines that are no longer practiced

---

[31]Short stories about Polish women often center on religious holidays (see Gladsky, 1997). Silverman (2000) also notes the importance of Easter and Christmas traditions as the backbone of Polishness in America.

but not completely forgotten. Talking about church rituals, Angel says, "You really miss it now, and everybody says the same thing, 'Why does everything have to be eliminated?' The May processions, it was just so much to it. And I think it just gave you a background or roots."

Their Polishness is a life they shared with others in a particular time and place. Fran's story centers on her childhood when her family lived on the Polish West Side, which provides a comfortable place to visit through storytelling on a fading Sunday afternoon. At the end of one such afternoon she said, "Every time you leave I am caught back in that place for days." The locale of Polishness. In that locale, she sees her mother in her large hats, plays in the park across from Sacred Heart Church, wakes on Sunday morning with her father sitting in a chair smoking a cigar and her mother in the kitchen frying *kiełbasa*. As an older woman remembering her childhood, Polishness brings her past into the present and connects her to generations of family.

Their ethnic history is a family history. Historians Roy Rosenzweig and David Thelen, in their book *The Presence of the Past* (1998), show how family histories give meaning to present-day selves. When I ask "What's Polish about you?" Caroline responds, "My love of flowers, my love of music, my love of color, my love of family." And she connects some of these values to her Polish grandmother's fiery red cannas and her lessons to talk about plants and not people. The Grasinski Girls use family history, whose members are Polish descendants, to define their life spaces and choices. Their values located in an ethnic childhood are also used at times to evaluate contemporary society.[32] When Polishness taps into the rhythms of childhood, for them a pleasant childhood, it becomes linked to an all-is-right-with-the-world feeling. Fran, describing a Polish Christmas celebration, said, "We just cried and we laughed and sang and they danced. They danced all these songs like Mom used to do, the *Oberek* and everything, it was just so wholesome. I didn't even want to put the television on when I came back. You know, it was just so good. Oh it was just real Polish!"

Ethnicity stretches into yesterday to provide routines for today's traditions, routines that connect us to the bloodlines swirling through concrete local places. Traditions bring the past into the present and the self into the family. We affirm our connections by acting out our traditions, which in our family means eating mounds of horseradish, wearing large hats, and pickling cukes.[33] Ethnicity also joins us at the hip.

CAROLINE: I can see, in Emily, I can see some of the Grasinski in her, and I can also see in Eddie, I can see that Grasinski smile, Grasinskis they all got that smile real big. They all got good smiles. And Annette's girl, Carrie, she's the one that we call "Grandma Helen the second." [chuckle] She looks like a Fifelski. She looks like one of Aunt Adele's, I don't know if you remember Antonia, do you remember Antonia? Oh, I keep thinkin' you know these people but you don't.

---

[32]John Bukowczyk writes that Polish Americans in the later generations found ethnicity "appealing because it touched a sensitive psychological chord, which had little to do with ethnic background per se, but had a lot to do with the more general need for roots. Mass society in the 1970s was a rather faceless place, conducive to an assortment of psychological and personality disorders: rootlessness, alienation, anomie"(1987:119). Silverman agrees that ethnic groups provide affective ties that help hold together splintered modern families; the folk culture "provides a sense of rootedness and stability in an era of economic and social uncertainty" (2000:5). Chrobot (1973) also argued that the ethnic revival in the 1960s and 1970s was a response to commercialism. But Bukowczyk counters that the revival itself has become commercialized as the ethnic culture was mass produced in buttons and slogans and Bobby Vinton and the Pope: "Ethnicity had become a purchasable and profitable commodity" to be bought and sold, made and eaten" (1987:119).

[33]Elizabeth Pleck (2000) argues that the immigrants enact rituals from the old country to help themselves adjust to the new country; and the descendants of immigrants engage in rituals to connect them to their immigrant ancestors.

They want me to know. They want me and their children and their children's children to know, to remember. Gendered, private ethnicity in the later generation is about connections and relations. Having family and knowing family are important to these women.

Polishness connects the generations of the family and the generations of the self (the old self to the young self). Ethnicity is a mediating process. Helen named her babies after her old Polish relatives and contemporary American songs. The sixth generation is connected to the first generation when the grandchild cries out to *Busia* for a hug. The fifth generation is connected to the second generation when the grandfather with the highball breath whirls his granddaughter around the wedding floor in the one-two-two polka. Great-aunt Adele played in a polka band, Angel played the accordion, and as a young girl I watched two women dancing together, holding onto each others' arms, laughing and twirling, and touching.

For the Grasinski Girls, Polishness is a wisp of a thread floating from the ribbon of one generation to the next. It is in the nuances of the social world that we detect the traces of ethnicity hidden in the third and fourth colors of the weave.

> CAROLINE: I remember when I was little, Grandma Grusczynski, you know, they never told us their names [laughter]. It was Wayland Grandma and country Grandma [laughter]. No names, I didn't have any names. Anyhow, this Wayland Gramma she'd come out by us and help Mom make *pierogi*. She's the one that taught Momma how to do a lot of her cooking. She'd make *pierogi*, [pause] and I can remember walking behind her in the yard, I'd just see a faint shadow, and she used to pick all the dandelion greens, you know, the little greens, she'd pick those up, bring them in the house and she'd cook 'em like that. And, she taught my mom how to make *czarnina* [duck blood soup]. But my mom didn't like baking. We make more *babkas* [cakes] and stuff than they did at that time.

In the later generations, ethnicity is something that has no name because it was not named, it is the shadow of a grandmother the child follows behind, it is what was taught (*czarnina*), what was refused (baking), what was reclaimed (*babka* making). Ethnicity is not a cover for whiteness, it is not a culinary recipe, an organizational membership, nor a vocabulary list. Ethnicity is an ethos, a soul, a connection, not to a community in some foreign land but to local spaces and generations, the generations of their selves and the generations of their families. And that's why women do it well. Ethnicity reaffirms their connections.

Polishness goes back to Hilliards and the West Side but not to Poland. They feel a connection to Frances's zinnias and hollyhocks and their mother singing *kolędy*. Their Polishness is not public identity, and they don't claim Polishness as some sort of ethnic revival. They don't wear "kiss-me-I'm-Polish" buttons or join anti-defamation groups. They don't feel a connection to Polish organizations. Polishness is an unspoken language that holds existential meaning, that signifies "this is me," this is who I say I am, a vestige of this family, the remains of this day. Like the incense at midnight mass, it wafts through the air and reminds us of whence we came; it's the familiarity of routines, the soak of tradition, the way they do it in Hilliards. This is who I am. A Grasinski.

Ethnic culture is in a constant state of construction. Ethnic rituals are altered as each generation, like a pianist who is a little tone deaf, reconfigures its cultural sonata—something new is intermingled with the old, grandma's recipe with her daughter's new ingredients gets resent as an e-mail, the seeds of a country grandma's peonies are replanted in the suburban backyards of her daughters and repotted on the urban apartment balcony of her granddaughter; the tatted-lace doily gets matted, framed, and hung on the wall. Like soil and recipes, ethnicity gets reworked so that even in the later generations we find threads, seeds, yeast, an old photo, the dimple in the chin, that laugh, the love of music that binds them to the generation before. But ethnicity is not about what gets passed down; rather it is about the process of passing down.[34] And that is family.

References

Alba, R. D. 1990. *Ethnic Identity: The Transformation of White America.* New Haven, CT: Yale University Press.

———. [1981] 1995. "The Twilight of Ethnicity Among American Catholics of European Ancestry." In N. Yetman (Ed.), *Majority and Minority: The Dynamics of Race and Ethnicity in American Life,* 5th ed. (pp. 420–429). Boston: Allyn & Bacon.

Bourdieu, P. [1979] 1984. *Distinction: A Social Critique of the Judgement of Taste,* R. Nice (Trans.). Cambridge, MA: Harvard University Press.

Bratt, J. D., and C. H. Meehan. 1993. *Gathered at the River: Grand Rapids, Michigan and Its People of Faith.* Grand Rapids, MI: Eerdmans Publishing Company.

Bukoski, A. 1999. *Polonaise.* Dallas, TX: Southern Methodist University Press.

Bukowczyk, J. 1985, Spring. "Mary the Messiah: Polish Immigrant Heresy and the Malleable Ideology of the Roman Catholic Church, 1880–1930." *Journal of American Ethnic History 5,* 5–32.

———. 1987. *And My Children Did Not Know Me: A History of Polish-Americans.* Bloomington: Indiana University Press.

———. 1996. "Polish Americans, History Writing and the Organization of Memory." In J. J. Bukowczyk (Ed.), *Polish Americans and Their History: Community, Culture and Politics* (pp. 1–38). Pittsburgh, PA: University of Pittsburgh Press.

———. 2002. "The Big Lebowski Goes to the Polish Wedding: Polish Americans–Hollywood Style." *The Polish Review 47*(2), 211–230.

———. 2003. "Hail Mary, Other of God: Sacred and Profane Constructions of Polish-American Womanhood." *The Polish Review 48*(2), 195–203.

Chrobot, Rev. L. 1973. "The Elusive Polish American." *Polish American Studies 30*(1), 45–53.

———. 2001. "Typologies of Polish American Parishes: Changing Pastoral Structures and Methods." *Polish American Studies 58*(2), 83–94.

di Leonardo, Micaela. 1987. "The Female World of Cards and Holidays: Women, Families, and the Work of Kinship." *Signs 12,* 440–453.

di Leonardo, Micaela. 1984. *The Varieties of Ethnic Experience: Kinship, Class and Gender Among California Italian-Americans.* Ithaca: Cornell University Press.

Erdmans, M. 1998. *Opposite Poles: Immigrants and Ethnics in Polish Chicago, 1976–1990.* University Park: The University of Pennsylvania State Press.

———. 2000. "Polonia in the New Century: We Will Not Fade Away." *Polish American Studies 57*(1), 5–24.

Galush, W. J. 1990. "Purity and Power: Chicago Polonia Feminists, 1880–1914." *Polish American Studies 57*(1), 5–24.

Gladsky, T. S. 1997. "Monika Krawczyk, Victoria Janda, and the Polonie Club." In T. S. Gladsky and R. H. Gladsky (Eds.), *Something of My Very Own To Say: American Women Writers of Polish Descent* (pp. 101–111). New York: Eastern European Monographs, Columbia University Press.

Gladsky, T. S., and R. H. Gladsky (Eds.). 1997. *Something of My Very Own to Say: American Women Writers of Polish Descent.* New York: Eastern European Monographs, Columbia University Press.

Greene, V. 1992. *A Passion for Polka: Old-time Ethnic Music in America.* Berkeley: University of California Press.

Ignatiev, N. 1995. *How the Irish Became White.* New York: Routledge.

Jacobson, M. F. 1995. *Song of Sorrows: The Diasporic Imagination of Irish, Polish, and Jewish Immigrants in the United States.* Cambridge, MA: Harvard University Press.

Kleiman, J. D. 1985. "The Great Strike: Religion, Labor, and Reform in Grand Rapids, Michigan, 1890–1916." Ph. D. dissertation, Michigan State University.

Kolinski, D. L. 1994. "Shrines and Crosses in Rural Central Wisconsin." *Polish American Studies 51*(2), 33–48.

---

[34]See also Edward Shils (1981), who uses the word *tradition* as a verb to refer to the process of passing down.

Krieger, S. 1996. *The Family Silver: Essays on Relationships Among Women.* Berkeley: University of California Press.

Koloski, Bernard. 1997. "Children's Books: Lois Lenski, Maia Wojciechowska, Anne Pellowski." In T. S. Gladsky and R. H. Gladsky, *Something of My Very Own To Say: American Women Writers of Polish Descent* (pp. 147–157). New York: Eastern European Monographs, Columbia University Press.

Kuznicki, E. M. 1978a, Spring–Autumn. "A Historical Perspective on the Polish American Parochial School. *Polish American Studies 35*(1–2), 5–12.

———. 1978b. "The Polish American Parochial School." In F. Mocha (Ed.), *Poles in America* (pp. 435–460). Stevens Point, WI: Worzalla Publishing Company.

Lieberson, S., and M. Waters. 1988. *From Many Strands: Ethnic and Racial Groups in Contemporary America.* New York: Russell Sage Foundation.

Lopata, H. 1976a. *Polish Americans: Status Competition in an Ethnic Community.* Englewood Cliffs, NJ: Prentice Hall.

———. 1976b. "The Polish American Family." In C. H. Mindel and R. W. Habenstein (Eds.), *Ethnic Families in America: Patterns and Variations* (pp. 15–40). New York: Elsevier.

———. 1994. *Polish Americans, Second, Revised Edition* (with a chapter by Mary Patrice Erdmans). New Brunswick: Transaction.

Lydens, Z. Z. 1976. *A Look at Early Grand Rapids.* Grand Rapids, MI: Kregel Publications.

Majewski, K. 1997. "Toward 'a Pedagogical Goal': Family, Nation, and Ethnicity in the Fiction of Polonia's First Women Writers." In T. S. Gladsky and R. H. Gladsky (Eds.), *Something of My Very Own To Say: American Women Writers of Polish Descent* (pp. 54–66). New York: Eastern European Monographs, Columbia University Press.

Nagel, J. 1994. "Constructing Ethnicity: Creating and Recreating Ethnic Identity and Culture." *Social Problems 41*(1), 152–176.

Napierkowski, T. J. 1983. "The Image of Polish Americans in American Literature." *Polish American Studies 40*(1), 5–44.

Napolska, Sr. M. R. CSSF. 1946. The Polish Immigrant in Detroit to 1914. In T. S. Gladsky and R. H. Gladsky (Eds.), *Something of My Very Own to Say: American Women Writers of Polish Descent* (pp. 87–99). New York: Eastern European Monographs, Columbia University Press.

Obidinski, E. 1985. "Beyond Hansen's Law: Fourth Generation Polonian Identity." *Polish American Studies 42*(1), 27–42.

Obidinski, E., and H. S. Zand. 1987. *Polish Folkways in America: Community and Family.* New York: University Press of America.

Pacyga, D. 1996. "To Live Amongst Others: Poles and Their Neighbors in Industrial Chicago." *Journal of American Ethnic History 16*(1), 55–73.

Pleck, E. H. 2000. *Celebrating the Family: Ethnicity, Consumer Culture, and Family Rituals.* Cambridge, MA: Harvard University Press.

Pula, J. 1980. "American Immigration and the Dillingham Commission." *Polish American Studies 37*, 5–31.

———. 1996. "Image, Status, Mobility and Integration in American Society: The Polish Experience." *Journal of American Ethnic History 16*(1), 74–95.

Radzilowski, T. 1974. "A View from the Polish Ghetto: Some Observations of the First Hundred Years in Detroit." *Ethnicity 1*(2), 125–150.

———. 1975, Spring. "Reflections on the History of Felicians in America." *Polish American Studies 32*(1), 19–28.

———. 1996. "Family, Women, and Gender: The Polish Experience." In J. J. Bukowczyk (Ed.), *Polish Americans and Their History: Community, Culture and Politics* (pp. 58–79). Pittsburgh, PA: University of Pittsburgh Press.

———. 1997. "Reinventing the Center: Polish Immigrant Women in the New World." In T. S. Gladsky and R. H. Gladsky, *Something of My Very Own To Say: American Women Writers of Polish Descent* (pp. 11–24). New York: Eastern European Monographs, Columbia University Press.

Roediger, D. R. 1991. *The Wages of Whiteness: Race and the Making of the American Working Class.* New York: Verso.

———. 1994. "Whiteness and Ethnicity in the History of 'White Ethnics' in the United States." In D. R. Roediger, *Towards the Abolition of Whiteness: Essays on Race, Politics, and Working Class History* (chapter 11). New York: Verso.

Rosenzweig, R., and D. Thelen. 1998. *The Presence of the Past: Popular Uses of History in American Life.* New York: Columbia University Press.

Rubin, L. B. 1994. *Families on the Fault Line: America's Working Class Speaks About the Family, the Economy, Race and Ethnicity.* New York: HarperPerennial.

Sandberg, N. C. 1974. "The Changing Polish American." *Polish American Studies 31*(1), 5–14.

Sanders, I., and E. Morawska. 1975. *Polish-American Community Life: A Survey of Research.* New York: Polish Institute of Arts and Sciences.

Savaglio, P. 1997. "Big-Band, Slovenian-American, Rock, and Country Music: Cross-Cultural Influences in the Detroit Polonia." *Polish American Studies* 54(2), 23–44.

Shils, E. 1981. *Tradition.* Chicago: University of Chicago Press.

Silverman, D. A. 2000. *Polish-American Folklore.* Chicago: University of Illinois Press.

Skendzel, E. A. 1983. "The Polanders." *Grand River Valley Review* (Spring–Summer), 2–11.

———. 1999. *The Grand Rapids St. Isadore's Story: A History Within a History, Centennial 1897–1997.* Grand Rapids, MI: Littleshield Press.

Sollors, W. 1986. *Beyond Ethnicity: Consent and Descent in American Culture.* New York: Oxford University Press.

Stone, E. 1988. *Black Sheep and Kissing Cousins: How Our Family Stories Shape Us.* New York: Penguin Books.

Symanski, E. 1964, July. "Polish Settlers in Grand Rapids, Michigan." *Polish American Studies XXI*(2), 91–106.

Symmons-Symonolwicz, K. 1983. "Is There a Polonian Culture?" *Polish American Studies* 40(1), 88–90.

Taras, P., A. T. Pienkos, and T. Radzilowski. 1980. "Paul Wrobel's *Our Way*—Three Views." *Polish American Studies* 37(1), 32–51.

Taras, P. A. 1982. "The Dispute Over Polonian Culture." *Polish American Studies* 39(1), 38–54.

Waters, M. 1990. *Ethnic Options.* Berkeley: University of California Press.

Wrobel, P. 1979. *Our Way: Family, Parish, and Neighborhood in a Polish-American Community.* Notre Dame, IN: University of Notre Dame Press.

Zand, H. S. 1958. "Polish American Holiday Customs." *Polish American Studies* 15(3–4), 81–90.

Ziolkowski, Sr. M. J., CSSF. 1984. *The Felician Sisters of Livonia, Michigan: First Province in America.* Detroit, MI: Harlo Press.

7

∎ ∎ ∎

The Mexican American Family

Rosina M. Becerra

INTRODUCTION

Mexican Americans are a highly heterogeneous population. Some trace their roots to the Spanish and Mexican settlers who first settled the Southwest before the arrival of the Pilgrims in New England, whereas others are immigrants or children of immigrants who began to arrive in large numbers by the beginning of the twentieth century (McWilliams, 1990). There is wide social differentiation and cultural variation among Mexican American families. Some factors include variability across regions (including Mexico) and changes over time. Mexican American families in various historical periods have adapted differently to economic and political forces, and family socialization patterns have responded differently to societal pressures (Baca-Zinn, Ertzen, and Wells, 2010).

The history of the Mexican American family is largely anchored in the context of the American economy. The Southwest's geographic proximity to Mexico and demand for low-wage labor have influenced the high concentration of the Mexican population in the southwestern states—in particular, California and Texas. Because of the continuous emigration from Mexico and the proximity to Mexico, Mexican Americans have regular interactions with first-generation immigrants. This proximity of Mexico to the United States and the amount of flow back and forth reinforces familial ties—and the family values—that span the two countries. Thus, the Mexican American family continues to maintain its strong cultural values, although change and acculturation are taking place (Becerra, 1983).

For these reasons, to understand the present-day Mexican American family, one must incorporate both the U.S.-born and Mexico-born populations. In this chapter the term *Mexican American family* means all families in the United States with Mexican origin (i.e., those of Mexican birth or parentage whether born in Mexico or the United States) because they are part of the same family.

HISTORICAL BACKGROUND

The history of the Mexican American people predates the incorporation of the Southwest into the United States. Native to the Southwest, the Mexican people have a history marked by conflict and colonization, first by the Spanish and then by Anglo Americans. This early history, perhaps because of the proximity of the southwestern states to the Mexico border, has left a legacy of conflict that is present today between Mexican Americans and Anglo Americans. The present position of Mexican Americans as a people, their family life, and the effects of their position on their family life can best be understood through a brief review of their history as Mexicans and as North Americans.

In 1821 Mexico achieved independence from Spain, which had colonized Mexico since the sixteenth century. Because the Spanish *conquistadores* (conquerors) were all men, they intermarried with the Mexicans and indigenous Indians. This mixed heritage of the Spanish, Mexican, and Indian is prevalent among today's Mexican Americans. The Spanish heritage, language, and other contributions of the indigenous cultures of the Indians and Mexicans constitute the foundation of the unique Mexican American culture. Because the areas that are now the southwestern states were originally established by the Spanish settlers and their Mexican/Indian children, their Mexican descendants already were native to these territories when they became part of the United States in the late nineteenth century (McWilliams, 1990).

During the nineteenth century, the Mexican government had opened the Texas territory to settlers under the condition that they pledge allegiance to Mexico and agree to become Catholics. The Anglo American settlers (mostly United States citizens), however, resisted these conditions. At the same time, Mexicans of the territory resisted Anglo American colonization through various forms of rebellion. The Southwest had been relatively isolated until the development of the railroad system ended that isolation. This southwestern region attracted large numbers of Anglo Americans. As the Anglo American population grew throughout the territory of Texas, so did rebellions against the Mexican government. Anglo Americans of the territory, however, whose numbers had soared, used the political process to pass laws favoring their group, and thereby stripping the indigenous Mexicans of what little wealth they had and relegating them to the lowest social and economic classes. Some wealthier Mexicans collaborated with the Anglo Americans to maintain their own positions in the new order (Acuna, 2010). These events set the stage for the conquest of the Texas territory and the rest of the Southwest.

In 1832, the Anglo American settlers in the Texas territory pressed Mexico to lift the restrictions on Anglo American immigration to Texas. Because of the economic trade that had been established between the territory of Texas and the United States, the Anglo settlers believed that separation from Mexico and statehood in the United States would be to their economic advantage. By 1835, 5,000 Mexicans resided in the Texas territory while the Anglo American population rose to 30,000. A full-scale rebellion escalated, and the Anglo Americans in Texas (with some Mexican supporters) declared war on Mexico. To squelch the rebellion, Mexican General Santa Ana led an army of approximately 6,000 men who marched from the interior of Mexico to arrive in San Antonio, Texas, in February 1836. One hundred and eighty-seven (187) Texans took refuge in the Alamo, a former mission, to confront Santa Ana's army. Texans lost the battle; however, a legend that grew out of that struggle continues today. The cry "Remember the Alamo" prompted President Andrew Jackson to send U.S. troops to assist the Texans because most of them were U.S. citizens (Acuna, 2010; Jansson, 2009).

Then in 1836 Sam Houston defeated Santa Ana at the battle of San Jacinto. This defeat ended the era of the Texas revolution, or Texas's war for independence. Fear of continued domination by Mexico prompted the annexation of Texas by the United States in December 1845. This act severed U.S. diplomatic relations with Mexico and paved the way for the Mexican-American War. The Mexican-American War (1846–1848) terminated with the Treaty of Guadalupe Hidalgo, in which Mexico accepted the Rio Grande River as the Texas border and ceded territory in the southwest to the United States for $15 million. The occupation of the southwest territory created the present-day states of California, New Mexico, Nevada, and parts of Colorado, Arizona, and Utah (Acuna, 2010; Jansson, 2009).

People of Mexican ancestry residing in Texas and the Southwest suffered overt economic, political, and social subordination as Anglo Americans began descending on the territory. This pattern was well established by the time the Mexican revolution drove thousands of Mexicans to the United States in the early 1900s.

Immigration and Population Growth

Between 1880 and 1910, the southwestern United States experienced rapid economic development and commercialization of agriculture. Mexican labor was highly sought by U.S. mining, railroad, and agricultural interests. During these three decades, the population of Mexican origin grew threefold as Mexican immigrants gravitated toward the region's growing demand for low-wage labor (McWilliams, 1990). The railroads played a crucial role in the expanding Mexican immigration because they were a rapid and a relatively easy means of transportation from central Mexico and a principal source of employment during the late nineteenth and early twentieth centuries. In 1909, workers of Mexican origin comprised 17 percent of the workforce of the nine large western railroads (Reisler, 1976).

Between 1910 and 1930, the Mexican population in the United States continued to grow rapidly. The 1910 Mexican Revolution and the Cristero Rebellion[1] (1926–1929) in Mexico served to increase Mexican migration to the United States. In addition, emigration from Mexico was spurred by a strong demand for labor, heightened by the entry of the United States into World War I (Acuna, 2010).

The 1930s were a period of widespread domestic unemployment, and the demand for unskilled labor decreased. By 1930, the population of Mexican origin exceeded 1 million persons. Anti-Mexican sentiment increased and swept through the Southwest, resulting in mass repatriations. Between 1929 and 1935, more than 415,000 Mexicans (some of whom were American citizens) were forcibly expelled from the United States in railroad cars back to Mexico. Another 85,000 left "voluntarily." As a result, between 1930 and 1940, the Mexican population dramatically declined, and 41 percent of Mexico-born persons actually returned to Mexico (Jansson, 2009; McWilliams, 1990).

During World War II, the United States again began to experience labor shortages in the Southwest. Agricultural interests sought and obtained government cooperation in the recruitment and importation of Mexican workers for agricultural labor. In 1942, the *bracero* program, originally conceived as a temporary wartime measure, was created. Agricultural growers pressured the government to both extend and expand this program throughout the 1950s. The program ended in 1964, following growing opposition by organized labor. During the twenty-two years of its operation, the *bracero* program recruited over 4 million workers, and at its peak over 400,000 Mexican workers were entering the United States annually. During this time, the Mexican population nearly doubled from 377,000 to 746,000 (Jansson, 2009; Reichert and Massey, 1980).

---

[1]The Cristero War (also known as the Cristiada) of 1926 to 1929 was an uprising against the Mexican government set off by religious persecution of Catholics.

After the *bracero* program was officially phased out, Mexican workers continued to enter the United States legally and illegally because U.S. businesses continued to actively recruit these low-wage workers. Between 1970 and 1980, legal and illegal migration, high fertility rates, and social and economic conditions in Mexico combined to produce a 64 percent increase in the U.S. population of Mexican origin. Over the decades of the 80s and 90s, almost one out of three of the foreign-born population in the United States were born in Mexico. Today Mexicans still account for 32 percent of all immigrants residing in the United States. More than half of the Mexican immigrants (52 percent) are undocumented; in addition, they comprise 59 percent of the almost 12 million undocumented immigrants in the United States (Passel and Cohn, 2009).

Today 30 million persons of Mexican origin or descent reside in the United States, representing 64 percent of the total Hispanic population (46 million). The 46 million Hispanics today represent 15 percent of the U.S. population. Mexican Americans are the fastest growing and the largest Hispanic ethnic group in the United States. The majority of the Mexican American population reside in the five southwestern states of Arizona, California, Colorado, New Mexico, and Texas. In 2008, 40 percent of the Mexico-born population were foreign born compared to the 12.4 percent in the population overall. Although 22 percent of all foreign-born Mexico-born individuals are now citizens, the majority (63 percent) of the immigrants from Mexico arrived in the United States after 1990 (Pew Hispanic Center, 2009).

The Civil Rights Movement and the Rise of Chicano Power

The 1960s, the era of the New Frontier and the War on Poverty, was a time of economic and political upheaval. Underrepresented and economically disadvantaged groups (often the same) organized to demand their civil rights and particularly to spotlight those issues that plagued individuals, families, and communities. The growing ferment of Chicano youth focused on inequities in education, the high rate of unemployment, the working conditions of low-wage workers, and the general poverty status of the Mexican American population.[2] This generation of Chicano activists, like members of many other groups, pressed for the rights they had been guaranteed by the U.S. Constitution, and particularly for the many rights guaranteed to the Mexican population historically in the numerous treaties between the United States and Mexico in exchange for the lands of the Southwest (Acuna, 2010; Jansson, 2009).

Four leaders formed the foundation of Chicano activism in the 1960s and 1970s. Each represented an area central to Mexican American concerns: Cesar Chavez and the United Farm Workers (a union addressing working conditions of farm and other low-wage workers); Reis Tijerina and the Alianza (a movement focusing on land grant claims in New Mexico); José Angel Gutierrez and La Raza Unida Party (a political party uniting Mexican Americans); and Rudolfo "Corky" Gonzales and the Crusade for Justice (a movement of Chicano self-determination). Through their efforts and that of many others, the growth of the Chicano population and the legacy of the Chicano Movement, mainstream political power, emerged in the late 1970s and early 1980s and has continued to grow. This movement had the effect of generating a new pride in the Spanish, Mexican, and Indian heritage of the Chicanos, and it gave rise to many Mexican American organizations to press for equal rights in numerous arenas of society.

---

[2]*Chicano* is used only in reference to Mexican Americans, not Mexicans living in Mexico. The literary and political movements of the 1960s and 1970s among Mexican Americans established *Chicano* as a term of ethnic pride. It has strong political associations.

Because of their sheer numbers throughout the United States, with major concentrations in the Southwest and the Midwest, Mexican Americans have become a political force. Since the advent of the Chicano movement, Mexican American families have increasingly become more involved in the political process. This developing political strength has given the Mexican American population a stronger voice and power base.

Since 1990, the political strength of the Mexican American population can particularly be seen in California where one-third of the state's population is of Mexican origin. Hispanics, mostly Mexican Americans, hold numerous state assembly and state senate seats. The Latino Caucus of the California Assembly is a powerful group whose voice is widely listened to in the political process.[3] In recent years, two speakers of the California Assembly have been of Mexican origin. Many of the mayors of several California cities (such as Los Angeles) are of Mexican origin. This representation of Mexican-origin politicians is also seen at the national level, particularly in the U.S. House of Representatives (Loretta Sanchez, Linda Sanchez, Xavier Becerra, and others).

The Hispanic vote, primarily Mexican American, carries great political clout in the Southwest as well as in states of the Midwest (e.g., Illinois). In the 2008 presidential election, the Hispanic vote was vital for carrying some states. To win the presidency, voters in states such as California and Texas, with large numbers of electoral votes, were critical in ensuring a win. The showing of Hispanic political strength in the 2008 presidential election has made Hispanics an important constituency to be courted (Lopez, 2008).

CHANGE AND ADAPTATION

Much has been written about the traditional structure of Mexican American families. Depending on the author, these structures appear rigid, cold, and unstable on one end of the continuum or warm, nurturing, and cohesive on the other end. The traditional structure of the Mexican family, however, grew out of the socioeconomic needs dictated by the agrarian and craft economies of Mexico. The traditional Mexican *familia* ("family") meant an extended, multigenerational group within which specific social roles were ascribed to specific persons. By dividing functions and responsibilities among different generations of family members, *la familia* was able to perform all the economic and social support chores necessary for survival in the relatively spartan life circumstances of the rural Mexican environment. Mutual support, sustenance, and interaction during both work and leisure hours dominated the lives of persons in these traditional Mexican families (Baca-Zinn, Ertzen, and Wells, 2010; Becerra, 1983; Griswold del Castillo, 1984).

Mexican American families tended to work and live in ethnically homogenous settings, minimally influenced by Anglo American culture. These communities supported the maintenance of Mexican familial structures as they might have been practiced in rural Mexico. The male took the role of authority figure and head of the household, and the female took the role of child bearer and nurturer. Like all family forms responding to particular economic and political forces, these ideals are undergoing modification under the new economic and political circumstances of life in the United States (Becerra, 1983).

---

[3]Historically, areas conquered by the Spaniards were called Hispania. These regions include Mexico, Central America, and most of South America where Spanish is the primary language, with the exception of Brazil. Individuals with origins in these countries are considered *Hispanic*. *Latino/Latina* is very close in meaning to Hispanic but also includes other countries, such as Brazil. The term is a descriptor for individuals with origins in countries where Romance languages (Spanish, Portuguese) are spoken. *Latino* is the term more widely used today.

The Contemporary Mexican American Family

The contemporary Mexican American family exhibits a blend of traditional values and adaptation to new environments and changing times. It is a product of the social, economic, and political milieu in which it resides. The ceremonies relating to life cycle rituals—birth, marriage, and death—that have been integral to the Mexican American culture still survive in greater and lesser degrees. These traditional rituals are sustained by families through ceremonies, often linked to the basic religious beliefs and values of the Mexican American culture. Rituals also highlight the role of the extended family and the conjugal family. The extent and elaboration of the rituals and ceremonies are often determined by the extent of acculturation and assimilation of the Mexican American family into the mainstream of American life. The large-scale urbanization of the Mexican American conjugal family has diminished the maintenance of extended family arrangements, and the extended family—*la familia*—is less central to the everyday life of today's Mexican American family (Baca-Zinn, Ertzen, and Wells, 2010; Williams, 1990).

FAMILY STRUCTURE AND FORMATION.   The Mexican American population is young, with a median age of twenty-five years in 2007, compared with the non-Hispanic population median age of thirty-six. About 52 percent of Mexican Americans are males compared with a male population of 49 percent for the entire U.S. population (Pew Hispanic Center, 2009). Because Mexico borders the United States, it facilitates male movement back and forth to seek work, leaving families behind in Mexico, perhaps accounting for the slightly higher number of Mexican American males than females.

In 2007, Mexican American families had a median household family income of $40,274 compared to the median of $50,595 for all U.S. families. The median annual personal earnings (per capita) for full-time year-round Mexican American workers aged sixteen and over was $25,298 versus $39,464 annually for non-Hispanic workers and $27,521 for individuals in other Hispanic groups. Related to these income levels is the fact that Mexican American families are significantly larger than all other ethnic or racial families in the United States. The mean number of persons in Mexican American families is 3.7 compared with 3.45 in other Hispanic family groups and 2.6 persons in White non-Hispanic U.S. families. The larger Mexican American family must be supported by a family income that is smaller than that of most other groups. That is one reason that 21 percent of Mexican American families live in poverty, a higher rate than for the general population in the United States of 12 percent (Pew Hispanic Center, 2009).

Occupationally, Mexican Americans are far more concentrated in blue-collar jobs (46 percent) than in white-collar jobs (35 percent). They are no longer concentrated in rural areas in agriculture and farming labor. Mexican American families are most likely to reside in large urban settings, working in low-wage service industries (health care, education, social services, food services, accommodations, hospitality) or in construction and retail trade. Immigrants are the most likely to be in the construction or food services industries while those born in the United States are more likely to work in health, education, and social services (Pew Hispanic Center, 2008).

Mexican Americans have the lowest median school years completed of any other group in the United States. Of individuals ages twenty-five and over, Mexican Americans are the mostly to have less than a high school education (23.7 percent) compared to all Hispanics (21.5 percent) and the United States as a whole (10 percent). In part, this phenomenon can be explained by the high rate of low or no schooling of persons who emigrate from Mexico looking for unskilled labor. Because this factor is compounded by the elevated high school dropout rate among Mexican Americans in general—which in some areas is as high as 45 percent—educational attainment is a major social problem for Hispanics in general and Mexican Americans in particular (Pew Hispanic Center, 2009).

English language proficiency is also a factor in both schooling and occupational opportunities. A majority of Mexicans (59 percent) speak English proficiently while 41 percent of Mexicans, ages five and older, report speaking English less than very well (or not at all), compared with 38.8 percent of all Hispanics (Pew Hispanic Center, 2009).

Marriage patterns among Mexican Americans are similar to those of other groups. Among those individuals aged 15 and over, less than half of Mexicans (49.3 percent) and Hispanics overall (47.3 percent) are married. These marriage patterns are slightly less than the rate of married individuals (50.2 percent) in the total U.S. population. In addition, the percentage of never-married Mexican Americans is similar to the Hispanic population in general but larger than for persons of non-Hispanic origin (37.7 percent compared to 30 percent) (Pew Hispanic Center, 2009).

Mexican Americans have a divorce rate of 7.5 percent compared to the non-Hispanic rate of 9.7 percent. Interestingly, however, the currently unmarried (divorced, separated, widowed) rate for Mexican Americans is 13 percent, 15 percent for Hispanics as a whole, and 19.6 percent for non-Hispanics (Pew Hispanic Center, 2009).

Of the 10.4 million Hispanic women ages 15 to 44 in 2007, 6.6 million were of Mexican origin. The fertility rate for Mexican American women (ages 15–44) in 2007 was 95.4 births per 1000, a rate significantly higher than among women 15 to 44 in the general population (64.4 per 1000). Women born in Mexico accounted for 40 percent of all births to foreign-born women ages 15–44 in 2008, even though they account for 27 percent of all foreign-born women of childbearing age (U.S. Census Bureau, 2007).

ASSIMILATION.   As Hispanic subgroups, particularly the foreign born, begin to blend into the total community or assimilate into their environment through various dimensions of structural integration (e.g., language, schooling, intermarriage), the socioeconomic profile moves closer to that of the socioeconomic profile of the population as a whole. Intermarriage, one of the strongest indicators of assimilation, seems to be widespread among U.S.-born Mexicans. In fact, more than one-third of married, U.S.-born Mexicans have non-Mexican spouses, with an overwhelming majority being non-Hispanic Whites (Duncan and Trejo, 2008). Duncan and Trejo (2008) indicate that the majority of Mexican Americans who intermarry tend to have higher levels of education and earnings. Thus, over a couple of generations Mexican immigrants assimilate to the degree that their identity and socioeconomic achievement are understated or fade from observation. As educational levels increase, residential segregation decreases and social mobility increases. As the Mexican American socioeconomic profile moves closer to the socioeconomic profile of the population as a whole, the assimilation process moves accordingly.

Social Issues

The Mexican American family, as considered in this chapter, incorporates both native and foreign-born individuals of Mexican origin currently living in the United States. Most Mexican American families contain both native and foreign-born family members who may differ by generational level. Nativity and generation are important for understanding some of the major social issues affecting Mexican American families. Mexican immigrants and U.S.-born Mexican Americans are distinct groups with different opportunities, but because of the familial ties and common origin, many researchers combine them and treat them as one group when analyzing some social issues. Although many social issues affect the well-being of all of these families, three broad areas of concern affect all Mexican American families in varying degrees based on nativity and generational level: (1) the education gap, (2) health care, and (3) immigration policy.

THE EDUCATION GAP.   In the United States, fewer Mexican Americans complete the least years of schooling than any other group. This educational deficit is central to understanding why Mexican-origin workers earn relatively low wages, are more likely to be in the lower socioeconomic strata of the society, and are the most likely to live below the poverty level.

Immigration plays a large role in the understanding of the Mexican–White high school graduation gap. The younger an individual is when immigrating to the United States, the better chance he or she has of completing high school. For example, those who arrived in the United States between the ages of 15 and 21 have high school completion rates of about 28 percent compared to those who arrive before the age of 5 and have completion rates closer to the U.S.-born Mexican Americans who have a graduation rate of 70 percent; however, the completion rate is still lower than for U.S.-born Whites (87 percent) and African Americans (79 percent) (Grogger and Trejo, 2002).

The national high school dropout rate (individuals have not completed high school and are not enrolled in school) for youth ages 16 to 19 is 10 percent. For White non-Hispanics, the dropout rate is 7 percent, and for African Americans it is 12 percent, compared to 25 percent for Mexican-origin youth. As previously noted, a significant proportion of teen Mexican school dropouts are more likely to be recent immigrants who may have never enrolled in school (Pew Research Center/Kaiser Family Foundation, 2004).

Mexican American student attrition is often attributed to their less favorable family and community circumstances. These youth are disproportionally represented in lower socioeconomic levels, are from families whose parents have not completed high school, and are twice as likely as Whites to reside in inner city areas with poor educational climates that undermine educational attainment (Pew Hispanic Center, 2004).

Yet even among high school graduates, achieving higher education is also at a low level. Among 18- to 24-year-old high school graduates, only 33 percent of Mexicans enroll in college. Several studies show that among Hispanic high school graduates, these students are less well prepared academically than their counterparts of other racial and ethnic backgrounds (Oakes, 2005; Swail, Cabrera, and Lee, 2004). Some of the reasons given by researchers for low college attendance and/or poor academic preparation of Mexican youth are low performance on standardized tests (Schmidt and Carmara, 2004), attendance in low-achieving K–12 schools (Fry, 2005), lack of information about college choice (Tornatzky, Cutler, and Lee, 2002), and most important, the cost of college (Pew Research Center/Kaiser Family Foundation, 2004).

For low-income Mexican American families, the financial considerations are major impediments to college attendance because family financial responsibilities often affect college enrollment decisions. Perhaps for this reason, Hispanics in general and Mexican Americans in particular are more likely to enroll in two-year institutions, which decreases four-year institutional participation (students are less likely to transfer to a four-year college) and, thus, has negative ramifications on degree completion (Saenz, 2002). Moreover, the undergraduate completion data show that Hispanics, of whom Mexican Americans are the majority, are about 50 percent less likely to complete a bachelor's degree than their White peers (Fry, 2004, 2005).

Thus, the educational deficit is a major predictor of many of the social issues affecting Mexican American families. This deficit affects wages and occupational achievement, which in turn affect the need and uses of other services such as health care and welfare use. Nativity plays a significant role by masking the achievements of the American-born population and downplaying the plight of many of the foreign-born population (Grogger and Trejo, 2002; Kao and

Thompson, 2003). Even considering nativity, however, the educational gap between U.S.-born youth of Mexican origin and non-Hispanic youth is of continuing social concern.

HEALTH CARE.   Access to health care is among the most critical social issues facing Mexican American families. Good health conditions increase with increased levels of education and family income. Clearly the key ingredient in achieving good health status is access to health care. Access to heath care, particularly to preventative or early medical care, is most often dependent on having health insurance. Among the uninsured, Hispanic persons (43 percent) were about three times as likely as non-Hispanic persons (15 percent) to have never had health insurance coverage. Reasons affecting lack of health insurance include lack of employer-provided insurance and low-wage employment that precludes buying private health insurance because of the cost to individual families (Centers for Disease Control, 2009; U.S. Census Bureau, 2007).

Immigrant status can and does affect access to health care, and it also influences differences in need for health care. For example, low-wage jobs are also related to higher exposure to occupational hazards because of working conditions. The higher birth rate among Mexican women also leaves them vulnerable to the need for prenatal care as well as other women's health issues, such as preventable cancers and domestic violence (de la Torre and Estrada, 2001).

Some major health concerns include early health seeking for prenatal care for pregnant women and girls. For example, of particular concern are Mexican American teens because, while the overall teen pregnancy and birth rates have declined in recent years, the decline in the Hispanic teen pregnancy and birth rate has been slower than for other racial and ethnic groups. In particular, among all Hispanic groups, Mexican-origin teens have the highest birth rate. In 2004, the teen birth rate for all Hispanics was 82.6 per 1000, while for Mexican American teens it was 93.2 per 1,000 (The National Campaign to Prevent Teen and Unplanned Pregnancy, 2006). Research shows that Mexican Americans average fewer prenatal visits than non-Hispanic Whites (8.6 versus 10.2 visits) and are less likely to have adequate care (Moore and Hepworth, 1994). With the growth of the Mexican American population and teen birth rate, access and adequacy of health care threaten the health outcomes for the Mexican American population.

Another major health area of concern among Mexican American families is type 2 diabetes. Mexican Americans are 2.5 times as likely as non-Hispanic Whites to develop diabetes (savvyHealth, 2000). Interestingly, however, Mexican American families are more likely than Mexicans living in Mexico to develop type 2 diabetes. Research shows that this difference is due to American-style diets and lack of exercise. The high level of fat in the Mexican American diet is more likely to lead to obesity and hypertension. If untreated, diabetes can lead to blindness, kidney failure, heart attacks, stroke, and amputations.

These are just two health areas among Mexican Americans that exceed the general rate in the U.S. population, suggesting the need for access to affordable and quality health care for this population.

IMMIGRATION POLICY.   Perhaps no topic is as emotionally laden for both Mexican Americans and non-Hispanics as immigration reform. For U.S.-born Mexican Americans the ties to their immigrant roots can be recent and may define many family members. Immigrants may be in the United States legally, or they may be undocumented. Immigrants generally come to America to seek a better life through economic opportunity. They may intend to remain to build a life in America, or they may intend to return to their families in Mexico.

The demand of American businesses for low-wage workers provides the "pull" for many Mexican workers. Immigration, both legal and unauthorized, is common because of Mexico's proximity, lack of employment in Mexico, and familial ties in the United States. The type of low-wage labor demanded further attracts the poorly educated, low-skilled individual seeking opportunities to support his/her family.

Debate is widespread regarding the costs and benefits of immigration. Borjas (1999) suggests that the benefits accrue to a few by increasing the wealth of the richest segment of society while maintaining the poorest people (the immigrant) in continuing poverty. He notes that today's immigrant is less skilled than in previous eras and, thus, more likely to become unemployed and need public assistance and other public services over time. In addition, less social mobility is seen in their children, who are likely to remain in poor, residentially segregated communities and increase the population of the urban poor. Thus, there can be high costs associated with unregulated immigration (Borjas, 1999).

On the other hand, immigrants, as others who preceded them, are changing the face of America. In so doing, new ways of interacting with diverse populations are encouraging a greater examination of a more racially and ethnically diverse society in the near future. The need to create educational and economic opportunity for all must receive more attention. The strain and backlash on native Mexican Americans because of Mexican immigration raises many dilemmas for all Mexican American families (Suro, 1998). The issue of renewed immigration policy must clearly be in the forefront of this decade's social agenda.

CONCLUSION

The Mexican American family continues to be modified by the social and economic pressures of American life. The proximity to Mexico provides a continual influx of Mexican nationals who serve to maintain familial and emotional ties to Mexican cultural values.

The urbanization over time of Mexican American families has had a profound effect on the family structure. Although a strong familial orientation continues as a value in Mexican American families, today they are less likely to be composed of extended kin in the same household. The supportive family system is characterized much more by voluntary interaction than by the necessity for economic survival that characterized rural environments of the past.

Because of the various patterns of immigration, the Mexican American population exhibits much heterogeneity. It spans the continuum of acculturation and assimilation, depending on the length of time in the United States, nativity (United States or Mexico), generational status, and intermarriage with other groups. Spanish is still spoken by most Mexican Americans, and the Mexican American native-born population is almost all proficient in English.

Nativity plays a role in most socioeconomic measures, such as educational attainment, occupational status, and household and individual income. U.S.-born Mexicans are much more likely to achieve higher levels of success that are closer to the White non-Hispanic population. Although there continues to be a gap, it varies as nativity is introduced into the equation. However, on many other measures, such as some health problems, U.S.-born Mexicans fare less well than their non-U.S.-born counterparts.

All these factors converge to continually modify the Mexican American family by changing the roles and expectations of all family members, U.S. born and immigrant. As more opportunities emerge, social forces affect family life, and responses to an economic and political structure occur, and the Mexican American family will continue to change and adapt to the forces around it. Although the traditional Mexican American family has changed and will continue to change, the family form among Mexican Americans that fuses the culture of its roots and that of its American homeland will endure.

References

Acuna, R. 2010. *Occupied America: A History of Chicanos* (7th ed.). New York: Prentice Hall.

Baca-Zinn, M., D. S. Ertzen, and B. Wells. 2010. *Diversity in Families,* 9th ed. New York: Prentice Hall.

Becerra, R. M. 1983. "The Mexican American: Aging in a Changing Culture." In R. L. McNeeley and J. L. Colen (Eds.), *Aging in Minority Groups* (pp. 108–118). Beverly Hills, CA: Sage.

Borjas, G. 1999. *Heaven's Door: Immigration Policy and the American Economy.* Princeton, NJ: Princeton University Press.

Centers for Disease Control (CDC). 2009. "Summary Health Statistics for the U.S. Population: National Health Interview Survey, 2008." Washington, DC: U.S. Dept. of Health and Human Services.

de la Torre, A., and A. Estrada. 2001. *Mexican Americans and Health: Sana! Sana!* Tucson: University of Arizona Press.

Duncan, B., and Trejo, S. 2008. "Intermarriage and the Intergenerational Transmission of Ethnic Identity and Human Capital for Mexican Americans," IZA Discussion Papers 3547. Bonn, Germany: Institute for the Study of Labor (IZA).

———. 2004. *Latino Youth Finishing College: The Role of Selective Pathways.* Washington, DC: Pew Hispanic Center.

———. 2005. *Recent Changes in the Entry of Hispanic and White Youth into College.* Washington, DC: Pew Hispanic Center.

Griswold del Castillo, R. 1984. *La Familia: Chicano Families in the Urban Southwest, 1848 to the Present.* Notre Dame, IN: University of Notre Dame Press.

Grogger, J., and S. Trejo. 2002. *Falling Behind or Moving Up? The Intergeneration Progress of Mexican Americans.* San Francisco: Public Policy Institute of California.

Jansson, B. S. 2009. *The Reluctant Welfare State,* 6th Ed. Belmont, CA: Brooks-Cole.

Kao, G., and J. S. Thompson. 2003. "Racial and Ethnic Stratification in Educational Achievement and Attainment." *Annual Review of Sociology 29,* 117–142.

Lopez, M. H. 2008. *The Hispanic Vote in 2008.* Washington, DC: Pew Hispanic Center.

McWilliams, C. 1990. *North from Mexico,* rev. ed. Westport, CT: Greenwood Press.

Moore, P., and J. T. Hepworth. 1994. "Use of Perinatal and Infant Health Services by Mexican American Medicaid Enrollees." *JAMA 272*(4), 297–304.

Oakes, J. 2005. *Keeping Track: How Schools Structure Inequality,* 2nd ed. New Haven, CT: Yale University Press.

Passel, J., and D. Cohn. 2009. *A Portrait of Unauthorized Immigrants in the United States.* Washington, DC: Pew Hispanic Center.

Pew Hispanic Center. 2004, January. "Fact Sheet: Latino Teens Staying in High School: A Challenge for All Generations." Washington, DC: USC Annenberg School of Communication.

———. 2008. *Mexican Immigrants in the United States, 2008.* Washington, DC: Pew Hispanic Center.

———. 2009. *Hispanics of Mexican Origin in the United States, 2007.* Fact Sheet, September 16, 2009.

Pew Hispanic Center/Kaiser Family Foundation. 2004. *National Survey of Latinos: Education, Summary and Chartpack.* Washington, DC: Pew Hispanic Center.

Reichert, J. S., and D. S. Massey. 1980. "History and Trends in U.S. Bound Migration from a Mexican Town." *International Migration Review 14,* 479–591.

Reisler, M. 1976. *By the Sweat of Their Brow: Mexicans in the United States, 1900–1940.* New York: Greenwood Press.

Saenz, V. B. 2002. *Hispanic Students and Community Colleges: A Critical Point for Intervention.* Los Angeles, CA: ERIC Clearinghouse for Community Colleges. ERIC Document Reproduction Service No. ED477908. www.eric.ed.gov/PDFS/ED477908.pdf (accessed April 3, 2011).

savvyHealth. 2000. "Health News: Mexican American Diabetes Studied." www.savvyHEALTH.com/db/newsview.asp?docid=4806 (accessed April 3, 2011).

Schmidt. A. E., and W. J. Camara. 2004. "Group Differences in Standardized Test Scores and Other Educational Indicators." In R. Zwick (Ed.), *Rethinking the SAT: The Future of Standardized Testing in University Admissions.* New York: RoutledgeFalmer.

Suro, R. 1998. *Strangers Among Us: How Latino Immigration Is Transforming America.* New York: Knopf.

Swail, W. S., A. F. Cabrera, and C. Lee. 2004. *Latino Youth and the Pathways to College.* Washington, DC: Pew Hispanic Center.

The National Campaign to Prevent Teen and Unplanned Pregnancy. June, 2006. "Fact Sheet: Teen Sexual Activity, Pregnancy and Childbearing Among Latinos in the United States." Washington, DC: The National Campaign to Prevent Teen and Unplanned Pregnancy. www.thenationalcampaign.

org/resources/pdf/Latinos_2006.pdf (accessed April 3, 2011).

Tornatzky, L., R. Cutler, and J. Lee. 2002. *College Knowledge: What Latino Parents Needs to Know and Why They Don't Know It.* Claremont, CA: The Tomas Rivera Policy Institute.

U.S. Census Bureau. 2007. June Current Population Survey, Selected Years, June 1994 to June 2006. Supplemental Table 7. Women 15 to 44 Years Old Who Had a Birth in the Last 12 Months and Children Ever Born Per 1,000 Women, by Nativity Status, Region of Birth, Citizenship Status, Race, Hispanic Origin, and Age: Selected Years, 1994 to 2006. www.census.gov/population/socdemo/fertility/cps2008/SupFertTab7.xls (accessed April 3, 2011).

Williams, N. 1990. *The Mexican American Family: Tradition and Change.* New York: Free Press.

8

···

The Cuban American Family

Zulema E. Suárez
Rose M. Perez

INTRODUCTION

At an estimated size of 1.7 million, Cuban Americans represent the third-largest group of Hispanic origin in the United States, after Mexicans and Puerto Ricans (Pew Hispanic Center, 2009). Most Cubans arrived in the United States following Fidel Castro's triumph to power in 1959. Those in the initial exodus following the revolution felt confident that their stay would be temporary, until things calmed down and life would return to normal. Over a half-century later, Cubans are still in the United States—the early Cubans, who sought to replicate their former way of life, the second generation whose roots are in the United States, and the newcomers who, although maintaining close ties with the island, have adapted to life in the United States. The journey to the United States has been brief for those fortunate enough to travel by air, and incessantly long for those traveling across the perilous Atlantic on makeshift boats and inner tubes. But regardless of when and how they came, Cubans' adaptation has been intertwined with emotional pain, hardship, and strife due to generational and ideological differences stemming from the sociopolitical divide between the two homelands: the one they left and the one that welcomed them. Migration has meant the loss of loved ones, of a way of life, and an incessant yearning to return to a paradise lost.

Still, the pain of exile has not deterred the exodus of hundreds of thousands of Cubans, representing as much as 15 percent of the island's population in 2008 from seeking personal, political, and economic freedom (Pew Hispanic Center, 2009; Portes and Bach, 1985). Because the early Cubans brought high human capital and achieved entrepreneurial success, Cubans have been christened a "model minority" and credited with elevating Miami to the international economic gateway to Latin America (De Haymes, 1997). Hence, this first wave came to be known as the "Golden Exiles." Although there is, typically, some truth to most stereotypes, this chapter describes a more complex and nuanced portrait of this diverse diaspora, highlighting selected contextual factors contributing to their incorporation.

Given the significant role of the family and of the enclave in the adaptation and incorporation of Cuban Americans to this country, we have found it useful to use a social capital framework to organize our discussion. We define social capital as the benefits accrued from membership in groups (familial or extra-familial) and social networks (Portes, 1998). These benefits may be tangible, like informal loans or job referrals, or intangible, like interpersonal trust. Moreover, although social capital is often viewed as positive, it can also have negative consequences, such as social exclusion and social control (Portes, 1998). Because the political conditions that have propelled Cubans to the United States have shaped their characterizations, incorporation, and ethnic identity, we start by acknowledging long-time connections with the United States, focusing on the most recent period since Cuba's 1959 revolution.

CHRONOLOGY OF THE EXODUS

Perhaps, because of the long history of early trade routes (Pérez, 2003), and the short 90 miles of ocean that divides the United States and Cuba, Cuban people have, historically, sought the assistance of the United States, and the United States has generally corresponded. In 1870, approximately 5,000 Cubans were living in this country, most having fled the Spanish colonizers governing the island at the time (Jimenez-Vasquez, 1995; Skaine, 2004). Later, the United States played an important role in shaping the sovereignty of that island-nation when, in 1898, the United States aided Cuba in gaining sovereignty from Spain. Similarly, the United States heard Cubans' plea for help after the 1959 revolution, when Fidel Castro declared that his regime would follow Marxist–Leninist ideology (Pedraza-Bailey, 1980). Dissenters of the island's new politics quickly sought asylum in the United States, and the United States welcomed them. In April 1961, a different fate befell Cuban exiles landing at the Bay of Pigs, in a U.S.-backed invasion to overthrow Fidel's government, when the Kennedy administration failed to send the promised air support and the invasion failed, leaving the fighters stranded.

Despite strict immigration restrictions by the island's government, Cubans continued to flee to the United States, largely, in what scholars call waves, four identifiable periods of mass migration coinciding with political tensions between the two countries. However, scholars have recently collapsed these four waves to two based on their similar demographic and social characteristics (Eckstein, 2009). In this chapter, we use the term *early exiles* to refer to Cubans arriving during the first two waves, and *recent exiles* to describe those entering in the latter two waves, after 1980. A closer examination of the contrast in social and demographic characteristics of the different waves of Cuban Americans should dispel popular perceptions of group homogeneity.

The Early Exiles

Most Cubans, regardless of class, initially supported Castro's revolution for the societal changes it promised (Eckstein, 2009), but after the euphoria of the revolution subsided and Castro's Communist ideology became evident, panic ensued. This frenzy sparked what would be one of the largest influxes of refugees in U.S. history. Cubans in the elite class, having the most to lose, were the first to leave after Fidel's nationalization of Cuban industry, agrarian reform laws, and the United States' severance of economic ties (García, 1996) immediately displaced them (Eckstein, 2009). Exiles from the first wave, spanning 1959 to 1962, were mainly high-skilled upper- and middle-class families (Suro and Escobar, 2006). After the United States closed its embassy in Havana in January 1961, another 150,000 came to the United States under a "visa waiver" program handled through the Swiss embassy (García, 1996). During those chaotic early days of the revolution, fearful that the new government would remove their children, middle- and upper-class families sent their offspring to the United States through a program sponsored by the Catholic Church. This program, later coined "Operation Peter Pan," placed 14,000 Cuban children with foster families and in orphanages throughout the United States while they awaited reunification with their families; unfortunately, many were never reunited (Skaine, 2004; Torres, 2003). This first phase of the emigration ended in October 1962, the time of the Cuban Missile Crisis.

Emigration continued despite stringent governmental constraints (Portes and Bach, 1985). Cubans on the island were living through changes that included the silencing of the Catholic Church, a collapse of the electoral system, and continued reform that extended to the most rural parts of the island (Eckstein, 2009). The next major wave, from 1965 to 1974, began with Fidel suddenly allowing anyone wishing to leave to be picked up by relatives via the port of Camarioca in the province of Matanzas (Eckstein, 2009; Suro and Escobar, 2006). This naval exodus brought to the United States 2,866 people on tugboats, yachts, shrimpers, and other floating devices from September to November 1965 (García, 1996), culminating in the Johnson administration's establishment of an airlift, also known as freedom flights, which transported to the United States 275,000 refugees from December 1965 to March 1972 (Wasem, 2009). Unlike the initial wave, who were primarily the elite class, about 40 percent of the airlift group were students, women, and children who were reuniting with their relatives (Bean and Tienda, 1987). During this time, the Cuban government began barring the migration of young men of military age, professionals, and technical and skilled workers to prevent a brain drain (Pedraza and Rumbaut, 1996). Hence, this wave was largely working class and employees, independent craftsmen, small merchants, and skilled and semiskilled workers.

The Recent Exiles

Although the government and people of the United States welcomed the early refugees, subsequent migrations have been controversial. Whereas the first Cuban migration to the United States has been characterized as politically motivated, recent ones are said to be economically induced (Portes and Bach, 1985). The third wave began with the 1980 Mariel boatlift (Suro and Escobar, 2006). Between April and September 1980, more than 125,000 residents left Cuba under extremely perilous and chaotic circumstances through a hastily improvised boatlift, via the port of Mariel (Skaine, 2004). Although thousands fled to join family members, Castro's government expelled some gay men and lesbians, people with criminal records (whether they had actually committed crimes or were dissidents), and other institutionalized persons. This political maneuver was Castro's retaliation because thousands of Cubans had broken into the Peruvian Embassy in April 1980 to seek political asylum (Ojito, 2006). This group came to be known as "social undesirables" who were not wanted by Cuba or the United States (Bach, Bach, and Triplett, 1982; Jimenez-Vasquez, 1995). They also came to be known pejoratively as "Marielitos," after the port of Mariel. Unlike the Golden Exiles, these were "children of the revolution."

A fourth wave of entrants, coming primarily by sea, began arriving during what Cuba called "the special period," coinciding with the 1989 collapse of Communism in Eastern Europe, especially in the Soviet Union. During that time, Cuba lost trade and economic subsidies needed for its survival. The tightening of the U.S. embargo in 1992 worsened the economic woes of the island (Suro and Escobar, 2006), triggering yet another major exodus of people, so desperate to leave the island that they left on *balsas* (rafts, tires, or other improvised vessels), fearless of the risks of death from starvation, dehydration, drowning, or sharks (Pedraza and Rumbaut, 1996). This group became known as *balseros*. For years, a volunteer rescue team, *Los Hermanos del Rescate* (Brothers to the Rescue), patrolled the ocean to rescue escapees. Approximately 5,791 *balseros* survived the trip to the United States between 1985 and 1992, but the most dramatic number of balseros—37,000—were rescued at sea during the months of August and September 1994 (Pedraza and Rumbaut, 1996). Massive protest riots in Havana during this time led Castro to order the Coast Guard to allow departures from Cuba's beaches (Pedraza and Rumbaut, 1996). The U.S. government, confronted with an apparently immense breach of national security, responded by redirecting these balseros to Guantanamo Bay Naval Station in Cuba. Up until an unexpected turn of events nine months later, the approximately 30,000 aspiring entrants lived in tents, anticipating that they would be returned to Cuba, as they had been told by U.S. personnel at Guantanamo.

To prevent exiles from risking their lives at sea, President William Clinton's administration developed a "wet foot/dry foot" policy, in which Cuban rafters found at sea, not firmly on U.S. soil, would be returned to Cuba (Wasem, 2009). The only exception would be if they claimed fear of persecution, since that would potentially qualify them as political refugees under the 1980 Refugee Act. On the other hand, Cubans intercepted on land may, after one year, adjust their status under the 1966 Cuban Adjustment Act (CAA), which allows Cubans entering the United States undocumented to become permanent residents at the discretion of the U.S. attorney general. This accord ended a longstanding American policy of granting refugee status to all Cubans rescued at sea; it required the United States to return anyone fleeing Cuba by boat to the island and to grant at least 20,000 immigrant visas to Cubans each year (Wasem, 2009). Still, Cubans continue to find creative ways to leave the island—some exiting through a third country and finding elicit ways to get to U.S. soil.

This chronological review of each of the four major waves demonstrates how each wave was driven by both similar and different political and social factors. At the same time, these four waves can be collapsed into two waves to differentiate betweens Cubans who grew up under capitalism (the Early Exiles) and those growing up under socialism (the Recent Exiles), as this has influenced their life experience, initial reception on arrival, and their adaptation (Eckstein, 2009). In the next section we discuss factors influencing the adaptation and incorporation of the Early and Recent Exiles and how demographic and ideological differences have influenced their intraethnic relationships and their place in the wider society.

CHANGE AND ADAPTATION

From the first Cuban exiles to the most recent, the vast majority arrived on U.S. soil without material or monetary possessions, due to Cuba's strict exit restrictions, and most did not speak English. Yet, clear migration and cohort differences have influenced the exiles' ability to adapt to life in the United States. Factors triggering each migration wave and differential receptions have contributed to the success of each group's incorporation into U.S. society.

Context of Reception

The social similarities between the Early Exiles and Americans, the former's desirable demographics, and their rejection of Communism earned them an exceptionally warm reception by the United States. The Early Exiles, who presumably had grown up under a capitalist system, migrated because they were unable or unwilling to adapt to the radical changes sought by

Castro's socialist government; their anti-Communist ideals resonated with the Cold War policies of the United States (Pedraza-Bailey, 1980). Although the Early Exiles did not carry much material baggage, they did come to the United States with deep bitterness stemming from Castro's declaration that he would run a Communist government. This perceived betrayal drove some of the Early Exiles to cut their emotional ties to Cuba and others to plot a counterrevolution to redeem the island.

The Early Exiles were known for their entrepreneurial talents and shared the ethics of individualism and work cherished in the United States, putting their skills and familiarity with market economics to work on U.S. soil (Portes, 1969). Predominantly of European stock (94 percent were White), they were from the upper, middle, and professional sectors of the population. Early Exiles were greeted with open arms and treated like the Golden Exiles (Eckstein, 2009; Suárez, 1993). To facilitate their incorporation into their new country and to reduce the burden on Miami, the U.S. government established a massive Cuban refugee program (Portes and Bach, 1985; Wasem, 2009). The program retrained selected groups of skilled and professional workers (i.e., teachers, college professors, doctors, optometrists, and lawyers) and provided resettlement assistance; aid, however, was contingent on relocation to areas with jobs, as government officials were concerned about the burden the refugees would place on Miami, the port of entry (Portes and Bach, 1985). However, the unskilled workers in this first wave were not eligible for training programs since they did not have transferable human capital (Pedraza-Bailey, 1980).

Adjustment to the United States, although not easy for any immigrant, is arguably easier for those who have human capital in the form of skills and education (Borjas, 1999), social capital, familiarity with U.S. culture, and massive federal aid. Although each successive wave brought people of lower socioeconomic, educational, and occupational levels than the Early Exiles, each subsequent wave still benefitted from the goodwill and social structures of the enclaves.

However, unlike the Early Exiles who glided into the country, the post-revolutionary Cubans who exited in 1980 through the Port of Mariel, the Marielitos, faced a dramatically different context of reception for a number of reasons. First, Castro's inclusion of people with criminal records and other institutionalized persons within this wave frightened exiles and Americans alike. That their entry coincided with a surge in drug-related gang crimes did not help their image either. Further, U.S. bureaucracies politically benefitting from public anti-immigrant anger added to the stigmatization of the Mariel entrants (Hamm, 1995). Although many of these concerns were unfounded, as only an estimated 16 percent of Marielitos had been incarcerated in Cuba (Fernández, 2007), it was too late for the cloud of negative public opinion that ensued. The Mariel group had already been stamped as "social undesirables," a stigma that has hindered their incorporation (Fernández, 2007).

But beyond the "social undesirables" stereotype, this group also had other stigmatizing identities that belied the Golden Exile" image: their class, their darker phenotype, their gender, and their having grown up under Fidel. At approximately 18 percent non-White, the Marielito group was "darker" than all preceding waves (Fernández, 2007). Their color especially made them even more undesirable to White Cubans and U.S.-born Americans, alike (Fernández, 2007). Mariel entrants were also younger, more likely to be single, and overwhelmingly working class, with close to 70 percent single males and blue-collar workers (mechanics, heavy equipment operators, carpenters, masons, and bus and taxi drivers). Unlike the early exiles, the Recent Exiles lacked both human and social capital; not only did they lack the training of the early groups, but their stigmatized status denied them the interpersonal trust needed to access social networks and social structures. And although these exiles were also eligible for federal benefits, the massive federal programs established when the early exiles arrived during the Golden Exile era no longer existed. With that said, many have disproved the Marielito stigma by becoming educators, businesspeople, artists, and journalists (Ojito, 2006). Many others, however, remain burdened by the Mariel stereotype. The latter face high levels of depression, incarceration, and economic adversity due to unemployment and discrimination (Fernández, 2007).

The latest arrivals from the 1994 flotilla have not transcended the stigma that began with the Mariel boatlift (Eckstein, 2009; Fernández, 2007). This group is tainted not only by the Mariel stigma but also because they grew up in Castro's Cuba (Eckstein, 2009). Indeed, the Early Exiles see these Recent Exiles as being so different that they are not identified as Cuban (Eckstein, 2009). According to one Early Exile, Recent Exiles lack basic moral understanding, which he attributed to the increased bartering arrangements, and even petty theft, existing in the Cuba of today due to the dire scarcities of goods on the island (Eckstein, 2009). For example, the Cuban Internet blogger Yoani Sánchez describes people desperately looting abandoned buildings for scarce building materials (Rohter, 2009). These perceived and actual differences have discouraged Early Exiles from helping Recent Exiles to incorporate.

In summary, differences and similarities are seen among the Early Exiles and the Recent Exiles. Although the different Cuban waves have benefitted from the United States' liberal immigration policies toward Cubans, not all have been welcomed.

Massive federal aid that helped the Golden Exiles to transfer their human capital to the United States played a key role in their successful incorporation. Although the Recent Exiles have also benefitted from federal aid, such as welfare, this has added to their stigma of being lazy and undesirable. This stigma has tarnished their credibility and deprived them of social capital within the Early Exile Cuban community (Fernández, 2007). Whereas the Early Exiles were socially similar to Americans, the Recent Exiles, having grown up under a socialist system, many were unfamiliar with the market dynamics of capitalism and had to learn unorthodox skills to survive within a repressive environment. However, as the Recent Exiles acculturate, their fate is yet to be determined.

Patterns of Settlement

With 68 percent of Cuban exiles living in Miami (Suro and Escobar, 2006), the prominence of the enclave in the adaptation of this group cannot be overlooked. Enclaves are considered a source of social capital, as members have privileged access to work and social opportunities that enable them to sustain their culture despite living in a "foreign" country. Although both the early Cubans and the Recent Exiles were dispersed on arrival to alleviate the economic burden on Miami (Fernández, 2007; Portes and Stepick, 1985), most have found their way back to Florida because it is so reminiscent of Cuba. Interestingly, three-quarters of the Recent Exiles have settled in Florida, despite experiencing rejection by the Early Exiles (Fernández, 2007). Residents of ethnic enclaves such as Miami and Hialeah, Florida, and West New York and Union City, New Jersey, have replicated, as much as possible, the communities they came from in Cuba to ease the pain and losses of migration as well as for economic reasons (Portes and Jensen, 1992; Prieto, 2009; Skaine, 2003).

STRENGTHS/BENEFITS OF THE ENCLAVE.   The enclaves benefit both the "haves" and "have-nots." For those who had enough economic and human capital to start their own businesses, the enclave provided an opportunity for economic mobility (Portes and Jensen, 1992), although this has been mostly true for men, as few Cuban women are self-employed. Enclaves also protect Cubans with lower levels of education and language proficiency from the stressors of functioning in an English-only environment (Rothe and Pumariega, 2008). Cubans who lack professional skills, regardless of migration wave, can easily go through life in the United States without speaking a word of English. They may have Cuban bosses and Latin American co-workers, shop at Cuban stores, and use Cuban health care professionals. During their leisure time, they can watch Spanish-language television and attend Cuban social, civic, and dance clubs. Enclaves also help to strengthen and maintain Cuban ethnicity and the intergenerational transmission of cultural traits (Rothe and Pumariega, 2008), as in the case of Cuban food and coffee, which can be found at stands at Miami International Airport and anywhere else in the city. In Miami, homesick Cubans can find "the soft clickety-click of a domino game, the sweet crunchiness of a granizado—a Cuban Snow-Cone—the nostalgic talk of boxing heroes" (Ojito, 1988). Spanish-language radio, print, and television media offer a rich selection of programs in Miami although many of these are widely available throughout the United States.

Children growing up within the enclave do not see themselves as a minority, as they are encased in an ethnic bubble that insulates them from exposure to other minority groups (Rothe and Pumariega, 2008). Many attend school with other Cubans and Latin Americans, who have since added to the population growth of Miami. Much of the after-school activities are offered by Hispanic teachers and coaches. The role models these children look up to—mayor, bank president, doctor, and lawyer—may all be Cuban. These Cuban children may go through life being unaware of their "minority" status: in their world, Cubans are the majority. Because of ethnic pride, Cubans have not easily succumbed to the negative programming minority group members are exposed to in U.S. society, resisting both the subtle and often blatant messages of inferiority and inadequacy projected by mainstream society to minority groups. According to the Pew Foundation 2006 National Survey of Latinos (Suro and Escobar, 2006), 45 percent of Cubans reported that discrimination was important, whereas significantly higher reports were provided by Central and South Americans (65 percent), Puerto Ricans (59 percent), and Mexicans (58 percent).

The enclave also helps to preserve cultural characteristics and expressions, though these may cause friction with co-ethnics. One typically Cuban characteristic, often misunderstood by outsiders, "is a sense of specialness that most Cubans have about themselves and their culture" (Bernal, 1984). This specialness, Bernal argues, may stem from the cultural fusion of European, African, and indigenous cultures, which has given rise to the *son*, a musical syncretization of Yoruban and Spanish lyrics; the rumba; the mambo; *charanga; guaguanco;* and the cha-cha-cha—all at the root of today's salsa music and popular ballroom dances. These Latin rhythms have gained increasing popularity among mainstream audiences through crossover Cuban artists such as Gloria Estefan, Jon Secada, and the late Celia Cruz. The popularity of Cuban music among mainstream audiences reaffirms young Cubans' pride in their cultural heritage. Within the enclaves, Cubans can, safely, use humor—*choteo*—without being misunderstood. According to Bernal (1984), *choteo* is a "typical Cuban phenomenon and a type of humor that has been defined as ridiculing and making fun of people, situations and/or things," and at one time "served as defensive function in the social reality of Cubans" (Bernal, 1984). In *choteo*, serious matters are markedly exaggerated and made light of through jokes. However, people from other ethnic groups and Latin American subgroups may perceive this behavior as inappropriate and disrespectful.

In summary, Cuban Americans who grow up in an enclave may be less acculturated, or more likely to be bicultural, than Cuban Americans living outside the enclave. On the other hand, the second-generation children, due to assimilation, and Recent Exiles, due to their different socialization under Communism, may reject the strong subculture of the early exiles, many of whom are now elderly. Ana Menéndez, Cuban American author of *In Cuba I was a German Shepherd,* highlights through fiction how the elderly play dominoes in enclave parks while reminiscing about their status back in Cuba. Many Cubans continue to dream about an illusive return to the island and maintain a strong sense of cultural identity with and fidelity to the motherland, or *la patria.* Preservation of the Spanish language and culture, however, may in the future extend to a wider pan-ethnic identity as Miami continues to grow and absorb more immigrants from throughout the Americas.

CHALLENGES OF THE ENCLAVE.   The enclave reinforces the retention of a Cuban identity and is a rich source of social capital, often touted as an asset; however, it is not without limitations (Portes, 1998). Enclaves may exercise social control and reduce the possibility of assimilation and economic incorporation. Enclave members decide who is allowed in and who is left out, as evinced by the Early Cubans' rejection of the Recent Exiles, and through the dictatorial enforcement of an anti-Castro political ideology. For Recent Exiles, overcoming the Mariel stigma has been difficult, both within the established Cuban American community and American society (Fernández, 2007; Portes, Clark, and Manning, 1985). And, while some have found jobs within the enclave, Recent Exiles, especially those exiting through Mariel, have experienced higher rates of unemployment and of looking for work (Aguirre, Saenz, and James, 1997, cited in Fernández, 2007:607). Although it is not clear why this is so, Fernández (2007) argues that the Mariel stigma has hindered this group's incorporation.

The enclave also exerts ideological control through the vitriolic anti-Castro "Cuba, sí, Castro, no" tone set by the Early Exiles, which has influenced Cuban political thought within the enclave and beyond, including U.S.–Cuba relations. For the Early Exiles, hating Fidel is so much a part of their soul that it has acquired religious significance, according to De La Torre (2004). For years, the Early Exiles were able to maintain an ideological stronghold that sanctified Cuba and demonized Fidel and anyone daring to deviate from this doctrine. In the past, "deviants," especially those who supported people-to-people relations with Cuba, were threatened, ostracized, and even killed (Eckstein and Barberia, 2002; Ojito, 2005). For example, in 1979 members of Omega 7, a U.S.-based Cuban terrorist organization, were found guilty for the shooting of exiles who had been arranging for Cuban Americans to travel back to Cuba (Ojito, 2005). This militant anti-Castro ideology has been controlling and intimidating of more liberal exiles, even within the same family (Ojito, 2005). With subsequent waves of exiles, who are less likely to support this ideology (Girard and Grenier, 2008), Cuban Americans of today are more ideologically divided, contributing to more intraethnic and intrafamilial conflict. Although the Early Cubans' vehemence toward Castro has at times created deadly intraethnic strife (Eckstein, 2009), on the positive side it has also given this group a unified platform. Cuban Americans have helped each other to gain political participation. They tend to vote for policies favoring the continuance of the Cuban embargo in hopes that Castro will either comply or collapse. They are noted for high voter registration and voting and have been partial to the Republican Party because of their "strident anti-Castro image" (Girard and Grenier, 2008). Paradoxically, although Cubans were exercising their right to vote, many have felt pressured to vote with one voice.

Enclaves, often equated with ghettos, are also believed to contribute to holding back assimilation and, in turn, economic progress (Chiswick, Miller, Barkan, and Kraut, 2008). Chiswick and Miller's (2002) research suggests that those living in the Miami enclave who do not learn English fare worse economically than those living outside of the enclave. Also, according to the Pew Hispanic Center (Sura and Escobar, 2006), Cubans who live in Florida, compared to those who live elsewhere, have a lower median income ($36,000 compared to $44,000) but a higher rate of home ownership (65 percent compared to 52 percent), except for Recent Exiles, who are more likely to live in rental properties, but such data are not adjusted for cost-of-living differences. However, it is impossible to determine whether a Cuban's earnings would be higher elsewhere because he or she cannot, by definition, live both inside and outside of the enclave simultaneously and because no research could possibly account for the number of variables that would need to be controlled. For Cubans, the choice to live in Miami is not economically driven, as they have often moved there from higher-wage areas; they live there because, we suspect, they want to feel closer to Cuba, culturally and geographically.

A strong Hispanic enclave, such as Miami's, increases Cubans' and co-ethnics' visibility and their potential threat to dominant groups. For example, Cuban Americans' steadfastness in retaining their ethnic culture has contributed to interethnic conflict. In 1980, shortly after the arrival of the Mariel entrants, a predominantly White commission passed an anti-bilingual ordinance. The law prohibited the use of "any language other than English, or promoting any culture other than that of the United States" (Editorial, 1993). Cubans faced this assault with rebuttal through the power of group unity. By organizing and running for elected office, Cubans gained enough votes to have the ordinance repealed in 1993. In a similar light, the Cuban community's failure to keep Elián González in Miami, the little boy whose mother died en route to the United States in 2000, was perceived as another assault that drove Cubans to support Republicans (Portes and Rumbaut, 2006). In turn, President George W. Bush rewarded Cuban Americans for their support by appointing several Cubans to positions in his government and by tightening the embargo on Cuba (Portes and Rumbaut, 2006).

In sum, whether or not cultural and language retention threatens a person's ability to assimilate or thrive economically (Chiswick, Miller, and Institute for the Study of Labor, 2002) is the subject of much discussion. Since speaking Spanish in Miami is almost a necessity, it is not surprising that 69 percent of Cuban American children (under age 18) and 89 percent of adults (age 18 and older) speak Spanish at home, which are rates higher than those of other Hispanic groups (Suro and Escobar, 2006). Of Cubans age 18 and older, about half speak English less than very well (Suro and Escobar, 2006). Arguably, concern for native language retention may more appropriately be dubbed as fear mongering by mainstream groups, considering that Spanish language retention has not deterred Cuban Americans from incorporating into the United States. Rather, because of their self-contained structures, linguistic retention, and mass media, enclaves provide alternative paths to incorporation into the social structures of U.S. society (Rodríguez, 2008).

The Family in Transition

If social capital is defined as the acquisition of benefits by virtue of membership in familial and other social networks (Portes, 1998), then people living in families would be expected to have greater social, emotional, and economic wealth. Many characteristics of the Early Exile Cuban American family have advanced the group's social capital and adaptation to this country. However, years away from Cuba and mainstream culture's investment in individualism, overworking, and materialism have threatened the value of family. Although Cuban Americans can still be said to have strong family bonds, family patterns and the values sustaining them seem to have weakened, as reflected in marriages and divorce rates.

FAMILY TIES.   *Familism,* a social value in which the family is given a position of ascendance over individual values, is a central characteristic of Latin American cultures and seems to have contributed to economic adaptation and to creation of the enclave. The Early Exiles migrated with their families and with the belief that the family had to stick together. Early Exile families, many of which were three generational, provided multiple incomes and caregivers for children while their parents worked. These family arrangements largely contributed to the early Cuban economic success story, as the family also played a central role in enclave development (Portes and Stepick, 1985; Rothe and Pumariega, 2008). According to Portes and Jensen (1992), although education and work experience were to a large extent important to building the enclave, Cuban enterprise was "a family affair" (p. 946). Women, who had been homemakers in Cuba, worked while their husbands built their businesses, and helped to manage them once they were built. Unlike the Early Exiles, however, most of the Recent Exiles (about 70 percent) were single, mostly men, who arrived without families, deprived of the advantage of multiple earners. In contrast, a small percentage of this group had family members in the United States who helped them to escape Cuba and to resettle. It is, therefore, not surprising that studies show that Mariel Cubans were more likely to exhibit "unstable" living arrangements (i.e., not with family) (Fernández, 2007). If, indeed, the family played such a pivotal role in the early Cubans' adaptation, it is not surprising that these recent waves are not doing as well.

The image of the early Cuban family working and living together has changed, however. Although the retention of the extended family was an economic necessity when Cubans first arrived in the United States, use of the extended family network primarily occurs during the first three years of migration (Chavira-Prado, 1994; Jimenez-Vasquez, 1995). Divisions, both ideological and cultural, between the Early Exiles and the Recent Exiles have translated to weaker family ties among the most recent arrivals. Cultural, or mind-set differences among waves create friction within families and the Cuban community. Older exiles see the newer Cubans, those who grew up under Castro, as inferior and different from them (Eckstein, 2009). Although the Recent Exiles risked everything to leave Cuba, they are not consumed by anti-Castro venom, as they migrated for primarily economic reasons, according to some scholars (Eckstein and Barberia, 2002). Unlike those who came to the United States in the early waves and place politics first, since they have been long reunited with family or grown distant from relatives in Cuba, recent arrivals are motivated by family ties. Whereas the Early Exile Cubans might favor continuing the embargo, Recent Exiles are less concerned about hurting Fidel than they are about supporting family members on the island.

Differences among the waves of Cuban exiles, along with acculturation to U.S. society, have contributed to changing marriage and divorce patterns of the group as a whole. Although most Cuban Americans live in married families, this group, like others in U.S. society, has experienced increased marital instability. The stresses of migration and societal change have added to a corresponding increase in the rate of divorce. Between 1960 and 1980, Early Exile marriages began to break up as a result of women's entry into the workforce and their assertion in the home (Bean and Tienda, 1987). Since then, divorce rates have continued to climb since then, to 12 percent in 2004; these rates are about the same as those of non-Hispanic Whites (11 percent) and higher than those of other Hispanics (7 percent) (Suro and Escobar, 2006). Hence, divorce no longer appears to bear the stigma that it once did. Moreover, the pressure to marry seems to have decreased. The number of never-married Cubans is on par with that of non-Hispanic Whites, both hovering at about 24 percent (Suro and Escobar, 2006).

Not surprisingly, marriage rates have also dropped since the mid-1990s. Only 52 percent of Cuban Americans ages 15 and over are married, a rate lower than that of non-Hispanic Whites (57 percent) (Suro and Escobar, 2006). There are differences among waves, however, with Early Exiles having higher marriage rates (61 percent) than the Recent Exiles (55 percent).

Foreign-born Cubans tend to have much higher marriage rates (58 percent) than those born in the United States (36 percent) (Suro and Escobar, 2006). This suggests that generational status and, possibly, acculturation to U.S. culture, as well as recentness of arrival, are correlated with lower marriage rates. Drawing on anecdotal evidence, we suspect that growing up under Communism, where religion has for years been shunned, may explain the informal rather than formal cohabitation agreements among Recent Exile couples we have observed.

Cuban American families in exile have unusually low fertility rates. Indeed, they have the lowest fertility among any other group—Hispanic, Black, or White. In 2000, there were 9.7 births of Cuban Americans per 1,000 total population, as compared to 25 for Mexicans, 18 for Puerto Ricans, and 12.2 for Whites (Sutton and Mathews, 2006). Cuban American women also have older age-specific birth rates (25–29) than Mexicans (20–24). These lower fertility patterns—which preceded migration with fertility in Cuba having declined prior to the revolution—reflect changed attitudes toward marriage and childbearing (Martinez, 2002). That Cuban American families had, and still have, unusually low fertility rates may have also contributed to the economic adaptation of the family, since women took less time out from work due to pregnancies.

Acculturation

Although adaptation to any new country is difficult, one of the most visible signs of acculturation is rate of intermarriage. Cubans are reported to have high intermarriage with the majority group (Qian, 2002). This trend started when Fidel Castro's prohibition of the migration of military-age males to the United States during the 1960s and 1970s forced Cubans to intermarry with White non-Cubans because of the shortage of males in exile (Nordheimer, 1988). Still, despite a better balance in the ratio of men to women in the second generation, and the high number of Cubans living within an enclave, the rate of out-marriage among Cuban Americans continues to climb. Between 1970 and 2000, Cuban Americans' intermarriage rate increased by 50 percent, from 8 percent to 12 percent (Lee and Edmonston, 2005). However, U.S.-born Cuban Whites are more than four times as likely as Cuban-born Whites to intermarry, according to an analysis of the 1990 Census (Qian, 2002). Another study found Cuban females to have higher rates of intermarriage than males (Jacobs and Labov, 2002). High rates of intermarriage may eventually weaken the strength of Cuban cultural traditions, signaling that acculturation is well underway.

As is the case with many immigrants, acculturation may be associated with psychological distress and anxiety (Rivera-Sinclair, 1997). For Cubans, adapting to the United States has meant embracing a culture and lifestyle that is faster, and more impersonal and individualistic, than what they had been accustomed to (Szapocznik et al., 1981). The rapid rate of change has caused dislocations for those who, in their eagerness to embrace American culture and to belong, have adapted too quickly. Particularly the young, who are in a greater rush to assimilate, cut themselves off from their roots and cultural heritage (Szapocznik et al., 1978). The problem of differential acculturation rates has also contributed to the isolation of some Cuban elderly from their children and their grandchildren, causing them to live independently (Martinez, 2002; Queralt, 1983).

Yet people living in bicultural environments may become maladjusted if they remain or become monocultural (Santisteban et al., 1981). Becoming bicultural enables Cuban Americans to interact within mainstream society while enjoying the social capital within the Cuban community. Perhaps a bicultural identity is associated with lower levels of anxiety among Cuban Americans because they do not need to feel guilty about privileging one culture over the other (Rivera-Sinclair, 1997). At the same time, although growing up biculturally is advantageous, it can also be a liability (Boswell and Curtis, 1984). For some Cuban Americans who were born on the island but grew up in the United States, this has led to an identity crisis—they feel neither completely Cuban nor completely American. Although part of both worlds, they also feel estranged from both.

Despite the early exiles' overbearing political ideology, today political views may vary more among the second generation and within families, with acculturation. Whereas one sibling may identify as Cuban and hold conservative political views, another sibling may identify as Cuban American and could not care less about American policies toward Cuba and politics in general (Eckstein, 2009). Jorge Mas Canosa, an old-school Cuban activist, and Jorge Mas Santos, his son, dramatically illustrate this vast-intergenerational political change. Although both led the Cuban American National Foundation (CANF), the elder was a hard-liner, and the younger a liberal who took the organization in radically different directions. CANF, originally dedicated to over-throwing the Cuban government and staunchly Republican, is now not only seeking ties with Cuba but is considered Democratic. While leading CANF, Mas Santos was willing to meet with Castro and his brother Raul and supported Miami's hosting of the Latin Grammy Awards, despite the inclusion of artists with ties to the Cuban government (Eckstein, 2009)—acts that would never have been considered in earlier times.

The recent waves, like the second generation, see themselves as more politically tolerant; although they may reject Castro's government, intellectually they may be open to socialist ideas and resentful of the ultra-reactionary attitude of the Early Exiles. Although weakened with time, hatred of Fidel is not dying with the Golden Exiles; rather, it is nurtured within the "institutional completeness" of the Miami enclave (Girard and Grenier, 2008). Research shows that Cuban Americans who spend more than half their life within the enclave are more likely to embrace anti-Castro ideology, but less so if they acquire news from English-language media, a possible sign of acculturation. However, having grown up under a dictatorship where no elections were held, Mariel and recent immigrants are not as politically active or involved in civic activities; they are also not driven to politics by the fervent anti-Castro ideology that catapulted the Early Exiles into the political scene, and they are significantly less likely to support this ideology (Eckstein, 2009).

Hence, with the second generation and the incorporation of the latest waves of Cubans and the birth of the third generation, the semblance of a unified Cuban voice is fading (Eckstein, 2009). This is evident in a 2004 survey conducted by the Institute for Public Opinion Research and Cuban Research Institute of Florida International University: 56 percent of Cubans support dialogue with the government on the island, an increase of 16 percent compared to the first poll conducted in 1991 (Suro and Escobar, 2006). Despite the typification of Cuban Americans as conservative Republicans, according to the 2006 National Survey of Latinos only 28 percent of Cubans belonged to that party, as compared to 15 percent of Mexicans and 11 percent of Puerto Ricans (Suro and Escobar, 2006). In that same poll, only 20 percent of Cubans, 50 percent of Puerto Ricans, and 29 percent of Mexicans and South Americans considered themselves Democrats (Suro and Escobar, 2006). Cubans are as likely to be Independents as they are Republicans (27 percent), as compared to 15 percent of Puerto Ricans and 34 percent of Central and South Americans (Suro and Escobar, 2006).

Current and Future Issues: Are Cuban Americans More Successful?

As there is truth to any stereotype—in this case, the model minority myth—Cuban Americans have been more economically successful than other Hispanic groups in the United States. This is misleading, however, since disaggregating income statistics reveals a mixed picture. At

$38,000 per year, aggregate Cuban American median household income is not much higher than that of the overall group Hispanics ($36,000) and is much lower than that of non-Hispanic Whites ($48,000) (Suro and Escobar, 2006). Further differences emerge when you look at native born compared to the foreign born, and across waves. The U.S.-born Cubans' median income of $50,000 exceeds that of non-Hispanic Whites by $2,000. However, looking at differences among waves, we find that Recent Exiles' median income (between $30,000 and $33,000) is much lower than that of the Early Exiles ($38,000) (Suro and Escobar, 2006). As noted, Cubans living in Florida have a lower income ($36,000) than those living outside of Florida ($44,000). This may be due, however, to more favorable market conditions in places with a smaller population of Cuban Americans (Davis, 2004). Home ownership among Cubans is higher (61 percent) than that of other Hispanic groups (47 percent) but lower than non-Hispanic Whites (74 percent) (Suro and Escobar, 2006). Still, these rates vary according to waves, with Early Exiles more likely to own homes (72 percent) than those who entered in the recent waves (about 50 percent).

Despite the relative success of Cubans, however, segments of the population are not exempt from poverty. Although poverty rates for Cubans tend to be lower than for other Hispanics, there are some exceptions. On aggregate, 13 percent of children (under age 18) have lower poverty rates than Hispanic children (27 percent). But, foreign-born Cuban children under age 17 have higher poverty rates (21 percent) than Hispanics (18 percent) and non-Hispanic Whites (7 percent). The poverty rate among working-age adults (ages 18–64), irrespective of nativity, is lower (11 percent) than that of other Hispanics (17 percent). However, the poverty rate more than doubles among Cubans, age 65 and older (24 percent) as compared with 18 percent of other Hispanics and 7 percent of non-Hispanic Whites. Post-1980 entrants are more likely to be unemployed 28 years after migration (Fernández, 2007).

Education

Cubans place a very high value on education. Education is considered an investment *que nadie te puede quitar* ("that no one can take from you"). For working-class Cubans, education is a way of joining the ranks of the middle class; for others, it is a way of recovering the status they had in Cuba; and for younger Cuban Americans it is a way to escape the low-wage work their parents endured. Whether in Cuba or in the United States, Cubans have received higher levels of education than the average Hispanic. According to 2004 statistics (Pew Hispanic Center, 2006), one quarter of Cubans age 25 and older have graduated from college, more than twice as many as other Hispanics (12 percent) but fewer than non-Hispanic Whites (30 percent). But, again, these rates differ according to nativity. Almost 40 percent of native-born Cubans have graduated from college, as compared to 22 percent of foreign-born Cubans. Although education has always been an important part of Fidel's government, the Mariel group has significantly lower college graduation rates among foreign-born Cubans as compared to 24 percent of the Early Exiles. It is interesting that, although the Cuban government has typically denied tourist or exit visas to its most skilled citizens to prevent a brain-drain, 26 percent of the more recent Cubans, those leaving the island after 1990, have graduated from college, a rate 4% shy of non-Hispanic Whites. It is probable that the higher educated Cubans were allowed to leave by way of the "visa lottery" system, which works by random selection (Wasem, 2007).

On aggregate, Cubans also have slightly higher high school graduation rates (almost 49 percent) than other Hispanics (47 percent) but not as high as non-Hispanic Whites (59 percent) (Suro and Escobar, 2006). Native-born Cubans are more likely to graduate from high school (54 percent) than are those born in Cuba (48 percent) (Suro and Escobar, 2006). But whether the overall higher educational attainment of Cubans will persist remains to be seen. According to a study of the second generation of Cuban children, the aspirations of Cuban children are higher among the more recent arrivals and begin to wane with length of time in the United States (Rumbaut and Portes, 2001, cited in Rothe and Pumariega, 2008:258). Surprisingly, the children of the Early Exiles, the most successful, of the émigrés, have the highest dropout rates and the lowest GPAs. Paradoxically, with time spent in the United States, the children of the most ambitious and successful exiles do not acquire the drive of their parents and begin to resemble the mainstream groups.

Race and Class

Racial issues were a serious problem in Cuba and are also a problem in the United States. Before the revolution, Cuba was a multiracial society plagued by prejudices and discrimination, as is the United States today. In pre-revolutionary Cuba, Blacks and other non-Whites were systematically excluded from the pinnacle of society (yacht and country clubs, elite vacation resorts and beaches, hotels, and private schools) (Eckstein, 2009; Ojito, 2000). Although Castro made these facilities available to all Cuban citizens regardless of color and class to enlist support, a half-century later sixty Black American intellectuals condemned the government's racism toward the island's large Black population in a "stinging" statement, "Acting on Our Conscience" (Padilla, 2010).

Since most of the early immigrants were White (94 percent of the first wave versus 82 percent of the Mariel wave), there are racial tensions between the newer and older immigrants (Fernández, 2007). In a series on race relations in Miami, Mirta Ojito (2000) a Cuban-born *New York Times* writer, chronicles the poignant story of two men, one White and one Black, who were best friends in Cuba but in Miami are "worlds apart" because of the racial divide. Indeed, most Cubans see themselves as White and reject being referred to as "people of color" by mainstream society. According to 2004 U.S. Census data, 86 percent of Cubans identified as White, compared to 60 percent of Mexicans, 53 percent of South and Central Americans, and 50 percent of Puerto Ricans (Suro and Escobar, 2006). White Cubans' tendency to marry non-Cubans rather than Black Cubans suggests that race is a stronger variable than ethnicity, although this assumption is speculative. For some Black Cubans, however, national identity supersedes racial identity (Prieto, 2009). At the same time, White Cubans are more prejudiced against American Blacks than against Black Cubans (Ojito, 2000); this is probably the only case in which ethnicity supersedes race.

But Cubans do not only discriminate by race, they also discriminate by class. Since as a result of the different waves, all social strata of the island are represented in the United States, whatever class differences existed in Cuba have been replicated, to a certain extent, in the United States. Therefore, class is a significant factor in understanding Cuban Americans. Although pre-Castro Cuba class differences may have eroded in the United States due to downward and upward mobility, upper-class Cubans may still see themselves as superior to lower classes (Eckstein, 2009). For example, a young Cuban American woman was rejected by her Cuban-born boyfriend's mother because she came from a working class, rural family in Cuba; that she was a doctoral candidate at a world-class university was irrelevant, because she was being judged by Cuba's social scale. Cuban Americans also look down on the newer exiles, no matter what their accomplishments, because having lived under Castro they are considered "guilty by association" (Eckstein, 2009).

CONCLUSION

With low-fertility rates, restricted emigration out of Cuba, high intermarriage rates, and an aging population, it is unclear whether the Cuban population in the United States will decline, or how changes in U.S.–Cuba relations would affect them. Like many exiles, we authors suspect that the doors to Cuba will one day reopen and, when they do, that Cuban Americans, while remaining firmly on U.S. soil, will look forward to strengthening long-lost transnational ties (Levitt, 2003) with their culture. In the meantime, how the Cuban family will continue to adapt and change hinges on the political moves between the United States and Cuba, as has been the case histori-cally. At the time this chapter was written, Fidel Castro was, reportedly, still alive, though barely, and had delegated power to his brother Raul Castro (Wasem, 2009). With the decline of the Golden Exiles' bitter anti-Castro hegemony, and an elected Democratic U.S. government, U.S.–Cuba relations are beginning to thaw, with a possible end to the Cuban embargo. This is a hoped-for change by younger Cuban Americans and by Fidel, as long as Cuba's sovereignty and public right to self-determination are not compromised (Prada, 2009). But after three failed attempts to relax political relations during the past thirty-five years, and with Cuba's "hopeful tenor" toward Obama ebbing (Lacey, 2009), change seems elusive and unlikely (Richter and Nicholas, 2009). Until that time, the chant of return to the island will continue to resonate in Cuban American enclaves, while for others the United States has become home.

References

Aguirre, B. E. R. Saenz, and B. S. James (1997) "Marielitos Ten Years Later: The Scarface Legacy." *Social Science Quarterly* 78(2): 487–507.

Bach, R. L., J. B. Bach, and R. Triplett 1982. "The Flotilla Entrants: The Latest and Most Controversial." *Cuban Studies/Estudio Cubanos* 2(12).

Bean, F., and M. Tienda. 1987. *Hispanic Population of the United States in the 1980s.* New York: Russell Sage Foundation.

Bernal, G. 1984. "Cuban Families." In M. McGoldrick, J. Giordano, and J. K. Pearce (Eds.), *Ethnicity and Family Therapy* (2nd ed., pp. 186–207). New York: Guilford Press.

Borjas, G. J. 1999. *Heaven's Door: Immigration Policy and the American Economy.* Princeton, NJ: Princeton University Press.

Boswell, T. D., and J. R. Curtis. 1984. *The Cuban-American Experience: Culture, Images, and Perspectives.* Totowa, NJ: Rowman and Allanheld.

Chavira-Prado, A. (Ed.). 1994. *Latina Experience and Latina Identity.* Houston, TX: Arte Publico Press.

Chiswick, B. R., and P. W. Miller. 2005. "Do Enclaves Matter in Immigrant Adjustment?" *City and Community* 4(1), 5–35.

Chiswick, B. R., P. W. Miller, E. R. Barkan, H. Diner, and A. M. Kraut (Eds.) 2008. "Immigrant Enclaves, Ethnic Goods, and the Adjustment Process." In *From Arrival to Incorporation: Migrants to the U.S. in a Global Era* (pp. 80–93). New York: New York University Press.

Chiswick, B. R., P. W. Miller, and Institute for the Study of Labor. 2002. "Do Enclaves Matter in Immigrant Adjustment?" Discussion paper.

Davis, C. 2004. "Beyond Miami: The Ethnic Enclave and Personal Income in Various Cuban Communities in the United States." *International Migration Review* 38, 450–469.

De Haymes, M. V. (1997). "The Golden Exile: The Social Construction of the Cuban American Success Story." *Journal of Poverty* 1: 65–80.

De La Torre, M. A. 2004. *Santería: The Beliefs and Rituals of a Growing Religion in America.* Grand Rapids, MI: Eerdmans Publishing Company.

Eckstein, S., and L. Barberia. 2002. "Grounding Immigrant Generations in History: Cuban Americans and Their Transnational Ties." *International Migration Review* 36(3), 799–837.

Eckstein, S. E. 2009. *The Immigrant Divide: How Cuban Americans Changed the US and Their Homeland.* New York: Routledge.

Eckstein, S. E., and L. Barberia. 2002. "Grounding Immigrant Generations in History: Cuban

Americans and Their Transnational Ties." *International Migration Review* 36(3), 799–837.

Editorial. 1993. "Board in Miami Repeals an English-Only Law," May 19. www.nytimes.com/1993/05/19/us/board-in-miami-repeals-an-english-only-law.html (accessed April 5, 2011).

Fernández, G. 2007. "Race, Gender, and Class in the Persistence of the Mariel Stigma Twenty Years After the Exodus from Cuba." *International Migration Review* 41(3), 602–622.

García, M. C. 1996. *Havana USA: Cuban Exiles and Cuban Americans in South Florida, 1959–1994.* Berkeley: University of California Press.

Girard, C., and G. J. Grenier. 2008. "Insulating an Ideology: The Enclave Effect on South Florida's Cuban Americans." *Hispanic Journal of Behavioral Sciences* 30(4), 530–543.

Hamm, M. 1995. *The Abandoned Ones: The Imprisonment and Uprising of the Mariel Boat People.* Boston, MA: Northeastern University Press.

Jacobs, J. A., and T. G. Labov. 2002. "Gender Differentials in Intermarriage Among Sixteen Race and Ethnic Groups." *Sociological Forum* 17(4), 621–646.

Jimenez-Vasquez, R. (Ed.) 1995. *Encyclopedia of Social Work,* 19th ed. Washington, DC: NASW Press.

Lacey, M. 2009, December 31. "In Cuba, Hopeful Tenor Toward Obama Is Ebbing." *New York Times.* www.nytimes.com/2009/12/31/world/americas/31cuba.html?_r=1 (accessed April 5, 2011).

Lee, S., and B. Edmonston. 2005. "New Marriages, New Families: US Racial and Hispanic Intermarriage." *Population Bulletin-Washington* 60(2).

Levitt, P. 2003. "Transnational Villagers." In *Race and Ethnicity: Comparative and Theoretical Approaches* (pp. 260–273). Berkeley: University of California Press.

Martinez, I. L. 2002. "The Elder in the Cuban American Family: Making Sense of the Real and Ideal." *Journal of Comparative Family Studies* 33(3), 359–375.

Nordheimer, N. 1988, April 13. "For Cuban-Americans, an Era of Change." *New York Times.* www.nytimes.com/1988/04/13/us/for-cuban-americans-an-era-of-change.html?pagewanted=allandsrc=pm (accessed April 5, 2011).

Ojito, M. 1988. "Miami Generation Feels Separate from Fellow Exiles." *Miami Herald,* December 27, p. x.

Ojito, M. A. 2000, June 5. "Best of Friends, Worlds Apart." *New York Times.* www.nytimes.com/2000/06/05/us/best-of-friends-worlds-apart.html (accessed April 5, 2011).

———. 2005. *Finding Mañana: A Memoir of a Cuban Exodus.* New York: Penguin Press.

———. 2006. *El mañana: Memoria de un Éxodo Cubano,* 1st ed. New York: Vintage Español.

Padilla, S. (2010, January 4). "African American Activists, Including Jeremiah Wright and Cornel West, Blast Cuba on Racism." *Los Angeles Times.* latimesblogs.latimes.com/washington/2010/01/african-american-activists-blast-cuba-on-racism.html (accessed April 5, 2011).

Pedraza, S., and R. G. Rumbaut. 1996. *Origins and Destinies: Immigration, Race, and Ethnicity in America.* Belmont, CA: Wadsworth.

Pedraza-Bailey, S. 1980. "Political and Economic Migrants in America Cubans and Mexicans." Unpublished Ph.D. dissertation, University of Chicago.

Pérez, L. A. 2003. *Cuba and the United States: Ties of Singular Intimacy.* Athens: University of Georgia Press.

Pew Hispanic Center. 2009. *Hispanics of Cuban Origin in the United States, 2007.* Washington, DC: Pew Hispanic Center.

Portes, A. 1969. "Dilemmas of a Golden Exile: Integration of Cuban Refugee Families in Milwaukee." *American Sociological Review* 34, 505–518.

———. 1998. "Social Capital: Its Origins and Applications in Modern Sociology." *Annual Review of Sociology* 24, 1–24.

Portes, A., and R. L. Bach. 1985. *Latin Journey: Cuban and Mexican Immigrants in the United States.* Berkeley: University of California Press.

Portes, A., J. Clark, and R. Manning. 1985. "After mariel: A Survey of the Resettlement Experiences of 1980 Cuban Refugees in Miami." *Cuban Studies/Estudios Cubanos* 15(2), 37–59.

Portes, A., and L. Jensen. 1992. "Disproving the Enclave Hypothesis: Reply." *American Sociological Review* 57(3), 418–420.

Portes, A., and R. G. Rumbaut. 2006. *Immigrant America: A Portrait* (3rd ed.). Berkeley: University of California Press.

Portes, A., and A. Stepick. 1985. "Unwelcome Immigrants: The Labor Market Experiences of 1980 (Mariel) Cuban and Haitian Refugees in South Florida." *American Sociological Review* 50(4), 493–514.

Prada, P. 2009, April 24. "Cuban-Americans Ponder What U.S. Should Do Next." *Wall Street Journal.* online.wsj.com/article/SB124052279417849941.html (accessed April 5, 2011).

Prieto, Y. 2009. *The Cubans of Union City: Immigrants and Exiles in a New Jersey Community.* Philadelphia: Temple University.

Qian, Z. 2002. "Race and Social Distance: Intermarriage with Non-Latino Whites." *Race and Society 5*(1), 33–47.

Queralt, M. 1983. "The Elderly of Cuban Origin: Characteristics and Problems." In R. L. McNeely and J. L. Cohen (Eds.), *Aging in Minority Groups.* Beverly Hills, CA: Sage.

Richter, P., and P. Nicholas. 2009, April 18. "U.S., Cuba mutually signal thaw in relations." *Los Angeles Times.*

Rivera-Sinclair, E. A. 1997. "Acculturation/Biculturalism and Its Relationship to Adjustment in Cuban-Americans." *International Journal of Intercultural Relations 21*(3), 379–391.

Rodríguez, N. 2008. "Theoretical and Methodological Issues of Latina/o Research." In H. Rodríguez, R. Sáenz, and C. Menjívar (Eds.), *Latinas/os in the United States: Changing the Face of América.* New York: Springer.

Rohter, L. 2009, October 18. "Yoani Sánchez: Virtually Outspoken in Cuba." *New York Times,* p. WK5, New York edition.

Rothe, E., and A. Pumariega. 2008. "The New Face of Cubans in the United States: Cultural Process and Generational Change in an Exile Community." *Journal of Immigrant and Refugee Studies 6*(2), 247–266.

Santisteban, D., Szapocznik, J., and Rios, A. (1981, June) *Acculturation/biculturalism: Implication for a mental health prevention strategy.* Paper presented at the Interamerican Congress of Psychology. Santo Domingo, Dominican Republic.

Skaine, R. 2003. *The Cuban Family: Custom and Change in an Era of Hardship.* Jefferson, NC: McFarland and Company.

———. 2004. *The Cuban Family: Custom and Change in an Era of Hardship.* Jefferson, NC: McFarland and Company.

Suárez, Z. E. 1993. "Cuban Americans: from Golden Exiles to Social Undesirables." In H. P. McAdoo (Ed.), *Family Ethnicity: Strength in Diversity.* (pp. 164–176). Thousand Oaks, CA: Sage.

Suro, R., and G. Escobar. 2006. National survey of Latinos: The immigration debate. Pew Hispanic Center Report.

Sutton, P., and T. Mathews. 2006. "Birth and Fertility Rates for States by Hispanic Origin Subgroups: United States, 1990 and 2000." *Vital and Health Statistics,* Series 21: Data on Natality, Marriage, and Divorce (57), 1.

Szapocznik, J., D. Santisteban, H. F. Spencer, and W. Kurtines. 1981. "Treatment of Depression Among cuban american Elders: Some Validation Evidence for a Life Enhancement Counseling Approach." *Journal of Consulting and Clinical Psychology 49*(5), 752–754.

Szapocznik, J., M. Scopetta, M. Aranalde, and W. Kurtines. 1978. "Cuban Value Structure: Treatment Implications." *Journal of Consulting and Clinical Psychology 46*(5), 961–970.

Torres, M. d. l. A. 2003. *The Lost Apple: Operation Pedro Pan, Cuban Children in the U.S., and the Promise of a Better Future.* Boston: Beacon Press.

Wasem, R. E. 2009, June 2. "Cuban Migration to the United States: Policy and Trends." Congressional Research Service, 7-5700, R 40566.

9

▰ ▰ ▰

The Puerto Rican American Family

Lirio K. Negroni

INTRODUCTION

This chapter focuses on Puerto Rican families residing in the United States. After a brief history of Puerto Rico and its relationship with Spain and the United States, the chapter focuses on a theoretical perspective of change and adaptation and issues related to migration, ecological contexts, acculturation, socioeconomic status and language that affect Puerto Ricans living in the United States. Changes and adaptation in family structure, child rearing, and care of elders also are discussed. The chapter concludes with a summary of strengths and contributions and suggestions for research.

DEMOGRAPHICS

The term *Puerto Rican* refers to individuals who self-identify as having a Puerto Rican origin, because either they were born in Puerto Rico or they trace their family ancestry to Puerto Rico (Pew Hispanic Center, 2010). A family is considered Puerto Rican if it self-identifies as Puerto Rican and some or all of its members identify themselves as Puerto Rican. Puerto Rican families residing in the United States also are referred to as stateside Puerto Rican families or Puerto Rican–American families. The ethnic cultural reality of Puerto Rican families differs from that of other Latino groups, given their sociopolitical history, racial and ancestral background, and the way they come into contact with U.S. society (Ramos, 2007). For example, of all the Latino groups, Puerto Ricans are the only ones who receive automatic citizenship at birth and do not encounter migration restrictions when they travel between the United States and Puerto Rico because Puerto Rico is a territory of the United States.

A total of 4.2 million individuals of Puerto Rican origin resided in the United States in 2008 (Pew Hispanic Center, 2010). Puerto Ricans are the second-largest Latino population living in this country. In 2008, they accounted for 8.9 percent of the total U.S. Latino population. Most Puerto Ricans (2.8 million) were born in the United States and one-third (1.3 million) were born in Puerto Rico. Therefore, it is not surprising that 8 in 10 Puerto Ricans (80.5 percent) report speaking English proficiently. With a median age of 29, Puerto Ricans are younger than the average age of the U.S. population and older than the average age of all other Latino groups. The majority of Puerto Ricans live in the northeast and southern regions of the country (Pew Hispanic Center, 2010). Another 4 million Puerto Ricans reside in the Caribbean. This group will be referred to as island Puerto Ricans.

Stateside Puerto Ricans have higher levels of education than the other Latino groups. The median annual personal earnings for Puerto Ricans ages 16 and older was $26,478 in 2008, which was higher than the median earnings for all U.S. Latinos of $21,488. Almost one-fourth of Puerto Ricans (22.6 percent) live in poverty, surpassing the general U.S. population average and that of all other Latino groups. Fewer Puerto Ricans (40.3 percent) are homeowners compared to other Latino groups (49.1 percent) and the U.S. population (66.6 percent) as a whole (Pew Hispanic Center, 2010).

Stateside and island Puerto Rican families are likely to comprise three to four members. In 2000, stateside Puerto Rican married couples with children younger than 18 years of age constituted 42 percent of all stateside Puerto Rican households, while more than one-fourth of the households were headed by females (Ramirez, 2004). Puerto Ricans are increasingly less likely than other Latinos to be married. In 2008, more than one-half (57.1 percent) of Puerto Rican women ages 15 to 44 who gave birth were unmarried. This rate was higher than the rate for all U.S. Latinas and U.S. women. As a young population, Puerto Ricans are more likely to create new families, but apparently changes are taking place regarding the stability of marriage versus consensual relationships.

HISTORICAL BACKGROUND

Puerto Ricans have a strong sense of national identity that emerged as early as the nineteenth century and that transcends political and class frictions. Three factors explain Puerto Ricans' pride and predicament: (1) their legacy of conquest and colonization of Spain and the United States, (2) their racial mix, and (3) their migration to the United States (Organista, 2007a).

Conquest and Colonization

Spain ruled Puerto Ricans for almost four centuries, since the Spanish arrival in 1493. The Spaniards were attracted by Puerto Rico's gold, fertile soil, and strategic location. They exploited and exterminated the native Taíno population and, to continue with their colonization, imported African slaves, whom they forced to work in the gold mines and farms (Negroni-Rodríguez and De La Cruz-Quiroz, 2006). Puerto Ricans pressured Spain for internal autonomy, which was granted in 1897 but lasted very briefly. Only a year later, Spain ceded the island to the United States as part of the Spanish-American War treaty. Once under U.S. possession, Puerto Rico became a military occupied territory until the United States instituted a colonial government. English became the official language, and the United States used the island to further its agricultural and industrial economic interests, depriving Puerto Ricans from their long-desired autonomy. Historians referred to the arrival of the United States as an invasion, and others documented how Puerto Ricans initially supported U.S. control with the understanding that it would facilitate their transition into an independent nation (Organista, 2007a).

As a result of the Foraker Act of 1900, free trade was established between Puerto Rico and the United States. In the first thirty years of U.S. possession, Puerto Ricans lost two-thirds of their land while the United States imposed higher taxes and credit restrictions; the Puerto Rican peso was devalued, and Puerto Rican farmers felt forced to sell their lands. The United States monopolized island industries and relegated Puerto Ricans to low-wage farm laborers. In 1917, the Jones Act granted Puerto Ricans U.S. citizenship. At the beginning of World War I, their new citizenship status placed Puerto Ricans under the obligation of serving in the U.S. military. Puerto Ricans have participated in all subsequent U.S. military involvements. Many Puerto Ricans have experienced the benefits and pains of being U.S. military families. They have lost loved ones, are coping with returned veterans who suffer the emotional and physical consequences of war, or are enduring both challenges.

Through the decades, Puerto Ricans have protested colonial exploitation and have continued to demand their independence. The leadership of Pedro Albizu Campos, a Puerto Rican lawyer, and the 1937 Ponce Massacre represent turning points in the development of a pro-independence national movement.

Luis Muñoz Marín is another important figure in the history of Puerto Rico. Although he favored independence, in exchange for opposing the independence movement, he negotiated the creation of a popular democratic party and a seat for Puerto Rico in the U.S. Senate. The United States gave him freedom to enact a reform that would combat poverty in the island. The years to come were characterized by a new political status for the island called the Estado Libre Asociado (commonwealth), which was accepted by many Puerto Ricans in the hope it would bring their country closer to independence. To this date, Puerto Rico is referred to as a U.S. commonwealth with the rights and responsibilities of a colony. On the island, one finds three major viewpoints about the desired political and economic status for Puerto Rico: statehood, independence, and commonwealth. Most Puerto Ricans prefer to maintain the status quo of a "commonwealth," while an increasing group favors the island becoming the fifty-first U.S. state. The group favoring the island's independence is the smallest.

Although politically divided, Puerto Ricans remain "culturally united in their assertion of their unique identity and need for greater control over their own fate" (Organista, 2007a:25–26; Rodríguez, 2002). The history of colonial government has affected Puerto Rican families' quality of life and has served to underscore Puerto Ricans' resiliency. This sense of struggle for freedom and affirmation of identity is present among Puerto Rican families residing in the United States. It seems to be experienced and manifested differently among generations. Puerto Ricans' views and positions are influenced by their level of acculturation and consciousness of past and existing oppression and discrimination. Electoral participation, an opportunity to effect changes, has increased in the last voting campaigns but still occurs in much lower numbers than the voting levels in Puerto Rico.

Racial Mix and Racism

For Puerto Ricans, race is a continuum of skin colors (Negroni-Rodríguez and De La Cruz-Quiroz, 2006). Even within the same family, members may present mixed skin colors and race distinctions dissimilar to those typical in the U.S. population. Longres (1974) raised the issue of racism's influence on Puerto Ricans in the United States, drawing attention to the threat that racism causes the Puerto Rican community. He asserted that the primary source of self-identity for Puerto Ricans was culture, not class or color. Therefore, for Puerto Ricans who were racially mixed, having to categorize themselves as either Black or White presupposed a problem.

Due to their skin color, Puerto Ricans experience a change in social status when treated with the racial standards predominant in the United States (Negroni-Rodríguez and De La Cruz-Quiroz, 2006). Once in the United States, Puerto Ricans may encounter discrimination due to their skin color. The color gradient of Puerto Ricans affect the way they are treated and the opportunities to which they may have access. This discrimination can contribute to their existing poverty and can limit their access to housing and education. It is not the same to be dark skinned in one's homeland—where national origin and a sense of community are shared—as it is to be dark skinned in a foreign land, isolated from loved ones and one's heritage, and with no entitlements (Falicov, 1998). Puerto Ricans' encounter with racism and discrimination may lead to their experiencing ethnic pride or ethnic shame, and to hoping to assimilate or isolate themselves from the dominant culture (Falicov, 1998).

Racism exists among Puerto Ricans, and it can be very subtle. Puerto Ricans and other Latino groups may encounter racism among each other as well. This racism may be connected to a variety of psychological factors, such as internalized racism. Occasionally, racial tensions manifest inside the family, which Falicov (1998) suggests may be a mask or deflector from other family problems.

Migration to the United States

Rodríguez (2002) explains that the U.S. occupation since the nineteenth century made Puerto Rico both politically and economically dependent. Puerto Rico's economy changed from a diversified subsistence economy of tobacco, cattle, coffee, and sugar to a sugarcane economy controlled by absentee American owners. By the 1920s, the cane-based industry had declined, but there was no U.S. reinvestment. The island's population kept growing, and high unemployment and poverty made Puerto Ricans desperate and determined to leave in search of a better life.

Puerto Rican migration to the United States began during the 1920s. People migrated mostly for economic reasons: to escape poverty and search for economic opportunities. Experts classify Puerto Rican migration into three major periods. In the first period, between 1900 and 1945, Puerto Ricans established themselves in New York City. By 1940, approximately 70,000 Puerto Ricans were in New York, and nearly 20 percent of the island's people had migrated (Maldonado, 1976). The second phase, between 1946 and 1964, is known as the "Great Migration." New Puerto Rican communities developed in areas such as New Jersey, Connecticut, Illinois, and other parts of the country (Rodríguez, 2002). Migration of Puerto Ricans peaked in the 1950s, a time of major transition in the United States as the nation moved from an industrial to a postindustrial society. Such change reduced job opportunities for unskilled and semiskilled poor people (Organista, 2007a). Many Puerto Ricans lost their jobs and faced increased poverty. The third period is known as "the revolving-door migration" and dates from 1965 to the present. By 1970, one-third of all Puerto Ricans resided in the United States, and half lived in New York City (Newman, 1978). Like Mexicans, Puerto Ricans came to the United States as farm workers and fell to the bottom of the economic ladder (Organista, 2007a); they also worked in textile and garment factories.

Today Puerto Ricans live in every U.S. state. In addition to economic need and hopes for a better life, Puerto Ricans also migrate to pursue an education, access health care services, solve personal problems, and/or initiate new ventures (Garcia-Preto, 2005). Skilled and technical workers and professionals are migrating from the island, causing a loss of human capital in Puerto Rico (Burgos, 2002). Back-and-forth migration continues, which helps families maintain connections with friends and extended networks, remain strongly identified with their culture, and maintain their cultural identity across generations. However, returned migration causes repeated ruptures and renewals, and the dismantling and reconstruction of family and community networks (Garcia-Preto, 2005).

CHANGES AND ADAPTATION

Puerto Rican families have been in the United States for almost a century. Through their struggles, they have demonstrated their resiliency capacity for change and adaptation. This section discusses the issues, problems, and concerns they have encountered and how they have responded to those challenges and difficulties to develop further, transform, and become an important force in both Puerto Rico and the mainland United States.

A Theoretical Perspective of Change and Adaptation

Puerto Rican families' change and adaptation can be explained from an ecological-systemic perspective. Ecological-systemic thinking considers the interdependence between individuals and their environments and the reciprocal influence they have on each other. It is through person–environment exchanges that the needs and goals of individuals, groups, and communities are met and their stressors solved (Gitterman and Germaine, 2008). A person-environment fit is the ultimate goal, one in which both individual and environment flourish. Life, relationship, and environmental stressors—and limited personal resources and/or optimal environmental conditions to adapt to or change those stressors—can lead to a poor person–environment fit. Individual development and functioning can be impaired as a result of a poor fit (Gitterman and Germaine, 2008). Environmental stressors such as demands for acculturation, poverty, and lack of networks influence the degree to which Puerto Rican families can fulfill their societal responsibilities. The ways families cope with these and other environmental demands and conditions can hinder or facilitate the well-being of family members and the family unit's survival as a social institution. Stateside Puerto Rican families encounter a wide range of expected and unexpected life stressors, including members' special developmental needs, losses, separations, and physical and mental illnesses, to name a few. At times, language and acculturation issues can affect members' ability to relate and communicate.

In dealing with different stressors, Puerto Rican families have coped in a number of ways. Individual members and families have adapted to conditions and circumstances in order to meet environmental expectations or to take advantage of environmental opportunities. History and current data show that Puerto Rican families have also become active in promoting changes in the physical and/or social environment to be more responsive to their individual and family needs and goals. They have also denounced societal forces such as oppression, discrimination, and social injustice. In helping Puerto Rican families with different stressors, service providers take two approaches. One approach has been to encourage and facilitate Puerto Rican families' adaptation and change. The other approach is to find ways to increase and/or develop opportunities and resources that are culturally responsive and socially just.

Puerto Rican families change and adapt in their search for well-being. According to Quiñones-Rosado and Barreto (2002), the process of achieving well-being should be both individual and collective. Individual well-being takes place in four dimensions: mental, spiritual, emotional, and physical. Collective well-being is influenced by four dimensions: political, cultural, social, and economic. Each of the individual and collective dimensions must be nurtured and fostered, ensuring that each gets proper attention and balanced care. The family plays a vital role in providing for the mental, spiritual, emotional, and physical needs of its members. Likewise, the family, as a system within a community and the key unit of society, plays a role in seeking and fostering the fairest and best possible political, cultural, social, and economic conditions in order to fulfill its protective and nurturing responsibilities. Puerto Rican families have changed and adapted to life in the United States by adapting individually and collectively; for example, within the family, individuals' attachments and connections to culture may be encouraged, while at the same time families coordinate and promote community activities and efforts that celebrate and maintain their culture.

Change and adaptation can also be examined through the analysis of Puerto Rican families' migration and cultural change, their ecological context, and their organization and life cycle (Falicov, 1998). The concept of the *family map* (Falicov, 1998) can be used to assess how these families make sense of their experience as a result of the change and adaptation taking place within their ecological context and daily life. Therefore, a Puerto Rican family map can change as the family copes with different life, interpersonal, and environmental stressors and seeks individual and collective well-being.

Puerto Rican Families' Core Values

To understand Puerto Rican families, it is necessary to examine the core values of the Puerto Rican culture. These values influence family functioning and organize family members' interactions and role performance. They include *familismo, personalismo, respeto, confianza, simpatia,* and *spirituality.* It is important to highlight that family members' identification with these values may vary. These within-family variations can be a source of stress and may challenge individual development and members' relationships.

Familismo refers to the importance of family to the individual and the community, as well as the interdependence among family members and among generations. Familismo incorporates attitudes and behaviors such as close contact, loyalties, and "a lifelong sense of the 'self-in-family' that serves as a psychosocial guide for family members with regards to their values, actions and identity in the world" (Organista, 2007b:142). Familismo stresses attachments and reciprocity with family members. Because of identification with familismo, participation is greater in family networks. Family needs take precedence over individual needs. This is an allocentric value by which "people understand themselves through others, emphasizing social relationships and highlighting group goals rather than individual ones" (La Roche, 2002:116, cited in Andrés-Hyman et al., 2006:695).

Children and parents may continue an intense interdependent relationship into adulthood, with children living with their parents even after adulthood. Their lifelong commitment to familismo prompts stateside Puerto Ricans to continue their financial support of family members who live in Puerto Rico or abroad. In times of crisis, Puerto Ricans turn to their families and other support systems first, seeking professional assistance only as a last resort.

Studies on Latinos indicate that some components of familismo, such as perception of the family as a support network, remain stronger even among the most acculturated Latinos/as. However, other elements, such as sense of family obligation and use of family as behavioral and attitudinal referents, may decrease with acculturation (Sabogal et al., 1987:408, cited by Organista, 2007b:167). Information is limited about how these findings apply specifically to Puerto Ricans. Their identification with familismo may vary and can be influenced by their travel back and forth between Puerto Rico and the United States.

Personalismo emphasizes the personal dimension of relationships (Organista, 2007b) and the establishment and preservation of cooperative and personal relationships (Cordero, 2008). Puerto Ricans prefer to relate on a personal rather than a formal level. An example of personalismo is friends and family dropping by each other's homes without announcing their visits, just for the sake of spending time together and having informal conversations. Greetings may involve a kiss and/or a hug among women and a handshake or touch on the shoulder among men. Physical touch is common while talking, and the conversational distance is much closer than in other ethnic groups. Personal communication may be preferred over e-mails and voice-mail messages. Individuals may make personal inquiries, extend invitations to family parties, and give small presents (Andrés-Hyman et al., 2006). Personalismo is tied to *simpatia,* which values smooth, pleasant relationships, and minimizing and avoiding confrontation and conflict (Organista, 2007b).

Respeto (respect) is linked to *dignidad* (dignity) and includes ceremonial requisites based on age, gender, socioeconomic position, and contextual interactions (Negroni-Rodríguez and Morales, 2001). Respeto acknowledges individuals' social worthiness (Garcia-Preto, 2005). Thus, it is not surprising Spanish includes two different words to address another person: an informal "you" (*tú*) and a formal "you" (*usted*). The formal "you" is used to convey respeto to older adults and individuals in positions of authority. Asking for *la bendición* (a blessing) is another way of conveying respeto to parents, grandparents, and other elder relatives in the extended family.

A hierarchy of *respeto* is headed by elders and parents because it is important to display social esteem and consideration for individuals—first as persons, and second based on age and social position. Elders and children, in particular, are highly regarded and socially esteemed (Cordero, 2008). The lack of respeto is viewed as a character defect.

The belief in the merit of humanity that derives from respeto may serve as a protective factor and a source of strength. When traditionally identified with respeto, individuals may avoid discussing problems that compromise dignity, may express disagreement indirectly, and may seek a provider's advice and recommendations because of her or his professional status (Andrés-Hyman et al., 2006). Children are expected to demonstrate respeto by avoiding direct contact with authority figures and strangers. Addressing adults by their first names may be considered disrespectful. Service providers seek to show respeto by conveying appreciation of the culture and investing in the language and traditions of their service recipients. First-, second-, and third-generation Puerto Ricans may have different views and expectations regarding respeto. These differences can be a source of stress and conflict within the family if they are not understood.

Confianza is the process of establishing social intimacy and trust (Cordero, 2008) or the capacity to maintain confidences (Falicov, 1998). It emerges through the gradual development of a relationship based on personalismo and when there is perceived mutual respect and acceptance (Negroni-Rodríguez and Morales, 2001).

For Puerto Ricans, life and nature are of great importance (Garcia-Preto, 2005), as is religion. Cultural sayings such as *Dios aprieta pero no ahoga* ("God will squeeze but will not choke you") and *No hay mal que por bien no venga* ("Nothing bad happens without something good coming from it.") suggest Puerto Ricans' ways of accepting fate and coping with what life brings (Garcia-Preto, 2005).

Puerto Ricans are likely to identify with the Catholic religion, although religious diversity has increased. They may also believe in *espiritismo* (spiritism), the belief in an invisible world in which evil and good spirits can harm or protect people. Through rituals and consultation with an *espiritista* (spiritualist), individuals can communicate with the spirits. An evidence of the practice of espiritismo by stateside Puerto Ricans is the existence of *botánicas*. Botánicas are herb shops in which espiritistas can purchase the different paraphernalia essential for espiritismo rituals and other religious practices (Torres-Rivera, 2005). Botánicas also serve as point of community contact.

Change and Adaptation Related to Migration

Puerto Ricans are not considered immigrants, given that the island is a U.S. property. Falicov (1998) proposes that Puerto Ricans are more representative of a "transmigrant" group in which

relationships cross geographic and cultural borders. Many Puerto Ricans are cultural and physical commuters. However "their uprooting and relocation to the mainland is equivalent to the
adaptation experiences of other Latin-American, Spanish speaking groups" (p. 41), and for that
reason their experiences must be examined and addressed. Once in the United States, families
have to cope with racism, oppression, the lack of acceptance of their cultural values, the loss of
support systems, and the need to adapt to the new environment. These challenges threaten individual self-esteem and self-image and affect family relationships.

Experts analyze the process of migration/immigration in three stages: pre-migration,
migration, and the transition process. Each stage involves planning, decisions, and activities,
which vary in duration and impact depending on numerous factors. Although findings cannot be
generalized, perhaps for Puerto Ricans the pre-migration process is not as intense and difficult as
for other Latino groups. If things do not work out in the United States, Puerto Ricans may be able
to return to the island. Still, there is a decision-making process they must go through—their reasons for leaving the island, what to leave, whom to leave behind, how to make the move, who will
be on the other side to help, and how to survive once in the United States. The migration itself
may not pose a major threat or challenge, since Puerto Ricans are U.S. citizens and they do not
need a visa to relocate to the United States. The most difficult stage may be the transition to a new
country, which has emotional, social, cultural, and economic ramifications. This transition may
lead to the uprooting of physical, cultural, and social meaning systems, and both psychological
and family difficulties (Negroni-Rodríguez and Morales, 2001).

Migration brings losses and gains for the family and for each individual family member.
In dealing with losses, effective coping is essential for well-being. Coping and adaptation depend
on many factors: individuals' internal strengths (cognitive, emotional, spiritual, and social); a
family's collective strengths; the availability of resources and supports; the presence and influential power of prejudice, discrimination, and oppression; and the migrant family's responses to
those existing conditions. Therefore, the migration experience may lead to changes in the family's perception of who they are and how they make sense of their reality or their family map.
Losses may include not being able to speak Spanish all the time; separations from significant
others and friends; a sense of feeling "lost" because home is not where it used to be; changes in
social status; loss of familiar sounds, smells, and views; loss of preferred social and recreational
activities; and loss of support networks. Once in the new environment, family members may
have to deal with gender-role expectations regarding independence, and issues around mar-
riage/relationships and child rearing.

Migration brings new challenges, such as having to make lifestyle changes necessitated by
different environmental conditions—for example, a different climate with four seasons—and the
need to master the English language for survival. Stateside Puerto Ricans can face stressors such
as lack of understanding of how different systems work (e.g., jobs, schools, banks, hospitals); new
views about child rearing; differences in cultural values; and how those differences mark relationships, status, and opportunities. There is an implicit demand to acculturate. The acculturation
process itself represents a major stressor and forces individuals, and thus the family, to deal with
issues around identity, language, lifestyle, values, and the need to survive versus the desire to protect one's identity. On the other hand, for some or all family members, migration can bring gains
such as the possibility for a better life; the opportunity to prove oneself to others; the chance to
gain self-esteem, self-confidence, and independence; and the acquisition of a new language.

Stateside Puerto Rican families may encounter lack of acknowledgment and welcome as
U.S. citizens. It can be stressful to explain your legal status when it is often questioned because of
the unresolved political status of Puerto Rico, and resented by other Latin American groups who

struggle to access the privileges of citizenship. Puerto Ricans have to cope with the way they are perceived and the way they perceive themselves (Garcia-Preto, 2005).

Not all Puerto Rican families are migrant families. Second- and third-generation Puerto Rican families may not have been affected by migration or acculturation, and the influence of these processes is felt in their interactions and relationships with Puerto Ricans from the first generation, who may still remain more connected to the culture. For these families, the issues may be different, centering on understanding, communicating, and relating to older generations; making decisions about their cultural priorities; raising children within two worlds; and safeguarding younger generations to develop and maintain a Puerto Rican identity and culture.

Change and Adaptation and the Physical and Social Contexts

Migration to the United States involves life in new surroundings. For migrant Puerto Rican families, the change may be experienced as shock. In some instances, and depending on the city of relocation, individuals may face difficulties adapting to four seasons, with extremes of cold temperatures, snow, and ice. Migrant families complain about the closed doors and dark buildings in the neighborhoods where they reside, which represent a sharp contrast to the light and openness where they lived in their native land (Burgos, 2002).

A range of factors and events within the socioeconomic and physical environment has led families to change their lifestyles and the way they organize themselves and relate (Martínez, 2007). Some examples include the church; educational, labor, and welfare systems; neighborhoods; and means of communication and globalization. The feminist movement has also contributed to changes in Puerto Rican families by denouncing inequality and oppression toward women. The new meaning ascribed to *divorce* as an alternative to terminate oppression and violence also contributes to changes in existing family structures, and therefore to the increase of single-parent households (Martínez, 2007).

In 2000, the census in Puerto Rico included, in the same category, family households defined by either legal or consensual arrangements. No longer would marriage be required as criteria for the creation of a family. The civil rights movements in Puerto Rico led to the development of public policy that enforced equal treatment and protection for both men and women. More specifically, new laws recognizing women's rights allowed women to have the social and legal means to achieve and maintain their safety. It is important to indicate that in Puerto Rico, the law recognizes grandparents as the primary resource to care for children in situations of maltreatment. Interestingly, by 2000 in Puerto Rico 133,881 Puerto Rican grandparents were legally in charge of their grandchildren younger than 18 years old (Martínez, 2007).

Development of science and technology creates new opportunities to organize family and has impacted Puerto Rican families. For example, increased use of contraceptives allows individuals to consider parenting as a personal choice and not as the primary purpose in marriage. These days, single individuals and same-sex couples can become parents. Sexuality is no longer seen as the means to reproduce a family but also as a part of personality with other functions as legitimate as having children. There is a new vision as to the role of individuals within a family, one in which each member will contribute based on their interests, experiences, plans, and commitments. Family has both instrumental and affective roles that contribute to members' development and, legally, protect all members who constitute it.

Interpersonal networks are important to Puerto Ricans (Negroni-Rodríguez and Bloom, 2004; Negroni-Rodríguez and Bok, 2004). They feel that people within the network are an extension of family and can be called on for help in times of crisis (Velez and Cole, 2008). For that reason, when

Puerto Ricans need help, they prefer to approach a specific person within the system whom they have met and trust. Also, they seek services that others within their network know and recommend.

Community-based networks are important to Puerto Rican families because of the support they provide. In different U.S. states, the Puerto Rican community has organized with the purpose of increasing and protecting its rights. Puerto Ricans have worked collectively to better address issues specifically related to their presence in the United States. In many cities, Puerto Rican community-based networks offer Puerto Ricans and other Latino groups access to resources and support within their own community. These networks foster a sense of trust among members that leads to a sense of belonging to an extended family (Magaña and Ybarra, 2010).

Puerto Ricans' sense of collectivism contributes to the success and survival of the family. First, many efforts within the community are focused on the success of the family rather than on individuals. It is this sense of collectivism that influences organizations and businesses to perform multiple roles when serving the community. From providing a forum for the exchange of information, providing services or facilitating access to them, sharing community-related news, and assisting in accessing other formal and informal support systems, these organizations and businesses play a vital role in meeting individual and family needs. In this way, these community institutions contribute to the empowerment of families (Magaña and Ybarra, 2010).

Some examples of Puerto Rican organizations and grassroots movements in the United States include the National Congress for Puerto Rican Rights, the National Institute for Latino Policy, the ASPIRA Association, the National Puerto Rican Coalition, the Puerto Rican/Hispanic Youth Leadership Institute, the Puerto Rican Forum, the Institute for Puerto Rican Policy, the Puerto Rican Legal Defense and Education Fund, the National Association of Puerto Rican and Hispanic Social Workers, Inquilinos Boricuas en Acción, La Casa de Puerto Rico, and the National Conference of Puerto Rican Women.

Acculturation and Its Effect on the Family

Acculturation has been conceptualized as a multidimensional, multilinear process of intrapersonal and sociocultural attachment to culture (Cabán-Owen, 2008). This multidimensional and multilinear process varies among individuals and across time. In a multilinear process, the migrant acculturates (or not) at different levels, patterns, and speeds in different domains—for example, language acquisition, relationships, and cultural traditions. As a process of psychological attachment, acculturation leads to changes in attitudes, beliefs, and behaviors (Cabán-Owen, 2008).

Awareness of the role of culture and the impact of acculturation in family life can facilitate Puerto Rican families' functioning, relationships, and ability to meet the individual and collective dimensions of their well-being. Puerto Ricans have been influenced by the cultures of several different ethnic groups, with the Taínos, Spanish, Africans, and Anglo-Americans considered the most influential. Through time, Puerto Ricans developed their own folklore, music, arts, and their own ways of living together. The new generations of Puerto Ricans living in the United States have been exposed to the history, language, and politics of the United States. They live lifestyles that differ from those of their Puerto Rican elders, but they still maintain their Puerto Rican identity. As Puerto Ricans become Americanized, they speak more English, their traditional ties to the family change, and their social behaviors change. Nevertheless, Puerto Ricans who can travel back to Puerto Rico frequently and who live within a Puerto Rican and/or broader Latino network feel less pressure to assimilate (Cabán-Owen, 2008).

Emerging theoretical views of acculturation contribute to a deeper reflection of the acculturation experience of Puerto Rican families in the United States. In her study with thirty Puerto

Rican migrant women, Cabán-Owen (2008) identified a wide range of acculturation experiences and noted that the traditional acculturation categories proposed by the literature, monocultural and bicultural, not always described these women's sense of cultural attachment. She proposes three new categories that better express the women's experiences of acculturation and reflect their sense of cultural identity and attachment: in-situ cultural, neo-cultural, and intransitive cultural. Although Cabán-Owen's findings cannot be generalized, they propose new hypotheses about how Puerto Ricans experience acculturation, how each of those cultural identifications manifests within the context of the family, and how they influence the way in which families relate and function. Also, the findings raise new questions about the factors that lead individuals to develop these cultural attachments.

Individuals with in-situ cultural identification remain strongly identified with their Puerto Rican culture but have developed skills and abilities to interact with communities other than the Puerto Rican. They continue to practice most of their own cultural traditions and also move with relative ease within the dominant culture. When expected to behave differently outside the home, they do so. These individuals choose to behave according to the dominant cultural expectations.

Puerto Ricans with a neo-cultural identification are constantly taking from both cultures. They feel part of both cultures at the same time and, at times, a part of neither (Cabán-Owen, 2008). In the literature, they might be described as "bicultural" (Cabán-Owen, 2008), but the bicultural concept implies sameness or equal parts taken from each culture. The thoughts, feelings, and actions of a Puerto Rican with a neo-cultural identification do not actually result in equal parts. Such individuals feel they have lost part of their culture of origin, but they do not feel they belong fully to either culture. In fact, they have developed their own cultural style (Cabán-Owen, 2008). This idea of a new cultural identity resulting from the integration of two or more cultures merits special attention in future research.

Puerto Ricans with intransitive cultural identification have formed cultural attachments to, and identify with, the dominant culture even though they may speak only Spanish. Interestingly, individuals with this identification have no practical knowledge of the dominant culture, nor have they made any behavioral adaptations to it. They develop perceptions of the dominant culture based on their limited verbal and nonverbal interactions, their observations and interpretation of this culture from a distance (Cabán-Owen, 2008). These participants perceive themselves as assimilated into the dominant culture. They are aware of their roots and may practice Puerto Rican traditions and culture, yet they are attached psychologically to the dominant group.

Stateside Puerto Rican families may comprise members who present one or more of these three proposed cultural identifications. Cultural attachments may vary among generations. First and second generations may resist weakening their attachments and connections, despite the forces pushing for a strong acculturation to the host society. Mainland-born second- and third-generation Puerto Ricans may still maintain their loyalty to the values and traditions of the Puerto Rican culture, but their attachments may not be as strong. In the second and third generations, English proficiency may be stronger; therefore, they may have greater access to resources, opportunities, and upward mobility. Individuals acculturate according to their needs. If their cultural attachments are not understood and validated by others within the family, there is potential for family conflict and a threat to the individual's well-being.

In the 1970s, experts began to examine the links between the stress of acculturation and the prevalence of mental health disorders (Torres-Matrullo, 1976). In her study with Puerto Rican women, the author found that levels of acculturation and education correlated with personality adjustment and psychopathology, and that traditional family-related values did not change with the degree of acculturation. By the 1980s, experts were concerned about the impact of stress on the Puerto Rican family and effective treatment interventions. They found that discrimination, inadequate support networks, and intergenerational conflicts were creating dysfunctional patterns (Canino, 1980).

It is difficult to generalize about whether a Puerto Rican family retains its traditional values, unless the family is assessed as a group and each family member's acculturation and adaptation are assessed and compared. Although there is much anecdotal evidence of the effects of acculturation on stateside Puerto Rican families, there have been very few studies on this subject.

Language

Most stateside Puerto Ricans speak some degree of English (Pew Hispanic Center, 2010). However, although English is taught in public and private schools in Puerto Rico, once in the United States, Puerto Ricans may have difficulty understanding colloquial English or speaking the English language with the proper accent. Thus, mastery of the English language becomes a challenge (Burgos, 2002). For Puerto Ricans living where Spanish is spoken all the time, the need to learn English is less critical, and chances are they will use children and other supports as interpreters.

For Puerto Ricans living where Spanish is spoken all the time, the need to learn English is less critical, and chances are they will use children and other supports as interpreters.

Poverty and Socioeconomic Status

Puerto Ricans are the most economically and socially disadvantaged group within the Latino groups in the United States. Census data from 2000 ranked stateside Puerto Ricans as the group with the lowest median income ($20,310) and the highest poverty rate (Organista, 2007a). In 2008, the median annual personal earnings for Puerto Ricans had increased to $26,478, slightly higher than the median earnings of $21,488 for all U.S. Latinos (Pew Hispanic Center, 2010). By 2008, more Puerto Ricans lived in poverty (22.6 percent) than others in the general U.S. population (12.7 percent) and other Latino groups (20.7 percent) (Pew Hispanic Center, 2010). In 2005, the percentage of Puerto Ricans who had completed a high school diploma (33.7 percent) was the highest of all groups in the United States (National Institute for Latino Policy, 2007). They were the second-lowest group to complete post-high school education (38.5 percent) (National Institute for Latino Policy, 2007). The rate of homeownership among Puerto Ricans (40.3 percent) is lower than the rate for other Latino groups (49.1 percent) and the U.S. population as a whole (66.6 percent) (Pew Hispanic Center, 2010). Despite some economic improvement, Puerto Ricans remain an economically disadvantaged group and face problems usually associated with high poverty levels. In addition, Puerto Ricans are younger than Anglo-Americans and have larger households. When combined, these statistics represent risk factors for poverty to continue.

Changes in Family Structure

The family is the foundation of Puerto Ricans' social structure. Family unity, welfare, and honor are of great importance (Garcia-Preto, 2005; Negroni-Rodríguez and Morales, 2001). Whether traditional or modern, Puerto Rican families still attribute a central role to the family in the lives of their members. Traditionally, family ties are strong and members' contact is frequent. More Puerto Ricans are getting married at an older age and having fewer children (Garcia-Preto, 2005). Marriage is considered the union of two families, so much so that when adult children form their own families, they attempt to remain in physical proximity to parents and other family members.

Traditionally, Puerto Rican families have been patriarchal, and *machismo* and *marianismo* values have been dominant. Machismo is about masculinity and male identity and how men are to carry out their functions not only within their families, but also in their communities (Torres, 1998). It has been associated with negative expressions such as dominance, patriarchy, authoritarianism, and physical and emotional aggression and oppressive behavior toward women and children. But it also has positive expressions such as self-respect and responsibility for protecting and providing for the family. Males are socialized to be brave, strong, virile, aggressive, autonomous, and honorable. Unfortunately, many Puerto Rican men adhere to exaggerated expressions of their maleness and engage in dominant and aggressive behaviors that cause themselves and their families' pain and emotional, economic, and physical damage. Marianismo is the counterpart to machismo and is associated with the Catholic cult dedicated to the Virgin Mary. It also can have positive expressions such as loyalty, compassion, and generosity. These qualities help to provide support to others and can contribute to women's empowerment (Torres, 1998). Women's socialization includes expectations of self-sacrifice in favor of their family, sexual repression, consideration of sex as an obligation to their husband, chastity until marriage, and conformity to husbands' behaviors.

Gender-role expectations of marianismo and machismo are becoming less influential, in particular for those Puerto Ricans residing in the United States. Women have joined the workforce and have increased their awareness of both their personal power and access to economic resources. The concept of *la nueva marianista* can well describe the new Puerto Rican woman who is independent, competent, assertive, self-assured, and empowered (Torres, 1998). Still, there might be stateside Puerto Rican women who are struggling with internalized marianismo— the traditional gender-role expectations of their families and communities—and their new roles and status. These women find themselves coping with feelings of guilt, confusion, betrayal, and sadness.

Depending on how socialized they are into machismo, Puerto Rican men living in the United States can suffer psychological stress and role strain if they find themselves unable to live up to their male identity. Drinking, gambling, fighting, and promiscuity are commonly reported manifestations of attempts to maintain manhood. Changes in gender-role expectations can cause conflict for couples, which may lead to separation or divorce when not dealt with adequately. Many couples find ways to redefine these internalized gender constructions, transition into new gender roles, and develop more egalitarian and mutually beneficial relationships. Less traditional marriages are more common in second- and third-generation Puerto Ricans.

An extended family system, *compadrazgo*, ascribes to a kinship (the *compadre* and *comadre*) the obligation of helping in the protection and care of children. The compadre who is the child's *padrino* (godfather) and the comadre who becomes his or her *madrina* (godmother) are expected to commit to assume parental responsibilities if the parents should become absent. Another important family commitment is *hijos de crianza*—children who are raised by their relatives as their own, but are not legally adopted (Garcia-Preto, 2005). It is not surprising to find an aunt or uncle or a close friend assuming the rearing of a child within the extended family system and referring to him or her as "my child." For stateside Puerto Rican families, the supportive role of this extended family system may have lessened as a result of acculturation and separation from support networks.

Puerto Rican families are quite diverse in typology and structures. Families can be identified as heterosexual, gay and lesbian, traditional with two parents and children, reconstituted with children, constituted by a single female or male adult and children, couples without children, families with adopted children, families with elderly members, elderly members living together, military and/or migrant families, or families formed in the United States. A family may comprise more than two generations. Grandparents are increasingly becoming heads of household and taking over the care and rearing of their grandchildren. More women are entering the paid labor force, and more children are becoming Americanized more quickly than their parents (Organista, 2007b). Each of the previous arrangements carries different dynamics and challenges and, as Falicov (1998) would say, a unique family map.

Puerto Rican families in the United States may have to cope with internalized demands, expectations, and/or stereotypes (Martínez, 2007). There are family arrangements that, because of cultural factors, are considered illegitimate and dysfunctional. For instance, there is a hidden shame associated with families constituted by second or third marriages. To be a stepfather and stepmother is linked with coming from a destroyed and failed family; single female-headed families are associated with disorganization and disintegration. Stereotyping these families takes away recognition of the challenges they face, and their strengths and resiliency. Society marginalizes and stereotypes families that do not meet the standards of the so-called "normal family" (Martínez, 2007). Puerto Rican gay and lesbian families are affected by homophobia and the cultural gender-based expectations regarding marriage and childbirth. For these families, moving to and/or raising their children in the United States may provide them more freedom and better access to supports. But for a lesbian Puerto Rican, the benefits of having her own family in the United States may occur at the expense of being disconnected from her family of origin if the family does not accept her sexual orientation.

Martínez (2007), in citing experts in the field, identified a new family arrangement, which the author calls the "modified nuclear family." In this family arrangement, individuals tied by blood, rituals, or friendships come to identify themselves as family, with the corresponding commitments and obligations, even though they may have other separate family groups to which they belong and with whom they live. In this arrangement, family exists as an affective and instrumental relationship that takes place without the need to live together or be tied legally or by blood.

Child Rearing and Challenges with Child Discipline

Child rearing among Puerto Ricans is influenced by cultural beliefs and socioeconomic conditions (Negroni-Rodríguez, 2003). A child is raised to be *una persona de provecho* (a person of moral goodness who fulfills his or her obligations) (Falicov, 1998; Organista, 2007b). In Puerto Rican families, child rearing is grounded on in the core values of *familismo, respeto,* and *confianza.* Children are born into an intergenerational and extended family system. In many families, not only will children have their parents, but they also will be sponsored by their padrino and madrina, who commit themselves to be there to supplement parental functions in case of need (Falicov, 1998). Puerto Rican mothers emphasize their children's ability to engage in appropriate intimate and nonintimate relatedness, which is very different from Anglo-American parents, who stress their children's capacity to express and assert themselves to get their needs met. Puerto Rican parents expect their children to be *bien educados* (well educated, meaning with good manners) and to feel *verguenza* (shame linked to respeto) (Organista, 2007b).

Puerto Rican parents may know about a wide range of disciplinary practices, but most frequently they use verbal approaches (reasoning, teaching, explaining, repeating, advising, warning, praising, reminding, encouraging, and negotiating), corporal punishment, and removal of privileges to manage children's behaviors, both to elicit compliance and to manage disobedience (Negroni-Rodríguez, 2003). Traditionally, parents raise their children to obey and respect them by not disagreeing or arguing a point (Organista, 2007b).

Parenting suffers when Puerto Rican families move to or from the United States. Experts have raised awareness among U.S. service providers of the importance of understanding Puerto Rican parents' views of appropriate child discipline and educating them about child discipline practices in the United States (Negroni-Rodríguez, 2003). Cultural variations in child discipline have motivated service providers to examine their assessment tools and intervention strategies and modify them to make them more culturally responsive. A study conducted by Matos et al. (2006) of island Puerto Rican parents of younger children with hyperactivity and behavior problems served as a model of how therapeutic interventions can be adapted, taking into consideration the role of cultural views. It also confirmed the importance of adapting interventions to the particular ethnic group with which they are used (Chartier, Negroni, and Hesselbrock, 2010). When child rearing techniques are imposed on parents, they may feel uncomfortable and reluctant to trust the service provider. Although findings could not be generalized, they raised further questions and issues affecting Puerto Rican families that service providers must consider when working with this population.

Problems can emerge when Puerto Rican parents use traditional rearing practices at home, while their children are exposed to different value orientations about behaviors and attitudes outside of the home. Children and youth may experience conflict and confusion and may struggle with expectations at home and those in other settings that are attuned to Anglo-American values. It becomes important for all family members to understand the value-orientation struggles they are dealing with and to view themselves within such a context.

Challenges for Elders and Their Families

Puerto Rican older adults residing in the United States comprise two groups: the cohort of persons who migrated since the 1940s and the cohort that has arrived in the last decades either accompanying relatives or reuniting with them. It seems that both cohorts have encountered difficulties to achieve upward mobility, economic opportunities, and freedom of choice (Ramos, 2007). They may have lived in the United States through times when racism and discrimination were more openly practiced (Ramos, 2007). Elders with an African heritage may have experienced additional burdens, given the prejudices against Black Americans (Aguirre and Turner, 1995, cited by Ramos, 2007:49). Older Puerto Ricans are mostly Spanish speaking, Catholic, single, with high school education or less, and foreign born (Lozano-Applewhite, 1998; Negroni-Rodríguez and Bok, 2004). They are more likely than other elder groups to live with their children or alone, and they are far less likely than other ethnic groups to enter nursing homes (Griffith, 2004). Their source of income may be Supplemental Security Income, Social Security, and/or public assistance programs (Lozano-Applewhite, 1998; Negroni-Rodríguez and Bok, 2004). In addition to facing declines in health, income, social status, and the loss of aging partners, friends, and family members, they are affected by poverty, health disparities, and their experiences of migration and acculturation, racism, and discrimination (Ramos, 2007, cited by Acosta, 2007; Stratton, Hynes, and Nepaul, 2009).

Because of familismo values, family members are expected and feel obliged to meet the needs and best interests of their older adults (Velez and Cole, 2008). This sense of obligation comes from a felt responsibility to reciprocate for the care and love they received. In Puerto Rico, 71 percent of older adults lived within the same household with family members. Those who did not live in the same household often lived nearby (U.S. Bureau of the Census, 2000, cited by Velez and Cole, 2008). Female family members may encounter a higher level of stress in caring for their elders, as they are the ones expected to provide most of the care. Caregivers who have English knowledge and know the U.S. system are more likely to access the services available to the elderly.

Acculturation and other factors can influence how Puerto Rican elders are cared for and treated. Some families lack awareness of the elder's value orientation about family and aging. Family members may not realize the challenges faced by their migrant elders as a result of their acculturation process. Sometimes the younger generations do not appreciate what it means for their elders to grow old in a new country and culture. This can be a source of stress and pain both for the elders—who may feel they are not as important to the family—and for the family. Stressors can trigger feelings of insecurity, fear, incompetence, frustration, anger, grief, and separation. Limited English proficiency can be a barrier to accessing medical and social services.

CONCLUSION

Political, cultural, social, religious, and economic structures serve as the foundation for life in the United States for Puerto Ricans. It is from this foundation that stateside Puerto Rican families have further developed and transformed. The strengths of Puerto Rican families include the importance they give to the family, their sense of community, their cultural pride, their spirituality and their natural support systems. Also, the values of familismo, personalismo, and respeto provide individual and group support. Still, Puerto Rican families struggle with various socioeconomic challenges, racism, and oppression. More awareness is needed of the powerful dynamics operating between them and their physical and social environments.

Institutional oppression has been a powerful force in Puerto Rican history, and it affects Puerto Rican families. It has been defined as "when members of dominant social groups systematically subordinate members of other groups for the purpose of maintaining access to, and control of, the resources in society" (Quiñones-Rosado and Barreto, 2002:65). Puerto Rican families must be able to perceive and understand oppression and its impact on their well-being, which cannot truly be felt until oppression is ended. Puerto Rican individuals—indeed all people— need to perceive oppression, acknowledge it, and name it. As individuals become skillful in observing and noticing oppression, they can begin to understand and look at it with a critical eye. Through this process, people gain consciousness, which leads them to respond to such oppression. This consciousness-in-action is the essence of empowerment and transformation (Quiñones-Rosado and Barreto, 2002).

Over time Puerto Ricans have expanded their political activism and promoted grassroots movements to defend their rights and improve their life conditions. Still, they face a lack of awareness, understanding, and acceptance of their status as migrants and their U.S. citizenship. One example of this lack of awareness is the U.S. Census Bureau's exclusion of island Puerto Ricans from many of its reports on Latinos (Falcón, 2009). Policy makers claim that by counting only stateside Puerto Ricans, the Census fails to provide an accurate profile of Puerto Ricans in the United States, thus limiting their access to the resources and opportunities they have earned as U.S. citizens (Falcón, 2009).

This chapter cannot end without acknowledging Puerto Rican families' many contributions to the well-being of the United States. Puerto Ricans have been recognized for their service and sacrifice in the U.S. Armed Forces. Puerto Ricans have distinguished themselves in the arts and in the fields of education, politics, science, business, and health, to name a few. Like other cultures, the Puerto Rican culture has enriched the United States by instilling more attention to values that bring families closer. Puerto Rican cuisine, music, and folklore have become part of the lives of many in the United States. The economic power of Puerto Ricans is rising. Puerto

Ricans occupy important positions within the federal Government, including NASA. Puerto Ricans have brought to the United States a perspective of race that challenged the U.S. Black and White duality (Fontillas, 1999). Because of their mixed race, Puerto Ricans do not fit in either category, and efforts to categorize these realities continue through the U.S. Census Bureau.

More knowledge is needed of the differences and similarities of island and stateside Puerto Rican families. In the health area, for instance, studies suggest that although island and stateside Puerto Ricans may suffer similar health problems, they differ in the prevalence of health conditions, health status, and access to health care (Ho, Quian, Kim, Melnik, Tucker, Jimenez-Velazquez, et al., 2006). Experts consider it necessary to explore the factors that for each group contribute to better health status and use of health care services (Ho et al., 2006).

Service providers and policy makers must pay attention to the changing social, political, and economic structures in Puerto Rico and how those affect stateside Puerto Rican families. They also need to gain insights into how social and economic changes in the United States affect both island and stateside Puerto Rican families. Furthermore, it is their duty to prevent and solve emerging social problems threatening the individual and collective well-being of Puerto Rican, as well as all other, families.

References

Acosta, H. 2007, June. "Cultural Competence and Older Latinos." Paper presented at the 2007 Annual Conference of the National Association of Puerto Rican and Hispanic Workers at Stony Brook University, Stony Brook, NY.

Aguirre, A., & J. Turner. 1995. *American Ethnicity: The Dynamics and Consequences of Discrimination.* New York: McGraw Hill.

Andrés-Hyman, R. C., J. Ortíz, L. M. Añez, M. Paris, and L. Davidson. 2006. "Culture and Clinical Practice: Recommendations for Working with Puerto Ricans and other Latinas(os) in the United States." *Professional Psychology: Research and Practice 37*(6), 694–701.

Burgos, N. 2002. "Voices of Hispanic Caribbean Women: Migration, Family and Work." In J. B. Torres and F. G. Rivera (Eds.), *Latino/Hispanic Liaisons and Visions for Human Behavior in the Social Environment* (pp. 157–174). New York: Haworth Social Work Practice Press.

Cabán-Owen, C. 2008. "A Study of the Acculturation Experiences of Puerto Rican Migrant Women: Manifestations and Meaning Making Process." Doctoral dissertation, University of Connecticut.

Canino, I. A. 1980. "Impact of Stress on the Puerto Rican Family: Treatment Considerations." *American Journal of Orthopsychiatry 50*(3), 535–541.

Chartier, K., L. Negroni, and M. Hesselbrock. 2010. "Strengthening Family Practices in Latino Families." *Journal of Ethnic and Cultural Diversity in Social Work 19*(1), 1–17.

Cordero, A. 2008. "Commonly Shared Latino Values/Norms/Practices." Unpublished handout distributed for teaching purposes, University of Connecticut School of Social Work.

Falcón, A. 2009, November. "Puerto Ricans and the 2010 Census: 'Si quieres frutos, sacude el arbol.'" "Si quieres frutos, sacude el arbol." *Hispanic New York Project: Community and Culture Daily Update.* hispanicnewyorkproject.blogspot.com/2009/11/puerto-ricans-and-2010-census-si.html (accessed April 6, 2011).

Falicov, C. J. 1998. *Latino Families in Therapy: A Guide to Multicultural Practice.* New York: Guilford Press.

Fontillas, J. 1999. *Political Evolution of Puerto Ricans in America.* www.fontillas.com/dpr.htm (accessed April 6, 2011).

Garcia-Preto, N. 2005. "Puerto Rican Families." In M. McGoldrick, J. Giordano, and J. K. Pearce (Eds.), *Ethnicity and Family Therapy* (3rd ed., pp. 242–255). New York: Guilford Press.

Gitterman, A., and C. B. Germain. 2008. *The Life Model of Social Work Practice: Advances in Theory and Practice.* New York: Columbia University Press.

Griffith, V. 2004. "Generations to Come: Research Examines Options for Latino Elders as Economic Realities Challenge Family Traditions." Feature Story.

Austin: University of Texas. www.utexas.edu/features/archive/2004/latino.html (accessed April 6, 2011).

Ho, G. Y. F., H. Quian, M. Y. Kim, T. A. Melnik, K. L. Tucker, I. Z. Jimenez-Velazquez, et al. 2006. "Health Disparities between Island and Mainland Puerto Ricans." *Rev Panam Salud Publica/Panam Public Health 19*(5), 331–339.

La Roche, M. J. 2002. "Psychotherapeutic Considerations in Treating Latinos." *Cross-Cultural Psychiatry 10*, 115–122.

Longres, J. F. 1974. "Racism and Its Effects on Puerto Rican Continentals." *Social Casework 55*(2), 67–75.

Lozano-Applewhite, S. 1998. "Culturally Competent Practice with Elderly Latinos." In M. Delgado (Ed.), *Latino Elders and the Twenty-First Century: Issues and Challenges for Culturally Competent Research and Practice* (pp. 1–15). New York: Haworth Press.

Magaña, S., and M. Ybarra. 2010. "Family and Community Strengths in the Latino Community." In R. Furman and N. Nego (Eds.), *Social Work Practice with Latinos: Key Issues and Emerging Themes* (pp. 69–84). Chicago: Lyceum Books.

Maldonado, R. M. 1976. "Why Puerto Ricans Migrated to the United States in 1947–73." *Graduate School of Business Administration Monthly Labor Review 99*(9), 7–18.

Martínez, L. 2007. "Familias y Exclusión: De la Verguenza al Orgullo." In R. Rosa Soberal (Ed.), *La diversidad cultural: Reflexión Crítica Desde un Acercamiento Interdisplinario* (pp. 159–183). San Juan, PR: Publicaciones Puertorriqueñas.

Matos, M., R. Torres, R. Santiago, M. Jurado, and I. Rodriguez. 2006. "Adaptation of Parent–Child Interaction Therapy for Puerto Rican Families: A Preliminary Study." *Family Process 45*(2), 205–222.

National Institute for Latino Policy. 2007, February. "Stateside Latinos 2005." *Latino Policy Data.* www.latinopolicy.org (accessed June 13, 2010).

Negroni-Rodríguez, L. K. 2003. "Puerto Rican Abusive and Non-Abusive Mothers' Beliefs About Appropriate and Inappropriate Child Discipline." *Journal of Ethnic and Cultural Diversity in Social Work 12*(4), 65–90.

Negroni-Rodríguez, L. K., and M. Bloom. 2004. "The Use of Natural Support Networks in the Promotion of Mental Health Among caribbean Women." *Journal of Social Work Research and Evaluation 5*(1), 31–40.

Negroni-Rodriguez, L., and M. Bok. 2004. "Understanding the Relationship Between Natural Support Networks, the Physical and Mental Health of latina Elderly and the Utilization and Satisfaction with Services: Findings Report." Unpublished internal document, University of Connecticut School of Social Work.

Negroni-Rodríguez, L. K., and G. De La Cruz-Quiroz. 2006. "Multicultural Welfare Practice with Latino Children, Youth and their Families." In N. A. Cohen, T. V. Tran, and S. Y. Rhee (Eds.), *Multicultural Approaches in Caring for Children, Youth and Their Families* (pp. 196–237). San Francisco, CA: Allyn & Bacon.

Negroni-Rodríguez, L. K., and J. Morales. 2001. "Individual and Family Assessment Skills with Latino/Hispanic Americans." In R. Fong and S. Furuto (Eds.), *Culturally Competent Practice: Skills, Interventions and Evaluations* (pp. 132–146). Boston: Allyn & Bacon.

Newman, M. J. 1978. "A Profile of Hispanics in the U.S. Workforce." *Bureau of Labor Statistics Monthly Labor Review 101*(12) 3–14.

Organista, K. C. 2007a. "The Americanization of Latinos." In K. C. Organista (Ed.), *Solving Latino Psychosocial and Health Problems: Theory, Practice and Populations* (pp. 3–38). Hoboken, NJ: John Wiley & Sons.

_____. 2007b. "The Latino Family." In K. C. Organista (Ed.), *Solving Latino Psychosocial and Health Problems: Theory, Practice and Populations* (pp. 141–179). Hoboken, NJ: John Wiley & Sons.

Pew Hispanic Center. 2010, April. *Hispanics of Puerto Rican Origin in the United States, 2008.* Washington, DC: Pew Hispanic Center. pewhispanic.org/files/factsheets/not58.pdf (accessed on April 6, 2011).

_____. 2009, July. "Fact sheet: Hispanics of Puerto Rican origin in the United States, 2007." Washington, DC: Pew Hispanic Center.

Quiñones-Rosado, R., and E. Barreto. 2002. "An Integral Model of Well-Being and Development and Its Implications for Helping Professions." In J. B. Torres and F. G. Rivera (Eds.), *Latino/Hispanic Liaisons and Visions for Human Behavior in the Social Environment* (pp. 57–84). New York: Haworth Social Work Practice Press.

Ramirez, R. R. 2004. "We the People: Hispanics in the United States, Census 2000 Special Report." CENSR-18. Washington, DC: U.S. Census Bureau. www.census.gov/prod/2004pubs/censr-18.pdf (accessed April 6, 2011).

Ramos, B. M. 2007. "Housing Disparities, Caregiving, and Their Impact for Older Puerto Ricans." *Journal of Gerontological Social Work 49*(1/2), 47–64.

Rodríguez, C. E. 2002. "Puerto Ricans: Immigrants and Migrants—A Historical Perspective." Beltsville, MD: Americans All National Education Program. www.americansall.com/PDFs/02-americans-all/9.9.pdf. The Education Web Site of the People of America Foundation (accessed April 6, 2011).

Sabogal, F., G. Marín, R. Otero-Sabogal, B. V. Marín, et al. 1987. "Hispanic Familism and Acculturation: What Changes and What Doesn't?" *Hispanic Journal of Behavioral Sciences 9*(4), 397–412.

Stratton, A., M. M. Hynes, and A. N. Nepaul. 2009. *The 2009 Connecticut Health Disparities Report.* Hartford: Connecticut Department of Public Health.

Torres, J. B. 1998. "Masculinity and Gender Roles Among Puerto Rican men: Machismo on the U.S. Mainland." *American Journal of Orthopsychiatry 68*(1), 16–26.

Torres-Matrullo, C. 1976. "Acculturation and Psychopathology Among Puerto Rican Women in the Mainland United States." *American Journal of Orthopsychiatry 46*(4), 710–719.

Torres-Rivera, E. 2005. "Espiritismo: The Flywheel of the Puerto Rican Spiritual Traditions." *Interamerican Journal of Psychology 39*(2), 295–300.

Velez, D., and S. A. Cole. 2008. "Culture, Place of Origin and Service Delivery for Latino Older Adult Immigrants: The Case of Puerto Rican Older Adults." *Journal of Gerontological Social Work 51*(34), 300–314.

10

■ ■ ■

The Dominican American Family

Ramona Hernández

INTRODUCTION

The following monograph presents an analytical overview of the Dominican family in the United States. The methodological approach used intertwines information about the family in the Dominican Republic and in the United States. Why the comparative approach? The review of the literature showed a very small number of studies focusing specifically on the Dominican family. It also showed that most of what we know about the Dominican family in the United States comes from studies where the family appears as a subtheme and not as a central topic. We also found that many of these studies make assumptions about the family in the Dominican Republic without relying on academic evidence, largely missing bibliographical consultation and references. The early works describing the family in the Dominican Republic are based on ethnographic work and participant observation undertaken in the rural areas. These works describe the Dominican family as it was experienced by the informants and observed by the researchers. Subsequent works of the 1980s change slightly from this methodological model by introducing analysis that were based on informants who had been selected through large probabilistic surveys taken in the Dominican Republic and the United States. But the academic bias on the analysis and assumptions advanced in this research persisted to the extent that the responses elicited from the informants continued to be the main sources of the analysis and very few pertinent bibliographical references with regards to works produced in the Dominican Republic are included. The newest research focusing on the Dominican family in the United States suffers from the same methodological favoritism of privileging interviews. This research also lacks reviews of scholarly knowledge about the family in the Dominican Republic in spite of that many researchers now depart from the notion of an existing perpetual link between Dominicans in the United States and the Dominican Republic through what is called transnational practices.

In this monograph I try to break away from the traditional methodological approach to the study of the Dominican family so far taken by most researchers. I conduct an examination of the literature concerning the Dominican family both in the United States and in the Dominican Republic, paying particular attention to major works that advanced descriptions and definitions about the family. I also rely on empirical data obtained from several sources, including the decennial census both from the United States and the Dominican Republic, as well as various national surveys conducted in the Dominican Republic that pay particular attention to the evolution of the family.

The chapter offers a comparative approach by describing the Dominican family in the Dominican Republic and in the United States. The comparative approach aids in the possibility of constructing an analytical description of the U.S. Dominican family that is more in consonance with an immigrant group who many feel continues to be attached to home cultural values while at the same time it goes through the adaptation process and forms families and establishes homes in the new land. Similarly, looking at both families in both places allows for the possibility of contextualizing U.S. Dominicans' cultural attachment, thinking specifically about whether the family recreates cultural norms and practices and holds values that no longer exist in Dominican society or that have changed or transformed. Finally, the comparative approach provides the opportunity to see to what extent Dominicans' interaction with the new social milieu, and their desires and aspirations, provide the space for the emergence of a Dominican family model that upholds cultural values and practices that are very similar or very distinct compared to other families, whether in the United States or in the Dominican Republic.

THE DOMINICAN FAMILY AND WOMEN

One may write about Dominican women without writing about the family, but it would be futile to do the opposite. The family is the most important agent of socialization, responsible for children's training in the tenderest years of life; as such, society relies heavily on the family to re-produce individuals who will conform to a collective mentality that permeates society and maintains its stability. Such a mentality rests on a cultural view and historical legacy that distinguish each society from the other.

When studying the family in Dominican society, an observer would note that the woman occupies the most prominent place in the family because the socialization of children revolves around her. Similarly, when the Dominican woman did not work outside the home for pay, she minded her home and ensured everyone's existence through orchestrating and taking full responsibility for the re-production of her household. When she later joined the labor force, she continued with her former duties or bought other women's labor to replace hers at home.

In Dominican society, the woman's centrality is learned through a popular culture in which the mother has no equal, for as the popular saying so clearly expresses, *"Madre sólo una y padre cualquiera"* ("Mother is only one, and father anyone"), a view possibly carried from the Tainos' time. Regardless of social class background, Dominicans would think of *la patria* (the motherland), their highest symbol of nationhood and identity, as the mother of all Dominicans, and they would never conceive la patria as their father, contrary to the prevalent use of the term in the United States. The fundamental role of women in Dominican society is also reflected in the fact that an important segment of Dominican homes is headed by single women.

Female headship is not a recent development in Latin American societies. Some authors trace its origins to colonial times, arguing that as much as 25 percent of colonial Latin America had homes headed by single women with absentee males (Wainerman and Geldstein, 1994). As indicated in Figure 10.1, in the Dominican Republic the proportion of homes headed by women has increased systematically from 1971 to 2002, from close to 20 percent to 35 percent. The increase in women's headship of homes has concomitantly generated a decline in men's headship of household. Figure 10.2 shows that in 1981 close to 80 percent of households in the Dominican

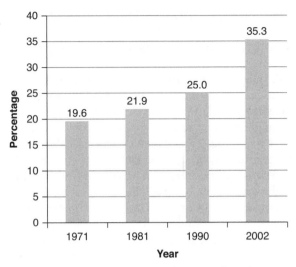

FIGURE 10.1 Homes Headed by Women in the Dominican Republic: 1971–2002

Sources: Data for 1971 and 1981 are based on La Problemática de las Jefas de Hogar; for 1990 based on Mujeres en Cifras; for 2002 based on Oficina Nacional de Estadísticas (ONE), Dominican Republic.

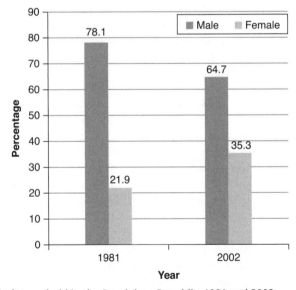

FIGURE 10.2 Head of Household in the Dominican Republic: 1981 and 2002

Sources: Data for 1971 and 1981 are based on La Problemática de las Jefas de Hogar; for 1990 based on Mujeres en Cifras; for 2002 based on Oficina Nacional de Estadísticas (ONE), Dominican Republic.

Republic were headed by men. By 2002, the proportion of homes headed by men had declined to less than 65 percent.

The high rates of female headship and its historic nature defy the perception of the Dominican family as a social space under the command of men and confirms more diversity and flexibility regarding leadership roles in the family. Pablo Tactuk (2007:1) correctly argues that

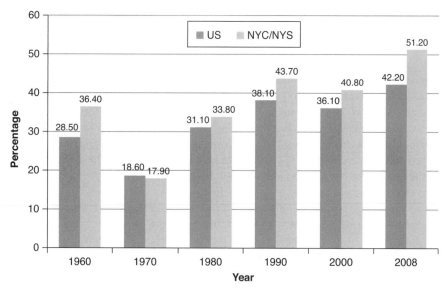

FIGURE 10.3 Dominican Female-Headed Households—United States vs. New York: 1960–2008

Sources: 1970 1% IPUMS; 1980, 1990, 2000 5% IPUMS; 2008 American Community Survey.

Note: 1970 only for New York State.

"women's increasing headship of homes is a social phenomenon that has changed the profile of many Dominican homes, *feminizing*[1] the basic structure of society: the family. Tactuk is not alone in his observation regarding the Dominican family. It has been argued that men's leadership role, particularly their role as economic provider, has become a myth in Latin America and the Caribbean, as a result of women's increasing participation in paid labor and the rise of homes and families headed by single women (Safa, 1995).

As we will see later, the female single-headed home does not disappear when Dominicans migrate to the United States, but on the contrary it intensifies (see Figure 10.3). Similarly, though the second generation has been increasing rapidly in the last two decades, still more than 6 in 10 Dominicans in 2008 were immigrants, and women not only initiate the migration process; they also predominate among those who leave for the United States.

DOMINICANS IN THE UNITED STATES

Dominican migration to the United States dates as far back as 1613 with Española's sailor Juan Rodriguez, the first nonnative person to settle in New York. Large contingents also came during the nineteenth century, particularly through the well-known port of Ellis Island through which over 5,000 Dominicans passed from 1892 to 1924, the year when this important port was officially closed. The largest waves came after the passage of the major immigration reform act of 1965 and the arrival into government in 1966 of President Joaquín Balaguer, who officially opened the doors for Dominicans to emigrate through the implementation of a new policy that generously issued passports for Dominicans to leave (Hernández, 2002).

---

[1]Author's translation from Spanish. Emphasis added.

Between the assassination of Rafael Leónidas Trujillo and the end of the 1980s, the Dominican Republic had implemented two economic development strategies: the import substitution economic model and the export-led economic model. Both economic models emphasized industrial production and dependency on foreign capital and integration into world markets. Both economic models managed to improve some macroeconomic indicators, such as higher level of production; increases in the level of exportations and importations; and a higher level of professional, technical, and industrial employment. As compared to the 1960s, for instance, Dominican society has experienced an incredible level of modernization as reflected in the multiplication of industrial establishments; the decreasing level of illiteracy to almost negligible levels; the increasing enrollment of students in schools and universities; the intensification in the construction of high-rises; the creation of a modern transportation system that connects the country from coast to coast via long highways; a first rail line in the city of Santo Domingo; modern ports in various cities; and five airports, four with international capacity, with several daily flights from and to Europe, Latin America, and the United States. Yet the irony is that economic development and modernization have resulted neither in better conditions for most Dominican families nor a more egalitarian distribution of economic resources.

For many Dominicans, neither the 1960s, nor the 1970s or 1980s, brought significant improvement to their lives. On the contrary, in the 1970s, 70 percent of Dominican families lost income in absolute terms. A decade later, 40.8 percent of children younger than five years of age were found to be malnourished, and the number of families who lived below the poverty level had doubled to 47 percent (Santana and Rathe, 1993:189). The 1980s have been called "the lost decade in Latin America," and this is the period when Dominican migration to the United States accelerated (Figure 10.4). Economic hardships for many families continued through the 1990s. In fact, in 1995 more than 7 in 10 families did not have their basic needs covered (Tejada Holguin, 1996). For most families their economic standing has changed little in the twenty-first century. In 2009, 40 percent of families in Dominican society still lived below the national poverty level, and only 13 percent of families were concentrated in middle-high and high annual incomes (Oficina Nacional de Estadísticas de la República Dominicana, 2007).

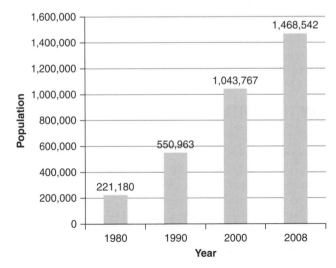

FIGURE 10.4   Dominican Population in the United States: 1980–2008
Sources: 1980, 1990, 2000 5% IPUMS; 2008 American Community Survey.

During the 1980s, migration from the Dominican Republic to the United States accelerated at an unprecedented level. A brief review of annual migration flow from the Dominican Republic from 1960 to 2008 reveals that emigration reached its peak in 1994, when over 42,000 Dominicans obtained U.S. permanent residence, and over 90 percent of them obtained it through the Family Reunification Act of 1965. These families packed their luggage and left in search of a better life. More than 1 in 2 of those who have left and continue to leave today are women. Dominican migration is a woman's affair for women dominate the movement and are the first ones to leave their country. Dominican migration is also a family affair, for the migration cycle is completed when a woman brings the rest of her family to reunite with her in the United States. As she reconstructs her family in the United States while pursuing her dreams, several questions come to mind: Does she manage to lift her family out of poverty in the United States? Does she continue to be the center of the family? And how do the cultural values she brought with her aid her in the socialization of the family? And finally, how much has the Dominican family changed in the United States as compared to the family in the Dominican Republic?

DEFINING THE DOMINICAN FAMILY: PATTERNS AND CHARACTERISTICS

Although research in Dominican studies has increased consistently during the last ten years, including a healthy growth in the number of doctoral dissertations, the number of studies focusing specifically on the Dominican family in the United States continues to be scarce. In a society where numbers matter, the lack of attention to the Dominican family is unjustified. In 1960, approximately 12,000 Dominican individuals were living in families distributed across the United States. Almost fifty years later, by 2008 the number of Dominican individuals living in families had grown to 813,015, reflecting a dramatic increase of almost 14,000 individuals per year, or a little over 1,000 per month (see Figure 10.5). In 1970, 90.5 percent of the individuals living

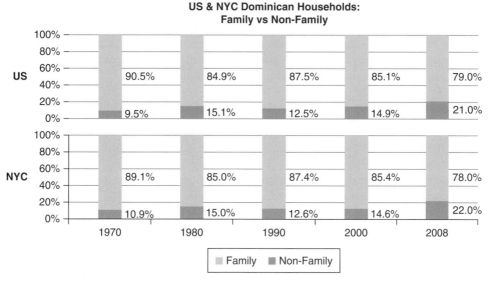

FIGURE 10.5 U.S. Dominican Households—Family vs. Non-Family: 1970–2008

Sources: 1980, 1990, 2000 5% IPUMS; 2008 American Community Survey.

TABLE 10.1   Dominican Individuals Living in U.S. Households: 1970–2008

# of Families	1970	1980	1990	2000	2008
1	47,400	149,440	283,314	542,574	702,514
2	5,700	14,860	52,973	120,052	84,470
3	1,200	2,800	12,221	24,103	16,654
4+	400	1,140	5,177	11,372	9,377
Total	54,700	168,240	353,685	698,101	813,015

Sources: 1970 1% IPUMS; 1980, 1990, 2000 5% IPUMS; 2008 American Community Survey.

in Dominican households were family members; in 2008, the percentage of family in households continued to be very high, at 79.0 percent (see Table 10.1).

Generally, most societies narrowly define the family based on an ideal type. In the United States, the family has been traditionally conceived as a middle-class, married couple living together with their unmarried children. In the Dominican Republic, the average family is defined as an urban, working-class, unmarried couple, living with children and other members of the couple's family (Tejada Holguin, 1996). In looking at the Dominican family in the United States, a few questions come to mind: How much does the Dominican family subscribe to the United States's ideal family type? How much does the U.S. Dominican family deviate from or adhere to the prevailing traditional family model left behind in Dominican society? Has migration to the United States provided space for the emergence of a Dominican family model that stands distinctively on its own, different from the ideal types in the United States and in Dominican societies? The following section addresses these and other questions through reviewing the different perceptions and definitions advanced concerning the Dominican family in the United States.

The current literature discussing the Dominican family in the United States concentrates on describing practices and beliefs that facilitate the construction of a typology of the Dominican family. A brief review of the literature reveals that observers have focused on three areas: adaptation, cultural retention, and parenting practices. Similarly, writings about the Dominican family can be divided into two large historical periods that may be organized arbitrarily following (1) a chronological order, (2) the volume of migration from the Dominican Republic, and (3) the theoretical understanding or the ideas explaining the Dominican family.

Assessment of Views About the Dominican Family Pre-1980

The first historical period of writings about the Dominican family extends from approximately the late 1960s to 1980 and the second from 1980 to the present. This section focuses on the first of these two periods.

Researchers writing about the Dominican family prior to 1980 describe a relatively small group who had relatively recently arrived. In contrast, those writing after 1980 described an enlarged group that included families that had already been living in the United States for over two decades, a generation of grown-up and U.S.-born Dominican children, they defined neighborhoods that were clearly marked and distinguished with Dominican symbols (businesses, organizations, associations, parades, names of streets, parks, schools, etc.). By 1980, U.S. Census data indicate that approximately 221,180 Dominicans were residing in the United States, and by 2008 that number had increased to 1,468,542 (see Figure 10.4). The overwhelming majority of the Dominican people emigrated between 1990 and 2000, pressured by the remnant negative economic effects of the 1980s. The 1980s were devastating years for the entire region of Latin America, which experienced prolonged economic slowdowns and increasing social instability. In fact, 297,190 Dominicans arrived between 1990 and 2000, an incredible amount as compared with the total of 173,304 for all those who had arrived before 1980 (Hernández and Rivera-Batiz, 2003). I argue that with the passing of time Dominicans have created a cultural identity that enables them both to resist and adapt—to act or develop practices and social behavior that are based on both pragmatism and an abstract memory that may or may not resemble what they left behind. Resisting and adapting are both part of a dialectical process of forces that are contrary but that produce, in the end, a historical legacy and a cultural identity unique to the Dominican people in the United States.

Most research focusing on the Dominican family prior to the 1980s is based on ethnographic research and included participant observations and interviews of members of the families who were selected using personal referrals or word-of-mouth. A general belief underlying most studies of this period is the view that Dominicans were capable of adapting to life in the United States and that they were pragmatic about it. Adaptation came through employment and securing a living in the new abode. Nancie L. González, one of the first to write about Dominicans in the United States, describes how easy it was for Dominican immigrants to integrate into the labor market of New York City. González adheres to the theoretical view in migration studies that explains the international migration of workers as a response to a demand for labor in the receiving society. Dominicans found jobs that, presumably, were readily available waiting for them. Referring to the jobs Dominicans found, González adds that "Puerto Ricans have been employed in these capacities in recent years, and we see a future trend in which Dominicans replace the former as they [Puerto Ricans] improve their economic status, intermarry with other Americans and lose their ethnic identity, or return to Puerto Rico (González, 1970:161–162).

González writes about Dominican peasants who are capable of saving in spite of their meager incomes because they lived modestly, below American standards, shared expenses, and saved to return to the Dominican Republic one day. In the minds of these peasants New York was the place to make money, not to raise children. In fact, the Dominican migrants studied by González leave children behind with members of the extended family (González, 1970:155). González also believes that uprooted Dominican peasants had a better chance of improving their lives in a large metropolitan and modern city, like New York City, than in a small one, such as Santo Domingo. She differentiates the options in the two cities by pointing out that "the structure of the very large metropolis permits . . . a kind of protective pluralism which the smaller city cannot. Individuals, depending on their previous life circumstances may then fit into one of several kinds of urban living patterns" (1970:170). In González's view, Dominican peasants are able to adapt to the new city because they are equipped with what she identifies as "techniques and social structures," abilities that perfectly matched with the new city's plurality. In the end, these techniques and social structures boil down to Dominican peasants' abilities to depend on primary relations—*family*—to survive in a strange environment, and on living in the present modestly, with a goal of living the future to the fullest.

Glenn Hendricks on his part also perceives migration from the Dominican Republic as a family affair. His *The Dominican Diaspora: From the Dominican Republic to New York City— Villagers in Transition* (1974) is the first book published about Dominican migrants in the United States. His contribution continues to be the more detailed account of Dominicans' everyday life, including parental practices, interfamily relations, adaptation to the United States, and relationship with the home country. Like González, Hendricks believes that Dominicans find jobs with relative ease. Once again, family and a network of known people, all coming from the same town, play an important role in helping Dominicans to incorporate into society.

According to Hendricks (1974), Dominicans' sense of family is reflected not only in their concrete support of sharing a small space with families doubled up and crammed together in a single-bedroom apartment, stoically, without conflicts due to the lack of space, and with elder siblings caring for the younger ones, but also in the fact that support and responsibility for one another do not involve only blood relatives but, rather, the entire Dominican community. They believe in the compounded family, or that members of the family include people who are not related by blood or by law. Both honor and shame are shared by the entire Dominican community; what happens to one happens to everyone; the family and the community "share any consequences of acts by one of its members" (Hendricks, 1974:103). The people observed and interviewed by Hendricks in New York City came from the same town he studied previously in the Dominican Republic, and most of them are related by blood, *compadrazgo*,[2] or friendship.

Though Hendricks's study was published only four years after González's, Hendricks notes that the Dominican family had undergone some cultural changes as it settled in New York. In New York, women who worked became presumably more independent from their husbands; those who did not work, however, became much more dependent on their husbands to deal with a society they did not know. And while Dominicans still preferred to live in consensual unions rather than legal marriage, immigration requirements were forcing them to legalize their marital relationship. Similarly, Dominican men's polygamous relationships with women were incompatible with the new life, in which a man often worked two jobs and was limited in his expenditures in order to send remittance and save to return home one day.

In general, the pioneering researchers observed that Dominicans (1) relied heavily on family and on co-national networks to adapt to U.S. society, (2) benefitted economically from migration to the United States and (3) remained connected to the Dominican Republic by sending remittances, visiting regularly, and keeping the dream of returning home. These are straightforward observations. An assessment of the cultural changes in these pioneering texts shows that Dominicans kept some social practices and upheld some values and disengaged from others which, as judged by the researchers, were unpractical and represented retrograde positions.

Assessment of Views About the Dominican Family Post-1980

Research published after 1980 continues to be mostly ethnographic, based on face-to-face interviews of family members and others who knew each other. As the decade progressed, ethnographic research introduced case studies and family-life history as sources of analysis.

Scholars of the post-1980 years continue to uphold certain views about the Dominican family advanced by the early researchers. Among the views is Dominicans' belief in the centrality of the family, consisting of those related by blood and those who were not. In *Through the Eye of the Needle: Immigrants and Enterprises in New York's Garment Trade* (1986), an ethnographic study looking at Dominican entrepreneurs, Roger Waldinger writes about Dominicans moving ahead of others, particularly native Blacks, because Dominicans leaned on a niche of employment that recruited heavily through word-of-mouth and supported members of their national group in detriment to others who were not part of that ethnic group.

Patricia Pessar, the most prolific Dominican migration scholar in the United States, pursues Hendricks's suggestions about Dominican women workers in New York. Her ethnographic

---

[2]Compadrazgo describes the relationship among parents and those who baptized—the godmother or godfather—the child. It is a religious precept and involves the highest level of trust and respect among the individuals involved. In the Dominican Republic, the godmother and the godfather are expected to take the role of the parents in the event that either one dies.

study surveys 55 Dominican households and 16 women garment workers. The households are classified as poor and middle-class. Pessar finds that "pooled household, rather than individual, income enables many of the Dominican garment workers to maintain what they perceived is a middle-class standard of living" (Pessar, 1987:112). The middle-class families are likely to have a low ratio of dependency and more than one wage earner. Poor households normally show a high ratio of dependency and fewer wage earners. In addition, middle-class households are found to have a "better diet, housing furniture, and use of leisure time" than poor households.

Pessar's opportune attention to gender issues continues to advance some of Hendricks's ideas regarding Dominican women's adaptation and change of their social behavior once settled in the United States. Pessar contends that with "Dominican settlement in New York . . . . There has been a movement away from the hegemony of one sex over decision making and control of domestic resources to a *more egalitarian division of labor and distribution of authority*" (Pessar, 1987:120).[3] Pessar argues that paid labor nurtured a feminist mentality among Dominican women; her buying power provided her with the opportunity to make decisions over the family. In effect, because she believed that returning home to the Dominican Republic would curtail her new freedom, she deliberately postponed the family return, going against the wishes of her husband, who wanted to return to resume control of his family: "Because wage work has brought immigrant women many personal gains, including greater household authority and self-esteem, they are much more active agents than men in prolonging the household's stay in the United States. When they left the Dominican Republic, most women looked forward to going back to live. This orientation has changed in New York" (1987:123).

Alejandro Portes and Luis L. Guarnizo (1990) undertake the major final piece of research underlying family and kinship relationships among Dominicans in the United States post. As its title indicates, *Tropical Capitalists: U.S.-Bound Immigration and Small Enterprise Development in the Dominican Republic* proposes the upward socioeconomic mobility in the United States through the development of an ethnic entrepreneurial sector. The authors emphasize the commercial sector of Washington Heights in New York City and its linkages to a similar operation in the Dominican Republic. Portes and Guarnizo describe the social relations among Dominicans in Washington Heights that in their estimation form the bases for the formation and the outcomes of the Dominican entrepreneur sector. They highlight the solidarity and trust among members of the immigrant community. The resulting outcome—that is, the thriving and expanding entrepreneurial sector—is perceived as social capital of the community that expands to the Dominican Republic with returnee migrants (Portes and Guarnizo, 1990).

Current research invariably departs from the view that the Dominican family is transnational (Duany, 1994; Guarnizo, 1994; Levitt, 2001; Levitt and Waters, 2002; Pantoja, 2005; Rodriguez, 2009). Within that framework, scholars have paid attention to what has been classified as transnational practices exhibited by Dominicans in their everyday life in the receiving society.

One of the first to describe the Dominican family as transnational was anthropologist Jorge Duany, who defines transnationalism as the construction of dense social fields across national borders as a result of the circulation of people, ideas, practices, money, goods, and information (Duany, 2008:2). In Duany's view, though many immigrant groups can be characterized as transnational, "few immigrant communities have developed such a large number

---

[3]Emphasis added.

and variety of transnational ties to their country of origin, and have maintained such strong ties over several decades, as Dominicans in New York" (2008:8). The description of Dominicans as the quintessential transnational group is supported by other major proponents of Dominicans as transnational people (Levitt, 2001; Kasinitz, Mollenkopf, and Waters, 2002; Sagás and Molina, 2004).

Transnational practices, on the other hand, refer to the carrying over of traditional cultural values, norms, and social practices associated with the home country and maintained in the United States. In the case of the Dominican family, scholars have identified a number of Dominican cultural values and practices that have been transported by Dominican immigrants to the United States. Salient among these cultural belongings are values such as *respeto, familismo,* religion, language, and practices such as *machismo* and *marianismo* (Bailey, 2002; Calzada, Fernandez, and Cortes, 2010:77; Guilamo-Ramos, Dittus, and Jaccard, 2007:17; Rodriguez, 2009). These cultural legacies have their origins in the larger culture of Latin America, and, as expected, have been also found in the United States.

Until recently, the term *transnational* was applied to just adult Dominicans. Children of Dominican ancestry born and raised in the United States were not taken into account in transnational studies. Similarly, neither young children born in the Dominican Republic who grew up in the United States nor Dominicans who severed their ties with the sending country were considered by transnational scholars. Of course, such an analysis inadvertently created a dichotomized Dominican family with parents and other members who were perceived as transnational and children and other members who were left out of the paradigm.

Tracy Rodriguez looks at young adolescents of Dominican descent who the author classifies as transnational (Rodriguez, 2009). Rodriguez studied 15 second-generation Dominicans, conducting formal life history interviews in their homes. According to Rodriguez, transnational practices among Dominican adolescents are reflected in various ways, among them that "the youth chose to interact primarily with other Dominicans and identify themselves as Dominicans" (2009, 26). In addition, Rodriguez emphasizes that young Dominicans have a strong desire "to learn more about the Dominican Republic in school. This desire was connected to another important theme that emerged: the [sic] role that language (i.e., bilingualism) plays in their transnational schooling identities" (2009, 26). Rodriguez's research with Dominican-born adolescents in the United States establishes a link between parents and children filling an important vacuum in the understanding of the Dominican family as transnational.

A few important issues should be noted here: Although Dominicans have been dispersing intensely throughout the United States since the early 1990s and their rate of growth elsewhere is today much higher than in New York, the bulk of the research on Dominicans continues to be undertaken in New York, particularly in New York City. Within New York City, the Bronx has emerged as the center of much of the research, replacing the historic neighborhood of Washington Heights in Manhattan (Calzada and Cortes, 2010). Similarly, a new cadre of scholars and practitioners associated with mental health and social services have joined in with research that is helping to expand and shape the field of Dominican studies. There is a great deal of consistency among the various groups of researchers regarding the cultural values and social practices associated with Dominicans in the United States. In general, the cultural heritage includes the same values and practices identified with the group and held over time, from the pre-1980s to the current works on transnationalism. Invariably, all scholars find that Dominicans are pressed by the urgency to go home, by a commitment to send remittance, and by a need to remain in constant contact with the Dominican Republic. And all researchers also stress the vital role family plays in enabling Dominicans to settle, survive, and move forward.

As noted, most of this research focuses on Dominican immigrants and rarely on the second generation. It would be interesting to see whether the second generation will continue their parents' practices of linkages with the Dominican culture and, particularly, with the Dominican Republic.

Evaluating the Impacts of the Cultural Legacies in the Dominican Family: The Good and the Bad

A group of scholars contends that some of the cultural values carried over and upheld by Dominicans enable them to successfully socialize their young children. In a study with Dominican and Mexican mothers of preschool children in the Bronx in New York City, Calzada and Cortes (2010) found, for instance, that these mothers' understanding and teaching of *respeto* to their children served as a mechanism to instill in the children tolerance and appreciation for others "*Respeto* is to be shown to all others, regardless of age or gender. Contrary to the traditional notion of *respeto* as strictly hierarchical, mothers described *respeto* as a broader construe in which respectful behavior towards peers is also important" (2010:81–82). A Dominican mother in the same study explains her views about the importance of respect in the following way: "One struggles so much to inculcate that respect of behaving well, of listening to their elders, of listening to their parents when we speak to them, that is the ultimate goal" (2010:81). As Calzada and Cortes suggest, this cultural value comes in handy in a society that, known for its lack of tolerance, has spent the last fifty years trying to overcome such a shortcoming.

Similarly, Guilamo-Ramos et al. (2007) stress the usefulness of familism in fostering a good relationship among Dominican and Puerto Rican mothers and their adolescent children. Valuing family helps members to be there for each other but, more important, it aids in avoiding the well-known wars in American culture between teenagers and their parents. Familism is explained through the understanding that family members must get along and be mutually supportive and responsible for each other. Guilamo-Ramos et al. point out that "Culturally competent social workers should understand the importance of family and the care-giving role for many Latina mothers . . . . Helping mothers and adolescents find ways to spend mutually rewarding time together can not only improve the parent-adolescent relationship, but can also help to alleviate any concerns mothers may have about not being able to spend more time with their adolescent children" (2007:27).

Scholars have found that Dominican families in the United States believe in holding on to Spanish and in transmitting it to their children. As with other Latino subgroups, encouraging children of Dominican descent to speak Spanish reinforces the sense of family—familism—here in the United States among the group as well as the links to family members and people in general in the Dominican Republic. Researchers believe that for Dominicans keeping the language means keeping the connection with the Dominican Republic, presumably emphasizing the transnational nature of the group (Duany, 2008).

Other scholars have argued that some of the cultural values upheld by Dominicans in the United States inhibit children's adaptation to American mainstream society and encourage sexist practices that are detrimental to women. Salient among these cultural traditions are *marianismo and machismo. Marianismo*, a description of women's character in Latin America that was first put forward by Stevens (1973) and that portrays women as faithfully devoted to Virgin Mary's moral standing and committed to follow a life in her image: of pure sexual chastity until marriage, of viewing herself primarily and foremost as a mother, as a wife devoted to her husband who controls and restricts her movements, as a caretaker, and as willing to commit enormous sacrifice in favor of her family and her marriage.

Machismo, on the other hand, in its popularized American version,[4] is the antithesis of *marianismo* and ascribes a number of unflattering traits to men in Latin American, describing them as chauvinistic, authoritarian, possessive, dictatorial, with a sense of superiority over women, and entitled to control women's life in general. Some observers argue that young women in Dominican families are driven into mental anguish by what they describe as a conflict between the imposition of Dominican cultural traditions carried over, particularly those associated with the binary *marianismo/machismo,* and the young women's desire to follow American culture, which is presumably free of the ills of *marianismo/machismo* (Inoa Vazquez & Gil, 1996). The American culture and the Dominican culture are perceived as representing two worlds, the first new and the former old. The common belief is that the two cultural worlds clash, and that young Dominican women who want to free themselves from restricting and imposing Dominican norms are caught in between and are pushed sometimes to commit suicide (Editorial, 2006).

The understanding among scholars is that the value of familism as understood and practiced by Dominicans involves a relationship among people that goes beyond blood-related members. According to these authors, the sense of family is intertwined with the community. In their eyes, thanks to this beyond-family solidarity, Dominicans find jobs, create jobs, take care of their children, pool their income together, presumably move ahead, and if not, enable themselves to survive as an interconnected ethnic group in the United States as well as the homeland. One could argue that the attachment to the home country—both physically through trips and remittance as well as through the abstract symbolism of Dominicans' insistence in preserving their cultural practices—laid the foundation of the next horizon in migration studies, transnationalism, which according to a new generation of scholars characterizes the Dominican people in the United States. But a question worth asking at this point is, to what extent are Dominicans in the United States holding on to cultural values and practices that have been transformed in Dominican society? If that is the case, how do we reconcile what Dominicans practice in the United States and what people practice in the Dominican Republic? Let us take, for instance, the values of familism and solidarity, which scholars believe are brought by Dominicans.

Scholars have described the social relationships among people in the Dominican Republic who are not related by blood but who consider themselves part of a big family. This extensive relationship among people is smartly described by anthropologist Tahira Vargas in *De la Casa a la Calle,* an ethnographic study of daily life of residents in a neighborhood in the city of Santo Domingo (Vargas, 1998). In her study Vargas found that "[i]n the social fabric, social relations weigh much more than individual practice. Which everyday life practices are performed individually? Almost none; they are almost imperceptible. The presence of networks in everyday life reflects this dynamic. One does not find relations or norms that isolate but on the contrary"[5] (1998:54).

---

[4]Although the origins of the term *machismo* may be traced to feminist writings in the United States during the 1940s, the use of the term in Latin America prior to the 1940s has various connotations, including a meaning applicable to male animals or plants as well as benign descriptions of men's social behavior (such as opening the door for a woman; sleeping to the side of the bed closer to the door to confront the potential robber who might enter the home's bedroom uninvited; when walking on the street, taking the side of the sidewalk closer to the road to protect the woman from potential accidents and from harassment; whenever stepping off the side walk, the man holds the woman delicately by the elbow to ensure that she does not trip and fall) and men's sexist behavior against women.

[5]Author's translation from Spanish.

Social networks among Dominican families have functionality, and Vargas clearly describes it through the use of a new concept that she believes captures the dynamics between mothers and children in the neighborhood. Vargas uses the term *medianamente solos* (partially alone) to refer to small children who are left alone in the house by their mothers, without the company of an adult, but whose mothers, however, believe that the children are not quite alone since they are being watched by the female and mother neighbors who live on the same street and who diligently keep an eye on the kids from their own homes while the mother of the kids is out (Vargas, 1998:111). The same author points out that the network of support is implicit in a collective understanding of norms and values that do not need to be written, verbalized, or expressed in any other formal way; they are expressed in everyday practice itself (1998:112).

The preceding depiction is what Hendricks (1974) described as what he observed among Dominicans in Vicente Noble (and itself a source of today's massive migration, highly gender specific, of Dominican women to Spain), the town in the Dominican Republic he studied, and the Dominican families he observed in Queens, New York. But the practice was common among rural Dominicans and the urban poor who often started as migrants in Dominican society. This practice was not common among the privileged social classes whose houses have always been quite detached one from another and have had doors that are hermetically closed to outsiders and backyards that are gated. Family practices have changed, although the concept of family may be as important as it used to be in the 1950s when Dominican society had fewer than 1 million people, the majority of them rural and subjected to a brutal dictatorship where most men and most women could not afford to even think about moving around without surveillance.

During the last fifty years, Dominican society has been characterized by rapid urbanization, industrialization, increasing inequality, and, consequently, increasing violence, just to mention a few changes. In 1950, the Dominican Republic had fewer than 2 million people, and by 1990 the population had increased to over 7 million. Homicides alone increased—for example, from 9.2 percent in 1984 to 22.8 percent in 2007 (Oficina Nacional de Estadísticas de la República Dominicana, 2010). All these changes have affected, if not the understanding of family, at least how family relations are practiced. Family may continue to be extended and compounded, but the extension may no longer expand to the street and the neighborhood. It is common sense today not to trust neighbors, for one does not know really who lives next door. Increasing population expands neighborhoods and leads to an inability of working people to get to know everyone who lives nearby. And the poor no longer keep their doors open for they are afraid of visitors who are not necessarily that friendly anymore. And of course, the incorporation of women into paid labor demands rearrangements for taking care of children that go beyond voluntarism and altruism.[6]

This is to say that whatever values Dominicans may have been holding and transmitting to their children in the United States may, in fact, represent values and practices that have gone and continue to go through a transformation process in the Dominican Republic. In addition, U.S. Dominicans may be transmitting a memorialized cultural legacy, with all of the implications that such an action may imply. The neighborhood in Santo Domingo Vargas (1998) described in her study has not been exempted from these transformations. On the contrary, Vargas studied an urban, working, low-class neighborhood, the kind of place that is most likely to be affected by the incorporation of women into free trade zones that generate a whole restructuring of neighborhood functioning. In other words, when a woman took a job that kept her a good ten hours away from home, she needed a social arrangement to take care of her children for longer—when formerly she

---

[6]In 1980, 31.1 percent of Dominican women worked, and by 1991 the percentage increased to 39.6 percent (Quehaceres, 1993).

did not work and had neighbors supervise her children for free while she went out for a short time. In fact, the new arrangement may have converted the neighbor into a paid worker whose job was to mind the children of mothers who went to work. Did solidarity among Dominicans disappear? What about Vargas's (1998) theory of children who were never alone but *medianamente solos* with adults present, particularly in relation to women's solidarity in the neighborhood? I believe that solidarity still exists among members of this neighborhood or among Dominicans for that matter. Without it, it would be virtually impossible to have a cohesive group that shares a common understanding. What needs to be understood, however, is how that solidarity reflects throughout time and changes rather than to assume a given manifestation in a quasi-fixed state.

Furthermore, evidence points to changes in how Dominicans in the United States organize themselves inside their homes. Figure 10.5 shows the percentage of Dominican families living in households in the United States and New York City from 1970, to 2008. In 1970, Dominican households were mostly composed of family members: 90.5 and 89.1 percent of Dominican households contained family members in the United States and New York City respectively. By 2008, those percentages had declined to 79.0 percent and 78 percent correspondingly. Similarly, the percentage of Dominicans residing in nonfamily households doubled during the same years for the United States as well as for New York City. Contrary to established wisdom, most Dominican households in the United States have been composed of a single family instead of extended and compounded families. Figure 10.6 compares number of families per household from 1970 to 2008 for both the United States and New York City. The comparison shows that there has been basically no variation regarding the number of families per household in the years under study. In 1970, in the United States almost 9 in 10 households were composed of one family and less than 2 in 10 had two families or more. In 2008, the number of families per household in the United States remained practically unchanged. Although households composed of a single family predominate in the United States between 1970 and 2008, the opposite is true for the Dominican Republic, where households are predominantly composed of extended and compounded families.

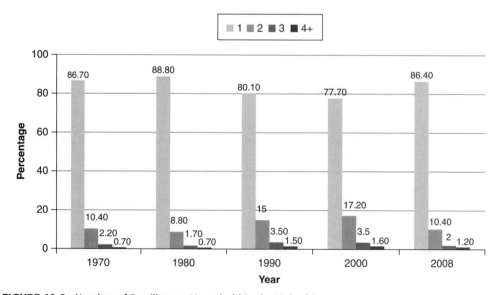

FIGURE 10.6 Number of Families per Household in the United States

Sources: 1970 1% IPUMS; 1980, 1990, 2000 5% IPUMS; 2008 American Community Survey.

Data from a national survey in the Dominican Republic confirms the following: Although over one-third of households in the lower social class were composed of extended and compounded families, almost 1 in 2 households in the middle and upper social classes had similar family compositions (Tejada Holguin, 1996:24).[7] The comparative analysis reflects that Dominican households in the United States appear to be transforming and adopting the nuclear family standard model of the United States and are moving away from the extended family standard model of the Dominican Republic.

Finally, Vargas's (1998) study includes an important observation about the limits of solidarity in the Santo Domingo neighborhood. When neighbors close their main entrance door, the action puts an immediate end to the solidarity shared with people in the street: "Closing the door produces an immediate rupture with a collective life in the street" (1998:148). Thus, what appears to be a quasi and idyllic place in terms of solidarity among people also has its mechanisms for creating distance. Dominican society has changed, and people have found themselves compelled to keep their main entrance door hermetically closed—as wealthy people do.

The reality of closed doors became more dramatic when Dominicans came to the United States. They went to live in urban neighborhoods, and the largest majority went to live in the most urban city of the United States, New York City. In New York City, they lived in buildings where they found an established culture of inside and outside, divided by a closed main door. Dominicans learned that the "police lock," which they renamed as *polilakar,* was the strongest lock of all and ensured their safety inside once the door was closed. They also learned that all visitors, family or not, needed to knock hard at the door to be heard and that no one opened the door before looking though the "magic eye." Life in New York City brought a new understanding to Dominicans: Although the unknown existed behind each door, the space outside the door was remarkably similar to the extent that the streets were dangerous and children were no longer allowed to play on it without adult supervision.

Yet in spite of this reality, the fact remains that Dominicans have managed to create vibrant communities that are distinctly marked with Dominican symbolism and where outsiders observe a sense of community and togetherness that many believe enables Dominicans to move forward as a group. This of course, seems to be in direct opposition to the distance among people nurtured by the new reality. For now let us say that an answer to the puzzle should include the experiences confronted in the new society, a culture left behind that no longer is what it used to be, and the needs and desires of the Dominican people to build a new life much better than the one they had.

Marital Status of Family and Gender Role: Cultural Legacy and Change

Glenn Hendricks (1974) predicted that immigration requirements were going to push Dominicans into formal marriage in the United States and away from the traditional consensual unions found in the Dominican Republic. Patricia Pessar (1987) argued that Dominican women acquire a feminist mentality when they migrate to the United States. The migration process allows women to leave behind in the Dominican Republic a life of male control. How much has marital status changed through time among Dominicans? And to what extent has women's mentality changed in the United States from conservative to feminist?

U.S. Census data show that Hendricks's predictions have not materialized (Table 10.2). From 1970 to 2008, the percentage of Dominican married households in the United States, with

---

[7]Extended family includes a nuclear family and family members of one member of the couple. Compounded family includes extended family and other members who may or may not be related by blood or document to the nuclear family.

TABLE 10.2 Marital Status of Dominicans in the United States and New York City: 1970–2008

	1970		1980		1990		2000		2008	
	USA	NYC	USA	NYC	USA	NYC	USA	NYC	USA	NYC
Married, Spouse Present	34.4%	35%	40.9%	38.3%	26.3%	23.6%	27.7%	25.4%	23.2%	19.5%
Married, Spouse Absent	3.7%	3.6%	7.9%	8.4%	6.5%	6.7%	6.2%	6.7%	5.5%	6.3%
Separated	3.2%	3.7%	6.5%	7.2%	5.6%	6.4%	5.6%	6.4%	4.8%	6.1%
Divorced	2.9%	2.8%	6.7%	7%	7.9%	8.1%	8.2%	8.4%	8.2%	8.5%
Widowed	2.2%	2.3%	3.7%	4%	2.4%	2.7%	2.2%	2.4%	3.1%	3.4%
Never Married, Single	53.5%	52.8%	34.3%	35.1%	51.3%	52.5%	50.2%	50.8%	55.3%	56.1%

Sources: 1970 1% IPUMS; 1980, 1990, 2000 5% IPUMS; 2008 American Community Survey.

Note: 1970 only for New York State.

spouse present or not, declined from 38.1 percent to 28.7 percent. Similar declines were seen in Dominican married households in New York City, with 38.6 percent in 1970 to 25.8 percent in 2008 (see Table 10.2). Although the rate of marriage has gone down, in general, the proportion of homes headed by a single person who has never married has been on the rise. In New York City, for instance, homes headed by a single person, never married, increased from 52.8 percent in 1970 to 56.1 percent in 2008 (Hernández & Rivera-Batiz, 2003; Hernández & Argeros, 2010).

When disaggregating by sex the "single-headed" or "never-married" Dominican families, one finds that the proportion of persons living in families headed by women is substantially higher than in any other marital category. Among Dominicans in the United States, almost 1 in 2 families in 1970 was headed by a single woman. The proportion was similar for New York City during the same year. In 2008, female single-headed families increased to 42.2 percent and 51.2 percent, respectively, for the United States and New York City. Yet, Dominicans are not alone in these patterns. While the overall percentage of households with married couples has been declining in New York City, households headed by single women have been on the rise, particularly among non-Hispanic Black and Puerto Rican women. It is difficult to assess from these numbers whether Dominicans are forming households according to patterns in New York or in the Dominican Republic since both places seem to follow similar trends in this regard. For now it may be safer to say that Dominicans seem to maintain certain family practices in the United States—such as single female head of household—which, as will be shown next, continue to prevail in the Dominican Republic and that are, at the same time, common in U.S. society.

To the liberating effects caused by living in the United States, I would like to juxtapose women's centrality in the Dominican family and, consequently, the mentality such a position may generate.

Regarding Pessar's (1987) suggestion concerning the liberating effects that living in the United States presumably bring to Dominican women, I would like to remind the reader of women's centrality in the Dominican family and, consequently, the mentality such a position may generate. In addition, as previously explained, in Dominican society the proportion of homes headed by women has increased dramatically in the last decades and now represents a significant proportion of Dominican families. As noted, while women's headship has risen, men's leadership has declined precipitously. These are drastic changes that have an impact on the entire fabric of society and transform people's mentality, including how they understand the family and the role each member plays.

The high rates and historic nature of female headship defy the perception of the Dominican family as a social space under the command of men and confirms more diversity and flexibility regarding leadership roles in the family. Pablo Tactuk (2007) correctly argues that "women's increasing headship of homes is a social phenomenon that has changed the profile of many Dominican homes, *feminizing*[8] the basic structure of society: the family" (2007:1). Tactuk is not alone in his observation regarding the Dominican family. Some have argued that men's leadership role, particularly the role as economic provider, has become a myth in Latin America and the Caribbean as a result of women's increasing participation in paid labor and the rise of homes and families headed by single women (Safa, 1995).

In 1995, anthropologist Helen Safa argued that female-headed homes promoted women's independence from men. Women's home headship, she argued, served as a platform for women to sharpen their decision-making-power skills as they were likely to make all the decisions on their own concerning the family or the entire household (Safa, 1995). Female heads of families may also represent the matrilocal family characterized by the emphasis placed on the bond

---

[8]Author's translation from Spanish. Emphasis added.

between mother and child over that of the father and child, women's important economic contribution to support the family, and the reduction of women's reliance on the male breadwinner (1995:56). Safa contends, however, that Caribbean "women have been unable to translate their importance at the domestic level into greater equality for women at the public level" (1995:56).

Prior to Safa's contentions regarding the limitations of women's control of the public sphere, sociologist Carmen Julia Gómez (1990) had theorized about the social impact of women's home-headship for patriarchal domination in Dominican society. Gómez formulates her ideas in a small book, *La problemática de las jefas de hogar: evidencia de la insubordinación social de las mujeres: magnitud, causas de su presencia y sus características,* published in 1990, in which she argued that the high prevalence of female-headed families/homes called for an explanation that perceived the phenomenon beyond the individual/personal decision and more as a social practice. Gómez contended that female headship as found in the Dominican Republic reflected a representation of a *social insubordination* that openly defied Dominican society's moral tradition that perceived matrimony as a sacrosanct value. For Gómez, *social insubordination* represented a collective manifestation of resistance against patriarchy domination (Gómez, 1990). Gómez has expanded Susan Brown's (1975) interpretation of Dominican women's preference for establishing consensual unions instead of legal matrimony by developing a frame of reference that permits the understanding of women's action from a larger context within Dominican society—the struggle between the sexes—and beyond the view of an action that results strictly from economic circumstances (Duarte & Gómez, 1987).

Finally, although socioeconomic changes (industrialization, urbanization, etc.) have undoubtedly contributed to the formation of homes headed by women in most societies, in the Dominican Republic the presence of this type of home is inherently connected to core cultural practices and norms. Anthropologist Susan Brown (1975), for instance, one of the first scholars to conduct research and write about rural women in the Dominican Republic, concluded that consensual union was a form of mating *preferred* and sustained by women who belonged to the poor social classes (1975:329). Legal matrimony was perceived as a permanent form of union but the consensual type was not. Brown's research sought to correct social scientists who condemned consensual union for presumably corrupting the moral fabric of the family. Brown said, "[M]y own research confirmed . . . that having various male mates in a serial fashion is a major means by which women cope with their difficult socioeconomic circumstances" (1975:324). In addition, the fact that those single women–headed homes are not among the poorest leaves one to conclude that this type of women's home not only openly challenges traditional views that postulate males as heads of homes but also indicates that the overall mentality of Dominican society must be influenced by women's ideas/ideals that value their kind, given the centrality of family in the socialization of individuals and women's role in Dominican family.

I would like to borrow Gómez's theory of "collective manifestation of insubordination" that provides an abstract frame of reference portraying women in the Dominican family as active agents in society, capable of undertaking subversive actions such as privileging informal unions over legal matrimony. This is to say that women in the Dominican family may or may not possibly transmit onto their children social practices that may be detrimental to women keeping them subordinated. No doubt Dominican women continue to exercise some control of their households in New York City, as reported by Hendricks (1974) and Pessar (1987) decades ago. The agency they saw among Dominican women was present in the homes they observed. Women's true colors have been shown as well by the fact that they are the first ones to migrate—hence they desire to control their return—and that they are likely to come from, or have been exposed to, families under the leadership of women rather than men.

THE BENEFIT OF MIGRATION AND ECONOMIC STANDING

As we have seen, most researchers have concluded that migration to the United States has pro-vided Dominicans with economic benefits. In the past I argued against what I thought was a mechanistic conclusion lacking an understanding of the mobility of workers within a capitalist orbit; I also thought it constantly reduced the value of workers and converted them into a redun-dant population that faced prolonged unemployment and high levels of poverty. I argued that migrant workers epitomized that process (Hernández, 2002). How have Dominican families really done economically since migration?

Figure 10.7 compares total family income for three Dominican household subgroups—married couple, female headed, and other—for the United States for various decades. Invariably, Figure 10.7 shows that married-couple households have higher income levels for all the years included than do female-headed households, which in turn have higher shares in the lower-income category (below $15,000). In 1980, for instance, 5 in 10 married-couple households in the United States had income of less than $15,000 per year as compared to almost 8 in 10 of the female headed and other householders. As expected, married-couple households also have three times more representation in the highest-income category ($75,000 and above) as compared to the two other householder groups.

Income measurement does not reveal much about the economic status of a group unless it is compared to other income of other groups. In addition, measuring per capita income provides a more accurate picture of the economic standing of the household since it takes into account the number of people who reside in the household as well as the total income. Table 10.3 categorizes the household income for various population groups in New York City for the years 1989, 1999, and 2007. It shows that Dominicans had a 16 percent increase in income in the 1990s, compared

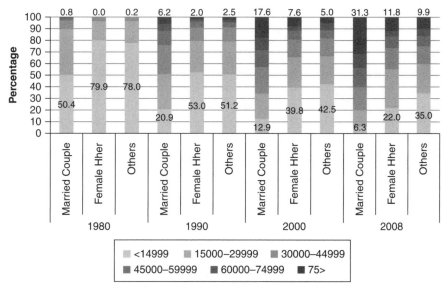

FIGURE 10.7 Total Dominican Household Income—United States: 1980–2008

Sources: 1980, 1990, 2000 5% IPUMS; 2008 American Community Survey.

TABLE 10.3   Mean Per Capital Household Income— New York City: 1989–2007

	1989	1999	2007
Dominicans	$ 8,659	$10,032	$15,516
NYC Overall	$21,991	$24,010	$27,859
Non-Hispanic White	$31,026	$37,391	$32,160
Non-Hispanic Black	$14,573	$15,367	$18,740
Non-Hispanic Asian	$18,189	$19,533	$30,480
Hispanic/Latino	$11,515	$12,500	$16,799

Sources: 1990, 2000 5% PUMS; 2008 American Community Survey.

to 9.2 percent for the New York City population overall. Still, Dominican income gains pale in comparison to those of the non-Hispanic White population, whose income per capita increased by over 20 percent in the 1990s. Even among Hispanics/Latinos, the per capita income of Dominicans was 25 percent lower in 1999 than the average for Hispanics/Latinos in New York. In 2007, the gains for Dominicans continued, showing a 54 percent increase, compared to 1999, the second-highest increase after non-Hispanic Asians who had an increase of 56 percent in the same year. But the income of Dominicans continued to be one-half of the income of non-Hispanic Whites and the *lowest* income of all the groups compared in 2007.

The comparatively low income of Dominican New Yorkers is reflected in high poverty rates. Table 10.4 compares the poverty rate for various groups and various years in New York City. As reflected in the table, about 1 of every 3 Dominicans in New York City lived in households with income under the poverty line. In fact, in each consecutive year compared, Dominicans had the highest proportion of families living below the poverty line in New York City.

The data presented in Tables 10.3 and 10.4 challenge the affirmation that migration to the United States has unequivocally been beneficial for Dominican families. Before Dominicans left, particularly during the largest wave of migration in the 1980s, between 30 and 40 percent of families lived below the poverty line in the Dominican Republic. When Dominicans arrived in the United States, especially to New York City where the largest majority went to live, the group faced unexpectedly high poverty levels and very quickly became the poorest group in the city (Ojito, 1997:B1). According to the U.S. Census Bureau, at least one-third of Dominican families have

TABLE 10.4   Family Poverty Rate—New York City: 1980–2008

Population Groups	1980	1990	1996	2008*
Dominicans	36.0%	36.6%	45.7%	28.0%
Total Overall Population	18.0%	17.2%	23.8%	17.6%
Non-Hispanic White	8.7%	8.2%	11.2%	10.4%
Non-Hispanic Black	28.3%	22.9%	33.1%	19.8%
Hispanic/Latino	35.0%	31.4%	37.2%	25.1%

Sources: 1980, 1990, and 1996, Hernández (2004:99); 2008, American Community Survey.

*A different methodological process was used to calculate the percentage for 2008.

been living below the poverty line for the past three decades (Hernández and Rivera-Batiz, 2003). But this data does not include, of course, those Dominicans who do not want to be counted and those who are systematically missed by census enumerators or analysts.

From a moral point of view, any poverty rate is high, for it embodies people whose basic needs are unmet. But the poverty rate for Dominicans is way too high for an immigrant group who most have described as doing well economically. It is that researchers miscalculated the economic standing of the Dominican people?

Scholars who have studied Dominicans in the United States evaluate the economic standing of Dominicans in the United States as compared to the previous economic status these Dominicans had when they lived in the native land. Scholars also think of social classes in the Dominican Republic and extrapolate the meaning of being poor or middle class there to Dominicans' present situation in the United States. Of course, the analogy is not accurate for it tells us very little, if anything, about how Dominicans—after migrating—compare to other groups in the society where they currently live and spend much of their life; nor does it tell us exactly what Dominican families have access to with the amount of income they generate. For now, we may conclude that migration to the United States has been beneficial to Dominicans to the extent that a proportion of them are doing relatively and progressively better, particularly when compared to other Dominicans who live in the United States. The hope is that the second generation will outperform their parents not only when compared to them—for their parents are in the lowest ranks of society—but when compared to other similar groups and other citizens of the United States, the society where they were born and will likely spend the rest of their lives.

TRANSNATIONAL PRACTICES AND ROOTING FIRMLY IN THE NEW ABODE

For some, what today is called transnational practices, or the concrete manifestations of attachment to home cultural values, have kept Dominicans from rooting firmly in the United States. Roger Waldinger (1986) found that the transient mentality among Dominican small business owners interfered with the group's ability to see itself as permanent settlers. Waldinger suggested that transience prevented Dominican entrepreneurs from achieving levels of success similar to the Chinese who were in the same line of business (1986:182–183). In the words of Sherri Grasmuck and Patricia Pessar (1991), transnationalism has kept Dominicans living in two places. They conclude, "The fact that our informants identified themselves as middle-class and drew on Dominican-based references in arriving at this self attribution is emblematic of the fact that Dominicans do indeed live between two islands"[9] (Grasmuck and Pessar, 1991:196–197). Living between two islands has negative consequences for it encourages Dominicans to supplant Manhattan's New York reality, the place where they live, for that of Dominican society, where they do not live.

Similarly, mental health practitioners believe that the Dominican family's attachment to the social practices of *marianismo and machismo* is detrimental to young Dominican women who want to assimilate into U.S. culture. The corresponding understanding among these observers is that U.S. culture is free of both social practices. That young Dominican women

---

[9]The phrase "two islands" makes reference to the island of Manhattan in New York City and the island of Española. Española is the name given by Spaniards to the island that today houses the Dominican Republic and the Republic of Haiti.

experience symptoms of depression and other mental disorders and diseases for which they seek help is a reality—and a discussion beyond the scope of this monograph. We are concerned here, however, with three issues: (1) a view of men and women in Dominican culture that does not match with the reality in Dominican society, (2) an oversimplification of Dominican culture, perceived as static and in which sixteenth-century beliefs remain constant among people, and (3) an overestimation of U.S. culture, seeing it as having progressed and banished all forms of sexist practices against women.

In the United States as well as in the Dominican Republic, control of a woman's body has been at the top of the list in the women's movement. The right to have or not have children has been a priority for women in their struggle. Today one finds that women in the Dominican Republic have a lot of control in deciding when and when not to have children. The national surveys on population and health reveal, for example, that a woman's own desire to have children, rather than her partner's desire or her religious convictions, explains her decision to refrain from using birth control. In 1991, 25.5 percent of women selected her "desire to have more children" as the reason behind her decision not to use any birth control methods as compared to 1.7 percent because of "partner disapproval" and 3.0 percent because of "religious beliefs." In 1996, responses remain similar, reflecting 25.9 percent, 2.5 percent, and 2.1 percent, respectively (República Dominicana Encuesta Demográfica y de Salud [ENDESA], 1991:61; 1996:65).

The fact that the decline in fertility has been accompanied by an increase in women's incorporation into the labor force, particularly in jobs related to industrial production in free trade zones, and that the decision to use or not to use birth-control methods has been in the hands of women, not those of their partners, enables us to create a picture of a Dominican woman who at least at the private level is much more in control of her body and her family. What remains to be seen is how much of that agency trespasses the limits of the larger Dominican society, whether in a subversive mode, as suggested by Gómez (1990), or in an open manner, though neither visible nor discussed, through the socialization of her children in the absence of their fathers (in homes headed by single women).

Although there are those who blame Dominican cultural values and social practices for keeping them unable to permanently establish themselves in the new society, others evaluate Dominicans' presumed cultural attachment as enabling the group to fit into U.S. culture. The latter describe a Dominican family that takes the best of its own cultural values and the best of U.S. cultural heritage and creates a new way to socialize the children. Calzada, Fernández, and Cortés (2010) explain that in the Dominican Republic *respeto* may be identified with children's straight-forward obedience and unquestioning attitude toward parents and elders, for instance, whereas Dominican mothers in New York, "in contrast to parents in their country of origins, are more likely to balance *respect* with communication" (Calzada et al., 2010:84). The balancing act of Dominican mothers with regard to an American cultural value (children's ability to question parents through communication) and a Dominican cultural value (children's unquestioned sense of respect for their parents) results in controlled assimilation[10] into U.S. culture and, in the eyes of the researchers, a process that in the end enables Dominican mothers to exercise valuable parenting skills.

Duany (2008) has argued that the Spanish language keeps Dominicans rooted in the cultural values of the home country. Other scholars have found that among the largest immigrant groups, second-generation Dominicans have the highest language retention level (Alba, 2004). In

---

[10]Some scholars argue that the second generation may assimilate into different segments of U.S. society (i.e., standard middle class, ethnic middle class, racial underclass).

general, keeping a second language is perceived as an asset. Of course, needless to say, we concur with those who see an added value in speaking two languages, particularly in a world of multiple contacts that seems to be obsessed with communication. It would be important to add that Dominicans may feel compelled for now also to keep the Spanish language because of pragmatic reasons. Census data indicate that in 2000 almost 1 in 2 Dominicans twenty-five years of age or older did not speak English well and that almost one-third of the same group did not speak English at all (Hernández and Rivera-Batiz, 2003). Not only is Spanish the only possible means of communication among family members who are likely to have a precarious grasp of English, but it is also the language for communicating with family members in the Dominican Republic, a country whose only language is Spanish. This is to say that practicing the language reminds us of transnational practices, but keeping the Spanish language is also an asset as it is for now the only way many Dominicans communicate among themselves, including many parents with their young children.

CONCLUSION

The Dominican family who left the Dominican Republic for the United States reconstructed life in the new country. Many families came with the intention of returning home after a finite period of time but ended up taking root and staying for good in a society that, coincidentally, was not necessarily hoping for these families to call the United States their home.

It is clear that women in Dominican society have been less passive and subordinated to men than what many thought they were. This is not difficult to see for oppression *always* carries resistance within. Obviously, there are *marianista* and *machista* practices in every society in which men continue to hold the larger share of power and resources, and some young Dominican women in the United States may be trapped by old patriarchal social norms and practices, as suggested by some practitioners. Yet when we consider Dominicans in the United States at large, these old traditions are not a replication of what their parents brought from home, crystallized in their memories as they may have been. And Dominicans' traditions in the United States have not escaped the inexorable dynamics of the new space and the passing of time.

Before migration, the Dominican family revolves around women. Women initiate the relocation of the family to the United States, and Pessar (1987) found that women control the return, and if not, they want to have a say about it. Similarly, in the United States a significant proportion of homes are headed by single women, and that, in effect, as has been argued, continues to give women centrality in their family. We hypothesize that, as in the Dominican Republic, the children of these families are likely to be raised in a more egalitarian manner in which children learn that women, not just men, also make decisions concerning the fate of the family.

As Calzada, Fernández, and Cortés suggest, Dominican mothers in New York City have found ways to adjust Dominican cultural values and practices into a new understanding that does not look like what they may once have practiced; nor does it look like what most Americans value and practice today. Dominicans in the United States have created their own cultural legacy, with its own sins and its own virtues. Creating something new as immigrants or children of immigrants does not have to imply that it is better or worse as compared to the Dominican Republic or the United States.

Migration has provided the Dominican family with the opportunity to reinvent itself within the constant endeavor that presupposes change, adaptation, and resistance to let go of what was once known. In the end that daily effort produces a U.S. Dominican family that is dynamic and continues to mold and shape itself according to space and time.

References

Alba, R. 2004. "Language Assimilation Today: Bilingualism Persists More Than in the Past, but English Still Dominates." Working Papers, Center for Comparative Immigration Studies, UC San Diego.

Bailey, B. 2002. *Language, Race, and Negotiation of Identity: A Study of Dominican Americans.* New York: LFB Scholarly Publishers.

Brown, S. E. 1975. "Love Unites Them and Hunger Separates Them: Poor Women in the Dominican Republic." In R. R. Reiter (Ed.), *Toward an Anthropology of Women* (pp. 322–332). New York: Monthly Review Press.

Centro de Investigación para la acción Femenina (CIPAF). "Mujeres Latinoamericanas en Cifras." Quehaceres, Año 13, Enero de 1993. Unidad de Investigación de República Dominicana, Proyecto Mujeres Latinoamericanas en Cifras, 1993. Santo Domingo, Republica Dominicana.

Calzada, E. J., and D. Cortes. 2010. "Incorporating the Cultural Value of Respeto into a Framework of Latino Parenting." *Cultural Diversity and Ethnic Minority Psychology 16*(1), 81–82.

Calzada, E. J., Y. Fernández, and D. E. Cortés. 2010. "Incorporating the Cultural Value of Respeto into a Framework of Latino Parenting." *Cultural Diversity and Ethnic Minority Psychology 16*(1), 77–86.

Duany, J. 1994. "El Impacto de la Inmigración Extranjera en el Mercado Laboral de Puerto Rico." *Homines 17* (1–2), 241–252.

———. 2008. *Quisqueya on the Hudson: The Transnational Identity of Dominicans in Washington Heights.* New York: CUNY Dominican Studies Institute.

Duarte, I., and C. J. Gómez. 1987. La familia en la República Dominicana: tendencias y caracteristicas. *Población y Desarrollo, VI* (20), 3–22.

Editorial. 2006, July 21. "Young Latinas and a Cry for Help." *New York Times.* www.nytimes.com/2006/07/21/opinion/21fri3.html (accessed April 16, 2011).

Gómez, C. J. 1990. "*La problemática de las jefas de hogar: evidencia de la insubordinación social de las mujeres: magnitud, causas de su presencia y sus características.*" Centro de Investigación para la acción Femenina (CIPAF). Santo Domingo, Republica Dominicana.

González, N. L. 1970. "Peasants' Progress: Dominicans in New York." *Caribbean Studies 10*(3), 154–171.

Grasmuck, S., and P. Pessar. 1991. *Between Two Islands: Dominican International Migration.* Berkeley: University of California Press.

Guarnizo, L. E. 1994. "Los Dominicanyorks: The Making of a Binational Society." *Annals of the American Academy of Political and Social Sciences 533,* 70–86.

Guilamo-Ramos, V., P. Dittus, J. Jaccard, M. Johansson, A. Bouris, and N. Acosta. 2007. "Parenting Practices Among Dominican and Puerto Rican Mothers." *National Association of Social Workers 52*(1), 17–30.

Hendricks, G. 1974. *The Dominican Diaspora: From the Dominican Republic to New York City—Villagers in Transition.* New York: Teachers College Press.

Hernández, R. 2002. *The Mobility of Workers Under Advanced Capitalism.* New York: Columbia University Press.

Hernández, R., and F. Rivera-Batiz. 2003. *Dominicans in the United States: A Socioeconomic Profile, 2000.* Dominican Research Monograph Series. New York: The CUNY-Dominican Studies Institute. (ongoing research of data from the U.S. Census Bureau, authors' tabulations).

———. 2004. "On the Age of the Poor: Dominican Migration to the United States." *Immigrants and Social Work: Thinking Beyond the Borders of the United States.* 87–107. The Hayworth Press.

Hernández, R., and G. Argeros. 2010. *Dominicans in the United States: A Socioeconomic Profile, 2010.* CUNY Dominican Studies Institute (ongoing research of data from the U.S. Census Bureau, authors' tabulations: on file with author). New York.

Inoa Vazquez, C., and R. M. Gil. 1996. *The Maria Paradox: How Latinas Can Merge Old World Traditions with New World Self-Esteem.* New York: G.P. Putnam.

Instituto de Estudios de Población y Desarrollo, (PROFAMILIA); Oficina Nacional de Publicación; Demographic and Health Surveys IRD/Macro International Inc. 1991. "Encuesta Demográfica y de Salud 1991 (ENDESA)." Santo Domingo, Republica Dominicana. 61.

Instituto de Estudios de Población y Desarrollo, (PROFAMILIA); Oficina Nacional de Publicación; Demographic and Health Surveys IRD/Macro International Inc. 1996. "Encuesta Demográfica y de Salud 1991 (ENDESA)." Santo Domingo, Republica Dominicana. 65.

Kasinitz, P., J. Mollenkopf, and M. C. Waters. 2002. "Becoming American/Becoming New Yorkers: Immigrant Incorporation in a Majority Minority City." *International Migration Review 36*(4), 1020–1036.

Levitt, P. 2001. *The Transnational Villagers.* Berkeley: University of California Press.

Levitt, P., and M. C. Waters (Eds.) 2002. *The Changing Face of Home: The Transnational Lives of the Second Generation.* New York: Russell Sage Foundation.

Ojito, M. 1997, December 16. "Dominicans, Scrabbling for Hope: As Poverty Rises, More Women Head the Households." *New York Times,* B1. www.nytimes.com/1997/12/16/nyregion/dominicans-scrabbling-for-hope-as-poverty-rises-more-women-head-the-households.html (accessed April 16, 2011).

Oficina Nacional de Estadísticas (ONE) de la República Dominicana. 2007. "Distribución geográfica de grupos socioeconómicos, 2002." Santo Domingo, República Dominicana.

Oficina Nacional de Estadísticas (ONE) de la República Dominicana. 2010. "La Seguridad Ciudadana en República Dominicana: Procesos y Contextos Socioeconómicos." Santo Domingo, República Dominicana.

Pantoja, S. 2005. *Religion and Education Among Latinos in New York City.* Boston: Brill Academic Publishers.

Pessar, P. R. 1987. "The Dominicans: Women in the Household and the Garment Industry." In Nancy Foner (Ed.). *New Immigrants in New York* (103–129). New York: Columbia University Press.

Portes, A., and L. Guarnizo. 1990. *Tropical Capitalists: U.S.-Bound Immigration and Small-Enterprise Development in the Dominican Republic.* Washington, DC: Working Papers, Commission for the Study of International Migration and Cooperative Economic Development.

Rodriguez, T. 2009. *Dominicanas entre La Gran Manzana y Quisqueya: Family, Schooling, and Language Learning in a Transnational Context.* Chapel Hill: University of North Carolina Press.

Safa, H. 1995. *The Myth of the Male Breadwinner: Women and Industrialization in the Caribbean.* Boulder, CO: Westview Press.

Sagás, E., and S. E. Molina. 2004. *Dominican Migration: Transnational Perspectives.* Gainesville: University Press of Florida.

Santana, I., and M. Rathe. 1993. *Reforma Social: Una Agenda para Combatir la Pobreza.* Santo Domingo, DR: Ediciones de la Fundación Siglo 21.

Stevens, E. P. 1973. "Marianismo: The Other Face of Machismo in Latin America," in: A. Pescatelo, *Female and Male in Latin America.* Pittsburgh, PA: University of Pittsburg Press.

Tactuk, P. 2007, December. "La Jefatura Femenina de Hogar en la Republica Dominicana: Un Estudio a Partir de Datos Censales," p. 1. Oficina Nacional de Estadística (ONE). www.one.gob.do/index.php?module=uploads&func=download&fileId=845 (accessed April 15, 2011).

Tejada Holguin, R. 1996. Las Familias Dominicanas: Un Rompecabezas Difícil de Armar. *Estudios Sociales XXIX*(105), 7–32.

Vargas, T. 1998. *De la Casa a la Calle: Estudio de la Familia y la Vecindad en Un Barrio de Santo Domingo.* Santo Domingo, DR: Centro de Estudios Sociales P. Juan Montalvo.

Wainerman, C., and R. Geldstein. 1994. "Viviendo en Familia: Ayer y Hoy." In C. Wainerman (Ed.), *Vivir en familia* (pp. 181–235). Buenos Aires: UNICEF/LOSADA.

Waldinger, R. D. 1986. *Through the Eye of the Needle: Immigrants and Enterprises in New York's Garment Trade.* New York: New York University Press.

11

■■■

The Korean American Family

Pyong Gap Min
Chigon Kim

INTRODUCTION

Koreans, along with Asian Indians and Vietnamese, comprise a new Asian immigrant group whose population in the United States has mushroomed since the passage of the liberalized immigration act in 1965. Between 1976 and 1990, annual Korean immigrants, numbering over 30,000, comprised the third-largest immigrant group in the United States. The vast majority of Korean Americans consist of post-1965 immigrants and their descendants. Since the early 1990s, the immigration of Koreans has gradually declined while an increasing number of second-generation Koreans have come of age, participating in the mainstream economy.

The Korean community in Los Angeles began to experience the emergence of 1.5- and second-generation Koreans after the 1992 Los Angeles riots. The Korean communities in New York and other cities have gradually witnessed the emergence of younger-generation Koreans in the twenty-first century.

In the previous two editions of *Ethnic Families in America*, Pyong Gap Min, the first author of this chapter, organized the material about the Korean-American family around the modernization theory of family systems by comparing Korean immigrant families with families in South Korea on one hand and native-born White American families on the other. He tried to show that Korean immigrant families generally stood in characteristics between traditional Korean families and modern postindustrial White American families. We still plan to make this two-way comparison. But the picture this time will not be as simple because family system and marital relations in South Korea have gone through radical changes over the last ten years or so. Now families in South Korea are more modern than White American characteristics in some indicators. This means that recent Korean immigrants may see more continuity in their family lives in the United States than the earlier Korean immigrants in the 1980s and early 1990s.

The other important changes in Korean Americans' family system and relations have much to do with the maturation of 1.5- and second-generation Koreans as young adults. When the first author was writing this chapter for the fifth edition of *Ethnic Families in America* in the mid-1990s, a small number of 1.5- and second-generation adults had established their own families. However, the number of younger-generation families has radically increased over the last fifteen years. Of course, native-born Korean families are likely to have lost many Korean family traditions rooted in the Confucian ideology. Yet as will be presented later in this chapter, a great deal of diversity in marital patterns is found among second-generation Korean families. Not much research has been conducted on younger-generation Korean families. In this chapter, we show the differences between Korean immigrant and younger-generation families based on U.S. Census data.

HISTORICAL BACKGROUND

Immigration and Settlement

The approximately 7,200 Korean laborers who moved to Hawaii between 1903 and 1905 to work on sugar plantations made up the first wave of Korean immigrants in the United States (Patterson, 1987). Although plantation owners needed more Korean workers in the first decade of the twentieth century, the Korean government was forced to stop sending any more laborers to Hawaii in 1905.[1] Before the Oriental Exclusion Act of 1924, approximately 2,000 additional Koreans moved to Hawaii and the West Coast. "Picture brides" of the pioneer male immigrants in Hawaii and political refugees engaged in the anti-Japanese movement comprised an overwhelming majority of the 1906–1924 Korean immigrants. Although the earlier Korean labor migrants on the West Coast intended to go back to Korea when they had made enough money, most of them and their picture brides remained in the United States permanently. However, most political refugees went back to their home country when Korea became independent of Japanese rule in 1945.

With an outbreak of the Korean War in 1950, the United States maintained close military, political, and economic relations with South Korea. The strong linkages between the two countries helped to resume the immigration of Koreans to the United States. About 15,000 Koreans immigrated to the United States between 1950 and 1964. Korean orphans adopted by American citizens and Korean women married to U.S. servicemen stationed in South Korea made up the vast majority of Korean immigrants during this period. The immigration of Korean adoptees and Korean "war brides" was expanded in the 1970s and 1980s, but it has moderated since the late 1980s as South Korea has significantly improved its economic conditions.

Despite nearly one hundred years of immigration history, the Korean population in the United States before 1970 was negligible. The 1970 U.S. Census enumerated the Korean population as 70,198. However, Korean immigration has accelerated with the enforcement of the 1965 Immigration Act as shown in Table 11.1. The number of annual Korean immigrants gradually increased from 1965, reaching close to 10,000 in 1970, hovering to about 30,000 in 1975, and peaking in the late 1980s with about 35,000 every year. More than 30,000 Koreans immigrated to the United States annually between 1976 and 1990, comprising the third-largest immigrant group, following Mexicans and Filipinos.

However, in the 1990s the annual number of Korean immigration dropped substantially below the level of 20,000 per year. Beginning in 2000, the number increased to over 20,000 but

---

[1]After its victory in the Russo-Japanese War in 1905, Japan made Korea its protectorate, gaining a free hand in influencing the Korean government. The Japanese government, to protect its own laborers in Hawaii, forced the Korean government not to send any more laborers there.

TABLE 11.1	Number of Korean Immigrants Every 5 Years between 1965 and 2008
Year	**Number of Korean Immigrants**
1965–1969	17,869
1970–1974	93,445
1975–1979	148,645
1980–1984	162,178
1985–1989	175,803
1990–1994	112,215
1995–1999	75,579
2000–2004	89,871
2005–2008	100,019

Source: Immigration and Naturalization Service, U.S. Department of Justice. *Annual Report of the Immigration and Naturalization Service, 1965–1978; Statistical Yearbook of the Immigration and Naturalization Service, 1979–2001;* Office of Immigration Statistics, U.S. Department of Homeland Security, *Yearbook of Immigration Statistics, 2002–2008.* Data on immigration are available online: www.dhs.gov/files/statistics/immigration.shtm

has never reached the 30,000 level. Several factors related to South Korea have contributed to the drastic reduction in the number of annual Korean immigrants: the significant improvement in economic conditions, social and political security associated with the end of military dictatorship and the popular election, and a significant reduction of fear of another war against North Korea. Publicity in South Korea about Korean immigrants' adjustment difficulties in the United States, especially the victimization of many Korean merchants during the 1992 Los Angeles riots, has also contributed to the reduction of Korean immigration. A better opportunity for their children's education or their own education is now a more important reason than a better economic opportunity for Koreans' decision to emigrate to the United States. In this connection, it is important to note that the majority of recent Korean immigrants are those who had entered the United States previously on nonimmigrant status and have changed their status as permanent residents (Min, 2006a:25). For example, there were 25,859 Koreans obtaining legal permanent resident status during fiscal year 2009. Of those, less than 20 percent were new arrivals and the remaining over 80 percent were status adjusters.[2]

As a result of the influx of Korean immigrants over the past forty years, the Korean population in the United States has witnessed a radical increase. As shown in Table 11.2, the 1970 U.S. Census counted slightly more than 70,000 Koreans. But the Korean population increased to over 350,000 in 1980, to nearly 800,000 in 1990, to over 1 million single-race Koreans and 1.2 million Koreans including multiracial Koreans in 2000.[3] Analysis of the 2008 American Community Survey data from IPUMS (Ruggles et al., 2008) estimated approximately 1.5 million, including 160,000 multiracial Koreans, which means that the Korean population increased more than twenty times

---

[2]Profiles on permanent residents are available online: www.dhs.gov/files/statistics/data/dslpr.shtm.
[3]Since, 2000 the U.S. Census Bureau has allowed people to choose two or more racial and/or ethnic categories in the racial classification question. Those who have chosen multiracial categories are children of interethnic and interracial marriages.

TABLE 11.2   Growth of Korean American Population, 1970–2008

	1970	1980	1990	2000	2008
Korean Alone	70,198	357,393	798,849	1,076,872 (87.7%)	1,372,152 (89.6%)
Korean in Combination	—	—	—	151,555 (12.3%)	160,033 (10.4%)
Total	70,198	357,393	798,849	1,228,427 (100.0%)	1,532,185 (100.0%)

Source: U.S. Census Bureau (1970 Census of Population, Table 192; 1980 Census of Population, Table 74; 1990 Census of Population, STF1-P007; 2000 Census of Population, SF1-PCT5). Available online: www.census.gov/prod/www/abs/decennial/

Note: The Korean American population in 2008 is estimated from the 2008 American Community Survey (Ruggles et al., 2008).

between 1970 and 2008. Despite the radical increase in the population, Korean Americans remain the fifth-largest Asian group, next to Chinese, Asian Indians, Filipinos, and Vietnamese. The Korean population is likely to share a smaller and smaller proportion of Asian Americans because the other countries that are major Asian sources of immigrants to the United States are sending much larger numbers of immigrants than is Korea.

The 2008 American Community Survey shows that approximately 23 percent of Korean Americans concentrated in the Los Angeles–Long Beach–Riverside area (see Table 11.3). With more than 300,000 Koreans, the Los Angeles metropolitan area is home to the largest Korean population outside of Korea. The high concentration of Koreans in the Los Angeles area is attributed

TABLE 11.3   Korean-American Population in Selected Metropolitan Areas, 2008

Metropolitan Area	Korean	
	N	%
Los Angeles–Long Beach–Riverside, CA CMSA	309,881	22.6
New York–Newark–Bridgeport, NY–NJ–CT–PA CMSA	183,249	13.4
Washington–Baltimore–Northern Virginia, DC–MD–VA–WV CMSA	86,039	6.3
San Jose–San Francisco–Oakland, CA CMSA	80,100	5.8
Seattle–Tacoma–Olympia, WA CMSA	60,694	4.4
Chicago–Naperville–Michigan City, IL–IN–WI CMSA	52,065	3.8
Atlanta–Sandy Springs–Gainesville, GA–AL CMSA	45,316	3.3
Honolulu, HI MSA	34,494	2.5
Dallas–Fort Worth, TX CMSA	31,258	2.3
Philadelphia–Camden–Vineland, PA–NJ–DE–MD CMSA	27,624	2.0
Total in these 10 metropolitan areas	910,720	66.4
Total in the United States	1,372,152	100.0

Source: 2008 American Community Survey from IPUMS (Ruggles et al., 2008).

Note: The estimates exclude multiracial Koreans. MSA and CMSA stand for metropolitan statistical areas and consolidated metropolitan statistical areas, respectively.

to various contributing factors, including the presence of a large Korean and other Asian populations since the 1960s, the convenience of air travel from Korea, active trade relations between Los Angeles and Korea, and mild weather.

Koreans in Los Angeles have created Koreatown, a Korean territorial community similar to Chinatown, approximately three miles west of downtown Los Angeles. In 2000, Koreans comprised only 20 percent of the population in Koreatown. Yet, covering about 25 square miles, Koreatown is the residential, cultural, commercial, and social center for the Los Angeles Koreans.

The second-largest Korean population center in the United States is the New York–New Jersey area with about 13 percent Korean Americans. The immigration of many medical professionals in the 1960s created the initial chance to bring more and more Koreans to that area (Kim, 1981). The Washington, DC, and San Francisco areas are the third- and fourth-largest Korean population centers in the United States. But these four metropolitan areas—Los Angeles, New York–New Jersey, Washington, DC, and San Francisco—experienced significant reductions in their share of the Korean population between 2000 and 2008. Chicago and Philadelphia experienced even higher levels of reduction in the share of the Korean population during the period. By contrast, Seattle, Atlanta, and Dallas achieved significant gains in the share of the Korean population during the first decade of the twenty-first century.

Korean History, Culture, Religions, and Family System

Korea is a peninsula extending northeast to Manchuria and southeast nearly to the southern island of Japan. Historically, the Chinese cultural influence spread southward to Korea and then to Japan. Thus, Chinese culture came to have a greater influence on Korea than on Japan, although Japan was also strongly influenced by Chinese culture. In fact, until recently the one dominating feature of Korean culture was the impact of Chinese culture, especially through Confucianism. Under the influence of the old Chinese culture, Chinese characters are still used in Korea, although they are less frequently used there than they are in Japan.

The Chinese Confucian cultural traditions have had such a deep influence on Korean society that it is almost impossible to understand the traditional Korean culture in general and the Korean family system in particular without understanding Confucianism. Concerned mainly with life in this world, Confucius provided several important principles that he advised people to follow for harmonious social relations. Five categories of interpersonal relations form the basis of his teachings on the duties and obligations of each individual. They are the relations between parents and children, between king and people, between the husband and the wife, between the older (brother or sister) and the younger (brother or sister), and between people. The significance of Confucianism for the Korean family system is clear because three of these five cardinal relations involve the family.

Confucius taught that parents and children should maintain mutual attitudes of benevolence. But, Confucianism, as applied to the Korean family system and social life, demanded children's one-sided obedience to and respect for parents and other adult members of the family. Children were required not only to pay the highest respect to their parents throughout their lives but also to fulfill their important obligations after their parents' deaths. The first son was supposed to live with his parents after his marriage, providing them with financial support and health care. Moreover, filial piety was extended after the death of a parent in the form of ancestor worship. Sons observed ritual mourning for three years after a parent died, and younger sons offered worshipful veneration to their ancestors. Filial piety is still considered one of the central norms in contemporary Korean society, with ancestor worship widely practiced.

Confucianism also emphasized a clear role differentiation between the husband and the wife. This principle helped to establish a rigid form of patriarchy in Korea. In traditional Korean society the husband was considered the primary breadwinner and decision maker in the family and exercised authority over his wife and children. The wife was expected to obey her husband, devotedly serving him and his family members and perpetuating her husband's family lineage by producing children.

In the traditional Korean society based on patriarchy and patrilineage, sons were considered more valuable and given more power than daughters. The first son very often attended important family meetings from which his mother was excluded. Interpersonal relations between brothers or sisters were regulated by Confucian ideology, which put emphasis on age as a basis of social hierarchy; older brothers and sisters were allowed to exercise a moderate level of authority over younger brothers and sisters. Because of this emphasis on age, sibling rivalry was not frequent in the traditional Korean family. Age was important not only for sibling relations but also for interpersonal relations in general. In social interactions, younger people were expected to be polite and respectful to older people even if the age difference was only five years.

Another major effect of Confucianism on Korean society was the adoption of the civil service examination, originally devised in China in the tenth century. The system, which was intended to bring men of intelligence and ability into government regardless of their social status, administered annual examinations based on Chinese literature and Confucian classics. Those who passed examinations were offered high government positions, giving them great power and economic rewards. This system helped to develop Korean parents' overemphasis on their children's education as the main channel for social mobility.

Korea had been strongly influenced politically and culturally by the Chinese. However, at the turn of the nineteenth century, three superpowers surrounding the Korean peninsula—Japan, China, and Russia—struggled for political control over Korea. When Japan won its war against Russia in 1905, it established its hegemony on the Korean peninsula. Japan annexed Korea in 1910, with its colonial rule lasting until the end of World War II. During the colonial period, the Japanese government tried to Japanize Korean society by ruthlessly repressing Korean culture and appropriating private and public lands. The Japanese military government also appropriated numerous young Koreans into military service and forced labor in the areas of the Pacific War and many young Korean women into military brothels. Because of this history, anti-Japanese sentiment in Korea is still strong, although South Korea normalized diplomatic relations with Japan in 1965.

Although Korea was liberated from Japan's colonial rule with Japan's defeat in the Asian and Pacific War in 1945, Korea has been politically divided into two halves, with South Korea under the influence of the United States and North Korea under the influence of the former Soviet Union and China. Koreans fought a civil war between 1950 and 1953, and the Korean War was the first major military confrontation between communists and anti-communists in the Cold War period. The Korean War ended in 1953, but military tensions in the Korean peninsula have continued until today. However, the end of the Cold War with the dissolution of the former Soviet Union, economic improvements, and diplomatic success achieved by the South Korean government in the 1990s have moderated military tensions during recent years and increased the possibility of a peaceful unification of the Korean peninsula in the near future. The close political, economic, and military linkages between the United States and South Korea since the Korean War have accelerated the American cultural influence in South Korea.

Buddhism is the largest religion in Korea, with two Christian religions (Protestantism and Catholicism) comprising the other important religions. Buddhism was transplanted by Chinese monks to Korea in the latter half of the fourth century. But it had not gained popularity in Korea

TABLE 11.4   Korean Immigrants' Self-Reported Religions in Korea and New York City, 2005

Religion	In Korea		In New York City	
	Number	%	Number	%
Protestantism	133	48.0	162	58.5
Catholicism	35	12.6	39	14.1
Buddhism	36	13.0	22	7.9
Other	1	.4	2	.7
None	72	26.0	52	18.8
Total	277	100.0	277	100.0

Source: Pyong Gap Min's 2005 Telephone Survey of Korean Immigrants in New York City (see Min, 2010:52).

until the late 1960s partly because of repression by the Chosun Dynasty and the Japanese colonial government and partly because of Korean temples' isolation in mountainous areas.

American missionaries, mostly Presbyterian and Methodist, brought Protestantism to Korea in the 1880s by establishing Christian schools and hospitals, whereas Korean intellectuals brought Roman Catholicism to Korea from Western missionaries in China in the 1760s (K. Min, 1988). But neither Christian religion was popular in South Korea until the late 1960s, partly because the Christian religious faiths and rituals collided with ancestor worship, the core of Confucian customs, and partly because the Japanese colonial government repressed the Christian religions during the colonial period. In 1962, only 2.8 percent of people in South Korea were Protestants, 2.2 percent were Catholics, and another 2.8 percent were Buddhists (Park and Cho, 1995:119). Before the 1960s, most Koreans had practiced Shamanism and ancestor worship, more traditional forms of religion.

However, the Christian populations, as well as the Buddhist population, have achieved a phenomenal increase over the last forty-five years. The most recent data show that Protestants and Catholics, respectively, comprised 20 percent and 7 percent of the population in South Korea, with Buddhists accounting for another 25 percent (Korea National Statistical Office, 2005). The gradual increase in the proportions of Koreans who have accepted the three adopted religions in South Korea since the late 1960s suggests that, as Koreans have improved their economic conditions and education, they have gradually replaced their more indigenous, traditional forms of religion (shamanism and Confucian ancestor worship) with more organized religions (Min, 2010:44).

Compared to the population in Korea, Christians are overrepresented among Korean immigrants. As shown in Table 11.4, in a 2005 survey of Korean immigrants in New York City conducted by the first author, the percentages of the respondents who were Protestant and Catholic before immigration were 48 percent and 13 percent, respectively, and only 13 percent answered that they were affiliated with Buddhism. These figures suggest that Korean immigrants have drawn largely from the Christian population in Korea. Christians are overrepresented among Korean immigrants in the United States for three major reasons. First, Christians are overrepresented among urban middle-class people in Korea, and Korean immigrants have largely drawn from this segment of the population.[4] Second, regardless of their class background more

---

[4]The two Christian populations are overrepresented in large cities, whereas Buddhists are overrepresented in rural areas.

Christians seem to have selectively chosen the U.S. emigration path because the United States is known to be a typically Christian country.

Many Koreans who were Buddhist or had no religion prior to their immigration are affiliated with Korean churches in the United States. Thus the Christian population has further increased in the Korean immigrant community. As shown in Table 11.5, in the same 2005 survey 59 percent of the respondents indicated Protestantism as their current religion, 14 percent chose Catholicism, and less than 8 percent selected Buddhism. These findings suggest that many former Buddhists and people with no religion attend Korean immigrant churches, especially Protestant churches. Two major factors have contributed to the great tendency for non-Protestant Korean immigrants to convert to Protestantism. One is the need of Korean immigrants to be affiliated with a Korean Protestant church for immigration orientations, fellowship, and other practical purposes. Since Korean Protestant churches provide their members with various services, fellowship, and cultural activities (Hurh and Kim, 1990; Min, 1992a), Korean immigrants, especially new immigrants, can benefit from their affiliation with a Korean church. Second, as Korean immigrant churches in the United States are heavily evangelical (Kim and Kim, 2001; Min, 2010), they aggressively try to recruit new members, usually new Korean immigrants.

KOREAN IMMIGRANT FAMILIES

Table 11.5 compares Korean immigrant families with families in Korea on the one hand and with native-born (non-Hispanic) White families on the other. As expected, overall we find that Korean immigrant families are more modern than families in Korea, but they are more traditional than non-Hispanic White families, with some notable exceptions.

In the previous edition of this book, the first author made the same type of two-way comparison based on the 1990 U.S. and Korean censuses. We also find that although native-born White families have not changed much between 1990 and 2005, both Korean immigrant families and families in Korea have experienced significant changes during the period. We can examine Korean immigrants' various aspects of family life, compared to the other two groups. In his chapter on the Korean American family included in the fourth edition of this book, the first author made the same type of comparison based on the 1990 U.S. and Korean censuses. In this chapter we also pay special attention to changes between 1990 and 2005 in Korean immigrant, Korean, and native-born White families.

Family Size and Composition

The first five rows in Table 11.5 provide data on family size and composition. As expected, Korean immigrants have on average a smaller household than the population in their home country but a slightly larger household than non-Hispanic Whites. A more noteworthy trend is that, although the non-Hispanic White household has not changed much in size between 1990 and 2005, both the Korean household and the Korean immigrant household have experienced significant reductions during the same period. We observe the same patterns in family size, too.

In the proportion of single-person households, Korean immigrants also are found between the two groups. The conspicuous trend again is that the proportion of single-person households has radically increased for both Korean households and Korean immigrant households between 1990 and 2005, whereas it has increased only a little (by 3 percent) for non-Hispanic White households. The radical increase in the proportion of single-person households in Korea and the Korean immigrant community was caused mainly by a great increase in the proportions of

TABLE 11.5 Selected Family Characteristics of White, Korean-Immigrant, and Korean Populations, 1990–2005

Characteristics	1990			2005		
	Non-Hispanic White	Korean Immigrant	Korean in Korea	Non-Hispanic White	Korean Immigrant	Korean in Korea
Average number of persons per household	2.5	3.3	3.7	2.4	2.6	2.9
Average number of persons per family	3.0	3.6	4.0	2.9	3.2	3.4
Single-person households	25.5%	13.3%	9.0%	28.4%	22.6%	20.0%
Average number of children per family	1.1	1.5	1.7	1.0	1.1	1.3
Average number of nonnuclear family members per family	.1	.3	.3	.1	.2	.2
Married-couple families	83.5%	84.0%	88.9%	81.0%	79.7%	79.5%
Female-headed families	12.3%	11.6%	10.8%	13.6%	12.4%	13.2%
Have own children in married-couple families	55.6%	79.9%	84.8%	49.6%	66.5%	75.3%
Number of divorced men per 1,000 men 15 years old and older	74	22	7	96	31	28
Number of divorced women per 1,000 women 15 years old and older	95	55	9	119	66	32
Labor force participation among urban women, 16 years old and over[a]	56.4%	55.8%	43.5%	58.8%	50.9%	48.5%
Labor force participation among urban married women, 16 years old and over[a]	57.6%	57.9%	33.2%[b]	59.2%	50.1%	39.1%[b]
Number of children ever born per 1,000 women 25–34 years old	1,233	1,088	1,387	1,193[c]	—	834
Number of children ever born per 1,000 women 35–44 years old	1,849	1,783	2,513	1,764[c]	—	1,799

Sources: U.S. Bureau of the Census, 1993a, Table 40; 1993b, Tables 41 and 44; 1993c, Tables 1, 2, and 4; 1990 Census 5-Percent Public Use Microdata Sample (PUMS), www.census.gov/census2000/PUMS5.html (accessed April 17, 2011); 2005 American Community Survey from IPUMS (Ruggles et al., 2008); Korean Bureau of Statistics, 1993, Tables 2-1 and 2-2; 1990 and 2005 National Population and Housing Census of Korea accessed from the Korean Statistical Information Service online (www.kosis.kr).

Note: Non-Hispanic and Korean immigrant households are defined by race and nativity of the householder, excluding multiracial cases.

[a] The labor force participation rate for Koreans in Korea includes those 15 years old and older, whereas for non-Hispanic Whites and Korean immigrants it includes those 16 years old and older.

[b] The 1990 data for the Korean married women in urban areas are from 1990 *Employment Structure Survey* (see Korean Women's Development Institute, 1994:Table 4-1-7), but the equivalent data in 2005 are not readily available. We approximate the 2005 data for married women in urban areas by using the administrative geographic unit, *dong*.

[c] Fertility data are from the Current Population Survey, June 2004 (see Dye, 2005).

elderly women living alone and unmarried adult children living separately from their parents. Many more unmarried adults in both Korea and the Korean immigrant community lived separately from their parents in 2005 than in 1990. Also, many more elderly people in Korea and the Korean community lived separately from their adult children in 2005 than in 1990.

We can observe a similar trend of change over time in the proportion of nonnuclear families. The average number of nonnuclear family members in both Korea and the Korean community in 1990 was 0.3, compared to 0.1 for non-Hispanic White Americans. The number of nonnuclear family members in both Korea and the Korean community decreased to 0.2 in 2005, whereas no change occurred in the number for non-Hispanic White families. Despite the significant reduction, both Korea and the Korean community still include extended families twice as large as White mainstream society. This indicates the enduring effect of Confucianism on kin ties among contemporary Koreans.

Family Stability

The next five rows in Table 11.5 show the differential levels of family stability among the three given groups and their changes between the two periods. In 1990, Korean immigrants have a slightly higher proportion of female-headed families than does the population in Korea, but they have a slightly lower proportion than non-Hispanic Whites. The proportion of female-headed families increased in 2005 for all three groups. But Koreans in Korea experienced the highest level of increase. In 2005, the population in Korea had a larger proportion of female-headed families than did the Korean immigrant population. This reveals a radical increase in the divorce rate in South Korea in the early 2000s.

Figures in the next two rows of Table 11.5 indicate the drastic increase in the divorce rate in Korea. Using the number of divorced persons per 1,000 people as an indicator of divorce, there was about a fourfold increase in divorce rate for both men (from 7 in 1990 to 28 in 2005) and women (from 9 to 32) in South Korea. But Korean immigrants experienced a moderate increase in the divorce rate—much less than Koreans in Korea—during the given period.

For all groups, a higher proportion of women were divorced in both periods. This is due mainly to the tendency of divorced women being less likely to get remarried than their male counterparts. But the gender difference in the divorce indicator is severe, especially for Korean immigrants in both periods. In 1990 the number of divorced women per 1,000 Korean immigrant women 15 years old and older (55) was 2.5 times as large as that of divorced men (22). The gender difference became somewhat moderated but remained significant in 2005 (66 versus 31). The great gender difference in the divorce indicator for Korean immigrants is due mainly to the fact that Korean women married to U.S. servicemen, composing a large proportion of Korean immigrant women, have an exceptionally high divorce rate (Kim, 1972).

Conjugal Role Differentiation

As noted, Confucianism emphasizes a strict role differentiation between the husband and the wife. Under the impact of Confucian family traditions, women in Korea, once they got married, usually stayed at home as full-time housewives, focusing on housework and child care. The exception is that most married women in rural areas engaged in farming. Since a significant proportion of the Korean population—a much larger proportion than in the United States— still engage in farming, it is important to use the labor force participation of married women in urban areas to compare it with those of Korean immigrants and native-born non-Hispanic White Americans.

As shown in Table 11.5, in 1990 44 percent of all Korean women 15 years old and older in urban areas participated in the labor force, with only 33 percent of urban married women working outside of the home.[5] We have noted the drastic changes in the Korean family system between 1990 and 2005. But Table 11.5 reveals that women's labor force participation rate, especially married women's labor force participation rate in South Korea achieved only a moderate increase during the same period. Of urban married women in Korea, 39 percent participated in the labor force in 2005, achieving only a 6 percent increase during the fifteen-year period. Given that urban women achieved a radical increase in their educational level in Korea between 1990 and 2005,[6] the moderate level of increase in the labor force participation rate of urban married women is surprising. No doubt, the Confucian patriarchal norm emphasizing the role differentiation between the husband and the wife is an important factor in the low labor force participation rate in South Korea relative to the United States and other Western countries. In addition, and probably more significant, the semireligious zeal for children's education has curtailed highly educated married women from working outside the home so they may concentrate on their children's education. Regarding this, it is important to note that the labor force participation rate of Korean urban married women with one or more children in school has not increased much during recent years (D. Kim, 2008).

In 1990, Korean immigrant married women show a much higher labor force participation rate (58 percent) than did their counterparts in Korea (33 percent). They had as high a labor force participation rate as native-born White married women in 1990. Most Korean immigrant married women in the labor force worked for the family business in 1990, as Korean immigrants had an exceptionally high self-employment rate (Min, 1996). Since many Korean immigrant women in the family business presumably did not report their work to the Census Bureau, the 1990 U.S. Census data underestimated the labor force participation rate of Korean married immigrant women. Results of a survey study conducted in 1988 by the first author indicated that 71 percent of Korean married immigrant women participated in the workforce, with most working long hours (Min, 1997). At that time, Korean immigrant women could find jobs somewhat easily in Korean-owned retail and service-related stores either as unpaid family members or employees of Korean-owned businesses (Min, 1998a). They usually worked as cashiers/salespersons, manicurists, or dry cleaners. By contrast, their husbands, although usually more highly educated, had more difficulty finding meaningful jobs. These factors explain why most married Korean immigrant women worked outside of the home. But other immigrant groups that did not develop significant immigrant businesses also showed higher married women's employment rates (Foner, 1999).

Although most Korean immigrant women worked for long hours outside the homes, their husbands did not much change their traditional patriarchal attitudes and thus did not help much at homes (Kim and Hurh, 1988; Lim, 1997; Min, 1992b, 1998a, 2001). Thus most Korean women overworked, participating in both paid work and housework extensively. Naturally, they suffered from stress and role strains (Min, 1992b, 1998a). Moreover, Korean immigrant women's

---

[5]By contrast, 64 percent of married women in rural areas, a much higher percentage, participated in the labor force. Because farmers comprise a significant percentage of married women workers in Korea, including all married women—farmers and non-farmers—can inflate the labor force participation rate of urban married Korean women who are comparable to Korean immigrant women. For this reason, we have analyzed only urban married women's labor force participation rate in Korea.

[6]The percentage of Korean women age 25 and older with associate or college degrees increased from 8.4 percent in 1990 to 25.4 percent in 2005 (Korea National Statistics Office, 2005).

increased economic role and their husbands' reduced socioeconomic status in the United States led to marital conflicts in many Korean immigrant families (Lim, 1997; Min, 1998a, 2001). The first author was so familiar with marital conflicts in Korean immigrant families in the 1990s that he made the main title of his 1998 book focusing on Korean immigrant families in New York City *Changes and Conflicts* (Min, 1998a). By "changes" he meant changes in Korean immigrant women's gender role behavior, and by "conflicts" he meant marital conflicts.

The 2005 data also show that Korean immigrant married women had a higher rate of workforce participation than their counterparts in their homeland. But the gap in the labor force participation rate between them became smaller in 2005 than in 1990. This is due to the fact that although more married women in Korea participated in the workforce in 2005 than in 1990, the labor force participation rate of Korean immigrant married women decreased during the period by 8 percent. We speculate that three major factors contributed to the drop in Korean immigrant married women's labor force participation rate between 1990 and 2005. First, as noted, contemporary Korean immigrants include many more temporary residents than do the Korean immigrants in 1990 and before. They include international students, employees of branches of Korean firms, and temporary workers. These Korean families seem to depend less on married women's earnings than the earlier permanent immigrant families. Second, the post-1990 Korean immigrants include a larger proportion of professional and managerial immigrants than the pre-1990 Korean immigrants, as the 1990 Immigration Act allowed for a significant increase in the number of professional and managerial immigrants and professional temporary workers. Many of these families probably can afford to live comfortably without the wife's extra earnings. Third, as will be shown, Korean immigrants in 2005 included a larger proportion of elderly people—most of whom were unlikely to participate in the labor force—than those in 1990.

The shrinking gap in labor force participation between married women in Korea and Korean immigrant married women in the United States suggests that marital conflicts related to sudden changes in women's gender role are now less prevalent than before. We do not have hard data available, as no one seems to have recently conducted research on this issue. But the first author's personal observations in the Korean community in New York suggest that Korean immigrant families at present have to deal with fewer marital conflicts than before. Also, more social service agencies are operational in large Korean communities than before, and they provide counseling for married couples with marital problems.

Fertility Rate

The bottom two rows of Table 11.5 provide data on number of children born per 1,000 as an indicator of fertility rate in the two given years for two age groups: 25–34 years old and 35–44 years old. In 1990, Korean immigrant women had a much lower fertility rate than women in Korea for both age groups. Korean immigrant women 35–44 years old, most of whom were past the peak childbearing age, had an average of less than two children, whereas their counterparts in South Korea had an average of 2.5 children. The former had even a smaller number of children than native-born non-Hispanic White Americans, and seem to have had a much lower fertility rate than Koreans for two main reasons. First, it was due to their much higher class background. By virtue of their selective migration, Korean immigrants, including women, had a much higher educational attainment than their compatriots in Korea. According to the 1990 U.S. Census data, 32 percent of Korean immigrants twenty-five years old and older completed a four-year college education, compared to only 9 percent of their counterparts in Korea.

Second, a high labor force participation rate of Korean immigrant married women served as a restrictive force to their fertility. A small proportion of married women in Korea worked outside the home in 1990, although many of them could depend on a cohabiting mother-in-law or a housemaid for child care. By contrast, most Korean immigrant married women needed to work long hours outside the home for economic survival, but they usually did not live with an elderly mother or mother-in-law who could help them with babysitting (Min, 1998a). Thus many Korean immigrant women had to delay pregnancy while undertaking their economic role. Women's economic role and fertility mutually influence each other. But for Korean immigrant women, their economic role seems to influence their fertility behavior more than the other way around.

Table 11.5 shows that Korea experienced a rapid drop in fertility rate between 1990 and 2005, from 2,513 to 1,799 for the 1,000 women 35–44 years old. Korea is known to be one of the few countries with the lowest fertility rates in the world (D. Kim, 2005). The trends of late marriage, gender equity orientation, women's increasing labor market participation, and labor market uncertainty have been indicated as major contributing factors to the rapid decrease in fertility rate in Korea as well as in other countries (D. Kim, 2005). But the rising cost of private education for children is the key causal factor unique to Korea (Suzuki, 2008).[7] Table 11.5 shows that the 35–44-year-old women in Korea had a slightly larger number of children in 2005 than their U.S. White American counterparts mainly because the women in their late thirties and early forties bore many children several years earlier. But when focusing on recently married women alone, those in Korea had a substantially lower fertility rate in 2005 than those in the United States. The 25–34-year-old women in Korea, consisting mostly of recently married women, had a much lower fertility rate (834 in 1,000 women) than their counterparts in the United States (1,193). Unfortunately, the U.S. Census did not give information about the number of children ever born per 1,000 Korean immigrant women for the two age groups in 2005. But Korean immigrant women are likely to have a lower fertility rate than native-born White American women. However, they may have a slightly higher fertility rate than women in Korea because the concern about the cost of private education for children here is not as strong a restrictive force as in their home country.

Child Socialization

Confucianism has probably had the most significant effect on child socialization practices in Korea. As previously noted, filial piety is a major element of Confucianism. As a consequence of the strong Confucian cultural tradition, child socialization in South Korea still places a great emphasis on children's obedience to and respect for parents and adults. Korean immigrant parents, the vast majority of whom completed their education in Korea, are more authoritarian than White American parents, although there are significant class differences in Korean immigrant parents' child socialization practices. The authoritarian child socialization technique was well documented in a survey in which Korean children and their mothers in New York City were asked to report their major complaints about their parents or children. The children respondents cited "restricting my freedom too much" and "too strict" as two of the most common complaints about their parents, whereas many mother respondents complained about their children "not respecting parents" and "talking back" (Min, 1995). Naturally, Americanized Korean children want to escape parental control and authority, leading to a high level of intergenerational conflicts.

---

[7]Korea spent the highest proportion (2.9 percent) of GDP on private education among Organization for Economic Co-operation and Development (OECD) countries (Suzuki, 2008:33).

But Korean immigrant parents have also gradually changed their traditional child socialization techniques as they are assimilating into the American culture. Based on focus group interviews, Choi and Kim (2010) indicate that Korean immigrants have realized the ineffectiveness of relying on absolute obedience to parents in the new setting and that they have therefore made some adaptations. Korean immigrant parents have reduced the use of corporal punishment as a method of discipline and have used affection and praise more often than parents do in Korea. According to Choi and Kim (2010:158), "Many feel more comfortable in expressing their love, care, and trust to their children nonverbally and indirectly." But the authors also claim that Korean parents have tried to maintain what they call "core domains" of Korean family socialization, such as respect for adults and adults eating first.

Another core element of Confucianism is its emphasis on children's education and social mobility through education. We noted in the previous section that parents in South Korea do everything possible to send their children to good colleges. Many Korean immigrants have chosen U.S.-bound emigration as a way of giving their children a better educational opportunity (B. L. Kim, 1978:189). As South Korea has achieved significant improvements in economic and social conditions over the past two decades, recent immigrants have tended to put more emphasis on a better opportunity for their children's education than their own economic opportunity in the United States. Many scholars have indicated that emphasis on children's education is what differentiates Jewish Americans from other White ethnic groups (Heilman, 1982; Sklare, 1971). However, an interview study of Korean immigrant and Jewish mothers showed that Korean immigrant parents may put more stress on their children's success in school than Jewish American parents do (Rose and Min, 1992). Over half of the secondary-school children of Korean mothers included in the study were found to attend private institutes specializing in mathematics and English, and/or to have received tutoring in those subjects during the previous summer, whereas 6 percent of Jewish students attended such programs. Among the Korean children 30 percent were also found to participate in extracurricular study programs at the time of the interview, in comparison to 11 percent of the Jewish children. The same study (Rose and Min, 1992) also found that the Korean mothers pressured their children to study longer hours after school and to get better grades than did Jewish mothers.

Not only Korean immigrants, but also other Asian immigrants, are known to provide their children with after-school cram sessions and to put extra pressure on them to do well in school (Louie, 2004; Zhou and Kim, 2006). Similar to Caribbean and other immigrant groups, not only their cultural sources but also their immigrant status contributes to Asian immigrants' overemphasis on their children's education. Since immigrants see more opportunities for their children's college education in the United States than in their home countries, they are more highly motivated than native-born Americans to provide their children with the best education possible.[8] In fact, as already indicated, many Korean and other immigrants have chosen U.S.-bound emigration to benefit their children's college education.

Given this motivation for immigration as well as selective migration, a comparative study of Korean immigrant parents and multigenerational native-born Jewish parents in children's education, whose findings are summarized in the preceding paragraph, seems to be problematic. First-generation Jewish immigrants may have put as much emphasis on their children's education as contemporary Korean immigrants. But we also like to point out that contemporary Korean and other Asian immigrants have advantages in their children's education over the Jewish

---

[8]According to a multivariate analysis, having immigrant parents is the most accurate predictor of school success (Kao and Tienda, 1995).

immigrants because of their very high class resources, higher than native-born White Americans. We need to consider all three of these factors—Asian cultural resources, immigrant status, and class resources—in explaining Korean and other Asian immigrants' overemphasis on children's education and Asian students' successful performance in school.

Gender socialization is another area in which Korean immigrant parents differ significantly from White American parents. We already noted that under the impact of Confucianism people in South Korea maintain a more traditional gender role differentiation than here in the United States. Closely related to a strict gender role differentiation, Korean parents practice conservative gender socialization. This traditional gender socialization, though somewhat moderated, persists today in the Korean community. Our personal observations strongly suggest that Korean immigrant parents treat boys and girls differently and assign different chores to them. Results of a comparative study of Korean and Jewish mothers also support these observations (see Rose and Min, 1992). Korean immigrant mothers were found to agree to the statements reflecting traditional gender stereotypes to a much greater extent than Jewish American mothers. Also, Korean mothers were found to be more traditional in assigning housework chores to boys and girls. For example, 63 percent of Korean immigrant mothers felt that "setting the table" should be done by girls, whereas all Jewish mother respondents said that it should be done by both boys and girls (Rose and Min, 1992:17).

Elderly Korean Immigrants' Adaptations

Elderly Koreans comprised less than 5 percent of the Korean immigrant population in 1990, as Korean immigrants drew largely from the young and middle-aged population in Korea (U.S. Bureau of the Census, 1993a). But the proportion of elderly people among Korean immigrants increased to 10 percent in 2005. Yet, it is not comparable to the proportion of White elderly people (14 percent) in the same year.[9] The rapid increase in the proportion of the elderly in the immigrant population is due to two factors: the increase in the immigration of elderly Koreans and the aging of Korean immigrants who came to the United States at earlier ages.

In traditional Korean society, elderly people usually lived with their first sons, as Confucianism emphasized the obligation of adult children to live with their elderly parents to support and take care of them. As recently as 1990, more than 70 percent of elderly people (60 years and older) in Korea lived with their children or other relatives, with only 8 percent living alone (Korea National Statistical Office, 2005:200). But the increasing tendency over the last two decades to adopt the nuclear family as a norm in Korea has significantly altered the living arrangements of elderly people. The proportion of the elderly population living in their child's or other relative's family decreased to 24 percent in 2005, with as much as 18 percent living alone (see Table 11.6). The change in elderly persons' living arrangements indicates a drastic change in family system in South Korea.

The percentage of Korean immigrant elderly persons who live in 2006 in the homes of their children or another relative was almost identical (25 percent) with that of the elderly in Korea. The majority of them lived with their spouse, with 17 percent living alone. The 1990 U.S. Census showed that 43 percent of elderly Korean Americans (including native-born Koreans) lived in the homes of their children or another relatives (Min, 1998b). Given that both the Korean foreign-born and native-born samples were included in the 1990 census data, the percentage for Korean elderly immigrants who cohabitated with their children or other relatives is likely to have been

---

[9]The elderly population is estimated from the 2005 American Community Survey data (Ruggles et al., 2008).

TABLE 11.6 Living Arrangements of White, Korean-Immigrant, and Korean Elderly Persons

Living Arrangement	Non-Hispanic White	Korean Immigrant	Korean in Korea
All elderly persons	30,153,332 (100.0)	101,289 (100.0)	4,365,218 (100.0)
Living as a family householder or his/her spouse	57.2	51.1	56.6
Living in his/her own child's family	5.1	22.8	22.4
Living in a family of a relative other than his/her own child	1.3	2.2	1.1
Living in a family of a nonrelative	.3	1.2	.4
Living in a nonfamily household	2.6	2.7	.4
Living alone	28.3	16.5	17.9
Living in a group quarter	5.2	3.5	1.1

Source: 2006 American Community Surveys from IPUMS (Ruggles et al., 2008) and 2005 National Population and Housing Census of Korea accessed from the Korean Statistical Information Service online (www.kosis.kr).

higher than 43 percent. These findings indicate that Korean elderly immigrants went through a radical change in their living arrangements between 1990 and 2006. Two major factors contributed to the change. First, a much higher proportion of elderly Korean immigrants in 2006 had their U.S.-born or U.S.-raised (1.5-generation) children than in 1990, whereas the vast majority of elderly Korean immigrants in 1990 had Korean-born and Korean-raised immigrant children. Naturally, it is more likely for elderly Korean immigrants to live with their immigrant children than with their American-born or American-raised children. Second, a cultural trend toward independent living among the elderly population also contributed to the change in the living arrangements of the elderly. The Korean elderly immigrants invited by their immigrant adult children during recent years try to live separately from their children after a few years of cohabitation with their children. Living separately from their children in Korea is even now a norm among the elderly.

Not surprisingly, a higher proportion (28 percent) of elderly Whites lived alone, with a much smaller proportion (only 6 percent) of them living with the families of their children or other relatives. More Korean elderly immigrants than White elderly people live with their children or other relatives for two practical reasons. First, since most Korean immigrants spend long hours working, they need to live with their elderly parents, who can take care of their children and housework. Many invited their elderly parents or mothers as visitors to help them at home even before they became naturalized citizens. Second, many Korean elderly immigrants invited as permanent residents cannot live separately from their children because of their severe language barrier and other adjustment difficulties. It is especially true of those settled in smaller Korean communities with no significant networks of elderly Koreans. A small, but substantially larger, proportion of Korean immigrant elderly persons live in group quarters than their elderly counterparts in Korea do.

But Korean elderly immigrants who live in a large Korean community, like the New York–New Jersey metropolitan area, can live separately from their children more easily because of strong Korean-language media, Korean-language elderly centers, and Korean elderly networks. There are several apartment complexes in the New York–New Jersey area where many Korean elderly people reside. Also, there are about ten elderly centers in the New York–New Jersey area, some of them social service agencies and others self-help elderly associations. They provide all kinds of services for elderly persons, including free lunch, paperwork, English-language education, and classes for naturalization tests. Along with several Korean churches and business associations, they also regularly offer parties and entertainments for all Korean elderly persons. Most of the approximately 600 Korean churches also arrange special tours called "filial tours" for elderly members, usually twice a year.

The first author included a chapter on "Adjustments Among the Elderly" in his book, *Change and Conflicts: Korean Immigrant Families in New York City* (Min, 1998a). In the chapter, he made a distinction between the immigrated elderly and the invited elderly. The immigrated elderly refer to those who immigrated in their middle years or younger and reached old age recently, whereas the invited elderly are those who immigrated to the United States recently (Min, 1998a:86). The elderly in the Korean community in 1990 consisted largely of the invited elderly who lived with their immigrant children, but the proportion and number of the immigrated elderly have greatly increased during recent years, as many Korean immigrants have reached elderly age. The distinction between the two groups of the Korean elderly is very important because they have different patterns of adaptations. The invited elderly usually do not have their own independent income source, as they have not worked much in the United States.

The majority of those Korean elderly persons who live with their children are invited elderly and thus do not have much income other than their supplementary Social Security income for naturalized citizens. But since most of the immigrated Korean elderly have worked for many years, they receive larger Social Security checks than the invited elderly, as well as pension and investment money (Min, 1998a:97). Many of them also continue to work in their own businesses after age sixty-five. Thus they are usually economically independent from their children. But they have more difficulty living with their 1.5- and/or second-generation adult children who have been educated in the United States and are very much acculturated to American society. Thus, few of the immigrated elderly live with their own children; although they are more satisfied with their economic conditions and with economic independence from their children than the invited elderly, they seem to be less satisfied than the invited elderly with the relationships they have with their children (Min, 1998a:99). First and foremost, the majority of second-generation Koreans are married to non-Korean partners (see Min and Kim, 1999), which makes it difficult for their parents to interact with their in-laws. Many immigrated Korean elderly persons feel lucky when their children marry Korean partners.

YOUNGER-GENERATION KOREANS' ADAPTATION IN FAMILY SYSTEM

It is about forty years since the mass immigration of Koreans started. Many native-born second- and 1.5-generation Koreans have grown up and established their own families. According to our analysis of the 2008 American Community Survey data (Ruggles et al., 2008), 27 percent of approximately 279,000 1.5-generation (those who immigrated to the United States at 12 or younger) Koreans ($N = 75,300$) and 16 percent of approximately 362,000 native-born Koreans ($N = 58,000$) were married. However, despite a rapid increase in younger-generation families, to our knowledge there is no major study of second-generation Korean families. Since no major study of younger-generation Korean families has been conducted, in discussing intergenerational changes in Korean American families we will depend partly on census data and partly on our speculations based on insiders' knowledge. Since the second generation seem to comprise the predominant majority of native-born Koreans, we will use in this section the second generation to refer to native-born Koreans.

As noted, Korean immigrants have gone through some changes in their family system in proportion to the length of their residence in the United States. But we expect to see more significant changes over generations. Not only native-born second- and higher-generation Koreans, but also those Koreans who came to the United States at early ages (the 1.5 generation), accompanied by their parents, are much more acculturated to American society than first-generation Korean immigrants. Moreover, although first-generation Korean immigrants are economically segregated in the ethnic economy as business owners or employees of co-ethnic businesses, younger-generation Koreans are predominantly in the mainstream economy (Min, 2006c). Thus younger-generation Koreans are likely to have lost much of the Confucian elements of the Korean family system that emphasize kinship ties, the importance of children's education, and subordination of wives to husbands.

Intergenerational Differences Based on Census Data

Table 11.7 shows the generational differences in family systems among Korean Americans based on the 2006–2008 American Community Survey data (Ruggles et al., 2008). As expected, Korean immigrants have a substantially larger household than native-born Koreans. But against our expectation there is not much difference in household size between the immigrant and 1.5 generations. The percentage of single-person households appears to increase over generations. The percentage of single-person households for 1.5-generation Koreans (29 percent) is almost identical with that of non-Hispanic Whites (28 percent in Table 11.5). It is smaller

TABLE 11.7   Family Characteristics of Korean Americans by Generation, 2006–2008

Characteristics	First-Generation Korean	1.5-Generation Korean	Native-Born Korean
Average number of persons per household	2.7	2.6	2.3
Average number of persons per family	3.2	3.3	3.1
Single-person households	22.3%	28.5%	35.9%
Average number of children per family	1.2	1.2	.9
Average number of nonnuclear family members per family	.2	.4	.4
Married-couple families	82.1%	75.6%	74.2%
Female-headed families	12.7%	12.9%	15.5%
Have own children in married-couple families	67.0%	72.0%	59.4%
Number of divorcees per 1,000 people 15 years and over	57	62	99
Women 16–64 years old who participate in the labor force	53.6%	68.1%	62.1%
Married women 16–64 years old who participate in the labor force	51.9%	70.7%	73.6%

Source: 2006–2008 American Community Surveys from IPUMS (Ruggles et al., 2008).

Note: Korean American households are defined by race and nativity of the householder, excluding multiracial cases; 1.5-generation Korean American refer to those who immigrated to the United States before age thirteen.

than that of second-generation Koreans (36 percent) but larger than that of Korean immigrants (only 22 percent). In addition, native-born Koreans have a smaller household size than first- and 1.5-generation Koreans, but there is not much difference in family size over generations. These findings suggest that native-born Koreans' smaller household size is due mainly to their much higher proportion of single-person households (36 percent) and partly to their smaller number of children.

We noted in the previous section that Korean immigrant families have an average of 0.2 non-nuclear family members per family, twice as much as native-born White families (0.1). Surprisingly, 1.5- and second-generation Korean families have twice as many non-nuclear family members (0.4) as Korean immigrant families. This surprising finding can be explained by two major factors: (1) two types of younger-generation Korean families having much smaller proportions of married-couple families[10] and (2) the possibility of many 1.5- and second-generation Korean unmarried young adults reporting themselves as heads of households, instead of their parents, to the U.S. Census Bureau.[11] When we compare the three generations while focusing only on married-couple families, first-generation Korean immigrant families are likely to have on average a larger number of non-nuclear family members than either of the younger-generation families.

Statistics in the middle columns in Table 11.7 are indicators of family stability. Native-born Korean families have a larger proportion of female-headed families than first- or 1.5-generation families. Consistently, when the number of divorcees per 1,000 people is used as an indicator of divorce rate, there seems to be a substantial increase in divorce rate over generations. But since there are radical differences in marriage rate among the three generations, we cannot use the same indicator of divorce to see the generational differences in divorce rate. Although about 70 percent of first-generation Korean immigrants 16 years old and over are married, only 28 percent of 1.5-generation Koreans and 17 percent of native-born Koreans are married. When such radical differences in marriage rate are found among the given generations, the ratio of married persons to divorced persons could be a more accurate indicator of divorce. When the ratios are assessed, we find that 1 for every 9.0 Korean immigrants is divorced. The ratios for the 1.5- and native-born generations are respectively 7.9 to 1 and 8.6 to 1. These figures suggest that the 1.5-generation has the highest divorce rate while the first generation has the lowest divorce rate.

As noted in the previous section, first-generation Korean women have a much higher divorce rate than their male counterparts mainly because Korean women married to U.S. servicemen have a greater tendency for divorce. When the unique effect on the divorce rate of Korean immigrants due to the intermarriage between Korean immigrants and U.S. servicemen is eliminated, the difference in divorce rate between first-generation Korean immigrants and younger-generations Koreans is actually greater than the above ratios may indicate. The higher divorce rate of younger-generation Koreans compared to first-generation Koreans seems to be due partly to the former's higher level of acculturation and partly to their higher intermarriage rate. As will be shown, an escalation in intermarriage rate occurs over generations among Korean Americans.

The final two columns in Table 11.7 have indicators of women's labor force participation rate. Naturally, regardless of their marital status younger-generation women participate in the

---

[10]Since 1.5- and native-born Korean families have much smaller proportions of married-couple families than Korean immigrant families, other types of non-nuclear families (consisting of two or more siblings or combining parents and unmarried adult children) are likely to comprise larger proportions of two types of younger-generation families.

[11]When unmarried younger-generation Koreans live with their parents, in most cases their parents are likely to be heads of households. But because of their fluency in English, younger-generation young adults may report themselves as heads of households to the Census Bureau.

labor force more actively than Korean immigrant women. Particularly among married women one finds a significant linear increase in the labor force participation rate over generations. Although only about half of Korean immigrant married women 16 to 64 years old work outside of the home, 71 percent of their 1.5-generation and 74 percent of their second-generation counterparts participate in outside-the-home economic activities. Younger-generation Korean women have much higher educational levels than Korean immigrant women.[12] Also, they are fluent in English and familiar with the American job market. Given these advantages for their employment in the general labor market, it is quite natural that three-fourths of married native-born Korean women participate in the labor force at working ages.

Intergenerational Differences Based on Our Insiders' Knowledge

In the preceding subsections, we discussed intergenerational differences in Korean American families based on census data. But there are many other significant intergenerational changes in Koreans' family life that we cannot capture using census data. Based partly on our deductive reasoning and partly on our insider's knowledge, we here summarize some of the significant intergenerational changes in Korean Americans' family life.

We previously noted that Korean immigrant women's increased economic role and their extremely long hours of work outside of the home contributed to their overwork and marital conflicts in Korean immigrant families. Although Korean immigrant women usually work in the family business or for a Korean-owned small business, younger-generation Korean American women mostly have professional and managerial jobs in the mainstream economy (Min, 2006c). Thus, they usually do not work long hours for their jobs. Moreover, younger-generation Korean husbands share more housework with their wives than Korean immigrant husbands. For these reasons, we expect younger-generation Korean marriages to be less conflict-ridden and involve more leisure activities other than paid work.

We also noted in the previous section that Korean immigrant parents place strong emphasis on their children's education as the main channel for social mobility. As previously noted, immigrant parents' focus on their children's education is common to other Asian and even Caribbean immigrants. Because Korean immigrants have high hopes for their own or their children's education, many of them may have chosen to emigrate to the United States. But second-generation Korean and other Asian parents, who complained about their parents' overemphasis on their education, are likely to put less stress on their children's good performance in school. The first author has known a third-generation Japanese American, with a Taiwanese immigrant wife, who often argues with his wife about child socialization. The Americanized husband said that his wife makes his children study too much at home while he wants to give them sufficient breaks after school. Given this intergenerational change in the level of motives for their children's education, third-generation Korean and other Asian Americans may experience intergenerational downward mobility when it comes to education.

We also expect to see a drastic intergenerational change in the authoritarian child socialization technique of most Korean immigrant parents. Confucian family norms require children to obey and respect parents. Thus, as noted, most Korean immigrant parents have used the authoritarian child socialization technique, which has led to a great deal of conflict with their children.

---

[12]According to the 2000 U.S. Census, 61 percent of native-born Korean women 25 to 64 years old completed four years of college education, compared to 39 percent of Korean immigrant women. In fact, native-born Korean women have a higher college graduation rate than their male counterparts (see Min, 2006b:91).

However, the American-born and American-raised younger-generation Korean parents who felt their parents had restricted their freedom too much during their childhood and adolescence are likely to adopt a more democratic technique, including allowing their children to "talk back" and listening to their children more patiently. In addition, they are expected to communicate with their children on a much more equal basis without exercising parental authority. Therefore, 1.5- and second-generation Korean families are likely to encounter a much lower level of intergenerational conflict. This intergenerational change may be applicable to most other immigrant groups.

Finally, kin ties is another area of Korean American family life that has gone through significant intergenerational transformations. As noted, Confucianism emphasizes kin ties and worship of ancestors covering three generations. Even in today's postindustrial Korea, most Korean adults participate in ancestor-worship rituals on important Korean cultural holidays for which not only brothers and sisters, but also second cousins, get together. The family- and relative-based chain migration has further strengthened Korean immigrants' kin ties. Min's (1984) study showed that Korean immigrants maintained stronger kin ties in the United States than in Korea. New immigrants need to depend on already settled brothers and sisters for their initial settlement and occupational adaptations. Especially because about half of Korean immigrants have family businesses, help from kin members is essential to new immigrants' business capitalization, business training, and operation (Min, 1988).

However, younger-generation Koreans, with some exceptions, are likely to maintain a lower level of kin ties outside of their own nuclear families than do their immigrant parents. They will not have a sense of obligation to financially support their elderly parents or siblings through financial difficulty. Moreover, since younger-generation Koreans find their occupations in the mainstream economy using their educational credentials, few of them understand the need for mutual help using collective resources, which has characterized their parents' adjustment to American society.

Patterns of In-marriage and Intermarriage

Younger-generation Koreans' higher levels of acculturation to American society compared to Korean immigrants contribute to radical changes in Korean Confucian family traditions. Moreover, their higher rates of intermarriage, especially intermarriages to White Americans, contribute to further modifications of Korean families. We are interested in Koreans' marital patterns in this chapter partly because it is an important topic related to Korean Americans' families and marriages. But we are also interested in generational and gender differences in marital patterns.

As shown in Table 11.8, there are radical generational and gender differences in Koreans' intermarriage rate. Only about 15 percent of first-generation Korean immigrants were married to non-Korean partners. There is a huge gender difference in the intermarriage rate among Korean immigrants. Only 3 percent of Korean immigrant men, compared to 24 percent of Korean immigrant women, are intermarried. As noted, many U.S. servicemen stationed in South Korea married Korean women there and subsequently brought their wives to the United States (Kim, 1972). The presence of many Korean women married to U.S. servicemen seems to have inflated the huge gender difference in the intermarriage rate of Korean immigrants. But even if these war-bride couples are eliminated, Korean immigrant women have a greater tendency to marry non-Korean partners than do their male counterparts. We can explain this tendency by indicating the two interrelated facts: (1) Korean immigrant men coming from very patriarchal traditions have difficulty living with American women and (2) many Korean immigrant women are attracted to American men, especially White men, to escape from Korean patriarchy. Korean

TABLE 11.8 Percentage Distribution of In-marriage and Intermarriage Patterns Among Married Korean Americans by Generation and Sex, 2006–2008

Marital Pattern	First-Generation Korean			1.5-Generation Korean			Native-Born Korean		
	Total	Male	Female	Total	Male	Female	Total	Male	Female
In-marriage	(85.5)	(96.8)	(76.5)	(47.4)	(62.9)	(35.3)	(38.8)	(45.1)	(33.2)
First-generation Korean spouse	80.1	92.0	70.6	27.0	38.5	18.0	10.0	14.3	6.1
1.5-generation Korean spouse	4.4	4.0	4.7	16.4	19.4	14.0	6.6	6.8	6.4
Native-born Korean spouse	1.0	.8	1.2	4.1	5.0	3.3	22.2	24.0	20.6
Intermarriage	(14.5)	(3.2)	(23.5)	(52.6)	(37.1)	(64.7)	(61.2)	(54.9)	(66.8)
Non-Hispanic White spouse	10.7	1.3	18.2	38.3	23.4	50.0	38.9	32.5	44.6
Other racial minority spouse	1.8	.5	2.8	6.2	5.9	6.4	12.2	11.2	13.1
Other Asian spouse	2.0	1.4	2.5	8.0	7.8	8.2	10.1	11.1	9.1

Source: 2006–2008 American Community Surveys from IPUMS (Ruggles et al., 2008).

Note: Numbers represent cell percentages in three-way contingency tables with generation, gender, and marital pattern.

immigrant men show the lowest intermarriage rate among all Asian male immigrant groups (Liang and Ito, 1999), which reflects Korean immigrants' strong patriarchal attitudes.

The intermarriage rate of Korean Americans increases rapidly over generations. Over half of 1.5-generation Koreans and more than 60 percent of native-born Koreans are married to non-Korean partners. Even for these younger-generation Koreans, women have a greater tendency to marry non-Korean partners. But the gender difference in intermarriage rate has been moderated over generations. Approximately 55 percent of native-born Korean men, compared to 67 percent of their female counterparts, have non-Korean marital partners. Younger-generation Koreans with non-Korean partners overwhelmingly have White partners, and their preference for White partners is more conspicuous for women. In particular, half of 1.5-generation Korean women— a higher proportion than for native-born Korean women—are married to White partners. In fact, the tendency of much more 1.5-generation Korean women than men to marry White partners largely explains their much higher intermarriage rate than their male counterparts. One major factor that facilitates younger-generation Koreans' marriages to White partners is their Christian background. Approximately 75 percent of younger-generation Koreans attended Korean Protestant or Catholic churches during their childhood (Min, 2010:130).

Table 11.8 includes a sample of all married Koreans. Native-born married Koreans include elderly second- and third-generation Koreans who grew up in small Korean communities in Hawaii and California before the influx of post-1965 Korean immigrants. Mainly due to the unavailability of Korean partners, they have a much higher intermarriage rate than post-1965 native-born Korean Americas (Harvey and Chung, 1980). Younger-generation Koreans who have grown up in large post-1965 Korean communities have an advantage in meeting co-ethnic marital partners, and thus they should have a lower intermarriage rate than the 61 percent for all native-born Koreans shown in Table 11.8. Our study of post-1965 native-born Asian Americans' marital patterns (Min and Kim, 2009) reveals that 54 percent of them were intermarried.

Previous studies that examined Asian Americans' marital patterns focused on intermarriage patterns (Lee and Fernandez, 1998; Liang and Ito, 1999). But there are different patterns of in-marriage depending on the generation of their partners. In our recently published article (Min and Kim, 2009), we first analyzed native-born Asian Americans' patterns of "cross-generational marriages," as well as patterns of their intermarriages. As shown in Table 11.8, almost all married first-generation Korean immigrants are married to other Korean immigrants, with about 5 percent married to 1.5- or second-generation Koreans. This trend is quite natural, considering that first-generation Koreans outnumber 1.5-generation and native-born Koreans by large margins. But more 1.5-generation Koreans (27 percent) are married to first-generation Korean immigrants than to Koreans of their own generation (16 percent). It is easy for 1.5-generation Koreans to meet Korean immigrants for dating. And many of them can marry Korean immigrants because they can speak Korean well and are familiar with Korean customs. By contrast, most in-married native-born Koreans are married to other native-born Koreans (22 percent), with only 10 percent of them married to Korean immigrants. Native-born Koreans too have no difficulty meeting Korean immigrant partners, but their linguistic and cultural differences seem to be a barrier to their cross-generational marriages.

Gender has an effect on patterns of in-marriage as well. More 1.5- and second-generation men tend to marry Korean immigrant partners than their female counterparts. In particular, there is a huge gender difference in 1.5-generation Koreans' marriages to first-generation Koreans. Thirty-nine percent of 1.5-generation Korean men, compared to only 18 percent of their female counterparts, have first-generation Korean marital partners. It is not difficult to understand why this gender difference has occurred. Americanized 1.5-generation Korean women with more egalitarian gender role orientations would be reluctant to choose Korean immigrant partners with more traditional gender role orientations. But many women from Korea with feminist orientations would prefer 1.5-generation Korean partners to Korean immigrant partners.

We have devoted a fair amount of space to discussing patterns of Korean Americans' inter-marriages and cross-generational in-marriages mainly because younger-generation Korean subgroups preserve Korean cultural and family traditions at different levels, depending on their partners' race or generation. Naturally, Korean intermarried families are less ethnic in their cultural and family lives than Korean in-married families. But 1.5- and second-generation Koreans married to Korean immigrants have huge advantages in preserving some Korean family traditions. In particular, Korean cross-generationally married families with immigrant women fresh from Korea are likely to socialize their children in Korean ways and maintain strong transnational ties to Korea.

References

Choi, Y. S., and Y. S. Kim. 2010. "Acculturation and the Family: Core and Peripheral Changes Among Korean Americans." *Studies of Koreans Abroad 21*, 135–190.

Dye, J. L. 2005. Fertility of American Women: June 2004. *Current Population Reports*, P20-555. Washington, DC: U.S. Census Bureau.

Foner, N. 1999. "Immigrant Women and Work in New York City, Then and Now." *Journal of American Ethnic History 18*, 95–113.

Harvey, Y. S., and S.-H. Chung. 1980. "The Koreans." In John McDermott et al. (Eds.), *People and Cultures of Hawaii* (pp. 135–154). Honolulu: University of Hawaii Press.

Heilman, S. 1982. "The Sociology of American Jewry." *Annual Review of Sociology 8*, 135–160.

Hurh, W. M., and K. W. Kim. 1990. "Religious Participation of Korean Immigrants in the United States." *Journal for the Scientific Study of Religion 29*, 19–34.

Kao, G., and M. Tienda. 1995. "Optimism and Achievement: The Educational Performance of Immigrant Youth." *Social Science Quarterly 76*, 1–19.

Kim, B. L. 1972. "Casework of Japanese and Korean Wives of Americans." *Social Casework 53*, 242–279.

———. 1978. *The Asian Immigrants: Changing Patterns, Changing Needs*. New York: Association of Christian Scholars in North America.

Kim, D. I. 2008. "The Effect of Children in School on Married Women's Labor Supply" [in Korean]. *Korean Journal of Labor Economy 31*, 73–102.

Kim, D.-S. 2005. "Theoretical Explanations of Rapid Fertility Rate in Korea." *The Japanese Journal of Population 3*, 2–25.

Kim, I. 1981. *New Urban Immigrants: The Korean Community in New York*. Princeton: Princeton University Press.

Kim, K., and W. M. Hurh. 1988. "The Burden of Double Roles: Korean Wives in the USA." *Ethnic and Racial Studies 11*, 151–167.

Kim, K. C., and S. Kim. 2001. "The Ethnic Role of Korean Immigrant Churches in the United States." In H.-Y. Kwon, K. C. Kim, and S. R. Warner (Eds.), *Korean Americans and Their Religions: Pilgrims and Missionaries* (pp. 71–94). University Park, PA: Pennsylvania State University Press.

Korean Bureau of Statistics. 1993. *A Comprehensive Analysis of the 1990 Korean Population and Housing Census (4-3): Korean Household and Family Types*. Seoul: Korean Bureau of Statistics.

Korea National Statistical Office. 2005. *2005 Social Indicators in Korea*. Seoul: Korea National Statistical Office.

Korean Women's Development Institute. 1994. *Social Statistics and Indicators on Women*. Seoul: Korean Women's Development Institute.

Lee, S., and M. Fernandez. 1998. "Trends in Asian American Racial/Ethnic Marriages: A Comparison of 1980 and 1990 Census Data." *Sociological Perspectives 42*, 323–342.

Liang, Z., and N. Ito. 1999. "Intermarriage of Asian Americans in the New York City Region:

Contemporary Patterns and Future Prospects." *International Migration Review 33*, 876–900.

Lim, I.-S. 1997. "Korean Immigrant Women's Challenge to Gender Inequality at Home: The Interplay of Economic Resources, Gender, and Family." *Gender and Society 11*, 31–51.

Louie, V. 2004. *Compelled to Excel: Immigration, Education, and Opportunity Among Chinese Americans*. Stanford, CA: Stanford University Press.

Min, K. 1988. *Hanguk Kidokgyohesa* [A History of Korean Christianity] (rev. ed.). Seoul: Korean Christian Publishing.

Min, P. G. 1984. "An Exploratory Study of Kin Ties Among Korean Immigrant Families in Atlanta." *Journal of Comparative Family Studies 15*, 59–76.

———. 1992a. "The Structure and Social Functions of Korean Immigrant Churches in the United States." *International Migration Review 26*, 1370–1394.

———. 1992b. "Korean Immigrant Wives' Overwork." *Korea Journal of Population and Development 21*, 23–36.

———. 1995. "Jaemi Gyopo Gajungeso-Eui Bumojanyo Gwange" [Parents-Child Relations in Korean Immigrant Families]. *The Academy Review of Korean Studies 18*, 119–136.

———. 1996. "The Entrepreneurial Adaptation of Korean Immigrants." In S. Pedraza and R. Rumbaut (Eds.), *Origins and Destinies: Immigration, Race, and Ethnicity in America* (pp. 302–314). Belmont, CA: Wadsworth.

———. 1997. "Korean Immigrant Wives' Labor Force Participation, Marital Power, and Status." In E. Higginbotham and M. Romero (Eds.), *Women and Work: Race, Ethnicity, and Class* (pp. 175–192). Newbury Park, CA: Sage.

———. 1998a. *Changes and Conflicts: Korean Immigrant Families in New York City*. Boston: Allyn & Bacon.

———. 1998b. "The Korean–American Family." In C. Mindel, R. W. Habenstein, and R. Wright, Jr. (Eds.), *Ethnic Families in America: Patterns and Variations* (4th ed.). Upper Saddle River, NJ: Prentice Hall.

———. 2001. "Changes in Korean Immigrants' Gender Role and Social Status, and Their Marital Conflicts." *Sociological Focus 16*, 201–220.

———. 2006a. "Asian Immigration History: Contemporary Trends and Issues." In P. G. Min (Ed.), *Asian Americans: Contemporary Trends and Issues,* (2nd ed., pp. 7–31). Thousand Oaks, CA: Pine Forge Press.

———. 2006b. "Major Issues Related to Asian American Experiences." In P. G. Min (Ed.), *Asian Americans: Contemporary Trends and Issues* (2nd ed., pp. 80–107). Thousand Oaks, CA: Pine Forge Press.

———. 2006c. "Korean Americans." In P. G. Min (Ed.), *Asian Americans: Contemporary Trends and Issues* (2nd ed., pp. 230–259). Thousand Oaks, CA: Pine Forge Press.

———. 2010. *Preserving Ethnicity Through Religion in America: Korean Protestants and Indian Hindus Across Generations*. New York: New York University Press.

Min, P. G., and C. Kim. 2009. "Patterns of Intermarriages and Cross-Generational In-marriages Among Native-Born Asian Americans." *International Migration Review 43*, 447–470.

Park, I. H., and L.-J. Cho. 1995. "Confucianism and the Korean Family." *Journal of Comparative Family Studies 26*, 117–135.

Patterson, W. 1988. *The Korean Frontier in America: Immigration to Hawaii, 1980–1916*. Honolulu, HI: University of Hawaii Press.

Rose, J., and P. G. Min. 1992. "A Comparison of Jewish-American and Korean Immigrant Families in Child Socialization." Paper presented at the Annual Meeting of the American Sociological Association, Pittsburg, PA.

Ruggles, S., M. Sobek, T. Alexander, C. A. Fitch, R. Goeken, P. K. Hall, M. King, and C. Ronnander. 2008. *Integrated Public Use Microdata Series: Version 4.0* [Machine-readable database]. Minneapolis, MN: Minnesota Population Center [producer and distributor].

Sklare, M. 1971. *America's Jews*. New York: Random House.

Suzuki, T. 2008. "Korea's Strong Familism and Lowest-Low Fertility." *International Journal of Japanese Sociology 17*, 30–41.

U.S. Bureau of the Census. 1993a. *1990 Census of Population, General Population Characteristics, United States* (CP-1-1). Washington, DC: U.S. Government Printing Office.

———. 1993b. *1990 Census of Population, Social and Economic Characteristics, United States* (CP-2-1). Washington, DC: U.S. Government Printing Office.

———. 1993c. *1990 Census of Population, Asian and Pacific Islanders in the United States* (CP-3-5). Washington, DC: U.S. Government Printing Office.

Zhou, M., and S. S. Kim. 2006. "Community Forces, Social Capital, and Educational Achievement: The Case of Supplementary Education in the Chinese and Korean Immigrant Communities." *Harvard Educational Review 76*, 1–29.

12

■ ■ ■

The Changing Vietnamese American Family

Thanh Van Tran
Phu Tai Phan

INTRODUCTION

The Vietnamese population in the United States has grown rapidly in the past three decades: from just over 100,000 in 1975 to 1,228,427 in the 2000 census. This is among the highest rate of change among all Asian American populations, and by the year 2020 the Vietnamese American population will make up 16 percent of all Asian American populations and will be the third-largest Asian American group after the Filipino and Chinese (Barringer, Gardner, and Levin, 1993; Bernstein, 2004; Gardner, Robey, and Smith, 1985). Most Vietnamese Americans are urban residents (95.4 percent) and have concentrated in major cities, with 9.8 percent in the Northeast, 8.5 percent in the Midwest, 27.4 percent in the South, and 54.3 percent in the West (Barringer et al., 1993; U.S. Census Bureau, 2000a).

The family is a fundamental social institution in every human society. It follows, then, that to understand the culture of a group or a society, one needs to understand the structure, evolution, and functions of the family in such a group or society. With this in mind, this chapter provides a comprehensive review of the Vietnamese family in American society. It focuses on the following areas:

1. The historical background of Vietnamese society
2. The traditional Vietnamese family in the context of history and culture
3. The history of immigration and resettlement
4. The present-day Vietnamese family in the United States
5. The processes of adaptation of the Vietnamese family in America from 1975 to 2000

HISTORICAL BACKGROUND

A well-known national legend has it that the Vietnamese people are children of the dragons and grandchildren of the fairies. According to this ancient legend, the son of the first Vietnamese king of the Xich Qui kingdom, Lac Long Quan, whose mother was a daughter of the dragons, married

Au Co, who was a daughter of the fairies. Au Co gave birth to 100 eggs that became 100 sons. Then Lac Long Quan decided to separate from Au Co, telling her they could not live together as a family because he came from the dragons and she came from the fairies. They agreed to split their family; he took fifty sons and moved to the seashore, and she took fifty sons and moved to the mountains. Lac Long Quan later made his first son the king of Van Lang, and he became the ancestor of the Vietnamese people (Dao, 1961; Do, 1962). This legend might be interpreted as a symbol of the first Vietnamese family conflict.

There are, in fact, different scholarly theories about the origin of the Vietnamese people. Some believe that the Vietnamese came from China; others theorize that the Vietnamese have Melanesian and Indonesian origins (Pham, 1960; Nguyen, 1967). Hinton (1985:91) suggests that "from their physical appearance, the Vietnamese appear to have a common ancestry with the Malays, Indonesians and Polynesians of Southern Asia, but there is a definite Mongolian element also present."

No matter what their origin is, the Vietnamese developed their own culture and national identity over thousands of years (Nguyen, 1967:2). In fact, Vietnamese school children have been taught that their country has over four thousand years of history. With new developments and advancements in genetic research and deoxyribonucleic acid (DNA) testing, anthropologists will soon determine the origin of Vietnamese people from a scientific perspective. Regardless of their origin, the Vietnamese have their own language and social institutions, including family, religion, education, and economic and political systems.

Historically, the Vietnamese people have been continuously subjected to domination, colonization, and invasion from outside forces, including a thousand years of Chinese domination and a hundred years of French colonization. In addition, they have been torn apart by political conflict within the nation itself (Nguyen, 1967; Marr, 1981). At the end of French colonization, Vietnam was divided into Communist North Vietnam and American-influenced South Vietnam, and war ensued immediately thereafter. The civil war between the North and South ended in 1975. In 1978, Vietnam invaded Cambodia and another war began (Hinton, 1985).

More than 1 million Vietnamese have fled their country, seeking asylum in the West since 1975. At present, a sizable Vietnamese population still emigrates to other countries to reunify with immediate relatives, to work as migrant workers overseas, and to study at foreign universities. Vietnamese living overseas have played major roles in the transformation of traditional Vietnamese society into the modern world during the twentieth century and will continue to do so in the future.

In 2009, Vietnam had an estimated population of 87 million, the fourteenth most populous country in the world, with an annual rate of population growth of .98 percent. The country had an infant mortality rate of 23 per 1,000, and life expectancy was 74 years for women and 69 years for men. Currently, Vietnam's per capita income is $2,800.00, making it 169th out of 229 countries that are ranked by the World Fact Book (CIA, 2008). Several ethnic groups make up the total population of Vietnam: the Vietnamese or the Kinh (86 percent), the Chinese, the Muong, the Thai, the Meo, the Khmer, the Man, the Cham, and mountain tribes (CIA, 2008; Hinton, 1985; U.S. Department of State, 1995). Ethnic minority groups in Vietnam have their own languages and cultures (Hickey, 1982; Kunstadter, 1967).

In religion, Vietnam has traditionally been a tolerant society. Religions practiced in this country include Confucianism, Buddhism, Taoism, Christianity (Roman Catholicism and Protestantism), Hoa Hao, Cao Dai, Animism, and Islam. There is no one national religion. At times Confucianism and Buddhism were considered the main national religions, but people were not forced to belong to any religion. Buddhism has the largest number of adherents because many Vietnamese tend to claim they are Buddhist if they do not belong to any particular organized religion.

In prehistoric times, Vietnamese society was a matriarchal tribal society. Then it developed into a simple feudal society in which the king was the head of the country. Under the king were chiefs of tribes, and each tribe had different family clans, with a clan head called the Truong Toc. In the feudal period, Vietnamese society was dominated by the male, who was also the head of the family.

During a thousand years of Chinese domination of Vietnam, the Chinese significantly influenced Vietnamese culture. However, most Vietnamese and Western historians agree that Vietnamese culture, although containing many similarities to Chinese culture, has managed to preserve its own unique national characteristics and identity (Dao, 1961; Do, 1962). The ability of the Vietnamese to preserve their unique identity under different external influences was determined by their will to fight against the invaders. Taylor (1983:xviii) explains that "no theme is more consistent in Vietnam history that the theme of resistance to foreign aggression." With such a long history, Vietnamese society accumulated many traditions that have been passed down from generation to generation.

Traditional Vietnamese Society

Although it is hard to describe traditional Vietnamese society exactly, Pham (1960) and other historians agree that, following the prehistoric period, it was similar in many ways to traditional Chinese society. The king occupied the highest social position. He was considered the Thien Tu ("son of God") and had absolute power. In the family, the head of a family also had absolute power. The two main social classes were the rulers and the ruled. The rulers were kings and their significant others. Among the ruled, there were four traditional occupations: scholar, farmer, artisan, and trader. Scholars held the most respected occupation in society. Because this social group had access to governmental positions, scholars could potentially help their entire family and their village. Not all scholars were appointed to serve the king; many remained in their villages as teachers or medicine men. Their sons usually continued the scholarly tradition of learning, preparing for the civil exams, and waiting for the chance to become mandarins, ministers or higher level of bureaucrats in the monarchist periods. Most of the population were farmers, including landowners and hired hands; a small number were artisans or traders. An old Vietnamese proverb states, "The scholar ranks first, and then the peasant; but when the rice fails and men run wildly about, then the peasant comes first and the scholar second" (Do, 1962:138).

In traditional Vietnamese society, the village was considered next in importance to one's family. Nguyen describes a traditional Vietnamese village as "a group of patriarchal families whose members shared the same family name" (1967:16). Moreover, in the past the village was the place where most Vietnamese were born, grew up, got married, and died. A typical traditional village is a combination of several extended families. In those villages, the larger the family, the more influential and powerful it tends to be. Traditional villages have their own cultures, deity, tradition, and laws.

Recent studies offer new revelations about the traditional Vietnamese village. It could be a single extended family-based type, with all village members belonging to an extended family system. Such single extended family-based villages often bear the names of their founders. Outsiders are excluded from these family-based villages. In some villages, outside people could only migrate to a village if they changed their family name and adapted the village family name. Other villages require that an outsider can live in the village if that person is adopted by the village. Many traditional villages are founded on public land where villagers farm the public-owned land and pay taxes to the government for use of the land.

The Traditional Vietnamese Family

In traditional Vietnamese society, the family is the center of an individual's life and activities. Toan Anh (1969), a well-known scholar of Vietnamese tradition and culture, notes that a Vietnamese person usually cares about his or her family more than about himself or herself. The word *family* in Vietnamese means a social entity that consists of all an individual's relatives, not just father, mother, and siblings. Some authors have argued that the traditional Vietnamese family was modeled after the traditional Chinese family in terms of its ethical and moral structure (Che, 1979; Pham, 1960; Toan Anh, 1969; Vuong, 1976). Others have stressed that the traditional family in Vietnamese culture is a dynamic concept that is not really capable of definition (Tran, 1991). Though Chinese culture has had deep influences on Vietnamese culture, the Vietnamese family has its own unique structure and culture.

The teachings of Confucius clearly define the power, position, responsibilities, and relationship of each member of a family. There are certain fundamental characteristics of the traditional family, such as domination by sex hierarchy (father–son relationship), by age hierarchy (the elderly have more power), the center of loyalty, and the cult of ancestor worship. An individual is expected to be loyal to his or her family and obey and respect elders. Parents are required to raise and educate their children. Children are required to take care of their parents when they become old or sick and to worship their parents when they die.

Tran (1991) discusses two typical traditional Vietnamese families—the scholar family and the peasant family—as they differ in economic and social factors. Scholar families enjoy high social status and respect from society and depend on the achievement of the male head of the family. If he is a success—that is, he passes exams and is appointed to serve the king—his family will receive salaries and be given public land. For traditional scholar families, family life and activities are centered around the men's studies and taking exams because, if he passes, it would secure the family's economic well-being. Scholars who do not pass exams or are not called to serve the king often stay in their villages as teachers or medicine men. Women are the key providers in scholar families. In classic Vietnamese literature, several scholars praised their wives for their economic support. A renowned classic Vietnamese scholar, Tran Te Xuong (1879–1907), who failed his exams and never had adequate means to support himself and his family, wrote several famous poems praising his wife as the key breadwinner of his family. The poems about his wife reflected the role of women in a traditional scholar family, especially those scholars who did not pass the civil exams. In the first two lines of the poem "Thuong Vo" ("Love for My Wife"), he writes:

> *Quanh nam buon ban o mom song*
> *Nuoi du nam con voi mot chong.*
>
> All year-round you engaged in petty commerce by the side of the river To feed all five children, and a husband Tran (n.d.)

Although valuable as historical artifacts about the role of women, such admission is rare in patriarchal societies such as traditional Vietnam.

The majority of traditional Vietnamese families are peasant families organized around agricultural seasons and activities. In a typical traditional village, most peasants do not own land. They work on public land or for more wealthy, landowning peasant families. Landless peasant families have to earn their living by doing things other than farming. Wealthy peasant families are typically self-sufficient and are able to hire outside labor. Most family activities in the traditional Vietnamese family are agricultural and related to farming.

Vietnamese Kinship System

The Vietnamese kinship system is a patrilineal, or male-oriented, kinship system (Hickey, 1964; Luong, 1984). The term for the kinship system in the Vietnamese language, *Ho,* describes an extended family system that includes both living and deceased members. The Ho consists of a combination of small families (*Nha*) of different generations. There are two types of Ho: *Ho Noi* and *Ho Ngoai*. The Ho Noi consists of all relatives on the father's side, and the Ho Ngoai consists of all relatives on the mother's side. Members of the third generation of the Ho Ngoai are allowed to marry each other. In his classic study, Spencer describes the Vietnamese kinship system as "bifurcate collateral in that it distinguishes paternal and maternal aunts and uncles from one another as well as from the parents" (1945:286).

Very little has been written about the Vietnamese kinship system. The available anthropological studies examine only the structural pattern of the kinship system (Benedict, 1947; Luong, 1984; Spencer, 1945), and there are few studies on the evolution, relationship, and function of the kinship system in terms of individual Vietnamese life situations. To better understand the traditional Vietnamese family, we must study the role and function of each member within the family unit.

The Head of the Family and the Father

In a traditional Vietnamese extended family, the head of the family is called the *Truong Toc*. The Truong Toc is the oldest male, and he is responsible for maintaining the patrimonial land, ancestral graves, and worship of the common ancestors. He makes decisions about matters related to the lives of the extended family.

The heads of the traditional Vietnamese nuclear family (*Gia Truong*) are the grandparents, if they are alive. Upon the death of the grandparents the father becomes the head of the family, and the eldest son will take over this position at the death of the father. Traditionally, the head of the family has absolute power over the members of his family. Toan Anh (1969) notes that the role of the head of the family is similar to the role of the king. Nguyen explains this further: "At the top of each family, the paterfamilias of *gia-truong* exercised an absolute authority over his wife and children. He had full power to act and command. He was invested with rights prevailing over those of the other members of the family" (1965:15).

The head of the family is responsible not only for the living members of the family but also for those who are deceased. His obligations are to take care of the living and to worship the spirits of the dead. Under traditional law, the head of the family also bears the legal responsibility for all members of the family. The law punishes a father for failing to prevent his children or other members of the family from committing crimes (Whitfield, 1976).

The Mother and the Wife

In traditional society, Vietnamese women, like Chinese women (Che, 1979; Toan Anh, 1969) have no power and fewer privileges than Vietnamese men. A Vietnamese woman is expected to obey her father when she is single and her husband after she gets married and to live with her eldest son when she becomes a widow. Morally, she is not expected to marry again after her husband dies. After her marriage, a Vietnamese woman is expected to live with her husband's parents until her husband is ready to have his own house, to obey them absolutely, and to serve and care for them. Her husband has the right to punish her if he thinks that she has done something wrong. She can be divorced by her husband under seven conditions: (1) if she disobeys her husband's parents, (2) if she cannot have children, (3) if she commits adultery, (4) if she is overly jealous, (5) if she has an incurable disease, (6) if she is garrulous, and (7) if she is a thief (Toan Anh, 1969). A husband is not permitted to divorce his wife under these three conditions: (1) if she has been in mourning for her husband's relatives for three years, (2) if she and her husband become rich after the marriage (they were both poor before their marriage), and (3) if no one will be available to take care of her if her husband divorces her (Phan, 1975). A woman cannot leave or separate from her husband; this act is viewed as a crime. The only areas in which a husband and wife have equal rights are properties and debts.

In many traditional villages, polygamy was common before the 1959 Family Act was passed by the National Assembly of the South Vietnamese government, making both polygamy and concubinage illegal (Hickey, 1964). At the same time, the North Vietnamese government also abolished polygamy in its national constitution (Nguyen, 1993). Under polygamy, the first wife in a family had more power than subsequent wives. The first wife could decide to find another wife for her husband if she felt that he needed one. The practice of polygamy exhibited some common characteristics: It often occurred among the rich; in families in which the first wife could not have children, especially sons; and in families that needed more people to work on the farm.

As a woman and a wife, a Vietnamese woman has very limited rights. She has to accept control by the men in her life: father, husband, and son. Vietnamese women in traditional society begin to gain some power when they become mothers. A mother holds the second rank in power in a family after the father. She can expect her children to obey and respect her, and she manages her family in the absence of her husband. Many Vietnamese mothers have raised and managed their families while their husbands were engaged in war(s). Indeed, as a result of Vietnam experiencing so many wars and turmoil during its history, Vietnamese women have had no choice but to assume the role of head of the family for much of its existence.

Children

The teachings of Confucius require children to obey and respect their parents. Children's piety for their parents is regarded as the most important moral obligation of children while their parents are alive and after they die (Phan, 1975). Vietnamese children must live with their parents until they are married and have their own house (Toan Anh, 1969); they are expected to contribute to the family economy, but they own nothing. When they are old enough, they are required to work and bring home their wages and salaries. In turn, the parents are obligated to provide for all of the children's needs, including helping them in adulthood with the purchase of a home whenever possible.

SOCIALIZATION.   The socialization process of Vietnamese children takes place in everyday life situations. The teachings of Confucius give the father the most responsibility in socializing children. One of the traditional principles of the role of the father is that of *Duong bat giao, phu chi qua*, which means that failing to raise a child appropriately is the mistake of the father. However, society tends to blame the mother for the child's misconduct or deviant behavior. An old Vietnamese saying, *con hu tai me*, means that a child is spoiled by the mother (Toan Anh, 1969). Mothers tend to take their children with them to visit neighbors and attend religious or social ceremonies in order to teach them how to deal with different people and how to behave in different social situations. Parents and the older siblings are expected to set good examples, respectively, for their children and younger siblings. Life experiences are passed down from grandparents to parents, from parents to older siblings, and from older to younger siblings.

Siblings

In the traditional Vietnamese family hierarchy, older people have more power than younger people. The eldest son in the family (*Anh Ca* or *Anh Hai*) is expected to assume more responsibility in taking care of the family after the death of his father. A Vietnamese proverb states, "The older brother has the same power as the father in the absence of the father." The older sister also has more power than her younger brothers and sisters. Siblings of the same parents are called *Dong Bao;* siblings of the same father but different mothers are called *Di Bao.* Siblings are expected to express mutual affection and protection for each other. When one is in trouble, the others are obligated to help. Vietnamese siblings are expected to share everything they have with each other while they live under the same roof. However, Vietnamese parents often think about their sons' education before that of their daughters. In traditional Vietnamese society, boys are educated, whereas females are often excluded.

Traditional scholars are all males because only male scholars take exams and are called to serve the king. Although female have been heads of the country in a couple of instances, no females were ever appointed as mandarins throughout the ancient periods of Vietnamese history.

The Elderly

As in many traditional societies (Keith, 1982) old age is respected and valued in traditional Vietnamese society (Toan Anh, 1965). The hierarchy of social status differs between government and village. In government, hierarchy is defined by position, whereas age determines social status in a village. The older the person, the higher the social status. For example, Le (1992) noted that in traditional village festivals the most important ceremony, Dai Te, was performed by seventeen or twenty-one men who were the elders or people with the highest education in the village. Although both elderly men and women are equally respected, the attendant social status is for men more than women.

Old people are respected because of their experience, skills, and knowledge. They are also respected because of their longevity. In Vietnamese culture, longevity is one of the three conditions of happiness after esteem (social status) and numerous children. When a person reaches fifty, sixty, and seventy years of age, his children must give him a reception at the village's communal hall to honor and celebrate his longevity. The older the person, the bigger the reception. The children have to prepare special food as thanks-giving gifts to the gods for their parent's longevity. The longevity reception is also a way for children to show appreciation to their parents and their willingness to take care of them in their old age. However, because Vietnam is a traditionally patriarchal society, old men have more power than their women counterparts. In many regions in Vietnam, if both elderly parents are alive, children often celebrate their father's longevity, not their mother's; the mother's longevity is celebrated if the father is dead.

The traditional civil code requires children to take care of their elderly parents. Those who mistreated their elderly parents are subjected to caning, with the maximum punishment of eighty lashes. However, the punishment is executed only if the elderly parent files a formal complaint against his or her children (Dao, 1961). It is unusual, however, for parents to bring their children to court for abuse and/or neglect, because of close social control and fear of losing face with neighbors and relatives. Contemporary Vietnamese family codes require that all children share equal responsibility in taking care of their parents when they are unable to take care of themselves. Grandchildren are responsible for their grandparents' economic well-being when they don't have the means or sources of support (Nguyen, 1993). A study of an ancient village in North Vietnam found a written village code of social conduct that specifically required all villagers to assist the elderly. The village law stated that anyone who met an elder on a street carrying heavy things must assist that person. Those who ignored such an elderly person were subjected to punishment (Phan, 1992).

Marriage

The ultimate goal of marriage in traditional Vietnamese society is to bear children (Toan Anh, 1965). According to the teachings of Confucius, marriage is a ceremony that allows a man to continue his family clan by having new children (Dao, 1961). Parents choose the marriage partner for their children. There is an old Vietnamese saying that "one needs to know the origin of the man or woman whom one would marry." It is also assumed that only parents have the proper knowledge to choose a wife or a husband for their children. Boys and girls are not allowed to date or choose their own mate. In traditional Vietnamese society boys are allowed to marry at sixteen years of age and girls at thirteen. However, in traditional scholar families, parents look for a wife for a student after his graduation.

Marriage is one of the most important events in a Vietnamese person's life. Traditionally, the marriage ceremony is complicated and colorful, encompassing five different traditional ceremonial events in the celebration (Toan Anh, 1965). The first ceremony, *Le Ban Tin*, is held after the parents and the son find the right girl in the village. The parents ask the *Ba Mai* (matchmaker woman) who knows the young woman's family to deliver a message about their desire to marry her to their son. The Ba Mai also observes the reaction of the young woman's family to the proposal and reports it to the young man's parents. The second ceremony, *Le Cham Ngo*, is held after the young woman's parents accept the proposal of the young man's parents and allow the young man and his parents to take a good look at the young woman and her family. In the third ceremony, *Le An Giam*, the young man's parents send someone with gifts to the girl's family to ask for her birth certificate. The fourth ceremony, *Le An Hoi*, requires both families to officially announce the engagement of their children. Between Le An Hoi and the wedding ceremony, the young man must practice *Sieu*, which means that he has to bring gifts to the girl's parents in March, May, August, and October, with each of these months representing a season. These gifts are often local agricultural products. Besides the Sieu, the young man is required to bring gifts to the young woman's house for special religious or social ceremonies, such as the *Tet* (New Year's day). In many traditional villages the young man has to work for the woman's family for a certain period of time and do anything that the girl's family wants. Last comes the wedding ceremony, *Le Than Nghinh* or *Le Hon Nhan*, in which the man's family brings the new daughter-in-law home. This is the most important ceremony, and it is complicated and costly. Often the entire village, including relatives and guests from the bride's family, is invited to the ceremony, and all expenses are paid for by the groom's family.

These wedding traditions vary from village to village or among geographical regions. Today marriage ceremonies have become simpler. People often practice only three ceremonies: the first meeting between the man's family and the woman's family, the engagement ceremony, and the wedding ceremony. In general, after the marriage ceremony, the young couple lives with the husband's family. The new daughter-in-law has to completely adjust and adapt to her husband's parents. She is expected to obey her husband's parents and to do everything to please them. The couple will live with the husband's parents until they are able to afford to live independently.

MARRIAGE TO FOREIGNERS.   Vietnam was under the domination of China for a thousand years followed by a hundred-year period of French colonization and twenty years of U.S. and

Soviet influence during the period of the Vietnam War. Though Vietnam has a long history of exposure to foreigners and foreign cultures, marriages with foreigners have been considered taboo. Traditionally, Vietnamese women were expected to marry men in the same village. An old Vietnamese saying states, "A woman is better off marrying the poorest man in her own village than the richest man in another village." This traditional attitude has had significant influence on the Vietnamese attitude toward women who marry foreigners. Toan Anh (1969) notes that there is more concern about women who marry foreigners than about men who do so. Although at times women from the royal family have married foreigners, general public opinion has been negative toward women who marry foreigners, especially Westerners.

Immigration History and Resettlement

The terms *Indochinese refugee* and *Southeast Asian refugee* have been used to refer to refugees who have arrived in the United States since 1975 from the three nations of Indochina: Cambodia (Kampuchea), Laos, and Vietnam. Although Indochinese refugees share some cultural, historical, and religious similarities, each is a unique group of people with their own language, nationality, ethnic identity, history, and culture (see Strand and Jones, 1985). Since they share a similar history of immigration to the United States, it is important to include all three nations in this discussion of immigration history and community development.

Unlike other Asian American groups with a long history of emigration to the United States, Indochinese refugees are one of the most recent immigrant groups, arriving in large numbers since 1975. Statistics show that before 1975 very few Indochinese immigrants were in the United States. Indeed, in the 1950s there were only 179 Indochinese immigrants; this population increased to 3,503 in the 1960s and 18,558 in 1974 (U.S. Department of Health and Human Services, 1985). The Vietnamese make up the largest subgroup of the Indochinese population in the United States.

On April 30, 1975, when the South Vietnamese government collapsed, more than 100,000 Vietnamese escaped from South Vietnam to avoid persecution by the North Vietnamese Communists. South Vietnamese soldiers, government officials, businessmen, religious leaders, students, fishermen, and people from every social class in South Vietnam risked their lives for a new, unknown refuge. The U.S. government quickly responded to the Vietnamese refugee crisis by ordering its navy in the Pacific to rescue Vietnamese refugees (Montero, 1979). Refugee centers were established to receive and process the first group of Vietnamese refugees arriving in America, even though at the time more than half of the American people believed that Vietnamese refugees should not be allowed to enter or remain in the United States (Deming et al., 1975). Schaefer (1979:122) describes the American perception of Vietnamese refugees in 1975:

> In almost all segments of the population—the college educated, the rich, the poor, Blacks, Protestants and Catholics—only the minority favored permitting the South Vietnamese to live in the country. Only the young, those under thirty, seemed to favor settlement but even a third of that group rejected the idea. Rejection was greatest among the working class where almost two-thirds opposed accepting South Vietnamese.

Despite this strong rejection by the American public against the settlement of Vietnamese refugees, the U.S. government felt a moral obligation to receive Vietnamese refugees in the aftermath of the Vietnam War (1975). However, the United States was not the only nation that gave political asylum to Vietnamese refugees; more than a dozen nations in the world also responded and took in Vietnamese refugees. It was the largest influx of refugees into the United States in history, and remnants of this immigration continues today.

Vietnamese refugees have concentrated and built their communities in specific areas of the country. Thus, despite the U.S. government's initial policy of refugee dispersement throughout the country, Vietnamese refugees engaged in secondary migration soon after their arrival. These secondary migrations resulted in large Vietnamese ethnic enclaves in California, Texas, and other urban areas in the United States.

The first wave of Vietnamese refugees who arrived in the United States in 1975 were well educated and have successfully adapted to American society. More recent Vietnamese refugees, however, have come from a lower socioeconomic level in Vietnam and tend to experience more socioeconomic problems than their first-wave counterparts (Strand and Jones, 1985). Nguyen (1985) identifies four types of Vietnamese refugees in the United States:

1. The first-wave refugees, who left South Vietnam at the end of the war in 1975 and tend to be more educated than the later refugees or immigrants
2. The second-wave refugees, also called the "boat people," who left Vietnam during the 1978–1979 period, among them ordinary people and many ethnic Chinese who fled the Vietnamese communist government's persecution of ethnic Chinese
3. The escapees who either organized their trips by way of boats to the Philippines, Thailand, Malaysia, Singapore, or Japan, or by walking across the borders of Laos and Cambodia to Thailand
4. The orderly departees, who emigrated since 1979 after the Vietnamese communist government agreed with the United Nations High Commissioner for Refugees to allow Vietnamese to join their immediate relatives, such as parents, spouses, children, and siblings abroad (In addition, the U.S. government also accepted its former employees in Vietnam.)

Since then, two special groups have been arriving in the United States: Amerasians and former political detainees and their families. Amerasians were the children of U.S. servicemen and Vietnamese mothers, and many of them were subjected to prejudice because of cultural attitudes and the new government's "re-education" of the masses. The Amerasian Homecoming Act of 1988 has brought more than 30,000 Amerasians and their families to the United States. Although some Amerasians have adjusted well into their new life in the United States, many of them have faced both mental and physical difficulties. Since many have had very little schooling in Vietnam, in America they have struggled with the mental health issues of abandonment, drug use, and a multitude of other problems, including acquisition of language skills. One example is the fact that despite being sons and daughters of American servicemen, Amerasians were not given automatic citizenship and many could not pass the citizenship test. It took almost twenty years with intense lobbying efforts for the Amerasian Paternity Recognition Act of 2003 to pass and provide Amerasians with citizenship (Amerasian Foundation, n.d.). For many, this law came too late, since many of them were now middle aged and job opportunities that came with citizenship were no longer available.

The former political detainees are people who were imprisoned in Vietnam because of their links with the former South Vietnamese governments or with the U.S. government. The majority of these people are men in their late forties or mid-fifties who have spent years in forced labor camps and now have a multitude of problems themselves, much the same way that returning U.S. veterans of war are afflicted with depression and posttraumatic stress disorder (PTSD). In the United States, these former political detainees became active in forming mutual aid associations and held anticommunist rallies, while actively working for human rights in Vietnam. Since most former political detainees came to the United States with their immediate family members, the

Vietnamese American community grew quickly. They and the Amerasians are unique groups of Vietnamese immigrants, who came with different backgrounds and expectations and have brought new life to Vietnamese American communities.

Since 1980, many Vietnamese communities have been developed and established throughout the United States. These communities offer newcomers all kinds of supports and services that the earlier Vietnamese refugees did not have. In addition, many recent immigrants were more prepared because they had time and knew their destination while their predecessors did not. For example, a well-educated former political detainee recalls his story:

> Once I knew I was permitted to come to America, I did everything I could to prepare myself and my family for the journey. I forced my children to learn as much English as they could. I myself got a job as a tourist guide for a travel agency so I could practice my English with English-speaking tourists. I also worked as a waiter in restaurants which catered to foreigners to practice my English (Tran, 1998).

But expectations and reality sometimes do not match. A middle-aged woman from a rural village who came to the United States to join her husband recalls:

> I knew I had to prepare myself to get a job in America. He (my husband) warned me that everybody needs a job here and it's not like working in a rice or coffee farm in my village. So I went to town to learn to sew and to operate sewing machines. Unfortunately there are no sewing jobs around here. And even if there were sewing jobs, I could not do it because things are different here. I need to learn English first. I wished I could learn English in Vietnam but there were no English classes in my village (Tran, 1998).

The Vietnamese American population has increased from just over 100,000 in 1975 to more than 1,508,489 million at the end of 2007. After three decades of settling in the United States, more than 77 percent of Vietnamese are now living in 10 states with 43.9 percent in California (see Table 12.1).

TABLE 12.1 Concentration of Large Vietnamese American Communities in 10 States: 2000

States with High Concentration	Percent
California	43.9
Florida	3.2
Georgia	2.4
Louisiana	2.1
Massachusetts	3.2
New York	1.9
Pennsylvania	2.1
Texas	11.1
Virginia	3.4
Washington	4.2
Total	77.5

Source: Authors' calculations using U.S. Census Bureau (2000b), 5 percent Public Use Microdata Sample (PUMS).

THE VIETNAMESE FAMILY IN AMERICA

Background

There is no doubt that the present-day Vietnamese family in the United States is the product of the traditional family in Vietnamese society. As in other traditional societies, one of the significant values of the traditional Vietnamese family is the mutual caring or concern among its members; the old saying "One drop of blood is much more precious than a pond full of water" means that one should always value one's relatives no matter who they are. As Bell (1985:30) notes, "All of the various explanations of the Asian Americans' success tend to fall into one category: self-sufficiency. The first element of this self-sufficiency is family." Although traditional family values continue to influence contemporary Vietnamese families, one should realize that changes in economic, sociocultural, and technological environments have modified the family structure, traditions, and values of overseas Vietnamese families. Vuong (1976:21–22) describes the Vietnamese family prior to arrival in the United States:

> It is a mini-commune where its members live and share together, a maternity center where children are born, a funeral home where funeral rituals are performed, a religious place where the family alter is set up to revere ancestors or observe rituals, a welfare center where assistance and social security services are rendered, a nursing home where the elderly are taken good care of, an educational institution where family and formal education is provided, a bank where money is available and a place where all members share the joys, the sadness, the enjoyments, the suffering of life.

Vuong's description of the Vietnamese family is an ideal one that is no longer true of many contemporary Vietnamese families, especially the Vietnamese American family. In the midst of a changing world, traditional values seem to be losing ground. Moreover, Vietnamese culture is very resilient and adaptable as expressed in an old saying, "Nhap gia tuy tuc." This means literally that when entering someone's house, you should follow their values and traditions. Hence, some of the changes have been voluntarily adopted by Vietnamese Americans.

A Vietnamese can always depend on family or relatives in time of need, and it is a moral obligation to support one's family and relatives. The responsibilities of an individual Vietnamese person to his or her family are the same no matter how far this person may live from his or her family. Haines, Rutherford, and Thomas (1981), who have studied the Vietnamese refugee family and community structure in the United States, note that the Vietnamese family has no geographical boundary; its members are bound together by traditional values and moral obligations.

The following is an example of a Vietnamese person's responsibilities toward his family even though he has been separated from them since his early teens:

> Tuan is a Vietnamese graduate student in his early thirties who came into the United States with his relatives twenty years ago. At the time, his parents' strategy was to send him first with relatives and stayed behind so that they could help him in case he is caught. His parents and siblings are still in Vietnam and despite Tuan's urging, the parents said they were too old to start a new life in America so they continue to stay in Vietnam. Tuan's siblings are now all married with multiple children and does not have the knowledge and resources to file for emigration to the U.S. Tuan carries great responsibilities because he is the only son who has opportunities to provide economic support to his family. As a graduate student, he is only able to get by but managed to send home at least $2,000 a year in the last several years. This source of income has tremendously improved the quality of life of his parents and siblings in Vietnam. However, he is scared to call Vietnam because every time he does, he learns that more money is required

because a relative is sick, someone is getting married, a nephew needs books for school, etc. He is concerned about whether he will be able to send home money forever, especially when he marries and has his own family. He does not say it, but because of these concerns, he has been afraid to get serious with women that he occasionally goes out with (Huynh, 2009).

Tuan's story is not an exception in the Vietnamese American and other overseas Vietnamese communities. Numerous Vietnamese persons of all ages and genders have continued to support their immediate and extended families even though they live far apart. However, not all Vietnamese persons feel the same sense of responsibility toward the well-being of other family members. The following case is an example of Vietnamese persons who place their own well-being before that of their family. The reader will notice that the husband–wife hierarchy in America is also in conflict:

> The Nguyen family is a well-to-do family who arrived in the United States in 1975. Mr. and Mrs. Nguyen have three children and all of them are college graduates with decent jobs. Mr. and Mrs. Nguyen have constantly been in conflict because they cannot agree on whether and how much they should send money to help their siblings in Vietnam. Mrs. Nguyen's philosophy is that she has to work very hard to maintain her family living standard; therefore, she is responsible only for her children. Mr. Nguyen has complained that his wife is extravagant in many respects. For example, he argues that she could use the money she spent on her jewelry to help his and her siblings in Vietnam. Mrs. Nguyen's rationale is that she bought expensive jewelry as an investment for her children. She will give them all of it when she dies. Mr. Nguyen has not been able to influence her in helping relatives and has been very resentful toward her. The problem is compounded because he feels she no longer respect his authority as head of the household (Tran, 1998).

In other families, conflicts often occur either because the wife or the husband has sent "too much" money to help his or her relatives in Vietnam. Although hard data are hard to come by, a perusal of any Vietnamese newspaper's version of "Dear Abby" will provide the reader with many anecdotes about financial disagreements because of extended family obligations (Viet Tribune Online, 2008). Long-distance family responsibilities are a source of family stress and conflict in many Vietnamese American families.

Characteristics of the Vietnamese American Family

The structure of the Vietnamese American family has changed significantly during the past three decades. For example, our analyses of the U.S. census data in 1980, 1990, and 2000 (U.S. Census Bureau, 1980, 1990, 2000b) have revealed significant changes in the various compositions and structures of the Vietnamese American family. In general, the Vietnamese American family size has decreased to an average of 4.3 in 2000 from 5.33 in 1980. In the 1980s, almost 60 percent (59.9 percent) of Vietnamese households had 6 or more members; this percentage has decreased to 51.7 percent in the 1990s and to 49.4 percent in the 2000s. The percentage of families with 1 or more children has decreased noticeably from 36.5 percent in the 1980s to 32.1 percent in the 1990s and 10.7 percent in the 2000s. Similarly, the percentage of married couples living in the same household also has decreased from 71.4 percent in the 1980s to 69.2 percent in the 2000s. However, the percentage of multigenerational Vietnamese families living in the same household remains as high as 17 percent in 2000 (Xie and Goyette, 2004).

Marital status is one of the powerful indicators of family structure. U.S. census data (2007) revealed that among the Vietnamese population age 15 years and older, 55.8 percent were married compared to 50.2 percent of the total U.S. population. Interestingly, the percent of divorced among Vietnamese population (5.7 percent) was half the percentage of divorced in the total population (10.5 percent). Vietnamese men age 15 and older had a significantly lower percentage of divorced (4.1 percent) compared to Vietnamese women (7.2 percent). Sex difference in the prevalence of divorced is slightly greater in the Vietnamese population than in the general total U.S. population (i.e., 9.3 percent for men and 11.7 percent for women). However, this prevalence of divorced was estimated for the entire population, including those who were never married (U.S. Census Bureau, 2007).

In terms of economic conditions, several positive changes have occurred in the past two decades. The median family income increased from $12,000 in 1980 to $30,000 in 1990, to $40,000 in 1999, and $54,048 in 2007. The percentage of families in poverty also decreased drastically from 35 percent in 1980 to 20 percent in 1999 and 11.3 percent in 2007. More Vietnamese Americans have completed a high school or a college education since 1980. For example, in 1980 only 14 percent of foreign-born Vietnamese had a college degree or higher, but this number increased to 27 percent in 2000. From an economic perspective, the Vietnamese American family has adjusted and adapted well to the mainstream American way. Changes in median family income, education, and percentage of families in poverty over the past three decades have demonstrated the economic success of the Vietnamese American family (Xie and Goyette, 2004; U.S. Bureau of Census, 2007).

The following case illustrates some family factors that contribute to the economic adaptation and success of the Vietnamese family in America.

> The Pham family arrived in the United States in 1975. This extended family has seven small families with thirty-seven people. The families first resettled in Iowa through the refugee sponsor program of the United States Catholic Conference (USCC). Because no sponsor could take the whole extended family in one community, they decided to settle in close proximity as adult members of the families found jobs in various local milk farm and food processing factories. This extended family stayed in Iowa for about two years. The head of the extended family, a strong and wise man, decided that the family had to move to an area with a larger Vietnamese population because some of the children in the families were ready to marry and there were not enough Vietnamese in Iowa for them to court. Accordingly, they moved to Southern California, the largest Vietnamese community in the United States. They stayed in California for two years, during which time some older children got married. Mr. Pham learned a trade, which later became the main source of economic stability for the whole extended family, by becoming an upholsterer though a public job training program.
>
> Because California was too expensive for the family to own a decent house, they decided to move to Texas in 1970 and have lived in the Dallas-Fort Worth metropolitan area ever since. Few Vietnamese Americans have done as exceptionally well as the Pham family. All of the children who arrived in the United States in their teens now have college degrees in engineering, business, and medicine. There are four medical doctors, three with masters' degrees. Children from other branches of this extended family also have done exceptionally well, and many graduated from colleges with advanced professional degrees in engineering, law, and medicine. Education attainment was the family's goal, and all activities of the family centered around the children's education, putting great pressure on all children to achieve. Mr. Pham demands great respect from his own children and members of his extended family. At the same time, he gave them a sense of direction and goals. Family ties and respect for education are the key for economic and educational success of the Pham family (Pham, 2009).

Although Mr. Pham's family appears to be an exception, other Vietnamese American families have done well because they were able to preserve their traditional family values while venturing into new areas of business. The last twenty years saw a boom in the manicuring industry for Vietnamese Americans. It has been estimated that of 311,725 manicurists in the United States in 2002, over 50 percent of them were of Vietnamese descent, compared to 10 percent African American and Hispanic combined (Ha, 2002). In California, more than 66 percent of manicurists are Vietnamese (Greenhouse, 2007). Well spread out in big and small, rural and urban communities in the United States, many manicuring salons are owned and operated by Vietnamese with great success. In fact, they are so spread out and successful that chances are very good that if one is new to a city and wants to find out about the local Vietnamese community, all that needs to be done is to find the nearest nail salon where chances are very good that either the workers and/or the owners are Vietnamese. One other indication of the Vietnamese American manicurists' strength and economic success is the fact that the United Food and Commercial Workers (UFCW) Union in San Jose, California, is trying to organize them to join their union (Porter et al., 2009).

Vietnamese American families pooled their resources to learn, train, and operate these manicuring salons that cater to mostly Caucasians, African Americans, and Hispanics. What is also interesting is the fact that even though manicuring is traditionally seen as "women's work," Vietnamese American men are now a sizable force in this industry. Although only 2.4 percent of the nation's manicurists (also called nail technicians) are male, it has been estimated that almost all of the males are of Vietnamese descent (Phan, 2003). Like families operating family businesses in other ethnic communities, the Vietnamese American community has found its niche in the "nail" business, and in these family-run businesses they are able to preserve their family values in a way that families who work apart cannot.

However, children of a number of Vietnamese American families are not as successful as those in the Pham family. The following two cases illustrate the lack of traditional family values and its impact on the children and family members:

> The Tran family arrived in the United States in 2000 under the sponsorship of Mrs. Tran's father. They have one son, 15 years old, and one daughter, who is 12. Once in the U.S., both parents went to work right away at local electronic assembly plants. Feeling that they came to the U.S. "too late" in comparison with his in-laws, Mr. Tran pushed himself to work hard so he could have what his in-laws has. He took on a second job, working a total of 16 hours a day. His wife also worked hard and took an additional part-time job to save for a new car. Unfortunately once they were able to save enough money, they bought the things they wanted but they continued to work the extra jobs convincing themselves that it was good because they can provide material things to the children. Two years into their resettlement, their son moved back to Vietnam without the parents' consent to live with his paternal grandparents because he felt there was no "family life." The daughter then became severely depressed and started acting out in sexually promiscuous ways. Against the repeated recommendations of counselors, the parents continued to work two jobs and blame their children for being "selfish" and did not understand why it was a problem that they themselves worked hard to provide for their children's needs (Tran, 2009).

The second case involves the family of a single mother whose husband died in Vietnam when she and four children came to the United States.

> Mrs. Hai came to the United States with four young children in 1999 after waiting 12 years with the sponsorship of her brother. Her husband died in Vietnam of cancer right before they got the visas to come to the U.S. As a single mother in her late thirties with little education and skills, she worked in a factory and moonlighted by sewing for a Vietnamese man who had a work contract with a local garment factory. Soon thereafter, she dated a man from work and

without the children knowing, he moved into the house and acted as stepfather to the children. He grew increasingly abusive to the children and the children mostly took it in silence until they reached adolescence, when the oldest boy dropped out of high school, held several odd jobs, and became an alcoholic. Two girls finished high school and got married early as a means of getting out of the house. The youngest boy was involved in drugs and had problems with the law. It was then that the boyfriend moved out. Economically, Mrs. Hai had been a successful woman. After several years of hard work and thrift, she now owns three houses, but she has never been happy because of her children's failures, which she now blames herself (Hai, 2009).

In contrast to the Pham family, the families of Mr. Tran and Mrs. Hai did not have a head of household who could provide guidance and moral support for the children. Unfortunately, family relationships in many Vietnamese American families have deteriorated because of economic pressures and lack of knowledge about the society.

Family Values

Many of the traditional values of the Vietnamese family are still held by the majority of Vietnamese now in America. However, the American economic system tends to force some changes. For example, Vietnamese children are becoming more economically independent, and many young Vietnamese are now able to work and bring home wages and salaries. Traditionally, the majority of this group would be nonproductive members of their families. If they were students, they would have to depend on their parents for financial support. In addition, many Vietnamese parents are aware of the fact that their children know more about America and Americans than they do; therefore, young Vietnamese are now allowed more freedom. Parents also no longer require their children to live with them until they get married, as they did in Vietnam. Many young Vietnamese, because of their job and career situations, now have to move away from home to work in another city or state. With communication and transportation technology available, the young Vietnamese are changing their attitudes toward dating and marriage. Boys and girls are allowed to go to parties at night without parental supervision.

Family members are still expected to help each other. However, there are some changes in the roles of family members as a result of external influences from the new sociocultural environment. Table 12.2 presents data on a small nonrandom sample from a Vietnamese community on the East Coast. The data reveal some differing attitudes about family values between children ($N = 53$) under 18 years old and their parents ($N = 56$). Data in Table 12.2 show that children often have different attitudes toward family values than their parents. Although the majority of Vietnamese parents agree with the four selected family values listed in Table 12.2, not all parents surveyed agree with this particular set of values.

The Vietnamese American Father

Despite cultural traditions, because of war and turmoil many Vietnamese refugee fathers spent their lives as soldiers in Vietnam. Their entire professional careers involved military service with perhaps one or two weeks of annual vacation with their family. A majority never played the role of full-time father or head of the family. They depended on their wives to take care of the family and raise the children. As a result, the Vietnamese father in America has had to learn how to adjust to American society and also to being a full-time father and husband. In addition, he had to learn to accept the fact that he has no absolute power over his family. His wife, likewise, is now able to get a job and bring home money. His children are living in a different culture; they think and act differently, and he finds that his use of the types of punishment that he could have used

TABLE 12.2 Agreement in Family Values Between Vietnamese American Children and Parents

Values	Children (*N* = 52) Percent	Parents (*N* = 56) Percent
A person should talk over important life decisions with family members before taking action		
Agree	62.7	90.4
Disagree	37.3	9.6
Family members should give more weight to each other's opinions than to the opinions of outsiders		
Agree	61.5	72.2
Disagree	38.5	27.8
If a person finds that the lifestyle he/she has chosen runs so against his/her family's values that conflicts develops, he/she should change		
Agree	57.7	76.4
Disagree	42.3	23.6
If possible, married children should live close to their parents.		
Agree	34.4	63.0
Disagree	64.6	37.0

Source: Tran (1998).

in Vietnam to correct or discipline his children is not always acceptable. The following case illustrates a situation that many Vietnamese American fathers have experienced.

> Mr. Do, an ex-official in the South Vietnamese Army, spent seven years in prison after the war like many other Vietnamese persons who were involved in the war. His wife and three children managed to escape Vietnam and were resettled in the United States in early 1980. The children were between the ages of 5 and 10 when they left. Mr. Do never spent more than a month with his children because he was a soldier during the war and a prisoner after the war. Mrs. Do decided to leave Vietnam when she saw no future for her children and herself after her husband was imprisoned without hope of release. She was told that he could be home after a short time in a reeducation camp, but years passed and she lost track of his locations because he had been transferred from place to place, and the family had no means to visit or support him. Mr. Do was finally released in 1987 and reunited with his family in 1992. When he arrived in the United States, his oldest son was 22 years old and the youngest one was 17. The children had grown up without their father and had very little connection with him emotionally. Unfortunately, the children also forgot the Vietnamese language and could no longer communicate with their father. Mr. Do was very upset and depressed, but he soon realized the fact and has learned to accept it bitterly. He blamed his wife for not knowing how to raise their children and letting them become too Americanized. He learned English but never feels comfortable speaking to his children. The family situation and environment are constantly tense (Tran, 1998).

More than 30 years after the Vietnam War, the generation of Vietnamese fathers who were involved directly in the war is now in their old age. More than 8 percent of Vietnamese American men are age 65 and older. Many are now grandparents. About 6.9 percent of older Vietnamese Americans lived with their grandchildren in 2007, and 20.0 percent cared for their grandchildren.

The major of Vietnamese American fathers (42.9 percent) are age 35 to 64 years and older (U.S. Bureau of Census, 2007). Postwar and young Vietnamese American fathers did not have to struggle to readjust to their ordinary family life and the new life in the United States as their father's generation did. However, this group of Vietnamese American fathers grew up in the United States lacking proper directions from their own fathers who came to the United States without or with very limited knowledge about U.S. society. Vietnamese American fathers age 25 and older are still behind in terms of education and economic achievements compared to the same age group of men in the total U.S. population. For example, 77.6 percent of Vietnamese American men in this age group were high school graduates or higher compared with 83.9 percent of men in the same age group in the total population. On average, Vietnamese American men earned an annual income of $53,492, which was $6,752 lower than the earning of men in the total U.S. population. However, among men 16 years and older, 32.7 percent of Vietnamese men held management, professional, and related occupations in 2007 compared with 31.6 percent of all men in the same age group in the total U.S. population. This is an important indicator of the professional and economic achievements of the new generation of Vietnamese American fathers.

It is difficult to describe a typical Vietnamese American new father. But it is safe to say that young Vietnamese fathers who are well educated in the U.S. education system are much more acculturated and assimilated into mainstream American society than those with less education. Educated fathers are more involved in their children's education and extracurricular activities than those who are still struggling to earn a living.

The Vietnamese American Woman and Mothers

Vietnamese women in America are in a process of transition. Either voluntarily and/or through economic necessity, most are in the job market. As a result, they are gaining increased status and power in the family because of the contributions they make to the family's economic resources. The U.S. Census Bureau (1993) reported that among Vietnamese people age 25 years and older, 53.3 percent of the women had a high school education or higher compared to 61.2 percent of the men. Women also made up a lower percentage (12.2 percent) of persons with a bachelor's degree than did men (17.4 percent). Overall, 55.5 percent of Vietnamese women age 16 and older were in the workforce, and 8.9 percent were unemployed. By 2007, 59.9 percent of Vietnamese American women age 16 and older were employed, and 29.7 percent of them were in management, professional, and related occupations compared with 31.3 percent of Vietnamese American men in the same age group. Among individuals age 25 and older, 24.0 percent of Vietnamese women had a bachelor's degree or higher compared to 29.7 percent of Vietnamese men. However, among adult Vietnamese Americans, 31.5 percent of men were enrolled in college or graduate school compared with 32.7 percent of women in 2007 (U.S. Bureau of Census, 2007). If this trend continues, Vietnamese women will surpass Vietnamese men in educational achievements. This is, indeed, a significant cultural change with respect to the traditional Vietnamese sex role. With women becoming more educated than men, the traditional view regarding sex roles within the Vietnamese American family will definitely change forever. Nevertheless, we still see gender inequality in terms of earnings. In 1999, on average, a Vietnamese women who worked full-time for the entire year earned 75 dollars for every 100 dollars earned by her male counterpart (Xie and Goyette, 2004).

Employed Vietnamese women are still expected to be good wives and mothers by taking care of their children, husbands, and homes. In many Vietnamese American families, even though both husband and wife work full time, the wife is expected to cook, clean the house, and take care of the children; the husband remains the dominant authority figure. The following case illustrates a typical traditional family:

> Mrs. Le is employed by a local sewing factory, where she works 40 hours per week and often works overtime. Her husband, Mr. Le, is a machinist employed by a local factory, who also works 40 hours per week. The couple has four children, all of school age. Every morning, Mrs. Le gets up early to cook breakfast (her husband only eats Vietnamese food) and prepares lunches for the children, her husband, and herself. In the evening, Mrs. Le hurries home to cook dinner. When she has to work overtime, her oldest daughter, a 16-year-old, prepares dinner for the family. Mr. Le never knows what is going on in the kitchen, but he would become angry if dinner were not ready at 7:00 p.m. Mrs. Le takes care of all domestic affairs, including controlling and planning the family budget. During the weekend, Mr. Le spends most of his time working with the Vietnamese Catholic community (attending meetings or other social activities) while his wife stays home and cleans the house or works in the garden (Tran, 1998).

The reader will note that because the wife takes charge of all domestic affairs, she is often termed the "general of the home" and has a certain amount of respect and control in the household, especially finances. Moreover, domestic labor gradually has become more equally divided among younger Vietnamese couples. Zhou and Bankston (2001) found that since traditional gender role expectations allowed parents to push girls harder than boys, Vietnamese young women are being pushed more than young men to achieve academically. Ironically, this academic achievement often results in economic independence, which in turns gives women independence in other areas. Data in Table 12.3 show some attitudes of adults age 18 and older about sex roles between men and women in Vietnamese American families. The data reveal that both men and women tend to agree on shared responsibilities between husband and wife. It is expected that sex roles within the Vietnamese American family will continue to change and will be similar to those in mainstream society.

Data from the 2004 American Community Survey reported that among Asian Americans age 15 to 50 years, Vietnamese women had the second-highest rate of fertility (72 out of every 1,000) after American Asian Indian women (74 out of every 1,000 women) (U.S. Bureau of Census, 2004). In the 2007 American Community Survey (U.S. Census Bureau, 2007), data revealed that about 6.5 percent of Vietnamese Americans women age 15 to 50 years had a birth in 2007 compared to 7.3 percent of women in the same age group in the total U.S. population (U.S. Census Bureau, 2004, 2007). The percentage of single mother families with children 18 years and younger in the Vietnamese American population (6.3 percent) is somewhat similar to the total in

TABLE 12.3   Attitudes Toward Sex Roles (*N* = 76)

Sex Roles	Female (*N* = 90) Percent	Male (*N* = 112) Percent
Men should share the work around the house with women, such as doing dishes, cleaning, and so forth		
Agree	58.0	63.0
Disagree	42.0	37.0
Important family decisions should be made jointly by a husband and wife		
Agree	85.9	83.0
Disagree	14.1	17.0

Source: Tran (1998).

the U.S. population (7.4 percent) in 2007. Although the percentage of the married population age 15 and older remained the same from 2004 to 2007, there has been a reduction in the birth rate among unmarried Vietnamese women from 15 to 50 years old. In 2004, the percentage of unmarried Vietnamese women with a birth in the previous 12 months was 16.2 percent, but it was reduced to 14.8 percent in 2007. The proportion of unmarried Vietnamese women who gave birth to a child in 2006 was 18.7 percent lower than that among unmarried women in the general population. These statistics could have profound impacts on the changing structure of the Vietnamese American family (U.S. Census Bureau, 2007).

Marriage

Vietnamese parents in America no longer make all decisions about their children's marriages. The relocation from Vietnam to America destroyed many traditional ceremonies that were part of the marriage celebration. Moreover, as many Vietnamese young people are more economically independent from their parents and more self-sufficient, they have more freedom to make decisions on all matters relating to their marriage. Parents and older members of the family still exercise important influence over their children's marriages, but their influence is not absolute. Most Vietnamese parents still expect their children to marry other Vietnamese rather than people of another race.

Vietnamese Americans tend to marry at a slightly older age (30 for men and 26 for women) than other Asian groups, but similar to Korean Americans (30 for men and 27 for women). Although interracial marriage is becoming increasingly more common, many Vietnamese parents try to influence their children to go to Vietnam to find their mates, especially in communities where there are relatively few Vietnamese. In 2000, 92 percent of married Vietnamese men were married to Vietnamese women compared with 86 percent of married Vietnamese women who were married to Vietnamese men. In general, interracial and interethnic marriage among Vietnamese Americans is relatively lower than other Asian American groups but greater than Asian American Indians. About 7 percent of Vietnamese American men are married to non-Vietnamese compared to 14 percent of Vietnamese American women who are married to non-Vietnamese (Xie and Goyette, 2004).

A curious and under-studied phenomenon is that of young Vietnamese going back to Vietnam to get married. Many of these marriages are arranged, whether through family and/or friends. This raises interesting questions about the level of acceptance of traditional cultural values by young people and how these young couples navigate seemingly different cultural worldviews.

In regard to the traditional goal of marriage, many young Vietnamese in America, unlike their parents, do not see bearing children as the ultimate goal of marriage. Birth control methods are becoming more widely used by many young Vietnamese, and this practice is affecting family size. However, young Catholic Vietnamese are still influenced by the teachings of their church on birth control as well as other issues. In Vietnam, before and during the civil war, a Catholic priest was the most powerful person in a Catholic village or town. However, more and more young Vietnamese are venturing into a new era of sexual freedom, and premarital sexual activities are increasingly common among young people. The size of families among young couples also tends to be smaller. In fact, many young couples are realizing that it is costly to have children in America and that their new standard of living does not allow them to have as many children as they might like to have. In this way the new economic environment has changed traditional values and practices pertaining to marriage among the younger generation of Vietnamese Americans.

Table 12.4 presents some information on marriage in the Vietnamese American family. The majority of Vietnamese women in the study tended to think that premarital sexual relationships are not acceptable. Men were more ambivalent about this issue than women. Birth control also appears to be a sensitive issue among Vietnamese Americans. Again, women were more likely to

TABLE 12.4 Attitudes Toward Marriage Issues (N = 176)

Sex Roles	Female (N = 90) Percent	Male (N = 112) Percent
Do you think it is all right for a man and a woman to have sexual relations before marriage?		
Yes	14.1	27.4
No	60.0	33.0
No ideas	25.9	39.6
Do you think birth control information should be made available to Vietnamese teenagers?		
Yes	15.7	34.9
No	61.4	37.6
No ideas	22.9	27.5
Do you think birth control information should be made available to Vietnamese adults?		
Yes	45.8	53.6
No	21.7	17.0
No ideas	32.5	29.5
Should Vietnamese couples divorce when they think they can no longer live together?		
Yes	23.6	27.2
No	25.8	34.2
No ideas	50.6	38.6

Source: Tran (1998).

oppose the idea of making information about birth control available to teenagers than were men. The majority of respondents were still ambivalent or against marital divorce.

We used U.S. Census Bureau data (1980, 1990, 2000) to track the changes in marital status among ever married people (excluding never married individuals form the estimates) across different age groups from 1980 to 2000. Individuals were grouped into three age groups: 21–39, 40–59, and 60 and older. Our analysis revealed that among individuals age 21 to 39, the prevalence of divorced was 1.6 percent for men and 4.4 percent for women in the 1980 census. This age group's prevalence of divorced increased to 4.6 percent for men and 6.2 percent for women in the 2000 census. Among individuals age 40 to 59, the prevalence of divorced was 2.0 percent for men and 3.8 percent for women in the 1980 census. However, the divorced rate increased to 5.9 percent for men and 8.8 percent for women in the 2000 census. Finally, among adults age 60 and older, the prevalence of divorced increased from 3.5 percent for men and 0.4 percent for women in the 1980 census to 4.9 percent for men and 5.1 percent for women in the 2000 census. Overall, it appears that the divorced rate among ever married Vietnamese Americans has increased continuously over the past three decades. Consequently, the configuration of the Vietnamese American family undoubtedly has been in transition and transformation as this population has acculturated into mainstream American society.

Socialization of Young Vietnamese Americans

Young Vietnamese Americans have less opportunity to interact with other young Vietnamese and older Vietnamese. In a state, such as California, or city with a high concentration of Vietnamese the opportunity to interact with other Vietnamese is naturally greater. However, many Vietnamese children quickly learn about America and Americans through a daily diet of television, and many

Vietnamese parents are very busy working and have little time to teach their children the Vietnamese language and culture. Vietnamese children are learning to become Americans on their own. In many Vietnamese American families, children communicate with each other in English and with their parents in broken Vietnamese and/or a combination of both English and Vietnamese. Less educated and less acculturated parents, in most situations, do not have enough knowledge about American culture to help their children. In fact, in cities with high concentrations of Vietnamese, tutoring centers flourish as Vietnamese feel inadequate to help their children so they work even harder to send their children to these tutoring centers after school. As a result, many young Vietnamese Americans spend even less time with their parents and tend to experience conflict between their parents' culture and the culture they learn from school and television. Dinh and Nguyen (2006) call this the parent-child acculturative gap and found that it is a predictor of poor parent-child relationships. Also, the communication gap between older parents and children in the Vietnamese family is becoming wider. Trinh (2006) found significant relationships for parenting style and intergenerational conflicts in the domains of family expectations, especially regarding education and career choice. Choi, He, and Harachi (2008) also found that intergenerational cultural dissonance directly predicts problem behaviors in Vietnamese American youths. Vietnamese children also experience conflict between their Vietnamese and American identities. Stonequist (1961) explains this phenomenon via the concept of the "marginal man." A "marginal person" stands on the edge of two cultures, torn between their differences. A marginal person cannot make up his or her mind to choose what culture is right for him or her: his or her parent's culture or the culture of the host society. Even so, a marginal person who attempts to assimilate to the host culture may experience rejection from members of the dominant group. More positive data have come out recently regarding the role of families regarding ethnic identity. Umana-Taylor, Bhatnot, and Shin (2006) found that "familial ethnic socialization" played a significant role in Vietnamese adolescents' ethnic formation. This process takes time on the part of the parents to socialize the children, and time is a luxury for many Vietnamese American parents who are constantly trying to make ends meet by working at two or three low-paying jobs at any given time.

Old Age in America

In 2007, approximately 128,161 older Vietnamese Americans were in the United States. This was about 8 percent of the total Vietnamese American population. Elderly Vietnamese women made up 50.4 percent of the older Vietnamese population. About 15.0 percent of Vietnamese Americans age 65 and older lived in poverty compared with 9.5 percent of older Americans. About 7 percent of elderly Vietnamese Americans lived in the same house with their grandchildren, and 20 percent of them provided care for their grandchildren. More than 41 percent of older Vietnamese Americans suffered from some types of physical disability (U.S. Census Bureau, 2007).

Elderly Vietnamese are isolated from not only American society but also their own family members. Most elderly Vietnamese in the United States are unable to speak English and cannot drive; they spend most of their lives at home alone (Tran, Ngo, and Sung, 2001). Even among those who speak English and live with their children, there is rarely an opportunity to talk to them because of the amount of time people spend working outside the home in America. Tran, Ngo, and Sung (2001) found that one of the most difficult things for an older Vietnamese American is to make friends and build a support system. This coupled with the inability to speak and understand English makes life "mute and deaf" for many elderly persons (Phan, 2008). The grandchildren of older Vietnamese Americans prefer to speak English rather than Vietnamese, and when they are at home they spend most of their time in front of the television rather than interacting with their grandparents. Elderly Vietnamese have lost the respect they would have had in traditional Vietnamese society, where their age status allowed them to pass down their knowledge to the younger generation. In America, most feel that their knowledge is useless. In most Vietnamese communities in the United States, churches and Buddhist temples are the only places for elderly Vietnamese to socialize. In Milpitas, California, for example, where there is a large Vietnamese community, many elderly Vietnamese Americans got each other to join a health club where many of them congregate each morning, more to socialize than to work out. Five miles from Milpitas, in San Jose, California, realizing that many Vietnamese Americans die without proper burials and mourners, elders got together and created the Concerned Members Club, which members join and pay dues to while they are living so the money for burial arrangements when they die is available (*Doi Moi Magazine*, 2009). This is similar to popular form of *hui* (a rotating credit system) that Asians often engage in to build up initial capital for business (Lindahl and Thomsen, 2002). Since Vietnamese American elders comprise one of the poorest groups among elderly Asian Americans, the popularity of the Concerned Members Club characterizes the anxiety and loneliness felt by many regarding their old age. In smaller communities, elderly Vietnamese are completely cut off from the outside world, and therefore many wish to return to Vietnam despite no longer having any form of social network or relatives there. However, for many, this remains an unfulfilled wish, and they feel stuck between the two worlds: America and Vietnam (Phan, 2008).

CHANGE AND ADAPTATION

The Vietnamese American family has gone through several stages of change and has been transformed into a different entity as Vietnamese Americans themselves change and adapt to their new identity and culture. In many Vietnamese American families, traditional values still have some influence on family members. However, lack of communication between parents and children in many families makes it hard to preserve and maintain traditional familial values, norms, and processes.

Communication Gap

Many Vietnamese parents are similar to first-generation Japanese American parents (Issei) in believing that if their children learn English and adopt American customs, they will become respected American citizens. Unfortunately, in many cases some young Vietnamese tend to favor English over Vietnamese and quietly rebel against their parent's culture, just as many Nisei (second-generation Japanese American) did (Knoll, 1982). In many Vietnamese American families, children prefer to speak English rather than Vietnamese and prefer to eat hamburgers or hot dogs rather than traditional Vietnamese food.

The communication gap between the elders and the youngsters in a family has become wider and wider. The older Vietnamese try to hang onto their traditional culture and values, whereas the youngsters are quickly learning the new dominant culture and absorbing American values. Many older Vietnamese parents cannot understand the new culture and the values that their children are absorbing at school and home through television. An extreme example of this is the case of Tila Tequila whose Vietnamese name is Thien Thanh Thi Nguyen. Tila became a sensation when she gathered the largest group of friends (1.5 million) on Myspace.com and went on to notoriety by starring in such reality TV shows as "A Shot at Love with Tila Tequila." When asked what her Vietnamese parents has to say about her notoriety, she replied that they have no idea because they don't watch TV and are always working (Grossman, 2006). Hence, in America many Vietnamese parents appear to be losing their authority. They cannot understand their children and do not know how to communicate with them. Their children have become Americanized too quickly and too soon. In the long run, the Americanization of Vietnamese children may have negative effects. As Gardner, Robey, and Smith (1985:39) suggest:

> In the past, Americanization has involved the absorption of values relating to schooling and work which encourage both individual success and national productivity. But the Americanization of Asian immigrants may have the opposite effect – reducing their exceptionally high level of dedication to learn or work.

Marital Conflicts

Vietnamese American husbands and wives most likely will experience more role conflict and role ambiguity in their marital relationship. In many traditional Vietnamese families, as mentioned, the husband rarely stayed home because he was a soldier. Now he plays the role of a husband and father and assumes more responsibilities in everyday family life. At the same time, he must deal with changes in his family status since many wives are now working outside of the home. He is no longer the sole breadwinner in the family (Nghe, Mahalik, and Lowe, 2003). As a result, the divorce rate probably will increase because many Vietnamese women are now free from their traditional social obligations and dependent status.

The data presented in Table 12.5, taken from interviews conducted among 116 adults age 18 and older, illustrate marital roles within the Vietnamese American family. The data indicate

TABLE 12.5 Marital Responsibilities ($N = 116$)	
Responsibilities	**Percent**
Care for sick children	
Husband	5.0
Wife	3.3
Both	91.7
Educate children	
Husband	1.7
Wife	1.7
Both	96.6
Manage family finances	
Husband	3.2
Wife	27.4
Both	69.4
Prepare dinner	
Husband	3.2
Wife	44.4
Both	52.4
Wash dishes	
Husband	1.6
Wife	35.5
Both	62.9

Source: Tran (1998).

that responsibilities which require social involvement, including health and education of the children, are expected to be shared by both men and women. However, domestic affairs are not evenly divided between husbands and wives. Most Vietnamese Americans still expect wives to do most of the domestic work.

CONCLUSION

In 2010, overseas Vietnamese communities and the Vietnamese community in the United States commemorated thirty-five years of resettlement in host societies. This was an unprecedented event for a people who traditionally have tended to stay in their own villages. When Vietnamese first arrived in the United States, many could not imagine what would happen in the ensuing years. Few people believed that they would return to visit their country or be reunited with their spouses and loved ones. Between 1980 and 1990, several anticommunist groups were formed in overseas Vietnamese communities with a common hope of overthrowing the Vietnamese communist government of Vietnam. Many anticommunist diehards had hoped that the U.S. government would eventually support their cause to fight for the freedom of Vietnam, and few Vietnamese Americans believed that the United States and Vietnam had finally normalized their diplomatic relations. In California and other areas with a large concentration of Vietnamese Americans, radio programs and newspaper were devoted to spreading anticommunist propaganda. It seems even today that the wound of war has not been healed for many Vietnamese adults, especially those who had been imprisoned and tortured by the Vietnamese communist regime.

One cannot talk about changes in the Vietnamese American family without talking about changes in the Vietnamese American community. Obviously, these two social institutions are intertwined. Most major Vietnamese communities started to form around 1980, after the first five years of resettlement. Though no systematic study has investigated the factors that contributed to the development of Vietnamese communities in the United States, no doubt religious beliefs have played a major role. Catholics and Protestants formed their communities around their local American churches, but Buddhists had a tougher time forming their communities because of the lack of Buddhist temples. However, there are now many well-established temples that draw thousands of Vietnamese and non-Vietnamese alike to services in major metropolitan centers in the United States.

The second major factor for the formation of these Vietnamese enclaves is socioeconomic. Vietnamese people tend to gather in a few concentrated geographical areas because of their social and economic needs. The symbols of these enclaves are ethnic Vietnamese restaurants, social service agencies, ethnic groceries, and other services. The largest Vietnamese community in southern California, Little Saigon, has earned its name on the official map and stands out as a major commercial and tourist center of Orange County. Vietnamese communities, like Little Saigon, offer everything from ethnic food to health, legal, and travel services.

Communication and media technologies have also facilitated the development of Vietnamese American communities. Several Vietnamese-language newspapers and magazines circulate in Vietnamese communities, and bookstores also serve the population. The development of Vietnamese word-processing software in the late 1980s provided tremendous help to Vietnamese communities wanting to link up throughout the United States and elsewhere. During the first decade of the twenty-first century, numerous Vietnamese Web sites have flourished on the Internet. One can find almost any type of information and services on the World Wide Web, and Vietnamese people and communities all over the world have been connecting with it. Vietnamese media and computers have linked Vietnamese Americans together to form a new type of community: the informational or cyberspace community.

Overall, Vietnamese Americans have adjusted and adapted relatively well to their host societies. Many have done exceptionally well. Vietnamese Americans have gradually entered many fields, including politics, education, business, health, military, and more. Between 1980 and 2007, Vietnamese Americans improved their economic conditions tremendously and showed significant gains in educational achievement. Among the four major Indochinese groups that have arrived in the United States since 1975, the Vietnamese have done much better than their Cambodian, Laotian, and Hmong counterparts. For example, the 2000 census data show that 26.9 percent of the Vietnamese population holds managerial and professional occupations compared to 17.8 percent of the Cambodians, 13.4 percent of the Laotians, and 17.1 percent of the Hmongs. The percentage of the Vietnamese population that lives below the 2000 poverty level is 16.0 percent, much smaller than the 29.3 percent of Cambodians, 18.5 percent of Laos, and 37.8 percent of Hmong (Reeves and Bennett, 2004).

Inevitably, the Vietnamese family will have to continue to change in order to survive. The critical issue is the direction in which the Vietnamese family will change and the degree to which it will adapt to American culture. Despite recent attacks on public bilingual education, many Vietnamese community leaders and parents seem to agree that preservation of the Vietnamese language is one of the major factors that will help to foster the development and maintenance of the Vietnamese American community. Efforts have been made in many Vietnamese communities to teach the Vietnamese language to children in hopes that in this way the younger Vietnamese will preserve traditional Vietnamese values and their ethnic identity. An ideal Vietnamese American family will be one that adopts American culture in order to survive but still preserves its traditional Vietnamese values and ethnic identity.

References

Amerasian Foundation. (n.d.). *Amerasian Laws.* amerasianfoundation.org/?page_id=9 (accessed April 18, 2011).

Barringer, H. R., R. W. Gardner, and M. J. Levin. 1993. *Asian and Pacific Islanders in the United States.* New York: Russell Sage Foundation.

Bell, D. A. 1985, July 15 and 22. "The Triumph of Asian-Americans." *The New Republic,* 30.

Benedict, P. K. 1947. "An Analysis of Annamese Kinship Terms." *Southwestern Journal of Anthropology 3,* 371–392.

Bernstein, R. 2004, June 14. "Hispanic and Asian Americans Increase Faster than Overall Population." Press Release. Washington, DC: U.S. Census Bureau.

Che, W. 1979. *The Modern Chinese Family.* Palo Alto, CA: R & E Research Associates.

Choi, Y., M. He, and T. Harachi. 2008. "Intergenerational Cultural Dissonance, Parent-Child Conflict and Bonding, and Youth Problem Behaviors Among Vietnamese and Cambodian Immigrant Families." *Journal of Youth and Adolescence 37*(1), 85–96.

CIA. 2008. "The World Fact Book: Vietnam." https://www.cia.gov/library/publications/the-world-factbook/geos/vm.html (accessed April 18, 2011).

Dao, D. A. 1961. *Vietnam van-hoa so cuong* [History of Vietnamese Culture]. Saigon, Vietnam: Nha Xuat Ban Phuong.

Deming, A., et al. 1975. "The New Americans." *Newsweek.* May 12, 32–41.

Dinh, K., and H. Nguyen. 2006. "The Effects of Acculturative Variables on Asian American Parent-Child Relationships." *Journal of Social and Personal Relationships 23*(3), 407–426.

Do, M. V. 1962. *Vietnam: Where East and West Meet.* Rome, Italy: Edizioni Quattro Venti.

Doi Moi Magazine. 2009. Concerned Members Club (Advertisement). San Jose, CA.

Gardner, R. W., B. Robey, and P. C. Smith. 1995. "Asian Americans: Growth, Change, and Diversity." *Population Bulletin 40,* 1–44.

Greenhouse, S. 2007, August 19. "Studies Highlight Hazards of Manicurists' Chemicals." *New York*

Times. www.nytimes.com/2007/08/19/nyregion/19nailside.html?_r=1&ref=nyregion (accessed April 18, 2011).

Grossman, L. 2006, December 16. "Tila Tequila." *Time Magazine.* www.time.com/time/magazine/article/0,9171,1570728,00.html (accessed April 18, 2011).

Ha, Duc. 2002, December 1. "Nghe lam nail tai My" ["The Nail Industry in America]. *Ngay Nay Minnesota Newspaper 324.*

Hai, H. 2009, April 16. Interview by Phu Phan. Personal Interview.

Haines, D., D. Rutherford, and P. Thomas. 1981. "Family and Community Among Vietnamese Refugees." *International Migration Review 15,* 310–319.

Hickey, G. C. 1964. *Village in Vietnam.* New Haven, CT: Yale University Press.

———. 1982. *Free in the Forest: Ethnohistory of the Vietnamese Central Highlands 1954–1976.* New Haven: Yale University Press.

Hinton, H. C. 1985. *East Asia and the Western Pacific 1985.* Washington, DC: Skye-Post.

Huynh, T. 2009, May 8. Interview by Phu Phan. Personal Interview.

Keith, J. 1982. *Old People as People: Social and Cultural Influences on Aging and Old Age.* Boston: Little, Brown.

Knoll, T. 1982. *Becoming Americans.* Portland, OR: Coast to Coast Books.

Kunstadter, P. (Ed.). 1967. *Southeast Asian Tribes, Minorities, and Nation* (vol. 2). Princeton, NJ: Princeton University Press.

Le, T. V. 1992. *Le hoi co Truyen* [Traditional Folk Festivals]. Ha Noi, Vietnam: Nha Xuat Ban Khoa Hoc Xa Hoi.

Luong, H. V. 1984. "'Brother' and 'Uncle': An Analysis of Rules, Structures, Contradictions, and Meaning in Vietnamese Kinship." *American Anthropologist 86,* 290–315.

Lindahl, J., and L. Thomsen. 2002. "Private Business and Socio-Economic Networks Relations in the Chinese in Ho Chi Minh City, Vietnam." In T. Menkhoff and S. Gerke (Eds.), *Chinese Entrepreneurship and Asian Business Networks* (pp. 129–155). New York: Routledge-Curzon.

Marr, D. G. 1981. *Vietnamese Tradition on Trial, 1920–1945.* Berkeley: University of California Press.

Montero, D. 1979. *Vietnamese Americans: Patterns of Resettlement and Socioeconomic Adaptation in the United States.* Boulder, CO: Westview Press.

Nghe, L. T., J. R. Mahalik, and S. M. Lowe. 2003. "Influences on Vietnamese Men: Examining Traditional Gender Roles, the Refugee Experience, Acculturation, and Racism in the United States. *Journal of Multicultural Counseling and Development, 31*(3), 245–261.

Nguyen, H. M. 1985. "Vietnamese." In D. W. Haines (Ed.), *Refugees in the United States: A Reference Handbook.* Westport, CT: Greenwood.

Nguyen, K. K. 1967. *An Introduction to Vietnamese Culture.* Tokyo, Japan: Centre for East Asian Cultural Studies.

Nguyen, T. G. 1993. *Luat hon nhan va gia dinh* [Marriage and Family Law]. Ha Noi, Vietnam: Nha Xuat Ban Chinh Tri Quoc Gia.

Pham, S. V. 1960. Viet su toan thu: *Tu thuong co den hien Dai* [Vietnamese History: From Ancient Times to the Present Day]. Saigon, Vietnam: Thu Lam An Quan.

Pham, T. 2009, March 16. Interview by Phu Phan. Personal Interview.

Phan, B. K. 1975. *Viet-Nam phong tuc* [Vietnamese Traditions]. Paris: École Française D'Extrême-Orient.

Phan, D. D. 1992. *Lang Vietnam: Mot so van de kinh te xa hoi* [The Vietnamese Village: Some Social and Economic Issues]. Ha Noi, Vietnam: Nha Xuat Ban Khoa Hoc Xa Hoi.

Phan, P. 2003. "Acculturation and the Occupational Choice of Immigrant Vietnamese Men.: Ph.D. thesis, University of Minnesota.

———. 2008. "The Perceived Intergenerational Relationship and Residency Choice of Older Vietnamese Americans. Unpublished raw data.

Porter, C., et al. 2009. "Over Exposed and Under-Informed: Dismantling Barriers to Health and Safety in California Nail Salons." California Healthy Nail Salon Collaborative.

Reeves, T. J., and C. E. Bennett. 2004. "We the People: Asian in the United States. Census 2000 Special Report." Washington, DC: U.S. Census Bureau. www.census.gov/prod/2004pubs/censr-17.pdf (accessed April 18, 2011).

Schaefer, R. T. 1979. *Racial and Ethnic Groups.* Boston: Little, Brown.

Spencer, R. F. 1945. The Annamese Kinship System. *Southwestern Journal of Anthropology 1,* 284–310.

Stonequist, E. V. 1961. *The Marginal Man.* New York: Russell & Russell.

Strand, P. J., and W. Jones, Jr. 1985. *Indochinese Refugees in America: Problems of Adaptation and Assimilation.* Durham, NC: Duke University Press.

Taylor, K. W. 1983. *The Birth of Vietnam.* Berkeley: University of California Press.

Toan Anh. 1965. *Nep cu: con nguoi Vietnam* [The Old Way: The Vietnamese People]. Saigon, Vietnam: Dai Nam.

———. 1969. *Phong Tuc Viet-Nam: Tu ban than den gia dinh* [Vietnamese Customs, from Individual to Family]. Saigon, Vietnam: Dai Nam.

Tran, D. H. 1991. "Ve gia dinh tryuen thong Vietnam voi anh huong Nho Giao" [The Traditional Vietnamese Family and the Influences of Confucianism]. In R. Liljestrom and T. Lai, *Nhung nghien cuu xa hoi hoc ve gia dinh Vietnam* [Sociological Studies of the Vietnamese Family]. Ha Noi, Vietnam: Nha Xuat Ban Khoa Hoc Xa Hoi.

Tran, Thanh V. 1998. "The Vietnamese American Family," in Charles H. Mindel, Robert W. Habenstein and Roosevelt Wright, Jr. (Eds.), Ethnic Families in America (4th edition) . New Jersey: Prentice_ Hall, Inc.

Tran, T. V., D. Ngo, and T. H. Sung. 2001. "Caring for Older Vietnamese Americans." In L. K. Olson (Ed.), *Age Through Ethnic Lenses: Caring for the Elderly in a Multicultural Society* (pp. 59–70). Lanham, MD: Rowman & Littlefield.

Tran T. X. n.d. "Thuong Vo" [Love for My Wife]. http://vi.wikisource.org/wiki/Th%C6%B0%C6%A1ng_v%E1%BB%A3 (accessed April 22, 2011).

Trinh, N. M. 2006. *Intergenerational Conflict in Vietnamese-American Families.* Master's thesis (M.S.), University of Delaware.

Umana-Taylor, A., R. Bhanot, and N. Shin. 2006. "Ethnic Identity Formation During Adolescence: The Critical Role of Families." *Journal of Family Issues* 27(3), 390–414.

U.S. Census Bureau. 1980. "Public Use Microdata Sample (PUMS)." www.census.gov/acs/www/data_documentation/public_use_microdata_sample (accessed April 18, 2011).

———. 1990. "Public Use Microdata Sample (PUMS)." www.census.gov/acs/www/data_documentation/public_use_microdata_sample (accessed April 18, 2011).

———. 1993. *U.S. Census: Research Guide.* University of Pennsylvania. gethelp.library.upenn.edu/guides/govdocs/census (accessed April 18, 2011).

———. 2000a. "Your Gateway to Census 2000." www.census.gov/main/www/cen2000.html (accessed April 18, 2011).

———. 2000b. "Public Use Microdata Sample (PUMS)." www.census.gov/acs/www/data_documentation/public_use_microdata_sample (accessed April 18, 2011).

———. 2004 "American Community Survey: Asians 2004." http://www.census.gov/prod/2007pubs/acs-05.pdf (accessed April 20, 2011).

———. 2007. "American Community Survey 2007. Population Group: Vietnamese Alone." factfinder.census.gov (accessed April 18, 2011).

U.S. Department of Health and Human Services. 1985. "Refugees Resettlement Program, Report to the Congress." Washington, DC: U.S. Government Printing Office.

U.S. Department of State. 1995. *Vietnam: Background Notes.* Washington, DC: U.S. Government Printing Office.

Viet Tribune Online. 2008. www.viettribune.com/vt/index.php?c=G-Ri (accessed April 18, 2011).

Vuong, G. T. 1976. *Getting to Know Vietnamese and Their Culture.* New York: Ungar.

Whitfield, D. J. 1976. *Historical and Cultural Dictionary of Vietnam.* Metuchen, NJ: Scarecrow Press.

Xie, Y., and K. A. Goyette. 2004. *The American People: A Demographic Portrait of Asian Americans.* New York and Washington, DC: Russell Sage Foundation & Population Reference Bureau.

Zhou, M., and C. L. Bankston III. 2001. "Family Pressure and the Educational Experience of the Daughters of Vietnamese Refugees." *International Migration* 39(4), 133–151.

13

■ ■ ■

The Chinese American Family

Morrison G. Wong

INTRODUCTION[1]

The Chinese have been residing in the United States in significant numbers for over 160 years. In 2000, 2,432,585 Chinese were residing in the United States—a 48 percent increase from the 1990 population (U.S. Census, 1993, 2000). Barring any major immigration reform, the number of Chinese in the United States is expected to continue to increase. Although they comprise just less than 1 percent of the total U.S. population, the Chinese Americans are the largest of the various Asian American groups. Despite their lengthy residence and their numbers, a review of the literature on the Chinese American family suggests that theories on their family life are almost nonexistent, and empirical studies are sparse and lacking. With the exception of a few early studies (Hayner and Reynolds, 1937; Lee, 1956; Schwartz, 1951), it is only within the last two decades that major contributions have been made to the literature on the Chinese American family (Glenn, 1983; Huang, 1981; Lyman, 1968), their marriage and intermarriage rate (Barnett, 1963; Beaudry, 1971; Burma, 1963; Chin, 1994; Ferguson, 1995; Kitano and Yeung, 1982; Lee and Fernandez, 1998; Lee and Yamanaka, 1990; Sung, 1987, 1990; Uba, 1990; Wong, 1989; Yuan, 1980), their child-rearing practices and sexual behavior patterns (Chao, 1995; Chen and Yang, 1986; Huang and Uba, 1992; Sollenberger, 1968), or identity and filial piety (Fuligini and Tseng, 1999; Fuligini, Tseng, and Lam, 1999; Fuligini, Yip, and Tseng, 2002; Uba, 1994). The delay in research on the Chinese American family may be due to a number of factors: (1) their small numbers and geographical concentration in major cities on the West and East Coasts, (2) their underrepresentation among social scientists to develop theories and carry out research on the Chinese family and lifestyles, and/or (3) the perception that the Chinese American family is not a "problem" in American society but, instead, bears a close resemblance to the White middle-class model—a hardworking, conforming, cohesive family that is the carrier of a traditional culture (Staples and Mirande, 1980; Sue and Kitano, 1973). For the most part, past and present research on the

[1]I would like to thank Janet Wong for all of her time, patience, and encouragement. Without her understanding, this project would never have been completed.

Chinese American family has focused on traditional Chinese cultural values and how they are manifested and modified in the Chinese family in America (Glenn, 1983). The portrayal of the Chinese American family includes such favorable characteristics as (1) a stable family unit, as indicated by low rates of divorce and illegitimacy (Huang, 1981), (2) close ties between generations, as shown by the low rates of juvenile delinquency (Sollenberger, 1968), (3) economic self-sufficiency, as demonstrated by the avoidance of welfare dependency (Light, 1972), (4) conservatism, as expressed by the retention of the Chinese language and customs (Braun and Chao, 1978), and (5) conservative sexual behavior (Huang and Uba, 1992). This chapter reviews, evaluates, extends, and synthesizes the literature on the Chinese family in the United States.

Before beginning the discussion, we wish to address several issues. First, just as there is no typical American family, there is no typical Chinese American family. The family variations within the culture are as wide as between cultures. It would be a gross simplification and inaccuracy to single out one Chinese American family form as representative of all Chinese American families. Instead, a greater understanding of the formation, development, and modifications of the Chinese American family necessitates looking at the different types of Chinese families that have and currently exist in the United States, realizing that even these are ideal types.

Second, although cultural factors have been emphasized in past research, the Chinese American family is a product of the complex interaction among structural factors (e.g., social, legal, political, and economic) and cultural factors. For example, although the cultural values of filial piety and respect for elders have been proposed as the major reason for the low juvenile delinquency rate among the Chinese during the first half of the twentieth century, an equally convincing argument can also be made that the Chinese custom of leaving the wife at home when the husband went to work, even to distant countries (cultural values), as well as the racist and exclusionist immigration laws that prevented Chinese females from entering the United States (structural factors), prevented the development of a significant Chinese American population, which may account for their low juvenile delinquency rate. The Chinese juvenile delinquency rate was low simply because there were very few juveniles.

Third, because both structural and cultural factors are constantly undergoing change, the Chinese American family is best viewed not as a static entity but as one also undergoing constant changes and adaptations. Knowledge and awareness of these various structural and cultural effects on the Chinese American family will result in a greater understanding of the changes and adaptations that the Chinese American family has undergone and will continue to undergo. It is within this framework that the Chinese family in the United States will be analyzed.

The discussion of the formation and evolution of the Chinese American family in the United States will be presented within the context of five historical periods with the understanding that there is considerable overlap between historical periods and family types. They are (1) the traditional Chinese family before their arrival in the United States, (2) the "mutilated" or "split household" Chinese family between 1850 and 1920, (3) the small producer Chinese family between 1920 and 1943, (4) the transitional Chinese American family between 1943 and 1965, and (5) the modern Chinese American family from 1965 to the present. Speculations on future changes and adaptations of the modern Chinese family in the United States are also offered.

THE TRADITIONAL CHINESE FAMILY

The Chinese American family, both past and present, has its foundation in the traditional family structure of China. Remaining unchanged for many centuries and encompassing a much broader connotation than the Western nuclear ideal consisting of only the conjugal unit of father, mother, and children, the traditional Chinese family also included the extended kinship groups and clan members (Sung, 1967:152).

The traditional family in China was patriarchal, with clearly defined roles. Males, particularly the father and eldest son, had the most dominant roles (Hsu, 1971a). Authority passed from the father to the eldest son whose authority and decisions were absolute. Females, relegated to a subordinate position, were expected to please and obey their fathers and, if married, were subordinate to not only their husbands but also their husbands' parents (Hsu, 1970; Kitano, 1985:223–224).

The traditional Chinese family was patrilocal; the married couple lived with the husband's parents. It was an extended family in which the grandparents, their unmarried children, and their married sons and their wives and children all lived under one roof. Ideally, the more generations living under the same roof, the more prestigious the family. The Chinese extended family structure provided an important function. In an agriculturally based economy, there was an urgent need for many workers to cultivate and till the land and harvest the crops. A nuclear family would be at a disadvantage in this economy. The extended family system was a much more suitable arrangement, providing the family with the much needed additional laborers as well as providing the members of the extended family with some degree of economic security.

Because of patrilocal residence, daughters were considered less valuable and less important than sons in the Chinese family. Parents felt that daughters were "spilled water," being reared at their expense only to be given away after marriage to another family (Lan, 2002; Sung, 1967:152; Thorton and Lin, 1994; Wolf, 1972). In some cases, particularly if the family was extremely poor, infanticide of the female child was practiced.

According to the Chinese system of patrilineal descent, the household property and land were to be divided equally among the sons, either at the father's death or upon the marriage of the youngest son. However, in exchange for the property and land, the sons were expected to reciprocate by sharing equally in the responsibility for the care and support of their parents in their old age (Fei, 1939; Hsu, 1971b; Ikels, 1985; Nee and Wong, 1985). Ancestor worship was practiced. It was believed that a Chinese male could achieve some sense of immortality only if his family line were continued (i.e., if he bore sons). One of the greatest sins that a man could commit was to die without having any sons to carry on the family line and perform the ancestor worship ritual of burning incense at his grave. As a consequence, the desire to have as many sons as possible was intense. Ancestor worship reflected the strength and importance of lineage solidarity, thus providing a link between the past and present (Hsu, 1971b).

Filial piety was a highly cherished value in the traditional Chinese family. It was a set of moral principles, taught at a very young age and reinforced throughout one's life, of mutual respect to those of equal status and reverence toward the dominant leader and one's elders. Duty, obligation, importance of the family name, service, and self-sacrifice to the elders, all essential elements of filial piety, characterized Chinese family relations (Fuligni et al., 1999, 2002; Ho, 1981; Hsu, 1971a; Kung, 1962:206; Shon and Ja, 1982; Uba, 1994).

As in many other agrarian-based societies, marriage was a family concern, not a private matter between a couple in love. Love was not a prerequisite for marriage and was highly discouraged. Because the bride lived with the husband's parents, the parents felt that they should have an important voice in the decision about who would live with them. The arranged marriage, another characteristic of the traditional Chinese family, is a classic case of not leaving such important decisions to the impetuous young. In many cases, the groom did not know who the bride was until after the wedding ceremony when the bride unveiled her face (Fong, 1968).

Because of the strong traditional bonds of the family, the Chinese peasants during this period may be characterized as "familist," lacking any sense of a developed national identity and valuing the family first and foremost (Fei, 1939; Johnson, 1962). The Chinese family entailed much more than a family in the Western sense. It was a link to a much larger chain of extended kinship and clan members, bringing large numbers of people together with a common bond, whether real or imagined, and promoting a sense of solidarity, security, and belonging (Liu, 1959; Yang, 1959).

The "Mutilated" or "Split Household" Chinese Family (1850–1920)

Although Chinese resided in the United States as early as 1785, the discovery of gold in California and the political and economic instability of China provided the major impetus to the immigration of a significant number of Chinese to the United States in the early 1850s (Chinn, Lai, and Choy, 1969:7; Hirschman and Wong, 1981; Lai and Choy, 1971:22). The Chinese practice and custom of expecting the emigrating men to leave their wives and children behind in China had three major consequences. First, it guaranteed that the emigrating sons would continue to send back remittance to their parents to support them in old age (Glick, 1980). Second, it instilled in the emigrating Chinese a sojourner rather than immigrant orientation. The single male or the husband who left his wife in China looked on his stay in the United States as temporary, as a sojourner, and evaluated American society primarily in terms of its economic opportunities. They sought to make and accumulate as much money as possible as quickly as possible to pay off debts and hoped to rejoin their family in China with a much higher status (Barth, 1964:157; Lyman, 1968; Siu, 1952). Third, it ensured a continual bond to the family and the village on the part of the emigrating men (Nee and Wong, 1985).

From their arrival in the 1850s until the 1920s, the overwhelming majority of the early Chinese immigrants were men. More than half of the arriving men were single, and those who were not often were separated from their wives and condemned to live a good portion of their lives as "bachelors" in Chinese communities scattered throughout the United States (Coolidge, 1909; Kingston, 1981; Lyman, 1968, 1977; Nee and Nee, 1973; Siu, 1952; Weiss, 1970). As a consequence, the majority of the early Chinese immigrants did not lead normal family lives. In fact, one can hardly speak of Chinese family life during this period because there were so few Chinese women (Glenn, 1983; Kingston, 1981; Lyman, 1968; Nee and Nee, 1973; Siu, 1952; Sung, 1967; Weiss, 1974).

Table 13.1 presents the sex ratio of the Chinese in the United States from 1860 to 2000. From 1860 to 1890, tremendous imbalance in the sex ratio existed among the Chinese, fluctuating from 1,284 to 2,679 Chinese men per 100 Chinese women! After 1900, the sex imbalance among the Chinese began to decline. However, in 1920 and 1930, when an American-born Chinese population began to emerge, the sex ratio was still highly imbalanced, ranging from 400 to 600 Chinese males per 100 females. Without a significant number of Chinese women, the formation of Chinese families was greatly hindered. The view of emigration solely as a temporary economic proposition, coupled with the Chinese practice of leaving the wife and children in China, resulted in a bizarre family structure among these early Chinese immigrants. In these "mutilated" families (Sung, 1967), or split household families (Glenn, 1983), the married Chinese males in the United States were physically separated from their wives and children in China. The economic or production function of the family was carried out by the Chinese males living in the United States, whereas other family functions, such as socialization of the young, were carried out by the wives and other relatives in the home village in China. In essence, many Chinese

TABLE 13.1 Chinese Population in the United States by Sex, Sex Ratio, Percentage Foreign Born, and Percentage Under 14 Years of Age: 1860–2000

Year	Total	Male	Female	Sex Ratio	Foreign Born (Percent)	Under 14 Years of Age (Percent)
1860	34,933	33,149	1,784	1,858	—	
1870	64,199	58,633	4,566	1,284	99.8	
1880	105,465	100,686	4,779	2,106	99.0	
1890	107,475	103,607	3,868	2,679	99.3	
1900	89,863	85,341	4,522	1,887	90.7	3.4
1910	71,531	66,856	4,675	1,430	79.3	
1920	61,639	53,891	7,748	696	69.9	12.0
1930	74,954	59,802	15,152	395	58.8	20.4
1940	77,504	57,389	20,115	286	48.1	21.1
1950	117,140	76,725	46,415	190	47.0	23.3
1960	236,084	134,430	100,654	135	39.5	33.0
1970	431,583	226,733	204,850	111	46.9	26.6
1980	812,178	410,936	401,246	102	63.3	21.1
1990	1,645,472	818,542	827,154	99	69.3	19.3
2000	2,432,585	1,176,913	1,255,672	94	70.6	17.7

Sources: Gardner, Robey, and Smith (1985); Glenn (1983:38); Lyman (1970:79); U.S. Census Bureau (1993, 2000).

men in the United States were family men without the presence of wives or family members. Obviously, this family form was not preferred but was tolerated because many Chinese males looked on their stay in the United States as temporary.

Racial and ethnic antagonism, coupled with White xenophobia against the early Chinese immigrants, culminated in the passage of the Chinese Exclusion Act of 1882. This act, the first national act that excluded a specific nationality group from immigrating, barred Chinese laborers and their relatives from entering the United States. Wives of Chinese laborers were denied entry into the United States by the same law that excluded their husbands (Kung, 1962:101; Lyman, 1974:87). Although Chinese custom prevented most women from joining their husbands, the Chinese Exclusion Act erected an official barrier to their coming. However, Chinese officials, students, tourists, merchants, and relatives of merchants and citizens were exempt from this exclusion. Because a Chinese wife was accorded the status of her husband, Chinese merchants were allowed to bring their wives from China with them. The shortage of women among the Chinese immigrants in the United States might have been mitigated if the Chinese had the opportunity to intermarry with the White population. However, the mutual peculiarities of dress, language, customs, and diet, the physical and racial distinctiveness, the mutually exclusive associations, prejudice and discrimination, and the enforcement of anti-miscegenation laws restricted the amount of intimate contact and interaction between the two groups, precluding any possibility of romantic involvement. As a consequence, Chinese laborers, faced with an unfavorable sex ratio, forbidden as noncitizens from bringing their wives, and prevented by laws in most western states from marrying Whites, had several options regarding their marital status. They could return permanently to China. If single, they could remain as bachelors during their stay in the United States or they could marry other minority group members, the law permitting. If married, they could remain separated from families except for occasional visits (Glenn, 1983) or they could set up a second household in the United States with another wife—a form of polygamy (Ling, 2000). Thus, for many Chinese immigrants, the establishment of a family in America was a near impossibility.

The 1888 Scott Act further exacerbated the plight of many Chinese laborers stipulating that they would be barred reentry into the United States if they left. Those Chinese laborers who wished to stay in the United States could look toward a future of only loneliness and isolation (Kung, 1962:101).

Table 13.2 shows the number of Chinese immigrants to the United States by time period and the dramatic impact the Chinese Exclusion Act and the Scott Act had on Chinese immigration. From first arrival in significant numbers in 1850, there was a continual and dramatic increase in Chinese immigration, reaching its peak of 123,201 Chinese immigrants during the decade of the 1870s, probably in anticipation of their impending exclusion from the United States. After the passage of the Chinese Exclusion Act, Chinese immigration declined precipitously. Only 10,242

TABLE 13.2 Chinese Immigrants[a] to the United States: 1820–2004	
Years	**Number of Immigrants**
1820–1850	45
1851–1860	41,397
1861–1870	64,301
1871–1880	123,201
1881–1890	61,711[b]
1891–1900	14,799
1901–1910	20,605
1911–1920	21,278
1921–1930	29,907[c]
1931–1940	4,928
1941–1950	16,709[d]
1951–1960	25,198[e]
1961–1970	109,771[f]
1971–1980	237,793
1981–1990	444,962
1991–2000	528,893
2001–2004	218,832

Source: U.S. Department of Homeland Security (2004).

[a]Beginning in 1957, includes Taiwan.
[b]In 1881 and 1882, before the Chinese Exclusion Act, 51,469 Chinese immigrated to the United States
[c]Before the Immigration Act of 1924, from 1921 to 1924, 20,393 Chinese entered the Untied States
[d]After various immigration and refugee policies were passed, about 15,341 Chinese immigrants entered the United States (1946–1950)
[e]The McCarran-Walter Immigration Act was passed in 1952.
[f]The 1965 Immigration Act was passed.

Chinese immigrated to the United States in the 1880s after passage of this act and 15,268 Chinese in the 1890s. With the restrictions placed on Chinese entering the United States and without the establishment of families in America, there were very few incentives for these early Chinese immigrants to invest in acquiring the social and cultural skills necessary to integrate or blend into American society (Siu, 1952).

Although immigration laws excluded the majority of Chinese from entering the United States, it did allow entry of relatives of United States citizens of Chinese ancestry. The 1906 San Francisco earthquake and fire destroyed not only most of San Francisco's Chinatown and much of the rest of the city but also most of the municipal records (including Chinese immigration and citizenship records). This provided a loophole by which the Chinese could immigrate to the United States. The "slot racket" or "paper son" form of immigration developed. Chinese residents would claim birth in the United States, and the authorities were powerless to disprove their contention. These American-born Chinese, whether actual or claimed, would then visit China, report the birth of sons who were considered American citizens, and thereby create entry slots. As American citizens, these "sons" were free to enter the United States. Years later, the slot could be used by a relative or the birth papers could be sold to someone wanting to immigrate. The purchaser, called a "paper son," simply assumed the name and identity of the alleged son. Under the terms of this type of immigration, the Chinese in America developed a long-term pattern of sojourning (Glenn, 1983; Kung, 1962; Lyman, 1974; Sung, 1967).

A limited number of Chinese women immigrated to the United States in the latter part of the nineteenth century (see Table 1). Those women who immigrated between 1850 and 1882 were either prostitutes or wives of the small group of Chinese merchants (Lyman, 1977:69; Nee and Wong, 1985). Chinese prostitution was an important element in the maintenance of the split household family, helping men avoid long-term relationships with women in the United States and ensuring that the bulk of their meager earnings would continue to support the family in China (Hirata, 1979). From 1882 to 1924, a period of restricted immigration, the few Chinese women who immigrated to America were usually married to merchants (Lyman, 1968).

For those few Chinese men who were fortunate enough to have resident wives in the United States, the old patriarchal Chinese family system continued. Values of the Old Country were stressed. The husband was expected to be obeyed by the wife. She was kept in seclusion by her husband, seldom ventured forth alone in the Chinese community, and almost never ventured beyond the community into White America. Obedience and filial piety to the patriarch were prime virtues and were often exhibited by children long after maturity. Parental control even extended to matters of courtship and mate selection. Marriages were always arranged, either by relatives living in China or in other Chinatowns in the United States (Hsu, 1971a; Kung, 1962; Lee, 1960; Lyman, 1968; Weiss, 1970, 1974:32–33). Men were expected to accept jobs under the direction or sponsorship of one's father or male relatives to provide economic support of the parental household (either in China or the United States) and to take care of the parents in their old age (Ikels, 1985).

In sum, Chinese custom and tradition, the sojourner orientation of the Chinese immigrants, and the imbalanced sex ratio all had profound consequences for the personal, social, and family life of the early Chinese in the United States. One consequence was the formation of the "mutilated" or split household family structure and the subsequent perpetuation of this Chinese family type by various racist and exclusionist immigration laws. Another consequence was that only a small number of Chinese immigrant families were able to be established in America during this early period. The emergence and maturation of a substantial second-generation Chinese American population was delayed for almost seventy to eighty years after the initial arrival of the Chinese immigrants.

The Small Producer Chinese Family (1920–1943)

Despite the numerous obstacles to family formation, a sizable second-generation Chinese population became increasingly evident in the major Chinatowns in the United States by the 1920s and 1930s. These early Chinese families consisted primarily of small entrepreneurs or former laborers who were able to accumulate enough capital to start their own business, either alone or with partners. They were involved in such family enterprises as laundries, restaurants, mom-and-pop grocery stores, and other small shops. The change in immigration status from laborer to merchant was of no small consequence for the Chinese. It allowed the new merchants to return to China and bring over their wives and children (Glenn, 1983; Nee and Wong, 1985). This is evident in the slight increase in Chinese immigration after 1900 (see Table 13.2). From 1920 to 1950, the percentage of Chinese born in the United States grew from 30 percent to a little over 50 percent of the total Chinese population in the United States. However, the sex ratio still remained highly imbalanced (see Table 13.1).

Two types of Chinese families predominated during this period. The first type, which was already discussed, was the mutilated or split household family. Chinese tradition was certainly one barrier keeping Chinese families separated. Another barrier was the discriminatory features of the Immigration Act of 1924. This act made it impossible for American citizens of Chinese ancestry to send for their wives and families. Even Chinese merchants, who previously were able to bring their wives to the United States, were denied this privilege. This law was later changed in 1930 to allow wives of Chinese merchants, as well as those married to American citizens before 1924, to immigrate to the United States (Chinn et al., 1969:24). The "mutilated" family remained one of the predominant forms of family life among the Chinese in the United States until the end of World War II, when more liberal immigration legislation was passed (Sung, 1967:156).

Another type of Chinese family, the small producer family, emerged during this period. This family type consisted of the immigrant and first-generation American-born family functioning as a productive unit (Glenn, 1983). All family members, including the children, worked in the small family business, usually within the ethnic economy. The business was profitable only because it was labor intensive and family members put in extremely long hours (Mark and Chih, 1982:66).

The small producer family had five distinctive characteristics. First, there was no clear demarcation between work and family life. Second, the family was a self-contained unit in terms of production and consumption. Third, although all family members participated in the family enterprise, there was a division of labor according to age and gender with gradations of responsibility according to capacity and experience. Fourth, it was labor intensive and family members were expected to put in extremely long hours. This was the only way such a family enterprise could be profitable (Mark and Chih, 1982:66). Fifth, there was an emphasis on the collective versus the individual (Glenn, 1983).

Children undertook a great deal of responsibility and gained considerable status at a very early age in the small producer family. They played a crucial role in carrying out the daily business and domestic affairs of the family because of their superior knowledge of English compared to their immigrant parents. They acted as mediators between their immigrant parents and the outside society, performing such tasks as reading and translating documents and business contracts, filling out bank slips, and negotiating with customers (Kingston, 1976; Lowe, 1943; Nee and Nee, 1973; Wong, 1950). Occasionally, this led to generational conflict.

Wives in the small producer Chinese family had much higher status compared to their traditional counterparts. As a result of limited immigration, the small producer family tended to be nuclear, consisting of husband, wife, and children. Consequently, wives did not have to contend with in-laws. Moreover, being more-or-less equal producers in the family business enabled Chinese wives to improve their position in the family and attain considerable autonomy and equality. Although the women did not have much economic power, they were considered the emotional centers of the household—the guardians of Chinese traditions and customs (Glenn and Yap, 2002).

The traditional Chinese family system lived in the minds of the older Chinese during this period. The Chinese American family was patriarchal, with the oldest living male theoretically being the master of the household. In actual practice, however, the opinion of the mother of the oldest living male carried considerable weight in major family decisions. In relations between parents and children, the father occupied the seat of authority and expected the children to obey without question. The practice of deferring to the wishes of the elders was strengthened by the difficulty of the children in finding employment outside of Chinatown, making them economically dependent on the older members of the family and clan. Patrilocal residence—married sons and their wives living with the son's parents—was still practiced among the Chinese in America during this period. The Chinese family conformed to traditional sex roles. A good husband was expected to be a good provider who not only earned the money but also spent it. A good, traditional Chinese wife in America was expected to spend very little money and rear as many children as possible—preferably sons (Hayner and Reynolds, 1937). However, there was considerable variation in this pattern. If the wife was born and educated in this country, her position in the family approximated the American pattern. Likewise, American-born Chinese children who were educated in American schools developed attitudes very similar to those of native-born children of European immigrant parents and other native-born Americans.

In sum, the shortage of Chinese women and various racist immigration policies resulted in the mutilated or split household family, which continued to be a predominant family form among the Chinese in America from the 1920s to the 1940s. Another type of Chinese family that emerged during this period was the small producer family. A distinguishing characteristic of this sizable second-generation Chinese American family was that the Chinese children divided their time between growing up as active participants in the small family enterprise serving the ethnic community and trying to get ahead in school. Despite the emergence of this new Chinese family form, the cultural link between the Chinese family in the United States and the traditional family in China was maintained, although there were signs of gradual weakening as the family members became more acculturated into American society.

The Transitional Chinese American Family (1943–1965)

The racist and exclusionist immigration policies in place during the early tenure of the Chinese in America played a major role in the resultant shortage of Chinese women in the United States and in the delay in the emergence of a second-generation Chinese population in the United States. Ironically, the liberalization and reforms of immigration policies during and after World War II were instrumental in partially rectifying past discrimination against the Chinese, which slowly led to the development and normalization of family life among the Chinese in the United States. In 1943, the Chinese Exclusion Act of 1882 was repealed, making Chinese immigrants, many of whom had been living in the United States for decades, eligible for citizenship. In recognition of China's position as an ally of the United States in World War II, a token quota of 105 persons per year was established for Chinese immigration. Although small, the quota did open the door to further immigration and had an impact on the future formation of Chinese families in the

United States. In 1945, the War Brides Act was passed, allowing approximately 6,000 Chinese women to enter the United States as brides of men in the United States military. In 1946, an amendment to this law put Chinese wives and children of United States citizens on a nonquota basis. The Displaced Persons Act of 1948 gave permanent resident status to 3,465 Chinese visitors, seamen, and students who were stranded in the United States because of the Chinese civil war. This same year saw the California anti-miscegenation law declared unconstitutional. In 1952, the McCarran-Walter Act was passed, eliminating race as a bar to immigration and giving preferences to relatives (Chen, 1980:211–213; Lee, 1956; Li, 1977a). The Refugee Relief Act of 1953 allowed 2,777 Chinese into the United States as refugees of the Chinese civil war. A presidential directive issued in 1962 permitted refugees from the People's Republic of China to enter the United States as parolees from Hong Kong. By 1966, approximately 15,000 refugees had entered under this provision. During the period from 1943 to the repeal of the quota law in 1965, Chinese immigration to the United States was overwhelmingly female with approximately nine females for every one male immigrant. Most of these women were alien wives of citizens admitted as nonquota immigrants (Sung, 1977; Yuan, 1966).

Although many of the Chinese male immigrants remained bachelors or separated from their wives during most of their lives in the United States, the liberalization of immigration policies after World War II enabled many mutilated or split household families to be reunited. Reform in immigration policies also encouraged Chinese men to return to Hong Kong in droves to find wives. The quest for a bride generally conformed to the age-old pattern of getting their family elders to find a mate for them through a go-between or matchmaker (Sung, 1967:156–157). The courtship was usually instantaneous, and complete strangers often married after knowing each other for as little as one week. These trans-Pacific marriages were characterized by a wide disparity in age—men in their thirties and forties marrying women between eighteen and twenty-two years old.

Tremendous differences also existed in the cultural upbringing between the partners—older, traditional men marrying younger, more modern women (Kitano, 1985:225; Sung, 1967:162). After their wedding, these newlyweds returned to the United States to ghetto conditions and a life of hardship in the urban Chinatowns of the West Coast. Despite the stress, strain, and cultural shock, these Chinese families usually remained intact. However, the relatively low divorce rate among the Chinese may be a result of marital discord and unhappiness generally being turned inward on the self, resulting in a high suicide rate.

For those Chinese families in which both spouses were native-born Americans, the family pattern approximated the American form, consisting of the husband, wife, and children and, occasionally, elderly parents. The parent–child relationship may be characterized as being situated somewhere between the strict formality of the traditional Chinese family and the high degree of permissiveness of the American (White) family (Sung, 1967:162, 176). The stranded Chinese who were displaced by the Chinese civil war in 1948 had family backgrounds strikingly different from the other Chinese in the United States. They were well educated, having attended teacher-training institutions and colleges in China and having received postgraduate education in the United States. Selection of a spouse was based more on individual preferences and love rather than the traditional reliance on or the decision of elders or matchmakers. These former students settled in the suburbs near the universities and research facilities where they ultimately found employment (Ikels, 1985).

The size of the Chinese families in the United States during this period was much larger than the general American population. Chinese families in New York's Chinatown had an average of 4.4 children compared with 2.9 children for White families (Liu, 1950). This difference may be the result of the Chinese value that a man's stature rose in direct proportion to the number of sons he sired and that women gained status by producing sons. It may also result partly from generational differences. Kwoh (1947) observed that if both parents were born in China, the median number of children in the family was 6.2; if both were American born, the median number was 3.2 children. Taken together, the average Chinese family had 5.5 children. As the Chinese became more Americanized and acculturated, the number of children in the Chinese family declined.

There are several general characteristics of the Chinese family during this period that hold regardless of the nativity or generational status. First, filial piety or loyal devotion to one's parents was still highly stressed, although in varying degrees. No matter how old a son was or how exalted his social position, his first obligation was to his parents.

Second, Chinese children were taught the concept of "face" at a very early age. If the children did something wrong, it was not just a personal matter between themselves and their conscience. They also brought dishonor and shame to their families, family names, and loved ones. The emphasis was not just on personal responsibility but also accountability to the family and kinship network. This served as a strong method of social control.

Related to the concept of face was the fact that the Chinese went to great lengths to keep their "dirty linen" within the family walls. Their infrequent use of social agencies and the common perceptions or misconceptions that the Chinese take care of their own help perpetuate the myth that the Chinese family was relatively problem free.

In sum, the liberalization of immigration policies after World War II slowly led to the transition of the Chinese families in the United States from split household or mutilated family to a more nuclear form. As Chinese families became more acculturated to American society, their family patterns began to closely resemble those of their American counterparts.

The Modern Chinese American Family: 1965 to the Present

The Immigration and Naturalization Act of 1965 had a profound influence on the family life of Chinese in America. Emphasizing family reunification, this act abolished the national-origins quota system established by the McCarran-Walter Act of 1952 and granted each country a quota of 20,000 immigrants per year. Since 1968, when the law went into effect, approximately 22,000 Chinese have immigrated to the United States through Hong Kong each year (Wong, 1985, 1986; Wong and Hirschman, 1983) (see Table 13.2). Unlike the pre-1965 immigrants who came over as individuals, most of the new Chinese immigrants are coming over as family groups—typically husband, wife, and unmarried children (Hong, 1976). A family chain pattern of migration developed whereby family members already in the United States would sponsor their relatives (Li, 1977b; Sung, 1977; Wong and Hirschman, 1983). Initially, many of these new immigrants usually settled in or near Chinatown so that they could trade in Chinese-speaking stores, use bilingual services, and find employment (Glenn, 1983).

Before discussing the characteristics of the various types of modern Chinese families, it may be informative to first briefly discuss some of the general social, demographic, economic, and family characteristics of the Chinese in the United States. A glance at Table 13.3 shows that in 2000, there are a slightly greater proportion of Chinese females to males. This is a relatively new phenomena occurring for the first time in 1990. As a consequence, the Chinese sex ratio was much more balanced than in previous decades and very similar to that of their White counterparts.

The Chinese population is slightly younger than the White population. This is evident by the much larger proportion of Whites than Chinese who were elderly. Although three-fourths of the White population resides in urban areas in the United States, these figures pale in comparison

TABLE 13.3   Social and Demographic Characteristics of the Chinese Family: 2000

	Chinese	White
Total Population		
% of U.S. population	0.9	80.6
Male	48.4%	49.0%
Female	51.6%	51.0%
Age		
Median	35.5 years	37.2 years
Under 5 years	6.1%	6.1%
18 years and over	78.7%	76.5%
65 years and over	9.7%	14.3%
Residence		
Urban	98.1%	75.2%
Rural	1.9%	24.8%
Nativity Status		
Native born	25.6%	93.3%
Foreign born	74.4%	6.7%
Marital Status		
Never Married	28.5%	24.0%
Married	63.1%	59.0%
Widowed	4.4%	7.0%
Divorced	3.8%	10.0%
Family Status		
Married	83.7%	81.8%
Male headed	5.8%	5.2%
Female headed	10.5%	13.0%
Grandparents as Caregivers		
Grandparents living with grandchildren	5.9%	2.5%
Grandparents responsible for grandchildren	18.6%	41.7%
Family Size	3.40	3.02
Language Spoken at Home		
All speak English	9.5%	83.5%
Some speak non-English language	15.2%	8.6%
All speak non-English language	75.3%	8.0%
Linguistically Isolated	33.1%	3.2%
Education (25 years and older)		
Less than high school	23.0%	16.4%
High school graduate	13.2%	29.5%
Some college	15.8%	28.0%
College graduate	24.2%	16.6%
Postgraduate	23.9%	9.4%

TABLE 13.3 *(continued)*

	Chinese	White
Occupation		
Manager, professional, and related	52.3%	35.6%
Service	14.0%	13.3%
Sales	20.8%	27.0%
Farm	.1%	.6%
Construction, extraction, maintenance	2.6%	9.8%
Production, transport, material move	10.4%	13.6%
Income		
Median family income	$60,058	$53,356
Per capita income	$23,756	$23,918
Families below poverty level	10.3%	6.3%
Family Income		
$0–$19,999	15.8%	11.8%
$20,000–$99,999	58.5%	71.3%
$100,000 or more	25.8%	16.9%

Source: U.S. Census Bureau, (2000).

to the overwhelming 98 percent of the Chinese living in urban areas, particularly areas with large Chinese communities on the West and East Coasts. As a consequence of continued high rates of immigration, about three-fourths of the Chinese population is foreign born, a proportion that has seen continual increase during the past few decades. Over 90 percent of the White population is a predominantly native-born population.

One of the stereotypes of the Chinese family is that it is very stable as evidenced by the low incidence of divorce. The data seem to support this stereotype. The Chinese were more likely to be never married than Whites because they are younger and also because they tend to marry at a later age. At the same time, a greater proportion of Chinese are married than Whites. The Chinese are about 2.5 times less likely to be divorced than the White population, 4 percent and 10 percent, respectively. A partial reason for this lower incidence of divorce may be due to immigrants being less likely to be divorced (Wong, 1986). They are also less likely than Whites to be widowed— partly because of the lower proportion of their older population.

Looking at family status, the Chinese and White population have very similar proportions of married, male-headed families, and female-headed families. Although the White population had a slightly higher proportion of female-headed families, the Chinese had slightly higher rates of those who were married and male-headed families.

When one thinks of the Chinese family, images of the extended family are conjured up, where two or three or even four generations live under the same roof. The data lend some support to this image. Although the proportion is small, Chinese grandparents are much more likely to live with their grandchildren (5.9 percent) than White grandparents (2.5 percent). Interestingly, over 40 percent of the White grandparents state that they are responsible for their grandchildren, compared to only about 20 percent of the Chinese grandparents. Moreover, the average family size of the Chinese was larger than the White population. This may be due to (1) grandparents living in the household, (2) adult children living at home because of the later time of marriage or because they are still pursuing an education, or (3) immigrant relatives needing a temporary residence until they can find their own place.

Only about 10 percent of Chinese households were households where all the members spoke English. About 15 percent of the Chinese households had members in which some spoke a non-English language. About three-fourths of Chinese households consisted of families in which all members spoke a non-English language. This compares with only about 8 percent of the White population. The large proportion of foreign-born Chinese with a lack of facility with the English language affects cross-generational communication as well as human capital for job opportunities.

Although many look upon the Chinese as a model minority, a racial/ethnic group that has succeeded in American society, a glance at their educational, occupational, and income characteristics presents some interesting and somewhat contradictory findings. The educational distribution of the Chinese is bimodal—that is, they tend to be overrepresented at both ends of the educational continuum. About half of the Chinese graduated from college compared to about a quarter of the White population. Even more impressive is that almost 25 percent of the Chinese have some postgraduate degree compared to about 10 percent of the White population. However, it should be noted that on the opposite end of the continuum, the Chinese are disproportionately represented among those with less than a high school education compared to their White counterparts, 23 percent and 16 percent, respectively.

The high educational achievements of the Chinese may be reflected in their occupational distribution. The manager and professional occupations were the modal occupational category for both Chinese and Whites. Over half of the Chinese compared to one-third of Whites were involved in these occupations. This high proportion of Chinese in this occupational category should be viewed with caution as managers in this category include those who work for major corporations in the Fortune 500 to those who work for small mom-and-pop grocery stores and restaurants in the ethnic community. Whites were more likely to be represented in sales (possibly due to their greater facility with the English language) and in construction, extraction, maintenance, production, transport, and material movement (occupations that tend to be highly unionized) than the Chinese.

The occupational distribution of the Chinese as well as their lack of facility with the English language may be partially reflected in their income statistics. The Chinese median family income of $60,058 was slightly higher than the $53,356 for Whites. This is partially explained by their high educational attainment and their disproportionate concentration in the manager, professional, and related occupations. However, a closer look at other income statistics shows that this advantage is partly due to the Chinese family being slightly larger than the White family. The per capita income shows that Chinese family members are at a slight disadvantage compared to their White counterparts. Moreover, Chinese families (10.3 percent) are much more likely to have family incomes below poverty level than White families (6.3 percent). The Chinese are disproportionately represented at both the lower and higher ends of the income distribution compared to their White counterparts.

The modern Chinese American family can be divided into four major types: old immigrant families, professional immigrant families (Glenn and Yap, 2002), American-born Chinese families, and biracial/bicultural Chinese families.

The old immigrant families have been referred to as the "ghetto or Chinatown Chinese" (Huang, 1981), "dual worker family" (Glenn, 1983), or the "downtown Chinese" (Kwong, 1987). They consist of the new immigrant Chinese families living in or near Chinatowns in the major metropolitan areas of the United States or the aging segment of the small producer or split households in the United States. Immigrating before 1965, the fathers typically started out as laborers but were able to save enough money to own their own business, such as small mom-and-pop grocery stores or restaurants. Most are still connected socially and economically to Chinatown and speak the same Toysan dialect (Glenn and Yap, 2002; Wong, 1985). Because of their lack of facility with the English language and/or the lack of transference of educational or occupational credentials from their country of origin, many experience downward mobility. Both husband and wife are more-or-less co-equal breadwinners in the family, usually employed in the secondary labor market or enclave economy—in the labor-intensive, low-capital service and small manufacturing sectors, such as tourist shops, restaurants, and garment sweatshops (Light and Wong, 1975; Wong, 1980a, 1983; Wong and Hirschman, 1983). However, unlike the small producer family, there is almost complete segregation of work and family life with parents and children being separated for most of the day. Moreover, it is not uncommon for parents to spend very little time with each other because of different jobs and job schedules—one parent having a regular shift (i.e., sweatshop) and the other parent having the swing shift (i.e., restaurant)—or with their children (Wong, 1983). The parents' fatigue, the long hours of separation, and the lack of common experience can undermine communication between the parents and between parents and their children. Chen (1980:227–228) vividly describes the lifestyle of these new immigrants:

> Penetrate, if you can, into the crowded tenements, and you will find families of four, five, and six living, working, playing, and sleeping in a single room. Pots, pans, and food must be taken to a community kitchen shared with other families. Privacy is a sometime thing. These facts speak for themselves: for all its gaiety, good humor, and indomitable spirit this area suffers from wide-spread poverty, high unemployment, substandard and overcrowded housing, inferior public services and facilities, and resulting grave health problems.

The frequent influx of new Chinese immigrants has helped preserve some of the old traditional ways. Parental authority, especially the father's, is more absolute, and the extended family, if present, plays a much more significant role than typically found in middle-class Chinese or White families.

A variant of the "ghetto" or "Chinatown" family are the "out of town" or "trans-Pacific" families. Many new and old Chinese immigrants returned to China, Hong Kong, or Taiwan to marry. As a result, the number of trans-Pacific marriages involving U.S. citizens and Chinese brides increased in the late 1970s and early 1980s—about 5,000 Chinese brides arrived in the United States annually in the late 1980s (U.S. Department of Justice, 1988, 1989). Like the brides of the reunited "mutilated families," shock and a sense of betrayal are probably the initial reactions of these new brides upon their arrival to the United States. They were shocked to learn that their husbands must wash other people's clothes, shocked at the heavy load of work of their husbands, and shocked at the heavy load of work they must bear. Many felt a sense of betrayal by their husbands for misinforming or misleading them as to their future lifestyles. The shock and sense of betrayal exacerbate the problems that these brides already face in accommodating and adjusting to their husbands and to American society (Chin, 1994).

The second type of Chinese family is the professional immigrant family, the scholar-professionals or the middle-class, white-collar, or professional Chinese American family that moved away from Chinatown to the surrounding urban areas and suburbs. The parents of these families were either international students who arrived in the 1940s and 1950s shortly after the Communist takeover of China or those who entered after passage of the 1965 Immigration and Naturalization Act. These "uptown" immigrant or American-born Chinese are more modern and cosmopolitan in orientation and view themselves as more American than Chinese (Huang, 1981;

Kitano, 1985:224; Weiss, 1970, 1977). The parents are highly educated with one, if not both, having a college degree and being involved in professional or white-collar occupations, serving the greater society rather than the ethnic community. Many of these immigrant scholar families are from Taiwan, seeking work at the many universities throughout the United States. Their relatively high socioeconomic status and high degree of acculturation to American society allow these Chinese to live fairly comfortable lives in the better parts of the city or in the suburbs (Kuo, 1970; Yuan, 1963, 1966). These Chinese tend to reestablish a Chinese community in the suburbs (Fong, 1994; Horton, 1995; Lyman, 1974:149), a situation that may be structurally termed "semi-extended." Originally nuclear in structure, the opening up of relations between the United States and China resulted in many families sponsoring their parents for immigration to the United States. Although grandparents prefer to establish their own household, many may live in the same building, block, or neighborhood as their children (Huang 1981:123). Many still will live with their children. An extended family form is developing among this family type (Glenn and Yap, 2002).

The American-born Chinese family constitutes the third family type. It was not until the 1940s that the majority of Chinese in the United States were native born. However, due to the increased immigration of Chinese since 1965, the American-born Chinese population represented a significant minority of the Chinese population by the 1980s. Differences in the timing of immigration to the United States has resulted in considerable diversity among this population, ranging from sons and daughters of first-generation immigrants to fourth- and fifth-generation American-born Chinese, descendants from the nineteenth-century pioneers. These American-born Chinese tend to be college educated and are able to find jobs and careers in the general economy, usually commensurate with their high educational achievements. Their housing is usually consistent with their relatively high occupational status and income—in predominantly White, middle-class neighborhoods and suburbs (Glenn and Yap, 2002; Kuo, 1970; Kwong, 1987; Yuan, 1966). These highly acculturated American-born Chinese families are more modern and cosmopolitan in orientation and view themselves as more American than Chinese (Huang, 1981; Weiss, 1970, 1974).

One last Chinese family type is the interracial and/or biracial/bicultural Chinese family. There has been a dramatic increase in the incidence of interracial marriages, particularly with Whites, among the younger generation during the past two decades (Barnett, 1963; Burma, 1963; Lee and Fernandez, 1998; Lee and Yamanaka, 1990; Staples and Mirande, 1980; Sung, 1990; Weiss, 1970; Wong, 1989). Approximately 33 percent of all marriages among the Chinese are intermarriages (marriage to someone other than a Chinese).

The vast majority of Chinese are married to Chinese partners. However, Chinese American males (89 percent) are slightly more likely than Chinese females (83 percent) to have Chinese spouses. Chinese men are slightly more likely to marry other Asians and Hispanics or Latinos than Chinese women. Chinese women are more likely than Chinese men to have White spouses. There were marked differences between the generations, with 1.5-generation (those who immigrated early in life) and second-generation Chinese Americans much more likely to out-marry than the general Chinese population. Interestingly, regardless of generational status, both Chinese men and women are more likely to have a White than an Asian, Black, or Hispanic partner.

Other trends in intermarriage include a strong inverse relationship between age and the proportion of those who intermarry (Yuan, 1980), more Chinese women than Chinese men intermarrying (Barnett, 1963; Hsu, 1971a; Liang and Ito, 1999; Sung, 1990; Wong, 1989; Yuan, 1980), and a strong positive relationship between generational status and incidence of intermarriage (Kitano and Yeung, 1982; Liang and Ito, 1999; Sung, 1990). Numerous explanations for these trends have been suggested: (1) dissatisfaction with the more traditional Chinese males' limited attitudes toward women by more acculturated Chinese women (Braun and Chao, 1978), (2) the inability of

TABLE 13.4 Percentage of Marriage Parents of Chinese by Sex and Generational Status: 2000

Total Population	Second and 1.5 Generation	
Chinese American Men		
Chinese partner	89.5	65.6
Other Asian	4.1	12.7
White	5.1	19.3
Black	0.1	0.2
Hispanic/Latina	1.4	2.6
Chinese American Women		
Chinese partner	83.0	55.0
Other Asian	3.3	10.8
White	12.0	29.9
Black	0.6	0.7
Hispanic/Latino	1.1	2.0

Source: Le (2009).

Chinese American males to relate positively to Chinese-White social/sexual situations (Huang and Uba, 1992; Weiss, 1970), (3) occupational, housing, social mobility, and acculturation of the Chinese, especially by generation (Hirschman and Wong, 1984; Kitano and Yeung, 1982; Lee and Yamanaka, 1990), (4) changes in the attitudes of the Chinese, as well as the dominant group and other minority groups regarding interracial marriages (Kitano and Yeung, 1982; Wong, 1989), (5) the social class position of the Chinese and the increasing dispersal of Chinese away from the Chinatown ghetto (Huang, 1981; Parkman and Sawyer, 1967; Wong, 1989), and (6) the perpetuation of the stereotype of the Chinese male as asexual and nerdy and the Chinese female as sexy, exotic, and knowing how to please her man (Shah, 2003; White and Chan, 1983; Sue and Sue, 1971). Whatever the reason, there is no question that there has been a dramatic increase in the incidence of intermarriage among the Chinese in recent years, particularly in the 1980s and early 1990s. One ramification of this increase is that it furthers the acculturation of the Chinese into American society and, hence, hopefully their greater acceptance on the part of the dominant group. However, intermarriage is not without its costs. A loss of ethnic traditions, heritage, and a distinct sense of Chinese identity resulting in "symbolic ethnicity" (Gans, 1979), and intergenerational strain and conflict between the Chinese parents and their interracially married children are but some of the most evident costs. Sung (1990:350) sums it up best when she states:

> There is no question that the children will experience problems of identity physically as well as culturally. The children will not look wholly like the mother or the father. The children will be teased and taunted and possibly excluded for no other reason except that they look different. They are quickly labeled half-breed, half-caste, or mixed bloods, all disparaging terms. In some homes, if one of the ethnic cultures is suppressed as if it should be covered up, the child is left wondering if one half of him/her is something to be ashamed of. In other homes, the parents cannot agree on how the children are to be brought up, so the off-springs are baffled and confused.

Regardless of the particular type, the modern Chinese American family has a lower fertility rate, fewer out-of-wedlock births, and more conservative or traditional attitudes toward the role of women than the White population (Braun and Chao, 1978; Monahan, 1977). Divorce is a rarity among the Chinese (Huang, 1981:122; Schaffer, 1984:351). It is not uncommon for unhappy Chinese couples to remain together for fear of public opinion, social disgrace, and social ostracism. However, among the younger generation brought up to believe in the American ideal of romantic love and personal happiness in marriage, the incidence of divorce has increased. The economic position of the husband and wife as co-breadwinners and/or their high socioeconomic position lends itself to a mutual sharing of responsibility and authority in the decision making of most aspects of family life (Sollenberger, 1968), although the wife usually assumes the role of helper rather than equal partner (Huang, 1981). In child rearing, the father maintains his authority and respect in the Chinese family by means of a certain amount of emotional distance (Shon and Ja, 1982:212). The mother does not interact with the children but commands and decides what is best for them, and the children are expected to obey (Huang, 1981; Sollenberger, 1968; Sung, 1967:165, 168–169). Although Chinese parents may be more indulgent with their young children than parents of the White American culture, discipline is much stricter (Petersen, 1978). Punishment is immediate and generally involves withdrawal from the social life of the family or the deprivation of special privileges or objects (Petersen, 1978), or it may involve physical punishment (Uba, 1994). Many Chinese parents will reward their children for their good behavior by simply not punishing them. After all, why should one reward behavior that is expected. As the child grows older, overt expressions of physical and emotional affection exhibited among family members, whether between the husband and wife or between the parents and children, are withdrawn. Many Chinese children have never seen their parents kiss or hug each other, nor are they expected to kiss or hug their parents (Huang, 1981:126). The public display of affection is considered in poor taste by many Chinese. Independence and maturity are stressed at a very young age, and the child is expected to behave as an adult. Aggressive behavior on the part of the young and sibling rivalry are not tolerated and are highly discouraged (Sollenberger, 1968). Older children are expected to be directly or indirectly involved in the socialization of their younger siblings—serving as role models of adult behavior. Chinese children are brought up in the midst of adults, not only their parents but also members of the extended family. As a consequence, they learn at a very early age socially approved patterns of behavior and also what others think of them. Instead of individual guilt governing their behavior (as is true of their White counterparts), the sense of face, or shame, to themselves and to their family acts as a major form of social control (Huang, 1981:124–125).

Chinese students are more sexually conservative than White students. A lower proportion of Chinese have engaged in premarital intercourse, and they put off physical intimacy longer than Whites (Espiritu, 2001; Huang and Uba, 1992; Tong, 2003). Explanations for these differences include (1) the need to feel more certain of an emotional commitment, (2) less positive body image of some Asian Americans, which may cause them to be more sexually modest, (3) lack of social acculturation, (4) the stereotype of Asian men as "nerdy" and socially inept, hence, making them undesirable dating partners, and (5) reflection of traditional Chinese culture's emphasis on modesty (Chen and Yang, 1986; Hsu, 1970; Huang and Uba, 1992).

Education is highly valued in the Chinese family, and parents will undergo extreme financial sacrifice and hardship so that their children can receive as much education as possible. This value on education may stem from numerous factors: (1) the parents' traditional Confucian respect for learning and that children are expected to do well in school and other endeavors in order to provide honor to their family (Chao, 1995; Fuligni and Tseng, 1999), (2) the realization that education is an avenue by which their children will gain security and a better life than they have, (3) the higher social status that the parents receive in the Chinese community if they have a college-educated or professional child, and/or (4) the demographic and high socioeconomic characteristics of the Chinese (Hirschman and Wong, 1986; Wong, 1980b). Education does not stop with the typical American school curriculum. Fearing a loss of Chinese heritage, many Chinese parents feel that their children should be instilled with knowledge about Chinese culture, traditions, customs, history, and language. As a consequence, in areas with a significant Chinese population, many native-born and foreign-born Chinese children attend Chinese school after American school or during the weekends (Fong, 1968).

Many believe that due to their adherence to the Confucian ethic of filial piety, Chinese children show greater concern and devotion toward their elders and that they are more likely to take care of their elder parents than average White children. The exact strength of this devotion compared with other ethnic groups and the veracity of this stereotype of the Chinese family is an empirical question for which limited data are available. One study found that family members are the primary source of assistance for the elderly Chinese and that it is only recently that they are seeking assistance from social service agencies and professional persons (Wong, 2001). Hirata (1975) found that approximately 90 percent of both native- and foreign-born Chinese youths and their parents indicated that they believed children should support their aged parents. Chinese children felt a strong sense of guilt and shame over what they considered inappropriate care for elderly parents, such as the placement of their elderly parents in nursing homes (Kalish and Moriwaki, 1973). Fuligni et al. (2002) found that Chinese adolescents from immigrant families spent more hours per day (1.25 hours) assisting and being with their families compared to White high school students (.7 hour per day). Chinese students also divided equally the amount of time spent on family obligations and on socializing with peers compared to their White counterparts, who spend from 80 percent to 100 percent more time with their peers. Fuligni et al. (1999) found that Chinese placed greater importance on treating their elders with respect, following their parents' advice, and helping and being near their families in the future than Whites. Knowledge that their parents' lack of facility with the English language may result in problems of adjustment, mistreatment, inadequate care, and a sense of isolation and alienation in nursing homes may contribute to the high degree of filial responsibility among the Chinese children (Wong, 1984, 2001).

Filial piety may act as a major form of social control. Many Chinese American children are taught at a very young age their obligation, not only to themselves, but also to their parents and other family members. Any behavior that may bring shame to them or their family is unacceptable. Hence, filial piety, in an indirect way, serves as a method of social control that is pervasive among Chinese American children (JWK International Corporation, 1978; Sue and Kirk, 1972). Recent research suggests a transformation away from the dictates of the Confucian ethic to greater gender and generational equality, especially among the Chinese middle-class (Espiritu, 1996; Tong, 2003).

In sum, instead of talking about the modern Chinese American family, it is probably more accurate to say that there are many different forms of the modern Chinese American family, each with its own particular characteristics, depending on the time and circumstance of arrival, generational status, and degree of acculturation. Moreover, there are probably many more variations within each of these forms than between them.

CHANGES AND ADAPTATIONS

The Chinese American family has undergone tremendous changes and adaptations during its 160 years in the United States—from the mutilated or split household family to the small producer family to the trans-Pacific marriage pattern to the diverse present-day Chinese American family structures. Many of these changes and adaptations were the result of complex interactions between cultural and structural factors. During the twenty-first century, the Chinese family will continue to change, modify, adapt, and transform according to the ebbs and flows of societal forces and the constraints and expansion of opportunities in American society.

The Chinese family in the United States is intensely involved in the process of urban socio-cultural changes and acculturation. One indicator of this process is the geographic dispersion of the Chinese away from the Chinatown areas and to the metropolitan areas and the suburbs (Fong, 1994; Horton, 1995). As Chinese children attend American schools and develop friend-ships with White American children, as they become more competent in English than in Chinese, as they become more acculturated, they will probably view themselves as more American than Chinese. With their high degree of acculturation, the younger Chinese Americans will probably face a clash of cultures and identity conflicts between themselves as primarily "American" and their appearance to others as "Chinese" or "Asian" (Chen, 1972, 1981; Chen and Yang, 1986; Fong, 1965, 1968, 2008).

> We ABC (American-born Chinese) were ridiculed by the old immigrants as "Bamboo Stick" for not being able to speak Chinese and not being accepted as "white people." We are not here. We are not there. White people consider us to be inferior to the educated Chinese from China because we lack the "exotic value." This is the reason why many of us do not want to socialize with the China-born Chinese American. We are different. Most of us are proud of the Chinese cultural heritage, but due to the pressure to assimilate and the lack of opportunity, we don't know much about the Chinese way. (Wong, 1982)

A number of Chinese American personality types have emerged ranging from the "banana" (yellow on the outside but White on the inside) who rejects or denies all aspects of being Chinese in order to try to appear completely American or White to the "radical" Chinese who may espouse a new Asian consciousness while rejecting the values of traditional Chinese and American culture (Sue and Sue, 1971; Chen, 1981). These personality types may further exacer-bate the generational conflicts between child and parent.

The acculturation of the second-generation Chinese also has additional consequences. There may be a gradual drift from the older generation that will result in a lack of communica-tion as well as a conflict in values between the older generation and their younger, more accultur-ated children (Fong, 1965; Fong, 1968; Jiobu, 1988; Wong, 2006). Noted one Chinese parent:

> Raising children does not do any good in this country. They leave when they are grown up. I seldom see them nowadays, with the exception of my youngest son who is running the factory in Chinatown. They are too independent in this country! They are selfish, too! (Wong, 1982:32)

The acculturation of the Chinese is also affected by immigration rates. Proficiency in English is a key to assimilation. People who speak English are more assimilated, not just because they can communicate with members of the dominant group but also because they can be more effectively socialized by the dominant culture (Jiobu, 1988; Ferguson, 1995). At least 75 percent of the Chinese in the United States speak another language other than English at home. Although one can make the argument that many of the Chinese are bilingual, and many are, about 24 per-cent of Chinese Americans do not speak English very well. Moreover, about 33 percent of Chinese American households considered themselves linguistically isolated (U.S. Census Bureau, 2000). With the continued influx of Chinese immigrants to the United States, we should expect an increase in the foreign-born population, in those not being able to speak English very well, and in those who live in linguistically isolated households. In essence, we should see the Chinese American, as a group, become less acculturated, at least in the short term. We can also anticipate a continued generational conflict between the values of the immigrant parents and their more Americanized children.

During the 1980s and 1990s, intermarriages among the Chinese were quite significant. Whether this rate will continue to increase, only the future will tell. There are several factors that may promote a continued increase in intermarriages among the Chinese. The emergence of a significant native-born Chinese population, who are highly acculturated, is one factor. The rate of out-marriages increases with each succeeding generation. Another factor is the dispersal of Chinese away from the segregated Chinatowns to the suburbs where they will come in contact with other ethnic and racial groups. However, some countervailing forces may slow down or even reverse the intermarriage rate for the Chinese. In 2000, about 75 percent of the Chinese American population is foreign born. Unless there is a drastic change in immigration policy, we can expect a continued influx and increase of Chinese immigrants to the United States, many who lack facility with the English language. Research suggests a much lower intermarriage rate among the foreign-born than native-born Chinese (Lee and Yamanaka, 1990; Wong, 1989) and that the greater the size of the Chinese population, the greater the probably of finding a spouse within one's group (Le, 2007). All these factors suggest the possibility of a decrease in the intermarriage rate among the Chinese in the United States in the future.

Change and adaptation were important elements in the formation and development of the Chinese family in the United States, and it is probably safe to say that they will continue to play important roles in the future. Although some people may regard the Chinese family as breaking down or undergoing social disorganization, as evidenced by the increase in acculturation, interracial marriages, and juvenile delinquency rates (Fong, 1968; Sung, 1967:185–186), one can view the recent changes and adaptations as essential elements of the greater process of modification and reorganization that has been occurring for the past 160 years and will continue to occur. The present-day Chinese family in the United States is much different from the Chinese families of the past. The continued influx in Chinese immigration to the United States and continued pressure to acculturate to American society, the generational conflicts between the immigrant parents and their native-born children, the differing identity formations of subsequent generations all suggest, with a high degree of certainty, that the Chinese American family will continue to successfully evolve, develop, and adapt from its present-day form.

References

Barnett, L. D. 1963. "Interracial Marriage in California." *Marriage and Family Living* 25(4), 425–427.

Barth, G. 1964. *Bitter Strength: A History of the Chinese in the United States, 1850–1870.* Cambridge, MA: Harvard University Press.

Beaudry, J. A. 1971, May. "Some Observations on Chinese Intermarriage in the United States." *International Journal of Sociology and the Family* 1, 59–68.

Braun, J., and H. R. Chao. 1978, Spring. "Attitudes Toward Women: A Comparison of Asian-Born Chinese and American Caucasians." *Psychology of Women Quarterly* (vol. 2, p. 195–201).

Burma, J. H. 1952. "Research Note on the Measurement of Interracial Marriage." *American Journal of Sociology* 57, 587–589.

———. 1963, May. "Interethnic Marriages in Los Angeles, 1948-59." *Social Forces* 42, 156–165.

Chao, R. K. 1995. "Chinese and European American Cultural Models of the Self Reflected in Mothers' Childrearing Beliefs." *Ethos* 23, 328–354.

Chen, Clarence L. 1972, Summer. "Experiences as an American in Disguise." *Newsletter of the Midwest Chinese Student and Alumni Services* 14(4), 4–8.

———. 1981, July 8. "An Asian American Approach to Confronting Racism." *East West: The Chinese American Journal 15*(27), 2, 5.

Chen, C. L., and D. C. Y. Yang. 1986. "The Self Image of Chinese American Adolescents: A Cross Cultural Comparison." *International Journal of Social Psychiatry 32*(4), 19–26.

Chen, J. 1980. *The Chinese of America*. San Francisco: Harper and Row.

Chin, K. L. 1994. "Out of Town Brides: International Marriage and Wife Abuse Among Chinese Immigrants." *Journal of Comparative Family Studies 55*(1), 53–69.

Chinn, T., H. M. Lai, and P. Choy. 1969. *A History of the Chinese in California: A Syllabus*. San Francisco: Chinese Historical Society of America.

Coolidge, M. 1909. *Chinese Immigration*. New York: Henry Holt.

Espiritu, Y. L. 1996. *Asian American Women and Men: Labor, Laws, and Love*. Thousand Oaks, CA: Sage.

———. 2001. "We Don't Sleep Around Like White Girls Do: Family, Culture, and Gender in Filipina American Lives." *Signs 26*, 415–440.

Fei, H. T. 1939. *Peasant Life in China: A Field Study of Country Life in the Yangtze Valley*. London: Routledge and Kegan Paul.

Ferguson, S. J. 1995. "Marriage Timing of Chinese American and Japanese American Women." *Journal of Family Issues 16*(3), 314–343.

Fong, S. L. M. 1965. "Assimilation of Chinese in America: Changes in Orientation and Social Perception." *American Journal of Sociology 71*(3), 265–273.

Fong, T. P. 1968. "Identity Conflict of Chinese Adolescents in San Francisco." In Eugene B. Brody (Ed.), *Minority Group Adolescents in the United States* (pp. 111–132). Baltimore, MD: Williams and Wilkins.

———. 1994. *The First Suburban Chinatown: The Remaking of Monterey Park, California*. Philadelphia: Temple University Press.

———. 2008. *The Contemporary Asian American Experience: Beyond the Model Minority*. Upper Saddle River, NJ: Prentice Hall.

Fuligni, A. J., and V. Tseng. 1999. "Family Obligation and the Achievement Motivation of Children from Immigrant and American-born Families." In T. Urdan (Ed.), *Advances in Motivation and Achievement* (pp. 159–184). Stamford, CT: JAI.

Fuligni, A., V. Tseng, and M. Lam. 1999. "Attitudes Toward Family Obligations Among American Adolescents with Asian, Latin American, and European Backgrounds." *Child Development 70*(4), 1030–1044.

Fuligni, A. J., T. Yip, and V. Tseng. 2002. "The Impact of Family Obligation on the Daily Activities and Psychological Well-Being of Chinese American Adolescents." *Child Development 73*(1), 302–314.

Gardner, R. W., B. Robey, and P. C. Smith. 1985. "Asian Americans: Growth, Change, and Diversity." *Population Bulletin 4*(14). Washington, DC: Population Reference Bureau.

Gans, H. J. 1979. "Symbolic Ethnicity: The Future of Ethnic Groups and Cultures in America." *Ethnic and Racial Studies 2*(1), 1–20.

Glenn, E. N. 1983. "Split Household, Small Producer and Dual Wage Earner: An Analysis of Chinese-American Family Strategies." *Journal of Marriage and the Family 45*(1), 35–46.

Glenn, E. N., and S. G. H. Yap. 2002. "Chinese American Families." In Ronald L. Taylor (Ed.), *Minority Families in the United States: A Multicultural Perspective* (pp. 134–163). Upper Saddle River, NJ: Prentice Hall.

Glick, C. E. 1980. *Sojourners and Settlers: Chinese Migrants in Hawaii*. Honolulu: University of Hawaii Press.

Hayner, N. S., and C. N. Reynolds. 1937. "Chinese Family Life in America." *American Sociological Review 22*(5), 630–637.

Hirata, L. C. 1975. "Youth, Parents, and Teachers in Chinatown: A Triadic Framework of Minority Socialization." *Urban Education 10*(3), 279–296.

———. 1979, Autumn. "Free, Indentured, Enslaved: Chinese Prostitutes in Nineteenth-Century America." *Signs 5*, 3–29.

Hirschman, C., and M. G. Wong. 1981. "Trends in Socioeconomic Achievement Among Immigrant and Native-Born Asian-Americans, 1960–1976." *Sociological Quarterly 22*, 495–513.

———. 1984. "Socioeconomic Gains of Asian Americans, Blacks, and Hispanics: 1960–1976." *American Journal of Sociology 90*, 584–607.

———. 1986. "The Extraordinary Educational Attainment of Asian-Americans: A Search for Historical Evidence and Explanations." *Social Forces 65*, 1–27.

Ho, D. Y. F. 1981. "Traditional Patterns of Socialization in Chinese Society." *Acta Psychologica Taiwanica 23*, 81–95.

Hong, L. K. 1976. "Recent Immigrants in the Chinese-American Community: Issues of Adaptations and

Impacts." *International Migration Review 10*, 509–514.

Horton, J. 1995. *The Politics of Diversity: Immigration, Resistance, and Change in Monterey Park, California.* Philadelphia: Temple University Press.

Hsu, F. L. K. 1970. *Americans and Chinese.* Garden City, NY: Doubleday Natural History Press.

———. 1971a. *The Challenge of the American Dream: The Chinese in the United States.* Belmont, CA: Wadsworth.

———. 1971b. *Under the Ancestors' Shadow: Chinese Culture and Personality.* Palo Alta, CA: Stanford University Press.

Huang, L. J. 1981. "The Chinese American Family." In C. Mindel and R. Habenstein (Eds.), *Ethnic Families in America* (xxth ed., pp. 115–141). New York: Elsevier.

Huang, K., and L. Uba. 1992. "Premarital Sexual Behavior Among Chinese College Students in the United States." *Archives of Sexual Behavior 21*(3), 227–240.

Ikels, C. 1985. "Parental Perspectives on the Significance of Marriage." *Journal of Marriage and the Family 47*(2), 253–264.

Jiobu, R. 1988. *Ethnicity and Assimilation.* Albany: State University of New York Press.

Johnson, C. 1962. *Peasant Nationalism and Communist Power: The Emergence of Revolutionary China.* Palo Alto, CA: Stanford University Press.

JWK International Corporation. 1978. "Summary and Recommendations of Conference on Pacific and Asian American Families and HEW-Related Issues." Annandale, VA: Author.

Kalish, R. A., and S. Moriwaki. 1973. "The World of the Elderly Asian American." *Journal of Social Issues 29*(2), 187–209.

Kingston, M. H. 1976. *Woman Warrior.* New York: Knopf.

———. 1981. *China Men.* New York: Ballantine.

Kitano, H. H. L. 1985. *Race Relations.* Englewood Cliffs, NJ: Prentice Hall.

Kitano, H. H. L. 1982. "Chinese Interracial Marriage." *Marriage and Family Review 5*(1), 35–48.

Kung, S. W. 1962. *Chinese in American Life: Some Aspects of Their History, Status, Problems, and Contributions.* Seattle: University of Washington Press.

Kuo, C.-L. 1970. "The Chinese on Long Island: A Pilot Study." *Phylon 31*(3), 280–289.

Kwoh, B. O. 1947. "The Occupational Status of American-Born Chinese Male College Graduates." *American Journal of Sociology 53*, 192–200.

Kwong, P. 1987. *The New Chinatown.* New York: Noonday Press.

Lai, H. M., and P. P. Choy. 1971. *Outlines History of the Chinese in America.* San Francisco: Chinese-American Studies Planning Group.

Lan, P.-C. 2002. "Subcontracting Filial Piety: Elder Care in Ethnic Chinese Immigrant Families in California." *Journal of Family Issues 23*, 812–835.

Le, C. N. 2007. *Asian American Assimilation: Ethnicity, Immigration, and Socioeconomic Attainment.* New York: LFB Scholarly Publishing.

———. 2009. "Interracial Dating & Marriage." Asian-Nation: Asian American History, Demographics & Issues. www.asian-nation.org/interracial.shtml (accessed April 19, 2011).

Lee, R. H. 1956, February. "The Recent Immigrant Chinese Families of the San Francisco-Oakland Area." *Marriage and Family Living 18*, 14–24.

———. 1960. *The Chinese in the United States.* Hong Kong, China: Hong Kong University Press.

Lee, S., and M. Fernandez. 1998. "Trends in Asian American Racial/Ethnic Intermarriage: A Comparison of 1980 and 1990 Census Data." *Sociological Perspectives 41*, 323–342.

Lee, S., and K. Yamanaka. 1990. "Patterns of Asian American Intermarriage and Marital Assimilation." *Journal of Comparative Family Studies 51*(2) 287–305.

Li, P. S. 1977a, Spring. "Fictive Kinship, Conjugal Tie, and Kinship Chain Among Chinese Immigrants in the United States." *Journal of Comparative Family Studies 8*(1), 47–63.

———. 1977b. "Occupational Achievement and Kinship Assistance Among Chinese Immigrants in Chicago." *Sociological Quarterly 18*(4), 478–489.

Liang, Z., and N. Ito. 1999. "Intermarriage of Asian American in New York City Region: Contemporary Patterns and Future Prospects." *International Migration Review 33*(4), 876–900.

Light, Ivan H. 1972. *Ethnic Enterprise in America.* Berkeley: University of California Press.

Light, I. H., and C. C. Wong. 1975. "Protest or Work: Dilemmas of the Tourist Industry in American Chinatowns." *American Journal of Sociology 80*, 1342–1368.

Ling, H. 2000. "Family and Marriage of Late-Nineteenth and Early-Twentieth Century Chinese Immigrant Women." *Journal of American Ethnic History 19*(2), 43–64.

Liu, C. H. 1950. "The Influence of Cultural Background on the Moral Judgment of Children." Ph.D. dissertation, Columbia University.

Liu, H-c. Wang. 1959. *The Traditional Chinese Clan Rules*. Locust Valley, NY: J. J. Augustin.

Lowe, P. 1943. *Father and Glorious Descent*. Boston: Little, Brown.

Lyman, S. M. 1968. "Marriage and the Family Among Chinese Immigrants to America, 1850–1960." *Phylon* 29(4), 321–330.

———. 1970. "Social Demography of the Chinese and Japanese in the U.S. of America." In Stanford M. Lyman (Ed.), *The Asian in the West* (pp. 65–80). Las Vegas, NV: Western Studies Center.

———. 1974. *Chinese Americans*. New York: Random House.

———. 1977. *The Asian in North America*. Santa Barbara, CA: Clio Press.

Mark, D. M. L., and G. Chih. 1982. *A Place Called Chinese America*. Washington, DC: Organization of Chinese Americans.

Monahan, T. 1977, January–June. "Illegitimacy by Race and Mixture of Race." *International Journal of Sociology and the Family 7*, 45–54.

Nee, V., and B. Nee. 1973. *Longtime Californ': A Study of an American Chinatown*. New York: Pantheon.

Nee, V., and H. Y. Wong. 1985. "Asian American Socioeconomic Achievement: The Strength of the Family Bond." *Sociological Perspectives 28*(3), 281–306.

Parkman, M., and J. Sawyer. 1967. "Dimensions of Ethnic Intermarriage in Hawaii." *American Sociological Review 32*(4), 593–607.

Petersen, W. 1978. "Chinese Americans and Japanese Americans." In Thomas Sowell (Ed.), *Essays and Data on American Ethnic Groups* (pp. 65–106). Washington, DC: Urban Institute Press.

Schwartz, S. 1951. "Mate Selection Among New York City's Chinese Males, 1931–1938." *American Journal of Sociology 56*, 562–568.

Shah, H. 2003. "'Asian Culture' and Asian American Identities in the Television and Film Industries of the United States," *Studies in Media and Information Literacy Education 3*: 3.

Shon, S. P., and D. Y. Ja. 1982. "Asian American Families." In M. McGoldrick, J. K. Pearch, and J. Giodano (Eds.), *Ethnicity and Family Therapy* (pp. 208–228). New York: Guilford Press.

Siu, P. 1952. "The Sojourner." *American Journal of Sociology 58*, 34–44.

Sollenberger, R. T. 1968, February. "Chinese-American Child-Rearing Practices and Juvenile Delinquency." *Journal of Social Psychology 74*, 13–23.

Staples, R., and A. Mirande. 1980. "Racial and Cultural Variations Among American Families: A Decennial Review of the Literature on Minority Families." *Journal of Marriage and the Family 42*(4), 887–903.

Sue, D., and B. Kirk. 1972. "Psychological Characteristics of Chinese American Students." *Journal of Counseling Psychology 19*, 471–478.

Sue, S., and H. Kitano. 1973, Spring. "Asian American Stereotypes." *Journal of Social Issues 29*, 83–98.

Sue, S., and D. W. Sue. 1971. "Chinese American Personality and Mental Health." In A. Tachiki, E. Wong, F. Odo, et al. (Eds.) with Buck Wong, *Roots: An Asian-American Reader* (pp. 72–81). Los Angeles: Continental Graphics.

Sung, B. L. 1967. *Mountain of Gold*. New York: Macmillan.

———. 1977. "Changing Chinese." *Societ 14*(6), 44–99.

———. 1987. "Intermarriage Among the Chinese in New York City." In *Chinese America: History and Perspectives 1987* (pp. 101–118). San Francisco: Chinese Historical Society of America.

———. 1990. "Chinese American Intermarriage." *Journal of Comparative Family Studies 21*(3), 337–352.

Thorton, A., and H. S. Lin. 1994. *Social Change and the Family in Taiwan*. Chicago: University of Chicago Press.

Tong, B. 2003. *The Chinese Americans*. Boulder: University Press of Colorado.

Uba, L. 1990. "Chinese American Intermarriage." *Journal of Comparative Family Studies 21*(3), 337–356.

———. 1994. *Asian Americans: Personality Patters, Identity, and Mental Health*. New York: Guilford Press.

U.S. Census Bureau. 1993. "1990 Census of Population. Social and Economic Characteristics of the Asian American Population." Washington, DC: U.S. Government Printing Office.

———. 2000. "Sample File 2 (SF2) and Sample File 4 (SF4) 100 Percent Data." Washington, DC: U.S. Government Printing Office.

U.S. Department of Homeland Security. 2004. "2003 Yearbook of Immigration Statistics." Washington, DC: U.S. Government Printing Office.

U.S. Department of Justice. 1988. *Statistical Yearbook of the Immigration and Naturalization Service*. Washington, DC: U.S. Government Printing Office.

———. 1989. *Statistical Yearbook of the Immigration and Naturalization Service*. Washington, DC: U.S. Government Printing Office.

Weiss, M. S. 1970. "Selective Acculturation and the Dating Process: The Patterning of Chinese-Caucasian Interracial Dating." *Journal of Marriage and the Family 32*, 273–278.

———. 1974. *Valley City: A Chinese Community in America.* Cambridge, MA: Schenkman.

———. 1977. "The Research Experience in a Chinese American Community." *Journal of Social Issues* 33(4) 120–132.

White, W. S., and E. Chan. 1983. "A Comparison of Self-Concept Scores of Chinese and White Graduate Students and Professional." *Journal of Marriage and the Family 32*: 273–278.

Wolf, M. 1972. *Women and the Family in Rural Taiwan.* Palo Alto, CA: Stanford University Press.

Wong, B. 1982. *Chinatown: Economic Adaptation and Ethnic Identity of the Chinese.* New York: Holt, Rinehart and Winston.

Wong, J. S. 1950. *Fifth Chinese Daughter.* New York: Harper and Brothers.

Wong, Morrison G. 1980a. "Changes in Socioeconomic Achievement of the Chinese Male Population in the United States from 1960 to 1970." *International Migration Review 14*, 511–524.

———. 1980b. "Model Students? Teachers' Perceptions and Expectations of their Asian and White Students." *Sociology of Education 53*, 236–246.

———. 1983. "Chinese Sweatshops in the United States: A Look at the Garment Industry." In Ida H. Simpson and Richard L. Simpson (Eds.), *Research in the Sociology of Work* (vol. 11, pp. 3, 7–79). Greenwich, CT: JAI Press.

———. 1984. "Economic Survival: The Case of Asian-American Elderly." *Sociological Perspective 27*(2), 197–217.

———. 1985. "Post-1965 Immigrants: Demographic and Socioeconomic Profile." In L. A. Maldonado and J. W. Moore (Eds.), *Urban Ethnicity: New Immigrants and Old Minorities. Urban Affairs Annual Review* (vol. 29, p. 51–71). Beverly Hills, CA: Sage.

———. 1986. "Post-1965 Asian Immigrants: Where Do They Come From, Where Are They Now, and Where Are They Going." In Rita J. Simon (Ed.), *The Annals of the American Academy of Political and Social Science* (vol. 487, pp. 150–168). Beverly Hills, CA: Sage.

———. 1989. "A Look at Intermarriage Among the Chinese in the United States in 1980." *Sociological Perspectives 32*(1), 87–108.

———. 2001. "The Chinese Elderly: Values and Issues in Receiving Adequate Care." In Laura Katz Olson (Ed.), *Age Through Ethnic Lenses: Caring for the Elderly in a Multicultural Society* (pp. 17–32). New York: Rowman and Littlefield.

———. 2006. "Chinese Americans." In P. G. Min (Ed.), *Asian Americans: Contemporary Trends and Issues* (pp. 110–145). Thousand Oaks, CA: Pine Forge Press.

Wong, M. G., and C. Hirschman. 1983. "The New Asian Immigrants." In William McCready (Ed.), *Culture, Ethnicity and Identity: Current Issues in Research* (pp. 381–403). New York: Academic Press.

Yang, C. K. 1959. *The Chinese Family in the Communist Revolution.* Cambridge, MA: Technology Press.

Yuan, L. Y. 1963. "Voluntary Segregation: A Study of New Chinatown." *Phylon 24*(3), 255 –265.

———. 1966. "Chinatown and Beyond: The Chinese Population in Metropolitan New York." *Phylon 27*(4), 321–332.

———. 1980. "Significant Demographic Characteristics of Chinese Who Intermarry in the United States." *California Sociologist 3*(2), 184–197.

14

■ ■ ■

The Japanese American Family

Arthur Sakamoto
ChangHwan Kim
Isao Takei

INTRODUCTION

The internment of Japanese Americans during World War II has become widely recognized as an infamous event in American history. Much research continues to be devoted to topics relating to or foreshadowing that historic episode. Indeed, in Asian American studies courses, Japanese Americans are implicitly portrayed as "the group that was interned" as if that incident of victimization were the most important characteristic defining this group.[1]

This popular representation is ironic because the internment of Japanese Americans was not the consequence of any of the actual activities of Japanese Americans at that time—that is, Japanese Americans did not *do* anything to cause the internment to occur. In defining Japanese Americans as being noteworthy mainly because of their internment history, the salient life activities and achievements of Japanese Americans themselves are being overlooked. Our decades of social interaction with Japanese Americans suggest to us that they tend to prefer to be recognized by *what they have done and have worked to accomplish* in their lifetimes and not by distant historical events that were beyond their immediate control or were never part of their own personal experience.[2]

---

[1]For example, in her extended study of Asian American identity, Kibria (2002) almost entirely omits Japanese Americans and simply states that they "were vilified and sent off to internment camps" during World War II. According to Tuan (1998:16), Japanese Americans are "indelibly marked by their wartime internment," which is said to "play a significant role in promoting a salient ethnic identity even among current generations with no direct internment experience." Meanwhile, the historical significance and impact of the heroic accomplishments of the 442nd Infantry Battalion during World War II—the most highly decorated unit in U.S. military history—have been largely purged from recent writings on Japanese Americans.

[2]Among Japanese and to a somewhat lesser extent nisei Japanese Americans, the Confucian norm toward (ostensible) humility generally prohibits boastfulness and the claiming of credit especially in regard to events that one did not put forth effort to bring about. The reticence that Japanese Americans who endured the internment often have toward discussing it is not due to "repression" (Bai, 1995:38) but the belief that victimization is not as significant as the notable accomplishments that Japanese Americans themselves have worked hard to achieve. For a discussion of related issues for Asian Americans more generally, see Sakamoto, Goyette, and Kim (2009).

In this regard, Japanese Americans have traditionally understood that their *agency* takes place within the social context of their families, which undergirds the experiences of their actual lives. Understanding this critical context has been hampered, however, by the lack of research on the Japanese American family in recent years. In this chapter, we begin to fill this research gap by providing an empirical analysis of the Japanese American family using current data.

HISTORICAL BACKGROUND

Many excellent discussions of Japanese American history and Japanese immigration to the United States are well known and widely available (Barringer, Gardner, and Levin, 1993; Daniels, 1988; Hosokawa, 1992; Kitano, 1976; Kitano and Daniels, 1995; Min, 2006; Nishi, 1995; Takahashi, 1997; Wilson and Hosokawa, 1980). For our purposes, immigration patterns and related demographic trends are the most directly pertinent factors. These trends form the immediate antecedents of the current diversity of contemporary Japanese American family patterns.

As discussed in detail in the aforementioned references, immigration from Japan may be distinguished from immigration from other Asian nations in that a significant Japanese American population was established in the early twentieth century, especially in Hawaii and California. These communities included many Japanese American families consisting of immigrant parents residing with their native-born, second-generation children. Whereas immigration laws relating to the Chinese (most notably the Chinese Exclusion Act of 1882) limited the significant development of a regular Chinese American family during this time period (Wong, 1995:69), the Gentlemen's Agreement of 1907–1908 curtailed the immigration of Japanese male laborers but specifically allowed for Japanese women to immigrate for the purpose of marrying Japanese men who were already established in the United States. For more than a decade afterward, the so-called "picture brides" arrived in the United States, and their fertility was substantial within a fairly short period of time (Barringer, Gardner, and Levin, 1993; Kitano, 1976).

By 1920, the Japanese American population was expanding while the Chinese American population was contracting due to the limited number of Chinese women in the United States (Barringer, Gardner, and Levin, 1993:39). Although further immigration from Japan and most of the rest of Asia was largely eliminated by the Immigration Act of 1924, by that time Japanese Americans had already formed stable communities that included a sizable subpopulation of second-generation offspring. Japanese Americans had become by far the largest Asian American group during the first half of the twentieth century.

Another distinctive feature of Japanese immigration is that its level in the post-1965 period is the lowest among the major Asian nations (Min, 2006:17). After the fundamental changes in the immigration laws that occurred in 1965, immigration from such countries as Vietnam, China and Hong Kong, India, the Philippines, and South Korea has numbered in the millions during the last few decades, but immigration from Japan has been far more limited (Min, 2006:17). As a result of the smaller stream of recent immigrants when combined with the substantial subpopulation of second-generation persons (as well as their offspring) from the twentieth century, Japanese Americans today are the only Asian American group that is primarily native born[3] (Sakamoto, Goyette, and Kim, 2009:258).

---

[3]Due to their high fertility, the Hmong in the last few years appear to have joined Japanese Americans as being the only primarily native-born groups among the specific ethnicities included in the Asian racial category as currently defined by the U.S. Census Bureau (Sakamoto, Goyette, and Kim, 2009:258).

By convention in this literature and among Japanese Americans themselves, foreign-born immigrants are often referred to as *issei* (i.e., "first generation" in Japanese). Their native-born second-generation children are known as *nisei* (i.e., "second generation" in Japanese). The offspring of the *nisei*, who are also usually native born, are known as *sansei* (i.e., "third generation" in Japanese).

The Classical Issei Family

Kitano and Kitano (1998:317) describe "the *issei* family" in reference to the first stream of issei immigrants who, as noted, began arriving in significant numbers during the 1890s. Those immigrants were largely motivated by economic opportunity, and as discussed by Kitano and Kitano (1998), they brought with them the cultural heritage of a more traditional Japanese society (i.e., associated with the Meiji era of the nineteenth century). Having roots in Buddhism and Confucianism, this culture emphasized group obligation over individualism, and behavioral obedience to authority over personal verbal expression (Reischauer, 1977; Smith, 1983). As summarized by Kitano and Kitano (1998:318), the issei family may be characterized by "interaction based on obligation, strong involvement in family relationships, priority of filial bond over conjugal bond, male dominance, rigid division of labor by sex, emotional restraint with emphasis on compassion, respect, consideration, stability, and little verbal communication." In comparison to more typical American families (even at that time), which may permit and even encourage democratic-style exchanges between parents and children, the issei family was more hierarchical, authoritarian, and patriarchal.

In addition, the Confucian tradition "emphasized that stable families ensured a stable society. The *ie* (i.e., the family lineage) structure endured over time and was of greater importance than the individuals constituting the unit; individual interest and goals were secondary to the larger unit" (Kitano and Kitano, 1998:313). This cultural orientation was implicit in the issei family and was more consistent with the traditional Asian concerns for interdependence and collectivism than with the European American emphasis on fostering independence and individualism in their children (Kim and Wong, 2002:185).

This Confucian heritage also promoted a concern for children to be disciplined and trained in such a way that they will most likely bring honor to the family by their being successful in some manner (Kim and Wong, 2002; Lyman, 1974). Bringing honor to the family is consistent with filial piety, obedience toward parental wishes, and parental authority; Japanese parents want to have successful children in that their high achievements are naturally viewed as a positive reflection on the parents themselves as well as on the ie. Conversely, "shame was one means of social control: Don't do things that will bring shame on the Kitano family and the Japanese community" (Kitano and Kitano, 1998:312). "Dedicating one's life to the advancement and good reputation of the *ie* was an obligation" (Kitano and Kitano, 1998:313).

This combination of Buddhist austerity and Confucian authoritarianism was, in practice, regularly punctuated by family breaks that provided some relief from the concerns for fostering discipline, training, and obedience that characterized the daily parenting styles of the issei. Family outings, special treats on weekends, community gatherings, festivals, and both American and Japanese holidays were often venues for the issei family to engage in some entertainment and relaxation (Kitano, 1976; Kitano and Kitano, 1998). While one rarely finds discussions of especially happy or romantic issei marriages from this period, the family environment from the perspective of the nisei commonly provided security, stability, and some relaxation in addition to the Meiji-era discipline. As stated by Kitano and Daniels (1995:74), "The phrase *kodomo no tame ni* ("for the sake of the children") connotes sacrificing one's own life for the next generation, and it was a common cultural ideal (if not explicit verbal expression) among the issei in the early Japanese American communities.[4]

The Educational Attainment of the Nisei

The classical issei family promoted discipline, security, stability, and a motivation for achievement that served as the foundation of the educational attainment of the nisei (Lyman, 1974). As described by Jiobu (1988) "The Japanese-American culture places a high regard on education and on the set of values contained within the Confucian ethic: hard work, sacrifice for the future, patience, and stoicism in the face of adversity." In the same vein, Kitano and Kitano (1998:312) note that "There was a strong emphasis on obedience, especially to the Caucasian teachers, to study hard, to keep quiet, and not to complain (*monku*)." In other words, the classic issei family became the social venue through which the *agency* of Japanese Americans was expressed by directing the nisei toward economic self-sufficiency, achievement, and high educational attainment. Indeed, the adoration of the high level of educational opportunity that is available in the United States (i.e., "an education befitting kings") was specifically cited in the "Japanese American Creed," which was symbolic of the attitudes of many issei and nisei during that era (Kitano and Daniels, 1995:64). Kitano (1976:39) similarly states that "the story of *issei* self-sacrifice to send their *issei* children to college is a common one in the Japanese-American community."

Although not adequately acknowledged in contemporary research on Japanese Americans, a high level of schooling has been a statistical reality as well as an important demographic characteristic of the nisei (Akiba, 2006; Bonacich and Modell, 1980; Chin, 2005; Featherman and Hauser, 1978; Flewelling and Hirabayashi, 1994; Hirschman and Wong, 1986; Kitano, 1976; Mare and Winship, 1988; Sakamoto, Liu, and Tzeng, 1998; Sakamoto, Wu, and Tzeng, 2000; Thomas, 1952). For example, Sakamoto, Liu, and Tzeng's (1998:233) analysis of the 1940 U.S. Census data finds that the mean years of schooling completed by nisei men in the labor force was 2.26 times higher than for Whites (which was substantial during that era of low educational attainment). High educational attainment is likely the single most important proximate determinant of the prominent social mobility of Japanese Americans during the twentieth century (Levine and Montero, 1973; Sakamoto and Furuichi, 1997).

The exaggeration of a group characteristic is often unwarranted in that doing so may promote a "stereotype" that ignores the substantial variability that typically exists within any demographic group, including Japanese Americans. Nonetheless, in the case of the nisei during the twentieth century, their average levels of schooling and occupational mobility are sufficiently high to warrant general recognition. O'Brien and Fugita (1991:105) even claim that the nisei represent "one of the most remarkable upward mobility processes in American history. The economic, educational, and professional achievements of the Japanese Americans rank as high or higher than any other ethnic group in this country." Although we do not seek to endorse hyperbole about phenomena that are not actually that well studied, the above-average socioeconomic achievements of the nisei are nevertheless statistically undeniable and are important to understanding the traditional Japanese American family.

On average, the educational level of the issei during the early part of the twentieth century was higher than that of African Americans, Italian Americans, Mexican Americans, and Native

---

[4]The Japanese phrase *kodomo no tame ni* ("for the sake of the children") is so common and well known that it has even been used as the title of a book, a movie, and a play.

Americans but lower than that of English Americans, German Americans, Irish Americans, and Scottish Americans (Darity, Dietrich, and Guilkey, 1997:302).[5] As of 1910, most issei were still primarily employed in low-wage agricultural work so that their mean occupational status was quite low and similar to that of African Americans (Darity, Dietrich, and Guilkey, 1997:302). The issei soon moved into small self-employed farming and related businesses, however, which improved their incomes to some degree (Nee and Wong, 1985). Nonetheless, when compared to Whites who had much greater economic opportunities during the first half of the twentieth century, the socioeconomic backgrounds of the nisei (in terms of the rural origins, educational levels, occupational status, and incomes of their issei parents) were usually somewhat less advantaged. Given their less advantaged origins, the higher educational attainment of the nisei during that time period is especially notable and is more formally evident in the multivariate statistical results of Featherman and Hauser (1978:449) and Mare and Winship (1988:190).[6]

Education and Traditional Japanese and Japanese American Families

As pointed out by Hirschman and Wong (1986:2), post-1965 Asian American immigration is selective toward persons with higher levels of education. In their careful study of attitudinal and socioeconomic variables, however, Goyette and Xie (1999:24) nonetheless conclude that "the socioeconomic approach is unsatisfactory as a *general* framework for explaining the educational achievement of Asian American children." Indeed, the aforementioned studies by Featherman and Hauser (1978) and Mare and Winship (1988) find that the educational differential between White and Asian American men is statistically increased after controlling for socioeconomic variables in data from the 1970s.[7] Consistent with the references regarding the educational attainment of the nisei during the first half of the twentieth century, Japanese Americans in the post-1965 era continue to obtain educational levels above those obtained by Whites (on average) with similar socioeconomic backgrounds (Takei, Sakamoto, and Woo, 2006; Xie and Goyette, 2004). In sum, several subcultural factors relating to the family probably facilitate the high educational attainment of Japanese American children, which *cannot be fully explained by socioeconomic variables alone* (Caudill and De Vos, 1956; Goyette and Xie, 1999; Kao, 1995; Kao and Tienda, 1995).

One subcultural factor may relate to the transmission of expectations associated with Japanese and other Asian families. Prior research on post-1965 Asian Americans finds that Japanese and other Asian American children have higher educational expectations and that these derive from the high educational expectations placed on them by their parents (Cheng and Starks, 2002; Goyette and Xie, 1999; Kao, 1995; Sun, 1998; Wong, 1990)—that is, Japanese and other Asian American families seem to be especially conducive to the transmission of parental expectations (regarding education) to their children.

---

[5]As stated by Kitano and Kikumura (1980:8), "the majority of Japanese [issei] immigrants came from middle and lower classes."

[6]Jiobu (1988) disputes the view that educational attainment was high among the pre–World War II cohort of nisei and that education fostered their labor market attainments and social mobility. Jiobu's (1988:363) analysis is flawed, however, because most nisei at the onset of World War II were too young to have completed their educational attainment, and because analyses of their occupational attainments and wages (as adults) clearly demonstrate the primary importance of their higher educational attainment (Levine and Montero, 1973; Sakamoto and Furuichi, 1997; Sakamoto, Liu, and Tzeng, 1998).

[7]The doublethink irony of some "multiculturalist" perspectives of racial and ethnic inequality is that they assume fundamentally structural explanations that generally omit the consideration of minority subcultural factors. Okihiro (1994:32–33) even chides other researchers who have attempted to understand some of the subcultural sources of the higher educational attainment of the nisei which has yet to be adequately explained.

In general, educational attainment is often believed to be more important in Japan than in the United States in terms of long-term socioeconomic rewards (Ishida, 1993; Ono, 2004; Sakamoto and Powers, 1995). According to Reischauer (1977:171), "the close link between academic achievement and success in life is taken for granted by everyone in Japan." The Japanese labor market is more highly stratified by educational credentials that have long-term and persistent effects years after graduation (Ishida, Spilerman, and Su, 1997). The intense competition for entering prestigious universities in Japan (known as "examination hell") reflects the lifelong socioeconomic consequences of this competition, and it gives rise to an entire industry of after-school tutoring services (i.e., *juku* or cram schools [Stevenson and Baker, 1992]). By contrast, in the American labor market, the significance of educational attainment seems to be somewhat more rapidly replaced by observed labor force experience and previous work history as more important proximate determinants of labor market attainments; the returns to educational attainment are more significantly mediated by the worker's most recent job experience since the American pay system more strictly emphasizes current job category and title per se (Aoki, 1988).

The greater significance of educational attainment for advancement in the stratification system undoubtedly reflects, at least in part, a higher cultural value that is placed on education in Japan. "Nothing, in fact, is more central in Japanese society or more basic to Japan's success than is its educational system" (Reischauer, 1977:167). According to Reischauer (1977:167), the historical source of this cultural emphasis derives from medieval China and is commonly associated with Confucianism that continues to permeate Japanese cultural values and ethics (Reischauer, 1977:214; Smith, 1983:31).

In contrast to American egalitarianism, Japanese society accepts social hierarchy as inevitable and natural and lacks the American cultural strains that foster latent anti-intellectualism and glorify the "self-made man" and the "common man" (Hofstadter, 1963; Reischauer, 1977:162). Educational attainment is accepted as a fundamental aspect of social hierarchy. Universities therefore have a more clearly defined status hierarchy in Japan, and teachers at all levels are referred to respectfully in daily conversation with a special honorific title (i.e., *sensei*, which literally means "teacher"). This title distinguishes them from other adults who are usually referred to by a common generic title (i.e., *san*, which may be translated as "Mr." or "Miss" or "Mrs." or "Ms."). Educators rather than political leaders are more frequently portrayed on Japanese currency.

The cultural significance of education undoubtedly carries over to some extent among Japanese Americans, at least among the nisei and possibly among the *sansei* as well. In a detailed study of both quantitative and qualitative research, Schneider, Hieshima, Lee, and Plank (1994:347) conclude that:

> Results suggest that the strongest continuity between Japanese Americans and other East-Asian Americans is the focus on values. This is perhaps most pronounced in the area of education. Like other East Asians, Japanese Americans value education for self-improvement, self-esteem, and as a means for social mobility. It is important to underscore that Japanese Americans, like other East-Asian groups, place a high intrinsic value on education, which some may argue is not representative of American values, which tend to stress education primarily for occupational mobility.

In short, a high cultural value placed on education—both for its intrinsic and extrinsic rewards—may be observed among Japanese Americans, which is consistent with the quote from Jiobu (1988) cited earlier.

A common phenomenon in Japanese and Japanese American families is the social role known as the "education mom" (i.e., *kyoiku mama* [Reischauer, 1977:172; Stevenson and Stigler,

1992:82]). Stated bluntly, Japanese (and other Asian) mothers are often highly dedicated to preparing their children for a college educational career because the educational success of their children brings honor and status to the entire family. More specifically, Japanese and other Asian mothers and fathers routinely have high educational expectations for their children, clearly convey this fact to them, and carefully invest in educational and social resources that enhance their children's academic achievements (Caplan, Choy, and Whitmore, 1991; Fejgin, 1995; Goyette and Xie, 1999; Hieshima and Schneider, 1994; Hirschman and Wong, 1986; Kao, 1995; Schneider and Lee, 1990; Sun, 1998).

For example, as documented by Sun (1998), Asian American parents save proportionately more of their income for their children's college, have fewer children, are less likely to single-parent, are more likely to have a computer at home for educational purposes, are more likely to have their children involved in "cultural capital activities" (e.g., music lessons, art museums, science camps), and are more likely to expect their children to attend college or graduate school. In turn, Asian American children are more likely to face disciplinary pressures for poor academic performance, to have limited and regulated television viewing, to have rules about grades and doing homework, and to spend more hours per week doing homework (Fejgin, 1995; Kao, 1995; Wong, 1990). While typically both parents support these practices, the role of the "education mom" is usually seen as having the major responsibility of organizing, scheduling, fostering, and deciding on all of the education-related activities and rules.[8]

A second common pattern among Japanese and other Asian Americans centers around child-rearing patterns that promote greater family identity and cohesiveness than is typical among mainstream White American families (Conner, 1974; Rothbaum, Pott, Azuma, Miyake, and Weisz, 2000). Underlying these patterns are Asian collectivist beliefs that people are more inherently the products of their social and family environments (Reischauer, 1977) rather than being somehow intrinsically "individuals" who have their own innate sources of uniqueness that must be respected and nurtured (Lareau, 2002). Asian parents' group-oriented beliefs lead them to place greater emphasis on shaping and molding their children into being what parents deem to be more ideally desirable rather than what their children may individually prefer to do with their lives.[9] Asian parents are therefore more likely to believe that their appropriate role is to push their children into achieving higher educational attainment—despite their children's own personal proclivities and individualistic interests—because Asian parents are more likely to believe that their primary parental responsibility is to promote the long-term interests of their children by shaping their personal development (rather than allowing their children "to just be themselves" or to experience "natural growth" [Lareau, 2002:752]).

In keeping with that cultural predisposition, Japanese and other Asian child-rearing patterns do not promote independence but rather accept dependency as being natural, normal, and inevitable. Indeed, Japanese child-rearing patterns foster greater psychological dependency in their children and forestall the development of a psychological sense of individualistic self-identity that is separate from their parents (Doi, 1971). Although Stevenson and Stigler (1992:74–80) discuss the apparently greater permissiveness of early child-rearing practices of Japanese parents in relation to enhanced educational attainment (arguing that it leads their children to develop a greater appreciation of learning as a reward or end in itself), the authors' discussion does not adequately recognize the consequences of this early socialization in fostering a closer psychological bond or emotional

---

[8]As stated by Alston and Takei (2005:152) in their discussion of the *kyoiku mama* role, "[Japanese] mothers are expected to push and aid their children in their studies. The mother is blamed if a child does not do well or falls behind in school."

[9]A related cultural notion in this regard is the Confucian idea of the perfectibility of man.

interdependence between mothers and their children (Ben-Ari, 1996; Doi, 1971; Reischauer, 1977:140–141; Rothbaum et al., 2000). Lacking a strong sense of self, Japanese children are more readily influenced by their parents' wishes and expectations (De Vos, 1973; Shimahara, 1986).

One relevant process in this regard is the practice of co-sleeping that has been traditionally practiced and considered normative in Japan and elsewhere in Asia (Caudill and Plath, 1974; Reischauer, 1977). It also appears to be commonly observed among Japanese Americans (Kitano, 1976:131). That is, Japanese and Japanese American parents routinely sleep in the same bed with their young children. Even if Asian children begin sleeping in their own bed, often it is in the same room as their parents. This practice is usually continued until the child is as old as twelve years of age. Co-sleeping reduces the child's independent sense of self and thereby facilitates a greater emotional dependency of children on their parents (Caudill and Plath, 1974).

The result is that Japanese and other Asian and Asian American families and children are comparatively less individualistic than White Americans (Bumpass, 1990; Kim and Wong, 2002; Rothbaum et al., 2000). In contrast to Japanese parents, White middle-class American parents typically train their children to sleep by themselves even as infants (McKenna, 1996). White middle-class American parents (in contrast to Japanese parents) are careful to promote independence in their children's behavior at a young age, such as encouraging exploratory physical mobility even as toddlers. White parents tend to encourage their children to feed themselves their own food despite the consequent mess that is often made by toddlers when learning to do this. In contrast to Japanese culture, independence and rugged individualism are traditional ideals (and may perhaps even be somewhat exaggerated) in American culture (Reischauer, 1977:135). The child-rearing practices of White middle-class Americans train children to be more independent, resulting in a greater psychological insulation from their parents' expectations regarding educational attainment.

Space limitations prevent a detailed discussion, but the Japanese cultural idea of *amae* (which has no adequate simple translation in English but is sometimes referred to as "permissiveness" or "being spoiled") further enhances the interdependence in the behaviors and feelings between Japanese individuals in primary relationships (Doi, 1971; Meredith, 1966). Amae is said to originate in Japanese child-rearing practices (Alston and Takei, 2005:20–21; Kumagai and Kumagai, 1986; Reischauer, 1977:141).[10] Although the extreme forms of "co-dependence" would be viewed as dysfunctional in most any society (Beattie, 1987; Borovoy, 2001), the greater cultural proclivity toward amae is considered normal in Japan and is likely to promote interdependence between Japanese parents and their children. Being more dependent on their children's success for their own self-esteem, Japanese and Japanese American parents are more inclined to seek to highly motivate their children, who are in turn more dependent on their parents' approval in their own self-evaluations. Amae thus facilitates the transmission of expectations for high educational achievement from Japanese and Japanese American parents to their children.

CHANGE AND ADAPTATION

Any analysis of modern families will invariably need to incorporate the realities of several rising trends that have influenced the living arrangements of a broad spectrum of Americans in the twenty-first century. First, there is an increased incidence of non-family households. Demographers traditionally define the family as two or more persons living together in a household unit who are related by blood, marriage, or adoption, but in the United States today many

---

[10]The feeling inherent in amae resembles that expressed by the American slang saying "Oh man, give me a break!" but is more subtle and childlike.

households do not fit this description. [11] For example, one-person households are more common now as many middle-aged persons have delayed or even abandoned marriage while many elderly persons have become more independent. Cohabitation (i.e., a couple living together before marriage, usually on a short-term basis as such) is another trend in modern societies. Gay/lesbian couples are an additional example of a non-family household to the extent that these unions are not legally recognized, which is usually the case in the United States Non-family households were less common during much of the twentieth century, but the recognition of these households in the twenty-first century would be far more realistic.

Two other trends among modern families include the increased incidence of divorce and non-marital fertility. Due to these two trends, many children today live in households headed by a single parent. In some cases, the children were born while his or her parents were married, but the parents later divorced. In other cases, the mother was never married and gave birth to the child (or adopted a child) outside of marriage. Thus, household structures are far more complicated and varied now than during the early twentieth century when the divorce rate among the issei is estimated to have been a mere 1.6 percent (Kitano, 1976:42).

During that period before World War II, racial intermarriage was actually illegal in many states (e.g., especially in the South) and was referred to as "miscegenation." Intermarriage among the issei and even nisei during that era was rare (2 percent and 4 percent, respectively [Nishi, 1995:128]). The legality of the "miscegenation laws" remained in effect until 1948 when they were struck down by the U.S. Supreme Court.

Since that time, racial intermarriage has steadily increased among Japanese Americans (Kitano, 1976:106–107; Nishi, 1995:128). In the Los Angeles area, which includes the single largest concentration of Japanese Americans, Japanese American intermarriage rose from 2 percent in 1924 to 49 percent in 1972. More recently using data from the 2000 U.S. Census, Xie and Goyette (2004:24) report an intermarriage rate of 49 percent for Japanese American women and 31 percent for Japanese American men. In short, high rates of intermarriage are a reality for contemporary Japanese Americans.

The biological children of Japanese Americans who intermarry are often described as bi-racial, and they may identify as such according to the racial classification scheme that is currently used by the U.S. Census Bureau (Takei, Sakamoto, and Woo, 2006). Across the generations, assimilation into mainstream America (in both cultural and biological terms) appears to be a significant trend (Takei, Sakamoto, and Woo, 2006). Descriptions of the contemporary Japanese American population may vary to some extent depending on whether bi-racial and multi-racial Japanese Americans are included as being part of the Japanese American population (Takei, Sakamoto, and Woo, 2006).

From a cultural point of view, another changing facet of contemporary Japanese American families is the nature of immigration from Japan. The issei of the early twentieth century were motivated primarily by economic aspirations; "In common with most immigrants, they wanted to better their lives" (Kitano and Kikumura, 1980:4). By contrast, contemporary issei may be less likely to be so primarily focused on economic opportunity and social mobility. Today's issei are a more eclectic group. Some may be motivated to leave Japan precisely to avoid some traditional element of Japanese society such as (by American standards) strict gender roles, extended family relations, seniority-based hierarchy in the workplace, or the limited acceptance of less conventional

---

[11]Households by definition exclude persons living in "group quarters," which are defined as living units that do not include a private kitchen for individual use (e.g., college dormitories, military barracks, prisons). Persons in group quarters are often specialized demographic groups that are excluded from our analysis due to space constraints and data limitation.

lifestyles or independent personalities. Many Japanese Americans who were born in Japan may have come to the United States as the spouse of a native-born American, often of another racial group—that is, intermarriage itself was associated with their process of migration to the United States or their legal capacity to reside here on a long-term basis. Other Japanese Americans may be sojourners who reside in the United States for only a year or two to receive advanced training or education or who are on an overseas assignment for a major Japanese corporation.

In addition, the nature of contemporary migration from Japan differs somewhat from the migration of the issei during the early twentieth century because Japan has undergone substantial modernization and cultural change since that time. After the total and demoralizing defeat associated with World War II, traditional Japanese practices, norms, and values lost much of their sway and ideological appeal (Fukutake, 1981). Advances in technology, communications, travel, and incomes have increased globalized interaction and have reduced the cultural isolation of the Japan. In short, modern issei immigrants are typically far removed from the austere Meiji-era culture described earlier.

Studying Contemporary Japanese American Families

In order to investigate contemporary patterns of the Japanese American family, we use data from the American Community Survey (ACS), which is administered by the U.S. Census Bureau and is representative of the entire household population of the United States. Our analysis pools together the surveys from 2005, 2006, 2007, and 2008 so that an adequate sample size of a comparatively small demographic group (i.e., Japanese Americans) may be obtained. Our results thus refer to the period from 2005 to 2008.

Table 14.1 describes the categorization of racial/ethnic groups that we have adopted for the purpose of studying the contemporary Japanese American family. Our investigation makes use of the information that is available in the ACS (U.S. Census Bureau, 2005, 2006, 2007, 2008). Following the official classification system currently in use by the U.S. Census Bureau, the ACS classification system identifies Japanese as one group within the Asian racial category. Being Japanese is thus a particular type of racial identity that is recognized in these data. Given our purposes, our analysis obviously needs to distinguish between Japanese and other Asians as is summarized in Table 14.1. Furthermore, foreign-born versus native-born Japanese are identified in order to more precisely address issues relating to assimilation, intermarriage, and immigration.

The ACS also allows individuals to have multiple racial identities in that an individual is permitted to identify with as many racial categories as desired. In general, only a tiny proportion of the overall American population identifies as bi-racial or multi-racial, but the proportion is somewhat higher among Asian Americans and other minority groups, which have smaller population sizes than Whites (Sakamoto, Kim, and Takei, forthcoming; Tafoya, Johnson, and Hill, 2004). Given the availability of multi-racial identity in these data, we separate out Japanese Americans who also identify with other racial categories. We use the term *bi-racial Japanese* to refer to such individuals, as is summarized in Table 14.1. By contrast, *single-race Japanese* refers to individuals who identify only as Japanese.

The ACS further allows for individuals to identify their "ancestry" that may be different from their racial identity. Two general sorts of ancestry are distinguished. The first is known as "Hispanic" or "Latino," which is referred to as an "ethnicity" in the ACS questionnaire. The other sort of ancestry is a more general self-identification (permitting the individual to write in some response) that is referred to specifically as an "ancestry" and is also provided in the ACS.

Following Takei, Sakamoto, and Woo (2006), we use this ACS information to identify persons who state that they are single-race Whites but who have Japanese ancestry. Although this

TABLE 14.1   Description of Major Racial/Ethnic Groups Used in the Analysis

Group (Abbreviation)	Description
Foreign-Born Japanese (FB-Japanese)	single-race Japanese, foreign-born
Native-Born Japanese (NB-Japanese)	single-race Japanese, native-born
Biracial Japanese (BR-Japanese)	bi-racial and multi-racial Japanese, native-born or foreign-born
Japanese Whites (J-White)	single-race, native-born Whites who claim some "Japanese ancestry"
Whites (White)	single-race, non-Hispanic, native-born Whites without "Japanese ancestry"
Immigrant Whites (IWhite)	single-race, non-Hispanic, foreign-born Whites without "Japanese ancestry"
Asians (Asian)	single-race, non-Japanese Asian, native-born or foreign-born (may be Hispanic)
Blacks (Black)	single-race, non-Hispanic African Americans, native-born or foreign-born
Hispanics (Hispanic)	single-race, non-Asian, native-born or foreign-born persons who identify as "Hispanic"
Others (Other)	all other racial/ethnic groups, foreign-born or native-born

Source: U.S. Census Bureau (2005–2008).

group is not included as part of the Japanese American population in official U.S. Census Bureau publications, Takei, Sakamoto, and Woo's (2006) analysis of the 2000 Census data reports that 102,200 non-Asian persons (most of whom identify as Whites) claim to have some Japanese ancestry but do not identify as Asian or Japanese as a racial group. These non-Asian persons with Japanese ancestry might possibly include, for example, those who have one Japanese grandparent or great-grandparent. Following Takei, Sakamoto, and Woo (2006), we refer to this group as "Japanese Whites" as summarized in Table 14.1.

Due to space limitations, a detailed analysis of other groups is beyond the scope of our study, but several major racial/ethnic categories are identified in our investigation. As described in Table 14.1, "Whites" refers to single-race, non-Hispanic, native-born Whites without any Japanese ancestry. "Immigrant Whites" refers to single-race, non-Hispanic, foreign-born Whites without any Japanese ancestry. "Asians" refers to single race, non-Japanese Asians who are either native born or foreign born. "Blacks" refers to single-race, non-Hispanic African Americans who are either native born or foreign born. "Hispanics" refers to single-race, non-Asian persons who are either native born or foreign born and who identify as "Hispanic" or "Latino." "Others" refers to the residual category (i.e., anyone not included in the prior categories, such as Native Americans and Pacific Islanders).

The particular household types that we identify in our analysis are shown in Table 14.2. Following up on our earlier discussion about changes in household patterns in contemporary

TABLE 14.2 Description of Japanese Household Types

Type	Notes
Non-Family Households	
One-Adult Household	Adult householder living alone; householder is FB-Japanese or NB-Japanese or BR-Japanese or J-White
Non-Family Household	Two or more adults in household but none are legally related by blood, marriage, or adoption; householder is FB-Japanese or NB-Japanese or BR-Japanese or J-White
Non-Marital Families	
FB-Japanese NM-Family	Non-marital family with FB-Japanese householder
NB-Japanese NM-Family	Non-marital family with NB-Japanese householder
BR-Japanese NM-Family	Non-marital family with BR-Japanese householder
J-White NM-Family	Non-marital family with J-White householder
Marital Families	
White-FB-Japanese Family	White and FB-Japanese married couple
White-NB-Japanese Family	White and NB-Japanese married couple
White-BR-Japanese Family	White and BR-Japanese married couple
White-J-White Family	White and J-White married couple
FB-FB-Japanese Family	FB-Japanese and FB-Japanese married couple
NB-NB-Japanese Family	NB-Japanese and NB-Japanese married couple
BR-J-White Family	Married couple consisting of: BR-Japanese and BR-Japanese; or J-White and J-White; or BR-Japanese and J-White
FB-NB-Japanese Family	FB-Japanese and NB-Japanese married couple
FB-BR-J-White Family	Married couple consisting of: FB-Japanese and BR-Japanese; or FB-Japanese and J-White
NB-BR-J-White Family	Married couple consisting of: NB-Japanese and BR-Japanese; or NB-Japanese and J-White
IWHITE-FB-Japanese Family	Immigrant White and FB-Japanese married couple
IWHITE-NB-Japanese Family	Immigrant White and NB-Japanese married couple
IWHITE-BR-Japanese Family	Immigrant White and BR-Japanese married couple
IWHITE-J-White Family	Immigrant White and J-White married couple
ASIAN-FB-Japanese Family	Asian and FB-Japanese married couple
ASIAN-NB-Japanese Family	Asian and NB-Japanese married couple
ASIAN-BR-Japanese Family	Asian and BR-Japanese married couple
ASIAN-J-White Family	Asian and J-White married couple
BLACK-FB-Japanese Family	Black and FB-Japanese married couple
BLACK-NB-Japanese Family	Black and NB-Japanese married couple
BLACK-BR-Japanese Family	Black and BR-Japanese married couple
BLACK-J-White Family	Black and J-White married couple
HISPANIC-FB-Japanese Family	Hispanic and FB-Japanese married couple
HISPANIC-NB-Japanese Family	Hispanic and NB-Japanese married couple
HISPANIC-BR-Japanese Family	Hispanic and BR-Japanese married couple

TABLE 14.2 *(continued)*

Type	Notes
HISPANIC-J-White Family	Hispanic and J-White married couple
OTHER-Japanese Family	All other types of married couples in which the householder or the spouse is FB-Japanese or NB-Japanese or BR-Japanese or J-White

Source: U.S. Census Bureau (2005–2008).

BR = Bi-racial, FB = foreign born, I = immigrant, J = Japanese, NB = native born, NM = non-marital

societies, our typology is more detailed than that considered by Kitano and Kitano (1998). First, we explicitly acknowledge one-adult households (i.e., adults living alone) as shown in Table 14.2. Second, we include non-family households. Third, our analysis identifies families that do not include a married couple, which we refer to as non-marital families. These families are most typically represented by single-parent households with children. Also included in this group, however, are other miscellaneous types of families consisting of related persons without children but no married couple (e.g., an adult son living with his elderly mother). In regard to the Japanese American population, non-marital families are broken down according to whether the householder (i.e., the reference person who is listed first in the questionnaire) is foreign-born Japanese (i.e., FB-Japanese), native-born Japanese (i.e., NB-Japanese), bi-racial Japanese (i.e., BR-Japanese), or Japanese White (i.e., J-White).

Our most detailed classification is used to identify household patterns among marital families (i.e., families that include a married couple). As shown in Table 14.2, twenty-seven different types of marital families are specified in our analysis. The first four of them refer to each of the four types of Japanese Americans intermarried with Whites (i.e., White-FB-Japanese family, White-NB-Japanese family, White-BR-Japanese family or White-J-White family).

The next six categories refer to marital families in which the couple consists of a particular match between the two spouses based on the four Japanese American types. The FB-FB-Japanese family includes a married couple in which both spouses are foreign born. The NB-NB-Japanese family includes a married couple where both spouses are native born. The BR-J-White family includes a married couple consisting of spouses who are BR-Japanese and BR-Japanese; or BR-Japanese and J-White; or J-White and J-White. The FB-NB-Japanese family includes a married couple in which one spouse is foreign born and the other spouse is native born. The FB-BR-J-White family includes a married couple consisting of spouses who are FB-Japanese and BR-Japanese; or FB-Japanese and J-White. The NB-BR-J-White family includes a married couple consisting of spouses who are NB-Japanese and BR-Japanese; or NB-Japanese and J-White.

As shown in Table 14.2, the next four categories refer to marital families consisting of couples in which a particular Japanese American type is intermarried with a foreign-born White (i.e., IWhite-FB-Japanese family, IWhite-NB-Japanese family, IWhite-BR-Japanese family, and IWhite-J-White family). Four categories are then included to refer to marital families consisting of couples in which a particular Japanese American type is intermarried with a (non-Japanese) Asian (i.e., Asian-FB-Japanese family, Asian-NB-Japanese family, Asian-BR-Japanese family, and Asian-J-White family). Next, intermarriage with African Americans is categorized (i.e., Black-FB-Japanese family, Black-NB-Japanese family, Black-BR-Japanese family, and Black-J-White family). Finally, intermarriage with Hispanics is categorized as well (i.e., Hispanic-FB-Japanese family, Hispanic-NB-Japanese family, Hispanic-BR-Japanese family, and Hispanic-J-White family). Other-Japanese family is the last category and simply refers to a residual grouping consisting of any marital family not explicitly mentioned (and either the householder or the spouse identifies as FB-Japanese, NB-Japanese, BR-Japanese, or J-White).

Contemporary Japanese American Family Patterns

The frequencies for these various household types are shown in Table 14.3. The frequencies are categorized in two separate groups: White households and Japanese American households. White households include non-family and non-marital family households in which the householder is White as well as marital family households in which the householder is White and the spouse is not Japanese. Japanese American households include non-family and non-marital family households in which the householder is Japanese (i.e., FB-Japanese, NB-Japanese, BR-Japanese or J-White) as well as marital family households in which either the householder or the spouse (or both) is Japanese (i.e., FB-Japanese, NB-Japanese, BR-Japanese or J-White).

In regard to one-adult households, Table 14.3 shows that they represent 27.93 percent of White households and 23.88 percent of Japanese American households. When using the household as the unit of analysis (i.e., rather than counting up the total number of individuals), one-adult households are the second largest category. As also shown in Table 14.3, non-family households represent 6.21 percent of White households and 5.43 percent of Japanese American households. Non-marital family households represent 11.37 percent of White households and 8.47 percent of Japanese American households. The largest category is the marital family household comprising 54.49 percent among White households and 62.22 percent among Japanese American households.

These foregoing statistics are consistent with our discussion regarding the greater tendency among mainstream Americans (relative to Japanese Americans) to value individualism, which results in less conformity to traditional ideals and established patterns. Compared to Whites, Japanese American households are more likely to be represented by the more traditionally normative family that includes a married couple. By contrast, White households are more likely to be represented by one-adult households, non-family households, and non-marital family households.

In regard to marital families among Japanese American households, the level of intermarriage with Whites is notable. The most common category among all Japanese American marital families is the White-FB-Japanese family with 10.27 percent. Another 7.9 percent are White-NB-Japanese families, which are followed by White-BR-Japanese families (i.e., 6.19 percent) and then White-J-White families (i.e., 3.67 percent). Whereas intermarriage between Whites and Japanese Americans was relatively rare and outlawed in many states before World War II, households represented by this pattern of intermarriage today constitute 28.03 percent (i.e., 10.27 percent + 7.9 percent + 6.19 percent + 3.67 percent) of all Japanese American households. In other words, intermarriages between Whites and Japanese Americans are now the most common household grouping as is evident in Table 14.3.

Many Japanese Americans do of course marry other Japanese Americans, but the patterns vary depending on the type of Japanese American. As shown in Table 14.3, the most common category of endogamous marriage is the NB-NB-Japanese family (i.e., 8.63 percent), which is the group that most closely resembles what Kitano and Kitano (1998:319) referred to as "the nisei family." That category is closely followed by the FB-FB-Japanese family (i.e., 7.23 percent), which is the modern-day representation of the "the issei family." Other patterns of intraethnic marriage (i.e., BR-J-White families, FB-NB-Japanese families, FB-BR-J-White families, and NB-BR-J-White families) are much fewer as is shown in Table 14.3. The total amount of endogamous

TABLE 14.3 Distribution of Household Types for White and Japanese Households

Type	Whites (%)	Japanese (%)
Non-Family Households		
One-Adult Household	27.93	23.88
Non-Family Household	6.21	5.43
Non-Marital Families	**11.37**	**(8.47)**
FB-Japanese NM-Family		2.11
NB-Japanese NM-Family		4.13
BR-Japanese NM-Family		1.69
J-White NM-Family		0.54
Marital Families	**54.49**	**(62.22)**
White-FB-Japanese Family		10.27
White-NB-Japanese Family		7.90
White-BR-Japanese Family		6.19
White-J-White Family		3.67
FB-FB-Japanese Family		7.23
NB-NB-Japanese Family		8.63
BR-J-White Family		0.77
FB-NB-Japanese Family		1.94
FB-BR-J-White Family		0.25
NB-BR-J-White Family		0.76
IWHITE-FB-Japanese Family		1.04
IWHITE-NB-Japanese Family		0.53
IWHITE-BR-Japanese Family		0.37
IWHITE-J-White Family		0.22
ASIAN-FB-Japanese Family		1.77
ASIAN-NB-Japanese Family		4.29
ASIAN-BR-Japanese Family		1.54
ASIAN-J-White Family		0.09
BLACK-FB-Japanese Family		0.70
BLACK-NB-Japanese Family		0.23
BLACK-BR-Japanese Family		0.29
BLACK-J-White Family		0.05
HISPANIC-FB-Japanese Family		0.74
HISPANIC-NB-Japanese Family		0.88
HISPANIC-BR-Japanese Family		0.73
HISPANIC-J-White Family		0.25
OTHER-Japanese Family		0.89
Total	100.00	100.00

Source: U.S. Census Bureau (2005–2008).

marriage is 19.58 percent (i.e., 7.23 percent + 8.63 percent + .77 percent + 1.94 percent + .25 percent + .76 percent) of all Japanese American households.

Although Okihiro (1994:34) asserts that Asian Americans and African Americans are "a kindred people," Table 14.3 indicates that intermarriage between Japanese Americans and Blacks is actually rare in terms of marital family types. Intermarriage between Japanese Americans and Hispanics also appears to be relatively infrequent. In regard to IWhites, only 1.04 percent of Japanese American households are IWhite-FB Japanese families, and the percentages for the other IWhite categories are even smaller.

The grouping of intermarriage that is somewhat more prominent is the marital family consisting of a Japanese American with another (non-Japanese) Asian. Table 14.3 shows that 4.29 percent of Japanese American households are Asian-NB Japanese families while 1.77 percent are Asian-FB Japanese families and 1.54 percent are Asian-BR Japanese families. Though much less common than intermarriage with Whites, intermarriage of Japanese Americans with other Asians does appear to be a recognizable pattern in these data.

Characteristics of Contemporary White and Japanese American Households

Table 14.4 displays some descriptive characteristics for White households in terms of basic demographic indicators, whereas Table 14.5 shows these characteristics for Japanese American households. The indicators include the proportion residing in the Pacific region (i.e., Hawaii, Alaska, Washington, Oregon, and California), the mean age of the householder, the mean number of children in the household, the mean household size (i.e., including children and adults), the proportion of householders with a bachelor's degree, the official poverty rate (as defined by the U.S. Census Bureau), the mean household income (with all incomes converted to the 2008 price level), and the proportion who are home owners. Table 14.4 shows that only about one in eight White households resides in the Pacific region, although the proportion is slightly higher among non-family households. By definition, one-adult households and non-family households do not include any children (i.e., the mean number of children for these two types of households is 0). One-adult households tend to be older, and they tend to have lower household incomes in part due to the fact they have (at most) only one earner in the household. Nonetheless, 60.12 percent of one-adult households own their own homes, and their poverty rate is lower than that of non-family households and non-marital families. By contrast, non-family households tend to be younger and are less likely to own their own homes.

Non-marital families have the highest mean number of children (i.e., 1.23) and the lowest proportion with a bachelor's degree (i.e., 19.3 percent). They also have a fairly high poverty rate (i.e., 17.4 percent). On average, marital families have slightly less than one child, the highest proportion of bachelor's degrees, the highest household income, the lowest poverty rate, the largest household size, and the highest proportion of home ownership.

Table 14.5 shows these statistics for Japanese American households. As we have described, the classification of Japanese American families is broken down in a more detailed manner. Readers should be aware, however, that the descriptive statistics in Table 14.5 for Asian-J-White families and Black-J-White families are unreliable due to the small sample sizes for these two relatively uncommon household categories.

The results shown in Table 14.5 indicate that most types of Japanese American households are much more likely than Whites to reside in the Pacific region. This location is especially prevalent for households with an NB-Japanese householder or spouse. Japanese language usage at

TABLE 14.4 Characteristics of Households by Type for Whites

Type	Pacific[1]	Age[2]	Children[3]	Size[4]	BA[5]	Poor[6]	Income[7]	Home[8]
One-Adult Household	0.126	57.257	0	1.000	0.291	0.148	40,868	0.601
Non-Family Household	0.163	38.868	0	2.235	0.323	0.190	74,256	0.481
Non-Marital Families	0.121	47.143	1.226	2.856	0.193	0.174	56,654	0.629
Marital Families	0.111	51.113	0.916	3.005	0.354	0.030	99,731	0.880

Source: U.S. Census Bureau (2005–2008).

[1]The proportion residing in the Pacific region (i.e., Hawaii, Alaska, Washington, Oregon, and California)
[2]The mean age of the householder
[3]The mean number of children in the household
[4]The mean household size (i.e., including children and adults)
[5]The proportion of householders with a bachelor's degree
[6]The official poverty rate (as defined by the U.S. Census Bureau)
[7]The mean household income (with all incomes converted to the 2008 price level)
[8]The proportion that are home owners

TABLE 14.5 Characteristics of Households by Type for Japanese

Type	Pacific[1]	Age[2]	Children[3]	Size[4]	BA[5]	Poor[6]	Income[7]	Home[8]	Japanese[9]
One-Adult Household	0.625	53.098	0	1.000	0.439	0.165	46,168	0.492	0.373
Non-Family Household	0.573	34.945	0	2.273	0.450	0.257	77,974	0.330	0.254
FB-Japanese NM-Family	0.548	53.781	1.067	2.700	0.273	0.108	65,127	0.674	0.647
NB-Japanese NM-Family	0.871	59.032	0.919	2.690	0.291	0.065	85,299	0.774	0.160
BR-Japanese NM-Family	0.618	42.819	1.190	3.068	0.253	0.193	61,269	0.527	0.067
J-White NM-Family	0.251	36.919	1.206	2.954	0.167	0.159	57,779	0.567	0.010
White-FB-Japanese Family	0.412	51.370	0.714	2.775	0.523	0.022	102,096	0.789	0.245
White-NB-Japanese Family	0.603	50.036	0.951	3.035	0.607	0.009	136,969	0.876	0.018
White-BR-Japanese Family	0.398	42.884	1.204	3.291	0.467	0.016	121,878	0.816	0.024
White-J-White Family	0.256	39.864	1.227	3.296	0.439	0.019	117,920	0.813	0.008
FB-FB-Japanese Family	0.418	45.223	1.054	3.101	0.702	0.064	110,834	0.382	0.935
NB-NB-Japanese Family	0.930	63.895	0.674	2.826	0.475	0.017	113,858	0.923	0.122
BR-J-White Family	0.587	47.735	1.343	3.529	0.504	0.068	107,637	0.769	0.045
FB-NB-Japanese Family	0.853	60.562	0.685	2.784	0.508	0.019	95,525	0.791	0.570
FB-BR-J-White Family	0.647	50.437	1.063	3.164	0.489	0.011	99,351	0.830	0.453
NB-BR-J-White Family	0.891	47.462	1.157	3.321	0.548	0.003	132,341	0.875	0.049
IWHITE-FB-Japanese Family	0.417	48.652	1	3.042	0.664	0.031	124,594	0.750	0.239
IWHITE-NB-Japanese Family	0.720	50.354	0.853	0.851	0.670	0.003	134,466	0.851	0.062
IWHITE-BR-Japanese Family	0.464	44.553	1.218	3.303	0.549	0.017	126,770	0.742	0.000
IWHITE-J-White Family	0.390	45.545	1.234	3.352	0.479	0.020	123,087	0.776	0.098
ASIAN-FB-Japanese Family	0.556	43.748	0.988	3.128	0.655	0.041	112,593	0.663	0.347
ASIAN-NB-Japanese Family	0.902	50.722	1.037	3.220	0.543	0.016	130,305	0.867	0.038
ASIAN-BR-Japanese Family	0.791	43.877	1.366	3.676	0.400	0.038	107,908	0.758	0.025
ASIAN-J-White Family	0.689	41.551	0.922	3.102	0.408	0.052	97,348	0.813	0.037
BLACK-FB-Japanese Family	0.368	47.388	0.900	3.025	0.301	0.027	77,955	0.602	0.330
BLACK-NB-Japanese Family	0.714	46.457	0.845	2.876	0.552	0.020	129,079	0.773	0.015

TABLE 14.5 *(Continued)*

Type	Pacific[1]	Age[2]	Children[3]	Size[4]	BA[5]	Poor[6]	Income[7]	Home[8]	Japanese[9]
BLACK-BR-Japanese Family	0.323	44.431	1.225	3.460	0.488	0.000	111,440	0.867	0.000
BLACK-J-White Family	0.000	36.689	1.105	3.784	0.000	0.464	40,935	0.536	0.000
HISPANIC-FB-Japanese Family	0.594	46.008	1.076	3.217	0.322	0.040	85,731	0.660	0.167
HISPANIC-NB-Japanese Family	0.794	45.267	1.324	3.491	0.384	0.006	121,105	0.877	0.008
HISPANIC-BR-Japanese Family	0.560	40.890	1.401	3.596	0.332	0.048	94,444	0.761	0.009
HISPANIC-J-White Family	0.306	39.932	1.654	3.841	0.313	0.013	104,605	0.772	0.008
OTHER-Japanese Family	0.631	45.552	1.100	3.227	0.390	0.050	101,730	0.741	0.114

Source: U.S. Census Bureau (2005–2008).

[1]The proportion residing in the Pacific region (i.e., Hawaii, Alaska, Washington, Oregon, and California)
[2]The mean age of the householder
[3]The mean number of children in the household
[4]The mean household size (i.e., including children and adults)
[5]The proportion of householders with a bachelor's degree
[6]The official poverty rate (as defined by the U.S. Census Bureau)
[7]The mean household income (with all incomes converted to the 2008 price level)
[8]The proportion who are home owners
[9]The proportion of householders who report speaking Japanese at home

home is relatively uncommon except for those households that have an FB-Japanese householder or spouse (Kim and Min, 2010). At one extreme, 93.5 percent of FB-FB Japanese families speak Japanese at home, but the much smaller 1.8 percent figure for White-NB-Japanese families is more typical of households that do not include an FB-Japanese.

In terms of the mean age of the householders, White-NB Japanese families are substantially older than White-BR-Japanese families who are in turn older than White-J-White families. The same general pattern is even more evident among non-marital families. Although only suggestive, these results are consistent with the assumption that J-White householders may tend to have a higher generational status than BR-Japanese householders who in turn may tend to have a higher generational status than NB-Japanese householders. The mean age of householders among NB-NB Japanese families is notably older (i.e., about sixty-four years) suggesting that many of these marriages may have occurred in earlier decades when racial intermarriage among the nisei was lower.

In general, Japanese American families tend to have above-average educational attainment. In regard to the most common marital family categories, the proportion with a bachelor's degree is 52.3 percent among White-FB-Japanese families, 47.5 percent among NB-NB Japanese families, 60.7 percent among White-NB-Japanese families, 70.2 percent among FB-FB Japanese families, 46.7 percent among White-BR-Japanese families, and 54.3 percent among Asian-NB-Japanese families (as shown in Table 14.5) in comparison to the substantially lower proportion of 35.4 percent among White marital families (as shown in Table 14.4). Our results seem largely consistent with the broad conclusion reached by Takei, Sakamoto, and Woo (2006) that Japanese Americans most closely associated with FB-Japanese tend to have higher levels of educational attainment. Takei, Sakamoto, and Woo (2006) further find high levels of educational attainment among persons who identify as Chinese-Japanese, which seems consistent with the above mentioned result for Asian-NB-Japanese families because intermarriage with Chinese is likely to be the most common type of Asian intermarriage for Japanese Americans (Takei, Sakamoto, and Woo, 2006).

Not surprisingly, other results in Table 14.5 indicate that Japanese American household types with high proportions of bachelor's degrees tend to have high household incomes and low poverty rates. For example, among NB-NB Japanese families, mean household income is $113,858 and the poverty rate is 1.7 percent. These results indicate a higher level of socioeconomic status than for White marital families whose mean household income is $99,731 and whose poverty rate is 3.0 percent, as shown in Table 14.4. In general, most types of Japanese American households have higher levels of socioeconomic attainments than Whites.

CONCLUSION

Researchers have become so fixated on the drama of the World War II internment that the general study of contemporary Japanese Americans themselves has been unfortunately neglected in recent years. We have sought to help fill this research gap by investigating the Japanese American family using recent demographic data. Our results indicate major changes since the time of the first half of the twentieth century that figured prominently in the now-famous descriptions of the classical issei family and the nisei family as provided by Kitano (1976). Indeed, the changes that have occurred since that era have been so substantial as to amount to nothing less than a radical transformation of Japanese American family patterns.

First of all, Japanese American family patterns reflect the trends of modern societies in general. One-adult households and non-family households have now become commonplace even though many of them would have been considered rather unusual in the early part of the twentieth century. Furthermore, racial intermarriage appears to have become the dominant pattern among Japanese Americans. Table 14.3 implies that 45.0 percent of marital Japanese American families involve intermarriage with a White. The percentage would be increased to 48.5 percent if foreign-born Whites (i.e., IWhites) were added to that figure.

By contrast, Table 14.3 indicates that only about 31.5 percent of marital Japanese American families refer to households where both spouses are Japanese American even after expanding the definition of that group to include bi-racial Japanese (i.e., BR-Japanese) and Whites who identify as having some Japanese ancestry (i.e., J-Whites). The modern equivalents of the classical issei and nisei families (i.e., the FB-FB Japanese family and the NB-NB Japanese family, respectively) represent only about 15.9 percent of marital Japanese American families. Even that modest figure is likely to decline in the near future because the elderly average age of NB-NB Japanese families suggests that more recent cohorts of NB-Japanese may be increasingly turning to intermarriage.

These findings suggest why the term *yonsei* (i.e., "fourth generation" in Japanese) has never really become popular in the Japanese American community. Although persons who are fourth-generation Japanese American certainly exist (i.e., the great-grandchildren of issei immigrants from Japan), these persons are likely to be multi-racial due to the high level of intermarriage that, in the contemporary period, often begins with the very first issei immigrants. Given this low level of endogamous marriage among Japanese Americans, only a very small proportion of fourth-generation descendents are likely to think of themselves as having a primarily Japanese heritage. For this reason, the Japanese term *yonsei* is unlikely to be viewed as being very appropriate for most fourth-generation descendents of issei immigrants.

At the same time, however, some preservation of Japanese American identity seems to be suggested as well by our results. The mere fact that many bi-racial individuals choose to be enumerated as being partly Japanese is itself indicative of the significance of this ethnic identity to those individuals. This point may be even more applicable to J-Whites who apparently seek to maintain some identity relating to Japanese Americans even as they enumerate themselves as single-race Whites. Given that the ACS questionnaire uses the word *ancestry* rather than *ancestries* (although multiple responses are considered acceptable), the existence of J-Whites is suggestive of a notable desire to be recognized as having some Japanese American heritage.[12]

In terms of what might be somewhat more precariously referred to as Japanese American subculture, our results are also suggestive of some continuation of traditional patterns. As was discussed, high levels of educational attainment have been a historic characteristic of Japanese Americans (at least among those who were schooled in the United States). Immigrant Japanese Americans have adapted to life in the United States by promoting the education of their children, which is facilitated by the cohesiveness of Japanese families. Contemporary Japanese Americans to some extent maintain this tradition by tending to have higher rates of college completion. In particular, Japanese Americans most closely associated with FB-Japanese tend to have the highest levels of educational attainment as was also investigated by Takei, Sakamoto, and Woo (2006).

An additional aspect of some enduring subcultural aspects of Japanese Americans is their greater propensity to intermarry with (non-Japanese) Asian Americans (i.e., Asians). That is, Japanese Americans are much more likely to intermarry with Asians than with African Americans, Hispanics, or immigrant Whites, even though each of these latter three groups are substantially larger than Asians in terms of population. Although non-Japanese Asian Americans

---

[12]As discussed by Takei, Sakamoto and Woo (2006), the actual number of "single-race whites" with some Japanese ancestry is likely to be underestimated in Census data.

are obviously not Japanese in terms of their ethnic heritage, some subcultural similarities between East Asian Americans and Japanese Americans are evident in their common tendencies to achieve high levels of educational attainment as well as perhaps other characteristics relating to family processes (Min, 1995; Sakamoto, Goyette, and Kim, 2009; Takei, Sakamoto, and Woo, 2006; Xie and Goyette, 2004).

In our view, this transformation of Japanese American family patterns should be viewed as welcome change associated with the more multicultural ethos that America has embraced in the twenty-first century. Gone is the era when complete "Anglo-conformity" or "hyper-assimilation" was required for access to opportunities for advancement in educational and labor market institutions (Takei, Sakamoto, and Woo, 2006). Any nostalgic yearning for the traditional family patterns of the twentieth century is clearly unwarranted because contemporary Japanese Americans now have much more freedom to identify and live according to their own preferences in regard to their own chosen ethnic identities, household arrangements, and socioeconomic attainments. Japanese Americans today are free to intermarry, and the fact that they do so in large proportions with the predominantly native-born members of the majority group (i.e., Whites) suggests that societal prejudice and discrimination against Japanese Americans—once exemplified by miscegenation laws—are no longer systematically endemic. Overall, these aspects of the racial and ethnic relations of the twenty-first century are consistent with Masaoka's (1942:3) prophetic vision of "that greater America which is to come" as well as with the *kodomo no tame ni* spirit of the issei and nisei ancestors of many contemporary Japanese Americans.

References

Akiba, D. 2006. "Japanese Americans." In P. G. Min (Ed.), *Asian Americans: Contemporary Trends and Issues* (2nd ed., pp. 148–177). Thousand Oaks, CA: Sage.

Alston, J. P., and I. Takei. 2005. *Japanese Business: Culture and Practices.* New York: iUniverse Inc.

Aoki, M. 1988. *Information, Incentives, and Bargaining in the Japanese Economy.* New York: Cambridge University Press.

Bai, M. 1995. "He Said No to Internment." *New York Times Magazine.* December 25, 1995, p. 38.

Barringer, H. R., R. W. Gardner, and M. J. Levin. 1993. *Asian and Pacific Islanders in the United States.* New York: Russell Sage Foundation.

Beattie, M. 1987. *Codependent No More: How to Stop Controlling Others and Start Caring for Yourself.* San Francisco, CA: Harper/Hazelden.

Ben-Ari, E. 1996. "From Mothering to Othering: Organization, Culture, and Nap Time in a Japanese Day-Care Center." *Ethos 24,* 136–164.

Bonacich, E., and J. Modell. 1980. *The Economic Basis of Ethnic Solidarity.* Berkeley University of California Press.

Borovoy, A. 2001. "Recovering from Codependence in Japan." *American Ethnologist 28,* 94–118.

Bumpass, L. 1990. "What's Happening to the Family? Interactions Between Demographic and Institutional Change." *Demography 27,* 483–493.

Caplan, N., M. H. Choy, and J. K. Whitmore. 1991. *Children of the Boat People.* Ann Arbor: University of Michigan Press.

Caudill, W., and G. De Vos. 1956. "Achievement, Culture and Personality: The Case of Japanese Americans." *American Anthropologist 58,* 1102–1126.

Caudill, W., and D. W. Plath. 1974. "Who Sleeps by Whom? Parent-Child Involvement in Urban Japanese Families." In T. S. Lebra and W. P. Lebra (Eds.), *Japanese Culture and Behavior: Selected Readings.* Honolulu: University of Hawaii.

Cheng, S., and B. Starks. 2002. "Racial Differences in the Effects of Significant Others on Students' Educational Expectations." *Sociology of Education 75,* 306–327.

Chin, A. 2005. "Long-Run Labor Market Effects of Japanese American Internment During World War II on Working-Age Male Internees." *Journal of Labor Economics 23,* 491–525.

Conner, J. W. 1974. "Acculturation and Family Continuities in Three Generations of Japanese

Americans." *Journal of Marriage and the Family 36,* 159–165.

Daniels, R. 1988. *Asian America: Japanese and Chinese in the United States Since 1850.* Seattle: University of Washington Press.

Darity, W., Jr., J. Dietrich, and D. K. Guilkey. 1997. "Racial and Ethnic Inequality in the United States: A Secular Perspective," *American Economic Review* 87:301–305.

De Vos, G. 1973. *Socialization for Achievement.* Berkeley: University of California Press.

Doi, T. 1971. *The Anatomy of Dependence.* Tokyo, Japan: Kodansha International.

Featherman, D. L., and R. M. Hauser. 1978. *Opportunity and Change.* New York: Academic Press.

Fejgin, N. 1995. "Factors Contributing to the Academic Excellence of American Jewish and Asian Students." *Sociology of Education 68,* 18–30.

Flewelling, S., and G. Hirabayashi. 1994. *Stories from a Pacific Northwest Japanese American Community.* Seattle: University of Washington Press.

Fukutake, T. 1981. *Japanese Society Today.* Tokyo, Japan: University of Tokyo Press.

Goyette, K., and Y. Xie. 1999. "Educational Expectations of Asian American Youths: Determinants and Ethnic Differences." *Sociology of Education 72,* 22–36.

Hieshima, J. A., and B. Schneider. 1994. "Intergenerational Effects on the Cultural and Cognitive Socialization of Third and Fourth Generation Japanese Americans." *Journal of Applied Developmental Psychology 15,* 319–327.

Hirschman, C., and M. G. Wong. 1986. "The Extraordinary Educational Attainment of Asian-Americans: A Search for Historical Evidence and Explanations." *Social Forces 65,* 1–27.

Hofstadter, R. 1963. *Anti-Intellectualism in American Life.* New York: Knopf.

Hosokawa, B. 1992. *Nisei: The Quiet Americans.* Niwot: The University Press of Colorado.

Ishida, H. 1993. *Social Mobility in Contemporary Japan.* Palo Alto, CA: Stanford University Press.

Ishida, H., S. Spilerman, and K.-H. Su. 1997. "Educational Credentials and Promotion Chances in Japanese and American Organizations." *American Sociological Review 62,* 866–882.

Jiobu, R. M. 1988. "Ethnic Hegemony and the Japanese of California." *American Sociological Review 53,* 353–367.

Kao, G. 1995. "Asian-Americans as Model Minorities? A Look at Their Academic Performance." *American Journal of Education 103,* 121–159.

Kao, G., and M. Tienda. 1995. "Optimism and Achievement: The Educational Performance of Immigrant Youth." *Social Science Quarterly 76,* 1–19.

Kibria, N. 2002. *Becoming Asian American: Second-Generation Chinese and Korean American Identities.* Baltimore, MD: Johns Hopkins University Press.

Kim, C., and P. G. Min. 2010. "Marital Patterns and Use of Mother Tongue at Home among Native-Born Asian Americans." *Social Forces 89,* 233–256.

Kim, S. Y., and V. Y. Wong. 2002. "Assessing Asian and Asian American Parenting: A Review of the Literature." In K. Kurasaki, S. Okazaki, and S. Sue (Eds.), *Asian American Mental Health: Assessment Theories and Methods* (pp. 185–201). New York: Kluwer.

Kitano, H. H. L. 1976. *Japanese Americans: The Evolution of a Subculture.* Englewood Cliffs, NJ: Prentice Hall.

Kitano, H. H. L., and R. Daniels. 1995. *Asian Americans: Emerging Minorities.* Englewood Cliffs, NJ: Prentice Hall.

Kitano, H. H. L., and A. Kikumura. 1980. "The Japanese American Family." In R. Endo, S. Sue, and N. N. Wagner (Eds.), *Asian Americans: Social and Psychological Perspectives* (pp. 3–16). Ben Lomond, CA: Science and Behavior Books.

Kitano, K. J., and H. H. L. Kitano. 1998. "The Japanese-American Family." In C. H. Mindel, R. W. Habenstein, and R. Wright, Jr. (Eds.), *Ethnic Families in America* (4th ed., pp. 311–330). Upper Saddle River, NJ: Prentice Hall.

Kumagai, H. A., and A. K. Kumagai. 1986. "The Hidden 'I' in Amae: 'Passive Love' and Japanese Social Perception." *Ethos 14,* 305–320.

Lareau, A. 2002. "Invisible Inequality: Social Class and Childrearing in Black Families and White Families." *American Sociological Review 67,* 747–776.

Levine, G., and D. Montero. 1973. "Socio-Economic Mobility Among Three Generations of Japanese Americans." *Journal of Social Issues 29,* 33–48.

Lyman, S. M. 1974. *Chinese Americans.* New York: Random House.

Mare, R. D., and C. Winship. 1988. "Ethnic and Racial Patterns of Educational Attainment and School Enrollment." In G. D. Sandefur and M. Tienda (Eds.), *Divided Opportunities: Minorities, Poverty, and Social Policy* (pp. 173–203). New York: Plenum Press.

Masaoka, M. 1942, April 5. "Conscience and the Constitution: Japanese American Citizen League Bulletin #142" (accessesd April 20, 2011).

McKenna, J. J. 1996. "Sudden Infant Death Syndrome in Cross-Cultural Perspective: Is Infant-Parent Cosleeping Protective?" *Annual Review of Anthropology 25,* 201–216.

Meredith, G. M. 1966. "Amae and Acculturation Among Japanese-American College Students in Hawaii." *Journal of Social Psychology 70,* 171–180.

Min, P. G. 1995. *Asian Americans: Contemporary Trends and Issues.* Thousand Oaks, CA: Sage.

———. "Asian Immigration: History and Contemporary Trends." In P. G. Min (Ed.), *Asian Americans: Contemporary Trends and Issues* (2nd ed., pp. 7–31). Thousand Oaks, CA: Sage.

Nee, V., and H. Y. Wong. 1985. "Asian American Socioeconomic Achievement: The Strength of the Family Bond." *Sociological Perspectives 28,* 281–306.

Nishi, S. M. 1995. "Japanese Americans." In P. G. Min (Ed.), *Asian Americans: Contemporary Trends and Issues* (pp. 95–133). Thousand Oaks, CA: Sage.

O'Brien, D. J., and S. S. Fugita. 1991. *The Japanese American Experience.* Bloomington: Indiana University Press.

Okihiro, G. Y. 1994. *Margins and Mainstreams.* Seattle: University of Washington Press.

Ono, H. 2004. "College Quality and Earnings in Japan." *Industrial Relations 43,* 595–617.

Reischauer, E. O. 1977. *The Japanese.* Cambridge, MA: Harvard University Press.

Rothbaum, F. M. Pott, H. Azuma, K. Miyake, and J. Weisz. 2000. "The Development of Close Relationships in Japan and the United States: Paths of Symbiotic Harmony and Generative Tension." *Child Development 71,* 1121–1142.

Sakamoto, A., and S. Furuichi. 1997. "Wages among White and Japanese American Male Workers." *Research in Social Stratification and Mobility 15,* 177–206.

Sakamoto, A., and D. A. Powers. 1995. "Education and the Dual Labor Market for Japanese Men." *American Sociological Review 60,* 222–246.

Sakamoto, A., K. A. Goyette, and C. Kim. 2009. "Socioeconomic Attainments of Asian Americans." *Annual Review of Sociology 35,* 255–276.

Sakamoto, A., C. Kim, and I. Takei. Forthcoming. "Moving Out of the Margins and Into the Mainstream: The Demographics of Asian Americans in the New South." In press in K. Y. Joshi and J. Desai (Eds.), *Asian Americans and the New South.* Athens: University of Georgia Press.

Sakamoto, A., J. Liu, and J. Tzeng. 1998. "The Declining Significance of Race Among Chinese and Japanese American Men." *Research in Social Stratification and Mobility 16,* 225–246.

Sakamoto, A., H.-H. Wu, and J. Tzeng. 2000. "The Declining Significance of Race Among American Men During the Latter Half of the Twentieth Century." *Demography 37,* 41–51.

Schneider, B., and S. Lee. 1990. "A Model for Academic Success: The School and Home Environment of East Asian Students." *Anthropology and Education Quarterly 21,* 358–377.

Schneider, B., J. A. Hieshima, S. Lee, and S. Plank. 1994. "East-Asian Academic Success in the United States: Family, School, and Community Explanations." In P. M. Greenfield and R. R. Cocking (Eds.), *Cross-Cultural Roots of Minority Child Development* (pp. 323–349). Hillsdale, NJ: Lawrence Erlbaum.

Shimahara, N. K. 1986. "The Cultural Basis of Student Achievement in Japan." *Comparative Education 22,* 19–26.

Smith, R. J. 1983. *Japanese Society: Tradition, Self, and the Social Order.* London: Cambridge University Press.

Stevenson, D. L., and D. P. Baker. 1992. "Shadow Education and Allocation in Formal Schooling: Transition to University in Japan." *American Journal of Sociology 97,* 1639–1657.

Stevenson, H. W., and J. W. Stigler. 1992. *The Learning Gap: Why Our Schools Are Failing and What We Can Learn from Japanese and Chinese Education.* New York: Simon & Schuster.

Sun, Y. 1998. "The Academic Success of East-Asian-American Students: An Investment Model." *Social Science Research 27,* 432–456.

Tafoya, S. M., H. Johnson, and L. E. Hill. 2004. *Who Chooses to Choose Two?* Washington, DC: Population Reference Bureau and the Russell Sage Foundation.

Takahashi, J. 1997. *Nisei/Sansei: Shifting Japanese American Identities and Politics.* Philadelphia, PA: Temple University Press.

Takei, I., A. Sakamoto, and H. Woo. 2006. "Socioeconomic Differentials Among Single-Racial and Multi-Racial Japanese Americans: Further Evidence on Assimilation in the Post-Civil Rights Era." Paper presented at the 2006 Population Association of America annual meeting, Los Angeles, CA.

Thomas, D. S. 1952. *The Salvage.* Berkeley: University of California Press.

Tuan, M. 1998. *Forever Foreigners or Honorary Whites? The Asian Ethnic Experience Today.* New Brunswick, NJ: Rutgers University Press.

U.S. Census Bureau. 2005. "American Community Survey." http://www.census.gov/acs/www.

———. 2006. "American Community Survey." http://www.census.gov/acs/www.

———. 2007. "American Community Survey." http://www.census.gov/acs/www.

———. 2008. "American Community Survey." http://www.census.gov/acs/www.

Wilson, R. A., and B. Hosokawa. 1980. *East to America: A History of the Japanese in the United States.* New York: Morrow.

Wong, M. G. 1990. "The Education of White, Chinese, Filipino and Japanese Students: A Look at 'High School and Beyond.'" *Sociological Perspectives 33,* 355–374.

———. 1995. "Chinese Americans." In P. G. Min (Ed.), *Asian Americans: Contemporary Trends and Issues* (2nd ed., pp. 58–94). Thousand Oaks, CA: Sage.

Xie, Y., and K. Goyette. 2004. *Asian Americans: A Demographic Portrait.* New York: Russell Sage Foundation.

15

▪▪▪

The Filipino American Family

Carl L. Bankston III

INTRODUCTION

A look at Filipino American family life is essential to any portrait of contemporary family diversity, since Filipino Americans make up a large and rapidly growing part of the population of the United States. As Table 15.1 indicates, the increase has occurred mainly since 1970 and has been the result of both immigration and of births of native-born Americans of Filipino background. In 2008, the U.S. Census Bureau estimated the Filipino American population at over 2,425,000, making Filipinos the third-largest Asian group in the United States after Chinese and Asian Indians. Filipino Americans are most heavily concentrated in California, which was home in 2008 to an estimated 1,172,324 people of this national group, or slightly under half of all the Filipinos in the United States. Hawaii's estimated 175,000 Filipinos made up a large proportion of that state's population, since they constituted close to one out of every seven people in the island state.

The Los Angeles–Long Beach metropolitan area in California held the largest concentration of Filipino Americans in 2008, since about 13 percent of all members of the group lived there, according to survey data from the U.S. Census Bureau (2008a). A little under 6 percent of Filipinos in the United States lived in the San Diego metropolitan area in 2008, followed by Oakland (5.5 percent), Honolulu, Hawaii (5.2 percent), and San Francisco–Oakland (4.5 percent) (Ruggles, Sobek, Alexander, et al., 2008).

Outside of the West, Filipinos were fairly widely distributed around the United States, though, and at least some people of Filipino ancestry could be found in most areas of the country. Over 100,000 people who identified themselves as Filipinos lived in the greater Chicago area in 2008, and large Filipino populations could also be found in the New York–Northeastern New Jersey region (about 80,000), Las Vegas in Nevada (over 71,000), the Seattle–Everett area in Washington (over 46,000), Washington, D.C. (over 45,000), and the Houston–Brazoria metropolitan area in Texas (over 36,000). Filipinos lived in every state, with the smallest numbers found in Wyoming (home to an estimate of 800 to 900) and Vermont (where 200 to 300 lived) (Ruggles et al., 2008).

TABLE 15.1   Filipino Immigration to the United States and Filipino Population in the United States: 1900–1990

Immigrants		Filipino American Population	
1901–1910	N/A	1910	2,767
1911–1920	869	1920	26,634
1921–1930	54,147	1930	108,424
1931–1940	6,159	1940	98,535
1941–1950	4,691	1950	122,707
1951–1960	19,307	1960	176,310
1961–1970	98,376	1970	343,060
1971–1980	360,216	1980	812,178
1981–1990	495,271	1990	1,645,472
1991–2000	505,553	2000	1,864,120
2001–2008	469,033	2008	2,425,697

Sources: Department of Homeland Security (2010); Gall and Gall (1993); U.S. Census Bureau (2000–2008).

The Philippines has been closely linked to the United States since the close of the nineteenth century, and people in the Philippines have a great familiarity with American culture, politics, and mass media. This has placed Filipino American families in a unique position with regard to questions of assimilation and adaptation to North America. It has not, however, erased their distinctive characteristics.

HISTORICAL BACKGROUND

The Philippines is an archipelago, a cluster of islands, located across the China Sea from mainland Southeast Asia. More than seven thousand of these islands are stretched over a distance of more than a thousand miles.

The geography of the Philippines has greatly influenced the nation's history. Mountains rise above dense forests, and many-colored coral reefs surround island beaches. This varied landscape makes the Philippines a beautiful place, but it also makes transportation and communication difficult. Over the centuries, the people of the Philippines have become a variety of regional groups, who often speak different native languages. Most of these are non-tonal, grammatically complex languages related to the Malay and Indonesian languages. Tagalog, spoken in the region around Manila, is now widely understood throughout the country as a consequence of mass communication. Ilocano, spoken in the northern part of the country, and Cebuano and Visayan, spoken in the central islands, are also spoken as first languages by many in the Philippines and by many first-generation Filipino Americans. The use of English is widespread, since English is the primary language of instruction in the schools.

The Philippines was a Spanish colony from the second half of the sixteenth century until the end of the nineteenth. Although Filipino languages adopted many Spanish words, Spanish never became a dominant language as it did in the Spanish colonies of the Americas. However, Filipinos received many cultural influences from Spain, including Catholicism, which continues to be the religion of most Filipinos. Muslims make up a substantial minority in the far south of the Philippines, where the Spanish were largely unable to extend their rule (Bankston, 2003).

The establishment and growth of the Filipino American population has been a consequence of American involvement in Southeast Asia. In 1898, the United States went to war with Spain. As a result of the American victory, the Americans took control of several Spanish colonies, including Cuba, Puerto Rico, and the Philippines. Filipino forces, already fighting for independence from the Spanish, put up fierce resistance to the American occupiers, but by 1903 the United States had established its control. The close connections between the two countries brought American-style education to the Philippines, familiarized Filipinos with American culture, and established the basis of future movement to the larger and wealthier country (Bankston and Hidalgo, 2007).

American domination also created an attitude toward the United States that is often described as a love–hate point of view. Education is highly prized within Filipino families, and Filipinos appreciate the system of widespread public schooling developed during the American period. They also enjoy American mass media and American popular culture. However, many Filipinos have not forgotten that the Americans arrived as conquerors, and the former resent the high-handedness of the latter. Filipinos have also been victims of American racial prejudice in the past, and sometimes continue to be victims of prejudice in the present (Bankston, 2006).

Migration Periods

A small number of Filipinos settled in Louisiana, south of New Orleans, during the first half of the nineteenth century. It is unclear how these individuals arrived, but they may have come over on Spanish ships. Some descendants of the Louisiana Filipinos still live around the New Orleans region and retain an identification with their ancestral homeland (Espina, 1988).

Aside from the early Filipinos in Louisiana, the history of migration from the Philippines can be roughly divided into three major periods. The first period lasted from the end of the first decade of the twentieth century to the beginning of World War II. A small number of Filipinos, known as *pensionados,* came to the United States as students under a government-sponsored program. However, immigrants in these years came primarily in response to the U.S. demand for cheap labor, especially in agriculture. Sugar plantations dominated the economy of Hawaii early in the century, and plantation owners were interested in finding hardworking field hands who would work for low wages. The Hawaii Sugar Planters Association (HSPA) began recruiting in the Philippines, and by 1946 the HSPA had brought a quarter million Filipinos to Hawaii. Farmers in California and canning factories in Alaska also started to recruit Filipino workers in large numbers. In 1924, the United States passed an immigration act that barred most Asian immigration but allowed Filipinos to continue to enter because the Philippines was an American territory. This spurred the increase of Filipino agricultural workers on the mainland by cutting off other sources of Asian labor (Choy, 2007).

An estimated 45,000 Filipinos reached the West Coast of the mainland United States during the 1920s. Improved transportation and refrigeration had made it possible to grow fruits and vegetables on large farms in one part of the nation for export to all other regions. The resulting demand for cheap agricultural labor on the West Coast resulted in rapid growth of the Filipino population on the mainland, from 5,603 people in 1920 to 45,372 in 1930 (Mangiafico, 1988).

Although most Filipino American families arrived in the United States after this first migration period, descendants of the agricultural workers who came in the early twentieth century retain memories of family life at this time. Connie Tirona, whose parents were born in the

Visayas and went to work in Hawaii before moving again to California, recalled the stories her parents told:

> They [Filipinos in the labor camps] would work from very early in the morning until late at night. They would leave for work before the break of dawn and return long after dusk. The women like my mother would do the cooking, and some of them would go to work in the fields along with the men. But again, they said there were some fun times when they would get together and have their famous cockfights. Among other things, they would make this fermented drink from coconuts. So, despite an oppressive work atmosphere, there was joy. (Tirona, 1995:66)

Between agricultural seasons, Filipino agricultural laborers often sought work as dishwashers, gardeners, and domestic workers in American cities. This led to the creation of Filipino communities in Chicago, New York, Philadelphia, and New Jersey during the 1920s and 1930s. In addition to farm work and work in canneries, Filipinos also found employment at sea, in the U.S. navy and the merchant marine. About five thousand members of the group worked as merchant marines, until the Merchant Marine Act essentially shut out Filipinos in 1936 by requiring that 90 percent of merchant marine jobs go to U.S. citizens (Mangiafico, 1988). The navy placed most Filipino servicemen as mess stewards, and this position became closely identified with Filipino ethnicity.

The second migration period can be dated from 1946, when the Philippines became politically independent of the United States, until the middle of the 1960s. The United States had established large military bases in the foreign colony, and many of the Filipinos admitted to the United States were women married to American servicemen. Filipinos who had become naturalized American citizens after the war were also able to petition to have family members enter the United States, so many immigrants in this period came as a result of marriage or family connections.

Filipino nurses began to comprise a significant portion of the migration flow in the years following World War II. The Exchange Visitor Program, established as part of the Education Exchange Act of 1948, enabled foreign nurses to come to the United States for two years of study and professional experience. Filipino nurses, with their American-style educations and English-language skills, were able to take this opportunity in much larger numbers than nurses from other countries. Barbara M. Posadas (1999:30) has observed that "from 7,000 nurses in the Philippines in 1948, the number surged to 57,000 in 1953." The migration streams from this second period flowed into the larger currents of the third period. The United States continued to hold military bases in the Philippines until 1991. The migration of spouses, both of military personnel and other American citizens, remained a major source of Filipino movement to the United States.

The third migration period began in 1965, when the United States passed a new immigration law that ended the discrimination against Asians in all previous immigration laws. The result was rapid growth in the Asian American population in general and in the Filipino American population in particular. As pointed out in this chapter's introduction, Table 15.1 shows that the decades from the 1960s onward have been a time of dramatic growth, both in immigration from the Philippines and in the total Filipino American population.

Demand for nurses in America led to continuing recruitment efforts in the Philippines during the third migration period, and Filipino nurses are still common in American medical facilities. Health care in general became an ethnic occupational niche. By the end of the twentieth century, Filipinos had become the single largest ethnic group among nurses in the United States. A survey conducted by the Commission on Graduates of Foreign Nursing Schools in 2001, found that 41 percent of its respondents had received nursing degrees in the Philippines (Berger, 2003). Choy (2007:562) reported that "between 1966 and 1985 at least 25,000 Filipino nurses migrated to the United States. By 1989, Filipino nurses made up the overwhelming majority (73 percent) of foreign nurse graduates in this country." In some large cities in the United States, nursing had become a stereotypical Filipino American occupation. At Montefiore Medical Center in New York, pediatrics instructor Clemencia S. Wong observed, "if you meet a Filipino girl and say, 'you're a nurse,' you're probably right" (Berger, 2003:B1). Pio Paunon, a male nurse manager at the same hospital, remarked, "if you meet a Filipino man he'll probably say 'my wife is a nurse'" (Berger, 2003:B1).

Nursing continued to be the most common occupation among heads of households containing Filipinos toward the end of the first decade of the twenty-first century (see Table 15.8 later in this chapter). By 2008, registered nurses and managers and administrators were the most common occupations among Filipino men in the U.S. labor force (each with about 3.3 percent of all the male workers in the group). Among Filipino American women, registered nurses accounted for an estimated 14.3 percent of all workers in 2008, followed by nurses aides, orderlies, and attendants (6.8 percent of Filipinas in the United States). The hospital industry, including doctors, nurses, and all others who work in hospitals contained 14 percent of all Filipino American workers in that year, 8.1 percent of men and 19 percent of women. Another 6.1 percent of men and 10.7 percent of women worked in other health care-related industries, such as health services and nursing and personal care facilities.

Family, however, was even more influential than the U.S. demand for workers in increasing the flow of immigrants. With the 1965 change in U.S. immigration policy, family reunification became the first priority in the admission of immigrants to the United States. As the Filipino American population grew, the numbers of people in the Philippines with immediate relatives who were U.S. citizens or relatives of legal permanent residents increased, so that family became a growing basis for migration. In addition, marriages to non-Filipinos were common. In addition to marriages between U.S. service personnel in the Philippines and Philippine citizens, marriages growing out of international matchmaking services (discussed below) and marriages resulting from transnational business and social networks helped to keep family at the center of movement from the Southeast Asian nation to the North American one.

FAMILY AS A BASIS FOR MIGRATION IN THE POST-1965 ERA

As shown in Table 15.2, by the twenty-first century family had become the primary route for legal migration from the Philippines to the United States. A clear majority (57 percent) of the people born in the Philippines who were admitted as legal permanent residents in 2008

TABLE 15.2 Numbers and Percentages of People Born in the Philippines Admitted to the United States as Legal Residents, by Broad Class of Admission, 2008

	Number	Percent
Immediate relatives of U.S. citizens	30,662	56.7%
Family-sponsored relatives	13,799	25.5%
Employment-based preferences	9,193	17.0%
Refugees and asylees	304	0.6%
Diversity	8	0.0%
Other	64	0.1%
Total	54,030	100%

Source: Department of Homeland Security (2010), Table 10.

received their visas as immediate relatives of U.S. citizens. By contrast, 44 percent of all the immigrants from various places in the world who entered the United States as legal permanent residents received their status because they were immediate relatives of citizens (not shown in Table 15.2). The close family connections between these two countries had become an important migration route.

Over one-fourth of the Filipinos who arrived with the legal permanent resident classification came as family-sponsored immigrants. Although substantial numbers were admitted for the sake of employment (over 9,000 in that one year), family ties accounted for 82 percent of the legal migration from the Philippines. Professional migrants, such as nurses, were numerous, in other words, but employment did not come close to family as a means of sending Filipino migrants to the United States.

Family has also played an essential part in undocumented migration from the Philippines. Networks of family and friends can provide support and assistance to those without legal permanent residence. The Immigration and Naturalization Service (now known as the United States Citizenship and Immigration Services) estimated that in 2000 there were 85,000 undocumented immigrants from the Philippines in the United States (Office of Policy and Planning, U.S. Immigration and Naturalization Service, 2003; Table 15.2). Most of the undocumented immigrants from the Philippines have arrived on tourist visas and simply remained after their visas expired. The term that Filipinos, both in the United States and the Philippines, use to describe undocumented immigrants in their group is *TNT,* which stands for the Tagalog term *tago nang tago* (roughly, "constantly hiding").

Immigration History and Gender

The migration history of Filipino Americans shaped their gender composition over the decades. Most of the Filipinos who came as labor migrants during the first period were men. In 1950, men made up three-quarters of the Filipino American population, according to estimates from historical census data. However, new immigrants were mostly women. Of the 19,307 Filipinos who were admitted to the United States from the Philippines from 1951 to 1960, 71 percent were women who were admitted as nonquota immigrants. By 1960, about 62 percent of Filipino Americans were men, and this went down still further to 54 percent in 1970. Although migration along family lines did bring many more men from the Philippines to the United States in the late twentieth century, marriage migration and the labor recruitment of occupations such as nursing meant that the female proportion grew steadily. By 2000, a majority (55 percent) of all Filipino Americans, including those born in the United States as well as immigrants, were women. Although women made up almost half (49 percent) of native-born Filipino Americans, women comprised 58 percent of the foreign-born, and these proportions continued at roughly the same levels through the census estimates of 2008.

FAMILY AND ETHNICITY

A high degree of out-marriage, especially among women, is one of the most distinctive characteristics of Filipino American families. Using data from the 2000 U.S. Census, Choy (2007:565–566) observed that "after Japanese Americans, Filipino Americans report the highest percentage (21.8) of people of mixed heritage among Asian Americans. However, because of their larger numbers, the more than half a million Filipino Americans of mixed heritage form the single largest contingent of mixed race Asian Americans." According to estimates from the American Community

TABLE 15.3   Racial/Ethnic Categories of Spouses of Married Filipino Americans: 2008

	Husbands of Filipinas	Wives of Filipinos
Filipino	55.3%	74.2%
White	25.9%	8.8%
Black	2.8%	0.2%
Other Asian	2.9%	2.7%
Other or not recorded	13.1%	14.0%
Total N of married individuals	660,558	516,396

Source: Ruggles et al. (2009).

Survey data of the U.S. Census Bureau (2008), shown in Table 15.3, nearly half (45 percent) of the married Filipina women in the United States had a non-Filipino spouse in 2008. Most of those non-Filipino spouses (26 percent) were White. Although Filipino American men were more likely than Filipana American women to marry within their own ethnic group, out-marriage rates were still high, with 11 percent married to a spouse in the White category. It should also be noted that relatively small percentages of both men and women were married to other Asians, suggesting that Filipino Americans were not marrying into a larger Asian identity in the United States. Only Hawaii, with its large Asian and Pacific Islander population, provided something of an exception to these general patterns. In that state, over 70 percent of both Filipino men and women were married to other Filipinos, only 9 percent of men and 12 percent of women were married to Whites, 8 percent of both men and women were married to other Asians, and 10 percent of men and 9 percent of women were married to people of other backgrounds, mostly Pacific Islanders and people of mixed backgrounds (figures for Hawaii are not shown in Table 15.3).

Mixed marriages mean racially and ethnically mixed families. Table 15.4 shows the identifications of fathers and mothers of children in family households in which at least one parent or a child was classified as a Filipino. Nearly 30 percent of children in a family that was at least partially Filipino American had a father who was non-Filipino, and over 10 percent of children in this type of family had a mother who was not a Filipina. Clearly, one of the consequences of the strong pattern of mixed Filipino American families has been the creation of a large mixed background population.

TABLE 15.4   Racial Categories of Parents of Children with at Least One Filipino Parent: 2008

	Mother Filipino, Father:	Father Filipino, Mother:
Filipino	57.5%	84.9%
White	19.2%	6.5%
Black	2.6%	0.2%
Other Asian	2.9%	1.8%
Other race/ethnicity	4.1%	2.7%
Parent not present	13.7%	3.9%
Total N of children	793,567	793,567

Source: Ruggles et al. (2009).

The frequency of marriage by Filipino Americans to non-Filipinos and the large numbers of mixed families mean that ethnic identification can often be complicated for people in Filipino American families. By subtracting estimates from the 2000 U.S. Census of people who claimed to be "Filipino Alone" and people "Filipino Alone or in Any Combination" one can calculate that over a half million people in the United States (522,000) were of mixed Filipino background at the end of the twentieth century.

Parental Race/Ethnicity and Ethnogenesis

Some authors have suggested that the growing size of the Asian American population may be leading to the creation of a general Asian American identity, as people of Filipino, Chinese, Japanese, and other Asian groups share common experiences and are categorized or stereotyped by non-Asian Americans (Lee and Fernandez, 1998; Lee and Yamanaka, 1990). This process, known as ethnogenesis, shows only a modest presence among Filipino Americans. Filipino Americans do participate in events such as Asian heritage festivals in many cities around the United States. Young Filipino Americans are often active in organizations such as Asian American student unions or clubs. However, in spite of the frequent out-marriage by members of this group, only a relatively small increase in the mixed heritage Filipino–other Asian population has occurred.

In 1950, when the Filipino American population still consisted mainly of men, only an estimated 1.7 percent of children in the United States with Filipino fathers had mothers from a different Asian group. By 2008, still only 1.8 percent of the children of Filipino American men had mothers of another Asian group. As the numbers and proportions of Filipina American women grew, the women did have relatively more children with non-Filipino Asian fathers, but the percentages remained fairly small. Combinations of Filipina mother/other Asian father increased from an estimated 1.0 percent in 1950 to about 3.0 percent in 1970, but then stayed at about the 1970 level through 2008 (Ruggles et al., 2008).

By contrast, mixed families with a White parent have been historically common among Filipino Americans. In 1950, when this was still primarily a male population, just under 10,000 people under the age of twenty-one who had a Filipino father (or about 42 percent) had a White mother. This shifted as the Filipina population increased, but still by 2008 only 6.5 percent of Americans with a Filipino father had a White mother. One in ten young people with a mother who was Filipina had a White father in 1950. By 1990, the proportion became one in five and the White father–Filipina mother pattern continued to account for about 20 percent of Filipino American families into the first decade of the twenty-first century (Ruggles et al., 2008).

Table 15.4 gives estimates of parental racial and ethnic categories of children (under 21) with at least one Filipino parent in 2008. As we can see here, Filipino–White couples made up about one-fourth of the parents of children with immediate Filipino backgrounds, with most of those being mothers. The statistics indicate that some version of assimilation through marriage and childbirth fits the Filipino American population more accurately than Asian ethnogenesis does. However, whether the children of Filipinos grow up in mixed Asian families or some other version of an ethnically or racially mixed family, questions of self-identification will be complicated by complex heritages.

These complex heritages have fairly deep roots in Filipino American history. Calculations from U.S. Census data, shown in Table 15.5, indicate that in 1950 close to two-thirds of those under twenty-one years of age living in the United States who had at least one Filipino parent in the household also had a non-Filipino parent. Although the percentages of children living in mixed households went down over the following two decades, their numbers went up because of

TABLE 15.5 Numbers and Percentages of Children in Filipino American Households with One Filipino and One Non-Filipino Parent: 1950 to 2008

	Number	Percentage
1950	13,130	61.8%
1960	41,321	44.8%
1970	52,300	36.3%
1980	118,840	36.2%
1990	179,486	37.5%
2000	224,918	37.7%
2008	291,073	41.0%

Source: Ruggles et al. (2009).

the growth of the population. Moreover, even at the lowest points, in 1970 and 1980, over one-third of Filipino American children lived in families that were mixed by race or ethnicity. Both the numbers and the percentages of children in mixed families increased in the late twentieth and early twenty-first centuries, so that an estimated four out of ten children in Filipino American families, or 291,000 individuals, lived with a non-Filipino parent by 2008.

In a recent article on children of intermarriage in Asian American families, Danielle Hidalgo and Carl L. Bankston (2010) report that "in conversations with multiracial Asian children and their parents, ambiguity and the fluid nature of racial identifications are central themes." The same children will, in different situations and with different groups of people, define themselves as belonging to a specific Asian group, as "Asian," and as belonging to the category of the non-Asian parent. Further, Hidalgo and Bankston observe, "the information multiracial Asian children receive from others about identity also appears to be highly varied and changeable." "A-thirteen-year old son of Filipino–White parents reported to one of the researchers that one day his friends saw his mother when she was picking him up at school. One of the friends later remarked to him, 'I always thought you were White!'" (Hidalgo and Bankston, 2010) In many mixed Filipino American families, ethnic identifications can be difficult, and the boundaries of race and ethnicity have become fluid.

It is difficult to generalize about how the parents of children in mixed families classify their children. In the American Community Survey of 2008, the way in which parents in these families most commonly identified their children on the census forms was "White and Filipino." Table 15.6 also shows us that a sizable minority of parents in mixed families categorized their children as "Filipino," although this designation was slightly more common in households in which the father was the Filipino. At the same time, though, significant minorities of parents classified their children according to the identification of the non-Filipino parent as "White" or "Black."

Hidalgo and Bankston (2010) maintain that the creation of a generation of mixed-background Asian American children is blurring the clear boundaries that separate Asians from other racial groups in the United States. It appears that many young people with Filipino American parents, in particular, are developing identities that may be Filipino, or generalized Asian, or Black, or White, depending on their neighborhoods, friendship groups, and changing personal circumstances. As a result, ethnic identification in Filipino American families appears to be in the process of becoming less of a dichotomy, distinguishing between members of the group and non-members, and more a matter of gradual shading from those with strong ethnic identifications to

TABLE 15.6 Racial Categories of Children with One Filipino and One Non-Filipino Parent: 2008

	Mother Filipina	Father Filipino
White and Filipino	38.0%	33.4 %
Filipino	17.6%	21.5 %
White	15.2%	12.2 %
Black and Filipino	5.5%	1.8 %
Chinese and Filipino	2.8%	3.1 %
Filipino and Other	2.7%	4.8 %
Other Asian Combination	2.4%	4.2 %
Black	2.3%	1.5 %
Other	13.5%	17.5 %

Source: Ruggles et al. (2009).

those who have been completely assimilated into larger population groups. Because of continuing immigration and continuing transnational ties between the Philippines and the United States, this is probably not leading toward a disappearance of Filipino American ethnicity but, rather, a perpetual indistinctness in its definition.

Marriage by Correspondence

Some of the mixed marriages involving Filipino Americans have been the result of correspondence through international matchmaking services or informal international networks. Women who meet their spouses through correspondence are often described as "mail-order brides." This phrase may be both unfair and anachronistic because it implies that women whose relationships with their husbands began through communication at a distance have been "ordered" as products and because the Internet has replaced the postal system as the primary means of establishing these relationships. In addition, couples who meet through correspondence or an international matching service must now meet in person before contracting a marriage. In January 1987, the marriage-fraud provision of the 1986 Immigration Act prohibited foreigners from coming to the United States to marry people they had never met. Therefore, men in the United States who intend to marry a Filipina usually must first travel to the Philippines to meet and make arrangements.

During the 1970s, the number of marriages between men in the United States and women in the Philippines began to increase rapidly. Filipino and American entrepreneurs set up introduction services to put American men in search of wives in contact with Filipinas in search of financially stable husbands. Most often, the international introduction services put potential spouses in contact with one another by marketing catalogs that contained photographs of the women with addresses and information. By the late 1990s, several of these catalogs were available by Internet as well as by regular mail, and in the early twenty-first century the Internet became the main means of establishing these transnational connections.

By the end of the twentieth century, approximately 19,000 women who could be classified as "mail-order brides" were leaving the Philippines each year to join husbands and fiancés abroad, with the United States as the primary destination. Tolentino (1996) estimated that about 50,000 women who he identified as mail-order brides were living in the United States by the middle of the last decade of the twentieth century. Around that time, the social scientist Concepción

Montoya (1997) identified Filipina "mail-order brides," who often established social networks among themselves, as a rapidly emerging American community.

A number of widely publicized incidents have reinforced the negative views some people hold regarding introductions and marriages by mail. In 1995, for example, a man in Seattle, Washington, had brought a wife he had met through mail to the United States from the Philippines. The marriage did not work out, and the wife sought a divorce. In response, the husband contacted the Immigration and Naturalization Service, claiming that his estranged wife no longer qualified for residency in the United States and should be deported to the Philippines. The woman, who had become pregnant with another man's child, was sitting in a Seattle courthouse waiting for a hearing on her residency status when her husband drew a gun and killed her and several of her friends (Bankston, 1999a).

Incidents like this one, although recipients of a great deal of public attention, do not represent most marital relationships initially established through correspondence. Women who owe their legal migration status to marriage with U.S. citizens are sometimes exploited by their husbands, and such women in a new country can be vulnerable. Cultural conflicts and conflicts of expectations can also trouble international marriages. Women from the Philippines often expect to have full control over matters having to do with the household, and they do not see themselves as imported servants but, rather, as full and equal partners in marital relationships. When their husbands expect to obtain exotic, subservient women from an imagined land, the marriages face serious difficulties. Although there is little information on the success rates of correspondence marriages, available evidence suggests that the horror stories of wife abuse are the exception rather than the rule and that many of these marriages do work out to the satisfaction of both parties. Contrary to many popular views, moreover, Filipinas who enter into transnational marriages through a correspondence or matchmaking service are generally educated.

Assimilation and Ethnic Networks

Even Filipinos who are not in mixed families experience some pull toward assimilation into the larger American society. The wide scattering of Filipino Americans around the United States, combined with their familiarity with mainstream American culture, has meant that they are sometimes almost invisible in American society, despite their large numbers. In hospitals employing many Filipino nurses or in the few identifiable Filipino neighborhoods, such as those in Los Angeles, they may stand out. Elsewhere, they often fit unobtrusively into the society around them. As new generations grow up in the United States, Filipino Americans become even less visible as an ethnic group, frequently in their own eyes as well as in those of other people. San Diego-born Ana Maria Cabato expressed her own confusion about being Filipino in American society: "[W]hen I was younger, I used to question my identity. 'Am I Filipino? Am I American?' Even my kids ask me that today, because you don't know what you are. . . . I never learned to speak Tagalog. I guess my parents were trying to prevent us from having an accent. And plus we had to conform with the majority" (Cabato, 1995:153).

Despite the frequent unobtrusiveness of the Filipino American identity, the members of this group have not simply melted into the larger society around them. While other Americans are often unclear about Filipinos as a distinct group, many non-Filipino Americans do see group members as somehow different, and "foreign." A Los Angeles Filipino interviewed by Rick Bonus remarked, "[M]any people think of us as foreigners or, sometimes, even strangers and visitors because they find it very hard to place us. We get mistaken for Chinese, Japanese, Korean, Thai.

We're Asians, but we're different Asians too. Some of them think we're black or Hispanic or even [American] Indians" (anonymous interviewee in Bonus, 2000:51).

The distinctiveness is also felt by Filipino Americans themselves. Although they do feel loyalty and attachment to the United States, they have a sense of themselves as belonging to a unique part of America, with a distinctive history and tradition. This sense of uniqueness is fostered by informal social networks and formal ethnic organizations. It is increasingly expressed through active participation, as Filipino Americans, in the political life of the United States.

Throughout the United States, Filipino American families maintain ties with each other. They frequently keep track of new Filipinos arriving in their communities, and ethnicity serves as a basis of friendship. Even Filipinos who are married to non-Filipinos will enjoy get-togethers where they can enjoy ethnic foods and speak Tagalog or other Filipino languages.

Filipino American families also maintain connections through a wide variety of organizations and clubs that affirm and express ethnic identities. Cabato, who asked questions about her identity as a Filipino and an American, found answers to some of those questions through a folk dancing group formed within a community organization:

> My parents, especially my dad, have always been very active in the community. That's how we got involved with PASACAT [Philippine American Society and Cultural Arts Troupe]. At the time . . . my dad was president of the Filipino American Community Association of San Diego, and he organized a three hour dance program that featured Philippine folk dancing. (Cabato, 1995:145)

The dance program organized through the community center became a regular separate group. Of this group, Cabato reported, "I discovered who I was, what it meant to be Filipino, through PASACAT" (Cabato, 1995:153). Other Filipino Americans have had similar experiences. Organizations such as the community center in San Diego have played a vital part in maintaining Filipino American identity throughout the nation. Posadas (1999:60) remarks that "an exhaustive examination of organizations and associations created by Filipino Americans would be a monumental, if not an impossible task." She observes that "as officers and members of innumerable associations, Filipino Americans define and redefine attachments outside of their family networks" (Posadas, 1999:60–61).

Cultural exhibitions, such as the folk dancing program that attracted Cabato, form one type of activity of Filipino American organizations. Other prominent activities include festivals, picnics, and beauty pageants. On December 30 each year, Filipino American community centers and clubs usually celebrate Rizal Day, which commemorates the execution of national hero José Rizal by the Spanish. Typical Rizal Day activities involve a banquet and a dance. July 4 is celebrated both as American Independence Day and as Philippine-American Friendship Day. Some Filipino Americans recognize July 4 also as Philippine Independence Day, since that was the day the United States recognized the Philippines as an independent nation. Others prefer to celebrate Philippine independence from Spain on June 12. Picnics are common ways of marking both July 4 and June 12.

Towns and cities across the Philippines hold beauty pageants. In the United States, these events became part of Filipino American community life in the difficult times before World War II (Mandel, 2003). Today, they serve to raise funds for community organizations and to reinforce ethnic identity and ethnic solidarity. On the financial importance of pageants, one newspaper reporter remarked of Filipino American pageants in Southern California, "these contests raise . . . I would say, thousands of dollars each year . . . and I can be sure that they spend about half a million dollars every year for their social gatherings in various hotels, restaurants, and meeting halls . . . if you count the rest of Southern California-based Filipino American organizations" (quoted in Bonus, 2000:121).

CHANGE AND ADAPTATION

Language and Assimilation

The use of English in the Philippine educational system and the widespread presence of American mass media in the Philippines mean that even new Filipino arrivals in the United States show high levels of English fluency. New Jersey Filipino American Oscar Ocampo remarked of his own experience, "It's easy for Filipinos to assimilate, and a big part of that is that we're so familiar with American culture. I was a freshman in college when I saw 'Love Story' with Ryan O'Neal and Ali McGraw. Today they have 'Who Wants to be a Millionaire?' with a Filipino host" (Crouse, 2003:L01).

Table 15.7 presents data on Filipino American language use. In 2008, only very small percentages of Filipino Americans did not speak English well, and one-third spoke only English. Among those who spoke languages other than English, Tagalog was most common, since over 61 percent of Filipinos reported speaking this at home. This should be interpreted with some caution, though, because even in the Philippines people often speak "Taglish," incorporating large amounts of English vocabulary into Tagalog grammar. Aside from Tagalog, Ilocano, the language most spoken in the far north of the Philippines, had the widest usage in Filipino American households. Far fewer Filipinos spoke Spanish, Visayan, or Cebuano (the latter two are the most important languages in the central part of the Philippines). It is difficult to say whether those who spoke Spanish did so because they came from the small minority of people in the Philippines who still speak with the language of the former colonial power or because they live in neighborhoods and households with Spanish speakers in places, such as Southern California. The data for ethnically mixed households, shown in the right-hand column, suggest that the latter explanation probably holds for at least some of the Spanish speakers.

TABLE 15.7 Language Abilities and Use of Filipino Americans: 2008

English Ability	All	Filipinos in Households with Non-Filipino Spouse or Parent	Children with Filipino Parent and Non-Filipino Parent
Speaks only English	32.4%	52.6%	87.8%
Speaks English "very well"	45.1%	35.2%	9.6%
Speaks English "well"	16.9%	10.6%	1.4%
Speaks English "not well"	5.2%	1.6%	1.2%
No English	0.4%	0.0%	—
Language spoken at home:			
Tagalog	61.0%	40.9%	7.8%
English	32.4%	52.6%	87.8%
Ilocano	3.3%	1.2%	0.2%
Spanish	1.3%	2.6%	2.4%
Visayan (Bisayan)	0.8%	1.3%	0.3%
Cebuano (Sebuano)	0.3%	0.5%	0.1%
All others	0.8%	0.8%	1.4%

Source: Ruggles et al. (2009).

Because mixed households are such a prominent characteristic of Filipino American families, Table 15.7 also gives information on language usage among those classified as Filipino Americans who have a non-Filipino parent or spouse. Note that the figures in this table do not include the children of one Filipino and one non-Filipino parent who are reported as "White," "Black," "mixed race," or some other categorization. Most of the Filipino Americans in ethnically mixed households spoke only English (52.6 percent). Even when there was a non-Filipino family member, though, the use of Tagalog or another non-English language was still fairly common.

The third column in this table includes all those under 18 with one Filipino parent and one non-Filipino parent, including children who were not themselves classified as Filipino for the census. Nearly nine out of ten (87.8 percent) spoke only English. Only about 8 percent of children of mixed parentage spoke Tagalog, and only about 2.5 percent spoke Spanish.

Family and Household Characteristics

Filipinos often describe themselves as having strong beliefs in families, particularly in traditionally structured families. Table 15.8 supports this view. By the last half of the first decade of the twenty-first century, over 71 percent of all Filipino Americans and over 79 percent of Filipino

---

TABLE 15.8 Selected Household and Family Characteristics of Filipino Americans, 2008

	All Filipino Americans	Under 18
Household type		
Married family	71.3%	79.4%
Single female family	16.3%	14.7
Single male family	6.0%	5.7%
Female living alone	2.9%	—
Male living alone	2.2%	—
Other	1.6%	0.1%
Average number of family members in household	3.8%	4.9%
Living in a three-generation household	17.9%	22.4%
Median household income	$94,710	$92,062
Median income of household head	$42,772	$45,828
Most common occupations of household heads		
Registered nurses	10.7%	12.9%
Nursing aides and attendants	3.9%	4.3%
Accountants and auditors	3.6%	3.1%
Managers and administrators	3.4%	2.8%
Computer analysts and Scientists	2.3%	2.6%
Educational credentials of household heads	51.8%	51.7%
Bachelor's degree	42.0%	43.1%
Master's degree	5.7%	5.2%
Professional degree	3.4%	2.8%
Doctorate	0.7%	0.5%

Source: Ruggles et al. (2009).

American children lived in two-parent married-couple families. By comparison, less than 70 percent of all American children lived in this type of household in 2008. Only very small proportions of this group lived alone in households or in non-household situations such as institutional settings (the "other" category in Table 15.8). About one-fifth of Filipino American children lived in a family headed by a single parent (mostly headed by women), whereas well over one-fourth of all American children lived with single parents (the figure for all Americans is not shown in Table 15.8, but it is taken from America's Families and Living Arrangements (U.S. Census Bureau, 2008b).

Consistent with this attachment to family life, Filipinos tend to have relatively large families and households by American standards. The Census Bureau placed average household size in the United States in 2008 at 2.62 individuals and average family size at 3.22 (the latter is larger because households may consist of single individuals). Table 15.5, based on American Community Survey data (U.S. Census Bureau, 2008), shows that the average number of family members in a household containing a Filipino was 3.22, and that the average number of family members in a family was 4.9.

Divorce rates tend to be low among Filipino Americans, a fact that Choy (2007) attributes partly to Catholic religious beliefs and partly to the American immigration policies that favor family reunification. The divorce rates for women in 2000 (8.2 percent) were higher than those for men (5.4 percent) (Choy, 2007). This disparity is undoubtedly a reflection of the fact that the marriage rate outside the group has been much higher for women than for men in recent years.

Cimmarusti (1996:207) has noted in an article on family therapy among Filipino Americans that "the most important structural factor about the Filipino-American family is that the nuclear family is likely to be part of a larger extended family system, or clan, which plays an integral part in the life of the family." On this point, the American Community Survey data (U.S. Census Bureau, 2008) does indeed show very high rates of living in three-generation households, such as households with grandparents, parents, and children under one roof. Among all Filipinos, 17.9 percent lived in a multigeneration household in 2008. Over 22 percent of Filipino American children lived in a multigeneration household.

The household financial situations of Filipino Americans tend to be better than those of most other Americans. The 2000 U.S. Census, for example, estimated the median household incomes of Filipinos in the United States at $60,570, compared to $51,908 for all Asians and only $41,994 for all Americans (U.S. Census Bureau, 2000). Table 15.8 gives calculations for Filipino Americans from the 2008 American Community Survey sample (U.S. Census Bureau, 2008), which placed the median incomes of households in which Filipino Americans lived at $94,710. The median incomes for all Asians in that year (available online at www.census.gov, the U.S. Census Bureau Web site) were estimated at $70,069 for Asians in general and at $52,029 for all Americans (U.S. Census Bureau, 2008). One should keep in mind that all of this information comes from samples and has some margin of error, but the differences are large enough to make it clear that Filipino Americans have not only adapted well to the economic environment of the United States but have generally managed to establish fairly affluent circumstances for their families.

Estimated median income for Filipino household heads was $42,772 in 2008. The gap between total household income and the income of heads indicates that much of the financial well-being came from having two or more earners per household. The prevalence of professional jobs among Filipino American parents has also been important in maintaining good family economic situations. Rumbaut (2008:208) has reported that "Filipinos have the lowest poverty rate of any major ethnic group in the United States" (a reflection of a large component of professionals, especially nurses, among those who migrate). Table 15.8 shows that registered nurses were, in fact, the most common occupation of heads of household in Filipino American families, followed by other generally well-paying professional occupations.

Most Filipinos in the United States live in households headed by well-educated people. A clear majority of Filipino Americans in 2008 were in households in which the household heads had bachelor's degrees or higher. About one out of every ten Filipinos in the United States resided in a household headed by an individual with a graduate or other advanced degree.

The households, then, show some distinctive characteristics, such as large and multigenerational families. The distinctiveness is frequently invisible to outsiders, though, because the professional occupations and relatively high incomes enable many members of this group to fit into middle-class American situations. Although Filipino families have some visibility in a few ethnic concentrations, such as in Los Angeles, they rarely stand out in the communities across the nation where adults may serve as nurses, accountants, or managers.

Cultural Values and Family Relations

Although Filipino American families often have relatively low visibility in American society, those are distinguished by identifiable cultural traits and attitudes regarding family and interpersonal relations. Filipino social relations are generally described as shaped by four fundamental cultural values that focus on obligations to others and harmony in personal relations (Bankston and Hidalgo, 2006). The first of these is known in Tagalog as *utang na loob* (pronounced OO-tahng nah loh-ohb), which can be translated as "moral debt." This is the type of obligation one has to a benefactor. Within families, Filipinos see children as owing a constant debt of respect and obedience to their elders, especially to their parents and grandparents. *Hiya* (HEE-yah) means "shame." People are ashamed when they fail to behave according to expected social roles, which are often thought of in terms of family relations even when they involve people who are not actually family members. This cultural value, like Utang na loob, reinforces the demand for respect within families. Children who fail to show respect for elders may be described as *walang hiya* (wah-LAHNG HEE-yah) or "shameless," a very strong term of disapproval.

Amor proprio (pronounced as in Spanish [ah-MOHR PROH-pree-oh]), a term drawn from the Spanish heritage of the Philippines, can be translated as "self-esteem." Filipinos generally believe that one should avoid direct criticism of others, especially in public places, for fear of offending the sense of amor proprio. *Pakikisama* (pah-KEE-kee-SAH-mah), or "getting along with others," is linked to amor proprio because it places importance on smooth interpersonal relations. This is linked to the emphasis on self-esteem because it dictates avoidance of conflict and confrontation. Within families, *pakikisama* means that individuals should always place the interests of the family and the maintenance of relations within the family first, and they should consider their own interests and desires as secondary.

Gossip, known as *tsismis* (pronounced CHEEZ-mees), is a very common means of maintaining social control within Filipino families and communities. People will avoid actions that may lay them open to being labeled as walang hiya because of the fear of being the target of gossip. Families will also want children to behave in a respectful and respectable manner out of concern that the family will be the subject of gossip. Since gossip takes place behind the backs of those discussed, it helps to maintain pakikisama in matters of disapproval by providing an outlet that avoids face-to-face confrontation (Cimmarusti, 1996).

Ideas about older and younger people are central in directing how family members express respectful, courteous relations. When a child greets an older person, such as a grandparent, the child will show respect by taking the elder's hand and bowing slightly to touch the back of the hand with the forehead.

Older brothers and sisters must not be treated as equals. They should be addressed as *kuya* ("big brother") and *ate* ("big sister"). Older friends, also, are often called kuya or ate. Children will call unrelated adults *tita* ("aunt") or *tito* ("uncle").

Extended families may, within this cultural context, also include people who are not relatives in a way that other Americans would generally recognize. Godparents or sponsors are virtual members of Filipino families, a cultural practice known as *compadrazgo*. When a child is due to be baptized, the mother and father will ask a number of men and women to stand as sponsors or godparents for the child. Two of the sponsors are recognized by the Church as the child's godparents, but Filipinos rarely distinguish between these two primary sponsors and the other secondary sponsors; all are referred to as the *ninongs*, if men, and *ninangs*, if women, of the child. Sponsors are regarded as being close to additional parents, and they are expected to help the child in any way they can, to give presents on birthdays and other major occasions, and to play key roles in religious confirmation and wedding ceremonies as well as in baptisms (Bankston, 1999b).

Since sponsors have an obligation to help children, people in the Philippines will often seek out powerful or influential individuals for this part. In the United States, however, it is much more common for close friends to act as sponsors, creating formal, customary ties among people who refer to each other as *compadre* or *copare* and *comadre* or *comare* (literally "co-father" and "co-mother"). Friends, even if they are not actually sponsors for one another's children, will often shorten these terms and address each other as *pare* or *mare*. Families with non-Filipino spouses and parents and those living in geographic areas away from large numbers of other Filipino Americans are often not observant in maintaining these kinds of extended family relations, but they will usually have people they regard as godparents or sponsors of children.

Sexuality

Filipino culture is traditionally relatively tolerant of sexual diversity among family members, and Filipino American families generally retain this tolerance. Same-sex relations are not regarded as the norm, but Filipinos tend to be accepting of "tomboy love," or relations between women, and of *bakla*, or relations between men. In a study of Filipino gay men in New York City, Manalansan illustrates Filipino concepts of homosexuality, and of the comparative openness of families on this issue with the following case:

> One informant who was born and raised in California said that a turning point in his life was when he went to the Philippines at the age of sixteen and his uncle introduced him to cross-dressing and other practices among homosexuals. That brief (month and a half) visit was to become an important element in the way he now socialized in the gay community. He seeks cross-dressing opportunities not only with other transvestites but with other Filipinos. He said that Filipino gay men did not cross-dress for shock value but for realness. He further mentioned that he was unlike those gay men who were into queer androgyny, consciously looking halfway between male and female. He and other gay men who cross-dressed attempted to look like real women. More important, despite the fact that he was raised speaking English at home, his friendships with other Philippine-born gay men has encouraged him to attempt to speak at least some smattering of the Filipino gay argot. (Manalansan, 2007:316)

This passage reveals a great deal about attitudes toward same-sex relations and about sex roles in general in Filipino culture and within Filipino American families. Although there is tolerance, there is also a great deal of stereotyping, especially of bakla, who are typically seen as feminine men, or transvestites, and are frequently regarded as humorous figures. Filipino Americans have some fairly strong ideas about gender roles. The reader will note that the men in this passage were trying "to look like real women." Moreover, there is a very definite ethnic gay subculture here, with its own norms of behavior and idioms.

Although most Filipinos are Catholic and disapprove of sex outside of marriage on religious grounds, children born to single parents are accepted as family members, both in the Philippines and in the United States (Tamayo-Lott, 2006). At the same time, though, Filipino Americans may often hold young women to traditionalized ideas of sexual purity, and expect their daughters to have stricter sexual standards than the parents perceive in American society at large. Espiritu has quoted a mother who expressed this attitude:

> I want my daughters to be Filipino especially on sex. I always emphasize to them that they should not participate in sex if they are not married. We are also Catholic. We are raised so that we don't engage in going out with men while we are not married And I don't like it to happen to my daughters as if they have no values. I don't like them to grow up that way, like the American girls. (Espiritu, 2001:415)

Youth Accomplishments and Problems

The relatively advantageous socioeconomic positions of many Filipino Americans, combined with a tradition of respect for educational credentials, has tended to produce fairly high levels of educational achievement and attainment among members of the younger generation. Gloria and Ho (2003) report that Filipino American children generally show higher levels of achievement than Black or White Americans do, but somewhat lower than some other Asian groups. Bankston (2006) has found that Filipino Americans have been represented at disproportionately large percentages among students admitted to the elite universities of California. Between 2006 and 2008, an estimated 56.2 percent of people ages 18 to 24 in Filipino American families were enrolled in college or graduate school, compared to 40.7 percent of all Americans in that age group (Ruggles et al., 2008).

Although there is evidence of impressive accomplishments among young people raised in Filipino American families, there are also some problems. Despite the familiarity of people in the Philippines with American society, the cultural values discussed still give older Filipino Americans, especially the foreign born, perspectives different from their children. One common source of conflict between Filipino parents and children is the insistence of parents on respect and obedience from children. Young people learn to emphasize the values of independence and self-assertiveness from their peers and from the larger American society. Older people often place importance on hierarchical lines of authority within families (Morales, 1974; Tamayo-Lott, 1980). As a result, there can be serious disagreement over the proper roles within families.

The problems resulting from gaps between generations can be a source of friction, but they usually do not create serious long-term problems. In some cases, though, the challenges of life in America can result in delinquency. Filipino youth gangs have appeared in the metropolitan areas that have large Filipino American populations. Alsaybar (1993) maintained that there were more than sixty Filipino American youth gangs in Los Angeles in the early 1990s. The reasons that Filipino American young people join gangs are complex. The most basic reasons, though, involve the challenges of American society, where youth gangs have become a problem among many ethnic and racial groups, combined with an alienation from parents that leads adolescents to identify with each other in delinquent subgroups, rather than with their elders (Bankston, 1998).

Transnational Families

Filipino Americans have been described as "transnational" because they maintain ties with both the United States and the Philippines (Espiritu, 2003). Most Filipino Americans have family members in both countries, and they will often visit the Philippines or even resettle there after years spent in the United States. This has led to the phenomenon of the *balikbayan* (BAH-lik-BAI-yan) or "return to the homeland," a term widely used to describe Filipinos going back after time spent in other countries. This return migration has been a large source of income for the Philippines, as well as a way of maintaining close ties between people in that country and Filipino Americans.

Balikbayans are expected to bring *pasalubong* (Pah-sah-LOO-bohng), or gifts, to all of their family members. To do this, they use large cardboard boxes, known as balikbayan boxes, and this has created business opportunities for companies specializing in shipping between the United States and the Philippines. Boxes often move in the other direction, as well, since Filipino Americans will bring back gifts to their family members in America and foods that they cannot find in North American shops and homes. The gifts going to the Philippines typically contain items that are expensive or difficult to find in that country. Tins of corned beef, Spam, and American chocolate are all common articles in balikbayan boxes.

The transnational links of Filipino American families help to counter the tendency toward loss of ethnic identity among generations raised in the United States because the families maintain contacts with relatives across the ocean. Parents in the United States will also frequently talk about sending older children back to study and live with relatives when the parents perceive problems in behavior or schooling, and sometimes families will actually take such steps (Agbayani-Siewert, 1990).

Filipino and American

The Filipino American family combines Filipino and North American influences in even deeper and more complex ways than do other ethnic families in the United States. The United States seized the Philippines at the very end of the nineteenth century and held it as a colonial possession until the middle of the twentieth, bringing American administration, institutions, and popular culture to the Southeast Asian cluster of islands. As a result, the United States exported itself to people in the Philippines. The colonial domination also brought Filipinos to the United States, though, so the transnational movement of ideas, goods, and people has influenced family life among Filipinos on both sides of the world.

The migration history has shaped Filipino American families in a significant way by affecting the gender composition of the population and intensifying a tendency toward out-marriage. By the beginning of the second half of the twentieth century, ethnically mixed families were already common among Filipino Americans, in part because of the predominance of men among people who had arrived in the United States as laborers. During the second half of the twentieth century, though, women began to make up most of the immigrants from the Philippines. The continuing American presence in that country, even after independence, encouraged marriages between American men and Filipinas. The U.S. demand for nurses, a profession with many more women than men, also helped to bring more Filipinas than Filipinos to the United States. Ethnically mixed marriages and children of mixed racial and ethnic background became a prominent trait of Filipino American families.

As family became a basis of migration in the years following 1965, the Filipino American population grew rapidly and transnational family connections were continually formed and strengthened. Thus, although the line between Filipino and non-Filipino became blurred through intermarriage and cultural sharing between the two nations, the movement of people back and forth across oceans also connected Filipino Americans to their origins in the Southeast Asian homeland. The arrival of Filipino immigrants through family preferences in the U.S. immigration system, family support networks for documented and undocumented immigrants in the United States, and returnees to the Philippines all helped to maintain families with genuine and lasting connections to both countries.

In the United States, Filipino American families on average have shown fairly high levels of socioeconomic achievement. They also have faced challenges, though, as they have sought to maintain distinctive cultural perspectives and deal with gaps between generations. They often have assimilated outwardly in many respects, and yet they have maintained ethnic networks and organizations. Filipino American families have continued to be distinguished by strong attachment to family life and to family relations.

As the Filipino origin population of the United States grows, both through immigration and through the growth of the number of native born, families distinguished by Filipino heritage and by ties to the Philippines will be an increasingly prominent part of American family life.

References

Agbayani-Siewert, P. 1990. "Filipino American Families: Practice Guidelines for Social Work Practitioners." Paper presented at the 36th Annual Meeting of the Council of Social Work Education, New Orleans, LA.

Alsaybar, N. 1993, June. "Lost in L.A.: Gangs, Pinoy Style." *Filipinas 10–11,* 67.

Bankston, C. L. III. 1998. "Youth Gangs and the New Second Generation: A Review Essay." *Aggression and Violent Behavior 3,* 35–44.

———. III. 1999a. "Mail-Order Brides." In C. L. Bankston III., and R. Kent Rasmussen (Eds.), *Encyclopedia of Family Life.* Pasadena, CA: Salem Press.

———. 1999b. "Filipino Americans." In C. L. Bankston III and R. K. Rasmussen (Eds.), *Encyclopedia of Family Life* (pp. 608–611). Pasadena, CA: Salem Press.

———. 2003. "Philippines." In C. Bankston (Ed.), *World Conflicts: Asia and the Middle East.* Pasadena, CA: Salem Press.

———. 2006. "Filipino Americans." In P. G. Min (Ed.), *Asian Americans: Contemporary Trends and Issues* (2nd ed.). Thousand Oaks, CA: Pine Forge Press.

Bankston, C. L. III, and D. A. Hidalgo. 2006. "Respect in Southeast Asian American Children and Adolescents: Cultural and Contextual Influences." *New Directions for Child and Adolescent Development 114,* 25–38.

———. 2007. "The Waves of War: Immigrants, Refugees, and New Americans from Southeast Asia." In M. Zhou and J.V. Gatewood (Eds.), *Contemporary Asian America: A Multidisciplinary Reader* (2nd ed.). New York: New York University Press.

Berger, J. 2003, November 24. "From Philippines, With Scrubs; How One Ethnic Group Came to Dominate the Nursing Field." *New York Times,* B1.

Bonus, R. 2000. *Locating Filipino Americans: Ethnicity and the Cultural Politics of Space.* Philadelphia, PA: Temple University Press.

Cabato, A. M. 1995. "PASACAT Became My Whole Life." In Y. L. Espiritu (interviewer), *Filipino American Lives.* Philadelphia, PA: Temple University Press.

Choy, C. C. (2007). "Philippines." In M. C. Waters and R. Ueda with H. Marrow (Eds.), *The New Americans: A Guide to Immigration Since 1965.* Cambridge, MA: Harvard University Press.

Cimmarusti, R. A. 1996. "Exploring Aspects of Filipino American Families." *Journal of Marital and Family Therapy 22,* 205–217,

Crouse, D. 2003, August 17. "American Dream Alive and Well." Hackensack (Bergen County), NJ: *The Record,* L01.

Department of Homeland Security. 2010. *2004-2010 Yearbooks of Immigration Statistics.* http://www.dhs.gov/files/statistics/immigration.shtm (accessed April 23, 2011).

Espina, M. E. 1988. *Filipinos in Louisiana.* New Orleans, LA: A. F. Laborde.

Espiritu, Y. L. 2001. "'We Don't Sleep Around Like White Girls Do:' Family, Culture and Gender in Filipina American Lives." *Sings: Journal of Women in Culture and Society 26,* 415–440.

Espiritu, Y. L. 2003. *Home Bound: Filipino American Lives Across Cultures, Communities, and Cultures.* Berkeley, CA: University of California Press.

Gall, S. B., and T. L. Gall. 1993. *Statistical Record of Asian Americans.* Detroit: Gale Research, Inc.

Gloria, A. M., and T. A. Ho. 2003. "Environmental, Social, and Psychological Experiences of Asian American Undergraduates: Examining Issues of Academic Persistence." *Journal of Counseling and Development 81,* 93–105.

Hidalgo, D. A., and C. L. Bankston III. 2010. "Blurring Racial and Ethnic Boundaries in Asian American Families." *Journal of Family Issue 31,* 280–300.

Lee, S., and M. Fernandez. 1998. "Trends in Asian American Racial/Ethnic Intermarriage: A Comparison of 1980 and 1990 Census Data." *Sociological Perspectives 41*(2):323–342.

Lee, S., and K. Yamanaka. 1990. "Patterns of Asian American Intermarriage and Marital Assimilation." *Journal of Comparative Family Studies 21,* 287–305.

Manalasan, M. F. 2007. "Searching for Community: Filipino Gay Men in New York City." In M. Zhou and J.V. Gatewood (Eds.), *Contemporary Asian America: A Multidisciplinary Reader* (2nd ed.). New York: New York University Press.

Mandel, S. 2003, January 26. "Memories of the Manong: Photos Offer a Rare Glimpse into Filipino American History. *Washington Post,* G07.

Mangiafico, L. 1988. *Contemporary American Immigrants: Patterns of Filipino, Korean, and Chinese Settlement in the United States.* Westport, CT: Praeger.

Montoya, C. 1997. "Mail Order Brides: An Emerging Community." In M. P. P. Root (Ed.), *Filipino Americans: Transformation and Identity.* Newbury Park, CA: Sage.

Morales, R. 1974. *Makibaka: The Filipino-American Struggle.* Darby, MT: Mountain View.

Office of Policy and Planning, U.S. Immigration and Naturalization Service. 2003, January. *Estimates of the Unauthorized Immigrant Population Residing in the United States: 1990 to 2000.* Washington, DC: Department of Homeland Security.

Posadas, B. M. 1999. *The Filipino Americans.* Westport, CT: Greenwood Press.

Ruggles, S., M. Sobek, T. Alexander, C. A. Fitch, R. Goeken, P. K. Hall, et al. 2008. "Integrated Public Use Microdata Series: Version 4.0" [Machine-readable database]. Minneapolis, MN: Minnesota Population Center [producer and distributor].

Rumbaut, R. 2008. "The Coming of the Second Generation: Immigration and Ethnic Mobility in Southern California." *The Annals of the American Academy of Political and Social Science 620,* 196–236.

Tamayo-Lott, J. 1980. "Migration of a Mentality: The Filipino American Community." In S. Sue, N. Wagner, and R. Endo (Eds.), *Asian Americans: Social and Psychological Perspectives II* (pp. 132–140). Palo Alto, CA: Science and Behavior Books.

———. 2006. Common Destiny: Filipino American Generations. New York: Rowman & Littlefield.

Tirona, C. 1995. "Sometimes I Am Not Sure What It Means to Be an American." In Y. L. Espiritu (interviewer), *Filipino American Lives.* Philadelphia, PA: Temple University Press.

Tolentino, R. 1996. "Bodies, Letters, Catalogs: Filipinas in Transnational Space. *Social Text 48,* 49–76.

U.S. Census Bureau. 2000. "Census 2000, Summary File 4 (SF4)." http://factfinder.census.gov/servlet/DTCharIterationServlet?_ts=321530144468 (accessed April 23, 2011).

U.S. Census Bureau. 2000–2008. *American Community Survey.* http://factfinder.census.gov/servlet/DatasetMainPageServlet?_program=ACS&_submenuId=&_lang=en&_ts= (accessed April 23, 2011).

U.S. Census Bureau. 2008a. "2008 American Community Survey Data 1-Year Estimates." http://factfinder.census.gov/servlet/ADPTable?_bm=y&-geo_id=01000US&-ds_name=ACS_2008_1YR_G00_&-_lang=en&-_caller=geoselect&-format= (accessed April 23, 2011).

U.S. Census Bureau. 2008b. "America's Families and Living Arrangements: 2008." www.census.gov/population/www/socdemo/hh-fam/cps2008.html (accessed April 21, 2011).

16

∎∎∎

The Asian Indian American Family

Uma A. Segal

INTRODUCTION

The economic, political, and social opportunities promised by life in the United States have drawn immigrants from numerous countries. Recently, the term Asian American that has been officially established by the U.S. Census Bureau and the Office of Homeland Security to include all Asians and Southeast Asians, now attempts to recognize the major differences as well as the cultural variations that exist within and among nations and races from Asia by further differentiation.[1] Nevertheless, there continue to be generalized and overwhelming perceptions in the public that Americans of Asian origin are similar in many ways, that they constitute a "model minority," are professionally successful, and, according to their own cultural notions of health, are well adjusted both emotionally and mentally. Despite this stereotype and its appreciation of the achievement orientation of many Americans of Asian origin and its recognition that a disproportionate number in this popu-lation is productive and contributive members of the United States, it is clear to those engaged in migration studies that transnational and transcultural adaptation is often a difficult and painful process. This chapter isolates one group of Asians in the United States, the Indian American from among the many within the Asian American population, exploring its immigrant experience.[2]

HISTORICAL BACKGROUND

Immigration Patterns

Although documentation of the presence of Asian Indian Americans dates back to 1790 in Massachusetts, and the U.S. Census did count one Asian Indian in the early nineteenth century, it

---

[1]See question #6 on 2010 U.S. Census form.

[2]Although identified as Asian Indian by the U.S. Census, the population prefers to self-identify as Indian American in recognition of its allegiance to the United States. The term *Asian Indian* will be used to identify the population during its early immigration experience, moving to "Indian American" when referring to the population of the latter part of the twentieth century and early twenty-first century.

was essentially in the latter part of that century that Asian Indians began migrating to North America in significant numbers. These were voluntary emigrants from India, primarily agricultural laborers from northwestern India (mostly Sikhs and some Muslims), who settled in California between 1899 and 1920 and numbered about 7,300 (Balgopal, 1995; Chandrasekhar, 1982). Perhaps because of cultural and/or economic reasons, which were reinforced by restrictive immigration laws, only men from China (Lyman, 1973), Japan (Ogawa, 1973), and India (Balgopal, 1995) entered the United States. During the years 1928–1946, Asian Indians were denied citizenship and further immigration was prohibited. Isolated from their families because of punitive immigration policies, 3,000 Asian Indians returned to India between 1920 and 1940. After the passage of the Immigration Act of 1946, Asian Indians were once again able to immigrate legally to the United States, but only at the rate of 100 per year. Between 1958 and 1965, only a few more Asian Indians came to the United States, and on the whole these were a small transient community of students, Asian Indian government officials, and businessmen, although there was a small number (4,756) of new immigrants (Leonhard-Spark and Saran, 1980).

While immigrants from India continue to enter the United States, an exceptionally large number of Asian Indian immigrants arrived in the mid-1960s with the liberalization of immigration policies and passage of the Immigration and Naturalization Act of 1965, which abolished national quotas and allowed in immigrants based on profession and skills. Many Asian Indians (henceforth referred to as Indians) came to the United States in the mid-1960s as students, most with intentions of returning to India, yet the majority remained with the opening of professional opportunities and established homes and families, particularly on the East and West Coasts as well as in several other metropolitan areas around the country. Although Indians may be found across the nation and in all states, this pattern remains relatively consistent as is evident in Map 16.1, which displays the current distribution of the foreign-born population of Indian origin.

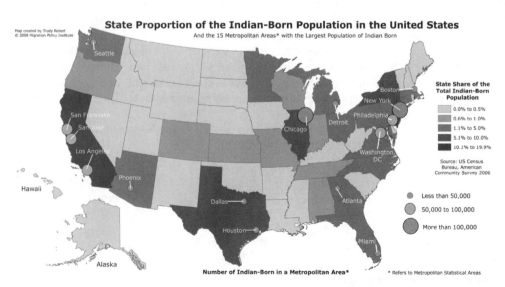

MAP 16.1 Distribution of the Foreign-Born Indian American Population: 2008

Source: Terrazas, A. 2008. "Indian Immigrants in the United States." Washington, DC: Migration Policy Institute. http://www.migrationinformation.org/Usfocus/display.cfm?ID=687 (accessed April 22, 2010). Used with permission.

TABLE 16.1   Major Asian and Other Foreign-Born Populations: 2008

Population	Single Race	Bi/multirace and Single Race Combined	Foreign Born	2nd+ Generation
All Asians*	13,413,976	15,281,043	9,211,303	6,069,740
Chinese	3,077,783	3,622,496	2,227,414	1,395,082
Indian	2,495,998	2,725,594	1,927,328	798,266
Filipino	2,425,697	3,088,000	1,653,820	1,434,180
Vietnamese	1,431,980	1,728,532	1,113,224	615,308
Korean	1,344,267	1,609,980	1,002,934	607,046
Japanese	710,063	1,298,890	441,681	857,209
Others				
White			18,569,693	
Black			3,081,782	
South American			1,847,115	
Central American			2,527,557	

*Includes other Asian groups.

Although the 2010 U.S. Census figures may provide more accurate data, the American Community Survey (2008)[3] indicates that among "single-ethnicity Asians," Indians are now the second-largest group following the Chinese and also comprise the second-largest number of foreign born (Table 16.1).

Between 1980 and 1990 the community grew 125.6 percent from 361,531 and the current figures of 2.7 million far surpass early projections of 2 million by 2050 (Bouvier and Agresta, 1985). Thus, as is evident from Table 16.1 and Figures 16.1 and 16.2 from the American Community Survey 2008, Indians comprise one of the fastest-growing Asian American groups, resulting not only from the arrival of new immigrants but also from the birth of the second generation.

Although little discussed, there is also a sizable unauthorized immigrant population from India. Unauthorized individuals may have entered the United States legally or illegally. In the former instance, they remain without permission after the term of their visa expires. In 2000, the

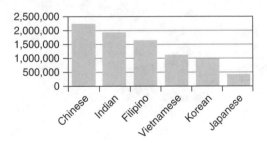

FIGURE 16.1   Major Asian Groups: Foreign Born

---

[3]The American Community Survey provides an annual estimate of the sociodemographic characteristics of the foreign born based on a sample of approximately three million households.

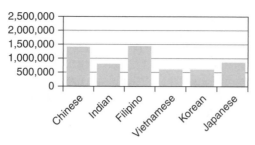

FIGURE 16.2 Major Asian Groups: Native Born

number of this population from India was estimated to be about 120,000 or 1 percent of the total unauthorized population. In 2009, it was estimated at 200,000 or 2 percent of the total unauthorized population and an increase of 64 percent. Unauthorized immigrants from India are the sixth largest in number, following groups from Central America and the Philippines (Hoefer, Rytina, and Baker, 2010). It is not clear to what extent this group is represented in the literature and data discussed in the remainder of the chapter.

Defining Characteristics of Indians in the United States

Indian migration is not new as this population has long sought better opportunities around the globe; however, the large wave that emigrated to the United States between the years 1965 and 1987 was highly educated and professional, distinctly different from the populations that emigrated to other countries and different also from other groups that have come to the United States. Indian immigrants to the United States during those two decades did not represent a cross-section of the Indian subcontinent; as a result of personal reasons for emigrating and restrictions on Asian immigration, most belonged to a select group seeking professional or advanced (graduate level) educational opportunities. Because India's educational system has a distinct British orientation, most Indians who came to the United States prior to 1985 were fluent in English with some exposure to Western values and beliefs, facilitating their entry into American society (Leonhard-Spark and Saran, 1980). Their facility in English, their high levels of education, and their professional skills enabled most to quickly establish themselves successfully in the United States, and because they tended to select residences based on convenience and locality rather than proximity to other Indians, few Indian ghettos in the late twentieth century existed in the United States.

Under the family reunification provision of the Immigration and Naturalization Act of 1965 (PL 89-236), U.S. citizens and permanent residents of Indian origin can sponsor their immediate family members for immigration. Many of the immigrants of the 1960s, 1970s, and 1980s are now citizens and/or permanent residents of the United States, are well established economically, and are in positions to sponsor relatives or recruit workers for their businesses. Many of these new immigrants are not as skilled as their sponsors.

The median income of Indians who immigrated between 1987 and 1990 dipped to one-fifth of that of pre-1980 migrants (Balgopal, 1995; Melwani, 1994). Despite this fact, the median family income in 2008 was $99,783, substantially higher than the U.S. median at $63,366. The per capita income of Indians is 29 percent higher than the national average, a 4 percent increase since 1990 when it was 25 percent higher (American Community Survey, 2008; U.S. Census Bureau, 1992).

Overall, the educational level of Indians over the age of 25 years is also high. The 2008 American Community Survey data show that in that year, 37.6 percent of Indians reported a graduate or professional degree, while the national average was 10.2 percent; 32.5 percent had a bachelor's degree (United States average was 17.5 percent); 9.4 percent had less than a high school diploma (national average was 15 percent). A significant proportion is employed in professional, scientific, and management positions (22.6 percent to the U.S. average of 10.4 percent) and in administrative positions or in education, health, and social services (22.9 percent to the U.S. average of 21.7 percent). More than 45,000 physicians of Indian origin are practicing in the United States, and another 15,000 medical students and residents are preparing to enter the profession (Sangal, 2008).

The influx of newcomers into a new country often strains the host country's cultural homogeneity and may be perceived as a threat to societal norms (Mayadas and Elliott, 1992; Mayadas and Segal, 1989). Although Indian Americans have generally been highly successful in their professional and business endeavors and are recognized as productive contributors to the U.S. economy, because of sociocultural differences between Indian and American societies, a marked distance continues to exist between long-established Americans and this group of naturalized citizens. The difference is further highlighted as intergenerational conflicts emerge between these immigrant professionals of the 1960s, 1970s, and 1980s and their American-born offspring (Segal, 2002).

Regardless of reasons for emigrating, all immigrants to a new country find adjustment to foreign values, expectations, and environment baffling. However, although European immigrants and their descendants faced cultural conflicts because their features are Caucasian and the color of their skin is white, their assimilation into the American mainstream was largely dependent on their individual decisions to adopt the American culture (Portes and Zhou, 1993) unlike the more recent immigrants from South America and Asia, who are always distinguishable because of their physical characteristics.[4] While the experiences of different immigrant groups from Asia vary in the extent to which they encounter overt discrimination, injustice, and oppression, their experience of acculturation in terms of value adjustment and orientation of family life tends to be similar. Immigrants often experience crises in identity, feeling isolated and alienated from both their culture of origin and the American culture (Sue, 1973). Such stress results in one of three reactions: (1) close adherence to the values of the culture of origin, (2) over-Westernization and rejection of Asian ways, or (3) integration of aspects of both cultures perceived as most amenable to the development of self-esteem and identity (Sue, 1973). Portes and Zhou (1993) propose a fourth response—segmented assimilation—in which a group engages in rapid economic advancement with the deliberate preservation of the immigrant community's values and tight solidarity. A study of relationships between acculturation-related demographics and cultural attitudes of a group of 105 Indians in the United States reported that 65 percent identified as being mostly Indian, 21 percent preferred an equal mix of Indian and American lifestyles, and 7 percent chose not to self-identify as Indian (Sodowsky and Carey, 1988).

Indian Demography and the Family

Located in South Asia, India's southern half is bordered by the Bay of Bengal and the Arabian Sea, and its northern portions border on Pakistan, China, Nepal, and Bangladesh. The country is

---

[4]Although not a focus of this chapter, immigrants from Africa are faced with another dilemma as they are often identified as African Americans although they do not share either the history or the culture of the latter.

1,269,340 square miles (3,287,590 sq km), slightly more than one-third the size of the United States, with an estimated population in 2009 of 1.17 billion, second only to that of China. Estimates in 2007 indicate that 30.8 percent of the population is below 14 years of age, 64.3 percent is between the ages of 15 and 64, and only 4.9 percent is age 65 and over (Central Intelligence Agency, 2010).

Regions across India are so diverse—with differences in phenotype, language (both spoken and written), culture, food, literature, art, music, and style of dress—that it could well be an "Indian Union" of several small nation-states. The population is ethnically diverse in religion (Hindus 80.5 percent, Muslims 13.4 percent, Christians 2.3 percent, Sikhs 1.9 percent, others 1.9 percent).

Although English has an associate status, it is the most used language for national, political, and commercial communications; Hindi, the official language, is spoken by about 41 percent of the population, with at least twenty-four other languages, each spoken by a million or more persons. It is believed that there are 1,652 Indian languages and dialects.

Politically, India is a secular federal republic and the world's largest democracy. The country received its independence from the British on August 15, 1947. With its twenty-eight states and seven union territories, it has a parliamentary government consisting of executive, legislative, and judicial branches and a universal suffrage age of eighteen years (Government of India, 2010).

The Traditional Indian Family

Most Indians base their family lifestyles on the following traditional values, beliefs, and expectations that appear to be common to most Asian cultures:

1. Asians are allocentric (group oriented), not idiocentric (self oriented), and the individual is expected to make sacrifices for the larger good of the group, more specifically, for that of the family (Hofstede, 1980; Segal, Segal, and Niemcyzcki, 1993; Segal, 2002; Triandis, Bontempo, Villareal, Asai, and Lucca, 1988).
2. Males are more valued than are females. In this clearly patriarchal society, men are heads of households, primary wage earners, decision makers, and disciplinarians. Women are subordinate and serve as caretakers; as children, they are groomed to move into and contribute to the well-being of the husband's family (Dhruvarajan, 1993; Mullatti, 1995; Segal, 2002).
3. Children are docile and obedient. They are expected to bring honor to their families by exhibiting good behavior and high achievement and contributing to family well-being. Children's mates are selected by the parents, often based on factors unrelated to the offsprings' emotional expectations. Choice of career is heavily influenced, if not dictated, by the family (Dhruvarajan, 1993; Dutt, 1989; Saran, 1985; Segal, 2002; Sinha, 1984).
4. High levels of dependency are fostered in the family. The female is expected to be dependent throughout her life—first on her father, then on her husband, and finally on her eldest son. Children are dependent emotionally, and often socially, on their parents throughout the parents' lives. Authority and respect for elders are paramount, and the family unit controls members in all areas of their lives. Traditionally, difficulties are handled within the family, whether these difficulties are familial, emotional, professional, financial, or health related (Segal, 2002; Sinha, 1984).
5. Two major concepts tend to permeate all significant relationships: obligation and shame. One is expected to be selfless and obligated to significant others, especially to parents and husbands, within the family. Nor should one's behavior ever bring shame upon oneself or one's family (Chatrathi, 1985; Segal, 2002; Sue, 1981).

Consistent with these patterns, the traditional Indian family system is that of the joint family, in which the family is strictly hierarchical, patriarchal, and patrilineal. Three or more generations may live together, with age, gender, and generation serving as the primary determinants of behavior and role relationships. Two or more family groupings of the same generation may be found in the joint family system as sons bring their spouses to the parental home. A high premium is placed on conformity. Interdependence is fostered, self-identity is inhibited (Sinha, 1984), and a conservative orientation, resistant to change, is rewarded. Despite the many changes and adaptations to a pseudo-Western culture and a tentative move toward the nuclear family among the middle class, this system is preferred and continues to prevail in modern India.

In the joint family, each child has multiple role models, and the supervision and training of children is shared by all family members. Whereas infants are generally overindulged, young children are reared in an authoritarian atmosphere in which autonomy is not tolerated (Mullatti, 1995). As children enter their teen and young adult years, guilt, shame, and a sense of moral obligation are used as the primary mechanisms of control. This control model has a positive aspect in providing a structure that maintains family integrity through a deep-seated belief in societal norms and an obligation to duty. Belief in the integrity of the group provides the family with a group identity and strengthens family stability, albeit at the cost of individual autonomy (Triandis et al., 1988). Western authors often overlook this aspect of Indian culture, which serves to bind the intergenerational family together (Segal, 1991).

Indian Adolescents

Biological puberty is considered the onset of adolescence; the end is marked by the integration of one's psychological identity and the establishment of a goal-directed life (Seltzer, 1982). In an individualistic society, adolescence extends over a long period and involves tasks that require considerable trial and error. Surmounting these difficulties and emerging as a well-functioning individual with a discrete self-identity can create high levels of stress, especially if adolescents' struggles to establish their identities are not understood or supported by significant adults.

The phenomenon of adolescence, as conceptualized in the West, is relatively absent for the Eastern teenager. Among Indians, the transitional period of adolescence is generally not recognized. Children continue to remain submissive to parents even after they get married, become employed, and leave the parental home (Segal, 2002). Because youth must always defer to age, the autocratic parent–child relationship tends to persist. Although each subcommunity may have a rite of passage with the onset of biological puberty to mark adulthood, there is no concurrent change in role, status, responsibility (Arredondo, 1984), or autonomy in decision making, and children accept parental authority throughout the latter's lifetime. The traditional family structure and norms do not reward competitiveness, achievement orientation, or self-orientation within the family. The welfare and integrity of the family supersedes individual self-identity (Sinha, 1984; Triandis, 1988).

THE MODERN "INDIAN AMERICAN" ETHNIC FAMILY

Mayadas and Elliott (1992) argue that key issues in the adjustment and integration of immigrants are the dimensions of economic advantage/disadvantage and cultural identity. They suggest that the immigrant group's socioeconomic status (including class, education, age, and gender) and cultural identity (language, religion, rituals, values, dress, food, art, music, and political affiliation) greatly impact acceptance by the host country, which, in turn, has implications for the adjustment, resocialization, and modification of values and beliefs of that immigrant group. Regardless of where Indians have migrated over the years (to the United States, England, Africa, the Caribbean, or the Far East), they have tended to move for economic reasons and not because they have been politically or socially oppressed in India. They have always maintained strong social, emotional, and cultural ties with their homeland; often return to visit India; and usually provide financial support to members of their families who remain in that country. Continued connections with the homeland are often evidenced by remittances, which in 2008 totaled $52 billion to India, surpassing amounts sent to any other country (Ratha, Mohapatra, and Silwal, 2009). Even emigrants who left India several generations ago for the United Kingdom, South Africa, and the Caribbean maintain a strong Indian cultural identity, and marital patterns have tended to remain endogenous.

This pattern is evidenced in the segmented assimilation (Portes and Zhou, 1993) of the more recent Indian immigrants to the United States. Collectively, they have advanced rapidly economically but have deliberately preserved traditional values and maintained tight community solidarity. This tendency has had significant implications both for their own integration into Western society and in the socialization of the second generation with its inevitable conflicts in balancing North American and Eastern values, beliefs, and lifestyles.

Family Structure, Family Behavior, and Ethnic Culture

Because the Indian immigrant group is a relatively new one in the United States, with members of the majority of the first generation now in their midlife years and with strong connections with their homeland, several family patterns have remained consistent with traditional ones. In fact, in an attempt to protect tradition, family patterns may not have experienced normal cultural evolution. Many immigrants arrived in the United States as married couples or family groups in the late 1960s and early 1970s; those who came as students returned to India to follow prescribed rules of arranged marriage. It is only in the late 1980s, when large numbers of second-generation Indians began achieving adolescence and adulthood, that traditional cultural values and practices were questioned, presenting conflicts of a nature the first generation had not envisioned. Furthermore, concerns about aging parents, many of whom still remain in India, and about their own retirement in a country into which they have not truly assimilated, are added issues that were not prevalent in Indians' early immigration experience. While some of these issues have been resolved for the first post-1965 wave of Indian immigrants as the second generation carved out its own path, newer immigrants arriving in large numbers with the H1B and L1 visas,[5] are, all over again, experiencing these conflicts. In 2008, Indians led all other countries with 38 percent of the H1B visa category and 17 percent for the L1 category. In this same year, Canada sent the second-largest group of H1B visa entrants at 5.7 percent, and the origin of the second-largest L1 entrants was the United Kingdom at 14 percent (Monger and Barr, 2009).

To understand the Indian family in the United States, it is advisable to look at role relationships within the family, demographic characteristics of the family, extended family relationships, and processes for the maintenance and transmission of the culture.

Family Roles

Most Indians who grew up and lived in a joint family system in India found themselves in a nuclear family after immigration to the United States because immigration policies permit only

---

[5]The H1B is a temporary visa for individuals in specialty occupations and their families, and the L1 is a visa for intracompany transfer.

spouses and children to accompany the young professional/student population. What does accompany these immigrants is the Indian patriarchal, paternalistic system, in which adult male members of the family continue to be the primary wage earners, decision makers, and protectors of the young, women, and the elderly. While a large proportion of immigrant Indian women are highly educated and professional women and who work outside the home, a fact that might suggest their emancipation from tradition, this assumption warrants discussion.

Regardless of the religious and cultural backgrounds of Indian families, perceptions of the role of women in the Indian family have been inculcated into the society through classical literature and throughout Indian civilization, and three pervasive models are prevalent: (1) Sita, the heroine of the *Ramayana,* who provides the feminine ideal of the chaste, self-sacrificing wife (Lebra and Paulson, 1984); (2) the powerful archetype—the Mother—who can be gentle or aggressive but ultimately is the supreme nurturer (Lebra and Paulson, 1984; Thomas, 1984); and (3) the dependent—first on her father, then on her husband, and finally on her son (Sinha, 1984).

India, with its diverse cultures, has always been a country of apparent dichotomies. The most obvious contradiction was reflected in the repeated election of a female prime minister, Indira Gandhi, in a highly patriarchal society. This dichotomy is still evident as one follows the significant and continuing roles women play in the current political environment. Perhaps the contradiction can be understood through alternative perceptions in the twentieth century. Mahatma Gandhi believed that women have stronger moral principles than do men, and Indira Gandhi was convinced that women's problems are associated with poverty, illiteracy, and lack of economic opportunities (Bumiller, 1990). Evident by its absence in the principles of these two prominent and influential political figures in near Indian history is the mention of gender inequality (Bumiller, 1990), especially in the home. Despite the Western belief that women's movements and higher social class increase gender equality (Dhruvarajan, 1993; Goode, 1982; Scanzoni, 1979), this equalization has not occurred in the Indian tradition. Thus, although women may become powerful in the political structure, they are still responsible for upholding the images of Sita/the pure, the Mother/the revered, and the dependent/fragile within the boundaries of the family.

These role models for women and the relationship between the genders persist today both in modern-day India and in the United States. Although many Indian immigrant women are encouraged into higher education by their families, it is frequently more to increase their attractiveness to successful eligible bachelors than to ensure their personal independence. Even though an educated wife increases the social status of a professional man, she is always aware that should she work, her professional responsibilities will always be subordinate to her family obligations. In a study examining the relationship between occupation and sex-role attitudes, findings indicated that there were no differences between homemakers and working women in their views of sex-role expectations, even among those who were aware of the inequities in the traditional role behaviors (Dasgupta, 1986). Indian immigrant families evidenced rigid division of roles, with women being primarily responsible for housekeeping, including cooking, cleaning, and child care, and men fulfilling the role of the primary breadwinner (Dasgupta, 1992). Dasgupta (1992) reported in her in-depth qualitative study that 80 percent of the women reported that their most important activities were to care for their husbands and children by cooking for them and "keeping the house," while the majority of the men felt their responsibility was to protect and provide for their families and make major family decisions in areas such as the children's education, home and car purchases, and family vacations.

Traditionally, especially among the middle classes, finances related to the maintenance of the home and the family have generally been managed by the women. Nevertheless, contrary to the belief that "money is power," Indian women are not the decision makers on major issues within the family. They may have input into decisions but generally defer to the will of the man. Interestingly, however, in the absence of a strong extended family network and domestic help, both of which are the norm for this socioeconomic group in India, Indian men in the United States are likely to help with the care of the children and with some of the household chores (Dasgupta, 1992). Nevertheless, as the term *help* implies, these are still clearly women's areas of responsibility. Across the board, both male and female respondents in Dasgupta's (1992:476) study concurred that

> the "ideal husband" . . . is friendly, understanding, affectionate, humorous, smart, educated, cooperative, a good companion, unselfish, a good provider and mild natured. . . . [the] `ideal wife' . . . is a good mother, understanding, supportive, a good homemaker, friendly and self-sacrificing. She . . . can share her husband's work, can take care of everybody and look after the well-being of the family.

Although the allocentric value orientation is clearly evident in role expectations for both men and women, it is worth noting that the term used by both genders to describe the ideal behavior for men is *unselfish,* while for women it is *self-sacrificing.*

While traditional male–female patterns persist in the immigrant generation, the patriarchy experiences considerable turmoil as the second generation reaches adolescence and adulthood. Whereas teenagers in India mature in a protected, unidirectional environment, their Indian counterparts in the United States grow up in a dual culture. Indian youth in the United States are faced with a critical need to establish their identities—not only in terms of moving into adulthood but also in determining their identity within the Indian and American cultures. Many of these children, and their parents, experience a turbulent adolescent period as a result of these conflicts (Segal, 1991).

Depending on the degree to which immigrant parents are willing or able to assimilate Western values, the second generation faces considerable value conflict, role conflict, and role discrepancies, often resulting in role partialization (Merton, 1957) during the adolescent and young adulthood phases of development. Especially because the parent generation retains traditional values and attitudes and is unaware of the conflict their children experience, it continues to exert pressure toward conformity (Saran, 1985*).*

Literature suggests that adolescents generally conform to their peer culture in lieu of parental norms (Blos, 1979; Segal, 1991; Seltzer, 1982). In a given society, the cumulative effect of parental/peer cultures provides continuity and impetus to the cultural evolution of society. However, when parents and peer group originate from different cultures, this continuity is often dramatically disrupted, giving rise to major intrafamilial conflict. Segal (1991) reports that at least five issues are identified by both parents and children as causing emotional difficulty within the family: control, communication, marriage, prejudice, and expectations of excellence.

1. ***Control.*** Many immigrant Indian parents do not recognize the ability of their children to make sound judgments and view their children's desire for independent decision making as cultural contamination that will eventually result in deviant behavior. To the children, this conflict represents a power struggle to which many respond with rebellion, verbal retaliation, or passive-aggressive behavior. Many exercise their freedom away from home, reinforcing their parents' fears of the adverse effects of independence.

2. ***Communication.*** Communication is often poor between the first and second generations. It tends to be unidirectional, flowing from parent to child, with the expectation that the latter will listen, attend, and agree. Children usually do not share personal concerns as they believe that parents will not listen, understand, or help. Both parents and children are cognizant of the poor communication between them.

3. *Marriage.* The major area of conflict appears to center on the relationship between young men and women. For the majority of Indian immigrant parents, marriages were arranged by their respective families. Although there are now some changes in India, dating then was not allowed, and immigrant parents have brought with them the twentieth-century Indian norms. Furthermore, even now, sexuality is not recognized, sex education (both at home and in school) is not available, and premarital sex is abhorrent. When Indian children in the United States seek permission to date, many parents fear dating will lead to sexual involvement. Thus, children who date—with parental knowledge—are the exception.

Parents' greatest fear is that the children will marry non-Indian Americans and thus lose their cultural identity, heritage, values, and mores. In India, people are expected to marry only within their own subculture and subcaste; therefore, the idea of marriage to a non-Indian is especially disturbing. The parents' fears are compounded by perceptions that most American marriages end in divorce.

Concerns about not being allowed to date, on the other hand, culminate in their fear of having a marriage arranged with someone unknown. Because most parents expect their children to marry Indians and the availability of partners in the Indian community in most cities in the United States is limited, arranged marriages are encouraged. However, to children reared in a country where individuals select their own spouses, thoughts of arranged marriage are alien and distressing.

4. *Prejudice.* Most first-generation Indians socialize only with other Indian immigrants. While they are well integrated with the dominant American society professionally, they tend to have few non-Indian friends. Consequently, prejudicial notions about American culture have had little opportunity for rectification. This lack of integration (Table 16.2) into American society suggests segmented assimilation (Portes and Zhou, 1993) and raises some important issues: Are Indians responding to underlying discrimination? Is American culture

TABLE 16.2 Areas of Non-integration

	Parental Preference	Family's Coping Strategy
Food	Indian, vegetarian	Two menus: Indian for parents, American for children
Clothing	*Sari, salwar kameez*	Parental garb: professional—Western; social—Indian; children's garb—contemporary American
Religion	Primarily Hinduism, some Islam	Organization of Hindu religion and practice in temples (normally, not an organized religion)
Language	Hindi or one of the numerous Indian languages	Poor mastery of Indian language by children; English primary in home
Friendship	Indian, preferably with those from the same region in India	Parents—minimal social contact with Americans; children—significantly more American friendships
Entertainment	Movies, eating out, dinner parties	Primary entertainment—large dinner parties with other Indians; children often excuse themselves

Source: Segal (1991).

so alien that distance is necessary to avoid contamination? Does retention of Indian culture supersede other factors? Whatever the parental reasons, children often view their parents as narrow minded and may respond by developing negative attitudes toward Indian culture.

Prejudicial attitudes of both parents and children create additional barriers to effective communication, making cross-cultural adjustment more difficult. In rural areas, because the Indian community is small, Indians must interact more with their American counterparts, allowing for the removal of some intercultural barriers.

5. ***Expectations of excellence.*** As a result of the high selectivity in immigration criteria, a large majority of Indians in the United States are professionals and high achievers. This "model minority" image is upheld as a standard for Indian youth. Success is expected because the behavioral norm is that "all Indians do well." However, unlike their parents, Indian children are not necessarily achievement driven. Although some may be outstanding in their performance, most will be average and a few will fail. Since perfection and excellence are expected, many average achievers perceive themselves as failures and experience low self-esteem. Moreover, these children may not receive intervention because seeking professional help is considered a sign of weakness and disgrace.

Despite these intrafamilial conflicts, inherent strengths within the family often support Indian children during critical periods. Most adolescents feel that despite the control exercised by their parents and the lack of communication, because of the training and guidance of parents they are firmly grounded in basic human values. Many have an unshakable confidence that their ties with the family are stable and permanent (Segal, 1991).

Demographic Characteristics of the Family

Data of the American Community Survey (2008) support the contention that the Indian lifestyle and philosophy are highly centered around the integrity of the family. Only 3.7 percent of Indian families in the United States have no husband present, and only 0.4 percent of Indian households consist of unmarried, or cohabiting, partners. Fertility rates in the United States appear to differ from those in India. While the majority of lower-class families in India may have large families of four or more children (Segal and Ashtekar, 1994) and the upper and middle classes may be limiting the number of their children to one or two (Segal, 1995), the norm of the Indian family in the United States appears to be two or three children. Perhaps this trend is an offshoot of family planning efforts in India in the 1970s and 1980s, when many of the first generation came to the United States and had as their slogan "*Do, ya theen bachchen, bus*" ("Two or three children are enough"). Younger generations of new immigrants seem to be having no more (but no less) than two children. Once again, concerns about family relationships may guide this decision. In India, relationships between first cousins are often as close as those of siblings. In the United States, where the support of extended families may not be readily accessible, most Indian families feel it important to ensure that their children have siblings to whom they can turn when they are adults and their parents are no longer living. Interestingly, the 2008 American Community Survey indicates that while 47,901 women of Indian origin gave birth in the twelve months preceding the survey, 1,563 of these (3.3 percent) were to unmarried women.

There appear to be no large-scale studies of the Indian population in the United States or representative data on the rates of marriage and/or divorce, yet observation suggests that marriage continues to be the preferred choice of lifestyle among Indians, and parents encourage their children (especially women) to marry while they are in their twenties. Most first-generation Indians, regardless of when they arrive in the United States, bring their spouses and children with them or return to India to marry according to family tradition. Therefore, changes in marriage patterns become most evident among the second generation of Indians. In India, partner preference is for someone from the same subgroup as oneself (culture, religion, region, caste). Ideally, parents in the United States would also select such Indian partners for their children, but because of limited choices they are likely to accept a partner from any Indian subgroup.

The actual choice of marriage partner is significantly affected by the process of mate selection permitted by parents. Oommen (1991) suggests that it is imperative not only to examine the family from without as part of a cultural tradition governed by society's norms, but also from within to understand its internal dynamics based on individuals' experiences and their psychosocial characteristics. Thus, while arranged marriages may be the norm, based on their own experiences and the extent to which they have accepted alternative options families may, or may not, opt to engage in the process of arranging marriages for their children.

If, consistent with tradition, an arranged marriage is expected by the first generation for its children, the family may follow a few established routes to the identification of a potential partner. The marriage partner may be sought either in the United States or in India, and parents inform their friends and family members that they are seeking a spouse for their child. They specify characteristics that may be important to them. In addition to looking for someone of the same subgroup, they may specify age, profession, food preference, interests, height, and even complexion of skin. In addition, parents may advertise in the matrimonial sections of any of the several Indian newspapers in the United States such as *India Abroad,* which has the widest circulation. Matrimonial websites such as www.Shaadi.com, www.iMilap.com, and www.Jeevansathi.com are becoming increasingly popular as young people are turning to them as links to other Indian singles contemplating marriage. The traditional arranged marriage occurred sight unseen between the couple; in the modern arranged marriage, however, both in India and the United States, appropriate potential partners are encouraged to meet and get to know each other. "Getting to know each other" is left to the discretion of the family, and the length of time, the frequency of contacts, and other details are based on the personal preferences of the particular family. Regardless of parental hopes, the man and woman can usually now decide whether they are suited for marriage.

The alternative is a "love" marriage, in which the couple meets, is attracted, and decides to get married after having established a relationship and engaging in an American-style courtship. Marriage partners are selected by the children themselves, and increasing numbers of parents are beginning to accept that if they choose to live in this country, such "love" marriages may be inevitable. Despite parental partiality toward an Indian spouse for the child, there is evidence of a rise in the number of intermarriages between Indians and Americans. This should not be surprising because second-generation children are in constant contact with non-Indians and, though they do have Indian peers, the choice of partners is relatively limited.

Observation over the last thirty years has revealed two interesting patterns: (1) Often second-generation Indian men will date American women, yet they will marry Indians—either those they have met and courted in the United States or those with whom their marriages have been arranged either in the United States or in India, and (2) frequently, second-generation Indian women will date American men and then marry them. It remains to be determined whether the men are more susceptible to the expectations of their parents or whether they perceive marriage to an Indian more consistent with familiar patterns and necessary to maintain traditional role relationships within the family.

Further observations on intermarriage suggest that, in general, Indian men who marry American women either assimilate into Western society or, alternatively, integrate their wives into the Indian ethnic group. Indian women, on the other hand, tend to balance the unique qualities of both cultures. Perhaps this is a function of the differing family relationships and norms. In Indian culture women are expected to leave their families of origin and become a part of the husband's family (Mullatti, 1995), whereas in American culture the woman's family maintains a strong presence even after the marriage. For Indian men, tradition may indirectly dictate that he integrate his wife into his family; if he is unable to fulfill this expectation, he might find it necessary to separate himself from his family. The Indian woman, however, who is socialized to compromise while taking care of her husband, may find the differing cultural expectations a surprisingly pleasant compromise as she participates in her husband's family but also has the option of including him in her own. The few studies that have addressed tradition and role relationships among Indians in the United States have focused on the immigrant generation. The time is ripe to study the experience of the second generation and the extent to which it has adopted, adapted, and/or rejected tradition.

One of the major concerns of Indian parents about intermarriages is an outgrowth of the fact that half of all marriages in the United States end in divorce within the first two years. In India, there is a general acceptance that divorce should be legally available (Desai, 1991); it is also believed to be objectionable (Chouhan, 1986; Singh, 1988), and a divorced individual, especially a woman, is highly stigmatized regardless of whether or not the divorce is based on mutual consent (Amato, 1994). Further, because a woman is expected to be self-sacrificing and devote herself entirely to her husband, people are inclined to blame the termination of the marriage on the wife (Kumari, 1989). Although both men and women receive emotional support from their respective families following marital separation, women are usually likely to receive less support than men from other sources (Amato, 1994). Divorced men are able to overcome the stigmatization, and it is often possible for them to remarry, while a divorced woman is often isolated and rarely remarries. There is a paucity of updated literature on divorce in India, which is becoming much more common in the twenty-first century; however, immigrant Indians may still adhere to the traditions of a time when they emigrated.

Given the perceptions of divorce and the future for the divorced person, the concerns that Indian parents voice about divorce rates in America are understandable. However, there are no indicators that intermarriages in the United States between second-generation Indians and Americans are ending in divorce any more frequently than marriages between Indians. Perhaps, therefore, the worries of parents may be unfounded. It is possible that those individuals who intermarry are more cognizant of potential problems and difficulties arising out of conflicting cultural expectations and, consequently, invest more effort in compromise and adaptation.

Extended Family Relationships

The extended/joint family system is the norm in India, but the familial structure favored by Indians in the United States is that of the nuclear family living in separate households. With changes in immigration laws and the naturalization of many Indians has come the sponsorship of family members, many of whom have been unmarried siblings or aging parents. While unmarried siblings initially reside with the sponsoring family, they soon establish themselves in separate households, either living alone or with other individuals. Even if they do remain with the family during their single years, they move as soon as they marry (Saran, 1985). Thus, it is rare to find two or more families living within the same dwelling. However, many make their residences in the same city or geographical area to maintain proximity to the family. There appear to be no studies that examine the size of the Indian population with extended family in the United States, although at least 9.3 percent of Indian households report the presence of relatives other than parents and children (American Community Survey, 2008), and it is rare to find an Indian in the United States who does not have at least one relative who has settled there.

Aging parents, often widows or widowers, compose another group that has come to join its children in the United States. These parents live with the immigrant generation, often making their home with the family of the eldest son, but travel between the residences of their children and spend extended periods of several months in the home of each. If both parents are alive, they may visit their children in the United States for four to six months at a time every few years, but most choose not to uproot themselves because there is little to occupy them in the United States. Furthermore, most find they are too dependent on their children, financially, socially, and for their transportation. Nevertheless, once they are widowed, and if most of their children are in the United States, they frequently emigrate from India. While they become an integral part of the family, their position of dependence and their lack of knowledge about Western society often obligates them to renounce their authority. Thus, although they retain their status and are told of decisions, they are only perfunctorily consulted. Since, increasingly, immigrant wives are working outside the home, most elderly parents—especially women—assume many of the household responsibilities. They provide child care, prepare the dinner before the family returns in the evening, and assume some of the lighter housekeeping duties. On the whole, however, since they lack a peer group, transportation, and an understanding of the culture, they are often isolated, alienated, and depressed.

Ties with other relatives, such as aunts, uncles, first cousins, and more distant cousins, are nurtured by Indian immigrants in order to maintain continuity and a sense of the family community. Families may travel to meet for festivals, important celebrations, rites of passage, and vacations; despite distances, traditional, extended family role relationships between family members are generally maintained. In addition to defining role relationships, the extended family provides financial, emotional, and social support to its members. Younger siblings, their spouses, and their children continue to consult older siblings, and younger generations are expected to show respect toward older generations through actions and words. Although it is understood that the immigrant family will support the parental generation, first-generation immigrants have fewer expectations that their own children will care for them as they age, and many are beginning to plan retirements without dependence on their children.

Although Indians have a strong sense of community and unite to maintain and transmit culture and values (Dhruvarajan, 1993), the ties with the community are limited to intense social contacts and are not associated with affective ties or long-term help (Dasgupta, 1992), which are an integral part of the relationship with the extended family. Thus, although the Indian community provides social interaction for its members as well as short-term mutual help in times of emergencies, death, and childbirth, there is little provision for long-term support. Consequently, when possible, Indian immigrants nurture relationships with extended family members; despite their dispersion throughout the United States, it is the extended family that provides the necessary ongoing emotional support and important affective ties.

Maintenance and Transmission of Culture

Although India is a multicultural country, it seems that certain patterns underlie all its cultures. The transmission of culture and values is inextricably interwoven with religious affiliation, and Indians define themselves simultaneously as Indian, as affiliated with a particular religion, and as belonging to a specific region of India. Religion prescribes not only the form of worship but also guides daily behavior, while the region usually identifies the language one speaks; the literature, art, and music one enjoys; the food one eats; and the clothing one wears. In the United States, if the community of Indians is small, it is united by its Indian heritage. As the community grows, it subdivides socially along regional and religious (Table 16.3) lines and also develops its own subgroup organizations for the maintenance and transmission of culture.

TABLE 16.3 Religions of India

Religion	N Percent[a]	Origination	Text	Fundamental Principle	Philosophy	Some Important Occasions
Hinduism	80.5	1500 B.C.	Vedas	A philosophy of life guided by Karma and Dharma	Cyclical nature of life, time. Good deeds result in a better rebirth, eventual release from rebirth and reunion with God.	Holi, festival of spring; Diwali, festival of lights honoring King Rama; Deshera, worship of Devi, goddess of Pantheon.
Islam	13.4	A.D. 570–632	Koran	Surrender to the will of God. God's functions: creation, sustenance, guidance, judgment.	Reforming the earth to benefit humanity, not self. Duties of profession of faith, prayer, alms giving, fasting, pilgrimage.	Muharram, day of mourning; Bakr Id, commemorating Abraham's obedience to God; Ramzan Id, feast following a month of daylight fasting.
Christianity	2.3	A.D. 3–30	Bible	Love of God and man	Call to discipleship and service. Ultimate reunification with God.	Christmas, birth of Christ; Good Friday and Easter, Christ's martyrdom and resurrection.
Sikhism	1.9	1469–1539	Adi Granth	Fuses elements of Hinduism and Islam—unity, truth, creativity of God and surrender to his will.	Advocates active service. Belief in transmigration and Karma, union with God through meditation.	Holi; Diwali; Baisakh, date of foundation of Khalsa—militant religious order; Gurupurab, birth of first and last Gurus.

TABLE 16.3 (*Continued*)

Religion	N Percent[a]	Origination	Text	Fundamental Principle	Philosophy	Some Important Occasions
Buddhism	0.8	563 B.C.	Tripitaka	The understanding and management of suffering	Management of human existence—material body, feelings, perceptions, predisposition and consciousness.	Buddha Jayanthi, Buddha's birth (only holiday recognized by Government of India).
Jainism	0.4	599–527 B.C.	Oral	Actions of mind, speech and body result in bondage and violence.	Eschew violence, free the soul. Better suffer injury than cause it.	Diwali; Mahavir Jayanthi, birth of Mahavir; Paryushana, end of rains and request for forgiveness.
Others (Judaism, Zoroastrianism, tribal religions)	0.6					

[a] The source for this data is Government of India (2001).

Indian culture is transmitted in various ways: (1) within the home, through the family, which often maintains strong Indian practices in role relationships, eating patterns, preferred music, and language; (2) through religious organizations or groups that meet in places of worship such as temples, mosques, churches, gurdhwaras, or individuals' homes; and (3) through formal classroom instruction on the history of the country and the religion, on language, and on literature and mythology. Female children are often enrolled early in dance classes because Indian girls traditionally have been expected to be trained in the dance, music, and song of the country. Boys, on the other hand, are generally exempt from initiation into this aspect of the culture, although an occasional child may learn to play an Indian instrument.

Major Indian artists, usually musicians and actors, often tour cities in the United States with large enough numbers of Indians to sponsor them. In addition, Indian movies often are shown in theatres around the country, and most cities with an Indian population usually have grocery and retail stores that serve Indian consumers. These stores also carry a very wide range of Indian movies, plays, and music on compact discs and DVDs. Second-generation children frequently accompany their parents to Indian social and cultural events and are usually exposed to Indian movies in the home—all of which contribute to the transmission of the culture.

Indians are also involved in ongoing community events that might be secular or nonsecular in nature. The secular celebrations take place on India's Independence Day (August 15) and on its Republic Day (January 26), when the country was formally established as an independent republic. These celebrations are often accompanied by music, dances, songs, plays, food, and fairs in which children either participate or assist. Since the large majority of Indians are Hindus, not only in India but in the United States, Indian community organizations tend to celebrate Hindu festivals such as Holi (a festival of spring) and Diwali (the festival of lights), while Indians of other religions (Muslims, Christians, and Jews) celebrate their nonsecular festivals with non-Indians of similar religions.

Transmission of Values

In addition to concerns about the transmission of culture, Indian immigrants are anxious to ensure that the second generation internalizes Indian values, many of which are allocentric and have been discussed previously in this chapter. The transmission of these values is also embodied in child-rearing patterns, reactions to dating, recognition of sexuality, acceptance of cross-cultural friendships, and emphasis on education.

Child rearing is primarily the responsibility of the mother, although discipline is often enforced by the father (Segal and Ashtekar, 1994). Infants and young children are usually overindulged; they are pampered, coddled, and allowed freedom in movement and behavior. As they reach middle childhood, they are expected to "be seen and not heard," and must be a source of honor and pride to their families through their appearance and their actions. Corporal punishment is acceptable discipline and, since it is still generally sanctioned even in the United States, is quite likely to be used by Indian Americans.

Children are an integral part of the Indian family unit in the United States; it is rare for social activities to exclude children. Almost all Indian gatherings and private parties are family occasions (Dasgupta, 1992); in the few instances when children are not invited, a significant number of families arrive with their offspring anyway. Furthermore, not until children are old enough to be away with their own friends does the parental couple go out on its own. It is unclear whether this practice arose because the family feels it is important to include children to socialize them or whether it is through a sense of protectiveness. This pattern is very inconsistent with the norm in India where children are often left at home with extended family members or domestic help while parents participate in social activities. It is less common to find an Indian American family that leaves its young children with babysitters, unless it is for work-related activities.

In addition to ensuring that children are exposed to Indian culture, parents are eager to ensure that children avail themselves of as many American extracurricular opportunities as possible, perhaps because these were not available as they, themselves, were growing up in India. Consequently, most Indian children participate on sports teams, learn musical instruments, engage in academic competitions, and enroll in additional enrichment programs. In high school, many are encouraged to participate on forensics and debate teams, assume leadership roles in the school's student council, and become a part of the larger community.

Despite the fact that most Indian immigrants have few American friends and encourage friendships between their children and other Indian children, they still feel it is important that their children receive status and respect in their school environments. As a result, they are becoming increasingly open to their children's friendships with Americans. With these friendships, however, comes the possibility of cultural contamination in the form of parties and dating and the threat of substance abuse and sexual activities.

Although most second-generation children are willing to accept most of the traditions and values of their parents, the most difficult rule for them to accommodate is prohibition of dating. While many American children are dating when they are fourteen and fifteen years old, most Indian children are not permitted to date, particularly if those children are female. Consequently, children often date without their parents' knowledge; when there are difficulties, however, they are unable to turn to the parents for support or guidance. Even if children do not date while they are living at home, they do begin to date when they leave home to attend college. When they do, they find that they are unfamiliar with the rules of the game in which their cohort is fairly adept; they may be more vulnerable and susceptible to abuse by their more experienced partners. This fact should be a cause for alarm for Indian parents, especially with the increasing information about the frequency of acquaintance rape and date rape among teenagers and college students (Hingson, Heeren, Winter, and Wechsler, 2005; Sampson, 2002).

Indians are generally inhibited when it comes to talking about sex and sexuality, especially with children. Sex education in India is unheard of, and in general even the professional group of immigrant Indians finds it difficult to overcome stereotypic responses and discomfort in discussing the subject with its children. Often, given the sex education children receive in school, they may be more knowledgeable on the subject than are some of their parents. The overriding concern of parents is that they must protect their children from becoming sexually active, especially their female children because this taints their purity. In this day of the rapid spread of sexually transmitted diseases, and with the terrifying knowledge that victims of the HIV/AIDS virus are growing rapidly in number among the teenage and young adult populations, precautions are warranted. Nevertheless, in many cases parents do not recognize their children's developing sexuality and the importance of keeping channels of communication open so that children do not find themselves grappling alone with difficult situations.

Since most Indian immigrants to the United States are professional people, a high premium is placed on secular education. In addition to the transmission of culture, this group of Indians stresses the necessity of a college degree, at the minimum. Many independent secondary (private-secular) schools report a disproportionate number of Indian students. Second-generation children are encouraged to study for professions in the medical field, in the sciences, or in business. There is less support for interest in the fine arts, humanities, and social sciences because these are not associated with success. Most Indians came to the United States to improve their quality of life, and this goal now encompasses their children; since professions in the fine arts, humanities, and social sciences are not financially rewarding, these fields are discouraged. Although this is beginning to change, because of the control mechanisms in place in the Indian family and the power of the parent–child relationship, children very often strive to fulfill parental expectations, even in choice of profession.

Thus, consistent with patterns for all immigrant populations (Parrillo, 1991), values are transmitted across generations through the family and through social and cultural organizations. They are modeled by parents as they socialize, discipline, and guide their children. High premiums are placed on the Indian culture, religion, allocentrism, and education. In this context, children are encouraged to be achievement oriented. In essence, segmented assimilation (Portes and Zhou, 1993) is endorsed.

CHANGES AND ADAPTATIONS

Maintenance of Culture

The Indian family, whether nuclear or extended, continues as a strong, viable unit that is cohesive and provides social, emotional, and financial support to its members. It is instrumental in transmitting Indian cultural norms and values to its children. With its increasing numbers, the community is able to consolidate its resources and provide organized vehicles for the transmission of norms and values to the second generation. Furthermore, despite the absence of Indian ethnic enclaves, close ongoing social contact with other Indian families ensures that children develop friendships with other second-generation Indians. Because of the shared experience of growing up in a multicultural environment, these friendships persist and complement friendships with children from other ethnic–cultural groups in American society.

Children of immigrants identify three themes in their expressions of cultural identity (Sue, 1979): (1) their sense of belonging versus estrangement (an increased sense of belonging in American culture results in increased self-esteem), (2) their identification with the new country's cultural values (the accommodation of their culture-of-origin values within the framework of American values provides stability and guidance and enhances the integrative process), and (3) their family and peer relations (to the extent that these are congruent, a synthesized identity emerges).

In urban metropolitan areas, the number of second-generation Indians is significant. Now, more so than in earlier decades, these adolescents and young adults have the option of meeting other Indians of like interests since the pool of potential friends is significantly larger. As they aim to establish their identities distinct from those of their immigrant parents and distinct from that of young immigrants of their own age, they have coined an acronym for themselves—the ABCDs—American-Born Confused *Desi*,[6] clearly indicating the struggle many encounter.[7] A large number weave their way through the process of adolescence by becoming "more American than the Americans" and gradually attempt to balance what they perceive to be the best of both cultures—that is, those elements most amenable to the development of self-esteem and self-identity (Sue, 1973). This attitude is dramatically different from the segmented assimilation perspective (Portes and Zhou, 1993) of the immigrant generation, which is protectionist about its culture while advancing economically.

Contemporary humanists in the dominant American society seek to understand ethnic diversity and multiculturalism and recognize the vast differences in the ethnocultural composition of the country. With the increasing realization that it is impossible for people of color to

---

[6]*Desi* is the Hindi vernacular for an Indian national.
[7]An acronym coined for the first generation is DCBA (*Desi* confused by America).

truly integrate into U.S. society, the country has evolved in its prescriptions for inclusion. The last few decades have seen the move from a belief in the melting pot theory (in which everyone blends into one indiscernible whole), through the salad bowl theory (in which separate groups maintain their differences but mix well with each other), to an understanding of the society as a mosaic (in which groups may be different, at times enmeshed with the dominant society, at other times maintaining a separation from it, preferring to remain with members of their own culture).

With more respect and acceptance accorded to differences, second-generation immigrants may not feel as great a need to reject their cultural heritage. This is apparent in the number of Indian high school students who are beginning to join Indian youth groups in several urban metropolitan areas of the country. In addition to providing social support for each other, these youth often assume responsibility for increasing awareness about the Indian culture among the non-Indian populations in their schools and communities. Much of the Hindu philosophy revolves around fulfilling duties toward family and occupations; on the whole, little emphasis is placed on service to the less fortunate. Nevertheless, many Indian youth groups around the country have also assumed community service activities, suggesting the incorporation of a very positive aspect of the American value system.

Numerous indicators suggest that second-generation Indian Americans continue to be, on the average, relatively high achievers, and most appear to be much more comfortable socially with their American counterparts than are their parents. Thus, they may serve as bridges between American and Indian cultures. With the acceptance of human diversity—and because they can often compete successfully academically, professionally, *and* socially in the dominant culture—increasing numbers are able to truly develop in a dual culture and integrate the superior qualities of both societies.

Race, Ethnicity, and Prejudice

Much of the future of the Indian ethnic group lies in the hands of the dominant culture. Although their numbers are large and they have been in the United States for three decades, Indians remain peripheral to discussions of American culture, experience, or history (Balgopal, 1995). Ironically, the restrictive legislation that permitted immigration of only professional Indians into the United States in the 1960s and 1970s had a beneficial effect for the Indian community: Those Indians who emigrated very rapidly became contributing members of society. Because most were influenced by the British through the Indian educational system, were fluent in English, and had some exposure to Western culture, pseudo adjustments in the United States were relatively easy. Moreover, since over the last five decades they have generally not established Indian enclaves, have not been socially and politically visible, and converse in English with other Indians at their place of work, they are less likely to be perceived as a threat to the status quo of American society. Nevertheless, the unfortunate events of September 11, 2002, and subsequent perceptions of immigrants with a phenotype similar to those of the perpetrators of the terror attacks on the World Trade Center in New York City and the Pentagon in Washington, DC, have made Indian Americans vulnerable to bigotry and hate crimes.

Because little has been understood about their culture, Indians have escaped the ongoing overt discrimination that other Asian groups have experienced in the United States and that Indians have experienced in other countries such as the United Kingdom and Canada. They have made unique contributions to several fields in the United States, and they continue to project a positive image there. Among their ranks are three Nobel laureate, naturalized American citizens of Indian origin: Hargobind Khorana for medicine in 1968, Subrahmanyan Chandrasekhar for physics in 1983, and Venkatraman Ramakrishnan for Chemistry in 2009. Table 16.4 provides a

TABLE 16.4   Some Indian American in the Limelight: 2005–2009

Year	Name	Achievement
2005	Zubin Mehta	Conductor, Opera House of the Ciutat de les Arts i les Ciències, Valencia
2005	Urvashi Vaid	Attorney, community activist, gay rights leader; Executive Director, ARCUS Foundation
2006	Vijay Iyer	Pianist, composer, writer; 2006 Fellow of New York Foundation for the Arts
2006	Indra Nooyi	CEO PepsiCo
2006	Beheruz Nariman Sethna	President of University of West Georgia; first Indian American president of an American university
2007	Bobby Jindal	Governor of Louisiana
2007	Shantanu Narayen	CEO Adobe
2007	Vikram Pundit	CEO Citigroup
2007	S.R. Srinivasa Varadhan	Mathematician, awarded Abel Prize by the Norwegian Academy of Science and Letters
2008	Raj Bhavsar	Gymnast, bronze medal winner with U.S. Olympic team
2008	Brandon Chillar	NFL player for the Green Bay Packers
2008	Sanjay Jha	Co-CEO Motorola
2008	Renu Khator	President of the University of Houston and Chancellor of the University of Houston System
2008	Neel Kashkari	Interim U.S. Assistant Secretary of the Treasury for Financial Stability
2008	Sunita Williams	Astronaut, NASA's Deputy Chief of the Astronaut Office
2008	Fareed Zakaria	Host of "Fareed Zakaria GPS"; Editor, *Newsweek International*
2009	Kiran Ahuja	Executive Director of the White House Commission on Asian American and Pacific Islanders
2009	Anju Bhargava	President Obama appointment on President's Advisory Council on Faith-Based and Neighborhood Partnerships
2009	Aneesh Paul Chopra	Federal Chief Technology Officer of the United States
2009	Sanjay Gupta	Emmy Award-winning chief medical correspondent for CNN; offered and declined position of Surgeon General in Obama administration—the position is still unfilled
2009	Norah Jones (Geethali Norah Jones Shankar)	Bi-racial singer-songwriter—sold more albums than any female jazz musician in the last decade
2009	Vivek Kundra	Federal Chief Information Officer (CIO) of the United States of America
2009	Kal Penn (Kalpen Modi)	Associate Director of the White House Office of Public Engagement
2009	Raju Narisetti	Managing Editor, *The Washington Post*
2009	Eboo Patel	President Obama appointment on President's Advisory Council on Faith-Based and Neighborhood Partnerships

TABLE 16.4 (*Continued*)

Year	Name	Achievement
2009	Rajiv Shah	President Obama appointment as head of United States Agency for International Development (USAID)
2009	Sonal Shah	Head of the new White House Office of Social Innovation
2009	Madhulika Sikka	Executive Producer of "NPR Morning Edition"
2009	Vinai Thummalapally	First Indian American Ambassador; Ambassador to Belize, nominated by President Obama and confirmed by the U.S. Senate
2010	Jhumpa Lahiri	Pulitzer Prize-winning author appointed by President Obama to the President's Committee on the Arts and Humanities
2010	Nikki Haley	Governor of South Carolina, first female Indian American to become governor

list of a small number of notable Indian Americans, in all walks of life, who have made headlines since 2005 through their contributions to mainstream society. Although this list includes some second-generation Indian Americans, the contributions of the many United States-born Indians in all disciplines are too numerous to include here.

With increases in the number of immigrants from India, decreases in the professional and educational levels of relative-sponsored (versus business-sponsored) new immigrants, and increases in the number of Indian-owned businesses, Indian Americans are becoming more visible and separate. The Asian American Hotel Owners Association reported in 2007 that 43 percent of the 47,000 hotels and motels in the country were owned by Indians, with 30 percent of those being independently run and not belonging to a chain (Yu, 2007), and they have been significant contributors to the world of software development and management.

In recent years, with the growth of the Indian community, Indians are beginning to feel a need to participate in the political process. The Association of Indians in America, a national organization focusing on the mainstreaming needs of Indians, was instrumental in the establishment of a separate category for Indian Americans for the 1990 U.S. Census. In addition, as is evident in Table 16.4, increasing numbers of Indians have been elected to political offices, and the Obama Administration has been particularly inclusive in involving minorities among its several appointees.

Because of Indians' greater visibility and activism in the political arena, recent years have seen dramatic increases in anti-Indian sentiment, especially in California, New Jersey and New York, which have the largest Indian populations. In the 1990s, groups emerged that called themselves the "Dot Busters" (in reference to the red *bindi* worn by many Indian women on their foreheads) and engaged in hate crimes[8] against Indians, attacking them in their homes and places of business. On a more subtle level, Indians had long experienced discrimination as they encountered the "glass ceiling," although this is beginning to change as is evidenced in Table 16.4.

Much of the fate of the Indian population and the transmission of its culture may be controlled by the group's level of acceptance by the dominant American society. Indians have proven

---

[8]Acts of violence perpetuated on people because of their race, religion, national origin, or sexual orientation.

their ability to cooperate and contribute to societal functioning; yet they have fiercely guarded their cultural heritage. Increases in overt discrimination will have significant impact on the behavior of second and subsequent generations of Indians. On the whole, the second generation is beginning to forge a new identity that allows it to integrate the best of both cultures and to function satisfactorily in both the Indian and American environments. Prejudice and fear of violence will threaten the synthesis of a healthy identity, and successive generations may reject one or the other culture.

Social Problems, Services, and Informal Support Systems

The high level of success of Indians in the United States, their image as part of the "model minority," and most of the discussion in this chapter obscure the social problems of isolation of the elderly, conjugal violence, intergenerational turbulence (Khinduka, 1992), and poverty (Balgopal, 1995) that are, of course, experienced by significant numbers of Indians. As noted, as the elderly population of Indians, retired and widowed parents of immigrants, arrive in the United States to be supported by the children as dictated by tradition, they find themselves increasingly isolated (Brown, 2009). Without access to financial resources, separated from their peer group and support systems in India, with little understanding of the American culture, with no familiar activities to occupy them, they remain at home while their children and grandchildren pursue their respective occupations. American senior centers are alien to them, and since Indians do not live in ethnic enclaves, access to other elderly Indians is practically nonexistent. Even if access were possible, many elderly may be from different regions and cultures of India, may not speak the same language, and may have little in common with each other.

The isolation of the elderly has received little attention, but the prevalence of conjugal violence among Indians in the United States is increasingly apparent as shelters for battered Indian women are established around the country. Although the highly educated and sophisticated population of Indian immigrants in the United States chooses not to acknowledge domestic violence, the first formal organization to provide protection and assistance to women experiencing conjugal violence, Manavi, was established in New Jersey in 1985. Since then, other agencies have been formed to offer similar services to Indian women in New York (Sakhi), Chicago (Apna Char), Philadelphia (SEWAA), Washington, D.C. (ASHA), Dallas (Chetna), and St. Louis (SAWERA) among others. In Indian culture, as in many others, women and children have been viewed as the property of males, and power has often been operationalized through violence and subjugation. It is surprising that domestic violence is evident in this professional population of Indians but is consistent with literature that suggests that family violence is not culture or class specific and is often evidenced in patriarchies (Dobash and Dobash, 1992).

Since the number of elderly Indians in the United States is still relatively low, since violence against women (and children) is hidden from public view, and since Indians have been most concerned about the enculturation of their children, the major areas of foci within the Indian family have been the behavior of the children and parent–child relationships. Even within these areas, issues that have been addressed are those of autonomy, mate selection, and career choice. There appears to be no information about teen pregnancies, abortion, or sexually transmitted diseases (including AIDS). There is little knowledge of the extent of drug usage or substance abuse, although these are significant problems in India, and while there may be a sizable gay and lesbian Indian population in the United States, as is evident in advertisements of publications in *India Abroad,* the group is not visible.

Indians traditionally have depended on their family networks to provide social, emotional, and financial support. In the absence of these supports, and because seeking help from mainstream or external resources is considered shameful, Indians often struggle in silence. For example, the American Community Survey (2008) reported that the poverty rate for Indian families in 2008 was 5.2 percent, and though lower than the overall rate of 9.6 percent, it is not negligible. Limited income has placed additional burdens and increased the isolation of many such Indian families, who often are not aware of external sources of support and emergency assistance. Balgopal (1988) suggests that since most Indians migrated to improve their economic condition, failure to do so often results in depression, alcohol abuse, psychosomatic problems, marital conflict and even suicide.

Most Indians are loathe to utilize the services of formal human service agencies. Mental health problems often manifest themselves as psychosomatic ailments such as chronic headaches, backaches, dizziness, and weaknesses. Physical ailments are comprehensible for the family, and physicians' services are much more acceptable than are those of mental health care professionals. Increasingly, however, through schools and doctors' referrals, social services and are able to make contact with families experiencing distress (Balgopal, 1995). Most effective, however, is the provision of services that mobilize the family's own resource network in addition to the formal networks of the heath care and social service delivery systems.

Clearly, since the Indian population has projected the image of the model minority, has apparently acclimated itself to its new environment, and has been silent about its needs, the issues and problems it faces are marginalized. Because Indians, like other Asians, prefer to keep concerns within the boundary of the family, they have not sought formal human services even in the absence of traditional informal support systems, including a viable and proximate extended family network. Since they have not come to the attention of mainstream human service agencies, the myth of the model minority is perpetuated, and few researchers in the social and behavioral sciences have seen a need to focus on their experiences, reinforcing the "squeaky wheel" phenomenon. Just as politicians are beginning to recognize that the Indian population is worth courting because of its size and overall economic power, the human service organizations will need to become cognizant of the growing problems and issues facing this population, which, unattended, can also in time impact the larger society.

CONCLUSION

This chapter has traced the experiences of one of the United States' newer and largest immigrant groups, the Indian American, over the last four decades. Perceived as part of the "model minority," this group numbers well over 1 million, is generally highly educated and professional, and has a strong commitment to family and the Indian culture. Major issues with which this group currently struggles are the transmission of culture to the second generation, support of its aging parents, most of whom remain in India, and planning for its own retirement. Indicative of its ties with its homeland, the immigrant generation is contemplating returning to India to retire, especially since it has not truly integrated itself socially into mainstream America. The major barrier to completing the circle of exodus and return to the native land is the realization that its dual-culture second-generation children are more at home in the United States than they would be in India; to maintain contact with them and with their grandchildren (or future grandchildren), the immigrant group will have to remain in the United States. It waits to be seen whether, as a group, this generation of immigrant Indians will find that the benefits of returning to India outweigh the benefits of retiring in the United States, the land that drew them with its promise of economic and professional opportunities.

References

Amato, P. R. 1994. "The Impact of Divorce on Men and Women in India and the United States." *Journal of Comparative Family Studies 25*(2), 207–222.

American Community Survey. 2008. Selected Population Profile in the United States. factfinder.census.gov (accessed April 22, 2011).

Arredondo, P. M. 1984. "Identity Themes for Immigrant Young Adults." *Adolescence 19*, 977–993.

Balgopal, P. R. 1988. "Social Networks and Indian American Families." In C. Jacobs and D. D. Bowles (Eds.), *Ethnicity and Race: Critical Concepts in Social Work* (pp. 18–33). Silver Springs, MD: National Association of Social Workers.

———. 1995. "Indian Americans." In R. L. Edwards (Ed.), *Encyclopedia of Social Work* (19th ed. (pp. 256–260). Washington, DC: NASW Press.

Blos, P. 1979. *The Adolescent Passage*. New York: International Universities Press.

Bouvier, L. F., and A. J. Agresta. 1985, May. "The Fastest Growing Minority." *American Demographics 31–33*. 46.

Brown, P. L. 2009, August 31. "Invisible Immigrants, Old and Left With 'Nobody to Talk To.'" *New York Times*. www.nytimes.com/2009/08/31/us/31elder.html (accessed April 22, 2011).

Bumiller, E. 1990. *May You Be the Mother of a Hundred Sons: A Journey Among the Women of India*. New York: Fawcett Columbine.

Central Intelligence Agency (CIA). 2010, April 7. *The World FactBook*. www.cia.gov/library/publications/the-world-factbook/geos/in.html (accessed: April 22, 2010).

Chandrasekhar, S. 1982. "A History of United States Legislation with Respect to Immigration from India." In S. Chandrasekhar (Ed.), *From India to America* (pp. 11–28). La Jolla, CA: Population Review Publications.

Chatrathi, S. 1985, September 13. "Growing Up in the U.S.: An Identity Crisis." *India Abroad 15*, 2.

Chouhan, I. 1986. *From Purdah to Profession: A Study of Working Women in Madhya Pradesh*. Delhi: B. R. Publishing.

Dasgupta, S. D. 1986. "Marching to a Different Drummer? Sex Roles of Indian American Women in the United States." *Women and Therapy 5*(2/3), 297–311.

———. 1992. "Conjugal Roles and Social Network in Indian Immigrant Families: Bott Revisited." *Journal of Comparative Family Studies 23*(3), 465–480.

Desai, M. 1991. "Research on Families with Marital Problems: Review and Implications." In TISS Unit for Family Studies (Ed.), *Research on Families with Problems in India* (vol. 2, pp. 337–373). Bombay: Tata Institute of Social Sciences.

Dhruvarajan, V. 1993. "Ethnic Cultural Retention and Transmission Among First Generation Hindu Indian Americans in a Canadian Prairie City." *Journal of Comparative Studies 24*(1), 63–79.

Dobash, R. E., and R. P. Dobash. 1992. *Women, Violence and Social Change*. New York: Routledge.

Dutt, E. 1989, October. "Becoming a 2nd Generation." *India Abroad 20*(2), 16.

Goode, W. J. 1982. "Why Men Resist." In B. Thorne (Ed.), *Rethinking the Family: Some Feminist Questions*. New York: Longman Canada.

Government of India. 2001. "Census Data 2001." www.censusindia.gov.in/Census_Data_2001/India_at_glance/religion.aspx (accessed April 22, 2011).

———. 2010. "States and Union Territories." www.india.gov.in/knowindia/state_uts.php (accessed: April 22, 2010).

Hingson, R., Heeren, T., Winter, M. and Wechsler, H. 2005. "Magnitude of Alcohol-Related Mortality and Morbidity Among U.S. College Students Ages 18–24: Changes from 1998–2001." *Annual Review of Public Health 26*, 259–279.

Hoefer, M., N. Rytina, and B. C. Baker. 2010. "Estimates of the Unauthorized Immigrant Population Residing in the United States: January 2009." Office of Immigration Statistics, Department of Homeland Security. www.sph.sc.edu/cli/2009%20unauthorized%20numbers.pdf (accessed April 22, 2011).

Hofstede, G. 1980. *Culture's Consequences*. Beverly Hills, CA: Sage.

Khinduka, S. K. 1992. "Foreword." In S. M. Furuto, R. Biswas, D. K. Chung, K. Murase, and F. Ross-Sheriff (Eds.), *Social Work Practice with Asian Americans* (pp. vii–ix). Newbury Park, CA: Sage.

Kumari, R. 1989. *Women-Headed Households in Rural India*. New Delhi: Radiant Publishing.

Lebra, J., and J. Paulson. 1984. "Introduction." In J. Lebra, J. Paulson, and J. Everett (Eds.), *Work and Women: Continuity and Change* (pp. 1–24). New Delhi: Promilla.

Leonhard-Spark, P. J., and P. Saran. 1980. "The Indian Immigrant in America: A Demographic Profile." In E. Eames and P Saran (Eds.), *The New Ethnics* (pp. 136–162). New York: Praeger.

Lyman, S. 1973. "Red Guard on Grant Avenue: The Rise of Youth Rebellion in Chinatown." In S. Sue and N. Wagner (Eds.), *Asian Americans: Psychology Perspectives* (pp. 22–44). Ben Lomond, CA: Science and Behavior Books.

Mayadas, N. S., and D. Elliott. 1992. "Integration and Xenophobia: An Inherent Conflict in International Migration." In A. S. Ryan (Ed.), *Social* Work *with Immigrants and Refugees* (pp. 47–62). New York: Haworth Press.

Mayadas, N. S., and U. A. Segal. 1989. "Asian Refugees in the U.S.: Issues in Resettlement." Unpublished manuscript, University of Texas-Arlington, Arlington, TX.

Melwani, L. 1994, January 31. "Dark Side of the Moon." *India Today,* 60c–60£.

Merton, R. K. 1957. "The Role-Set: Problems in Sociological Theory." *British Journal of Sociology 8,* 106–120.

Monger, R., and Barr, M. 2009. "Nonimmigrant Admissions to the United States: 2008, Annual Report." Office of Immigration Statistics, Office of Homeland Security. www.dhs.gov/xlibrary/assets/statistics/publications/ois_ni_fr_2008.pdf (accessed: April 22, 2011).

Mullatti, L. 1995. "Families in India: Beliefs and Realities." *Journal of Comparative Family Studies 26*(1), 11–26.

Ogawa, D. 1973. "The Jap Image." In S. Sue and N. Wagner (Eds.), *Asian Americans: Psychological Perspectives* (pp. 3–12). Ben Lomond, CA: Science and Behavior Books.

Oommen, T. K. 1991. "Family Research in India: Issues and Priorities." In TISS Unit for Family Studies (Ed.), *Research on Families with Problems in India: Issues and Implications* (vol. 1, pp. 19–30). Bombay: Tata Institute of Social Sciences.

Parrillo, V. N. 1991. "The Immigrant Family: Securing the American Dream." *Journal of Comparative Family Studies 22*(2), 131–145.

Portes, A., and M. Zhou. 1993. "The New Second Generation: Segmented Assimilation and Its Variants." American Academy of Political and Social Science. *Annals 530,* 74–96.

Ratha, D., Mohapatra, S. and Silwal, A. 2009. "Migration and Remittance Trends 2009. *Migration and Development Brief 11.* siteresources.worldbank.org/INTPROSPECTS/Resources/334934-1110315015165/MigrationAndDevelopmentBrief11.pdf (accessed: April 22, 2011).

Sampson, R. 2002. *Acquaintance Rape of College Students,* Washington, DC: U.S. Department of Justice. www.cops.usdoj.gov/pdf/e03021472.pdf (accessed April 22, 2011).

Saran, P. 1985. *The Indian American Experience in the United States.* New Delhi: Vikas Publishing House, PVT. Ltd.

Sangal, P. 2008. "American Association of Physicians of Indian Origin." PowerPoint presentation. www.aapiusa.org/uploads/files/docs/AAPI_Activities.ppt#352,5,Slide5 (accessed April 22, 2011).

Scanzoni, J. 1979. "Social Processes and Power in Families." In W. R. Burr, R. Hill, F. I. Nye, and I. L. Reiss (Eds.), *Contemporary Theories About the Family* (vol. 1). New York: The Free Press.

Segal, M. N., U. A. Segal, and M. A. P. Niemcyzcki. 1993. "Value Network for Cross-National Marketing Management: A Framework for Analysis and Application." *Journal of Business Research 27,* 65–84.

Segal, U. A. 1991. "Cultural Variables in Indian American Families." *Families in Society 74*(4), 233–242.

———.1995. "Child Abuse by the Middle Class? A Study of Professionals in India." *Child Abuse and Neglect 19*(2): 213–227.

———. 2002. *A Framework for Immigration: Asians in the United States.* New York: Columbia University Press.

Segal, U. A., and A. Ashtekar. 1994. "Detection of Intrafamilial Child Abuse: Children at Intake at a Children's Observation Home in India." *Child Abuse and Neglect 18*(11), 957–967.

Seltzer, V. C. 1982. *Adolescent Social Development: Dynamic Functional Interaction.* Lexington, MA: D.C. Heath.

Singh, K. B. K. 1988. *Marriage and Family System of Rajputs.* Delhi: Wisdom.

Sinha, D. 1984. "Some Recent Changes in the Indian Family and Their Implications for Socialization." *The Indian Journal of Social Work 65,* 271–286.

Sodowsky, G. R., and J. C. Carey. 1988. "Relationships Between Acculturation-Related Demographics and Cultural Attitudes of an Asian-Indian Immigrant Group." *Journal of Multicultural Counseling and Development 16*(3), 117–136.

Sue, D. W. 1973. "Ethnic Identity: The Impact of Two Cultures on the Psychological Development of Asians in America." In S. Sue and N. Wagner (Eds.), *Asian-Americans: Psychological Perspectives* (pp. 140–149). Ben Lomond, CA: Science and Behavior Books.

———. 1979. "Eliminating Cultural Oppression in Counseling." *Journal of Counseling Psychology 23,* 419–428.

————. 1981. *Counseling the Culturally Different.* New York: John Wiley.

Thomas, P. 1984. *Festivals and Holidays of India.* Bombay: D. B. Taraporevala & Sons.

Triandis, H. C., R. Bontempo, M. J. Villareal, M. Asai, and N. Lucca. 1988. "Individualism and Collectivism: Cross-Cultural Perspectives on Self-ingroup Relationships." *Journal of Personality and Social Psychology 19,* 323–338.

U.S. Census Bureau. 1992. "1990 Census of the Population-General Population Characteristics." Washington, DC: U.S. Government Printing Office.

Yu, R. 2007, April 9. "Indian-Americans Book Years of Success." *USA Today.* www.usatoday.com/money/smallbusiness/2007-04-17-indian-hotels-usat_N.htm (accessed April 22, 2011).

17

The African American Family

Dwain A. Pellebon

INTRODUCTION

The African American family as a social system within an ethnic group is complex, dynamic, and varied. Writing a chapter on the African American family is daunting as one examines the massive literature on African American demographics, history, culture, social dynamics, and challenges. This chapter is a focused description of the contemporary African American family using current literature and theory. First, I describe African emergence in the United States and how history impacts current cultural conditions. Current national and regional population data, along with recent migration patterns, are summarized. I look at African American family households demographically in terms of family types, adult presence, marital status, and children. Before discussing African American culture, I define foundational terms necessary to understand the conceptual framework. After these definitions, I devote a significant portion of the chapter to describing several traditional African American cultural features. These provide the bases for describing the African American family system—structure, norms, role, and rules. Finally, I discuss the current influences and social implications of politics, economics, racism, and education on the African American family.

HISTORICAL EMERGENCE IN THE UNITED STATES

Though Africans were present in the territories known as the United States of America for over 250 years, the status and condition of Africans were not significantly different before and after the framers signed the Declaration of Independence in 1776. In a mass and sanctioned exploitation of human capital, Africans were slave property for the benefit of Europeans and European Americans; African slaves provided the labor necessary to achieve their economic goals (Manning and Mullings, 2009a).

Africans experienced slavery's inhumanity at all levels: individual, family, and community. The dominant slave system and its supporters exercised control over any behavior and cultural expression believed contrary or resistant to U.S. economic gain. Slave owners systematically deprived men, women, and children of their physical, psychological, and social well-being unless such qualities were useful for slavery.

The same principles of health and well-being applied to working livestock were applied to slave chattel. One principle of preserving a slave "livestock" was the need for reproduction. One latent, possibly unanticipated, effect of this need was forming family units within the confines of the slave community. According to Blassingame (1972:78–79), the African family did exist and adapt:

> The family, while it had no legal existence in slavery, was in reality one of the most important survival mechanisms for the slave. In his family he found companionship, love, sexual satisfaction, sympathetic understanding of his sufferings; he learned how to avoid punishment, to cooperate with other blacks, and to preserve his self-esteem.

Even with the cruelty and confines of institutionalized slavery, Africans adapted to survive, giving rise to a slave community. Parallel with the imposed slave identity, other social identities were developing as a natural response to a repressive environment. Cultural memories, the desire for relationships, self-protection, anger, retribution, spiritual meaning, and learning to respond to this hostile environment shaped new social identities. With these human characteristics, Africans developed strategies to cope, adapt, and resist. Unavoidable outcomes of repression are informal social structures of family, spiritual expression, and social community. In cooperation with many non-Africans, Africans organized resistance with the vision of social and economic goals based on the belief in their eventual freedom from slavery (Blassingame, 1972; Manning and Mullings, 2009a).

It is important to recognize the remarkable adaptation of Africans to institutional slavery. It is equally important to recognize how historical slavery influences present-day racism and relations between European and African Americans (Manning and Mullings, 2009a). For civilized people to enslave other humans, a negative view of the enslaved population was necessary. According to Bar-Tal (1990), delegitimization justifies mistreating a less powerful out-group. European Americans used three of the five delegitimization methods to reinforce the belief of their innate superiority: group comparison, dehumanization, and trait characterization. In *group comparison*, Europeans juxtaposed themselves to the African, and the noted differences reinforced their existing negative views. Slave owners exploited any contrasts in culture, spirituality, phenotype, and social organization to justify ascribing the term *slave* to the out-group. Europeans used *dehumanization* to present African differences as evidence of inherent inferiority or subhuman characteristics. In more concrete form, *trait characterization* of the out-group characterizes every observable African feature in negative and unacceptable terms. The result is the complete removal of European American empathy for African suffering because of the idea that they were not human beings.

Each ethnic group's history and emergence in the United States provide a foundation for understanding that group's current condition and relative social standing. Most African Americans are descendants of slaves who developed unique cultural worldviews and patterns of adaptation (Carter, 1991). This began with enslavement and continued through post-slavery periods of reconstruction, institutional segregation, the northern migrations of African Americans, and the civil rights movement, and it continues to the present day.

DEMOGRAPHICS

General Population

In 2004, the U.S. population was reported to be 288,281,000, and of that population African Americans comprised 12.5 percent, numbering over 36 million.[1] European Americans totaled

---

[1]This chapter was written just before the 2010 U.S. Census was undertaken, so the 2004 Census and 2009 Census supplements inform this section.

TABLE 17.1   U.S. Population by Age and Ethnicity for African and European American Respondents

	Total Population		African American		European American	
	Number (000s)	Percent	Number (000s)	Percent	Number (000s)	Percent
Both sexes	22,281	100.0	36,121	12.5	57,286	19.8
Under 5 years	19,940	6.9	3,040	8.4	11,288	5.8
5 to 14 years	40,812	14.1	6,388	17.7	24,160	12.4
15 to 24 years	40,652	14.1	5,880	16.3	25,363	13.0
25 to 34 years	39,201	13.6	5,041	13.0	23,900	12.2
35 to 44 years	43,573	15.1	5,403	15.0	29,560	15.2
45 to 54 years	41,068	14.2	4,715	13.0	30,219	15.5
55 to 64 years	28,375	9.8	2,778	7.7	22,048	11.3
65 to 74 years	18,238	6.3	1,604	4.4	14,519	7.5
75 to 84 years	12,850	4.5	1,014	2.8	10,773	5.5
85 years and over	3,571	1.2	257	0.7	3,043	1.6

Note: African American refers to those who identified as Black, African American, Negro, or African on the census survey. *European American* refers to those who identified as White, not Hispanic.

Source: U.S. Census Bureau. 2004. "U.S. Interim Projections by Age, Sex, Race, and Hispanic Origin." www.census.gov/population/www/projections/usinterimproj.

67.5 percent, numbering near 195 million. Other ethnic groups accounted for 19.8 percent and numbered over 57 million people (U.S. Census Bureau, 2006a). Calculating continued population changes, the U.S. Census Bureau projects the 2010 U.S. population has increased to over 308 million. African Americans are estimated to have increased to 13.1 percent; European Americans (not Hispanic) to have decreased to 65.1 percent; Hispanic Americans (of any race) rising to 15.1 percent; and, all remaining ethnic groups totaling 7.6 percent of the overall population (U.S. Census Bureau, 2004).

Returning to the 2004 data, Table 17.1 (U.S. Census Bureau, 2006b) shows cohorts collapsed into age groups with a 10-year age span (e.g., 15–24 years old), with exceptions at early childhood (5 years and under) and older adults (85 years and older). The percentage comparisons are of total population to African Americans to European Americans. Two noteworthy observations are at the youngest and oldest populations. Of people 15 years old and younger, African Americans were a larger percentage (26 percent) of the population compared to European American (18.2 percent). This likely reflects both the higher fertility (U.S. Census Bureau, 2000) and mortality rates (Arias, 2007) of African Americans compared to European Americans.

Based on 2010 estimates, data on sex populations with all ethnic groups combined, females at 51 percent outnumber males (48.9 percent). When looking at ethnicity, sex populations vary across groups. African Americans are the only group with a female majority (13.1 percent) over males (11.9 percent). European Americans are close to even with both females and males at 67.6 percent, with the remaining ethnic groups showing a male majority (20.5 percent) over females (19.2 percent). With a national population percentage of 14.0 percent, Hispanic Americans were the largest ethnic group percentage in the "other" category (U.S. Census Bureau, 2004). Though the differences are not staggering across groups, relative populations by sex and ethnicity may be a critical statistic when one examines the status of African American men. Within the context of a patriarchal society, a small male population within a 13 percent overall ethnic population has social and economic implications about family development.

Migration Pattern

Throughout U.S. history African Americans have had migration shifts. There was a moderate migration northward after the Civil War. In 1879, the planned Kansas Exodus after the reconstruction period showed a historic migration caused by aversive social, economic, and political experience in the post-reconstruction South. In the late nineteenth and early twentieth centuries, data showed shifts in migration from rural to urban areas in the South, North, and West in hopes of finding economic and improvements. In the decades leading up to the 1950s, migration demonstrates various patterns and shows variation; however, the general dispersion pattern continued to the North and Midwest. The far West (California) shows significant population growth of African Americans resulting from the constant migrations (Johnson and Campbell, 1981). By 1970, the U.S. Census reported that 53 percent of African Americans resided in the South, 39.4 percent in the North (including Northeast and North Central), and 7.5 percent in the West (U.S. Census Bureau, 1975).

From 1970 to 2004, there have been notable shifts in African American migration in the United States. Based on census data, African Americans have continued migration from the South, leaving a densely populated North. Of those African Americans living in the U.S. mainland, 37.8 percent remain mainly populated in the South. The northern population has also seen a shift toward the Midwest, with the northeast population reducing from 39.4 percent in 1970 to 24.6 percent in 2004. The Midwest reports have an African American population of 20.3 percent. The population in the West has increased at a lesser rate, from 7.5 percent in 1970 to 9.9 percent in 2004 (U.S. Census Bureau, 2006b). Consistent with the general African American population, within each region African American females outnumber males (see Table 17.2).

TABLE 17.2   U.S. Population by Region, Sex, and Ethnicity

Region and Sex	African American		European American		Other Ethnic Americans	
	Number (000s)	Percent	Number (000s)	Percent	Number (000s)	Percent
Male						
Total	16,794	11.9	95,451	67.6	28,982	20.5
Northeast	3,006	11.6	19,117	73.6	3,837	14.8
Midwest	3,096	9.7	25,555	80.3	23,899	12.2
South	9,115	18.0	32,030	63.4	9,359	18.5
West	1,577	4.8	18,743	56.9	12,598	38.3
Female						
Total	19,327	13.1	99,423	67.6	28,303	19.2
Northeast	3,611	13.0	20,317	73.2	3,815	13.8
Midwest	3,400	10.6	26,561	80.6	2,885	8.8
South	10,510	19.8	33,397	63.0	9,127	17.2
West	1,706	5.1	19,148	57.4	12,476	37.4

Note: *African American* refers to those who identified as Black, African American, Negro, or African on the census survey. *European American* refers to those who identified as White not Hispanic.

Source: U. S. Census Bureau. 2006b. "Population by Sex and Age, for Black Alone and White Alone, Not Hispanic: March 2004." Current Population Survey, Annual Social and Economic Supplement, 2004, Racial Statistics Branch, Population Division. www.census.gov/population/socdemo/race/black/ppl-186/tab21.txt.

African American Family Demographics

This section defines African Americans adults as people 18 years of age and older. The 2009 Census supplement shows over 27 million African American adults with over 9 million family households. Of these adults, 41.9 percent have never married, 40.2 percent are legally married, 11.4 percent are divorced, and 6.5 percent are widowed. The average African American family size is 3.3 persons with 1.19 children under 18 years of age. When collapsing family size into three groups (i.e., 2–3 people, 4 people, and 5 and more people), the two- to three-person family is the largest of all family groups (See Table 17.3). Of all family types, legally married householders are the largest group (46.8 percent), with 50.3 percent having members 18 years of age and younger. However, the married family percentage decreases to 35 percent when subtracting absent and separated spouses. With that adjustment, single female householders become the largest family type (44.4 percent), with 75 percent having members 18 years of age and younger. Male single householders have the smallest family percentage (8.6 percent), with 54 percent having members 18 years of age and younger (U.S. Census Bureau, 2009a). Because African American families may define a family member more broadly than biological children, all household members 18 years and younger are included in the preceding percentages. Based on this data, single-parent female-headed families of two to three people, with children under 18 years of age, are the most typical African American family structures. By approximately 10 percentage points, the two-parent married families of two to three people, with children under 18 years of age, are the next most typical.

Nonetheless, single-parent female-headed households being the most common family structure compared to any other ethnic group does not suggest a cultural resistance to marriage or partnering. McGinnis (2003) found that African Americans are more likely to cohabitate, have lower education, and achieve lower income levels. Despite the higher cohabitation rate, from a cost–benefit perspective African American men perceive fewer negative costs and more benefits to marriage compared to other ethnic males. In separate studies, King (1999a, b)

TABLE 17.3   African American Family Households by Type, Number, and Percentage

Type of Household	Household Number (000s) and Percentage (%)	Household Size			Families with Members 18 Years of Age and Younger (%)[b]
		2–3 people (%)	4 people (%)	5 people (%)	
Married[a]	4,386 (46.8)	59.1	21.5	19.2	50.3
Female head	4,159 (44.4%)	70.5	16.9	12.4	75.1
Male head	912 (8.6%)	80.0	11.4	7.9	54.1
All families	9,357 (100%)	66.0	18.6	15.2	61.6

Note: African American refers to those who identified as Black, African American, Negro, or African on the census survey. *Head* refers to "householder," which is the person designated as the reference person to whom the relationship of all other household members is recorded.

[a] The married category in this table includes both separated and absent spouses.

[b] This percentage includes all family members under age 18, not only the parents' own children.

Source: U.S. Census Bureau. 2009. "Family Households/1, by Type, Age of Own Children, Age of Family Members, and Age, Race and Hispanic Origin/2 of Householder: 2009." Current Population Survey, 2009 Annual Social and Economic Supplement." www.census.gov/population/www/socdemo/hh-fam/cps2009.html (accessed April 28, 2011).

surveyed 172 African American males and 317 African American females, and both samples showed an overall positive attitude toward marriage. King noted age and income effects, showing age and income as being positively related with perception of marriage in both samples. A study of 268 African American college students found the perception of parental marriage satisfaction influenced attitudes; however, high religious commitment positively influences attitudes toward marriage regardless of the parents' experience (Martin, 2003). Sassler and Schoen (1999) studied 393 African Americans and also found that males and females have positive attitudes about marriage. So-called traditional perceptions of gender roles had a differing effect—that is, a positive association between traditional roles and marriage for males and an inverse relation between these variables for females. However, having a positive attitude toward marriage is not a high predictor of marriage. Sassler and Schoen (1999:157) conclude:

> We find attitudes do not account for the large racial differences in marriage rates. Despite a more positive view of how their lives would improve if they were married, Black women are no more likely to wed than White women with equivalent attitudes. Our results suggest that economic variables explain a larger share of racial differentials in marriage rates. Economic uncertainty among Black men even if employed full-time remains a significant facet of the Black experience

MARRIAGE AND PERSONAL EARNINGS. Of the more than 11 million married African American adults, there are more married males (50.6 percent) than married females (48.7 percent). These percentages do not differentiate a spouse's presence in the household. Looking at spousal presence, 33.5 percent of married adults live with a spouse, compared to 6.7 percent of married adults without a spouse (separated and absent combined) in the household (U.S. Census Bureau, 2009a).

The role of personal earnings is one economic variable that may influence marital status (Table 17.4). With personal earnings collapsed into three range groups ($0 to $24,999; $25,000 to $74,999; and $75,000 and over), and comparing married African American females living with a spouse to those with an absent spouse, the percentage of females living with a spouse was much higher at every earnings level: $24,999 and less (77.3 percent); $25,000 to $74,999 (82 percent); and $75,000 and above (93 percent). Looking at the same comparison of married African American males, the percentages of males living with a spouse were even higher: $24,999 and less (81.3 percent); $25,000 to $74,999 (90.9 percent); and $75,000 and above (96.2 percent). These percentages indicate that a vast majority of African American married couples live in one household, and those percentages increase with higher personal earnings.

These are much higher percentages of married couples in comparison to households with absent spouses. However, when only looking at married households with a spouse present, male and female differences emerge that may be related to personal earnings. With their personal earnings below $25,000, a higher percentage of females (58.3 percent) lived with a spouse compared to males (44.3 percent). With their personal earnings between $25,000 and $74,999, a higher percentage of males (44.5 percent) lived with a spouse compared to females (37 percent). At the latter earnings level, the female percentage was lower by 21.3 percent compared to a male percentage increase of less than 1 percent. With their personal earnings at $75,000 and above, again a higher percentage of males (11.1 percent) lived with a spouse compared to females (4.6 percent). These data suggest the likelihood that a female having a spouse in the household may be influenced by her personal earnings. In contrast, the likelihood of a female spouse in the household may be less influenced by male earnings until it reaches above $75,000. (See Table 17.4.)

TABLE 17.4 Personal Earnings of Married African Americans by Sex: 200

	Married Adults (18 Years and Older) with Spouse Present							Married Adults (18 Years and Older) with Spouse Absent						
	Males		**Females**					**Males**		**Females**			
Personal Earnings	**Number (000s)**	**Percent (%)**	**Number (000s)**	**Percent (%)**			**Personal Earnings**	**Number (000s)**	**Percent (%)**	**Number (000s)**	**Percent (%)**
$0.00–$24,999	2,040	44.3	2,554	58.3			$0.00–$24,999	469	45.8	748	67.7
$25,000–$74,999	2,049	44.5	1,620	37.0			$25,000–74,999	204	19.9	333	30.1
$75,000 and over	513	11.1	202	4.6			$75,000 and over	20	1.8	15	1.3
Total	4,601	100.0	4,376	100.0			Total	1,022	100.0	1,104	100.0

Note: African American refers to those who identified as Black, African American, Negro, or African on the census survey. Of the total African American married adult population, those living in a household with a spouse is 33.5 percent, those without a spouse (by separation and absence) in the household is 6.7 percent.

Source: U.S. Census Bureau. 2009. "Marital Status of People 15 Years and Over, by Age, Sex, Personal Earnings, Race, and Hispanic Origin, 2009 Current Population Survey, 2009 Annual Social and Economic Supplement." www.census.gov/population/www/socdemo/hh-fam/cps2009.html.

Looking only at married households with an absent spouse, other male and female differences emerge that may be related to personal earnings. With their personal earnings below $25,000, a higher percentage of married females (67.7 percent) had absent husbands compared to married males (45.8 percent) with absent wives. With their personal earnings between $25,000 and $74,999, again a higher percentage of married females (30.1 percent) had absent husbands compared to married males (19.9 percent) with absent wives. At that higher level of earnings, both female and male percentages of not having a spouse at home lowered—by 37.6 percentage points for females and 25.9 percentage points for males. With their personal earnings at $75,000 and above, again a higher percentage of males (1.9 percent) had absent wives compared to females (1.3 percent) with absent husbands. These data suggest that for both males and females the percentage of absent spouses may be inversely related to personal earnings.

Numerous variables, of which income is one, influence family structure and choices to remain with a married spouse. Because the highest percentage of females were in the lowest personal earning range, a focus on married women's participation in the labor force may provide some insight. Specifically, could lower participation rates in the labor force influence marital choices? I looked at 2008 Census data of African American women whose total family income was less than $25,000 and compared those who were in the paid labor force to those who were not in the paid labor force (U.S. Census Bureau, 2009b).

Of all married African American females, those with total income less than $25,000 who participated in the labor force were 6.0 percent compared to 28.1 percent who did not participate in the labor force. Considering the low total income, I assert this labor participation disparity is not by choice. Therefore, unemployment places women in an economic disadvantage regarding choices related to adult relationships: marriage, remaining married, cohabitation, or remaining single. When doing the same comparison only among families with less than $25,000 income, 69.5 percent of those married women did not participate in the labor force (U.S. Census Bureau, 2009b). Female unemployment may partially explain the inverse relationship between female income and having a husband present in the household.

SINGLE HOUSEHOLDS AND PERSONAL EARNINGS.   A majority of African American adults are unmarried, or married without a spouse present, compared to married adults who live together. Of the over 16 million unmarried (widowed, divorced, and never married) adults, there are more unmarried females (57.8 percent) than unmarried males (42.1 percent). There are over 11 million never married adults (41.9 percent), of which 43.3 percent are male and 40.7 percent are female. However, there are 15 percent more females in a single status of some type compared to males (U.S. Census Bureau, 2009c).

Unlike the previous comparison where married couple households far outnumbered those with absent spouses, single adults far outnumber married persons living as couples. Males and females are proportionally similar within the three personal earning ranges. With their personal earnings below $25,000, the percentage of single females (72.5 percent) are 2 percentage points higher than males (70.5 percent). With their personal earnings between $25,000 and $74,999, the percentage of single males (26.9 percent) is slightly higher than single females (25.2 percent). With their personal earnings at $75,000 and above, again the percentage of males (2.5 percent) is slightly higher than single females (2.3 percent). Most notable is that over 70 percent of all single African Americans are below 133 percent of the federal poverty line for a family of three. Looking within each earning range for an earnings gap by sex, the pattern is similar across all three ranges. Females have a higher percentage at each level; however, the gap narrowed as personal earnings increased. (See Table 17.5.)

TABLE 17.5 Personal Earnings of Single Adult African Americans: 2009

Never Married and Unmarried Adults (18 Years and Older)

| Personal Earnings | Males | | Females | | Sex Totals for Each Earning Range | | | |
	Number (000s)	Percent (%)	Number (000s)	Percent (%)	Totals	Male Percentage	Female Percentage	Sex Earnings Gap
$0.00–$24,999	2,754	70.5	6,718	72.5	11,472	41.4	58.5	17.1
$25,000–$74,999	1,815	26.9	2,336	25.2	4,151	43.7	56.2	12.5
$75,000 and over	171	2.5	214	2.3	385	44.4	55.5	11.1
Total	6,740	100.0	9,266	100.0				

Note: African American refers to those who identified as Black, African American, Negro, or African on the census survey.

Source: U.S. Census Bureau. 2009. "Selected Characteristics of Families by Total Money Income in 2008." Current Population Survey, 2009 Annual Social and Economic Supplement. www.census.gov/hhes/www/cpstables/032009/faminc/new01_006.htm.

AFRICAN AMERICAN CHILDREN.   This section defines African American children as individuals 17 years of age and younger. The 2009 U.S. Census supplement (U.S. Census Bureau, 2009a) shows there were over 11 million African Americans under 18 years of age in the United States. Of those children, 53.6 percent lived with a single mother (50.2 percent) or single father (3.4 percent) without another parent. The second-largest percentage of children (38.1 percent) lived with two parents in a household. This household could consist of parents of differing combinations in relation to the children. Of these households 91.1 percent were married parents. Looking closer at the children in the two-parent category, 31.0 percent lived with their biological parents (married or not); 4.8 percent had one biological parent and one stepparent; and 1 percent were children of adoptive parents. In addition, 3.3 percent lived with a single father who may or may not have been living with another adult. The remaining 8.3 percent of children lived in a family without either biological parent. (See Table 17.6.)

Grandparents are the most prominent non-parent relative living with households with children. Therefore, I looked at grandparents' presence in homes with children along family type and income. Of children living with a single mother, grandparents (one or both) were present in 15.1 percent of the families, and the grandparent(s) were the householder(s) in 65.1 percent of those families. With children living with both parents, grandparents (one or both) were present in 3.5 percent of the families, and the grandparent(s) were the householder(s) in 30.6 percent of those families. With children living with a single father, grandparents (one or both) were present in 13.8 percent of the families, and the grandparent(s) were the householder(s) in 65.3 percent of those families. Children living with grandparents only were 4.6 percent of the total. When looking at family income, the percentage of present grandparents is higher as the annual income is higher: below $25,000 (11.2 percent); $25,000 to $74,999 (15.2 percent); and above $75,000 (17.5 percent). Based on these data, the majority of African American children are being parented in a never-married single-mother household followed by households with married parents. The most typical African American family is a female householder with two to three persons of which one to two members are children. The next most typical family type is a two-parent family of two to three persons of which one to two members are children (U.S. Census Bureau, 2009d).

TABLE 17.6   African American Children by Presence and Type of Parents

Family Type	Number of Children Under 18 Years of Age (000s)	Percentage of Children Under 18 Years of Age (%)
Mother only	5,644	50.2
Both biological parents	3,485	31.0
Biological parents and stepparent	645	4.8
Grandparents only	513	4.6
Father only	37	3.4
Other relatives only	257	2.3
Nonrelatives only	141	1.3

Note: African American refers to those who identified as Black, African American, Negro, or African on the census survey.

Source: U.S. Census Bureau. 2009. ""Living Arrangements of Children Under 18 Years/1 and Marital Status of Parents, by Age, Sex, Race, and Hispanic Origin/2 and Selected Characteristics of the Child for All Children: 2009" Current Population Survey, 2009 Annual Social and Economic Supplement." www.census.gov/population/www/socdemo/hh-fam/cps2009.html.

TRADITIONAL AFRICAN AMERICAN CULTURE

Analysis of African American Ethnicity

Classifying humans into social groups, such as race or ethnicity, for study is not an academic given. Davis (1997) would suggest that ethnicity is an invalid social construct used to disguise an otherwise varied array of individual personality patterns. Even among those who accept ethnicity and race as valid constructs, there is controversy about approaches used to study African American families (Asante, 2003; Graham, 1999; Hattery and Smith, 2007). Scholars often reference E. Franklin Frazier's (1939) study as the foundational work that identified slavery as the institution which destroyed African family structures. Franklin asserted that slavery had a pervasive and enduring negative effect on the ability of African Americans to establish their own families. Social concerns of poverty, maternal family structures, criminality, and personal pathology were all outcomes that would be enduring patterns.

Following passage of the Civil Rights Act, Moynihan (1965) completed his controversial report of *The Negro Family: The Case for National Action.* This study reported that African American poverty created a culture harmful to behavior patterns, resulting in a weakened family. In response, African American sociologists decided the study applied a culturally inappropriate analysis to understand the African American family (Heiss, 1975; Hill, 1972). In addition, the European American family was an inappropriate basis of comparison (Allen, 1978; Staples, 1971). Afrocentric writers responded even more forcefully with charges of racism and Eurocentric hegemony (Nobles, 1978). Black-strengths advocates believed these scholars did not understand African American family culture, or how these structures are healthy adaptations from African culture within a racist society. However, Wilson (1987) believed the Black-strengths response to the Moynihan report (1965) caused liberal sociologists to minimize their research on African American poverty to avoid racist labels. Wilson suggested that societal structures, job erosion, and the lack of successful African American male role models shaped a socioeconomic underclass.

From the Black-strengths response of the 1970s until today, a significant body of knowledge on African American family culture (Hattery and Smith, 2007; Hill, 1998; McAdoo, 2007; Staples, 1971; Taylor, 2002) and racial/ethnic identity (Cross, 1995; Pellebon, 2000; Phinney, 1990) has continued. This chapter synthesizes prominent ideas from the literature into a summary of the present-day African American family.

CONCEPTUAL FRAMEWORK.   This chapter describes traditional African American culture and family using a systems approach. The systems approach examines interactions and impacts of social systems at all levels of society—micro (individuals and family), mezzo (groups, neighborhoods, organizations), and macro (large communities, society, culture, political movements). This framework assumes these social systems interact and shape one another, creating feedback loops from which each social system dynamically responds (Anderson and Carter, 1999). Such a holistic approach is conceptually suitable to study ethnic families (Julia, 2002), and necessary when describing the African American family (Allen, 1978; Hill, 1998; McAdoo and Younge, 2009).

CONCEPTUAL DEFINITIONS.   According to Sánchez and Loredo (2009), there are two polar tendencies of constructionism—subjective and objective. Subjectivism assumes concepts have no objective reality, but the subject defines a construct's meaning through experience. In contrast, Sánchez and Loredo (2009) assert that objectivism recognizes the existence of social constructs within categories.

Social constructions in this chapter are more philosophically driven by objectivism (e.g., ethnicity, class, and family), whereas others, such as race, are subjective. Several central constructs in the chapter presume to exist in reality, but their meanings are subjective. Therefore, the author's frame of reference defines the terms *majority/minority, race/racial identity, ethnicity/ ethnic identity, acculturation, and family.*

Majority *or minority is a literal reference to an ethnic group's population size and/or power status in the United States relative to European Americans.* Some suggest the term *minority* is inappropriate when applied to African peoples because they are a global numeric majority compared to Europeans (Asante, 2003). While recognizing this point, I accurately use these terms as qualified. Thus, African Americans are both a numeric and power minority in the United States compared with European Americans.

Race *is a socially reinforced, artificial social identity derived from qualifying and classifying humans based on phenotypic differences or ancestral bloodline.* This definition stresses race as an environmentally reinforced social construct. The subject observes objective observable physical features or knows the object's racial ancestry. If one believes race a reality, these observations preserve the belief. Ultimately, race is not an objective reality because there is no logically valid argument to support it (Parrillo, 2006). The biological argument that inheritable phenotypic features are de facto racial categories may appeal to anyone predisposed to the belief. However, the fallacy is exposed when it is noted that greater phenotypic variation exists within racial groups than across groups (Omni and Winant, 1986). Also, racial categories are not stable because they change over time. Despite compelling philosophical and empirical arguments against the notion of race, it remains a belief in the United States. Many believe the dominant group uses race as a tool to preserve power (Hattery and Smith, 2007).

Racial identity *is the affirmation or belief that one belongs to a racial group based on one's perceived possession of racial features and/or ancestry.* Individuals decide the importance of racial identification based on personal beliefs. Subjectivism drives this definition because racial membership is an individual's opinion.

Though racial classification is most commonly based on observable features (i.e., skin color, hair texture, nose shape, bone structure, and body shape), an individual may racially identify without having the ascribed racial features. For example, a New Orleans Creole's phenotypic features may infer a greater genetic contribution of his or her White French ancestors compared with her or his Black African ancestors. Though the person appears White, he or she theoretically has a choice of racial identity: A person can racially identify as White if his or her African ancestry is undisclosed and the person adopts European American culture; inversely, a person can racially identify as Black if she or he accepts and/or discloses African ancestry. Though society pressures racial classification, there are some circumstances in which racial identity is fluid and individually determined.

Ethnicity *(or ethnic identity) is a self-defined identity based on a perceived degree of connection and/or adherence to a culturally defined group's social norms, values, and traditions.* Ethnicity is group identity based on common cultural traditions and practices, rather than phenotypic likenesses (Parrillo, 2006). Of course, there are ethnic groups who have similar features that are distinguishable from other ethnic groups, but culture drives ethnic identification. Nevertheless, many in the United States consider African American ethnicity and race as synonymous. I suggest three social reasons have contributed to the overlap:

1. African and European American cultures existed within institutionalized racial segregation for most of the last two hundred years. One significant difference was that Blacks had to adapt to European American laws and institutions, whereas Whites had no practical reason to adapt to African American culture (Parrillo, 2006). This resulted in two cultural groups structurally separated and upheld by racial category.

2. European American stereotypes of Blacks were so negative, demeaning, and dehumanizing that two latent effects were felt in African American communities. First, a cultural identity was necessary to survive in a racist society. Second, the reactive anger to White hatred influenced many Africans Americans from taking part in European American culture. Such a pervasive attitude served to maintain the already relatively closed boundaries between African and European American cultures. Some believed adopting broad American norms equated psychological Whiteness, rejected African heritage, and/or inferred identification with the oppressor (Ogbu, 2008).

3. European Americans so internalized racist stereotyped beliefs that African Americans meeting mainstream cultural expectations either went unrecognized or were considered exceptions to the rule. A too often expressed comment by European Americans when an African American publicly speaks at his or her education level typifies the point. To remark "He was very articulate" implies a surprising observation, whereas educated European American speakers are well spoken. This is the European American variation of "Blacks being White."

African Americans are not a monolithic group, and all ethnic groups have relative degrees of cohesion and cultural practices among its members. That stated, this chapter identifies those values and family norms in traditional African American culture based on the literature. In addition, these descriptions apply to African American descendants of U.S. African slaves. It is impossible to account for the extensive cultural variation among African immigrants, African-descended immigrants, and African Americans who form families with non-African Americans.

For many of the reasons described, the terms *African American* and *Black* remain interchangeable (Hattery and Smith, 2007). It is equally important to understand that *American* and *White* are interchangeable terms in European American culture. Having *White* as a correlate term for *American* provides a racial frame of reference for the dominant culture to lay claim to Americanism. The logic flows: European Whites founded the United States of America; White colonists forged the original American culture; therefore, immigrants (or subjugated groups with granted American rights) must become cultural Americans. The immigrant acculturation literature seldom discusses the implicit psychological orientation that true Americans are White. This orientation assumes non-White citizens are by default legal, but not cultural, Americans. This cultural pattern explains the second-class treatment of all non-White Americans throughout U.S. history regardless of the ability to adopt dominant cultural practices.

In this chapter, the terms *African American* and *European American* refer to ethnicity, not race. With the understanding that the terms *Black* and *White* are both racial and ethnic, these terms are used for race or racial identity. This deliberate distinction is a literary device to disentangle race and ethnicity.

Cultural Adaptation and Definitions.   Cultural adaptation in the United States is a sociopolitical dynamic between dominant and less powerful ethnic groups. Each U.S. ethnic group's history, unique cultural tendencies, and current intergroup relations interact to shape adaptation strategies. Either U.S. ethnic groups converge with the dominant group, resist identification with European Americans, or cannot integrate into the mainstream (Parrillo, 2006). In Gans's (1997:875) discussion of reconciling two schools of thought on acculturation, he asserted, "if assimilation and acculturation are distinguished, acculturation" will be a more rapid process than assimilation. In other words, acculturation does not need action from the dominant group, whereas assimilation requires dominant group acceptance. As long as the dominant group actively prevents or limits ethnic minority access to American institutional power, learning the dominant culture will always precede, but not ensure, acceptance.

For African Americans, emigration models of acculturation are inadequate to explain cultural adaptation (Taylor, 2002). Park's (1949) theory of an immigrant's full integration and acceptance into a host society does not account for racial construction as a sociopolitical strategy to oppress. With the assumption that African Americans must culturally adapt while facing racial discrimination, a conceptual distinction between acculturation and assimilation emerges. Because race is a social identifier to prevent access to dominant group power, unaccepted racial groups by definition cannot assimilate. The following terms reflect the influence of race to cultural adaptation in the United States context:

Acculturation is the degree an immigrant or ethnic minority person adopts and identifies with the ethnic majority group's culture (language, social norms, values, and traditions). I defined this term from the perspective of an ethnic minority person's adaptation to the dominant culture. Such adaptation is a process on a continuum of acculturation assuming some aspects of European American culture are essential to engage in social systems built by the dominant culture (e.g., schools, legal and political systems).

Enculturation is the degree a person preserves the ethnic identity and practices of one's traditional culture. Enculturation assumes one's ethnic identity as distinct from the dominant culture and other minority ethnic groups. Whether a first- or later-generation emigrant, or descendant of a U.S.-conquered or enslaved ethnic group, cultural difference from the dominant culture is relative. The following section describes how African Americans remain culturally distinct from other ethnic groups. In that context, an enculturated family is one that preserves "traditional" cultural values.

Assimilation is the complete acculturation to another culture so the person is indistinguishable from other members of the new culture. This definition is one of absolute cultural adaptation to a different culture within a given societal context. For example, in the United States assimilation into the dominant culture requires individuals with White features to acculturate and access the social systems commonly used at their given socioeconomic status. This can take place without concern of ethnic discrimination. However, race-based stereotypes restrict African Americans from assimilating into the dominant U.S. culture.

Biculturality is the functional adaptation to a second culture while significantly maintaining the ethnic identity and practices of one's traditional culture within a society. Similarly, *multiculturality is the functional adaptation to more than two other cultures within a society.* These terms are the alternatives to assimilation for African Americans. By these definitions, all African Americans acculturate to some degree because they must interact with the dominant culture at some level. By definition, the bicultural African American effectively participates in both cultures. Three factors shape the balance of enculturation and acculturation in the United States: (1) social access to other African Americans, (2) the need to access predominantly European American institutions, and (3) one's commitment to the African American cultural collective. To reiterate, biculturality or multiculturality does not assume lessened identification with African American ethnicity. Mostly, such acculturation reflects the use of knowledge and methods adopted from the dominant culture for practical reasons. However, theoretically a person could both acculturate to other cultures and reject one's traditional culture. For African Americans, this strategy risks some form of social marginalization.

"Family is a set of people with whom you share social, physical, and/or financial support" *(Hattery and Smith, 2007:11).* This goes beyond the census definitions. It does not reflect the broadest range of people identified as family, but it includes people without qualifying household presence, biological relation, or marriage. Therefore, this definition is suitable in fitting the literature's descriptions of the varied family structures found in African American culture.

African American Cultural Features and Family Tendencies

African American cultural features vary by family and uniquely interact to influence acculturation (Scott, 2003). Eight prominent African American cultural features and tendencies are described in this chapter: the cultural collective, ethnic socialization and pride, prominence of motherhood, firm child-rearing strategies, social justice orientation, stylistic cultural expressiveness, assertive communication, and spirituality. Though other ethnic groups share similar cultural tendencies, it is how these features interrelate that makes them uniquely African American (Scott, 2003).

CULTURAL COLLECTIVE.   *The cultural collective is a functional network of people based on their shared views of history, culture, group experience, and struggles in a social environment of prejudice, discrimination, and socioeconomic disparities.* These beliefs create informal kinship networks at the interpersonal, family, community, and societal level (Green, 1981). At the interpersonal level, communicating cultural pride and identification reflects membership in the collective. Showing respect and preference toward African Americans are expressions of the collective membership. Expressing preference within the collective demonstrates support of, not prejudice against, other groups. For example, traditional African Americans who do not know one another will feel compelled to greet or socialize in a mixed setting. In greeting, they use expected cultural handshakes, verbalizations (e.g., "Whassup?"), and/or familial references such as "Brotha" or "Sista" to an otherwise stranger (Smitherman, 2000). These social gestures represent the psychological connection to, and awareness of, a cultural family.

The extended family demonstrates collective awareness an instrumental and expressive support of one another. A common instrumental role is seeking concrete help from a grandparent, uncle/aunt, adult brother/sister, and/or other family members. An example of expressive support would be genuine empathy for arrested or incarcerated family members. Though a criminal or civil law may have been broken, it is often the view that the family member deserves continued support to counter a racially biased criminal justice system (Hattery and Smith, 2007). According to Denby (2002), *communalism* guides families toward interdependence in support of the African American community and recognizes their interconnection (Boykin, 1983). Mezzo-level social systems, such as historically African American churches, colleges, universities, and businesses, provide African American families with psychological, educational, economic, and leadership opportunities (Hill, 1998). These social systems also promote cultural awareness and pride across all social systems within the community. Considering the array of systemic cultural and economic supports, the African American community social system has the most impact on family functioning and ethnic identity (Crowder and Teachman, 2004).

To gain insight into the African American cultural collective, it is helpful to examine the European American counterpart. A widely held impression among European Americans is that their lives represent a societal norm or American national identity (Devos, Gavin, and Quintana, 2010). In contrast to African Americans, most European Americans do not recognize their dominant cultural collective. For example, in a cultural diversity course for social work majors, I survey the students each semester, asking "What is your ethnicity?" Most of the European American students provide one of three answers: White (racial, not cultural), I do not know, or one or more European ancestries to which they have no cultural connection. In fact, some students will literally state that "White people don't have a culture." European Americans do not view themselves as a cultural collective because their geographic, economic, and political dominance distorts their social perception, and their ethnicity is not confronted with the challenges of societal discrimination. African Americans recognize this cultural reality because their lives are continuously impacted by discrimination and the many systemic differences with European American culture.

The African American cultural collective at the societal level is more diffuse compared to the family and community social systems. It operates as a social network of commonality that expresses itself socially in the arts and popular culture. The collective is also a mechanism for group protection in the political realm (Scott, 2003). An analogy of the latter is the "collective self-defence" statement of the North Atlantic Treaty Organization (NATO), which declares an attack on one member is an attack on all its members (NATO, 1949:Article V). African Americans are relatively united on sociopolitical issues such as the role of government, race relations, education, health care, and social justice. Bositis (2008) surveyed 750 African Americans in a national poll and found that only 4.0 percent of African Americans consider themselves Republicans. Though this demographic exists for several reasons, one factor is that the African American collective remembers the role of Republican conservatism in its support of segregation and racially charged political rhetoric. The cultural collective also systemically maintains in-group cohesion at a societal level. A recent example of societal-level self-protection was the controversy surrounding Bill Cosby's public criticism of impoverished African American families. In an address given to the NAACP, Cosby asserted that social problems faced by African Americans reflect behavioral choices that can be averted. Though there were disagreements with Cosby's assertions on objective grounds (Dyson, 2005; Manning and Mullings, 2009b), there was also a visceral group protection response (Campbell, 2005). Two concerns were that political adversaries can now use the views of an African American icon to dismiss institutional racism and stigmatize African American families. Such a cultural violation required a response from African Americans in a position to correct someone of Cosby's status. From politics to popular culture, and at all social system levels, the African American cultural collective exists in response to a social environment in which politics, race, culture, and economics intersect.

ETHNIC SOCIALIZATION AND PRIDE.   The African American cultural collective cannot exist without the ethnic socialization process. According to Denby (2002:32), "Building [ethnic] pride, self-respect, and a strong sense of [ethnic] identity are key components in cultivating the family unit." Pellebon's (2000) study of ethnic identity development among adolescents showed African Americans as having higher levels of ethnic identification compared to Latino or European Americans. One explanation for the heightened level of ethnic awareness among African American adolescents is ethnic socialization to counter negative stereotypes. Stereotypes regarding laziness, criminality, promiscuity, and lack of intelligence ascribed to Blacks have been part of the European American ethos for more than two hundred years. Though some persons in every ethnic group exemplify these traits, European American dominance grants European Americans the unique ability to define such behaviors among European Americans as deviant exceptions to the norm. However, when an observed "deviant behavior" matches an African American stereotype, many Americans conclude it to be a racial expectation. Regardless of a dominant group's power to establish broad perceptions of others, ethnic minorities have their own sense of history, heroes, achievements, and future visions. These are the foundation for promoting ethnic pride and respect.

Ethnic socialization also provides information about out-group prejudice and racism. Elementary-age children understand that observable differences between social groups can result in differential treatment (Bigler and Liben, 2007). African Americans understand this experientially, thus family and friends prepare African American youth for the inevitable experience of discrimination. According to Rivas-Drake, Hughes, and Way (2009:559), "Such messages may attenuate the potentially negative consequences of ethnic or racial discrimination for ethnic identity, or alternatively, [not doing so] may exacerbate such negative consequences by leaving youth unprepared for it." Therefore, inculcating ethnic pride is necessary for successful African American adaptation in the United States. Evidence of this positive outcome was found in research showing self-esteem among African American adolescents as being equal or higher compared to European Americans (Denby, 2002). Those surprised at these findings underestimated the effect of family socialization, which anticipates the negative societal messages about African Americans and replaces these messages with positive ethnic messages (McAdoo, 1985). Another function of ethnic socialization is to equip the next generation to resist anticipated racism. Two socialization tactics in the overall strategy for self-protection against racism are telling family stories and teaching behavioral responses to racism:

> *Family or personal stories.* Parents, other adults, and peers share their own experiences to provide personal examples of social observations. For example, upon hearing an actual account of police brutality, a hate crime, or discrimination, someone may have a personal story to share with the younger members as a learning tool. The current generation remembers and passes on to the next generation. Personal stories also provide youth with insight into racial dynamics and examples of responses in concrete scenarios.

> *Teaching behavioral responses to racism.* Members of oppressed groups survive in hostile social environments because they adapt to its demands while maintaining dignity and worth. Herman-Stahl, Stemmler, and Petersen (1995) describe two general strategies for coping with a stressful environment, each involving a cognitive and behavioral set. The *avoidance coping* strategy minimizes conflict. Cognitively the person understands the power differential and concludes that the most adaptive behavioral set is avoiding potentially punishing circumstances. The *approach coping* strategy engages the environment by challenging the circumstance. Whether or not a power differential is recognized, this perception does not deter active resistance or engagement. If there is a power difference, the engagement outweighs the potential risk.

In the segregated U.S. South, African Americans more often relied on avoidance coping responses because European Americans had a clear power advantage in most social contexts. African Americans behaved in a more subdued fashion when interacting with Whites because noncompliance could lead to serious consequences. Examples of such behavior would be to not look into the eyes of a White adult, being mindful of respectful language, nonverbal self-awareness, and forgoing walking paths or seats to Whites. These were only some of the necessary adaptive responses during the segregation era. Now that second-class citizenry is no longer overtly institutionalized; the avoidance coping strategy is no longer prevalent. However, changes in racist expression do require a new set of African American adaptive behaviors.

Adaptation to a combination of overt and covert racism requires a more sophisticated strategic use of both approaching and avoidance coping responses (Scott, 2003). Foundationally, children and adolescents are socialized about the means (e.g., education, saving money) and values (e.g., hard work, never quitting, and having goals) related to socioeconomic success in the United States. The means and values work together with the idea that an effective strategy to combat racism is to acquire power. Socioeconomic empowerment can then be used to bring social justice to the African American community. Because European American males dominate U.S. institutions, African Americans watch how European Americans work in these institutions. In other words, African Americans are taught to be bicultural at a functional level to navigate European American social systems. In settings where European American power shapes the social norms, speaking standard American English, wearing traditional European American clothing, and developing social shrewdness are components of biculturalism (Ogbu, 2008).

Social assertiveness is an approaching coping response to a racist environment. Examples of everyday interactions requiring assertiveness include direct communication, using passion, standing up for oneself, and/or responding to inferred and explicit racism. Because African Americans are stereotyped as violent, one risk of assertiveness is the possible out-group interpretation that such assertiveness is racial aggression. Particularly for youth, some circumstances requiring assertive behavior could potentially have serious consequences (Scott, 2003). Another part of the socialization process is learning to assess social circumstances. For example, many African Americans use the avoidance coping response of restraint during a traffic stop by law enforcement. In contrast, the same person may use the approaching response of advocating for a promotion or pay raise. In every social setting, African Americans carefully assess differential treatment to determine whether the response is a matter of circumstance or probable racial discrimination. These are only some examples of many adaptive measures taught to children and adolescents to help them function in a potentially discriminatory environment as seen through an African American cultural lens.

PROMINENCE OF MOTHERHOOD. The European American tradition of motherhood is based on the marriage of a head-of-household male to a female (working inside or outside the home) whose primary role is to nurture dependent children within a nuclear family. This family structure does reflect some African American households. If this was the typical African American experience, motherhood would not be a unique cultural feature. However, history shows motherhood for women of African descent has always been more convoluted than middle-class cultural fiction (Roberts, 1995; Winbush, 2000). In early American history, slavery imposed unusual expectations of motherhood. Under inhumane circumstances, and without the supports of legal marriage, African women socialized their own children to slavery and nurtured other slave children when their mothers were unable; some were forced to nurture and serve their enslaver's children. Even under these conditions, slave motherhood was scrutinized by men to meet unrealistic standards. Roberts (1995) recounts the story of a slave named Hannah who fled the plantation with her five-year-old daughter to avoid repeated rape but left her infant behind. The slave owner decried her choice to leave the infant as "inhumane" because it violated his social expectations of slave nurturance and submission (p. 195). Freedom from slavery was a viable maternal option for Hannah because she knew a network of African women would care for her infant.

African American women are no longer plantation slaves, but motherhood's role continues to function in a complex environment pressured by sexism's double standards, racial stereotypes, and economic disparities. In addition, the percentage of female heads of household is significantly higher compared to any other major ethnic group in the United States. This characteristic ensures that African American females (particularly economically) must go beyond European American middle-class scripted roles. According to Denby (2002:32), these roles include "nurturer, financial provider, teacher, caregiver, and community and family stabilizer." These "are indicative of the self-reliance, resourcefulness, and strength . . . in Black motherhood." It is evident that any woman able to function under these conditions is admirably strong and resilient. Unfortunately, those accolades do not compensate for the social conditions of lower wages, higher poverty rates, higher depression rates, and fewer economically stable partners forcing her remarkable adaptation (Collins, 1991; Taylor, Seaton, and Dominguez, 2008; Winbush, 2000). Though these conditions are evidence of sexism, European American feminism inadequately analyzes African American motherhood for four interrelated reasons: (1) African American women face a multiple intersection of gender, race, and class oppression, (2) analyzing patriarchy only as male dominance does not account for the racial oppression of African American males, (3) survival within the cultural collective is more male/female interdependent than for European Americans, and (3) motherhood is socially constructed from stereotypes culturally unique to African American women (Collins, 1991; Roberts, 1995). Therefore, African American solutions for increased female power in the larger patriarchy must be holistic and culturally applicable.

How African American mothers function under these conditions is what makes motherhood in African American families both noteworthy and culturally unique. African American motherhood can be observed in the reciprocal functions of supportive social networks, community mothering, and symbolic power. Supportive social networks are blood and nonblood connections between African American women. Within the cultural collective, sisterhood and motherhood are mutually supportive systems because both roles require similar emotional, spiritual, psychological, structural, and economic resources (Winbush, 2000). In social networks, the resourcefulness to obtain support and the nurturance of sisterhood are prominent expressions of African American motherhood. Community mothering allows for "bloodmothers" and "othermothers" (including blood relatives) to share parenting responsibilities within the African American community (Collins, 1991:121). This shared parenting strategy allows for the most efficient use of resources available within a geographic or networking community. Because community parenting is cultural, traditional African American families of all economic classes and family types may engage in some degree of shared parenting. However, community mothering is also practiced out of necessity; therefore, lower-income families probably use community mothering with more frequency. Fluidity of parental responsibility and accepting nonblood children as kin are the prominent expressions of African American motherhood. Finally, the symbolic power of motherhood is the abstract image that embodies the beliefs of African American women as mothers. According to Collins, "the controlling images of the matriarch, the mammy, and the welfare mother and the practices they justify are designed to oppress" (1991:120). Well-intentioned scholars from the strengths perspective responded with a counterimage of the "super strong Black mother" based on attributes of devotion, self-sacrifice, and unconditional love (1991:118). Collins's compelling analysis points out that out-group negative stereotypes and in-group glorification remain attributions that ignore the multiple oppressions faced by African American women.

Similarly, this chapter highlights the prominence of African American motherhood based on cultural uniqueness: resourcefulness, community nurturance, fluidity of parental responsibilities, and accepting nonblood children as kin. These themes take on a center of power within the African American family based on female networks with the reverence of motherhood as a centered principle. Unfortunately, these remain observations of female adaptation strategies in the context of an oppressive social environment.

FIRM CHILD-REARING STRATEGIES. Parenting styles within the context of any family system result from a combination of family dynamics, social and financial support, and social demographic factors (Belsky, 1984; Bluestone and Tamis-LeMonda, 1999; Garbarino and Kostelny,

1993). In African American families children are culturally valued (Denby, 2002; Hoffman and Manis, 1979). Even among low-income mothers in stressful environments, children are considered to be emotionally fulfilling as well as enhancing marital relationships and continuing the family name (Roxburgh, Stephens, Toltzis, and Adkins, 2001).

Several authors describe many child-rearing behaviors and strategies in African American families. Denby (2002) identifies two child-rearing strategies used in traditional African American families: shared parenting and firm discipline. African Americans share parenting responsibilities within the family system, which includes persons living inside and outside the home. Therefore, the parent/caregiver–child family subsystem is broad and fluid. The parenting in this system could include extended biological family members such as grandparents, uncles, aunts, older cousins. Persons not related biologically also fulfill expressive and instrumental roles for children. Their roles vary based on geographic proximity and perceived family closeness.

Firm discipline can be described as the "firm, caring, and uncompromising" approach to discipline (Denby, 2002:31). Despite the assertion that firm discipline is a function of culture, degrees of harsher physical and verbal discipline practiced by African American mothers vary based on education, economic class, maternal depression, and emotional strain (Hill and Sprague, 1999; Kelley, Sánchez-Hucles, and Walker, 1993). Findings from these studies indicate working and middle-class mothers use less firm combinations of parenting behavior. In fact, "harsh" physical punishment is shown to be infrequent, regardless of socioeconomic status (Horn, Cheng, and Joseph, 2004).

The literature identified three dominant patterns of child-rearing practiced in African American families—power assertive, material–social consequence, and child centered. Within each pattern there is overlap of parenting behaviors from other patterns, but each has its dominant characteristics. A typical combination of "power assertive" child-rearing includes physical punishment (e.g., spanking, physically removing a child), verbal correction and direction (e.g., yelling, sarcasm, threats of punishment, demand of immediate compliance), and nonverbal expressions that manage children and teenagers. Of those parents who use physical punishment, two findings are worth noting: First, the use of spanking increases the likelihood of behavioral problems over time, and second, maternal emotional support mitigates this outcome, demonstrating an inverse relation between future behavior problems and maternal emotional support (McLoyd and Smith, 2002). The "material and social consequences" pattern relies on isolation (e.g., time-outs), verbal reminding, and removing privileges; this pattern does not include direct reasoning as a primary parenting behavior. The "child-centered" pattern uses direct reasoning, interactions responsive to the child's perceived need, and overall less restrictive responses to misbehavior; physical punishment is infrequently used in this pattern (Bluestone and Tamis-LeMonda, 1999).

As stated, verbal correction is complementary to the parent's general child-rearing strategy. However, this writer suggests that verbalizations used to direct and correct children and adolescents are uniquely cultural. Verbal correction is often spontaneously expressed through a parenting variation of *signifyin',* "which depends on double meaning and irony, exploits the unexpected, and uses quick verbal surprises and humor" (Smitherman, 2000:260). Compared to a more lecturing approach, this technique is effective because it reduces the effect of habituation on the young listener. The combination of humor, surprise, and varied inflections effectively gains the child's or adolescent's attention and is not perceived as demeaning because there is a cultural context to understand the implicit message. However, within the "power assertive" complement, some verbalizations, such as sarcasm and verbal threats of punishment, can be misinterpreted by non–African Americans as emotionally demeaning or literal threats of harm. It is more likely the case the expression was a degree of hyperbole in order to make a point. For example, one may hear a parent say to a noncompliant child, "If you don't turn off that television and come here, I will knock you into tomorrow." There may be an implicit threat that some form of physical punishment may follow continued disobedience, but typically these are not literal threats of violence. In varied combinations, these techniques work together to build a model of stern parenting balanced with nurturance and protection.

SOCIAL JUSTICE ORIENTATION.   *A social justice orientation is a clear position of relating to and empathizing with persons who face discrimination or oppression.* As described in the previous section, African American socialization reframes the social context through which children see themselves. Contextualizing discrimination as social injustice creates a view of good versus evil. For children, this concrete reframe mitigates the anxiety of anticipated discrimination while developing in-group cohesion. From adolescence to adulthood, the cultural reframe becomes more complex, abstract, and generalizable. This results in a unique perspective because current experiences of oppression are contextualized in family and formal history. Family stories and knowledge about U.S. slavery, the civil rights movement, and sacrifices of historic African Americans (e.g., Harriett Tubman, W.E.B. DuBois, Martin Luther King, Jr., and Malcolm X) confirm the experiences. African American socialization and the experience of oppression within an inspiring historic context support development of a heroic sense of self and a social justice orientation (Knox, Fagley, and Miller, 2004). Three expressions of this orientation include a heightened sensitivity to injustice, social empathy, and the willingness to advocate:

> *Sensitivity to injustice.* Sensitivity to injustice is the heightened level of understanding of the effects of unjust treatment. Having experienced discrimination, African Americans have the capacity to readily recognize most forms of injustice and presume similar negative effects.

> *Social empathy.* If an oppressed group believes injustice is based on group membership, that group has the capacity to develop empathy for the oppressed. An important factor in developing empathy is whether the group identifies with the target of discrimination. African Americans will likely identify with other U.S. ethnic minority groups with a history of racial oppression. For example, African Americans have a more positive attitude toward Hispanics compared to European Americans (Shin, Ellison, and Leal, 2008). A relatively positive attitude toward the ethnic group should predispose African American empathy under conditions of perceived oppression. In contrast, high religiosity and homonegativity likely lessen African American identification with the gay community, thereby resulting in less empathy regarding marital discrimination (Negy and Eisenman, 2005).

> *Willingness to advocate.* Empathy precedes action to advocate on the behalf of others. Though African American willingness to advocate may vary depending upon the group and circumstance, history shows the cultural collective does broadly advocate for social justice. The movement led by Martin L. King Jr. was a national example of African Americans framing civil rights as universal. Recently, the Black Radical Congress met to discuss the future of progressive politics in the United States and set an agenda for the twenty-first century. Included were representatives of Black nationalist movements, the Black Panther Party, and other groups typically categorized as "militant" by many Americans. The documented Freedom Agenda demonstrates the willingness to advocate for others based on the understanding of social and economic injustice:

We will struggle for a society and world in which every individual enjoys full human rights . . . and in the United States equal protection of the Constitution and of all the laws. We seek a society in which every individual—regardless of color, nationality, national origin, ethnicity, religion, sex, sexual orientation, age, family structure, or mental or physical capacity—is free to experience "life, liberty, and the pursuit of happiness." (Manning and Mullings, 2009b:595)

Within the cultural perspective of social justice, African Americans reflect upon their own experiences and use this energy to seek justice beyond the collective. Heightened sensitivity to understand oppression, the potential for empathy, and social action on the behalf of other groups are interrelated components of this cultural feature.

STYLISTIC CULTURAL EXPRESSIVENESS.   Suggesting the existence of cultural world views implies observable differences in attitudes, speech, and behavior. What creates the uniqueness of style in traditional African American cultural behaviors? The relative differences are understood within the context of three interrelated cultural expressions: physicality, spontaneity, and rhythm. References available online provided adequate definitions:

- *Physicality* is an orientation "involving or characterized by vigorous bodily activity."
- *Spontaneity* is an expression "coming or resulting from a natural impulse or tendency; without effort or premeditation."
- Rhythm is a "movement or procedure with uniform or patterned recurrence of a beat." (www.dictionary.com)

Every individual has these innate potentials; however, culture modulates the intensity of these expressions. These expressions are notably present in African American music (soul, rhythm and blues, jazz, rap, and hip-hop), flamboyance in sports (Muhammad Ali, Deon Sanders, and the Harlem Globetrotters), church behavior (gospel worship, chants, and spiritual dance), and African American communication. I use African American communication here to show the three cultural expressions.

Two primary parts of communication are language and nonverbal expressions. Regarding the spoken word, social context and audience modulate the voice used with its unique cadence, tone, and nonverbal pattern. By time an African American reaches adulthood, she or he may have had to learn many voices, such as professional jargon, spiritual speech, and three dialects of English—Standard American, African American vernacular, and European American vernacular (Campbell, 2005). Cultural expressions of physicality, spontaneity, and rhythm differ from each voice, but the African American vernacular English (AAVE) provides a clear example of cultural style.

Before describing the cultural expressiveness of AAVE, I present an introductory discussion of how it has simultaneously created controversy and cultural copying. European American teens, politicians, commercials, and journalists use and exploit AAVE (Smitherman, 2000). When used by European Americans (in the upper middle class), these expressions provide disposable benefit. European American parents can earn "cool points" with his or her teen by using phrases such as "24/7" and "chill" to get his or her attention. The KFC Corporation used the phrase "phat degrees" as a marketing gimmick to describe chicken (Campbell, 2005). However, the novelty of AAVE fades if one suggests it replace Standard English in the European American home or professional setting.

Considering the many negative connotations associated with AAVE, why does the dominant culture tacitly borrow from its lexicon? First, words and phrases from AAVE are cultural representations of materials, symbols, moods, and experiences for which Standard English has no adequate expression (Smitherman, 2000). Therefore, European Americans may notice AAVE's unique cultural expressiveness and swagger, or "coolness," not found in Standard English. Verbal communication uses the physicality of head movement, facial expression, and body language to complete the message. The female side-to-side head movement (i.e., rollin' her neck) expresses disagreement; eye cutting expresses dissatisfaction; or a person "collar popping" expresses pride, all adding emphasis and emotion to the communication (Johnson, 1971). The timing of each expression is important for the optimal social reaction. Like an art form, not everyone can do it. Consider the skills needed for signifyin'—a "ritualized verbal art in which the speaker puts down, needles, talks about (signify on) someone, to make a point or sometimes just for fun" (Campbell, 2005:260). In this verbal duel, the winner needs more spontaneity to comment with more wit, humor, and sometimes rhyme than the challenger. Finally, the rhythm related to the delivery of each example is as precise as a comic's punch line.

From everyday conversations to storytelling, AAVE has a unique cadence and rhythm recognized by those using the language. Even in slavery, noted Blassingame (1972:20), "storytelling" as an art form included acting [physicality and spontaneity], singing [rhythm and spontaneity], and gestures [spontaneity and physicality].

ASSERTIVE COMMUNICATION.   Traditional African Americans communicate qualitatively differently from most European, Hispanic, Native, and Asian Americans. As noted, assertive communication helps African Americans respond to racism. In the previous section, I provided verbal and nonverbal examples of cultural expressiveness within the African American Vernacular English. This section describes distinct African American communication patterns regarding relative directness, emotional content, nonverbal communication, tone, confrontation, and the use of humor (Kochman, 1983).

African Americans use both direct and indirect forms of communication contingent upon the specific target, audience, and social context. However, relative to other ethnic groups, African Americans more frequently use direct interpersonal communication (Kochman, 1983; Spears, 2001). Direct communication refers to using words (literal or symbolic) that reflect actual thought, verbalizing experienced emotion, and using dramatic nonverbal action (Booth-Butterfield and Jordan, 1989). Though cultural metaphors and symbolism are technically indirect messages, the speaker expects the meaning to be understood by the listener. Certain AAVE phrases—such as "Tell it," "Word is bond," "Don't you even go there," "straight up," and "keepin' it real"—express the cultural importance of directness (Smitherman, 2000). Speaking directly also reflects personal strength and integrity because such speech is open to challenge. One summarizing metaphor is expressed in Aaron Neville's classic 1966 soul hit, "Tell It Like It Is," where he sings, "If you want somethin' to play with, go and find yourself a toy." Avoiding straightforward speech indicates the speaker is weak and wasting the hearer's time.

In contrast, African Americans may be less comfortable interacting with outgroups who use indirect communication. In social situations in which European Americans must interact with African Americans, European Americans tend to use avoidance coping tactics. One avoidance tactic is using indirect language in a manner that intentionally misleads. Examples of verbal avoidance responses experienced by African American are false compliments, partial disclosures of important information, insincere reassurances, distortions, and vague language. In time African Americans recognize the pattern and begin to depend less on the literal words and to listen more for the veiled messages. In addition, a person who appears to withhold emotional expressions appears disingenuous (Kochman, 1983).

Verbal frankness allows freedom in emotional, nonverbal, and tonal expressiveness. In some American Indian or Asian cultures, this assertive style may feel disrespectful, and in European American culture these may feel threatening (Spears, 2001). Speech with passion (spontaneity) and expressive nonverbal movements (physicality) produces higher volume, frequent inflection change, and irregular timing (Kochman, 1983). An anecdote that illustrates volume and timing was a family visit I made to New Orleans in 2004. As I sat in my aunt's rectangular den, approximately eleven adults engaged in different small group conversations. Having been away from a predominantly Creole or African American setting for many years, the conversation initially felt loud and confusing. With the sudden realization that this was normal, I forced myself to attune to the pattern. Within minutes the voices began to separate, and the pattern was easier to follow—in other words, I remembered. As I considered my experience, it also made theoretical sense. In a social context in which competing conversations are acceptable, the speakers' volume would naturally increase and they would eventually habituate to the higher volume. I keep that experience as one concrete reminder of cultural difference in communication.

The preceding story also depicts how African American speech patterns include speaking out of turn (Booth-Butterfield and Jordan, 1989). This does not mean two people talking simultaneously; however, there is overlap when one person ends and the other begins. Also, it would not be rude to interject with a comment of agreement or disagreement (e.g., "Amen!" or "Say what?") when someone is speaking. If a listener suddenly interrupts and the comments are accepted by other listeners, he or she may take over the conversation. In a culture that expects assertive communication, interjection and interruptions are a normal part of communication. Another feature of assertive communication is confrontation. An African American will look another in the eyes and ask a confronting question, expecting an immediate and direct response (Kochman, 1983). There are cultural norms regarding the appropriate time and place for a confrontation. But when the time and place is right, African Americans will confront one another to get to "the truth of the matter" (Smitherman, 2000).

In addition, the intensity of assertive and direct communication is balanced with the high level of humor experienced in everyday conversation. Making fun of each other, laughing out loud, and telling humorous stories promote engagement and continued interest in the conversation. Even a formal meeting presents opportunities for humor and wit. Of course, not all African Americans have the same gift of humor. Some use humor while others are the audience, but humor is an acceptable component of communication. Direct verbal/nonverbal communication, emotional expression, differences in tone and volume, confrontation, and humor in communication all have their place in the African American communication style. Some of these expressions could be interpreted as uncomfortable or rude by other cultural standards. That is why African Americans code-switch both language and style depending upon the people present (Booth-Butterfield and Jordan, 1989).

SPIRITUALITY. African Americans are more likely than members of any other racial or ethnic group to report their religious affiliation. Most African Americans identify themselves as Christian Baptists, and of all ethnic groups 6.9 percent (92 percent African Americans) report affiliation to a historically Black church (Pew Forum on Religion and Public Life, 2008). This devotion to Christianity may seem counterintuitive, considering its historic role of social control and justification for slavery. During U.S. slavery Christianity served at least three functions: Slaveowners used biblical passages (1) to justify slavery, (2) to reduce rebellion by using biblical examples of Christian submission; and (3) to inculcate the believe that their suffering was a predestined part of their natural experience—in other words, that God will reward their hope under suffering in the afterlife. However, a spiritual mix of African ritual and Christian doctrine had latent effects unanticipated by slave owners. All social systems organize, and within this spiritual system at least six organizing social functions emerged: (1) mechanisms for emotional/psychological support and adjustment, (2) opportunity to develop oral and written English skills, (3) insight into the enslaver's culture from knowing the master's religion, (4) structure for social roles based on group beliefs, (5) a psychological support system provided by faith and love teachings, and (6) a transcendent belief in hope that could be applied to the natural world. For many, Christianity helped to organize a social system of resistance, as not all slaves wanted to wait until the afterlife for freedom (Blassingame, 1972).

Many scholars believe that Christianity was incorporated into general spiritual beliefs already held by African slaves (McAdoo, 1997; Nobles, 1978). Jules-Rosette (1980) identified six features of African spirituality that emerged from the West African religions: (1) the link between the natural and the supernatural, (2) human intervention in the supernatural world that can occur through possession and spiritual contact, (3) music being important to invoke the supernatural, (4) strong ties between the world of the living and the dead that define the scope of community, (5) the participatory verbal performance/call-response pattern between the minister and congregation, and (6) the primacy of both sacred and secular verbal performance. Many modern Christian denominations still practice some of these features. For example, most historic African American churches use the call-response pattern first noted in the eighteenth century. Pentecostals believe they can be filled with the Holy Spirit in a manner that resembles spiritual possession, being able to speak prophetically to the congregation "while shoutin and undergoing spirit possession" in an unknown spiritual language (Campbell, 2005:278).

In the traditional African American Church, religion is relevant to the everyday experience of these social systems and remains a concrete source of political, civic, social, material, and psychological support for communities. The African American Church promotes psychological well-being, moral development, and existential meaning, and it connects the spiritual with the material (Jang, Borenstein, Chirigoga, et al., 2006; Mattis and Watson, 2009; McAdoo and Younge, 2009). Religious African Americans are spiritually based—in other words, the social world has spiritual meaning (Pellebon, 1999). In any given conversation, African Americans will use spiritual terms to describe or comment on everyday matters. Biblical quotes and spiritual phrases express feelings of joy, concern, love, and lament. With a sensed link between the natural and supernatural, it also follows that spirituality and social justice are inseparable.

The previously described expressions of spontaneity, physicality, and rhythm are all observable in African American worship (Campbell, 2005; McAdoo, 1997). Testifying is a spontaneous and rhythmic verbal "affirmation to the power and truth of something" (Campbell, 2005:279). Choir gospel music has a unique call-response cadence, more intense percussion, changing rhythm, and more physicality than other Christian forms of worship. Again there is evidence that these expressions may have roots in African dance. Blassingame (1972:20) quotes an Englishman's description of Ibos dancing during the slavery era:

> The dancers range themselves and begin slow rhythmic movements, unconsciously swaying their heads in time with the music. As the dance proceeds they appear intoxicated with the motion and the music, the speed increases and the movements become more and more intricate and . . . executed in perfect time.

Any discussion of African American spirituality should include three non-Christian spiritual worldviews. African Americans developed both Afrocentricity's Njia and the Nation of Islam, and African American membership in Islam in noteworthy. Though their memberships are significantly less than historically Black churches, these spiritual worldviews have support within the African American community because they advocate some degree of these perspectives: social activism, ethnic pride, economic autonomy, and Christianity as oppressive (Mazama, 2002). I described Afrocentricity's spiritual component in a previous study:

> Asante (2003) developed a belief system referred to as Njia. Translated as "The Way," Njia is the collective expression of the Afrocentric worldview which is grounded in the historical experi-

ence of African people. . . . Njia represents the inspired Afrocentric spirit found in the traditions of African-Americans, and the spiritual survival of an African essence in America (p. 30). Asante concretely organizes the reconstructive attitudes, values, and behaviors into ten quarters of teachings for a total of 234 precepts to learn and internalize. . . . Practicing Njia in whole is central to developing the fullness of Afrocentricity. (Pellebon, 2007:186)

W. Fard Muhammad (referred to as "the Master" by the Nation) founded the Nation of Islam in the United States on July 4, 1930. He then mentored the Honorable Elijah Muhammad to begin the religion until the Master's disappearance in February 26, 1934 (Young, 2001). Some of their basic beliefs are to honor the teachings of the Honorable Prophet Elijah Muhammad, follow the Koran, and accept truths (as they appear) of the Bible. The Nation of Islam believes Africans are Allah's chosen people because of the oppression and suffering experienced at the hands of slave masters. Instead of a resurrection of the physically dead as in Christianity, they stress a mental resurrection to the knowledge of Islam. In essence they are Black nationalists, seeing socioeconomic self-sufficiency and racial separation as the solution for American oppression. Because of the Nation of Islam's visible community presence and Malcolm X's notoriety among European Americans, the Nation had significant influence in African American communities during the civil rights movement (Manning and Mullings, 2009c).

Finally, a significant number of African Americans practice Islam. Islam combines certain history and tenets of Judaism and Christianity reconceptualized into a new religion by the founding prophet Muhammad in the seventh century (Parrillo, 2006). The Muslim population worldwide is approximately 1.3 billion people, and the United States is home to an estimated Muslim population of over 4 million. Of Muslims in the United States, 1.2 million (30 percent) are African American.

SOCIAL AND ECONOMIC CHALLENGES

Discussion of the African American family must include the largest and most impactful macro systems. Though the holistic perspective assumes systems at all levels affect each other, the macro social systems have more energy and power to alter smaller systems. This section describes racism, presents the public perception of discrimination, and provides evidence that racism still impacts African Americans. With racism and discrimination as social context, the section describes the current conditions of political power, education attainment, and income related to education for African Americans.

Racism and Discrimination

Racism as a general concept conveys differential attitudes and/or treatment of a person or group based on racial prejudice. According to Miller and Garran (2008:28), racism exists "along a spectrum, with many different types and forms." Within this spectrum, racism manifests at different levels (individual, group, and institutional), in approach (overt and covert), and with varied frequency and intensity. Evidence of racism across the spectrum demonstrates that African American families face a still hostile socioeconomic environment. This section describes varied perceptions about racism followed by examples showing that racism remains a significant challenge in the United States.

During slavery and segregation, racism at all levels was an openly accepted practice throughout the United States. Those who supported or opposed racism readily agreed that the practices existed. From the passage of the Civil Rights Act of 1964 until today, several social realities co-developed: Some racist attitudes lessened (e.g., 43 percent of European Americans who voted in 2008 supported Barack Obama), a new generation of Americans lived unexposed to formal and legalized racism, actual racists adopted new strategies to express their prejudices, and nonracist egocentrics learned that race can be exploited for personal gain. These developments have created an environment whereby it is difficult to describe the impact of racism to nonracists. This is evidence of the obvious—European Americans are not a monolithic ethnic group regarding the perpetuation of racism. Segments of the dominant group are racist, nonracist, and complicated variations of people not easily classified. Bona fide racists clearly understand the dynamic. They know their immediate social support is among some family members and friends. In addition, numerous racist organizations use print and electronic media to refine and reinforce racist beliefs. Outside these safe circles, racists identify each other indirectly by displaying symbols with double meanings (e.g., the Confederate battle flag), listening for inferred racism during casual conversations, and joining mainstream political movements able to accommodate racist attitudes without being openly racist.

Because covert racism is so complex and dynamic, determining the actual magnitude of racism is impossible. An unfortunate and latent effect of covert racism is the growing perception that racial discrimination is no longer a social problem in the United States. The Pew Research Center (2009) showed a growing gap between African and European Americans when asked whether African Americans experience "a lot" of discrimination (p. 4). A significantly higher percentage of African Americans (43 percent) agreed compared to European Americans (14 percent). Compared to 2001, African American perceptions were steady compared to a 20 percent drop among European Americans. Pollingreport.com compiles numerous surveys regarding social issues, and the following data are from this source (PollingReport.com, 2010). A 2008 Newsweek poll asked 1,042 European American voters why unsuccessful African Americans "cannot get ahead." Consistent with the aforementioned Pew poll, 67 percent believed African Americans were responsible for their own condition compared to 18 percent who believed discrimination was the primary cause. One explanation for this perception is that European Americans seldom experience racial discrimination. A 2008 CBS/New York Times poll asked respondents if they ever experienced racial discrimination. The percentages of persons having at least one experience were much higher for African Americans (68 percent) and Hispanic Americans (56 percent) compared to European Americans (26 percent). Finally, a Washington Post/ABC News poll asked, "If you honestly assessed yourself, would you say that you have at least some feelings of racial prejudice?" The majority of European Americans (65 percent) reported not having any racial prejudice; in fact, 4 percent more African Americans admitted to at least some prejudice (Pollingreport.com, 2010).

European American perceptions that racism is not a social problem, with most claiming to have no racial prejudice, may contribute to the lessening stigma of expressing racist attitudes. For example, coincidentally while writing this paragraph, CNN news (CNN Justice, 2010) reported an unidentified male used the public address system in a New Jersey Wal-Mart Supercenter to announce "All Blacks need to leave the store." More compelling examples are reported public remarks against the first African American president of the United States. During 2008 Republican campaign rallies, shouts of "Terrorist!" and "Treason!" and "Kill him!" were noted expressions of abhorrence toward candidate Barack Obama. Even in highly controlled social situations, underlying racial motives arose against this African American president. During a 2009 speech to Congress, President Obama asserted that reformed health care would not cover illegal immigrants, for which South Carolina Representative Joe Wilson shouted, "You lie!" Even Wilson's Republican colleagues acknowledged that the remark was embarrassingly uncivil toward a speaking president (CNNPolitics.com, 2009). Internalized racial attitudes, not political differences, provided Wilson with a sense of social permission to display such anger. It is not surprising that death threats made against President Obama increased by 400 percent after his election compared to those made against President George W. Bush (Kessler, 2009).

More serious than interpersonal incivility and threats, Americans still engage in interpersonal racial violence. According to FBI statistics 72 percent of all racially motivated hate crime victims were African Americans, up from 66.3 percent in 2001 (Federal Bureau of Investigation, 2008). The Southern Poverty Law Center's (2010) Web site reported active hate group chapters in 573 U.S. cities—Neo Nazi (163), White Nationalists (133), Skinheads (124), Ku Klux Klan (86), and Neo Confederates (67). This count did not include other groups who might find African Americans objectionable—for example Christian right and anti-immigrant groups. Hate groups that target African Americans have increased after electing the nation's first African American president. This is not evidence of more racism; instead it shows that existing racists are more willing to express their views and take action. Most Americans are not members of organized hate groups, but their prevalent existence demonstrates a continuum of racist beliefs, attitudes, and practices. Racial prejudice is undoubtedly a factor in measurable social and economic disparities between African and European Americans (Miller and Garran, 2008).

POLITICAL POWER. Ethnic groups in the United States primarily achieve social progress through political means. Grassroots organizing, campaign fund-raising, framing the issue, and effective communication influence decision makers. But politicians ultimately propose and vote on policy designed to achieve social change meaningful to African Americans. Progressive European Americans have often worked toward political objectives important to African Americans. Therefore, African American political power cannot be measured only by the number of racially identifiable persons in political office. Politicians must actively support political agendas believed to benefit African Americans. That stated, African American representation in national political office is an important indicator of ethnic political power.

In the executive branch, for the first time in American history an African American is president of the United States. One of many factors contributing to his election was a political platform articulated to represent the interests of all Americans. His campaign promised to end the Iraq War, save the economy, reform health care, strengthen education, and develop a new energy strategy for the future (Obama for America, 2010). These political issues were larger than any ethnic group concern; yet, African Americans strongly embraced his candidacy. Within the president's first year of office, progressives perceived him as moderate and overconcerned with bipartisanship. On the other hand, radical conservatives and some Republican politicians labeled him as socialist, racist, Muslim, dictatorial, and an illegal immigrant elected to office. Such unsupported rhetoric becomes racial because each label infers invokes the stereotype that African American males are dangerous. Many who believed these labels used President Obama's call for health care reform to organize like-minded individuals to form the so-called Tea Party Movement, now a legitimized caucus of the Republican party (Washingtonpost.com, 2011a). It is remarkable that the election of an African American president can create such an abrupt and dramatic sociopolitical response. In the end, President Obama's historic signing of health care reform into law was also a remarkable political achievement, arguably demonstrating his political acumen and clout.

Even if the Obama presidency is relatively successful, the future of another African American being elected U.S. president is difficult to predict. One certainty about this presidency is that the role of race in politics will be magnified by 2012. One example is the unprecedented demand, by so-called Birthers within the Tea Party, for President Obama to show an original birth certificate to prove he met requirements to be elected president. Initially a 2008 campaign issue, it is an early 2012 presidential campaign issue personified by possible Republican candidate Donald Trump. On April 27, 2011, President Obama released his long form birth certificate out of a concern that the issue has overshadowed more important issues (Washingtonpost.com, 2011b).

The legislative branch reveals how looking at the election of one president may exaggerate African American political power. The U.S. Congress has 638 members (538 House Representatives and 100 Senators). Currently, African American representation in Congress is far below the 12.8 percent African American percentage in the U.S. population. Only 39 African Americans (7.0 percent) are in the House of Representatives, and only one is in the Senate (1.0 percent), leaving 29 states without even one African American congressional representative. Of the states without African American Representatives, five have a higher than 10 percent African American population. With such small numbers in Congress, African Americans formed the Congressional Black Caucus (CBC) as one mechanism to develop political strategies to address issues important to African Americans (Congressional Black Caucus Foundation, 2009). Since the CBC's founding in 1971, only one U.S. Congressman, Representative J. C. Watts of Oklahoma, chose not to join the Black Caucus.

The U.S. Supreme Court provides an example of political representation being more salient than racial presence. As the only African American justice, Clarence Thomas's court rulings have been consistent with Republican conservative positions. Though an African American, he does not represent African American political power in the highest U.S. court. At the state level, Deval Patrick of Massachusetts is the only African American governor. In conclusion, having an African American president may misrepresent the significance of national political power held by African Americans in the United States. The inability to elect more traditional African Americans into national offices presents future challenges to having African American perspectives and enhancing the well-being of African American families.

EDUCATIONAL ATTAINMENT AND INCOME.   A clear social challenge with quality-of-life implications for African American families is educational attainment. This section compares African American educational attainment and yearly earning to European Americans. According to the U.S. Census (2008), among all African American adults, 18 percent have an eleventh-grade education or less compared to 13.6 percent European Americans. African American males have the highest percentage in this category (19.5 percent) with European American females having the lowest percentage (12.7 percent). High school dropout rates are also higher for African Americans (8.4 percent) than European Americans (5.3 percent). Not having at least a high school diploma places one at high risk for unemployment; nationally 44.5 percent of high school dropouts are unemployed with clear differences by ethnicity. The unemployment rate for African Americans without a high school diploma is 14.5 percent compared to 8.2 percent for European Americans. For those able to maintain yearlong employment, the median income for those without a high school diploma is $21,744 (U.S. Department of Labor, 2008).

The U.S. economy does not produce manufacturing jobs that once provided high school graduates with meaningful employment. In fact, many high school graduates find the job opportunities similar to when they were students (Kilborn, 1994). According to the U.S. Census (2008), among all African American adults, 34.9 percent have a high school education compared to 31 percent of European Americans. African American males again have the highest percentage in this category (36.8 percent) with European American females having the lowest percentage (30.8 percent). The unemployment rate for African Americans (9.3 percent) with a high school diploma is almost twice that of European Americans (5.1 percent). For those able to maintain yearlong employment, the median income for those with a high school diploma is $29,664 (U.S. Department of Labor, 2008). However, considering the single-parent household and the median income differences between African and European Americans, this increase has less of an impact on African American families.

Completing a bachelor's or higher college degree significantly impacts immediate earnings potential and the potential for upward mobility. According to the U.S. Census (2008), among all African American adults, 17.1 percent have at least one college degree compared to 27.2 percent of European Americans. African American males have the lowest college degree attainment percentage (15.0 percent) compared to all comparison groups: European American males (27.9 percent), European American females (26.9 percent), and African American females (18.1 percent). The median incomes for college graduates are considerably higher than those with less education: bachelor's degree at $48,579, master's degree at $59,184, and professional/doctorate degree at $73,208 (U.S. Department of Labor, 2008). In addition, African Americans had a 2008 median family income of $34,218, significantly less than a single earner with a bachelor's degree. The data indicate that the opportunity for quality education and access to college is necessary for African American families to improve their quality of life.

CONCLUSION

The strengths of African Americans lie in a dynamic, yet unique, culture. Eight of many cultural features of traditional African Americans were described as researched from the literature. The development of an African American cultural collective reflects the group's sense of fit and adaptation to the social environment. African American families survive by adapting cultural strategies of child rearing and socialization, of which cultural pride is an important focus. The unique challenges of African American motherhood reflect the complex roles that have emerged over the last two hundred years. Though African American females have adapted admirably, educational and economic disparities must narrow for the notion of motherhood to be truly self determined. The distinctiveness of style and expression makes culture unique and interesting. African American mannerisms and assertiveness are observable characteristics at all social levels. African American spirituality and belief in social justice reflect a developed social empathy arising from generations of social oppression. Though these cultural features are generalizations, many of these unique characteristics are present in many traditional African American families.

Each ethnic family group in the United States has unique vulnerabilities and challenges. As the African American population grows well beyond 36 million by 2010, the questions regarding family structure will increase. Will rates of single-parent, predominantly female-headed, households continue to increase? If so, is absentee parenting with extended family and community supports a viable strategy over the next several decades? With fertility rates rising, what are the implications for a new generation of African American children in a nation where education is failing lower-income children of all ethnic groups? These are only a few of the questions that remain a concern of a nation whose overall well-being will be influenced by these challenges.

Regardless of the developing family structure, the data indicate that the African American family is vulnerable. African Americans will face important decisions regarding relationships between men and women that will permanently impact the next generation. Clearly there are economic benefits to two-parent families, but the reality that African American men have significantly lower wages and less educational attainment complicate marital and parenting choices. Other challenges facing African Americans are the high rates of arrests and criminal dispositions, and the disproportionate incarceration rates, particularly for males. Unemployment, poverty, drug addiction, violence, and disparities in health/mental health are major social issues with immediate and future consequences for African American communities nationwide (Hattery and Smith, 2007). Finally, the election of the first African American president appears to have unleashed an insidious form of covert racism. Historically, African Americans have adapted, and the African American family has survived. An important final question is whether survival remains an acceptable outcome for the African American family in the United States of America.

References

Allen, W. R. 1978. "The Search for Applicable Theories in Black Family Life." *Journal of Marriage and the Family 40*(1), 117–129.

Anderson, R. E., and I. Carter. 1999. *Human Behavior in the Social Environment: A Social Systems Approach* (5th ed.). New York: Aldine De Gruyter.

Arias, E. 2007. "United States Life Tables, 2004." *National Vital Statistics Reports 56*(9). Hyattsville, MD: National Center for Health Statistics.

Asante, M. K. 2003. *Afrocentricity: The Theory of Social Change* (revised and expanded). Chicago: African American Images.

Bar-Tal, D. 1990. "Causes and Consequences of Delegitimization: Models of Conflict and Ethnocentrism." *Journal of Social Issues 46*(1), 65–81.

Belsky, J. 1984. "The Determinants of Parenting: A Process Model." *Child Development 55*, 83–96.

Bigler, R. S., and L. S. Liben. 2007. "Developmental Intergroup Theory: Explaining and Reducing Children's Social Stereotyping and Prejudice." *Current Directions in Psychological Science 16*(3), 162–166.

Blassingame, J. W. 1972. *The Slave Community: Plantation Life in the Antebellum South*. New York: Oxford University Press.

Bluestone, C., and C. S. Tamis-LeMonda. 1999. "Correlates of Parenting Styles in Predominantly Working- and Middle-Class African American Mothers. *Journal of Marriage and Family 61*(4), 881–893.

Booth-Butterfield, M., and F. Jordan. 1989. "Communication Adaptation Among Racially Homogenous and Heterogeneous Groups." *The Southern Communication Journal 54*, 253–272.

Bositis, D. A. 2008, October 21. "Joint Center for Political and Economic Studies: 2008 National Opinion Poll." www.jointcenter.org/publications_recent_publications/national_opinion_polls/2008_national_opinion_poll (accessed April 23, 2011).

Boykin, A. W. 1983. "The Academic Performance of Afro-American Children." In J. T. Spence (Ed.), *Achievement and Achievement Motives: Psychological and Sociological Approaches* (pp. 321–371). San Francisco: Freeman.

Campbell, K. E. 2005. *Gettin' Our Groove on: Rhetoric, Language, and Literacy for the Hip Hop Generation*. Detroit, MI: Wayne State University Press.

Carter, R. T. 1991. "Cultural Values: A Review of Empirical Research and Implications for Counseling." *Journal of Counseling & Development 70*(1), 164–173.

CNN Justice. 2010, March 20. "Teen Arrested in Wal-Mart Racial Announcement Incident." www.cnn.com/2010/CRIME/03/20/walmart.racial.remark/index.html (accessed April 23, 2011).

CNN Politics. 2009, September 10. "Joe Wilson Says Outburst to Obama Speech 'Spontaneous'." www.cnn.com/2009/POLITICS/09/10/obama.heckled.speech/index.html (accessed April 23, 2011).

Collins, P. H. 1991. "Black Women and Motherhood." In V. Held (Ed.), *Justice and Care: Essential Readings in Feminist Ethics* (pp. 117–135). Boulder, CO: Westview Press.

Congressional Black Caucus Foundation. 2009. "Congressional Black Caucus Directory: 111th Congress." www.cbcfinc.org/cbc/cbc-members.html.

Cross, W. E., Jr. 1995. "The Psychology of Nigrescence: Revising the Cross Model." In J. G. Ponterott, J. M. Casas, L. A. Suzuki, and C. M. Alexander (Eds.), *Handbook of Multicultural Counseling* (pp. 93–122). Thousand Oaks, CA: Sage.

Crowder, K., and J. Teachman. 2004. "Do Residential Conditions Explain the Relationship Between Living Arrangements and Adolescent Behavior?" *Journal of Marriage and Family 66*(3), 721–738.

Davis, R. A. 1997. *The Myth of the Black Ethnicity: Monophylety, Diversity and the Dilemma of Identity*. Greenwich, CT: Ablex Publishing Corporation.

Denby, R. W. 2002. "African American Family Values." In N. Benokraitis (Ed.), *Contemporary Ethnic Families in the United States: Characteristics, Variations, and Dynamics* (pp. 29–36). Upper Saddle River, NJ: Prentice Hall.

Devos, T., L. Gavin, and F. J. Quintana. 2010. "Say 'Adios' to the American Dream? The Interplay Between Ethnic and National Identity Among Latino and Caucasian Americans." *Cultural Diversity and Ethnic Minority Psychology 16*(1), 37–49.

Dyson, M. E. 2005. *Is Bill Cosby Right?: Or Has the Black Middle Class Lost Its Mind?* New York: Basic Civitas Books.

Federal Bureau of Investigation (FBI). 2008. "Hate Crimes." www.fbi.gov/hq/cid/civilrights/hate.htm (accessed April 23, 2011).

Frazier, E. F. 1939. *The Negro family in the United States.* Chicago: University of Chicago Press.

Gans, H. J. 1997. "Toward a Reconciliation of Assimilation and Pluralism: The Interplay of Acculturation and Ethnic Retention." *International Immigration Review 31*(4), 875–892.

Garbarino, J., and K. Kostelny. 1993. "Neighborhood and Community Influences on Parenting." In T. Luster and L. Okagaki (Eds.), *Parenting: An Ecological Perspective* (pp. 203–236). Hillsdale, NJ: Erlbaum.

Graham, M. 1999. "The African-Centered Worldview: Developing a Paradigm for Social Work." *British Association of Social Work 29*(2), 252–267.

Green, V. M. 1981. "Blacks in the United States: The Creation of an Enduring People." In G. Castile and G. Kushner (Eds.), *Persistent Peoples: Cultural Enclaves in Perspective* (pp. 69–77). Tucson: University of Arizona.

Hattery, A. J., and E. Smith. 2007. *African American Families.* Thousand Oaks, CA: Sage.

Heiss, J. 1975. *The Case of the Black family.* New York: Columbia University Press.

Herman-Stahl, M. A., M. Stemmler, and A. C. Petersen. 1995. "Approach and Avoidant Coping: Implications for Adolescent Mental Health." *Journal of Youth and Adolescence 24*(6), 649–665.

Hill, R. 1998. "Understanding Black Family Functioning: A Holistic Perspective." *Journal of Comparative Family Studies 29*, 15–25.

Hill, R. B. 1972. *The Strength of Black Families.* New York: Emerson Hall.

Hill, S. A., and J. Sprague. 1999. "Parenting in Black and White Families: The Interaction of Gender with Race and Class." *Gender and Society 13*(4), 480–502.

Hoffman, L. W., and J. D. Manis. 1979. "The Value of Children in the United States: A New Approach to the Study of Fertility." *Journal of Marriage and the Family 41*, 583–596.

Horn, I. B., T. L. Cheng, and J. Joseph. 2004. "Discipline in the African American Community: The Impact of Socioeconomic Status on Beliefs and Practices." *Pediatrics 113*(5), 1236–1241.

Jang, Y., A. R. Borenstein, D. A. Chirigoga, K. Phillips, and J. A. Mortimer. 2006. "Religiosity, Adherence to Traditional Culture, and Psychological Well-Being Among African American Elders." *The Journal of Applied Gerontology 25*(5), 343–355.

Johnson, D. M., and R. R. Campbell. 1981. *Black Migration in America: A Social Demographic History.* Durham, NC: Duke University Press.

Johnson, K. R. 1971. "Black Kinesics: Some Non-Verbal Communication Patterns in the Black Culture." In L. Samovar and R. Porter (Eds.), *Intercultural Communication: A Reader* (pp. 181–189). Belmont, CA: Wadsworth.

Jules-Rosette, B. 1980. "Creative Spirituality from Africa to America: Cross-cultural Influences in Contemporary Religious Forms." *Western Journal of Black Studies 4*(4), 273–285.

Julia, M. 2002. "Ethnicity and Gender." In M. Julia (Ed.), *Constructing Gender: Multicultural Perspectives in Working with Women* (pp. 1–10). Belmont, CA: Brooks/Cole.

Kelley, M., J. Sánchez-Hucles, and R. R. Walker. 1993. "Correlates of Disciplinary Practices in Working- to Middle-Class African American Mothers." *Merrill-Palmer Quarterly 39*, 252–264.

Kessler, R. 2009. *In the President's Secret Service: Behind the Scenes with Agents in the Line of Fire and the Presidents They Protect.* New York: Random House.

Kilborn, P. T. 1994, May 30. "For High School Graduates, a Job Market of Dead Ends." New York Times. www.nytimes.com/1994/05/30/us/for-high-school-graduates-a-job-market-of-dead-ends.html?pagewanted=1 (accessed April 23, 2011).

King, A. E. O. (1999a). "African American Males' Attitudes Toward Marriage: An Exploratory Study." *Journal of African American Studies 4*(1), 71–89.

———. 1999b. "African American Females' Attitudes Toward Marriage: An Exploratory Study." *Journal of Black Studies 29*(3), 416–437.

Knox, P. L., N. S. Fagley, and P. M. Miller. 2004. "Care and Justice Moral Orientation Among African American College Students." *Journal of Adult Development 11*(1), 41–45.

Kochman, T. 1983. *Black and White Styles in Conflict.* Chicago: University of Chicago Press.

Manning, M., and L. Mullings. (2009a). "Foundations: Slavery and Abolitionism, 1768–1861. In M. Manning and L. Mullings (Eds.), *Let Nobody Turn Us Around: An African American Anthology* (pp. 1–7). Lanham, MD: Rowman & Littlefield.

———. (2009b). "The Future in the Present: 1975 to the Present." In M. Manning and L. Mullings (Eds.), *Let Nobody Turn Us Around: An African American Anthology* (pp. 343–352). Lanham, MD: Rowman & Littlefield.

———. (2009c). "We Shall Overcome: The Second Reconstruction, 1954—1975." In M. Manning and L. Mullings (Eds.), *Let Nobody Turn Us Around: An African American Anthology* (pp. 343–352). Lanham, MD: Rowman & Littlefield.

Martin, M. L. 2003. "African American College Students and Their Attitudes Toward Marriage." Doctoral dissertation, Miami University, Ohio. drc.ohiolink.edu/handle/2374.OX/18558?show=full (accessed April 23, 2011).

Mattis, J. S., and C. R. Watson. 2009. "Religion and Spirituality." In H. Neville, B. Tynes and S. Utsey (Eds.), *Handbook of African American Psychology* (pp. 103–115). Thousand Oaks, CA: Sage.

Mazama. M. A. 2002. "Afrocentricity and African Spirituality." *Journal of Black Studies 33*(2), 218–234.

McAdoo, H. P. 1985. "Racial Attitude and Self-Concept of Young Black Children Over Time." In H. P. McAdoo and J. L. McAdoo (Eds.), *Black Children* (pp. 213–242). Newbury Park, CA: Sage.

McAdoo, H. P. 1997. "Upward Mobility Across Generations in African American Families." In H. P. McAdoo (Ed.), *Black Families* (3rd ed.), (pp. 139–162). Thousand Oaks, CA: Sage.

———. 2007. *Black Families.* (4th ed.). Thousand Oaks, CA: Sage.

McAdoo, H. P., and S. N. Younge. 2009. "Black Families." In H. Neville, B. Tynes, and S. Utsey (Eds.), *Handbook of African American Psychology* (pp. 103–115). Thousand Oaks, CA: Sage.

McGinnis, S. L. 2003. "Cohabiting, Dating, and Perceived Costs of Marriage: A Model of Marriage Entry." *Journal of Marriage and Family 65*(1), 105–116.

McLoyd, V. C., and J. Smith. 2002. "Physical Discipline and Behavior Problems in African American, European American, and Hispanic Children: Emotional Support as a Moderator." *Journal of Marriage and Family 64*(1), 40–53.

Miller, J., and A. M. Garran. 2008. *Racism in the United States: Implications for the Helping Professions.* Belmont, CA: Brooks/Cole.

Moynihan, D. 1965. *The Negro Family: The Case for National Action.* Washington, DC: U.S. Government Printing Office.

Negy, C., and R. Eisenman. 2005. "A Comparison of African American and White College Students' Affective and Attitudinal Reactions to Lesbian, Gay, and Bisexual Individuals: An Exploratory Study." *The Journal of Sex Research 42*(4), 291–298.

Nobles, W. 1978. "Toward an Empirical and Theoretical Framework for Defining Black Families." *Journal of Marriage and the Family 40,* 679–688.

North Atlantic Treaty Organization. 1949, April 4. *The North Atlantic Treaty.* www.nato.int/cps/en/nato-live/official_texts_17120.htm (accessed April 23, 2011).

Obama for America. 2010, March 25. "Organizing for America." [Issues]. www.barackobama.com/issues/index_campaign.php (accessed March 10, 2010).

Ogbu, J. U. 2008. "Collective Identity and the Burden of 'Acting White'." In J. U. Ogbu (Ed.), *Minority Status, Oppositional Culture, and School* (pp. 29–63). New York: Routledge.

Omni, M., and H. Winant. 1986. *Racial Formation in the United States: From the 1960s to the 1980s.* New York: Routledge & Kegan Paul.

Parrillo V. N. 2006. *Strangers to These Shores: Race and Ethnic Relations in the United States* (8th ed.). Boston: Allyn & Bacon.

Park, R. E. 1949. *Race and Culture.* Glencoe, IL: Free Press.

Pellebon, D. A. 1999. "Understanding the Life Issues of Spiritually-Based Clients. *Families in Society 80*(3), 229–238.

———. 2000. "Influences of Ethnicity, Interracial Climate, and Racial Majority in School on Adolescent Ethnic Identity." *Social Work in Education 22*(1), 9–20.

———. 2007. "An Analysis of Afrocentricity as Theory for Social Work Practice." *Advances in Social Work 8*(1), 169–183.

Pew Forum on Religion & Public Life. 2008, February. "U.S. Religious Landscape Survey—Religious Affiliation: Diverse and Dynamic." religions.pewforum.org/pdf/report-religious-landscape-study-full.pdf (accessed April 23, 2011).

Pew Research Center. 2010, January 12. "Blacks Upbeat About Black Progress, Prospects: A Year After Obama's Election." [Report]. pewresearch.org/pubs/1459/year-after-obama-election-black-public-opinion (accessed April 23, 2011).

Phinney, J. S. 1990. "Ethnic Identity in Adolescents and Adults: Review of the Research." *Psychological Bulletin 108,* 499–514.

Pollingreport.com. 2010. "Race and Ethnicity." [Opinion Poll]. www.pollingreport.com/race.htm (accessed April 23, 2011).

Rivas-Drake, D., D. Hughes, and N. Way. 2009. "A Preliminary Analysis of Associations among Ethnic-Racial Socialization, Ethnic Discrimination, and Ethnic Identity Among Diverse Urban Sixth Graders." *Journal of Research on Adolescence 19*(3), 558–584.

Roberts, D. E. 1995. "Race, Gender, and the Value of Mothers' Work." *Social Politics 2*(2), 195–207.

Roxburgh, S., R. C. Stephens, P. Toltzis, and I. Adkins. 2001. "The Value of Children, Parenting Strains, and Depression Among Urban African American Mothers." *Sociological Forum 16*(1), 55–72.

Sánchez, J. C., and J. C. Loredo. 2009. "Constructivism from a Genetic Point of View: A Critical Classification of Current Tendencies." *Integrative Psychological and Behavioral Science 43*, 322–339. doi: 10.1007/s12124-009-9091-1

Sassler, S., and R. Schoen. 1999. "The Effect of Attitudes and Economic Activity on Marriage." *Journal of Marriage and Family 61*(1), 147–159.

Scott, L. D., Jr. 2003. "Cultural Orientation and Coping with Perceived Discrimination Among African American Youth." *Journal of Black Psychology 29*(3), 235–256. doi: 10.1177/0095798403254213

Shin, H., C. D. Ellison, and G. Leal. 2008, July. "Derogation, Disrespect, and Discomfort: The Contact Hypothesis and Attitudes Toward Hispanics and Immigration." Paper presented at the annual meeting of the American Sociological Association Annual Meeting, Boston.

Smitherman, G. 2000. *Black Talk: Words and Phrases from the Hood to the Amen Corner.* Boston: Houghton Mifflin Company.

Southern Poverty Law Center. 2010, March. "Hate Map." www.splcenter.org/get-informed/hate-map (accessed April 23, 2011).

Spears, A. K. 2001. "Directness in the Use of African American English." In S. L. Laneheart (Ed.), *Sociocultural and Historical Contexts of African American English*(pp. 240–260). Philadelphia: John Benjamins.

Staples, R. 1971. *The Black Family: Essays and Studies.* Belmont, CA: Wadsworth.

Taylor, R. D., E. Seaton, and, A. Dominguez. 2008. "Kinship Support, Family Relations, and Psychological Adjustment Among Low-Income African American Mothers and Adolescents." *Journal of Research on Adolescents 18*(1), 1–22.

Taylor, R. L. 2002. *Black American Families.* In R. L. Taylor (Ed.), *Minority Families in the United States: A Multicultural Perspective* (3rd ed., pp. 19–47). Upper Saddle River, NJ: Prentice Hall.

U.S. Census Bureau. 1975. "Historical Statistics of the United States, Colonial Times to 1970, Bicentennial Edition, Part 1, 1999 to 2010: Methodology and Assumptions." Washington, DC: Government Printing Office.

———. 2000, January. "Projected Fertility Rates by Race, Origin, and Age Group." www.allcountries. org/uscensus/83_projected_fertility_rates_by_race_origin.html (accessed April 23, 2011).

———. 2004, March 18. "U.S. Interim Projections by Age, Sex, Race, and Hispanic Origin." www.census. gov/population/www/projections/usinterimproj (accessed April 23, 2011).

———. 2006a, March. "Population by Sex and Age, for Black Alone and White Alone, Not Hispanic: March 2004." www.census.gov/population/socdemo/race/black/ppl-186/tab1.html (accessed April 23, 2011).

———. 2006b, March. *Current Population Survey, Annual Social and Economic Supplement, 2004, Racial Statistics Branch, Population Division.* www.census.gov/population/socdemo/race/black/ppl-186/tab21.txt (accessed May 2, 2011).

———. 2008, March. "Educational Attainment." www.census.gov/population/www/socdemo/education/cps2008.html (accessed April 23, 2011).

———. 2009a. "Living Arrangements of Children Under 18 Years/1 and Marital Status of Parents, by Age, Sex, Race, and Hispanic Origin/2 and Selected Characteristics of the Child for All Children: 2009 Current Population Survey, 2009 Annual Social and Economic Supplement." www.census.gov/population/www/socdemo/hh-fam/cps2009.html (accessed April 23, 2011)

———. 2009b. "Selected Characteristics of Families by Total Money Income in 2008. Current Population Survey, 2009 Annual Social and Economic Supplement. www.census.gov/hhes/www/cpstables/032009/faminc/new01_006.htm (accessed April 23, 2011).

———. 2009c. "Marital Status of People 15 Years and Over, by Age, Sex, Personal Earnings, Race, and Hispanic Origin, 2009 Current Population Survey, 2009 Annual Social and Economic Supplement." www.census.gov/population/www/socdemo/hh-fam/cps2009.html (accessed April 28, 2011)

———. 2009d. "Children/1 with Grandparents by Presence of Parents, Sex, Race, and Hispanic

Origin/2 for Selected Characteristics: 2009. Current Population Survey, 2009 Annual Social and Economic Supplement." www.census.gov/population/www/socdemo/hh-fam/cps2009.html (accessed April 28, 2011)

U.S. Department of Labor, Bureau of Labor Statistics. 2008. "Education Pays." [Employment Projections]. www.bls.gov/emp/ep_chart_001.htm (accessed April 23, 2011).

Washingtonpost.com. 2011a. "Senate Tea Party Caucus holds first meeting without some who had embraced banner." [Postpolitics]. www.washingtonpost.com/wp-dyn/content/article/2011/01/27/AR2011012706966.html (accessed April 27, 2011).

Washingtonpost.com. 2011b. "Obama produces his detailed birth certificate." [Postpolitics]. www.washingtonpost.com/politics/obama-produces-his-birth-certificate/2011/04/27/AFFISyxE_story.html (accessed April 27, 2011).

Wilson, W. J. 1987. *The Truly Disadvantaged*. Chicago: University of Chicago Press.

Winbush, G. B. 2000. "African American Women." In M. Julia (Ed.), *Constructing Gender: Multicultural Perspectives in Working with Women* (pp. 11–34). Belmont, CA: Brooks/Cole.

Young, M. 2001, August 1. "What's in a Name? The Problem with the 'Nation of Islam.'" [Islam is different from Nation of Islam]. www.islamfortoday.com/nationofislam.htm (accessed April 23, 2011).

18

∎∎∎

The Native American Family

Robert John

INTRODUCTION

As the indigenous people of the Western Hemisphere, Native Americans[1] have a long and rich historical past. Depending on the source one consults, it has been estimated that during the period of contact with European cultures anywhere from one million (Kroeber, 1939) to seven million (Thornton, 1987) to as many as 18 million (Dobyns, 1983) Native Americans were living north of what is now Mexico. The diversity of this population is an overriding characteristic, reflected by a high degree of linguistic and cultural variation. At the time of contact with European cultures, around 300 languages were spoken. Few scholars, however, have attempted to estimate the number of separate groupings or "tribes" that existed, and no accurate estimate is possible.

Because the number of groupings was large, for most of the twentieth century anthropologists attempted to summarize the cultural practices and reduce the cultural complexity to a few cultural types. Toward this end, modern anthropologists have divided North America into ten to twelve different culture areas. However, this division is based largely on material artifacts and the modes of subsistence in a given geographical area rather than social organization or a people's way of life, including their family relationships.

The task of reducing Native American societies to relatively few cultural types has been made more difficult because diverse family practices existed not only within each culture area but within each group so that a wide variety of family practices were common and accepted. Indeed, according to Driver (1969:222), "almost all of the principal variants" of marriage and family practices can be found among American Indian groups. Those practices found among American Indians include bride price, bride wealth, bride service, and dowry; arranged marriage and betrothal; interfamilial exchange marriage and adoptive marriage; bride abduction and elopement; cross-cousin and parallel-cousin marriage; patrilocal, matrilocal, neolocal, avunculocal, and bilocal residence patterns; patrilineal, matrilineal, bilateral inheritance and descent; infanticide;

---

[1]I use the terms *Native American, Indian,* and *American Indian* interchangeably throughout this chapter to denote all aboriginal people, whether American Indian, Alaskan Native, Eskimo, or Aleut.

primogeniture; monogamy, polygyny and temporary polyandry; premarital and extramarital sexual relations; divorce; temporary marriage; trial marriage; wife lending; spouse exchange; sororate and levirate marriage; couvade; adoption; patriarchy, and matriarchy.

Obviously, the degree of diversity within Native American populations has been greatly reduced since first contact, largely because of the extermination of many groups through the introduction of European pathogens, including smallpox, measles, chickenpox, influenza, scarlet fever, malaria, typhus, typhoid fever, diphtheria, and other infectious diseases that by all accounts were more devastating to native cultural practices than warfare. An indication of the degree of impact can be recognized by the fact that nearly half of the aboriginal languages are now extinct, and within the United States 564 American Indian and Alaska Native tribes and villages are currently federally recognized (Echo Hawk, 2009). It has been estimated that more than 300 hundred tribes are "nonrecognized" (Indian Country Today, 2008; Office of Federal Acknowledgement, 2008), mainly in the eastern states and California, as the federal government fails to acknowledge them as American Indian entities and from which it withholds benefits. Although many of these tribes are in the arduous and complex legal process of petitioning to be recognized by the federal government (Nazzaro, 2005), the inescapable fact is the dramatic reduction of Native American population and peoples since the time of Columbus when sustained contact with European cultures began.

During most of the twentieth century, attempts to force acculturation to Anglo-European practices has resulted in the further reduction of the range and diversity of American Indian family practices. The influences with the greatest impact on Native American family practices that have played a major role in bringing about change include the intrusive nature of formal education, missionary activities, federal policies to force individual landholding, expropriation of Native Americans' land base, economic exigencies on reservations, intermarriage with other groups, and federal government inducements to relocate to urban areas. More recently, the overweening influence of American popular culture on Native American youth has also contributed to a convergence of Native American values and practices with the Anglo-European mainstream. However, despite nearly five hundred years of destructive contact with Anglo-European cultures, important differences in family practices persist among Native Americans.

NATIVE AMERICAN FAMILIES AFTER WORLD WAR II

Academic research on the status and needs of Native American families continue to lag far behind research on other minority families, and scholarship remains erratic, idiosyncratic, and meager. It is a jigsaw puzzle with at least half of the pieces missing. Moreover, much of the research on crucial topics is dated. One need only contrast the amount of information available about other minority groups, much less middle-class whites, to realize the relative paucity of information on Native American families. Indeed, the difference is easily seen when one looks at the model of family life believed to describe Whites and American Indians and the theoretical concepts used to explain current Native American family practices.

Coming out of the "isolated nuclear family" debate that dominated family studies during the immediate post–World War II era, the "modified extended" family model has been established as characteristic of White family life since 1965 (Brody, 1995). However, studies of Native American family life have not achieved a similar level of understanding. If any model of Native American family life is offered at all, it is the "extended family" model, a family form that has never been universally practiced by American Indians (Driver, 1969). This model is largely the legacy of anthropological studies that have shaped our conceptualizations of Native American family life to the present.

Indeed, if one looks at works on family life published during the post–World War II period, one must conclude that Native Americans were studied exclusively by anthropologists. Based on this anthropological perspective, in comparison to the family structure of White Americans, the opposite presumption was thought to characterize the family life of Native Americans. As examples of cultures that were not fully modernized, family life was presumed to approximate forms typical of "primitive" societies (see Queen and Adams, 1952).[2] It is true that the existence of extended family structures among many Native American groups was well documented in the anthropological literature, but very little of that literature was of recent origin, having been written during the prolific era of ethnographic studies that ended with the Great Depression. This situation of viewing Native Americans as living in an unchanging "ethnographic present" began to alter during the late 1960s when researchers began to study Native Americans from other perspectives and with other research questions in mind.

During the 1960s, the rapid pace of change within American society that had taken place since World War II was apparent among Native American cultures too, and scholars adopted a generalized version of acculturation theory in order to explain changes that were evident in Native American family practices. The two characterizations of Native American family life derived from anthropological studies—that extended families are the norm and that families can be classified according to degree of acculturation—persist as the twin themes of Native American family studies.

Although studies of various aspects of Native American family life have appeared during the last twenty-five years, these studies do little to clarify precisely what is occurring within Native American families as a whole. This fundamental problem is illustrated by a dual tendency to characterize Native American family life as based on the existence of extended families that integrate all generations into a cohesive Native American family, along with a general acknowledgment of the importance of culture change in modifying family practices. For example, Schweitzer (1983:173) acknowledged the tension between continuity and change in Native American family life:

> The most important social structure which operates within the Indian community remains that of the family. It is the family which provides the framework in which the elderly Indian occupies roles which constitute the most important area of power and prestige for old people. . . . If prestige accrues in any context just for the sake of being old it is in the family.[3]

In one of the few studies to challenge the prevailing consensus, Manson and Pambrun (1979:92) questioned whether the common view of elders' position in Native American family and community life may be a stereotype.

> The popular image of Indian elders places them in their children's homes, caring for young, respected in turn, and totally dependent upon these circumstances for a sense of self-worth and fulfillment. Communities presumably provide social and psychological support by seeking their counsel and apprenticing members to them to preserve rare skills and valued knowledge. The relevant literature is dated, limited theoretically as well as substantively, and provides no insight into this image.

---

[2]An interesting reflection, and perhaps a sign of academic irrelevance in shaping social policy during the 1950s, is the divergence between how academics and politicians viewed Native Americans. Although academics continued to treat Native Americans as examples of "primitive" societies, the federal government was busy terminating Indian groups because of a belief that many groups were already, and all groups should and would be, assimilated into the American cultural mainstream.

[3]It is important to recognize that the family life of Native Americans may be the residual institution of their societies that has been most resistant to change. Other native institutions, notably political, economic, educational, and even religious institutions, were decimated long ago, having been changed through violence or legal force. Today, American popular culture is the dominant force challenging American Indian cultural practices.

As these authors recognized, we have no definitive research to give a measure of certainty to our knowledge of the current status of Native American families or how Native American families are changing.

Native American Family Typologies

Based on fieldwork conducted on a reservation band of coastal Salish in the mid-1950s, Lewis (1970:87 ff.) advanced a tripartite model of family life. Lewis categorized Salish families as following the "old Indian ways," "between old and new," or as following "new ways" based on an assessment of the degree of acculturation derived from family lifestyles and values. The characteristics that distinguished the group following the "old Indian ways" included extended family households, use of Indian language, participation in tribal religious practices, low educational attainment and little value placed on formal education, a communal family economy with minimal participation in wage labor, low and tolerant supervision of children, and the importance of grandparents in child rearing. At the other extreme, families following "new ways" were characterized by nuclear family households, higher educational attainment and value on education, more material possessions, steady employment in wage labor, Christian religion, more contact with Whites, strict supervision of children, and intermarriage outside of tribal boundaries. Despite these differences, Lewis does make clear that this more acculturated group has not severed all participation in traditional Native American cultural practices, and she rejects the influence of intermarriage as a special determinant of style of family life, largely because a great deal of "admixture" with Whites had occurred before tribal rolls were created.

Wagner (1976), however, has claimed that, rather than being a cause of assimilation, intermarriage reflects the degree of assimilation that has already taken place. Based on a sample of seventeen urban Indian women, Wagner constructed a typology that, like others, is divided into three categories based on degree of acculturation. Wagner (1976:219) identified these as

> Tradition-oriented (those who adhere to traditional values, including a de-emphasis of material possessions, and seek to preserve or revitalize their culture); . . . Transitional (those who identify with their ancestral group but evidence more of the values of the dominant culture . . .); and . . . American middle-class (those whose cultural identification is with the dominant society but who identify themselves as Indians).

All those among the traditional group had married other Indians; had strong ties to their families, reservation, and tribes; adhered to values that were distinctly Indian; and had social lives centered around other Indians. Degree of Indian blood, however, was not found to be a factor in acculturation or intermarriage. The factors that were most significant in acculturation were the presence of a White father or grandfather; "an Indian parent who deliberately chose to abandon his cultural heritage" (Wagner 1976:227); and White schoolteachers, schoolmates, and clergy. According to Wagner, having a White husband represented another "potent maximizing agent."

Miller and Moore (1979), on the basis of a longitudinal study of 120 American Indian families in the San Francisco Bay area, constructed a four-category typology of Native American "modes of adaptation" based on the degree to which the families she studied exhibited Indian or White values and behaviors. Miller and Moore (1979:479) identified the four groups as:

> Traditional, in which the person clings to Indian values and behaviors; Transitional, where the individual adapts to white means and ends . . .; Bicultural, in which the person is able to hold onto Indian values and means and is also able to adapt to white ends without considering them the primary value structure; and Marginal, whose individuals are anomic in both worlds.

The most recent effort to create an American Indian family typology (Red Horse, 1988) has suggested a six-category continuum of family types[4] based on preferred language (native or colonial), religious beliefs (native, pan-Indian, Christian), attitudes about land (sacred or utilitarian), family structure (extended, fictive, nuclear), and health beliefs and behaviors (native health practices vs. Anglo-European health practices). According to Red Horse, the Traditional Indian family speaks Indian, has an extended family system and a sacred view of the land, practices the native religion, and retains native health beliefs and practices. The Neotraditional family has many of the same characteristics as the traditional family type but has converted or integrated elements of a new religion into its native spiritual beliefs and rituals, including new healing rituals, remedies, or spiritual healers to deal with health problems. The Transitional family is described as having suffered a geographic dislocation (i.e., moving to an urban environment) that has disrupted the transmission of the native language to younger generations, extended family ties and native religious practices. Although daily life generally is based on non-Indian family practices and forms, this family type attempts to maintain cultural connection with the extended family, native spiritual practices, the native homeland, and native health beliefs and practices through frequent trips to the cultural community. Within the Bicultural family most native elements have been replaced in daily practice by Anglo-American forms (English, nuclear family structure, non-Indian religion, view of nature, and health care practices), although people in this family type maintain a generic Indian identity. The Acculturated family type is indistinguishable from Anglo-Americans in beliefs and practices and has severed all ties to native culture. The Panrenaissance family type has passed through the loss of native culture and is engaged in an attempt to renew Indian beliefs and practices although in pan-Indian or hybrid form.

With this latest formulation, Red Horse has moved away from his claim (Red Horse, Lewis, Feit, and Decker, 1978:69) that "extended family networks represent a universal pattern among American Indian nations." Although this statement may have been *generally* true of most Native American groups in the past, it is not true of the present. Promotion of the continued existence of extended families may serve to reinforce an important generic Native American cultural value, albeit increasingly in an ideological manner. For example, based on a series of illustrative vignettes, Red Horse (1997) discusses traditional American Indian family values in an attempt to promote a strengths perspective that remains a theme evident among some contemporary American Indian families. Although some portion of Native American families fit this characterization, many more provide little evidence of adhering to these cultural traditions.

Despite weaknesses in existing data, there is little doubt that extended families are most important on recognized Indian lands and that historical evidence, case studies, population statistics, and empirical research suggest that Native American extended family structures, regardless of how they are defined, continue to weaken, particularly among the growing urban Indian population that constitutes more than two-thirds of all American Indians. Of the family types identified by Red Horse (1988), only three (Traditional, Neotraditional, and Transitional) continue to exhibit extended family values and behaviors, although with less fidelity to the Native American ideal as one moves along the continuum. The remaining three Native American family types reveal values and behaviors closer to Anglo-Americans or, at best, other American ethnic groups, who are also experiencing the harsh pressures borne by a mass, commodified, acquisitive, technological, competitive, invasive, hegemonic American culture.

---

[4]In a previous conceptualization, Red Horse, Lewis, Feit, and Decker (1978:69) offered a typology of "three distinct family patterns" among urban Chippewas ("traditional," "bicultural," and "pan-traditional").

Given this inconsistent evidence, one is tempted to conclude with Staples and Mirande (1980:168) that there "is no such institution as a Native American family. There are only tribes, and family structure and values will differ from tribe to tribe." Although this has always been true, as the feminist reconceptualization of family studies has shown, there is no such institution as "the family" among other groups in the United States either.

The error of comparing Native American families with a nonexistent isolated nuclear family believed to be typical of Whites makes it easy to identify an important between-group difference that distinguishes Native American families. However, the actual differences in family values and behaviors are more extensive and subtle. As Red Horse (1980a) has suggested, many Native American families are more firmly based on *interdependence* than Anglo families. Indeed, a good deal of evidence supports this somewhat more modest conclusion. For instance, Tefft (1967:148) found that Shoshone and Arapaho youth "place many more job restrictions on themselves than whites by refusing to seek jobs for which they are qualified very far from the reservation." Lewis (1970) also found a similar self-imposed limitation among the Salish in the mid-1950s. There is evidence to suggest that this is still true.

In addition, Witherspoon (1975) provided ample detail of the interdependence of "traditional" Navajo family's economic activities and kinship expectations (see also Lamphere, 1977). Interdependence also extends to child-rearing activities. Ryan (1981:28) characterized child rearing in traditional American Indian families as a "total family process" in which a number of relatives, rather than just the parents, provide guidance and instruction, although he states that it is being less utilized today.

Red Horse provided further support for this conclusion in revealing a difference between Indian and Anglo intergenerational family relations. Red Horse (1980a:464) contends that "eventual retirement, with self-responsibility apart from the mainstream of family, serves as a life goal in a nuclear model. Ego identity in extended family models, however, is satisfied through interdependent roles enacted in a family context."[5] Hennessy and John (1995:222–223) also found interdependence to be an important feature of caregiving situations in Pueblo families.

> In American Indian families, total dependence is no more valued than total independence. With a highly dependent elder sometimes family harmony can be reestablished through encouraging greater personal autonomy and ability to contribute to the group that are the central features of family interdependence.

If we are to refine our model of Native American family life, then studies of Native American family networks are essential in order to advance our understanding of contemporary Native American families. Although now somewhat dated, Guillemin (1975) has written the best account of family networks among a group of Native Americans. Her qualitative research on the Micmac of the Canadian maritime provinces and Boston provides the most complete portrait of the operation of what Red Horse (1980b) characterized as "interstate extended families." She describes the network processes she witnessed that link Micmac family members and their friends within a highly mobile but tribally based "community" grounded in the ethic of sharing resources, which extends over much of New England.

Despite this very rich portrait of Micmac extended-family operation, Guillemin (1975:246ff.) also describes a group of Micmac, which she characterized as few in number, that

---

[5]For example, see Cantor (1980), Mercier and Powers (1984), Powers, Keith, and Goudy (1981), Troll (1978), or Ward (1978) on the normative value Anglos place on independence. In fact, McKinlay, Crawford, and Tennstedt (1995) found that disabled elders in need of assistance acknowledged using formal services in order to maintain independence rather than asking family for help and feeling dependent. Few American Indian elders would feel the same way.

lives outside or, at best, on the margins of Micmac community life. These urban "spin-offs" include people who have married outside the tribe; elders; people with tuberculosis, heart disease or drinking problems; and vagrants; as well as another group of families who live in neighborhoods where few Indians reside and restrict their extended family and peer group contacts more in line with family patterns of the cultural mainstream.

Another study of Native American family support networks (John, 1991b) investigated the availability and proximity of kin and the frequency of nine common family activities with each child and sibling among Prairie Band Potawatomi elders living on a rural reservation in the Midwest. This study attempted to understand each elder's total matrix of interaction with his or her children and siblings, how gender and marital status affected contact, and the equity of their relationships. Although a majority of Prairie Band Potawatomi elders had frequent contact with their children and siblings, John (1991b) found that 11 percent of these elders did not have a living child or sibling and 32 percent did not have a child or sibling living on or near the reservation. This suggests that key members of the extended family do not exist or live too far away to provide much assistance for a significant proportion of Prairie Band Potawatomi elders. John (1991b) concluded that ritualistic contact may be the most important type of interaction when a conjugal pair exists. However, children and siblings do appear to mobilize resources in the event of greater need, but until a need exists they serve a largely symbolic purpose.

Native American Family Change

Currently, the American Indian population is, and should continue for some time to be, one of the fastest-growing and youngest subpopulations in the United States. For the 2000 decennial census, the method of collecting data and categorizing the American Indian population changed, making direct comparison with previous decennial census data impossible (Ogunwole, 2006).[6] The primary change was the ability of individuals to self-identify with multiple "racial" or ethnic ancestries instead of only one.[7] Based on the new categories, in 2000 there were 2.7 million people (U.S. Census Bureau, 2010) who claimed to have only American Indian ancestry (designated as the American Indian "alone" population by the Census Bureau). Another 1.5 million identify themselves as American Indian and some other ethnicity. This figure for the American Indian "in combination" population is

---

[6]Scholars of the American Indian have been heavily reliant on the decennial census to know more about the basic features of the American Indian population however it has been defined. Unfortunately, the detailed results of the 2000 Census were not published, and decennial census data will no longer collect detailed information from any population. This detailed data collection effort has been replaced by the ongoing American Community Survey. Over time, this source of data should prove more useful for anyone interested in the American Indian population because several years of data can be combined to provide accurate and reliable estimates of the characteristics of the American Indian population and to avoid the common practice of combining the American Indian population into the "other race" category or ignoring it altogether when results are reported. For all intents and purposes, the U.S. Census Bureau has defined American Indians as the "American Indian alone" population. In most cases, this is the group that is considered American Indian in the bureau's reports. Far less is reported about people who identify themselves as American Indian in combination with another race.

[7]Race is a social construct (i.e., something that does not exist but was invented by humans because it served a purpose, in this case a nefarious one). The term has no fixed meaning, no determinant biological or genetic basis, no fixed set of physical characteristics, and it exists because we continue to use it in our everyday discourse and academic writings as if it were real. Very few social and behavioral scientists, biologists, or geneticists continue to suggest that it has scientific value, let alone any social value. Even the Census Bureau, one of the chief perpetuators of the continued use of the concept, now routinely includes the following statement to acknowledge that it is used because the U.S. Office of Management and Budget requires it: "The concept of race as used by the Census Bureau reflects self-identification by people according to the race or races with which they most closely identify. These categories are sociopolitical constructs and should not be interpreted as being scientific or anthropological in nature. Furthermore, the race categories include both racial and national-origin groups."

substantially less than the 6.8 million people who claimed to be of partial Native American ancestry in the 1990 Census (Passel, 1996), a figure that was virtually the same as it was in 1980 (U.S. Office of Technology Assessment, 1986; cf. Eschbach, 1993). Greater detail about ethnic ancestry in 2000 (Grieco and Cassidy, 2001) reveals that 98 percent of census respondents identified only one racial heritage, and only 7 million people identified as having two or more racial heritages. This same study documents that 24 percent of people who claim multiple racial heritages identify themselves as American Indian and some other group, an implausible figure for a number of reasons.

This new classification system used by the U.S. Census does nothing to settle issues raised about the accuracy of American Indian census data that have been an area of debate among demographers for some time (Harris, 1994; Passel, 1976; Passel and Berman, 1986; Snipp, 1989). Passel (1996) investigated the 255 percent growth in the American Indian population that occurred between 1960 and 1990 and concluded that the increase is demographically impossible without substantial immigration, which cannot be the case for American Indians. In large part, this enormous growth occurred because of a change in census enumeration procedures beginning in 1960 through use of self-identification to classify the race of the respondent. Passel (1996) estimated that one-third of the total Indian population in 1990 had adopted a new self-identification as an American Indian between 1960 and 1990. Plausible reasons for the change in ethnic identity are discussed in Nagel (1995). However, natural increase and greater efforts to accurately count the Native American population are also responsible for the population increase. This problem is still evident in the discrepancy between population estimates and the basic demographic processes of births, deaths, and migration (U.S. Census Bureau, 2010:9).

Rapid population growth occurred between 1960 and 1990 in tandem with urbanization and a geographic redistribution of the Indian population to states that had few Indians in 1960 (Eschbach, 1993; Passel, 1996). Both demographic shifts have been greatly influenced by changing ethnic identification. As Eschbach (1993) has shown, almost all of the redistribution of the Native American population (particularly to California and the eastern states) is attributable to new self-identification as a Native American rather than migration. Based on his findings, Eschbach dismissed the reservation-to-city migration model as only a minor factor in understanding Native American demographic change.

Despite the growth and redistribution of the Indian population to urban areas, census data reveal that Native Americans continue to be the most rural of any ethnic group in the United States. Two-fifths (43 percent) of the American Indian alone population resides in nonmetropolitan areas, another 25 percent live in central cities, and the remaining 32 percent live in metropolitan areas outside central cities (U.S. Census Bureau, 2000). These same data classify approximately 40 percent of the American Indian alone population as rural. In comparison, only 21 percent of the U.S. population was classified as rural.

Slightly more than one-third of the Indian alone population (36 percent) lives in what are labeled American Indian or Alaska Native areas. In 2000 (U.S. Department of Commerce, 2003b) approximately 21 percent of the Indian population lived on American Indian federal reservations or trust land, 9 percent lived in tribal areas of Oklahoma, approximately 3 percent lived in areas (outside Oklahoma) that are inhabited by a federally or state-recognized tribe, and 2 percent lived in an Alaska Native Village Statistical Area. In 2009, 72 percent of all American Indians were living west of the Mississippi River (U.S. Census Bureau, 2010). Only two states east of the Mississippi River (New York and North Carolina) had more than 100,000 American Indians in the state, and five states (California, Arizona, Oklahoma, New Mexico, and Texas) had the largest number of Native Americans, together accounting for 46 percent of the total American Indian alone population (U.S. Census Bureau, 2010).

We have very few indicators of the extent to which American Indian cultural traditions are being preserved with American Indian families. Only approximately one-third of the American Indian population lives on or near identified Indian areas. Even if one concedes that a significant portion of the urban population maintains effective ties with their tribal community, substantial numbers of people who have a marginal connection to an American Indian cultural tradition still claim an American Indian identity. Liebler (2004) also explores this issue by an examination of non-response to the tribal affiliation question on the 1990 Census, which was left blank by 11 percent of American Indians. According to Liebler (2004:318)

> American Indians who are especially *likely* to report their tribe have American Indian ancestry, live with an American Indian who reported his or her tribe, speak an American Indian language or live with someone who does, live in a nonmetropolitan area, and/or live in an Indian state.

By 2000, Ogunwole (2002) found that 21 percent of the American Indian alone and 33 percent of the American Indian in combination population did not specify their tribal membership. Based on research conducted in a midsize city in Michigan, Jackson (2002) provides an interesting account of how an American Indian identity continues to be contested within American Indian urban communities because of the questionable connection some who identify as American Indian have to identifiable tribal communities and their perceived lack of experience and proficiency with a specific Indian culture. The main theme and title of her book hinges on the notion that some claim it (an Indian identity), but our elders lived it (an authentic American Indian cultural experience).

The only readily available proxy for the most essential feature of American Indian culture—the transmission of a tribal language—reveals that American Indian languages are being transmitted by, at best, less than one-third of the American Indian population and less than 15 percent of the American Indian in combination population. Ogunwole (2006) documents that 72 percent of the American Indian alone population only speaks English in the home, 18 percent speak a language other than English in the home (but also speak English very well), and 10 percent only speak a non-English language at home but speak English less than very well. Among the American Indian in combination population these same figures are 85 percent English only, 9 percent non-English at home but also speak English very well, and 6 percent no English at home and speak English less than very well. These data suggest that 78 percent of the total self-identified American Indian population is assimilating to some degree through the English language, 14 percent are fully bicultural, and 8 percent are not connected to American culture well enough to feel comfortable with English. Teufel-Shone et al. (2005) identify less use of the tribal language among a small tribe of Arizona American Indians as one of the elements of ongoing cultural oppression that may add stress to the family environment and negatively influence family interaction.

FERTILITY.   Regardless of whether one identifies as an American Indian alone or in combination with one or more other groups, the median age of the American Indian population is significantly younger than the general population. The median age of the U.S. population is 36.7 years compared to 31.1 for the American Indian alone population or 30.3 for the American Indian in combination population (U.S. Census Bureau, 2009). Based on U.S. Census data from 2000, Ogunwole (2006) reports that the median age of the American Indian population living in American Indian areas (25.2) is even lower.

There is also an important gender difference in the median age of the American Indian and non-Hispanic White population. According to U.S. Census Bureau (2001) data, the median age of female American Indian alone population (28.9) is almost 11 years less than the median age of the non-Hispanic White population (39.8), and there was a 10-year difference among males in the two populations. The significance of this difference is that a substantially higher proportion of American Indian females are in their prime childbearing years.

Findings between 1980–1982 and 2002–2004 for American Indian women in the IHS Service Areas (IHS, 2008) reveal that the pattern of fertility by age has changed little during the period. Fertility is highest among Native American women 20–24 years old, followed by the 25–29 age group, with the 15–19 age group with the next highest fertility rate (although roughly half that of 20–24 year olds), followed by 30–34 year olds. Despite somewhat lower fertility rates among teenage Native American females compared to Native American women in their 20s, this evidence documents that a substantial proportion of American Indian fertility (18.2 percent) is attributable to adolescent childbearing. In contrast, the proportion of White adolescent childbearing is approximately half the level among American Indians (9.4 percent). U.S. Census data for 2007 (U.S. Census Bureau, 2010) documents that the birth rate among American Indian teenagers is 59.3 per 1,000 women, slightly less than the rate for Black teenagers (64.9 per 1,000 women) but significantly higher than among Whites (38.8 per 1,000 women). However, the highest rate of teenage childbearing is among Hispanic teenagers (81.8 per 1,000 women).

These data reveal that American Indian women are far less likely to delay childbearing than White women. IHS data (IHS, 2008) corroborate this finding. Compared to Whites, very few American Indian women wait until age 30 to have their first child. From 2002 to 2004, only 8 percent of first births among American Indian women residing in IHS areas were to women age 30 and older compared to almost 27 percent among White women (IHS, 2008). These data also reveal that far fewer Indian women wait until age 25 to have their first child. Only 22 percent of first births among American Indian women were to women age 25 and older compared to half of first births among White women (51.1 percent). U.S. Census data (Dye, 2008) reveal that American Indian women had the second-highest birth rate in 2007 (68 births per 1,000 women) compared to 74 births per 1,000 women among Hispanics. Non-Hispanic Whites had the lowest birth rate at 50 births per 1,000 women.

Compared to every other ethnic group, American Indian women on average continue to have their first child at a younger age, giving them many more years of potential childbearing than women from other groups. According to Mathews and Hamilton (2009), the average age at which U.S. women have their first child increased by 3.6 years between 1970 and 2006 from 21.4 to 25.0 years. The average age of childbearing has increased among all identifiable ethnic groups. However, the American Indian population has the youngest average age at first birth (21.9 years), 6.6 years less than Asian or Pacific Islander women whose average age at first birth is 28.5 years. Although the average age of childbearing has increased among all groups, the rate has slowed since 1990 and increased the least (.6 year) for American Indian women.

During the twentieth century fertility among American Indians has declined, although American Indian fertility is still higher than it is in the general population. According to the latest figures (IHS, 2008), the American Indian birth rate for 2002 to 2004 among women in the IHS Service Area (20.8 per 1,000 population) was 50 percent higher than the rate among Whites (13.6 per 1,000 population). In a study of children ever born (parity) to married women ages 15–44, Thornton, Sandefur, and Snipp (1991) documented that fertility patterns between 1940 and 1980 were similar to the United States pattern, although Native American fertility was somewhat higher during each decade than among Whites. Overall, as with the White population, American Indian fertility increased during the postwar baby boom years but has shown an overall decline between 1940 and the present.

TABLE 18.1 Children Ever Born to Women Ages 35 to 44 by Place of Residence: 1990

Number of Children	American Indians		Non-Hispanic Whites	
	Urban	Rural	Urban	Rural
No children	14.9%	10.4%	22.0%	13.3%
1 child	16.6%	12.5%	17.4%	15.5%
2 children	27.9%	26.7%	35.5%	38.6%
3 children	20.7%	22.1%	17.3%	21.4%
4 children	10.6%	14.4%	5.5%	7.6%
5 or more children	9.2%	13.9%	2.4%	3.5%

Source: U.S. Department of Commerce (1993): Tables 54, 56.

During 2002–2004, American Indian women in the IHS Service Area were no more likely than White women in the general population to have a low birthweight baby (IHS, 2008), a fact also confirmed for the American Indian population as a whole for 2007 (U.S. Census Bureau, 2010). In comparison, during 2002–2004 American Indian women in the IHS Service Area (11 percent) were slightly more likely than White women (10 percent) to have a high birthweight baby, a fact that the IHS speculates may be attributable to more diabetic pregnancies among American Indian women (IHS, 2008).

Although somewhat out of date, Table 18.1 documents the number of children ever born to American Indian and non-Hispanic White women ages 35 to 44 by urban and rural residence. Unfortunately, there is no more recent information on this issue. This table provides an indication of desired family size and fertility among women who are nearing completion of their childbearing years. Although urban Indian women were more likely than rural Indian women to be childless, and fewer of them have had five or more children, their fertility pattern is quite similar to that of rural non-Hispanic White women until the two highest categories. In contrast, urban non-Hispanic White women have sharply lower fertility than the other groups.

Using data collected from 1989–1992, a study of childbearing (North, MacCluer, Cowan, and Howard, 2000) documented the average number of pregnancies (5.9) and average number of live births (5.3) among postmenopausal American Indian women residing in Arizona, Oklahoma, North Dakota, and South Dakota. This study found that the youngest cohort in the study (women born between 1940–1949) had significantly fewer pregnancies and live births than the other three older 10-year cohorts. Overall, approximately one-third of these women underwent a surgical procedure that ended fertility. This study also documented that the average age of surgical menopause was 40 years compared to an average of 47 years for women who underwent natural menopause. Additional evidence provided by this research reveals that the use of oral contraceptives increased dramatically for each 10-year cohort, from around 1 percent among the 1910–1919 cohort to 54 percent among the 1940–1949 cohort. For each of these measures of fertility, Indian women from Oklahoma were significantly different from Indian women from the other three states. On average, Oklahoma women had fewer pregnancies and live births, and they were more likely to use birth control and undergo surgery to end childbearing. Oklahoma women also had higher educational attainment and higher income than women from other states. Both of these characteristics were significantly associated with lower fertility among Indian women in the four states.

Childbearing entails a certain amount of risk to mother and child. American Indian maternal death rates for women in the IHS Service Area in 2002–2004 (11.1 per 100,000 live births) remain 1.3 times the U.S. White rate (8.7 per 100,000). Despite dramatic reductions in maternal death rates since the IHS assumed responsibility for Indian health in the mid-1950s and the creation of special programs aimed to improve maternal and child health, this health disparity continues to exist. Similarly, American Indian infant mortality rates have decreased by 67 percent since 1972–1974, but American Indian infant mortality in 2002–2004 within the IHS service population (8.3 per 100,000 live births) remains nearly 1.5 times the rate among the U.S. White population (5.7 per 100,000). The IHS (2008) reports that most of this disparity is attributable to higher postneonatal mortality (28 days–11 months) among American Indians with a rate 2.3 times the U.S. White rate. The two leading causes of infant mortality among American Indians are (1) congenital malformations, deformities, and chromosomal abnormalities and (2) sudden infant death syndrome (SIDS). The biggest discrepancy between American Indian and White infant mortality rates (2.8 times) is for SIDS during the postneonatal period. In a similar study of infant mortality trends among American Indians from 1989–2000, Tomashek, Qin, Hsia, et al. (2006) attribute the higher postneonatal death rates to the home environment and need for better primary care and explicitly identify reduction of parental smoking and exposure to environmental tobacco smoke to address the SIDS death rate.

Tyson, Higgins, and Tyson (1999) conducted a case-control study of pregnancies matched by age and tribe of all births in the IHS Santa Fe Service Unit (SFSU) between 1980–1985 to determine the effect of lack of prenatal care, family dysfunction, and a range of undesirable neonatal health outcomes. This study is important because none of the women experienced barriers to prenatal care that are typical of poor women in the United States. Therefore, failure to seek prenatal care could not be attributed to the lack of financial resources or other external service barriers. Family dysfunction was determined by one or more of six dysfunctional markers within the last two years, including children adopted or placed out of the nuclear family, children under protective surveillance, physical abuse of the mother by the father, denial of pregnancy, alcoholism in the mother or father, or maternal suicide attempt. Neonatal health outcomes included low birth weight, very low birth weight, and level II and III newborn intensive care (NBIC) days.

Only 3 percent of the pregnancies during the period received no prenatal care, 41 percent obtained prenatal care in the first trimester, 40 percent in the second trimester and 17 percent in the third trimester. Compared to the rest of New Mexico and the United States, the rates of low birth weight, very low birth weight, and neonatal deaths in the SFSU were lower, suggesting that free universal access to care does make a difference. However, the 3 percent of pregnancies with no prenatal care resulted in one stillbirth, the only fetal alcohol syndrome newborn, 11 percent of low birth rate babies, 18 percent of very low birth rate babies, 24 percent of level II NBIC days, and 41 percent of level III NBIC days. The most dramatic differences in adverse birth outcomes occurred among the women who did not obtain prenatal care and experienced one or more of the six markers of family dysfunction. This group of 33 births resulted in almost all of the adverse birth outcomes among women with no prenatal care. Tyson et al. (1999:117) conclude that the "combination of both factors constitutes a much more potent risk for adverse neonatal outcome in this population than does NPC alone."

Thornton et al. (1991) have shown that ethnic identity and intermarriage affect fertility. Since 1940, fertility has been higher among American Indians married to another American Indian, compared to Indians who have married someone from another ethnic group. Using 1980 census data, Thornton et al. (1991) also documented higher fertility among females who identify themselves as American Indian compared to fertility among women who claim some degree of Indian ancestry, while the fertility of women who identify themselves as Indian but who claim multiple ancestry was in between. For these authors, each of these categories represents degrees of assimilation. Using 1990 Census data, Eschbach (1995) found a strong relationship between marriage to another American Indian and mean number of children ever born. Indian couples averaged 3.41 children ever born compared to 2.36 children ever born to an Indian wife and non-Indian husband, and 2.21 children to a non-Indian wife and Indian husband.

A recent study (Urban Indian Health Institute [UIHI], 2010) adds a substantial amount of information to our understanding of the reproductive behaviors of the urban American Indian population about which very little is known. This study conducted an analysis of the 2002 National Survey of Family Growth that enabled a comparison of the reproductive behaviors and outcomes of a sample of urban American Indian women (N {equal} 299) with their urban non-Hispanic White counterparts. This is a watershed study because it investigates a range of reproductive issues in the large and growing urban American Indian population and establishes a baseline for future comparison.

There was no difference between age at first menarche or average age at first sex between American Indians and non-Hispanic Whites. Both groups reported first menarche around 12.5 years and first sexual intercourse at approximately 17.5 years. Approximately one-third of both American Indian and non-Hispanic White women between 15–24 years of age initiated sexual activity at age 15 or younger, and only approximately 10 percent of both groups of women waited until age 20 to initiate sexual activity. However, in contrast to non-Hispanic White women, approximately twice as many American Indian women (28 percent) had their initial sexual intercourse with someone who was four to six years older than they were, and another (14 percent) had their first sexual experience with someone who was seven or more years older. This means that approximately 41 percent of the first sexual partners of urban American Indian women are four or more years older compared to 22 percent among urban non-Hispanic White women.

The UIHI (2010) study asked women 18–44 years of age about non-voluntary sexual intercourse. These researchers found that non-voluntary first sexual intercourse was more common among urban Indian women than among non-Hispanic Whites. Non-voluntary first intercourse was nearly twice as common among urban American Indian women (14 percent to 8 percent), and this non-voluntary intercourse occurred before age 15 to approximately one-third of the women from both ethnic groups who had this type of experience. The three most common types of force reported by women in both ethnic groups, which were experienced by more than half of each group, were feeling pressured by words or actions without threats, doing what they were told because the male was bigger or older, and being physically held down. However, the only statistically significant between-group difference was being physically hurt or injured, which was twice as common among non-Hispanic White women (29 percent). More generally, approximately 21 percent of urban American Indian women 18–44 years of age reported being forced to have sexual intercourse during their lifetime, a proportion only slightly larger than among non-Hispanic White women (20 percent). The only statistically significant between-group difference in the type of force used was the greater likelihood that non-Hispanic White women were given alcohol or drugs during the episode.

The UIHI (2010) study also found the risk of pregnancy at first sex was much greater among urban Indian women. Only 48 percent of urban American Indian women used any method of birth control at first sex compared to 69 percent of non-Hispanic White women, and urban American Indian women 15–19 years old (13 percent) were far less likely than non-Hispanic White women of the same age to be using any method of birth control (35 percent). Furthermore, among urban women who had never given birth, American Indian women (63 percent) were far less likely than their non-Hispanic White counterparts (49 percent) to be using any form of birth control.

All these behaviors lead to earlier and more childbearing among urban American Indian women than non-Hispanic Whites. Overall, the average number of pregnancies was slightly higher among urban Indian women (2.1) than non-Hispanic White women (1.7). This difference is largely attributable to the significantly higher number of American Indian women who have had three or more pregnancies. The UIHI study found that there is a similar difference between American Indian and non-Hispanic White women in the number of births. The average number of births to urban Indian women (1.5) is significantly higher than among non-Hispanic White women (1.1). Once again, the major difference is the higher proportion of urban Indian women who have had three or more births. Urban Indian women were more likely than non-Hispanic Whites to have had three or more births even after controlling for age, marital status, poverty, and health insurance status. In fact, 51 percent of urban American Indian women between 35–44 years of age had three or more births compared to 26 percent among non-Hispanic White women of the same age. Among urban Indian women, lower levels of educational attainment were associated with three or more pregnancies.

The UIHI (2010) study also investigated unintended and mistimed pregnancies. Approximately 70 percent of both urban American Indian and non-Hispanic White women are currently at risk of having an unintended pregnancy. When asked if they had ever had an unintended pregnancy, approximately 31 percent of urban American Indian women, compared to only 21 percent of non-Hispanic White women, said that they had experienced an unwanted or mistimed pregnancy. Among urban American Indian women, 69 percent said that their pregnancy was intended (had occurred at the right time, later than they wanted, or that they did not care about the timing), 25 percent admitted that they had a pregnancy that occurred too soon, and 6 percent said that they had experienced an unwanted pregnancy. In contrast, 79 percent of non-Hispanic White women said their pregnancies were intended, 16 percent said they had experienced a mistimed pregnancy, and 5 percent had experienced an unwanted pregnancy. Mistimed pregnancies were exceptionally common among urban American Indian women 25–34 years old. Based on a multivariate analysis that controlled for cohabitation status, American Indian women were 54 percent more likely to have experienced an unintended pregnancy than non-Hispanic White women.

On balance, the UIHI data suggest that the primary reasons urban Indian women begin childbearing at an earlier age and have more pregnancies, unintended pregnancies, births, and abortions is because they do not practice effective birth control. Results presented in the UIHI study rule out that these fertility outcomes are related to different sexual practices or behaviors. The UIHI study found that 82 percent of all urban American Indian women and 65 percent of unmarried urban American Indian women were sexually active at the time they were surveyed, figures that are identical to non-Hispanic White women in the study. Moreover, on average, urban American Indian women reported fewer lifetime sexual partners (4) than non-Hispanic White women (6), and there was no between-group difference among unmarried women in the average number of sexual partners during the last year. Since this study also documents that similar proportions of both populations were fecund and urban American Indian women were no more likely than non-Hispanic White women to have experienced a stillbirth, miscarriage, or ectopic pregnancy, the only remaining reason for these differences in reproductive outcomes is less effective use of available contraceptive methods (for whatever reason).

OUT-OF-WEDLOCK CHILDBEARING.   Given the high rates of teen and unintended pregnancies, births are to unwed mothers in many cases. The historical trend and full extent of out-of-wedlock childbearing among American Indians is not known. The evidence suggests that out-of-wedlock childbearing has increased, and it is relatively common since in most tribes little or no stigma is attached to having a child whether a woman is married or not. Bock (1964:144) characterized the attitude toward illegitimacy among reservation Micmac in Canada as "matter-of-fact and tolerant," although he stressed that legitimacy was still considered the norm by the community as it had been prior to contact with European cultures. His study of illegitimacy from 1860 to 1960 on this Micmac reservation found a 20 percent incidence of illegitimacy throughout the period.

More recent research has indicated that the prevalence of out-of-wedlock childbearing has been increasing among Native Americans and is now more than three times as high as Bock's estimate. According to a study by the U.S. Department of Health and Human Services (1995), 55.8 percent of American Indian births in 1993 were to unmarried women, nearly three times the rate among non-Hispanic Whites (19.5 percent). By 2007, 65.3 percent of births among American Indian women were to an unmarried female (U.S. Census Bureau, 2010), although the rate is now only approximately twice as high as among the White population (34.8 percent). Previous evidence from New Mexico and South Dakota (U.S. Office of Technology Assessment, 1986) has shown that there is some regional, and probably tribal, variation in out-of-wedlock births. Census data (U.S. Department of Commerce, 1993) suggest that out-of-wedlock birth is higher among rural Indian women than among urban Indian women, especially among women ages 15–24.

Guillemin (1975:219) found that a "pattern of pregnancy and the birth of the eldest child out of wedlock followed by a marriage to a man who was not necessarily the father of that first child" had been prevalent among the Micmac for some time. This explanation fits the cross-sectional fertility data that show a "marriage lag" (i.e., a number of women have children first and get married later). Since birth can and frequently does precede marriage and the likelihood of ever getting married is quite high regardless of previous childbearing, marriage eventually catches up with fertility.

Guillemin (1975:226) identified cultural reasons for this pattern by noting that among the Micmac "a woman's ability to have children is a mark of her strength and value and there is really no one to shame her for having had a child out of wedlock." An Ojibway woman characterized the importance of childbirth at the same time that she reinforced the normative value placed on marriage.

> Giving birth was considered a woman's sacred role. She attained dignity in the process of giving birth, no matter who she was. Even if a girl was known to be irresponsible, if she married someone more respected than she and then gave birth, she'd redeem herself. (Katz, 1995:259)

Clearly, the cultural importance of the mother role easily outweighs the secular preference that marriage precede childbearing. The interdependent nature of Native American families makes it possible to absorb an event like this without undue travail.

CONTRACEPTION AND BIRTH CONTROL.   Very little systematic research has been conducted on contraception and birth control among American Indians. Some evidence suggests that American Indians, especially youth, make less use and have less knowledge of contraception. For example, Haynes (1977) found that unwed teenage Arapahoe and Shoshone girls 15–19 years old comprised 37 percent of the females who did not practice contraception on the Wind River Reservation. A study by Davis and Harris (1982) of 288 rural New Mexico youths ages 11–18 showed that Native American adolescents incorrectly answered significantly more questions about sex, pregnancy, and contraception than did Anglo or Hispanic youth. Davis and Harris (1982:490) reported that the Native American youth were "the least informed, both in test scores and self-reported knowledge of the sexual vocabulary terms presented."

Evidence from past research suggests that abortion was not considered a justifiable method to avoid childbearing. Liberty, Hughey, and Scaglion (1976) explored Seminole and Omaha attitudes toward abortion. Although approval of abortion was generally higher among the urban residents of both tribes, and fewer urban women were undecided on their attitude toward abortion given a particular situation in which an abortion may be contemplated, women in both reservation and urban environments held similar opinions with few exceptions. Both urban and reservation women disapproved of abortion simply because the couple could not afford another child, did not want another child, or were not married. A majority of Omaha women in both reservation and urban environments and urban Seminole women approved of abortion if the pregnancy seriously endangered the health of the mother, if there were good reasons to believe the child would be deformed, or if the woman had been raped. Reservation Seminole women also approved of abortion if the mother's health was seriously endangered but were less certain that fetal deformity or rape was an adequate justification, although opinion on these last two issues was equally divided with a large proportion of women who were undecided.

These research findings are complemented by a study of the use of surgical procedures to avoid childbearing among the Navajo and Hopi. Consistent with the attitudes toward abortion expressed in the studies just discussed, Kunitz and Slocumb (1976) found that the incidence of induced abortions among Navajo and Hopi women was lower than it was for the general population of Arizona and New Mexico. Overall, there was almost no difference between the two tribes in the rate of induced abortions. However, induced abortions varied greatly by age group. Navajo women made relatively uniform use of induced abortion regardless of their age whereas induced abortions among the Hopi increased with the woman's age. Hopi women ages 40–49 had the highest rate of induced abortions (approximately 5.5 times the overall rate among Navajo and Hopi women in general).

The most recent research (UIHI, 2010) about the reproductive health behaviors of urban American Indian women 15–44 years old ($N = 299$) suggests that attitudes toward abortion may have changed or that attitudes are not consistent with behaviors. For example, Gutierres and Barr (2003) found that Native American women drug users recruited from Phoenix drug treatment programs ($N = 28$) were less likely than White or Hispanic women to endorse abortion as an appropriate end to an unwanted pregnancy. However, the results of the nationally representative UIHI (2010) study found that the number of urban American Indian women who reported having two or more abortions (10 percent) was almost double the prevalence among non-Hispanic White women. More detailed examination of these results revealed that there was no difference between urban American Indian and non-Hispanic White women who have never had an abortion. Moreover, urban White women were somewhat more likely than urban American Indian women to have obtained one abortion. However, the major between-group difference was the significantly higher proportion of urban American Indian women who have had two or more abortions. This finding is a bit surprising because, as these authors note, access to abortion services may be more restricted for urban American Indian women because of their dependence on publicly funded health care services and strict federal limitations on funding abortion services.

Overall, the current prevalence of sterilization among Native American women is not known. Kunitz and Slocumb (1976:19) acknowledge the controversy that arose over the use of sterilization procedures on American Indian females during the 1970s, stating that there "has been considerable feeling on the part of some individuals that the Indian Health Service has engaged in unethical practices in some areas by performing sterilization procedures without informed consent or after exerting undue pressure on patients." Indeed, these authors report that over 90 percent of bilateral tubal ligations are performed on postpartum patients, and that females are far less likely to undergo the operation at other times. This leads to the possible conclusion that females may be more willing to agree to sterilization while the painful experience of childbirth is fresh in their memory and may make a decision that they will later regret. Haynes (1977) found that the controversy over sterilization was associated with a reluctance to use contraceptives among Arapahoe and Shoshone females. Federal investigation of these practices (General Accounting Office [GAO], 1976) resulted in changes in IHS procedures to prohibit sterilization of individuals younger than 21 years of age, improved procedures to ensure adequate informed consent including the signature of a witness, and required a 72-hour waiting period for sterilizations that were not medically necessary.

Although these studies of the use of sterilization are dated, the recent study of the reproductive health among urban Indian women ages 15–44 in 2002 (UIHI, 2010) documented that female sterilization remains a common contraceptive method. Overall, among women who had ever had sexual intercourse, 27 percent of urban American Indian females compared to only 16 percent of non-Hispanic White females report they have been sterilized and female sterilization was higher among American Indians regardless of age, region of residence, or insurance status. As might be expected, this study documented that female sterilization increases with age. Two-thirds of urban American Indian women ages 40–44 report that they have used female sterilization to end childbearing compared to less than one-third of non-Hispanic White women. This report also documents that urban American Indian women living at or below the federal poverty level were more likely than those living above poverty to use female sterilization.

In comparison to use of sterilization procedures among females, Kunitz and Slocumb (1976:9) found that "vasectomies are virtually never done on Hopi and Navajo men." Warren et al. (1990) also found no male sterilization among the sexual partners of a sample of reservation and urban Indian women in Montana (and only 4 percent of each sample of women reported use of a condom as a contraceptive device). The UIHI (2010) study confirms that male sterilization (vasectomy) is not a common method of contraception. Only 6 percent of American Indian females who had ever had sexual intercourse report that male sterilization was ever used as a contraceptive method compared to 17 percent of non-Hispanic White women. If one considers the current method of contraceptive use, male sterilization is even less common among American Indian females. Among women who are currently using a method of contraception, fewer than 3 percent report that they rely on male sterilization to avoid pregnancy. In contrast, approximately 12 percent of non-Hispanic White women who are currently using contraception are using male sterilization to avoid pregnancy. Whether or not males share concern about contraception, pregnancy, and childbearing, this evidence strongly suggests that Native American females bear the brunt of the responsibility to avoid pregnancy and childbearing.

MARITAL STATUS.   The Table 18.2 reveals the current marital status of the American Indian alone, American Indian in combination, and the non-Hispanic White population. The major differences are in marital status between both American Indian populations and non-Hispanic Whites. In fact, there are only minor differences between the American Indian alone and American Indian in combination population. Regardless of gender, far fewer American Indians are currently married, and far more have never been married. Across all groups, significantly more females are widowed than males. However, widowhood is substantially higher among non-Hispanic Whites. These data support the idea that American Indian females tend to marry at a younger age than American Indian males, who tend to delay marriage for a variety of reasons. Marital disruption—whether through separation, widowhood, or divorce—is more common among American Indian females than American Indian males.

TABLE 18.2   Marital Status by Ethnic Group (15 Years and Older): 2007–2009

Marital Status	American Indian Alone		American Indian in Combination		Non-Hispanic White	
	Male	Female	Male	Female	Male	Female
Currently married	39.6%	38.1%	40.2%	37.6%	55.8%	52.0%
Widowed	2.6%	7.9%	2.4%	8.0%	2.8%	11.0%
Divorced	11.3%	14.2%	14.3%	17.1%	10.1%	12.2%
Separated	2.8%	3.8%	2.6%	3.5%	1.4%	1.7%
Never married	43.7%	36.1%	40.5%	33.8%	29.8%	23.1%

Source: U.S. Census Bureau (2009).

INTERMARRIAGE.   Although intermarriage has taken place since first contact with European cultures, intermarriage has also changed contemporary Native American family life. Although less than 1 percent of marriages in the United States in 1970 were between individuals from different "racial" groups (U.S. Census Bureau, 1998), American Indians were the least likely of six groups (Clayton, 1979) to practice endogamy. This relatively high prevalence of intermarriage is reflected in the fact that overall American Indians were involved in 27 percent of all interracial marriages in 1970, most commonly between an American Indian and White person. In comparison to intermarriage with Whites, Black/American Indian intermarriage is far less common, which is consistent with some suggestive findings by Feagin and Anderson (1973) at an all-Indian high school that prejudice against Blacks was expressed by a majority of students there despite extremely limited contacts with them. Without a personal experience on which to base their opinion, this finding reveals the influence of American culture in shaping this attitude during this period of American history.

Figures available from the decennial U.S. Census for subsequent years (Eschbach, 1995; Sandefur and Liebler, 1996; U.S. Office of Technology Assessment, 1986) reveal that intermarriage increased substantially since 1970 so that by 1990 around 60 percent of currently married Native Americans were married to someone from another ethnic group. Using 1990 census data, Eschbach (1995) documented a pronounced age difference in intermarriage among four cohorts of American Indians. Among currently married American Indians, 65 percent under the age of 25, 61 percent ages 25–44, 57 percent ages 45–64, and 52 percent ages 65 and older were married to a non-Indian.

Sandefur and McKinnell (1986) have suggested that some portion of the increase in intermarriage is the result of a change in self-identification between 1970 and 1980, a process that has also been shown to affect the intergenerational transmission of an American Indian ethnic identity (Eschbach, 1995). However, there are significant differences in intermarriage between urban Indians and Indians living in rural areas, and important regional differences in intermarriage (Eschbach, 1995; Snipp, 1989). Endogamy is much lower among urban Native Americans and among Native Americans who live in regions that have experienced the largest increases in the Indian population because of a change in self-identification than it is among Native Americans residing on identified reservations (Eschbach, 1995; John, 1988a; U.S. Department of Commerce, 1986). Eschbach (1995) documented that approximately three-quarters of currently married American Indians who live in twenty-three states were married to someone from another race.

TABLE 18.3 Households by Family Type and Ethnicity: 2007–2009

Household Type	American Indian Alone	American Indian in Combination	Non-Hispanic White
Family households	68.6%	63.1%	64.8%
With own children under 18 years	35.0%	31.1%	26.8%
Married-couple family	40.0%	40.1%	52.3%
With own children under 18 years	18.5%	17.5%	20.1%
Female householder, no husband present, family	20.8%	17.2%	8.9%
With own children under 18 years	12.3%	10.5%	4.9%
Nonfamily households	31.4%	36.9%	35.2%
Male householder	16.0%	17.3%	16.0%
Living alone	12.4%	13.6%	12.5%
Not living alone	3.5%	3.7%	3.5%
Female householder	15.4%	19.5%	19.2%
Living alone	12.6%	16.2%	16.3%
Not living alone	2.8%	3.3%	2.8%
Average household size	3.03	2.66	2.44
Average family size	3.65	3.32	3.02

Source: U.S. Census Bureau (2009).

Within each "marriage market" there are only minor differences in the marital practices of Indian males and females (John, 1988a; Lee and Edmonston, 2005; Sandefur and Liebler, 1996; Sandefur and McKinnell, 1986). According to Eschbach (1995:94), except for a limited number of states in which American Indians tend to live in enclave communities, "in the remainder of the United States the Indian population is amalgamating rapidly." As Yellowbird and Snipp (1994:188) pointed out, "[T]he data on marriage patterns raise the prospect that Indians, through their spousal choices, may accomplish what disease, western civilization, and decades of Federal Indian policy failed to achieve."

HOUSEHOLD COMPOSITION.   Table 18.3 classifies everyone as living in either a family household or a nonfamily household and documents the household composition among the American Indian alone, American Indian in combination, and the non-Hispanic White population. On average, American Indians live in significantly larger households and live in larger families than non-Hispanic Whites. Overall, these data also suggest that extended family household arrangements are uncommon among the American Indian population. The major between-group differences are that far fewer American Indians reside in married-couple families, more live in female-headed families, and more Indian households contain children. The only pattern that appears to favor the American Indian alone population is that fewer female householders live alone (12.6 percent) compared to the non-Hispanic White population (16.3 percent).

A major change in American Indian household composition and family life is documented in census data collected over the last forty years. Census data document a steady increase in the prevalence of American Indian families maintained by women since 1970. Research conducted during this period has also established that female-headed families with no husband present are more common in urban areas. Leaving out non-family households, according to census data for 1990 (U.S. Department of Commerce, 1992), 29.4 percent of urban family households were female headed with no husband present compared to 24.7 percent of rural Indian family households. Naturally, this increase in female-headed families has been at the expense of other family forms, and the percentage of married-couple families among American Indians decreased between 1980 and 2007–2009 (U.S. Census Bureau, 2009; U.S. Department of Commerce, 1983).

An increase in female-headed families has occurred in the general population as well, but the proportion of female-headed families with no spouse present among American Indians (20.8 percent) is more than double the proportion among the non-Hispanic White population (8.9 percent). This appears to be a new adaptation to American society. Although a number of authors, past and present, have commented that marriage and divorce among Native American groups has always been more casual (Christopherson, 1981; Guillemin, 1975) and not fraught with guilt, recriminations, trauma, or adverse effects on extended family life, including affinal relations (Heinrich, 1972), this elevated rate of female-headed families does not appear to be a continuation or legacy of traditional cultural practices since remarriage, except by elders, was common for both men and women in the past.

Another change in American Indian family life is documented by census data. Among the groups studied based on categories employed by the 2000 U.S. Census, households headed by an American Indian alone were the most likely to be unmarried-partner households (Simmons and O'Connell, 2003; see also UIHI, 2010). Among American Indian alone households 16 percent were composed of an unmarried couple, 2.2 times the prevalence among non-Hispanic Whites. Another 1.3 percent were unmarried-partner households that are occupied by a same-sex couple with an American Indian alone household head, a proportion similar to most other identifiable groups in the U.S. population. This study also reveals that unmarried-partner households are younger than married-partner households, which is consistent with previous findings that these unions may be trial or short-term arrangements.

Sandefur and Liebler (1996) documented the decrease in the percentage of Indian children under 18 years of age who reside with two parents that has occurred between 1970 and 1990. In 1970, more than two-thirds (68.6 percent) of Indian children under 18 resided with two parents compared to slightly more than half (54.4 percent) in 1990. In contrast, 70 percent of children in the general population were residing with two parents in 1990. Sandefur and Liebler (1996) also show that fewer children on Indian reservations live with two parents (48.8 percent) as well as the considerable tribal variation in this family characteristic on the ten largest Indian reservations (ranging from a low of 35.2 percent on the Pine Ridge Reservation to 57.2 percent on the Navajo Reservation).

Sandefur and Liebler (1996) articulated a number of reasons for concern about the increase in female-headed families among American Indians since family structure affects the ability of the family to accomplish central functions and has a detrimental effect on the life chances of the children. According to Sandefur and Liebler (1996) female-headed families have fewer economic resources, have lower access to parental resources, experience an unavoidable alteration of the parent–child relationship, and have lower access to community resources because of less residential stability. Although they suggest that cultural influences also play a role, Sandefur and Liebler (1996) associated the increase in female-headed families to increases in the proportion of women who have never married (primarily because of a delay in age at first marriage) and an increase in divorce.

INCOME AND POVERTY.   Low income and disproportionate rates of poverty are chronic problems facing American Indian families. As seen in Table 18.4, American Indian median family

TABLE 18.4   Income by Type of Householder and Ethnicity: 2006–2008

	American Indian Alone	American Indian in Combination	Non-Hispanic White
Median family income	$42,428	$50,887	$70,399
Married-couple families	$57,220	$64,531	$78,667
Male householder, no spouse present	$33,542	$38,940	$49,151
Female householder, no spouse present	$23,824	$26,685	$36,029
Per capita income	$17,063	$19,368	$32,045

Source: U.S. Census Bureau (2008).

income is uniformly less than income among non-Hispanic Whites regardless of household composition. Median family income of the American Indian alone population ($42,428 in 2006–2008) was nearly $28,000 a year less than the median family income of the non-Hispanic White population (U.S. Census Bureau, 2008), and per capita income among American Indians was approximately half the amount among non-Hispanic Whites. Within each population, it is clear that living in a married-couple household confers significant economic benefits, and households headed by an American Indian female are particularly disadvantaged financially compared to American Indian married-couple families and non-Hispanic Whites regardless of household type. In 2006–2008, the median family income of American Indian female householders with no husband present ($23,824) was less than half of the median income of American Indian married-couple families ($57,287) and two-thirds that of non-Hispanic White female householders with no husband present ($36,029).

Sadly, poverty among the American Indian population is relatively common and has been so for some time (Gregory, Abello, and Johnson, 1996; John and Baldridge, 1996; Trosper, 1996). As documented in Table 18.5, one-quarter of all individuals who identified themselves as having only American Indian ancestry and one-fifth of the American Indian in combination population lived below the federal poverty level in 2006–2008 (U.S. Census Bureau, 2008). American Indian families also experience poverty. Nearly 21 percent of all American Indian alone families were living below the poverty level in 2006–2008, making Indian families 3.4 times as likely to be impoverished as non-Hispanic White families. With one exception, the American Indian in combination population is intermediate to the American Indian alone population and non-Hispanic Whites on these measures of poverty status.

Several authors (Guillemin, 1975; Miller and Moore, 1979) explain that the accumulation of wealth is difficult for Native Americans, in part because of the nature of their work experience but also because of the ethic of sharing with others within the family network. This inability to accumulate wealth is best documented currently in the median value of owner-occupied housing units, which represents the largest asset held by most Americans. In 2007–2009 (U.S. Census Bureau, 2009), the median home value of the American Indian alone population ($119,700) was much less than the American Indian in combination population ($153,800) and approximately 60 percent that of non-Hispanic Whites ($193,400).

Previous research has established that an even more somber picture emerges if one looks at just those Native Americans living in rural environments. Poverty, even according to official figures, is pervasive. According to the U.S. Census Bureau (2008), 28.6 percent of the rural Native

TABLE 18.5 Poverty Rate for Families and Individuals by Ethnicity: 2006–2008

	American Indian Alone	American Indian in Combination	Non-Hispanic White
All Families	20.9%	14.9%	6.1%
With related children under 18 years	28.1%	21.7%	9.7%
With related children under 5 years	31.3%	26.7%	11.8%
Married-couple family	10.8%	6.2%	3.1%
With related children under 18 years	14.3%	8.3%	4.0%
With related children under 5 years	14.2%	7.2%	4.2%
Female Householder, No Spouse Present	39.4%	34.0%	21.7%
With related children under 18 years	46.1%	42.4%	30.1%
With related children under 5 years	52.1%	52.1%	42.2%
All People	25.3%	18.8%	9.2%
Under 18 years	32.8%	23.0%	10.7%
18 to 64 years	22.6%	16.8%	9.0%
65 years and over	19.5%	12.9%	7.7%
People in families	22.5%	15.7%	6.3%
Unrelated individuals 15 years and older	38.2%	32.0%	21.0%

Source: U.S. Census Bureau (2008).

American alone population was living in poverty in 2006–2008 compared to 23.1 percent of their urban counterparts. These data also reveal that poverty is uniformly worse in rural environments regardless of age or gender. However, children are particularly disadvantaged in this regard. For example, 36 percent of rural American Indian children under 18 years of age were living in poverty compared to 30 percent of urban American Indian children. Other age groups also experience higher levels of poverty in rural environments. Fully 25 percent of rural American Indians 18 to 64 years old experience poverty compared to 21 percent of urban Indians of the same age, and 23 percent of rural elders over age 65 experience it compared to 17 percent of urban elders. Once again, American Indian females are particularly disadvantaged compared to males regardless of urban or rural setting. Among rural American Indian females, 30 percent lived in poverty in 2006–2008 compared to 27 percent of American Indian males. The comparable figures for urban Indian females and males were 26 percent and 21 percent respectively.[8]

As income figures suggest, unemployment among Native Americans 16 years of age and older is another pervasive problem with a direct impact on family life. The 2007–2009 American

---

[8]Calculations made by author using American Community Survey data from 2006–2008 (U.S. Census Bureau, 2008).

Community Survey (U.S. Census Bureau, 2009) reported that unemployment among the American Indian alone population was 7.9 percent and 7.7 percent among the American Indian in combination population compared to 4 percent among non-Hispanic Whites. Unfortunately, the standard U.S. Department of Labor (DOL) definition only counts people who are not employed but are actively seeking work. Undoubtedly, this figure, like the ones for poverty rates for the Indian population, is an underrepresentation of the extent of this social problem because a disproportionate number of American Indians would not be counted as unemployed since there is little point in actively seeking work in environments like Indian reservations where few employment opportunities exist. The DOL labels these individuals as "discouraged workers."

If one only counts the population that is in the labor force, the picture is much worse. Unemployment rates among the American Indian alone population (13.1 percent) and the American Indian in combination population (12.4 percent) is at least double the rate among non-Hispanic Whites (6.2 percent). Here, females in all groups are slightly less likely to be unemployed, probably because they receive lower wages as the previous income figures attest. Undoubtedly, some of the differences in labor force participation are attributable to higher rates of disability among American Indians. According to data collected for the civilian population between 16 to 64 years old for 2005–2007 (U.S. Census Bureau, 2007), 20.9 percent of the American Indian alone population and 27.3 percent of the American Indian in combination population compared to only 12.4 percent of non-Hispanic Whites experience a disability.

The effects of employment or unemployment on Native American family life have not been adequately studied. Bock (1964) found that periods of unemployment were associated with high rates of premarital pregnancy among the Micmac between 1860 and 1960. Oakland and Kane (1973) studied the relationship between working mothers and child neglect among the Navajo. They were interested in whether the growth in women's participation in wage labor was linked to child neglect as was maintained by popular opinion at a local Indian Health Service Unit. Oakland and Kane (1973:849) concluded that "child neglect was not . . . closely related to the mother's age, education, [or] employment, but the significant factors appeared to be marital status and size of family." Oakland and Kane (1973:852) concluded from their research that "close and extended family ties remained intact" even when mothers secured wage labor, although extended family supports were not universally available.

Witherspoon corroborates the impact of wage labor on Navajo subsistence residential units in one area of the large Navajo reserve. Witherspoon documents that neolocal residence patterns are now typical and that there was little neolocal residence before wage labor became an option. Change has occurred, but like Henderson (1979), Witherspoon emphasizes the Navajo-like character of these adaptations. According to Witherspoon (1975:78),

> the traditional subsistence residential units are continuing to function much the way they have for a long time. At least half of the younger people, however, are not living in these units but are supporting themselves in other ways. . . . Thus, the new economic and residence patterns are not destroying the old patterns; they are just supplementing them.

Witherspoon also illustrates the important difference between household composition and residential proximity as measures of Native American family life. Witherspoon found that 64 percent of the subsistence residential units were composed of three or more generations. However, household composition was overwhelmingly nuclear. Seventy-eight percent of the households were two-generation households, 13 percent were three-generation households, and 9 percent contained one generation. Current data from the U.S. Census Bureau cannot address the issue of whether, or the degree to which, extended families continue to function based on residential proximity. Current data reveal that household size among American Indians is not substantially larger than among non-Hispanic Whites.

An interesting longitudinal study of the salutary effects of tribal economic development and no longer living in poverty on the mental health of American Indian children can be found in Costello, Compton, Keeler, and Angold (2003). This study found that American Indian children who lived in families that had never been poor (who exhibited a low level of psychiatric symptoms) as well as those who lived in families that had always been poor (who exhibited a significantly higher level of psychiatric symptoms) did not experience a significant change in psychiatric symptoms after a casino opened and began providing per capita payments to tribal members. In contrast, the Indian children who were lifted out of poverty by the economic resources provided by the casino (14 percent of the Indian families) experienced a 40 percent decrease in behavioral symptoms related to conduct and oppositional disorders. After the casino opened, children who were lifted out of poverty were no different from children who had never experienced poverty on the number of behavioral symptoms, and both of these groups had significantly lower symptoms than the children who remained in poverty. In fact, the children who were persistently poor actually experienced an increase in behavioral psychiatric symptoms after the casino opened that approached statistical significance (p {equal} .06). Additional weight is given these results because the same improvement in psychiatric symptoms was found among White children from the area (10 percent of White families) who were lifted out of poverty at the same time (although the change was not directly attributable to resources from the casino). Based on these findings and other evidence, employment opportunities, increased economic resources, and subsequent reduction of poverty should be a priority to improve the health of the Indian population.

Life Course

CHILDHOOD.   Research on the Native American life course has tended to focus on childhood. A good deal of attention has been devoted to the subject of the state's intervention into Native American family life through the routine placement or adoption of Indian children into non-Indian families (Blanchard and Barsh, 1980; Blanchard and Unger, 1977; Brieland, 1973; Byler, 1977; Edwards, 1978; Edwards and Egbert-Edwards, 1989; Fanshel, 1972; Fischler, 1980; Garcia, 1973; Goodluck, 1993; Ishisaka, 1978; Red Horse, 1982a; Red Horse, Lewis, Feit, and Decker, 1978; Unger, 1977).

Claiming that this policy contributed to the further destruction of Native American cultures by disrupting the socialization process whereby children learned tribal values and customs, this debate and attendant political efforts were particularly intense in the mid-1970s and led to the enactment of the Indian Child Welfare Act (ICWA) of 1978 (P.L. 95–608). This legislation limited the rights of states to intervene in Native American family life by giving tribes the right to protect the welfare of Indian children as an aspect of tribal sovereignty and self-determination.

Under the authorization provided by this legislation (Pipestem, 1981) many tribes have established tribal agencies and judicial procedures to oversee the placement of Indian children within the tribe (preferably with a family member). As a consequence, the child's tribe now has legal jurisdiction in these cases. Pipestem (1981:60) has stated that the preponderance of cases in which the ICWA has protected children are in circumstances of "neglect, what we call dependent and neglected cases, where there is a substantial amount of chemical abuse by the parents." Edwards and Egbert-Edwards (1989) noted that although progress has been made in the areas of adoption and tribal jurisdiction as a result of the ICWA, implementation and compliance with all of the Act's stipulations have been uneven. Based on a nationwide survey conducted in January

1986, Edwards and Egbert-Edwards (1989) reported that the number of American Indian children in substitute care represented more than three times their relative percentage in the total child population. More important, although the number of children in substitute care from other races decreased, the number of American Indian children in substitute care *increased* 25 percent between 1980 and 1986. Just under half of the 9,005 children in substitute care lived in homes where one or both parents were Native American.

More recent studies of the ICWA provide a mixed portrait of the degree to which it has accomplished its intended goals. One study (Limb, Chance, and Brown, 2004) of 49 placements in a southwestern state revealed that 83 percent of the cases complied with the provisions of the ICWA. These authors concluded that there was a cooperative relationship between the state and tribes and a high level of compliance with the ICWA. Another recent study takes a different view (Cross, 2006).

Another line of research on childhood has focused on the socialization process in Native American cultures (Boggs, 1956; Brendtro, Brokenleg, and Van Bockern, 1991; Downs, 1964; Guillemin, 1975; H. Lefley, 1976; H. P. Lefley, 1974; Lewis, 1981; Miller and Moore, 1979; Ryan, 1981; Schlegel, 1973; Tefft, 1968; Underhill, 1942; Williams, 1958). According to Downs (1964:69), the socialization process among the Navajo operates on the principle of "the inviolability of the individual," a system that operates by "light discipline, by persuasion, ridicule, or shaming in opposition to corporal punishment or coercion." I would interject that to some interpreters this would appear to mean "permissive." Lewis (1981:104) has stated that the lack of corporal punishment is attributable to the respect that is "at the very center of a person's relationship with all others starting with the child's relationship to the family." Brendtro et al. (1991:8) pointed out that "adults will respect children enough to allow them to work things out in their own manner." Supernatural sanctions (Lefley, 1976; Ryan, 1981; Williams, 1958) are also used to control behavior.

Underhill (1942), Boggs (1956), Williams (1958), Guillemin (1975), and Miller and Moore (1979) have stressed that much of the socialization process among Native Americans is nonverbal, with communication by stern looks or simply ignoring inappropriate behavior. In addition, children are supposed to learn by observing others (by example), to share with others, to not make unreasonable or selfish demands, to show deference to everyone older than themselves, to take responsibility for themselves and others in the family, and to contribute to the group from an early age.

Tefft (1968) investigated changes in the socialization practices and values of the Wind River Shoshone and found what amounts to a generation gap between people over fifty years old and younger people. According to Tefft, the values of older Shoshone were more "Indian-oriented" than the values of their adult children. Tefft (1968:331) found that among people over fifty years old, "Collateral, Past, Subjugation-to-Nature, and Being Orientations predominated . . . while Individual, Future, Over-Nature, and Doing Orientations predominated" among their children. He attributed this difference to a shift in the agents of socialization that have had the greatest influence on the formation of values of each of these generations. Respondents in the oldest generation identified their parents and grandparents as most influential in their lives. In contrast, their children mentioned representatives of White institutions (White schoolmates, teachers, church leaders, or neighbors).

Tefft (1968) concluded that socialization practices have changed from "cohesive and structured" households characterized by high dominance–high support parent–child relations in which the older generation grew up to the "loosely structured" households with low dominance–low support parent–child relations of the younger generations. My own research

(John, 1985:305 ff.) among Prairie Band Potawatomi elders confirms, at least, the perception of similar changes in child-rearing practices as well as values and behaviors of younger generations. A composite portrait of these changes can be summarized as follows: Back when these elders were growing up the family was much closer, was more organized and protective, combined discipline with permissiveness better than today, and had the advantage of having parents (particularly the mother) around the home.

H. Lefley (1974) and H. P. Lefley (1976) studied the effects of the socialization process on self-esteem among the Seminole and Miccosukee tribes of Florida. These two tribes were chosen because they are closely related and represent more- and less-acculturated groups, respectively. Lefley wished to determine the effects of acculturation on a child's self-esteem, which she defined as "a sense of identity, worthiness, and self-acceptance as a human being" (Lefley, 1976:387). She posited that members of the less-acculturated Miccosukee tribe would have higher self-esteem because greater cultural integrity would provide a higher level of social integration that would be more conducive to the development of psychological health. Results confirmed her hypothesis. In fact, both mothers and children in the less-acculturated Miccosukee tribe had significantly higher self-esteem. However, some within-group differences were also evident. Girls were significantly higher in self-esteem and perceived parental love in both tribes. In addition, Lefley found that boys' self-concept was significantly correlated with perceived parental love, while girls' self-concept was positively correlated with their mothers' self-concept. Rotenberg and Cranwell's (1989) research on cross-cultural differences in self-concept, however, questions the appropriateness of conventional measures of self-esteem for Indian children. They point out that, although there are definite differences between White and Indian children, the attributes measured are probably not equally important to the two groups.

The basic idea advanced by Lefley's research is the destructive impact that acculturation has on self-esteem and the unfortunate prognosis that the intrusive agents of socialization in American culture will further increase the likelihood that younger members of relatively traditional groups will experience lowered self-concepts. Miller (1981) also viewed a number of these agents of socialization as powerful and insensitive forces shaping American Indian family life. In a study of the effects of one such institution, Metcalf (1976) concluded that religious and federal boarding schools undermined self-esteem as well as maternal behaviors among Navajo women in adulthood. Metcalf (1976:543) stated that "a disruptive school experience had significant detrimental effects on the women's measured levels of commitment to the maternal role, their attitudes toward their children and family life, and their sense of competence as mothers." This, in turn, negatively affected their children's self-esteem. A vivid illustration of the negative influence boarding schools had on parenting and children's self-esteem is provided by a Menominee/Lithuanian woman, whose father had ended up in boarding school and "was not able to be a good parent because he had no experience of parenting" (Katz, 1995:133). She also pointed out that "the elders were not able to protect the generation of Indians who grew up in boarding school" (Katz, 1995:132).

ADOLESCENCE.   Another modern American stage of the life course, adolescence, is much in evidence among Native Americans. The problems of American Indian adolescents, such as alcohol and drug use, suicide, risky sexual behaviors, and difficulties with identity and self-esteem, have been well-researched and publicized (Berlin, 1987; Blum, Harmon, Harris, Bergeisen, and Resnick, 1992; Dinges, Trimble, and Hollenbeck, 1979; Dodd, Nelson, and Hofland, 1994; May, 1987, 1996; Rutman, Park, Castor, Taualii, and Forquera, 2008). Indeed, Liu, Gail, Kinsman, and Khalid (1994:336) have summarized what is known about this period of the life course in the following manner: "Native American adolescents have an increased incidence of high-risk behaviors such as pregnancy, childbearing, school dropout, alcohol abuse, substance abuse, and mental health problems such as depression, suicide, anxiety, low self-esteem, alienation, and running away."

Unfortunately, no community, regardless of how remote, is immune from these changes in adolescent behavior. For example, Christopherson (1981) recognized that adolescence had arrived on the largest and, in many ways, most traditional of the reservations. Christopherson (1981:105–106) pointed to "alcohol, glue and gasoline sniffing, venereal disease, and a variety of delinquent behaviors" as evidence of adolescence among the Navajo. However, he did not estimate the prevalence of these behaviors. More recent research (Bachman et al., 1991) has documented the extent of the drug problem in a nationwide sample of American adolescents. Native American high school seniors were found to have had the highest prevalence rates for use of most illicit drugs, alcohol, and cigarettes of the six ethnic groups studied. The nationally representative survey was administered to more than 200,000 high school seniors between 1976 and 1989. Between 1985 and 1989, 8.2 percent of Native American male and 4.3 percent of female seniors reported daily use of marijuana/hashish during the thirty days prior to the survey. In addition, 10.1 percent of the males and 5.4 percent of the females reported daily use of alcohol; 18.4 percent of the males and 23.4 percent of the females reported smoking half-a-pack or more of cigarettes daily. The authors point out that these prevalence rates may very well be underreported for the total age cohort since Native American dropout rates are very high, and the surveys did not include youths who dropped out of school prior to the late spring of their senior year.

One of the known consequences of alcohol abuse among females is fetal alcohol syndrome (FAS) and fetal alcohol effect (FAE). Probably the most poignant and personal account (Dorris, 1989) is a natural history of a family's struggle with this issue through the difficulties experienced by an adopted son. Summarizing a large body of academic research on Indian alcohol use, May (1996) has shown that the prevalence of FAS/FAE varies greatly from tribe to tribe and that most FAS/FAE problems occur in children born to a "rather limited subset of women who are heavy drinkers" and who tend to live in areas (including urban areas) characterized by low community cohesion. Kunitz and Levy (1994:235) also have shown that the women most at risk of giving birth to a child with FAS/FAE had "severe personality or real-world problems" and that the family environment directly influenced women's drinking behaviors for better or worse. Consistent with this pattern, one of the few behavioral risk assessments of American Indian women (Warren et al., 1990) documented that 36.4 percent of their sample of urban Indian women compared to only 14.0 percent of the reservation sample had consumed alcohol during their last pregnancy.

On a more positive note, Bachman et al.'s (1991) analysis did show an overall decrease in use of marijuana, alcohol, and cigarettes by Native American seniors from 1976 to 1989. Unfortunately, this downward trend does not apply to adolescent suicide rates. May (1987) reported that the suicide rates for Indian males vary significantly between tribes. However, the overall suicide rate for 1990 to 1992 reported by the IHS (1995) for American Indian males ages 15–24 was almost three times (60.8 per 100,000) that of White males (21.9 per 100,000) in the same age group. Although the suicide rate has declined since then, the most recent evidence (IHS, 2008) reveals that the suicide rate among American Indian males in the IHS Service Areas between ages 15–24 (51.9 per 100,000) is still three times higher than among White males ages 15–24 (17.0 per 100,000).

Berlin (1987) attributed the high incidence of suicide to chaotic family structures resulting from divorce and disruption and to family disruption from death or alcoholism. He associated suicide rates to the degree of cultural tradition maintained by a tribe (i.e., the more traditional the tribe, the lower the rates of suicide). Berlin gave the existence of a functioning extended family substantial credit for the maintenance of tribal traditions. Levy and Kunitz (1987) add weight to the idea that the family may be the most important factor in self-destruction, reporting that suicides cluster within families more than within particular tribes.

LaFromboise and Bigfoot (1988) surmised that several cultural values and beliefs contribute to the high suicide rate among Native American youth. The idea that death is a part of the circle of life as opposed to a terrible event to be feared, the traditional emphasis on personal autonomy and choice, the idealization of the deceased at giveaways, and some tribes' belief in reincarnation may all fail to act as deterrents to suicide. In addition to these factors, LaFromboise and Bigfoot (1988:147) claimed that

> Continuous periods of mourning within close-knit extended families due to suicide, homicide, and accidental deaths coupled with the daily hassles of long-term poverty, social and political tension, unavailability of employment and underachievement in education understandably undermine an Indian adolescent's coping efforts.

In addition, according to LaFromboise and Bigfoot (1988), suicide rates among American Indian adolescents may be underreported. Their list of reasons include the use of automobiles as "suicide weapons" or the reporting official's unwillingness or inability to classify the death as a suicide. For instance, the death may be classified as a homicide, when in fact the adolescent who was killed instigated an incident with the intent of suicide.

Although these extreme behaviors have received much attention, we must not let them skew our perceptions of Native American youth. Berlin (1987:229) also emphasized that "some tribes and pueblos have suicide rates that are the same as or lower than the present White adolescent suicide rate," and Dodd et al. (1994) explained in detail many incidents that are interpreted negatively by non-Indian teachers and counselors, when in fact Indian adolescents are exhibiting positive self-concept and high self-esteem in a culturally prescribed manner.

Berlin (1987) noted that the prevention of suicide has become a top priority in many tribes and summarized several successful intervention programs. The use of tribal elders to help mitigate the loss of parental involvement and early nurturant figures in the lives of Native American adolescents have been especially effective. LaFromboise and Low (1989) have also identified possible interventions in managing the multitude of problems faced by Indian adolescents. They noted that Indian youth expect practical advice from counseling, not the reflective analysis that most conventionally trained counselors are taught to administer. The use of extended family, which they defined liberally as those persons who are influential and supportive in the adolescent's life, can be crucial in designing an effective intervention strategy for Indian youth. In each case, it appears to be the involvement of respected and caring individuals in the adolescent's life that delineates success from failure in the counseling process.

A large national study conducted among 11,666 American Indians in the seventh through twelfth grades in the 1990 National American Indian Adolescent Health Survey (Borowsky, Resnick, Ireland, and Blum, 1999), although not fully representative of the American Indian adolescent population, provides the most comprehensive data on suicide attempts and the risk and protective factors influencing this behavior among American Indian adolescents. Based on self-report, this study found that 21.8 percent of girls and 11.8 percent of boys in the sample had attempted suicide.

This study investigated a large number of risk and protective factors that have been found to influence suicidal behavior. Based on a separate multivariate analysis for boy and girls, Borowsky and colleagues (1999) identified eleven risk factors and four protective factors for girls and twelve risk factors and three protective factors for boys. The top two risk factors associated with suicide attempts by both girls and boys were a friend attempted or committed suicide and experiencing somatic symptoms (using a scale of questionable reliability that included five items: headaches, breathing problems, stomach problems, allergies, or nerves). Among girls, marijuana use, having a family member who attempted or committed suicide, and alcohol use rounded out the top five risk factors. For boys, experiencing sexual abuse, having a family member who attempted or committed suicide, and having health concerns during the past month completed the top five risk factors associated with an attempt. The three most powerful protective factors for both boys and girls were being able to discuss problems with family or friends, better emotional health during the past month (a reliable nine-item scale that included such items as feeling secure, rested, relaxed, cheerful, satisfied, in control), and family connectedness (a highly reliable five-item scale that included perceived caring by parents and family, family understands and pays attention, and has fun with family). A fourth protective factor for girls but not boys was having access to a school clinic or nurse. Borowsky et al. (1999) conclude that increasing protective factors will be more effective than decreasing risk factors in reducing suicide attempts among American Indian youth.

An analysis of Youth Risk Behavior Survey data for 1997–2003 (Rutman et al., 2008) from a sample of urban American Indian youth ($N = 513$) in the ninth to twelfth grades documents the extent and severity of a range of suicidal behaviors among these adolescents. Reporting on their thoughts and behaviors during the most recent twelve months, 27.9 percent of these urban American Indian youth admitted that they seriously considered committing suicide, 25.2 percent said that they had made a plan to commit suicide, 20.7 percent said they attempted to commit suicide, and 10.9 percent said that they were injured as a result of their suicide attempt. These latest figures are a menacing alarm about the extraordinary threat suicide poses to American Indian youth and the special need for public health efforts to address this problem.

ADULTHOOD AND MIDDLE AGE.   Adulthood and middle age have received very little attention. Christopherson (1981:106), quoting a study by the Office of Indian Education, characterized gender differences among the Navajo that I believe are relatively common among Native Americans in general. There is a tendency among females to settle down at an early age while "males . . . do not reflect qualities of sociological adulthood until their very late 20s or early 30s. Until then, males typically defer marriage, maintain their peer-group orientations, and have very little job stability" (see also Guillemin, 1975). This is undoubtedly related to the scarcity of employment opportunities on reservations as much as any other factor. When young Indians do settle down, as in American society in general, mate selection is based on romantic love.

Despite this similarity, there are attitudinal differences between Native American and other youth toward marital practices. Edington and Hays (1978) conducted a comparative study of the difference in family size and marriage age expectation and aspiration of Anglo, Mexican American, and American Indian youth living in rural New Mexico. They found that Native American youth wanted more children (mean 2.90) and expected to have more children (mean 3.05) than Anglo (2.30 and 2.49, respectively) or Mexican American (2.71 and 2.87, respectively) youth. Based on his analysis of 1980 census data, Snipp (1989) concluded that two to three children was the preferred number of offspring among American Indian women.

Edington and Hays (1978) also found that the ages at which American Indian youth wanted to marry (mean 23.4 years) and expected to marry (mean 23.2 years) were higher than the responses from the other two groups. On balance, however, Edington and Hays concluded that Native American youth were less certain of their desires and expectations regarding marriage and procreation because of a higher rate of non-response than Anglo or Mexican American youth. These attitudes and preferences appear to be confirmed by the latest data presented previously in this chapter.

Very little is known about husband–wife interaction among Native Americans. Only one such study (Strodtbeck, 1951) compared ten Navajo, Texan, and Mormon couples on how they interacted during decision making and whose opinion prevailed when asked to characterize families in their community. Strodtbeck hypothesized that Navajo women, because of their economic power and independence gained through the control of property, would win more of the decisions than either Texan or Mormon women. This hypothesis was confirmed by his study. Strodtbeck also discovered that the character of the dyadic interaction was very different among the Navajo couples. According to Strodtbeck, Navajos had a tendency to minimize analysis.

Navajos gave opinion, evaluation, and analysis acts during the solution of their differences only one-half as frequently as the Mormon and the Texan group. As a result they required, on average, fewer acts per decision (8 in comparison with 30 for the other groups), and the reasoning and persuasion in their protocols seemed extremely sketchy. They did not emphasize the arguments that might bear on the issue, they tended to reiterate their choices and implore the other person to "go with them," "go together," or simply consent. This is in marked contrast with the other couples who appeared to feel that they had to give a reasoned argument to show that they were logically convinced, even when they were giving in to the other person (Strodtbeck, 1951:473).

Without commenting directly on this study by Strodtbeck, Witherspoon (1975) corroborates the relative lack of verbal interaction during the decision-making process among Navajos. Because of the emphasis on unity, cooperation, and consensus in Navajo family life, when important decisions need to be made, feelings, attitudes, and decisions are sensed rather than verbally expressed. Serious matters are seldom dealt with at the level of speech, and important decisions are seldom discussed. Decisions are felt and sensed before they reach a verbalized conclusion. According to Witherspoon (1975:98), family members think over the situation until one of their number "has the sense of the group" and then offers a suggestion to the group that either resolves the issue or results in further deliberations. Because the Navajo live and work together closely, over the years they "learn to communicate with each other without the use of language."

This nonverbal approach extends to other tribes as well as other areas of family life. Quoting one of her informants, the first strength of Indian families identified by Miller and Moore (1979:457) was that "[r]elatives 'help without being asked. It's just our way.'" Elders, too, do not feel that they should have to ask for assistance but that family members, tribal officials, and service workers should be able to sense their needs and respond to them (John, 1988a, 1991b).

Guillemin (1975) provided a reasonable explanation for the nonverbal capabilities of American Indians when she characterizes the socialization process of Micmac children. "Micmac children learn by observation and are not subjected in the family to intense verbal instruction. Younger children are expected to imitate their older siblings in the basics of eating, toilet training, and general physical dexterity without individual instruction" (Guillemin, 1975:94–95). Williams (1958) and Underhill (1965) also documented this approach among the Tohono O'Odham (Papago).

Little is known about contemporary gender roles among Native Americans, in part because the lives of ordinary American Indian women have received so little attention (John, Blanchard, and Hennessy, 1997). Although there were a few exceptions, gender relations prior to contact with European Christian cultures tended to be egalitarian in nature (Allen, 1986; Bonvillain, 1989; Green, 1980; Gutiérrez, 1991; LaFromboise, Heyle, and Ozer, 1990; Tsosie, 1988). These writers share the view that Native American women in general, and older Native American women in particular, had much higher status prior to contact with European Christian culture. This body of literature persuasively argues that contact with patriarchal European Christian culture undermined the status of women, especially in the public sphere, although the line between these two spheres was less demarcated within traditional American Indian societies. This status change also influenced gender roles in Native American cultures.

Coming from cultures that traditionally had rigid gender roles,[9] contemporary Native Americans have experienced gender role changes that parallel those that have taken place in American culture in general. Although American Indian women still have primary responsibility for home life, there is evidence that men and women have modified their gender role behaviors toward the androgynous norms of American society as a whole. Based on a small sample from Los Angeles during the early period of gender role change, Price (1981) characterized the primary emotional concerns of women as largely expressive and men as instrumental. Price found that women were more concerned with kinfolk, family, marriage, and sexual relations, and men were more concerned with employment, money, success, and material matters. Guillemin (1975) characterized other aspects of gender roles during the period, including same sex confidants and peer groups.

More recently, an examination of the division of household labor among 28 two-parent Navajo families living in a rural area just off the reservation (Hossain, 2001) found that mothers spent significantly more time than fathers on cleaning and on food- and child-related tasks, although fathers were involved in these matters and spent approximately 75 percent as much time as mothers on these activities. In addition, mothers were more invested in activities that reflected commitment to their family (such as willingness to help other family members), cohesion (such as sacrificing for the family), and communication (sharing feelings and concerns). Hossain (2001) found that both parents were equally involved in household maintenance activities.

Another issue concerning gender roles is role change. The few scholars who have studied this issue differ on whether men's or women's roles have changed the most. Some observers of the Navajo (Christopherson, 1981; Witherspoon, 1975) have suggested that men's gender roles have changed more than women's because women continue to exercise economic power in subsistence residential units that have been the basis of the Navajo tribal economy for over a century. Blanchard (1975), however, has maintained the opposite for the Navajo, and Aginsky and Aginsky (1947:84) described a complete role reversal among the Pomo from a "man-authoritarian culture to a woman-authoritarian culture."

Blanchard claims that Protestant sects have afforded women new gender roles and statuses to compensate for the loss of roles and prestige that have accompanied economic change. Blanchard (1975) found that Navajo women who had joined either of the Protestant churches on

---

[9]A particularly misguided interpretation of American Indian gender roles can be found in Gonzales (1994). Indeed, because of the value Native American cultures placed on personal autonomy and taking direction from communion with the spirit world, one could say that personal forms of deviant behavior were institutionalized in native cultures. These types of personal deviance include "contraries," berdaches (individuals assuming the dress, social status, and role of the opposite sex), women warriors, healers, and "chiefs" (Allen, 1986; Garcia, 1994; Jacobs, Thomas, and Lang, 1997; Lang, 1998; Roscoe, 1991; Williams, 1986). Red Horse (1997) aptly characterized American Indian cultures as nonjudgmental and inclusive primarily because of respect for nature and a common belief that everything happened for a purpose. The type of deviance that could not be tolerated was deviance that threatened group survival (e.g., young hunters giving chase to a herd of buffalo before the signal was given by the hunt leader). The conceptualization of gender roles was rigid but not strictly tied to an individual's biological sex. Regardless of the sex of the role occupant, the role was open to anyone who was willing to practice the role in the prescribed manner. Women warriors were to perform the role set of men, and men who wished to be wives were to perform the role set of women.

the Ramah Reservation had twice the formal education, were twice as likely to work outside the home, were more likely to have lived and worked off the reservation, were more likely to live in a neolocal situation and in smaller households, were more likely to have fewer children, and were less likely to honor traditional social obligations than their more traditional counterparts. On balance, however, I would have to conclude that men have experienced the greatest role change, as the patriarchal family has given ground to Indian women's educational, economic, and political achievements, and successful efforts to provide for their family regardless of whether they have the support of a male partner.

DOMESTIC VIOLENCE.   There is a broad consensus that violence against Indian women was rare in traditional Indian societies and in most cases would have resulted in some form of family retribution or formal punishment of the perpetrator. This no longer appears to be true. One recent, and growing, area of concern is violence against Indian women, including domestic violence, sexual assault, and stalking. The National Violence Against Women Survey (Tjaden and Thoennes, 2000) documents that approximately one-third of American Indian women (34 percent) are raped during their lifetime compared to 18 percent of women in general. This study also found that American Indian women report the highest prevalence of experiencing a physical assault (61 percent) during their lifetime. Using the same data, Tjaden and Thoennes (1998) also report that American Indian men and women report the highest lifetime prevalence of being stalked of the five ethnic groups included in the study. However, American Indian women (17 percent) were more than three times as likely to report being stalked as American Indian men (5 percent). Although there is supporting evidence for these or higher rates from other studies (Evans-Campbell, Lindhorst, Huang, and Walters, 2006), Tjaden and Thoennes (2000) caution that we do not know if American Indians are more willing to reveal these experiences than other groups.

A broader study of crime among American Indians (Perry, 2004) reported that the annual rate of rape or sexual assault among American Indians 12 years and older during 1992–2001 was 5 per 1,000 persons, more than double the rate among Whites. This same study reported that 59 percent of rapes and sexual assaults were perpetrated by a person known to the victim, including an intimate partner or family member (25 percent) or acquaintance (34 percent). The remaining 41 percent of perpetrators were strangers. According to this study, 78 percent of American Indian victims of rape or sexual assault identified the perpetrator as White. In contrast to rapes and sexual assaults, 66 percent of murders among American Indians were committed by an American Indian relative or acquaintance.

A more circumscribed study of domestic abuse among 691 American Indians 13 years or older from Zuni Pueblo revealed that approximately 30 percent experienced some type of domestic partner violence in the past 12 months (Perry, 2004). Most of these incidences of domestic abuse were committed against women. Emotional or psychological abuse (44 percent) was slightly more common than physical abuse (38 percent), followed by threats (13 percent), stalking (5 percent) or sexual assault (1 percent). Alcohol or drug use by the offender was implicated in 69 percent of the incidents, and nearly one-third of the incidences of abuse were committed by someone who lived with the victim. Most of these crimes were not reported to the authorities.

A study of homicides of women in New Mexico between 1990–1993 (Arbuckle et al., 1996) found that approximately half of the murders (46 percent) in the state were committed by a male intimate partner. American Indian women comprised 25 percent of the homicide victims during the period and had the highest rates of both domestic-violence and non–domestic-violence homicide, approximately 2.8 times the rate among non-Hispanic White and Hispanic women.

Using data from seven Indian states from the 2003 National Survey of Children's Health, Probst et al. (2008) provide some insight into family situations that potentially lead to instances of domestic violence within American Indian families. This study examined how disagreements typically were handled in American Indian ($N = 1,015$) and White families. Violent disagreement (such as hitting or throwing things) and heated disagreement (limited to engaging in heated argument or shouting at least some of the time) were contrasted with calm disagreement (the residual category). The prevalence of both of the more extreme types of disagreement was similar between American Indian and White families. Among American Indians 8.4 percent reported violent disagreements, and another 30.6 percent reported heated disagreements. This study estimated that approximately 40 percent of American Indian children live in households where heated arguments or violent disagreements take place. Here too, a similar proportion of White children have the same experience. Several factors were associated with the more extreme forms of disagreements. Having three or more children in the home was associated with both violent and heated disagreements among American Indians. Apparently, however, this was not related to lack of financial resources since none of the measures of economic well-being (income, education, or having health insurance) were significantly associated with these behaviors. Parents' fair or poor mental health was strongly related to heated disagreements (but not violent ones). Overall, parenting stress was associated with both forms of severe disagreements (but more strongly associated with violent disagreements), and among American Indian parents, parenting stress was associated with having a child with special health care needs and if at least one parent assessed their health as fair or poor. Although a number of potentially important limitations of this study were recognized, this study is the first large-scale look at how family status and process variables may influence domestic violence.

ELDERS.   Another body of recent research on the life course has investigated the other end of the life cycle. The nature of the research that has been conducted during the last thirty-five years has changed greatly from anthropological accounts and issues to more practical investigations (John, 1988a), the goal of which is to improve the quality of life of Native American elders. For the most part, this applied social policy research has investigated the current status, service needs, and service use of Native American elders (Barón, Manson, Ackerson, and Brenneman, 1990; Bell, Kaschau, and Zellman, 1978; Brown, 1989; Edwards, Egbert-Edwards, and Daines, 1980; Hennessy and John, 1996; John, 1988b, 1991a, 1994, 1995; John and Baldridge, 1996; John, Hennessy, Roy, and Salvini, 1996; Johnson and Taylor, 1991; Joos and Ewart, 1988; Kramer, 1991; Kramer, Polisar, and Hyde, 1990; Kunitz and Levy, 1991; Lefkowitz and Underwood, 1991; Manson, 1989a, 1989b, 1993; Murdock and Schwartz, 1978; National Aging Resource Center on Elder Abuse, 1989; National Indian Council on Aging, 1981, 1983; Red Horse, 1982b). The general findings are that American Indian elders experience a number of disadvantages in old age compared to the general population.

However, there are significant differences between urban- and reservation-aging American Indians in their current status and need for services, as well as the mix of support they receive from informal and formal sources. Based on a nationwide sample of Indian elders over age 55 (John, 1991a), it is possible to characterize urban and reservation differences in current status. Without doubt, the deprivation experienced by aging reservation Indians is substantially greater than among urban Indians. In general, the reservation group is poorer, has greater financial concerns, supports more people on their income, has fewer social contacts, has somewhat lower life satisfaction, and is in poorer health.

As is true of the general population, the greatest service needs for both groups of elders are for non-personal (i.e., housework, shopping, transportation) rather than personal (i.e., bathing, dressing, eating) assistance. The top four activities of daily living for which both urban and reservation groups need ongoing assistance are help with housework, transportation, using the telephone, and going shopping, and the foremost unmet need of both groups is for information and referral assistance. However, the levels of need are substantially greater in rural environments (John, 1991a).

Sources of assistance also differ between urban and rural settings. In comparison to urban Indians, family members are more salient as direct and sole service providers to reservation residents. In addition, family members of reservation residents are more likely than their urban counterparts to share service responsibility with formal sources of support. In contrast, urban residents rely more on formal social services to meet their needs. Despite these differences, family is important in providing services for both reservation and urban Indians although the relative demands on the family network are greater on reservations because of fewer formal service options (John, 1991a).

The issue of the existence and extent of the family support network is important during all periods of the life course, but it is especially important to the well-being of children and frail elders. Among Native Americans, the absence of family support has been linked to child abuse and neglect (Metcalf, 1979; Oakland and Kane, 1973), adolescent pregnancy (Y. Red Horse, 1982), psychological disturbances (Fox, 1960), and problems adapting to urban life (Metcalf, 1979; Miller and Moore, 1979). More recently, elder abuse and neglect within American Indian families has been acknowledged (Brown, 1989; Carson, 1995; Carson and Hand, 1999; Maxwell and Maxwell, 1992; National Aging Resource Center on Elder Abuse, 1989). Although the full extent of elder abuse and neglect is not known, Brown's study (1989) among a random sample of 37 Navajo elders ages 60 years and older found that the most frequent type of abuse was being left alone when the elder needed help, followed by financial exploitation, and that elder abuse was associated with the suddenness of becoming dependent, having mental problems, and the personal problems of the caregiver. Instances of abuse and neglect contrast sharply with two common forms of intergenerational family caregiving that are important expressions of extended family support.

Among American Indian families in which extended family relationships are present, the grandparent–grandchild relationship is of special importance (Bahr, 1994; Ball, 1970; John, 1988a; Lewis, 1981; Ryan, 1981; Tefft, 1968; Schweitzer, 1999). Indeed, the grandmother is the center of American Indian family life, and she holds the family together. Although Medicine (1981) cautioned that the literature may popularize the role of grandmother at the expense of the broader kin group, many authors have described the grandmother's role as primary caregiver for grandchildren, especially on reservations (Bahr, 1994; Bradford and Thom, 1992; Crow Dog and Erdoes, 1990; Fisher, 1980; Green, 1992; Shomaker, 1989).

Because of the tendency among American Indians to begin childbearing at a very early age, it is common for a woman to be a grandmother by the time she is forty years old and often by the time she is in her mid-thirties. Although motherhood is an important transition in the life course, marking the status of becoming a woman, grandmotherhood is an even more important transition because of the additional responsibilities a woman assumes. Recognizing that not all grandmothers live up to the cultural ideal, Bahr (1994:245) succinctly characterized the ideal Apache grandmother as a woman who has entered "the full strength of her maturity."

Among American Indians, young women who have children, especially teenagers, frequently have little inclination or preparation for motherhood, and some irresponsibility is anticipated and tolerated (Bahr, 1994; Metcalf, 1979), as long as it does not endanger the well-being of the child. Generally, the young woman looks to her mother for assistance and training and frequently passes a great deal of responsibility for the care of the child to her mother. On occasion the grandmother takes over rearing one or more grandchildren because she or other family members feel that the child is not being raised properly or the parent(s) decide that it will benefit the child (Guillemin, 1975; Miller and Moore, 1979; Shomaker, 1989). A child may also go to live with a family member who needs help or if a family member would like to have a child around (Shomaker, 1989; Underhill, 1965). It is also possible for a child to ask to live with grandparents, a request that is honored if not a manifest impossibility. Bahr (1994) concluded that her respondents considered Apache children disadvantaged if they did not have a grandmother able to provide whatever care was needed.

Despite the centrality of grandmotherhood in the family life of American Indians, very few scholarly studies have investigated the topic. Most studies have been limited to a single location or tribe. A useful compilation of anthropological accounts, most of which were conducted in the mid-1980s, that address continuity and change in the lives of grandmothers from several tribes can be found in Schweitzer (1999). Schweitzer states that a universal trait of grandmothers across these studies is their involvement in child care and child rearing. According to Schweitzer (1999:9–10) "their roles in the enculturation of children have always been important, but today their participation in the welfare of future generations may be especially crucial." Grandmothers, and elders in general, are entrusted with the important task of transmitting tribal culture to younger generations. Many times, they attempt to accomplish this under less than ideal circumstances, including when they are full-time caregivers as well as when they have limited or episodic contact with their grandchildren.

Shomaker (1989, 1990) produced two closely related works about grandmothers that provide some insight into the grandmother's role among the Navajo. In the first article, Shomaker (1989) characterized the circumstances surrounding the placement of one or more grandchildren ($N = 98$) with their grandmother. In the great preponderance of cases, the child was provided care because of family problems that the grandmother was unwilling to let adversely affect her grandchild. The situations that most commonly precipitated the placement of grandchildren included "a deficit in parenting skills" that created an "unhealthy living environment for the grandchildren" (36 percent of the cases); a change in the parent's lifestyle, including death of a parent, an off-reservation job or remarriage (32 percent of the placements); a family workload that was too heavy for the mother, who was often unwed and unable to provide adequate care (18 percent of the cases); and the "grandmother's needs" (14 percent of the cases). In this last instance, grandchildren were sometimes given to the grandmother as a sign of respect, if the grandmother was lonely, or if she expressed a desire to raise another child. In the later article, Shomaker (1990) claimed that grandchildren were transferred to the care of grandmothers on the conscious expectation that this would secure care in old age when the grandmother became frail. However, her previous work had shown that only a small percentage of fosterage cases (14 percent) occur because the child will meet a need of the grandmother, a motivation that was also not the typical reason for care among Apache grandmothers (Bahr, 1994). Shomaker admitted (1989, 1990) that this expectation rarely resulted in care by the grandchild in later life.

Far less is known about the personal relationship between grandmothers and grandchildren. Citing work by Leighton and Kluckhohn (1948), Shomaker (1989:6–7) characterized the grandmother–grandchild relationship as "very warm, loving, solicitous, and indulgent." The degree to which this is typical, whether and how this may differ from tribe to tribe, or how it conforms to a similar stereotypical grandmother role in American culture is yet to be fully investigated, although Bahr (1994) has offered several points of contrast between one Anglo-American grand-mother type and the ideal Apache grandmother.

Based on a study of only 28 grandparents living in 17 households composed of elders who had returned to tribal homelands from urban areas, Weibel-Orlando (1990) identified five common and sometimes overlapping grandparenting styles among American Indians. These were the "cultural conservator" grandparent (35 percent of the households), who eagerly seeks to care for grandchildren for extended periods of time in order to socialize them into American Indian lifeways; the "custodial grandparent" (18 percent of the households), who is thrust into this care-taking situation because of family disruption; the "ceremonial grandparent" (12 percent of households), who has face-to-face interaction with grandchildren at regular intervals such as holidays, birthdays and other special occasions; the "distanced grandparent" (18 percent of households), whose visits are infrequent and reflect the growing divergence between the values and lifestyles of some portions of urban and reservation populations; and the "fictive grandparent" (18 percent of households), who forms relationships with non-kin because of the lack or absence of biological grandchildren.

Data from the 2000 U.S. Census provide some indication of the prevalence of having a grandparent co-reside with grandchildren (Simmons and Dye, 2003). Among the American Indian alone population ages 30 years and older, 8.0 percent were living with at least one grand-child under the age of 18. Among American Indians, co-residence appears to be for the sake of the child rather than a normative cultural pattern or for the sake of the elder. Among most of the American Indian grandparents who were living with one or more grandchildren (56.1 percent), the grandparent was responsible for meeting most of the basic needs of the grandchild(ren). This contrasts with the pattern among Asians and Hispanics, in which co-residence is less likely to result in caregiving responsibility for grandchildren. As other evidence presented in the report suggests, the vast majority of grandparents (94 percent) who acknowledge primary responsibility for the grandchild are the householder or spouse of the householder, and one-third of grandpar-ent caregiver households do not contain the child's parent(s). This study also documents that among American Indian grandparents this arrangement is relatively permanent. Among American Indian grandparent caregivers, 40 percent had cared for their grandchildren for five years or more, 13.9 percent for three to four years, 22.5 percent for one to two years, and only 23.5 percent had been providing care for less than one year.

A recent descriptive study using U.S. Census data from 2000 (Fuller-Thomson and Minkler, 2005) provides a snapshot of American Indian custodial grandparents age 45 and older. For American Indians and any population in which there is a substantial amount of teenage childbearing, the choice of only considering the characteristics of a grandparent over age 45 is curious and not justified. Therefore, some caution is required in making too much of these find-ings since these authors acknowledge that approximately 17 percent of American Indian custo-dial grandparents were dropped from their sample because they were younger than 45.

According to this study (Fuller-Thomson and Minkler, 2005), the prevalence of custodial grandparenting among American Indians over age 45 was 5.8 percent, a figure comparable to the prevalence among African Americans but significantly greater than among non-Hispanic Whites (1.3 percent). In most cases, the grandparent was raising one grandchild (63 percent). However, 26 percent were raising two grandchildren, and 11 percent were raising three or more grandchildren.

This article reveals that, compared to American Indians of the same age, American Indian custodial grandparents age 45 and older are less likely to be in the labor force and are more likely to be female; less educated; live in a larger household; live in overcrowded households; speak little or no English; identify themselves as American Indian only; live on a reservation; live in poverty; receive public assistance or Food Stamps (Supplemental Nutrition Assistance Program); experience severe vision or hearing problems; and experience functional impairment in walking, climbing stairs, or lifting. Clearly, some of these characteristics are attributable to their caregiving status (including having a larger household, living in poverty, and receiving Food Stamps or public assistance). One especially troubling finding of this study is that many custodial grandparents who were living in poverty and eligible for public benefits such as Food Stamps, Supplemental Security Income, or public assistance did not receive them.

The other important example of intergenerational family caregiving is elder care. Consistent with tribal values that emphasize familial obligations and interdependence (Red Horse, 1980a), the extended family remains the primary and often sole provider of long-term care for functionally impaired relatives, especially among rural American Indians (John, 1988a). However, because of the pervasive lack of formal long-term care services, family members often undertake extreme demands in caring for and preventing the institutional placement of an elderly relative (Manson, 1989b; 1993). As John (1991b:46) has pointed out:

> It is true that American Indian families continue to provide most of the care elders receive, but American Indian families are not immune to the stresses and strains that can compromise their ability to care for American Indian elders. Indeed, there are a variety of threats to the informal support system among American Indians.

John and Huntzinger (1994) outlined the variety of these threats to the informal family support system that most Indian elders currently rely on. In addition to disruptive cultural influences from the educational system, missionary efforts, mass media; declining fertility, and the necessity for young adults to seek employment in distant urban areas, restrictive program requirements and eligibility guidelines undermine extended family support (John, 1991b). This last problem is especially apparent in programs such as Supplemental Security Income that count total household income rather than personal income in the determination of program benefits. In this case, elders are penalized economically for practicing a widely held American Indian cultural value to live in an extended family unit.

In a qualitative study of family caregiving among Pueblo Indians, Hennessy and John (1995) highlight the culturally patterned attitudes toward dependency and the expectation, ready acceptance, and assumption of the role of primary family caregiver to a frail elder, especially by Pueblo women. For these caregivers ($N = 33$), providing care to functionally dependent elders was a significant expression of their identity as American Indians and reflected the importance of interdependence within the extended family and the tribe that continues into infirm old age.

Although not without difficulty, the attitudes expressed by these caregivers (Hennessy and John, 1995) suggest that different cultural values in the perceptions of family elder care contribute to a higher, or at least qualitatively different, threshold of burden than among White caregivers. These Pueblo caregivers confirmed experiences of role strain, interpersonal tensions and conflict within the family, feelings of apprehension and uncertainty about managing care, problems in dealing with psychosocial aspects of care, perceptions of detrimental effects on personal health and well-being, and feelings of burden. On the other hand, they did not feel that their caregiving responsibilities resulted in social constraints, limitations on personal freedom or privacy, or embarrassment. Pueblo caregivers did express a variety of frustrations with the caregiving situation, including family members not contributing to the caregiving effort or their criticisms of the primary caregiver's efforts, frustration with the care recipient's lack of cooperation or what were considered unreasonable and unneeded demands for care, and frustration with the lack of medical and social service resources.

An expanded study of caregiving within this same population (John, Hennessy, Dyeson, and Garrett, 2001) examined the features of caregiver burden among Pueblo caregivers ($N = 169$). A central concern of the research was to evaluate the level of perceived burden and identify the types of burden experienced by Pueblo caregivers. This study concluded that caregiver burden is common, multidimensional, and consists of several types of burden. Based on a factor analysis of responses to the burden interview, this study found that caregiver burden among Pueblo caregivers is composed of four dimensions: role conflict (the classic and ubiquitous form of burden), negative feelings toward the care recipient, lack of caregiver efficacy such that they would not be able to sustain caregiving much longer, and guilt that they were not doing everything they could for the care recipient. Two of these dimensions of burden—negative feelings and guilt—were unexpected. Negative feelings were unanticipated because expressing them contradicts the cultural ideal of providing for other generations without reservations, misgivings, or complaints. However, guilt was the most common form of caregiver burden and was especially surprising among these caregivers because it exists even when they are performing a culturally valued prescribed role under less than ideal circumstances.

Another study of Pueblo family caregiving (John, Hennessy, Roy, and Salvini, 1996) described other aspects of the caregiving situation among a group of impaired elders and their primary family caregivers ($N = 73$), including the identity and characteristics of the caregivers, the types of problems associated with the care needs of these elders (e.g., impairments in the ability to carry out activities of daily living, memory and behavioral difficulties), the types and extent of assistance provided by these family caregivers, the formal services used by the care recipients, and the perceived sources of burden in caring for an elder with cognitive and/or physical impairments.

Overall, although some caregivers and their families had worked out an acceptable caregiving arrangement, in many cases it was clear that the family arrangement was fragile or in need of periodic maintenance. In some instances, the caregiving system was in evident danger of exhausting the family's resources to provide care, particularly if the health of the caregiver or elder deteriorated further. Two factors emerged as important elements in establishing a satisfactory caregiving arrangement among Pueblo caregivers, including organizing caregiving into a predictable routine with a known magnitude of demands, and stabilizing family relationships around the caregiving situation through a consensual family process. Hennessy and John (1995) found that mobilizing family support to assist with elder care appears to be a salient, if not unique, consideration important to the success of caregiving in Pueblo Indian families.

Despite the obvious difficulties and the lack of access to essential long-term care services, Hennessy and John (1996) found a strong cultural mandate to provide elder care. However, a number of formal services would alleviate some of the strains and burdens experienced by these family caregivers. Caregiver training and support groups, enhanced care coordination or case management, adult day care and respite care, and family counseling or mediation were the supportive services most needed by these caregivers.

This series of studies strongly supports a general conclusion that extended family support networks continue to be extremely important to the well-being of American Indian elders, especially on rural reservations. However, the idea that the mere existence of an extended family is sufficient to meet the needs of elders places a number of them at risk, since the extended family is not a universal feature in the lives of either rural or urban American Indians. In fact, John and Huntzinger (1994) estimated that the proportion of American Indian elders in both urban and rural environments who are without an adequate family support network ranges from 16 percent to 20 percent. The clear implication of the research on family caregiving is that a comprehensive, responsive, and culturally sensitive community-based aging services system must be created if American Indian elders are to have the same kind of caregiving alternatives that are now available to the general population.

Unfortunately, the lack of formal services and a number of other barriers to service use are a significant problem among American Indian elders. As is true of other minorities (Federal Council on the Aging, 1980; National Indian Council on Aging, 1981), Native American elders, in general, have very low formal service utilization. Although the family's role as a direct service provider is well documented, scholarship has also suggested that the Native American family network is an important source of indirect assistance as well—that is, the family network is also instrumental in facilitating formal service use by family members. According to Murdock and Schwartz (1978), the availability of and contact with family members is an important factor in both the perception of needs and the use of services. In fact, they claim that "family structure is clearly related to objective indicators of need: the smaller the family unit, the greater its financial and housing needs" (Murdock and Schwartz, 1978:476–477). Murdock and Schwartz (1978:480–481) conclude that "children may assist elderly persons by both creating greater awareness of the needs for and availability of services, and in directly obtaining the required services."

Although Murdock and Schwartz (1978:481) stated their conclusion in a tentative manner, they suggested that "extended families serve to increase the mechanisms for service usage as well as the sources of information concerning services," or further that "levels of use as well as awareness . . . appear to be increased by living in a couple or in an extended family setting" (Murdock and Schwartz, 1978:479).[10] In their view, family members are not only the primary caregivers within the support network but also serve an indispensable mediator role between family members and alien service bureaucracies. Whether as direct provider or intermediary, then, the existence of an extended family network is no less crucial now compared to the not-too-distant past when such arrangements were the sole source of support of Indian family members.

CHANGE AND ADAPTATION

Among the industrialized nations, the United States remains one of the few without a formal pro-family policy. Moroney (1980) succinctly characterized the existing bias evident in social policy in the United States, a bias that is attributable to precisely the prevailing ideology and social interests arising from the concrete social location of most politicians and social planners. According to Moroney (1980:33–34):

> [M]ost social policies are oriented to individuals and not to families. Furthermore, when the object of the policy is the family, invariably it defines the family as nuclear. To shift policy development so that the modified extended family is explicitly included would require a major reorientation. . . . If successful, such a reorientation could result in policies that set out to maximize available resources, the natural resources of the family, and the resources of the social welfare system. Such an approach begins with a search for ways to support families by complementing what they are already doing—intervening directly and indirectly, but not interfering.

---

[10]Murdock and Schwartz (1978) are right to emphasize the important intermediary role of family members in service utilization. However, my research (John, 1986) suggests that this role is more important on reservations than it is in urban environments, primarily because of smaller households and fewer intact marriages among urban Indians. This does not contradict their findings since their study was of reservation Sioux. It does question the generalizability of their findings to urban environments. However, even on reservations, the role of family members as direct service providers is more important than their mediator role.

Without doubt, pressures to modify Native American family life in the direction of the patterns of the cultural mainstream will continue. By and large the greatest influences on Native American families are the same as for Americans as a whole. The capitalist political economy sets the conditions of employment and indirectly shapes the family structure and relationships within it for the ever increasing number of people who wish to pursue American-style success. Generally, such success can be achieved only at the sacrifice of family life.

The United States asks everyone to make a mutually exclusive choice: dedicate yourself to your work or your family. Although this statement may continue a controversy within family sociology since it denies the ideological but mythical belief that American culture is family oriented, the sad truth is that family structures in the United States are fragile, temporary, and shrinking in size and importance. Any number of social trends attest to the truth of this statement: high rates of divorce, the institutionalization of cohabitation and singlehood, prenuptial agreements, childbearing by unmarried women, the dramatic increase in the number of female-headed families, the escalation of women's labor force participation, the economic pressures that encourage dual wage-earner families, the increasing number of people of all ages who live alone, declining fertility, the rise of voluntary childlessness, the delay of marriage and childbearing, and greater reliance on assisted living facilities and nursing homes to provide care to the elderly. I should make it clear that my intent in listing these trends is neither for the purpose of making any invidious comparison with other family practices past or present nor to make any moral judgment on these practices. Rather, the trends are symptomatic and reveal something about how family life has changed in response to the U.S. political economy and culture.

Indeed, each of these trends can be explained as a rational response to the political economy and American culture. Children, from a strictly economically rational viewpoint, are unalloyed economic liabilities for an entire lifetime. Economically rational behavior dictates delaying childbearing, having only one or at most two children, or not having children at all. Working women and dual wage-earner families have become a necessary response to the steady decline in the standard of living in the United States that has occurred since the early 1970s. Concomitant development of a focus on self and immediate gratification (whether these are labeled narcissism or hedonism), so promoted by commodified, pre-packaged American mass culture, is consistent with most of these trends. I raise these issues not in order to call for sacrifice or devotion to some presumed duty. I merely wish to recognize these family trends as the most likely response and consequence of living in American society, and the fact that the absence of a comprehensive governmental pro-family policy fails to adequately mitigate the negative influences that the political economy has on family life. Most recently, we can add the near collapse of the world economy, the stunning loss of retirement savings (among the 50 percent of Americans fortunate enough to belong to a pension plan), the foreclosure crisis, globalization and outsourcing, a jobless "recovery," and renewed efforts to reduce, privatize, or eliminate government social safety net programs. Each of these events portends devastating consequences for American families in general and American Indian families in particular.

The impact of the political economy on family life is most clearly evident in the dire financial position of most female-headed families, and the fact that the impoverished in our society are disproportionately children, women, minorities, and elders. Each of these groups is now under renewed attack with the changes that have been implemented in welfare, a range of affirmative action policies, debates about the merits of extending unemployment benefits to people who experience long-term unemployment, and discussions of how to "save" Medicare (by some form of the reduction of benefits) and Social Security (by cutting benefits and increasing the retirement age) or, more ominously, doing away with both programs through privatization, personalization, vouchers or other euphemism. The lack of an adequate pro-family policy (or even the idea that one is needed) means that structural changes in the American economy can be dealt with through public exhortations that plenty of jobs exist and go unfilled as well as through cutbacks in public financial, housing, medical, and food support in the face of growing poverty, hunger, homelessness, and deficiencies in medical care in the United States. Likewise, the consequences of decisions made in corporate boardrooms to shut down operations or move them to another state or country are not seen to have large costs that families must ultimately absorb.

Despite the fact that Native American families are not immune to the larger social structural forces in operation in the United States, Native American families continue to exhibit a unique character attributable to long-standing cultural differences from American culture as a whole. Indeed, Native Americans continue to exhibit a great deal of cultural diversity and divergence from the American cultural mainstream. Culture change has occurred as the result of contact with Whites but not to the degree that some observers would have us believe. The recognition by several researchers that even when Native American family practices have a formal resemblance to Anglo-European practices there is something distinctively Native American in the way in which that practice is experienced should make academics circumspect in their use of an acculturation paradigm to explain family change among Native Americans. The rebirth of Native American cultural pride and the concomitant invigoration of tribal entities, clearly a direct outgrowth of the Red Power movement of the 1960s and, more recently, the resources accumulated by lucrative tribal business enterprises including gaming operations, have protected substantial numbers of Native Americans from total acculturation and assimilation.

However, it is true that Native American elders are more exclusively "Indian-oriented" than middle or younger generations. Among the middle and younger generations the best description of their value orientations would be "bicultural," having knowledge of two different cultural worlds and being able to operate in either one. Family practices have also changed. Although extended families remain the cultural ideal among Native Americans, in reality, extended families are not universal and within families that exhibit extended family characteristics there are prodigal sons and daughters who have moved outside the sphere of routine extended family operations. Nonetheless, it is true that Native American families are based more on interdependence and consanguine ties compared to the independent and conjugal emphasis within Anglo society.

The extent to which Native Americans adopt, resist, or adapt in modified form the family practices of the cultural mainstream depends on a number of factors. Certainly, some groups will have an advantage over others in retaining the cultural grounding of their tribal family practices. Among these, tribes that maintain or expand their land base (i.e., their cultural community) will have an advantage over tribes that do not have a community locus. Similarly, the largest groups will fare better than small ones in preserving their cultural heritage and unique family practices. Furthermore, tribes that succeed in building a tribal economy capable of sustaining their cultural community will have an advantage over tribes with weak and dependent economies. In addition, groups that maintain tribal spiritual practices and teach their children the tribal language will fare better than other groups.

However, the forces of change and cultural homogenization at work in American society as a whole will also have an effect on Native Americans. In addition to the American political economy, a number of other factors will pressure Native Americans toward practices of the cultural mainstream. American popular culture, education grounded in Anglo-European intellectual ways of knowledge, institutions or social movements (like Christian churches or the women's movement) that consciously or unwittingly undermine Native American values and practices, continued intermarriage with other ethnic groups, and urbanization present challenges to Native

Americans. How Native Americans respond to these external pressures remains to be seen, but their history of cultural resilience suggests that they will be able to absorb them and adapt their family practices to meet their own cultural needs.

References

Aginsky, B. W., and E. G. Aginsky. 1947, October. "A Resultant of Intercultural Relations. *Social Forces 26*(1), 84–87.

Allen, P. G. 1986. *The Sacred Hoop: Recovering the Feminine in American Indian Traditions.* Boston, MA: Beacon Press.

Arbuckle, J., L. Olson, M. Howard, J. Brillman, C. Anctil, and D. Sklar. 1996. "Safe at Home? Domestic Violence and Other Homicides Among Women in New Mexico." *Annals of Emergency Medicine 27*(2), 210–215.

Bahr, K. S. 1994. "The Strengths of Apache Grandmothers: Observations on Commitment, Culture and Caretaking." *Journal of Comparative Family Studies 25*(2), 233–248.

Ball, E. 1970. *In the Days of Victorio: Recollections of a Warm Springs Apache.* Tucson: University of Arizona Press.

Barón, A. E., S. M. Manson, L. M. Ackerson, and D. L. Brenneman. 1990. "Depressive Symptomatology in Older American Indians with Chronic Disease: Some Psychometric Considerations." In C. C. Attkisson and J. M. Zich (Eds.), *Depression in Primary Care: Screening and Detection* (pp. 217–231). New York: Routledge.

Bachman, J. G., J. M. Wallace, P. M. O'Mally, L. D. Johnston, C. L. Kurth, and H. W. Neighbors. 1991, March. "Racial/Ethnic Differences in Smoking, Drinking, and Illicit Drug Use Among American High School Seniors, 1976–89." *American Journal of Public Health 81*(3), 372–377.

Bell, D., P. Kasschau, and G. Zellman. 1978. "Service Delivery to American Indian Elderly." In J. P. Lyon (Ed.), *The Indian Elder: A Forgotten American (Final Report on the First National Indian Conference on Aging).* Albuquerque, NM: National Tribal Chairmen's Association.

Berlin, I. N. 1987. "Suicide Among American Indian Adolescents: An Overview." *Suicide and Life-Threatening Behavior 17*(3), 218–232.

Blanchard, E. L., and R. L. Barsh. 1980. "What Is Best for Tribal Children? A Response to Fischler." *Social Work 25*(5), 350–357.

Blanchard, E. L., and S. Unger. 1977. "Destruction of American-Indian Families." *Social Casework 58*(5), 312–314.

Blanchard, K. 1975. "Changing Sex Roles and Protestantism Among the Navajo Women in Ramah." *Journal for the Scientific Study of Religion 14*(1), 43–50.

Blum, R., B. Harmon, L. Harris, L. Bergeisen, and M. Resnick. 1992. "American Indian-Alaska Native Youth health." *Journal of the American Medical Association 267*(12), 1637–1644.

Bock, P. K. 1964. "Patterns of Illegitimacy on a Canadian Indian Reserve: 1860–1960." *Journal of Marriage and Family 26*(2), 142–148.

Boggs, S. T. 1956. "An Interactional Study of Ojibwa Socialization." *American Sociological Review 21*(2), 191–198.

Bonvillain, N. 1989. "Gender Relations in Native North America." *American Indian Culture and Research Journal 13*(2), 1–28.

Borowsky, I. W., M. D. Resnick, M. Ireland, and R. W. Blum. 1999. "Suicide Attempts Among American Indian and Alaska Native Youth: Risk and Protective Factors." *Archives of Pediatric and Adolescent Medicine 153*, 573–580.

Bradford, C. J., and L. Thom. 1992. *Dancing Colors: Paths of Native American Women.* San Francisco: Chronicle Books.

Brendtro, L. K., M. Brokenleg, and S. Van Bockern. 1991, Winter. "The Circle of Courage." *Beyond Behavior 2*, 5–12.

Brieland, D. 1973. "Far from the Reservation: The Transracial Adoption of American Indian Children." *Social Service Review 47*(2), 310–11.

Brody, E. M. 1995. "Prospects for Family Caregiving: Response to Change, Continuity, and Diversity." In R. A. Kane and J. D. Penrod (Eds.), *Family Caregiving in an Aging Society: Policy Perspectives* (pp. 15–28). Thousand Oaks, CA: Sage.

Brown, A. S. 1989. "A Survey on Elder Abuse at One Native American Tribe." *Journal of Elder Abuse and Neglect 1*(2), 17–37.

Byler, W. 1977. "Removing Children—Destruction of American-Indian Families." *Civil Rights Digest 9*(4), 19–27.

Cantor, M. H. 1980. "The Informal Support System: Its Relevance in the Elderly." In E. F. Borgatta and N. G. McCluskey (Eds.), *Aging and Society: Current Research and Policy Perspective* (pp. 131–144). Beverly Hills, CA: Sage.

Carson, D. K. 1995. "American Indian Elder Abuse: Risk and Protective Factors Among the Oldest Americans." *Journal of Elder Abuse and Neglect 7*(1), 17–39.

Carson, D. K., and C. Hand. 1999. "Dilemmas Surrounding Elder Abuse and Neglect in Native American Communities." In T. Tatara (Ed.), *Understanding Elder Abuse in Minority Populations* (pp. 161–184). Philadelphia: Brunner/Mazel.

Christopherson, V. A. 1981. "The Rural Navajo family." In R. T. Coward and W. M. Smith (Eds.), *The Family in Rural Society* (pp. 105–111). Boulder, CO: Westview Press.

Clayton, R. R. 1979. *The Family, Marriage, and Social Change* (2nd ed.). Lexington, MA: D. C. Heath.

Costello, J. E., S. N. Compton, G. Keeler, and A. Angold. 2003. "Relationships Between Poverty and Psychopathology: A Natural Experiment." *Journal of the American Medical Association 290*(15), 2023–2029.

Cross, S. L. 2006. "Indian Family Exception Doctrine: Still Losing Children Despite the Indian Child Welfare Act." *Child Welfare Journal 85*(4), 671–690.

Crow Dog, M., and R. Erdoes. 1990. *Lakota Woman*. New York: Grove Weidenfeld.

Davis, S. M., and M. B. Harris. 1982. "Sexual Knowledge, Sexual Interests, and Sources of Sexual Information of Rural and Urban Adolescents from Three Cultures." *Adolescence 17*(66), 471–492.

Dinges, N. G., J. E. Trimble, and A. R. Hollenbeck. 1979. "American Indian Adolescent Socialization: A Review of the Literature." *Journal of Adolescence 2*, 259–296.

Dobyns, H. F. 1983. *Their Number Become Thinned: Native American Population Dynamics in Eastern North America*. Knoxville: University of Tennessee Press.

Dodd, J. M., J. R. Nelson, and B. H. Hofland. 1994. "Minority Identity and Self-concept: The American Indian Experience." In T. Brinthaupt and R. P. Lipka (Eds.), *Changing the Self: Philosophies, Techniques, and Experiences* (pp. 307–336). Albany: State University of New York Press.

Dorris, M. 1989. *The Broken Cord*. New York: Harper & Row.

Downs, J. F. 1964. *Animal Husbandry in Navajo Society and Culture*. Berkeley: University of California Press.

Driver, H. E. 1969. "Larger Kin Groups, Kin Terms." In H. E. Driver (Ed.), *Indians of North America* (2nd ed., pp. 242–267). Chicago: The University of Chicago Press.

Dye, J. L. 2008. "Fertility of American Women: 2006" [Current Population Report, P20–558]. Washington, DC: U.S. Census Bureau.

Echo Hawk, L. 2009, August 11. "Indian Entities Recognized and Eligible to Receive Services from the United States Bureau of Indian Affairs." *Federal Register 74*(153), 40, 218–240.

Edington, E., and L. Hays. 1978. "Difference in Family Size and Marriage Age Expectation and Aspirations of Anglo, Mexican American and Native American Rural Youth in New Mexico." *Adolescence 13*(51), 393–400.

Edwards, E. D. 1978. "The Destruction of American Indian Families." *Social Work 23*(1), 74.

Edwards, E. D., and M. Egbert-Edwards. 1989. "The American Indian Child Welfare Act: Achievements and Recommendations." In J. Hudson and B. Galaway (Eds.), *The State as Parent: International Research Perspectives on Interventions with Young Persons* (pp. 37–51). Dordrecht, Netherlands: Kluwer Academic Publishers.

Edwards, E. D., M. Egbert-Edwards, and G. M. Daines. 1980, Spring. "American Indian/Alaska Native Elderly." *Journal of Gerontological Social Work 2*(3), 213–224.

Eschbach, K. 1993. "Changing Identification Among American Indians and Alaska Natives." *Demography 30*(4), 635–652.

———. 1995. "The Enduring and Vanishing American Indian: American Indian Population Growth and Intermarriage in 1990." *Ethnic and Racial Studies 18*(1), 89–108.

Evans-Campbell, T., T. Lindhorst, B. Huang, and K. L. Walters. 2006. "Interpersonal Violence in the Lives of Urban American Indian and Alaska Native Women: Implications for Health, Mental Health, and Help-Seeking." *American Journal of Public Health 96*(8), 1416–1422.

Fanshel, D. 1972. *Far from the Reservation: The Transracial Adoption of American Indian Children*. Metuchen, NJ: Scarecrow Press.

Feagin, J. R., and R. Anderson. 1973. "Intertribal Attitudes Among Native American Youth." *Social Science Quarterly 54*(1), 117–131.

Federal Council on the Aging. 1980. "Policy Issues Concerning the Elderly Minorities: A Staff Report"

[DHHS Publication No. (OHDS) 80–20670]. Washington, DC: U.S. Government Printing Office.

Fischler, R. 1980. "Protecting American Indian children." *Social Work* 25(5), 341–349.

Fisher, D. (Ed.). 1980. *The Third Woman: Minority Women Writers of the United States.* Boston: Houghton Mifflin.

Fox, J. R. 1960. "Therapeutic Rituals and Social Structure in Cochiti Pueblo." *Human Relations* 13(4), 291–303.

Fuller-Thomson, E., and M. Minkler. 2005. "American Indian/Alaskan Native Grandparents Raising Grandchildren: Findings from the Census 2000 Supplementary Survey." *Social Work* 50(2), 131–139.

Garcia, D. W. 1973. "Far from the Reservation: Transracial Adoption of American Indian Children." *Social Work* 18(1), 125.

Garcia, M. 1994. "A Higher Power of Their Understanding: Cheyenne Women and Their Religious Roles." In V. Demos and M. T. Segal (Eds.), *Ethnic Women: A Multiple Status Reality* (pp. 17–24). Dix Hills, NY: General Hall, Inc.

General Accounting Office (GAO). 1976. "Investigation of Allegations Concerning Indian Health Service" [Letter]. archive.gao.gov/f0402/100493.pdf (accessed April 24, 2011).

Gonzales, J. L. 1994. "The Native American Family." In *Racial and Ethnic Families in America* (pp. 287–315). Dubuque, IA: Kendall/Hunt.

Goodluck, C. T. 1993. "Social Services with Native Americans: Current Status of the Indian Child Welfare Act." In H. P. McAdoo (Ed.), *Family Ethnicity: Strength in Diversity* (pp. 217–226). Newbury Park, CA: Sage.

Green, R. 1980. "Native American Women." *Signs: A Journal of Women in Culture and Society* 6(2), 248–267.

———. 1992. *Women in American Indian Society.* New York: Chelsea House Publishers.

Gregory, R. G., A. C. Abello, and J. Johnson. 1996. "The Individual Economic Well-being of Native American Men and Women During the 1980s: A Decade of Moving Backwards." In G. D. Sandefur, R. R. Rindfuss, and B. Cohen (Eds.), *Changing Numbers, Changing Needs: American Indian Demography and Public health* (pp. 133–171). Washington, DC: National Academy Press.

Grieco, E. M., and R. C. Cassidy. 2000. "Overview of Race and Hispanic Origin. (Census 2000 Brief)." Washington, DC: U.S. Census Bureau.

Guillemin, J. 1975. *Urban Renegades: The Cultural Strategy of American Indians.* New York: Columbia University Press.

Gutierres, S. E., and A. Barr. 2003. "The Relationship Between Attitudes Toward Pregnancy and Contraception Use Among Drug Users." *Journal of Substance Abuse Treatment* 24(1), 19–29.

Gutiérrez, R. A. 1991. *When Jesus Came, the Corn Mothers Went Away: Marriage, Sexuality, and Power in New Mexico, 1500–1846.* Palo Alto, CA: Stanford University Press.

Harris, D. 1994. "The 1990 Census Count of American Indians: What Do the Numbers Really Mean?" *Social Science Quarterly* 75(3), 580–593.

Haynes, T. L. 1977. "Some Factors Related to Contraceptive Behavior Among Wind River Shoshone and Arapaho Females." *Human Organization* 36(1), 72–76.

Heinrich, A. 1972. "Divorce as an Integrative Social Factor." *Journal of Comparative Family Studies* 3, 265–272.

Henderson, E. 1979. "Skilled and Unskilled Blue Collar Navajo Workers: Occupational Diversity in an American Indian Tribe." *Social Science Journal* 16(2), 63–80.

Hennessy, C. H., and R. John. 1995. "The Interpretation of Burden Among Pueblo Indian Caregivers." *Journal of Aging Studies* 9(3), 215–229.

———. 1996. "American Indian Family Caregivers' Perceptions of Burden and Needed Support Services." *The Journal of Applied Gerontology* 15(3), 275–293.

Hossain, Z. 2001. "Division of Household Labor and Family Functioning in Off-Reservation Navajo Indian Families." *National Council on Family Relations* 50(3), 255–261.

Indian Country Today. 2008, October 3. "Indian Recognition of Non-recognized Tribes." *Indian Country Today.* www.indiancountrytoday.com/opinion/editorials/30272599.html (accessed September 17, 2010).

Indian Health Service (IHS). 1995. "Trends in Indian Health 1995." Rockville, MD: Author.

———. 2008. "Trends in Indian Health: 2002–2003 Edition." Rockville, MD: Author.

Ishisaka, H. 1978. "American Indians and Foster Care: Cultural Factors and Separation." *Child Welfare* 57(5), 299–308.

Jackson, D. D. 2002. *Our Elders Lived It: American Indian Identity in the City.* DeKalb: Northern Illinois University Press.

Jacobs, S.-E., W. Thomas, and S. Lang (Eds.). 1997. *Two Spirit People: Native American Gender Identity, Sexuality, and Spirituality.* Urbana: University of Illinois Press.

John, R. 1985. "Aging in a Native American Community: Service Needs and Support Networks Among Prairie Band Potawatomi Elders." Unpublished doctoral dissertation, University of Kansas, Lawrence.

———. 1986. "Social Policy and Planning for Aging American Indians: Provision of Services by Formal and Informal Support Networks." In J. R. Joe (Ed.), *American Indian Policy and Cultural Values: Conflict and Accommodation* (pp. 111–133). Los Angeles: American Indian Studies Center, University of California.

———. 1988a. "The Native American Family." In C. H. Mindel, R. W. Habenstein, and R. Wright, Jr. (Eds.), *Ethnic Families in America: Patterns and Variations* (3rd ed., pp. 325–363). New York: Elsevier.

———. 1988b. "Use of Cluster Analysis in Social Service Planning: A Case Study of Laguna Pueblo Elders." *Journal of Applied Gerontology* 7(1), 21–35.

———. 1991a. "Defining and Meeting the Needs of Native American Elders: Applied Research on Their Current Status, Social Service Needs, and Support Network Operation. Vol. 1: Urban and Rural/Reservation American Indian Elders: A Reanalysis of the 1981 National Indian Council on Aging Nationwide Sample." (Final Report, Administration on Aging Grant #90AR0117/01). Lawrence: University of Kansas Gerontology Center.

———. 1991b. "Family Support Networks in a Native American Community: Contact with Children and Siblings Among the Prairie Band Potawatomi." *Journal of Aging Studies* 5(1), 45–59.

———. 1994. "Health Research, Service and Policy Priorities of American Indian Elders." In C. M. Barresi (Ed.), *Health and Minority Elders: An Analysis of Applied Literature 1980–1990* (pp. 136–161). Washington DC: American Association of Retired Persons.

———. 1995. *American Indian and Alaska Native Elders: An Assessment of Their Current Status and Provision of Services.* Rockville, MD: Indian Health Service.

John, R., and D. Baldridge. 1996. *The NICOA Report: Health and Long Term Care for Indian Elders.* Washington, DC: National Indian Policy Center.

John, R., P. H. Blanchard, and C. H. Hennessy. 1997. "Hidden Lives: Aging and Contemporary American Indian Women." In J. M. Coyle (Ed.), *Handbook on Women and Aging* (pp. 290–315). Westport, CT: Greenwood Press.

John, R., C. H. Hennessy, T. B. Dyeson, and M. D. Garrett. 2001. "Toward the Conceptualization and Measurement of Caregiver Burden Among Pueblo Indian Family Caregivers." *The Gerontologist* 415(2), 210–219.

John, R., C. H. Hennessy, L. Roy, and M. Salvini. 1996. "Caring for Cognitively Impaired American Indian Elders: Difficult Situations, Few Options." In G. Yeo and D. Gallagher-Thompson (Eds.), *Ethnicity and the Dementias* (pp. 187–203). Washington, DC: Taylor & Francis.

John, R., and P. Huntzinger. 1994. "The Legacy of the Columbian Exchange: A Policy Analysis of American Indian Aging at the Quincentennial." *The Southwest Journal on Aging* 9(2), 23–30.

Johnson, A. E., and A. K. Taylor. 1991. "Prevalence of Chronic Diseases: A Summary of Data from the Survey of American Indians and Alaska Natives" (AHCPR Publication No. 91–0031). Rockville, MD: Agency for Health Care Policy and Research.

Joos, S. K., and S. Ewart. 1988. "A Health Survey of Klamath Indian Elders 30 Years After the Loss of Tribal Status." *Public Health Reports* 103(2), 166–173.

Katz, J. (Ed.). 1995. *Messengers of the Wind: Native American Women Tell Their Life Stories.* New York: Ballantine Books.

Kramer, B. J. 1991. "Urban American Indian Aging." *Journal of Cross-Cultural Gerontology* 6(2), 205–217.

Kramer, B. J., D. Polisar, and J. C. Hyde. 1990. "Study of Urban American Indian Aging" (Final Report, Administration on Aging, Grant #90AR0118). City of Industry, CA: The Public Health Foundation of Los Angeles County.

Kroeber, A. L. 1939. *Cultural and Natural Areas of Native North America.* Berkeley: University of California Press.

Kunitz, S. J., and J. E. Levy. 1991. *Navajo Aging: The Transition from Family to Institutional Support.* Tucson: The University of Arizona Press.

———. 1994. *Drinking Careers: A Twenty-Five-Year Study of Three Navajo Populations.* New Haven, CT: Yale University Press.

Kunitz, S. J., and J. C. Slocumb. 1976. "The Use of Surgery to Avoid Childbearing Among Navajo and Hopi Indians." *Human Biology* 48(1), 9–21.

LaFromboise, T. D., and D. S. Bigfoot. 1988. "Cultural and Cognitive Considerations in the Prevention of American Indian Adolescent Suicide." *Journal of Adolescence* 11(2), 139–153.

LaFromboise, T. D., A. M. Heyle, and E. J. Ozer. 1990. "Changing and Diverse Roles of Women in American Indian Cultures." *Sex Roles* 22(7/8), 455–479.

LaFromboise, T. D., and K. G. Low. 1989. "American Indian children and Adolescents." In J. T. Gibbs, L. N. Huang, et al. (Eds.), *Children of Color: Psychological Interventions with Minority Youth* (pp. 114–147). San Francisco: Jossey-Bass.

Lamphere, L. 1977. *To Run After Them: Cultural and Social Bases of Cooperation in a Navajo Community.* Tucson: The University of Arizona Press.

Lang, S. 1998. *Men as Women, Women as Men: Changing Gender in Native American Cultures.* Austin: University of Texas Press.

Lee, S. M., and B. Edmonston. 2005. "New Marriages, New Families: U.S. Racial and Hispanic Intermarriage" (Population Bulletin, Vol. 60, No. 2). Washington, DC: Population Reference Bureau.

Lefkowitz, D. C., and C. Underwood. 1991. "Personal Health Practices: Findings from the Survey of American Indians and Alaska Natives" (AHCPR Pub. No. 91–0034. National Medical Expenditure Survey Research Findings 10, Agency for Health Care Policy and Research). Rockville, MD: Agency for Health Care Policy and Research.

Lefley, H. 1976. "Acculturation, Child-Rearing and Self-esteem in Two North American Indian Tribes." *Ethos* 4(3), 385–401.

Lefley, H. P. 1974. "Social and Familial Correlates of Self-esteem Among American Indian Children." *Child Development* 45(3), 829–833.

Leighton, D., and C. Kluckhohn. 1947. *Children of the People: The Navaho Individual and His Development.* Cambridge, MA: Harvard University Press.

Levy, J. E., and S. J. Kunitz. 1987. "Suicide Prevention Program for Hopi Youth." *Social Science and Medicine* 25(8), 931–940.

Lewis, C. 1970. *Indian Families of the Northwest Coast: The Impact of Change.* Chicago: University of Chicago Press.

Lewis, R. G. 1981. "Patterns of Strengths of American Indian Families." In J. G. Red Horse, A. Shattuck, and F. Hoffman (Eds.), *The American Indian Family: Strengths and Stresses* (pp. 101–111). Isleta, NM: American Indian Social Research and Development Associates, Inc.

Liberty, M., D. V. Hughey, and R. Scaglion. 1976. "Rural and Urban Omaha Indian Fertility." *Human Biology* 48(1), 59–71.

Liebler, C. A. 2004. "American Indian Ethnic Identity: Tribal Nonresponse in the 1990 Census." *Social Science Quarterly* 85(2), 310–323.

Limb, G. E., T. Chance, and E. F. Brown. 2004. "An Empirical Examination of the Indian Child Welfare Act and Its Impact on Cultural and Familial Preservation for American Indian Children." *Child Abuse and Neglect* 28(12), 1279–1289.

Liu, L. L., B. Slap Gail, S. B. Kinsman, and N. Khalid. 1994. "Pregnancy Among American Indian Adolescents: Reactions and Prenatal Care." *Journal of Adolescent Health* 15(4), 336–341.

Manson, S. M. 1989a. "Long-term Care in American Indian Communities: Issues for Planning and Research." *The Gerontologist* 29(1), 38–44.

———. 1989b. "Provider Assumptions About Long-term Care in American Indian Communities." *The Gerontologist* 29(3), 355–358.

———. 1993. "Long-term Care of Older American Indians: Challenges in the Development of Institutional Services." In C. M. Barresi and D. E. Stull (Eds.), *Ethnic Elderly and Long-term Care* (pp. 130–143). New York: Springer.

Manson, S. M., and A. M. Pambrun. 1979. "Social and Psychological Status of the American Indian Elderly: Past Research, Current Advocacy, and Future Inquiry." *White Cloud Journal* 1(3), 18–25.

Mathews, T. J., and B. E. Hamilton. 2009. "Delayed Childbearing: More Women Are Having Their First Child Later in Life" [NCHS Data Brief, No. 21]. Hyattsville, MD: National Center for Health Statistics.

Maxwell, E. K., and R. J. Maxwell. 1992. "Insults to the Body Civil: Mistreatment of Elderly in Two Plains Indian Tribes." *Journal of Cross-Cultural Gerontology* 7, 3–23.

May, P. A. 1987. "Suicide and Self-destruction Among American Indian Youths." *American Indian and Alaska Native Mental Health Research* 1, 52–59.

———. 1996. "Overview of Alcohol Abuse Epidemiology for American Indian Populations." In G. D. Sandefur, R. R. Rindfuss, and B. Cohen (Eds.), *Changing Numbers, Changing Needs: American Indian Demography and Public Health* (pp. 235–261). Washington, DC: National Academy Press.

McKinlay, J. B., S. L. Crawford, and S. L. Tennstedt. 1995. "The Everyday Impacts of Providing Informal Care to Dependent Elders and Their Consequences for the Care Recipients." *Journal of Aging and Health* 7(4), 497–528.

Medicine, B. 1981. "American Indian Family: Cultural Change and Adaptive Strategies." *Journal of Ethnic Studies* 8(4), 13–23.

Mercier, J. M., and E. A. Powers. 1984. "The Family and Friends of Rural Aged as a Natural Support System." *Journal of Community Psychology* 12(4), 334–346.

Metcalf, A. 1976. "From Schoolgirl to Mother: The Effects of Education on Navajo Women." *Social Problems 23*, 535–534.

———. 1979. "Family Reunion: Networks and Treatment in a Native American Community." *Group Psychotherapy, Psychodrama, and Sociometry 32*, 179–189.

Miller, D. L. 1981. "Alternative Paradigms Available for Research on American Indian Families." In J. G. Red Horse, A. Shattuck, and F. Hoffman (Eds.), *The American Indian Family: Strengths and Stresses* (pp. 79–91). Isleta, NM: American Indian Social Research and Development Associates, Inc.

Miller, D. L., and C. D. Moore. 1979. "The Native American Family: The Urban Way." In E. Corfman (Ed.), *Families Today: A Research Sampler on Families and Children* (pp. 441–484). Washington, DC: U.S. Government Printing Office.

Moroney, R. F. 1980. "Families in Perspective." In *Families, Social Services and Social Policy: The Issue of Shared Responsibility* (pp. 19–50). Rockville, MD: U.S. Department of Health and Human Services.

Murdock, S. H., and D. F. Schwartz. 1978. "Family Structure and the Use of Agency Services: An Examination of Patterns Among Elderly Native Americans." *The Gerontologist 18*(5), 475–481.

Nagel, J. 1995. "American Indian Ethnic Renewal Politics and the Resurgence of Identity." *American Sociological Review 60*(6), 947–965.

National Aging Resource Center on Elder Abuse. 1989. "American Indians and Elder Abuse: Exploring the Problem." Washington, DC: National Association of State Units on Aging.

National Indian Council on Aging. 1981. "Indian Elderly and Entitlement Programs: An Accessing Demonstration Project." Albuquerque, NM: Author.

———. 1982. "Access: A Demonstration Project, Entitlement Programs for Indian Elders" (Final Report). Albuquerque, NM: Author.

Nazzaro, R. M. 2005. "Timeliness of the Tribal Recognition Process Has Improved, but It Will Take Years to Clear the Existing Backlog of Petitions (GAO-05–347T)." Washington, DC: U.S. General Accountability Office.

North, K. E., J. W. MacCluer, L. D. Cowan, and B. V. Howard. 2000. "Gravidity and Parity in Postmenopausal American Indian Women: The Strong Heart Study." *Human Biology 72*(3), 397–414.

Oakland, L., and R. L. Kane. 1973, May. The Working Mother and Child Neglect on the Navajo Reservation." *Pediatrics 51*(5), 849–853.

Office of Federal Acknowledgement. 2008, September 22. "Number of Petitioners by State." www.bia.gov/idc/groups/public/documents/text/idc-001212.pdf (accessed April 24, 2011).

Ogunwole, S. U. 2002. "The American Indian and Alaska Native population: 2000 [Census 2000 Brief]. Washington, DC: U.S. Department of Commerce.

———. 2006. "The American Indian and Alaska Native Population: 2000." Washington, DC: U.S. Department of Commerce.

Passel, J. S. 1976. "Provisional Evaluation of the 1970 Census Count of American Indians." *Demography 13*(3), 397–407.

———. 1996. "The Growing American Indian Population, 1960–1990: Beyond Demography." In G. D. Sandefur, R. R. Rindfuss and B. Cohen (Eds.), *Changing Numbers, Changing Needs: American Indian Demography and Public Health* (pp. 79–102). Washington, DC: National Academy Press.

Passel, J. S., and P. A. Berman. 1986. "Quality of 1980 Census Data for American Indians." *Social Biology 33*(3–4), 163–182.

Perry, S. W. 2004. "American Indians and Crime" (NCJ 203097) [A BJS Statistical Profile, 1992–2002]. Washington, DC: U.S. Department of Justice.

Pipestem, F. B. 1981. "Comments on the Indian Child Welfare Act." In J. Red Horse, A. Shattuck, and F. Hoffman (Eds.), *The American Indian Family: Strengths and Stresses* (pp. 53–69). Isleta, NM: American Indian Social Research and Development Associates, Inc.

Powers, E. A., P. M. Keith, and W. J. Goudy. 1981. "Family Networks of the Rural Aged." In R. T. Coward and W. M. Smith (Eds.), *The Family in Rural Society* (pp. 199–217). Boulder, CO: Westview Press.

Price, J. A. 1981. "North American Indian Families." In C. H. Mindel and R. W. Habenstein (Eds.), *Ethnic Families in America: Patterns and Variations* (2nd ed., pp. 245–268). New York: Elsevier.

Probst, J. C., J.-Y. Wang, A. B. Martin, C. G. Moore, B. M. Paul, and M. E. Samuels. 2008. "Potentially Violent Disagreements and Parenting Stress Among American Indian/Alaska Natives Families: Analysis Across Seven States." *Maternal Child Health Journal 12*, S91–S102.

Queen, S. A., and J. B. Adams. 1952. *The Family in Various Cultures.* Chicago: J. B. Lippincott.

Red Horse, J. G. 1980a. "Family Structure and Value Orientation in American Indians." *Social Casework 61*(8), 462–467.

————. 1980b. "American Indian Elders: Unifiers of Indian Families." *Social Casework* 61(8), 490–493.

————. 1982a. "Clinical Strategies for American Indian Families in Crisis." *The Urban and Social Change Review* 15(2), 17–19.

————. 1982b. "American Indian and Alaskan Native Elders: A Policy Critique." In E. P. Stanford and S. A. Lockery (Eds.), *Trends and Status of Minority Aging* (pp. 15–26). San Diego, CA: San Diego State University Center on Aging.

————. 1988. "Cultural Evolution of American Indian Families." In C. Jacobs and D. D. Bowles (Eds.), *Ethnicity and Race: Critical Concepts in Social Work* (pp. 86–102). Silver Springs, MD: National Association of Social Workers.

————. 1997. "Traditional American Indian Family Systems." *Families, Systems & Health* 15(3), 243–250.

Red Horse, J. G., R. Lewis, M. Feit, and J. Decker. 1978, February. "Family Behavior of Urban American Indians." *Social Casework* 59, 67–72.

Red Horse, Y. 1982. "A Cultural Network Model: Perspectives for Adolescent Services and Para-professional Training." In S. Manson (Ed.), *New Directions in Prevention Among American Indian and Alaska Native Communities.* (pp. 173–185). Portland: Oregon Health Sciences University.

Roscoe, W. 1991. *The Zuni Man-Woman.* Albuquerque: University of New Mexico Press.

Rotenberg, K., and F. Cranwell. 1989. "Self-concept in American Indian and White Children." *Journal of Cross-Cultural Psychology* 20(1), 39–53.

Rutman, S., A. Park, M. Castor, M. Taualii, and R. Forquera. 2008. "Urban American Indian and Alaska Native Youth: Youth Risk Behavior Survey 1997–2003." *Maternal and Child Health Journal* 12(Suppl. 1), S76–S81.

Ryan, R. A. 1981. "Strengths of the American Indian Family: State of the Art." In J. G. Red Horse, A. Shattuck and F. Hoffman (Eds.), *The American Indian Family: Strengths and Stresses* (pp. 25–51). Isleta, NM: American Indian Social Research and Development Associates, Inc.

Sandefur, G. D., and C. A. Liebler. 1996. "The Demography of American Indian Families." In G. D. Sandefur, R. R. Rindfuss, and B. Cohen (Eds.), *Changing Numbers, Changing Needs: American Indian Demography and Public Health* (pp. 196–217). Washington, DC: National Academy Press.

Sandefur, G. D., and T. McKinnell. 1986. "American Indian Intermarriage." *Social Science Research* 15, 347–371.

Schlegel, A. 1973. "The Adolescent Socialization of the Hopi Girl." *Ethnology* 12(4), 449–462.

Schweitzer, M. M. 1983. "The Elders: Cultural Dimensions of Aging in Two American Indian Communities." In J. Sokolovsky (Ed.), *Growing Old in Different Societies: Cross-cultural Perspectives* (pp. 168–178). Belmont, CA: Wadsworth Publishing Company.

————. (Ed.). 1999. *American Indian Grandmothers: Traditions and Transitions.* Albuquerque: University of New Mexico Press.

Shomaker, D. J. 1989. "Transfer of Children and the Importance of Grandmothers Among the Navajo Indians." *Journal of Cross-Cultural Gerontology* 4, 1–18.

————. 1990. "Health Care, Cultural Expectations and Frail Elderly Navajo Grandmothers." *Journal of Cross-Cultural Gerontology* 5, 21–34.

Simmons, T., and J. L. Dye. 2003. "Grandparents Living with Grandchildren: 2000" (Census 2000 Brief). Washington, DC: U.S. Department of Commerce.

Simmons, T., & O'Connell, M. 2003. "Married-Couple and Unmarried-Partner Households: 2000" (Census 2000 Special Reports). Washington, DC: U.S. Department of Commerce.

Snipp, C. M. 1989. *American Indians: The First of This Land.* New York: Russell Sage Foundation.

Staples, R., and A. Mirande. 1980. "Racial and Cultural Variations Among American Families: A Decennial Review of the Literature on Minority Families." *Journal of Marriage and the Family* 42(4), 157–173.

Strodtbeck, F. L. 1951. "Husband-Wife Interaction over Revealed Differences." *American Sociological Review* 16(4), 468–473.

Tefft, S. K. 1967. "Anomy, Values and Culture Change Among Teen-age Indians: An Exploratory Study." *Sociology of Education* 40(2), 145–157.

————. 1968. "Intergenerational Value Differentials and Family Structure Among the Wind River Shoshone." *American Anthropologist* 70(2), 300–333.

Teufel-Shone, N. I., L. K. Staten, S. Irwin, U. Rawiel, A. B. Bravo, and S. Waykayuta. 2005. "Family Cohesion and Conflict in an American Indian Community." *American Journal of Health Behavior* 29(5), 413–422.

Thornton, R. 1987. *American Indian Holocaust and Survival: A Population History Since 1492.* Norman: University of Oklahoma Press.

Thornton, R., G. D. Sandefur, and C. M. Snipp. 1991. "American Indian Fertility Patterns: 1910 and 1940 to 1980." *American Indian Quarterly* 15, 359–367.

Tjaden, P., and N. Thoennes. 1998. "Stalking in America: Findings from the National Violence Against Women Survey." (Research in Brief). Washington, DC: U.S. Department of Justice.

———. 2000. "Full Report of the Prevalence, Incidence, and Consequences of Violence Against Women: Findings from the National Violence Against Women Survey." Washington, DC: U.S. Department of Justice.

Tomashek, K. M., C. Qin, J. Hsia, S. Iyasu, W. D. Barfield, and L. M. Flowers. 2006. "Infant Mortality Trends and Differences Between American Indian/Alaska Native Infants and White Infants in the United States, 1989–1991 and 1998–2000." *American Journal of Public Health* 96(12), 2222–2227.

Troll, L. E. 1978. "The Family of Later Life: A Decade Review." In M. M. Seltzer, S. L. Corbett and R. C. Atchley (Eds.), *Social Problems of the Aging: Readings* (pp. 136–164). Belmont, CA: Wadsworth.

Trosper, R. L. 1996. "The Individual Economic Well-being of Native American Men and Women During the 1980s: A Decade of Moving Backwards." In G. D. Sandefur, R. R. Rindfuss, and B. Cohen (Eds.), *Changing Numbers, Changing Needs: American Indian Demography and Public Health* (pp. 172–195). Washington, DC: National Academy Press.

Tsosie, R. 1988. "Changing Women: The Cross-currents of American Indian Feminine Identity." *American Indian Culture and Research Journal* 12(1), 1–37.

Tyson, H., R. D. Higgins, and I. Tyson. 1999. "Family Dysfunction and Native American Women Who Do Not Seek Prenatal Care." *Archive of Family Medicine* 8, 111–117.

Underhill, R. M. 1942. "Child Training in an Indian Tribe." *Marriage and Family Living* 4(4), 80–81.

———. 1965. "The Papago Family." In M. F. Nimkoff (Ed.), *Comparative Family Systems* (pp. 147–162). Boston: Houghton/Mifflin.

Unger, S. (Ed.). 1977. *The Destruction of American Indian Families.* New York: Association on American Indian Affairs.

Urban Indian Health Institute (UIHI). 2010. "Reproductive Health of Urban American Indian and Alaska Native Women: Examining Unintended Pregnancy, Contraception, Sexual History and Behavior, and Non-voluntary Sexual Intercourse." Seattle, WA: Author.

U.S. Census Bureau. 1998. "Race of Wife by Race of Husband: 1960, 1970, 1980, 1991, and 1992." www.census.gov/population/socdemo/race/interractab1.txt (accessed April 24, 2011).

———. 2000. "Census 2000 Summary File 2 (SF 2) 100-Percent Data." factfinder.census.gov/servlet/DatasetMainPageServlet (accessed April 24, 2011).

———. 2001. "Population by Age, Race, and Hispanic or Latino Origin for the United States: 2000 (PHC-T-). www.census.gov/population/www/cen2000/briefs/phc-t9 (accessed April 24, 2011).

———. 2007. "2005–2007 American Community Survey 3-Year Estimates." Retrieved February 2, 2011, from U.S. Census Bureau: factfinder.census.gov/servlet/DatasetMainPageServlet?_program=ACS&_submenuId=datasets_2&_lang=en.

———. 2008. "2006–2008 American Community Survey 3-Year Estimates." factfinder.census.gov/servlet/DatasetMainPageServlet?_program=ACS (accessed April 24, 2011).

———. 2009. "2007–2009 American Community Survey 3-Year Estimates." factfinder.census.gov/servlet/DatasetMainPageServlet?_program=ACS&_submenuId=datasets_2&_lang=en (accessed April 24, 2011).

U.S. Census Bureau. 2010. "Statistical Abstract of the United States: 2011" (130th ed.). Washington, DC: Author. www.census.gov/compendia/statab (accessed April 24, 2011).

U.S. Department of Commerce. 1983. "General Social and Economic Characteristics: 1980." Washington, DC: U.S. Government Printing Office.

———. 1986. "American Indians, Eskimos, and Aleuts on Identified Reservations and in the Historic Areas of Oklahoma (Excluding Urbanized Areas). 1980: Census of Population" [Part 2, Sections 1 and 2]. Washington, DC: U.S. Government Printing Office.

———. 1992. "General Population Characteristics, United States." Washington, DC: U.S. Government Printing Office.

———. 1993. "Social and Economic Characteristics: United States." Washington, DC: U.S. Government Printing Office.

———. 2003a. "Summary social, economic, and housing characteristics: Part 1" (PHC-2–1). (2000 Census of Population and Housing). Washington, DC: Author.

———. 2003b. "Summary Social, Economic, and Housing Characteristics: Part 2" (PHC-2–1). (2000 Census of Population and Housing). Washington, DC: Author.

U.S. Department of Health and Human Services. 1995. "Report to Congress on Out-of-Wedlock

Childbearing" (DHHS Pub. No. [PHS] 95–1257). Washington, DC: U.S. Government Printing Office.

U.S. Office of Technology Assessment. 1986. "Indian Health Care." Washington, DC: U.S. Government Printing Office.

Wagner, J. K. 1976. "The Role of Intermarriage in the Acculturation of Selected Urban American Indian Women." *Anthropologica 18*(2), 215–229.

Ward, R. A. 1978, October. "Limitations of the Family as a Supportive Institution in the Lives of the Aged." *Family Coordinator 27,* 365–373.

Warren, C. W., H. I. Goldberg, L. Oge, D. Pepion, J. S. Freidman, S. Helgerson, et al. 1990, Spring. "Assessing the Reproductive Behavior of On- and Off-Reservation American Indian Females: Characteristics of Two Groups in Montana." *Social Biology 37*(1–2), 69–83.

Weibel-Orlando, J. 1990. "Grandparenting Styles: Native American Perspectives." In J. Sokolovsky (Ed.), *The Cultural Context of Aging: Worldwide Perspectives* (pp. 109–125). New York: Bergin & Garvey.

Williams, T. R. 1958. "The Structure of the Socialization Process in Papago Indian Society." *Social Forces 36*(3), 251–256.

Williams, W. L. 1986. *The Spirit and the Flesh: Sexual Diversity in American Indian Culture.* Boston: Beacon Press.

Witherspoon, G. 1975. *Navajo Kinship and Marriage.* Chicago: University of Chicago Press.

Yellowbird, M., and C. M. Snipp. 1994. "American Indian Families." In R. L. Taylor (Ed.), *Minority Families in the United States* (pp. 179–201). Englewood Cliffs: Prentice Hall.

19

■ ■ ■

The Jewish American Family

Charles H. Mindel
Bernard Farber[1]
Bernard Lazerwitz

INTRODUCTION

This chapter is about Jewish American families. To be Jewish in America is to be a member of a religious faith, a follower of Judaism, but also importantly it means to share a sense of "people-hood," an ethnicity, with a widespread number of people sharing a distinct cultural identity. In one effort to define the basic fundamental values of the Jewish people, it has been stated that "Judaism is more than a religion; it demands identification with the Jewish people as a whole, with its historical homeland, and a familial closeness with Jews of all kinds everywhere. Jews, whether by birth or by choice, must consider themselves links in a great chain of Jewish tradition, a *shalshelet* ("chain") that stretches across the generations binding Jews across time and into the future" (American Jewish Committee, 1997).

This duality has often presented confusion to many, especially non-Jews, who cannot decide whether Jews are a religious group, or a "nationality," or an ethnic group. On the wider global stage, though the Jewish religion can be traced back to the ancient Israelite Jews, the Jewish religion is practiced by people of diverse racial and ethnic backgrounds—a result of the continual historical process of conversion to Judaism. Thus, Jews throughout the world can be considered descendants of converts as well as direct descendants of ancient Israelite Jews. In the United States, there tends to be less of this ethnic diversity since most American Jews are descendants of Ashkenazic Jews—that is, European, especially eastern European, Jews.

---

[1]Dr. Bernard Farber passed away on May 5, 2000. These words from his 2001 obituary express our feelings perfectly: "Bernard Farber was truly one of the grand old scholars of family sociology. He was blessed with the keenest intelligence and a wonderful sense of humor. Bernie wrote eloquently about the family for decades and lived a life that made others lives better. It was a great honor to know him—a man who left the world a much better place and enriched our discipline with his intellect."

Worldwide, Judaism currently embraces approximately 13 million followers, concentrated mainly in a few key areas throughout the world. The two largest populations of Jewish people are found in the United States with a Jewish population estimated at between 5 million and 6.5 million, and in Israel with approximately 5.5 million (National Jewish Population Survey, 2000–2001; Saxe, Tighe, Phillips, and Kadushin, 2007). Although these two countries constitute about 80 percent of the Jewish population, Jewish people are to be found in societies all over the globe. Another 12.5 percent can be found in European countries and Canada. The remainder are spread all around the world in small numbers (American Jewish Committee, 2007).

Some of these smaller groups represent historical entities that have largely disappeared and are now remnants of settlements that had been of some size in the past. These include populations of Arab and Yemeni Jews as well as Jews of Persian origin. The largest groups of non-Caucasian Jews included Jews from Ethiopia; there were also small Jewish communities such as the Kaifeng Jews of China (now mostly assimilated), and Jewish communities in India. Until 1960, a community of cave-dwelling Jews was said to exist in southern Libya. A community in Burma claimed to be Jews, and reports and legends abound about African, Native American, and other tribes claiming Jewish ancestry. A twentieth-century convert community, the Abayudaya Jews, lives in Uganda.

HISTORICAL BACKGROUND

Jews have been in America since the colonial period, though they began arriving in large numbers only about one hundred years ago. The immigration of Jews to America has occurred in several major historical waves involving people from four national locations: Sephardic Jews, originally from Spain and Portugal; German Jews from the Germanic states; Eastern European Jews, largely from Poland and Russia but also from Romania, Hungary, and Lithuania; and most recently, sizable numbers of Jews from the former Soviet Union. These four waves of immigration are important because they define distinct cultural patterns that tend to distinguish Jewish communities in America.

Immigrants from the nearly destroyed Sephardic, German, Eastern European, and Soviet Jewish communities differed for a variety of historical, cultural, and economic reasons. Descendants of migrants from Eastern Europe, constituting by far the largest number of America's Jews, probably constitute more than 90 percent of Jewish Americans. The Sephardic and German Jews are and have been important not for their numbers but largely because of their social position and influence. The impact on American culture of Jews from the former Soviet Union is as yet unknown, although they, along with other new immigrants in New York City, are making their presence felt. Only the future will tell the extent to which they influence the American Jewish community or the larger American culture.

The Sephardic Jews

The earliest Jewish settlement in America occurred in 1654 in what was then New Amsterdam (now New York City), a colony of the Dutch West India Company. The Jews who settled there followed a circuitous route, ultimately traceable to the large medieval Jewish population of Spain and Portugal. However, the Jews were not particularly welcome in New Amsterdam. Peter Stuyvesant, the governor, resisted, arguing that "none of the deceitful race be permitted to infest and trouble this new colony" (Golden and Rywell, 1950:13). However, the Dutch West India Company decided to allow the Portuguese Jews to live in New Netherlands "provided the poor among them shall not become a burden to the Company or the community but be supported by their own nation" (14). From this beginning there continued a steady flow of immigration of Sephardic Jews and, increasingly, German Jews, who numbered approximately 15,000 in 1840.

The German Jews

The middle of the nineteenth century, from approximately 1840 to 1880, saw a second wave of Jewish immigration, mostly German Jews. Conditions in Germany—or, to be more accurate, the collection of Germanic states—were quite inhospitable to Jews and non-Jews alike at mid-century. Anti-Jewish medieval laws of oppression were enacted, especially in Bavaria, that among other items provided for heavy, discriminatory taxation; designated areas to live in; restricted occupations; and limited the number of Jewish marriages. These conditions prompted many German Jewish single men to leave for America to seek opportunity. In the later part of the nineteenth century, when these laws were relaxed, immigration of German Jews slowed down to a trickle (Glazer, 1957; Weinryb, 1958).

Many German Jewish immigrants started out as peddlers, an occupation that did not require great skill or large capital investment. They spread out all over America and gave many non-Jews their first glimpse of a Jewish face. Originally starting out with a backpack, they traversed the countryside. If they were reasonably successful, they would graduate to a horse and wagon. If they were able to accumulate a little money, they might open a dry goods store in one of the many towns and cities in which they traded. These were the origins of what later became the great clothing and department stores in America, such as Altman's, Bloomingdale's, Bamberger's, Goldblatt, Nieman-Marcus, Macy's, The May Company, Maison Blanche, Stix, Baer & Fuller, and others.

The importance and influence of the German Jews is crucially linked to their spectacular financial success. Although certainly not all German Jews became wealthy, the rise of several families, many of whom started out as peddlers, had enormous implications for the status of Jews in America. Some became important figures in banking and finance in a period of American history when industrialization was just beginning and there was a need for large amounts of capital to feed the growing industrial base.

The German Jewish influx into America was great enough to overwhelm the Sephardim in numbers. By 1848, 50,000 Jews were in America, and by 1880 an estimated 230,000 who were largely German Jews (Sklare, 1958).

Eastern European Jews

It was, however, the arrival of the Jews from Eastern Europe that has had the greatest impact on Jewish American life. Beginning around 1881 and largely ending by 1930, almost 3 million Jews immigrated to America. These individuals and families, though Jewish like their American counterparts, were in fact of another world. Whereas the Germans came from an "enlightened" modern society in which Jews were more often than not integrated into German culture, the Eastern European Jews came from a milieu in which a feeling of cultural homogeneity was strongly entrenched. A set of Jewish values and attitudes prevailed, including religious devotion and observance.

Most of the 5 million Jews of Russia and Poland had been restricted from the time of Catherine the Great to an area established for them known as the "Pale of Settlement." Jews were generally not allowed to settle in the interior of Russia and were limited to this area. Extending from the shores of the Baltic south to the Black Sea, the Pale has been described (except for the

Crimea) as a 313,000 square mile, monotonously flat, sand-arid prison (Manners, 1972:30). Within this area approximately the size of Texas, 808 *shtetlach* (small Eastern European towns *sing. Shtetl*), each of which was perhaps two-thirds Jewish and 94 percent poor, were the social limit in which Jews lived, survived, and "attained the highest degree of inwardness . . . the golden period in Jewish history in the history of the Jewish soul!" (Manners, 1972:31).

The concentration of Jews in these areas for hundreds and hundreds of years led to the development of a culture and civilization grounded in biblical and Talmudic teachings that remained unchanged to a remarkable degree until the twentieth century. Those who migrated from this society to America and elsewhere have, on the whole, become prosperous; those millions who remained, including most of the devout, were, for the most part, destroyed.

The mass migration of Eastern European Jews began in the 1880s and continued at a high level until the passage of restrictive U.S. immigration laws in 1924. The chief instigating factors that started the massive flow were imperial Russia's governmentally inspired *pogroms* focused on devastation and destruction, specifically of Jews, in 1881. Pogroms consisted of ransacking, burning, rape, and assorted violence committed in the towns and villages of Russia. The government, driven by an overwhelming fear of revolution, used pogroms as a form of diversion and weapon against dissenting minorities (Manners, 1972).

Beginning in 1882, new laws, the so-called May laws, were issued by the Czar that severely restricted Jewish rights, such as they were. Thousands were forced to leave their homes, especially those who resided in the interior of Russia. These laws and their extensions left most Jews no choice but to emigrate, mainly to America. Some went to Palestine, others went to other parts of Europe, but 40,000 came to the United States in 1881 and 1882. Another 62,000 came in 1888, and by 1906 the number was up to 153,000 per year (Manners, 1972:57).

The pogroms and restrictive laws that forced the migration of Russian Jews were but the final chapter of a long process of disintegration of Jewish communities that had been going on for more than a century. Antagonisms and tensions had been developing within for a long time. Of more importance were the effects from the world outside the shtetl. Industrialization and the decline of the feudal system came late to Eastern Europe, but by the nineteenth century its effects were being felt there as well. By the time of the pogroms in the late nineteenth and early twentieth centuries, social change, social disintegration, and demographic expansion had already come to this traditional society.

The arrival of this mass of people was a mixed blessing to Jews already established in the United States, especially to the German American Jews, who feared for their recently achieved middle-class status. However, native-born Jews and Americans in general took a compassionate though largely condescending view toward the newly arrived poverty-stricken immigrants (at least until 1924, when the U.S. Government, in the throes of a xenophobic isolationist wave, passed a restrictive immigration law).

Relations between the older, established Jews, primarily German American Jews, and the newly arrived Eastern European Jews were nevertheless difficult. The German Jews were interested in helping the immigrants in order to "Americanize" them so they would not be a source of embarrassment. They saw the idiosyncratic dress and speech and poverty of their fellow Jews as reflecting unfavorably on themselves and believed that the quicker these newcomers became indistinguishable from the rest of America, the better. Americanization was made more difficult by the fact that the Eastern European Jewish immigrants clustered together in distinct urban neighborhoods, especially in the American Northeast and particularly in New York City.

Though the Eastern European Jewish immigrants tended to be less observant and traditional than their counterparts who remained in Europe, the religious institutions established by them in America were traditional Orthodox recreations of the institutions that existed in Eastern Europe. The immigrants did not recognize Reform Judaism as it was practiced by native-born, predominantly German Jews; to them, it was unacceptable. "They are Jews," declared Rabbi Dr. Issac Meyer Wise, the leading light of Reform Judaism. "We are Israelites." The Russian Jews said with equal assurance, "We are Jews. They are *goyim* [Gentiles]" (Manners, 1972:76).

One important ingredient in the continuing vigor of Orthodox Judaism in America was the immigration during the Hitler and post–World War II years of numbers of Orthodox Chassidic Jews. The Chassidic groups, organized around a particular charismatic leader (a *rebbe*, or *Tzaddik* ["righteous one"]) are identified by the location in Europe from which they originated. These groups, which stress a communal life and close-knit group cohesion, were generally found in the New York area, often in old neighborhoods, although they are now frequently found in many parts of the country. One group, however, the Skverer Chassidim, has established its own town, New Square, in the suburbs of New York City, in which they have attempted to recreate the traditional life of the Eastern European Jew. The impact of these groups has been to bring new life into what was a disappearing branch of Judaism. The close ties of the members and the emotionalism of the religion as they practice it are attractive to many young people who have been seeking more emotion in their religious practice. Others who have not become members of Chassidic groups have borrowed much of the emotional content of this movement and put it into their own observance.

Jews from the Former Soviet Union

A smaller fourth wave of immigration from the former Soviet Union emerged in the 1980s. Estimated to be at least 700,000, these refugees from the former Soviet empire have taken up residence in the United States, with roughly half residing in the New York City area (Kliger, 2004; Saxe et al., 2007). The largest number came from what is now Ukraine and Russia. Because of Soviet policies, they comprise a largely secular group with little knowledge of Jewish religious and cultural traditions. Russian Jews tend to see religion as more of a cultural, traditional, or philosophical concept and are attracted to the religion because it is the religion of their ancestors (Kliger, 2004). Unlike previous waves of Jewish immigrants, this group is highly educated, with 65 percent having college degrees and 10 percent having advanced degrees, a figure higher than American Jews in general (AJC, 2000; Kliger, 2004). However, despite the higher educational levels, the National Jewish Population Survey (NJPS) 2000–01 (NJPS, 2004) survey found significant levels of poverty in this population, with 27 percent living below the poverty level as compared with 4 percent for other Jewish households and 11 percent for other immigrant groups (NJPS, 2004).

Traditional Eastern European Jewish Life

It has been estimated that today more than 90 percent of America's Jewish population is, or is descended from, immigrants from Russia and Eastern Europe who arrived between 1880 and 1930. Because their arrival has been relatively recent, family patterns that existed in Europe and were brought to the United States can still be expected to have an impact on present-day Jewish American family lifestyles. Many of the values commonly associated with the Jewish people found their expression in how people lived their daily lives in the small and large cities and towns of Eastern Europe.

At the risk of presenting an overly simplistic and stereotypical picture of Jewish life in the early twentieth century in Eastern Europe, we offer here a description of family life in the shtetl, where large numbers of Jews lived.[2] This description is an attempt to draw a picture of life at a time before the events of the twentieth century began crashing down on this population. It should also be remembered that not all Jews lived in shtetls; many lived in urban areas and cities. Late nineteenth-century Europe was a cauldron of change, and conflict. By the time of the mass migrations in the early decades of the twentieth century, major upheavals in Poland, Russia, Germany, and the Balkans had reduced the world of the shtetl to a remnant of the past. After the Holocaust, it was as if it had never existed.

SOCIAL ORGANIZATION.   The shtetl was a poor place, a place of unpaved streets and decrepit wooden buildings. It is said that there was no "Jewish" architecture; instead, the most noticeable features of the dwellings were their age and their shabbiness (Zborowski and Herzog, 1952:61). Occupationally, the Jews were generally tradespeople—dairymen, cobblers, tailors, butchers, fish-mongers, peddlers, and shopkeepers.

If the marketplace was the economic center of the shtetl, the synagogue was the heart and soul of the community. It was impossible to escape and separate the religious from the secular. Religious values infiltrated all aspects of life; every detail of life was infused with some religious or ritual significance.

Chief among the values of the shtetl and Jewish culture was the value of learning. One of the most important obligations of a devout Jew was and remains to study and learn. To obey the commandments of the scriptures, one must know them, and one must study them to know them. Studying and learning the Torah[3] became the most important activity in which a man could involve himself—and it was more important than earning a good living. Every shtetl of reasonable size contained schools of various levels, including the *cheder* for boys as young as three and four years of age. A learned young man was considered the most highly prized future son-in-law. In fact, it was considered prestigious for a father-in-law to support his new son-in-law for the first few years of marriage if the son-in-law was bright, so that he could devote himself to full-time study.

The stratification of the shtetl was based in large measure on learning and the tradition of learning in one's family. Shtetl Jews were either *sheyneh yidn* (beautiful Jews) or *prosteh yidn* (common Jews). The position of a person in this status hierarchy was, ideally, dependent on learning, but wealth played an important part in determining the sheyneh. A third quality, *yichus*, a combination of family heritage in learning and wealth, was also an important criterion in deter-mining social position. A person with great yichus was able to claim many ancestors of great worth, particularly in learning and philanthropy. To have yichus was very prestigious.

Life in the shtetl was guided by written codes of behavior that derived from the Talmud and other religious sources. These standards ideally had the effect of regulating behavior of all Jewish residents of the shtetl, sheyneh and prosteh alike. It is in these codes of behavior and the folklore, proverbs, and other customs that grew up around the shtetl that we find the unique cultural basis for Jewish family life, important aspects of which still have an impact today.

---

[2]Much of this discussion of shtetl family structure comes from Landes and Zborowski (1968) and Zborowski and Herzog (1952).

[3]Torah literally refers to the Pentateuch, the Five Books of Moses, or the written scriptures. However, Torah has come to mean much more, including remaining portions of the Old Testament as well as the whole of the commentaries and interpretations on the Pentateuch, known as the oral law, or the Talmud. In addition, the numerous codifications and newer commentaries that appeared during the Middle Ages, such as the works of Maimonides, have also come to be included under this rubric. In essence, Torah means all the religious learning and literature, including and surrounding the Holy Scriptures.

MARRIAGE.   Duties and roles for men and women were carefully detailed in traditional writings, and chief among these was the injunction that a man and woman marry. It was said, "It is not good for man to be alone." Marriage in the shtetl was traditionally arranged by the parents of the young couple, frequently through the use of a matchmaker *(shadchen)*. It was assumed that the "parents always want the best for their children" (Zborowski and Herzog, 1952:275), and the children went along with the match.

Because marriage was considered such an important institution—indeed, a commandment *(mitzvah)*—there was great pressure for marriage and families to remain united. In fact, because divorce reflected badly on one's family and stigmatized the individuals involved, it was a relatively rare occurrence. Marital stability was related to a dominant orientation in Jewish family life, *sholem bayis* (domestic harmony or peace). Only when maintaining a satisfactory family equilibrium became impossible and the sholem bayis was broken was divorce considered. The relative infrequency of divorce indicates that adaptations of many kinds occurred with some frequency.

FAMILY ROLES.   The injunction that a man should study, learn, and promote the book-learning tradition had important implications for the functioning of the husband in the family. The husband or father was often remote from most domestic concerns. If he was a scholar, much of the economic responsibility for the home was left to the wife. The husband's primary responsibility was in the spiritual and intellectual sphere; only the men were taught to read, speak, and write Hebrew, the sacred language; women who were literate spoke and read Yiddish.[4]

In reality, women often played a dominant role in family life and in the outside world. There was a high degree of interchangeability in family roles, and wives were trained to be ready to assume the economic burdens of supporting the family. Women often had wide latitude and opportunity for movement to conduct business or seek employment, and in time of emergency or need, they were able to partake in any number of "male" activities. It has been argued that as a consequence of their subordinate status, women were less regulated than men, and therefore they were able to partake in all activities that were not expressly forbidden to them. As a result, they quite often had greater freedom than men, who were bound up very tightly in a highly regulated way of life (Landes and Zborowski, 1968:81).

Basic to the Eastern European Jewish family with its wide range of rights and obligation was parental love. Seldom demonstrated verbally or physically after the child was four or five years old, parental affection, especially from the mother, was felt to be an unbreakable bond. "No matter what you do, no matter what happens your mother will love you always. She may have odd and sometimes irritating ways of showing it, but in a hazardous and unstable world the belief about the mother's love is strong and unshakable" (Zborowski and Herzog, 1952:293). The Jewish mother's love was expressed by and large in two ways: "by constant and solicitous overfeeding and by unremitting solicitude about every aspect of her child's welfare" (Zborowski and Herzog, 1952:293). Both paternal and maternal love contained the notions of suffering and sacrifice for the sake of the children. It was said that "she kills herself in order to bring up her children and

---

[4]Yiddish, a Middle High German dialect written in Hebrew characters, was the common *mamaloshen* (mother tongue) of most Eastern European Jews. Its use can be traced back a thousand years, and though Yiddish varied in form and pronunciation in different parts of western and eastern Europe, it provided a common language for Jews across all national boundaries and was a crucial factor in maintaining the unity of this branch of the Jewish people. The other major Jewish branches are the Sephardim, who spoke a dialect of Spanish written in Hebrew characters, and the Oriental Jews, who usually used Arabic.

care for her husband as well, who also becomes like a child in the family. Her conduct was understood and tolerated by her children, who nostalgically idealized it when they got older; she was remembered as a 'loving despot.'" (Zborowski and Herzog, 1952:297).

Affection among the shtetl Jews, as previously mentioned, was not expressed with kisses and caresses after a child reached age four or five and especially not in public. However, a mother was more likely to be demonstrative to her son and a father more demonstrative to his daughter. Furthermore, though much contact between members of the opposite sex, such as between brother and sister, was restricted by avoidance etiquette, there was virtually no avoidance between mother and son. It has been claimed that "though marital obligations are fulfilled with the husband, the romance exists with the son" and that "when the son marries, he gives the wife a contract and the mother a divorce" (Landes and Zborowski, 1968:80–88).

The father related to his daughter in a similar way as the mother related to her son, only not with quite the same intensity. With his daughter, he was undemanding and indulgent. A father, however, was a distant figure for the most part, one to whom great respect was owed. He was a particularly remote, authoritarian figure for the boy, whose growth into a "Jew" and a *mensch* ("whole person" or adult) was the father's responsibility.

The shtetl was viewed as an extended family. At the very least, Jews consider themselves to be ultimately related as the "Children of Israel," and often, because of extensive intermarriage within the shtetl, they were closer than that. In any case, there were strong obligations and pressure to maintain close ties to kin. Particularly strong was the obligation to take care of elderly parents, although there was great reluctance on the part of the elderly parent, especially the father, to accept aid.

THE MODERN AMERICAN JEWISH FAMILY

Jewish families have lived in the United States since before its founding, and it is nearly 135 years since the start of massive Jewish immigration from Eastern Europe. With the passage of time, American Jews have become highly "Americanized." However, each successive historical era has generated or magnified concerns about Jewish family life. The immigrant family was concerned about maintaining its traditional family forms in the face of the demands and expectations of modern industrial society. Since World War I, when 70 percent of the Jewish population lived in the Northeast, dispersion has been another factor adding to the problem of maintaining traditional family life; by 2008, only 44 percent remained in the Northeast. Along with these concerns, Americanization brought with it reasons to control fertility and to encourage women to enter the labor force in large numbers. As a result, levels of fertility have fallen significantly below the number required merely to replace the older generation. Operating together, these factors have resulted in an explosion in the prevalence of intermarriage between Jews and non-Jews in recent decades.

The Jewish Population in the United States

Estimating the number of Jewish people in the United States is not a simple matter. Since the U.S. Census does not ask questions on religion, nongovernmental estimates have been undertaken by private groups. The most well known of these is the National Jewish Population Survey (NJPS) sponsored by the United Jewish Communities (UJC), the most recent of which was completed in 2000–2001. Though it has been criticized for a variety of methodological problems, it remains the largest study of its kind and is the standard reference on the size of the Jewish population in the United States as of the beginning of the twenty-first century.

One of the most interesting and problematic issues in any study estimating the number of Jews in America, is the answer to "What is a Jew?" Is being Jewish simply being a member of a religion, or is it membership in an ethnic group? How do we define religious membership in the Jewish religion? Does membership in a synagogue congregation make one Jewish? What about self-identification (i.e., just calling oneself Jewish)? Traditional Jewish law uses the definition of a Jew as a person born to a Jewish mother. Thus, if you were born to a Jewish father and Gentile mother you are not Jewish under this definition (this is practiced in Israel and affects the legitimacy of many marriages there). What about converts? Many non-Jewish partners undergo a lengthy conversion procedure to convert to Judaism upon marriage, and traditionally they are regarded just as Jewish as those born Jewish. However, conversion procedures vary by Jewish denomination and not all conversions are mutually accepted between denominations. What about those people "born" to a Jewish mother or people "born" Jewish who don't practice the religion, don't go to synagogue, and might go to a Christian or a Unitarian church or perhaps are atheists? Are they Jewish?

This is always a vexing problem for researchers and other people concerned with the state of the Jewish people. A definition that is too restrictive—for example, counting only those people born to a Jewish mother—will produce a smaller count than one that includes a father who was born Jewish but was raised in a Christian setting, which is likely to produce a higher count. In addition, such calculations will produce a varying if not incorrect assessment on the state of the Jewish community.

The NJPS, for its part, tried to be as inclusive as possible, and in both its NJPS 1989–1990 and 2000–01 (NJPS, 2004) studies defined a Jew

"as a person:

- whose religion is Jewish, or
- whose religion is Jewish and something else, or
- who has no religion and has at least one Jewish parent or a Jewish upbringing, or
- who has a non-monotheistic religion, and has at least one Jewish parent or a Jewish upbringing." (NJPS, 2004)

The NJPS 2000–01 (NJPS, 2004) study estimated the Jewish population to be 4.3 million who were Jewish by religion or had no religion and considered themselves to be Jewish; plus 800,000 people of Jewish background; and an additional 100,000 thought to live in institutional settings. These numbers result in a total estimated population of Jews and persons of Jewish background of 5.2 million. This estimate represented a significant reduction in the size of the Jewish population compared to the previous survey (NJPS, 1989–1990) and a substantial decline from what was predicted based on natural growth and increases due to Jewish immigration. (NJPS, 2004; Saxe et al., 2007).

Differing definitions of *Jewish* and other more technical methodological concerns on undercounting have spurred researchers to reexamine the size of the population. Scholars at Brandeis University in 2007, concerned with an inexplicable decline in the number of Jews from the NJPS 1989–1990 study to the one in 2000–01, undertook a project whose goal was to verify or correct the estimates provided by NJPS and develop methods that can be used to monitor changes in the American Jewish population (Saxe et al., 2007).

The Brandeis group used a new methodology that synthesized ("meta-analyzed") data from 37 national studies funded by government and private agencies in order to reestimate the size and characteristics of the population. Analyzing each of these surveys independently yielded a wide range in estimates of the percentage of the total U.S. population that identified as Jewish by current religion. Estimates ranged from a low of under 1 percent to a high of nearly 3 percent, compared to the NJPS 2000–01 (NJPS, 2004) estimate of 1.5 percent. They concluded that NJPS underestimated the total population, in particular because it failed to count substantial numbers of young and middle-aged individuals. They state:

- The U.S. adult Jewish population, defined in terms of religion, is at least 3.5 million. This estimate is more than 15 percent higher than that indicated by NJPS 2000–01 (NJPS, 2004).
- The total number of Jews in the United States, using definitions that parallel NJPS's "core Jewish population" is likely greater than 6 million individuals and possibly as high as 6.4 million. These estimates include those who identify by criteria other than religion. Based on NJPS 2000–01 (NJPS, 2004), a conservative estimate of the proportion of Jews of "no religion" is more than 20 percent above the estimate of those who identify religiously. Other studies specifically suggest that this adjustment should be more than 25 percent. In addition, an adjustment needs to be made for individuals in institutional settings—students in dormitories, in hospitals or similar settings, or in the military. We estimate these numbers at between 250,000 and 350,000.
- An additional group, perhaps 1 million more than the 6 to 6.5 million estimated to be Jewish by NJPS criteria, might be considered Jewish based on their Jewish family backgrounds. In most cases, these individuals are the children of intermarried parents. Including these individuals would bring our estimate to between 7 and 7.5 million individuals. More broadly, the present static analysis does not take into account the dynamic impact of family changes—and doing so is a priority (Saxe et al., 2007).

AGE STRUCTURE OF THE JEWISH POPULATION.   The NJPS 2000–01 (NJPS, 2004) study indicates that the American Jewish population is older than it was in the 1990 study and compared to the U.S. population in general. They found that the median age of the Jewish population is 42, five years older than the median age in the 1990 study. The NJPS study also found 20 percent of the Jewish population to be children compared to 21 percent 10 years earlier and 26 percent for the total U.S. population in 2000. The elderly, 65 years or over, were 19 percent of the Jewish population, as compared to 17 percent in 1990 and 12 percent for the total U.S. population in 2000.

Traditionalism in Religion

Because European Jewish social structure and characteristics are historically the foundation of the American Jewish family, one is tempted to use the number of generations in America as an index of Americanization of the Jewish family. However, Jewish denominational preference incorporating historical change, gives a more accurate characterization of lifestyle trends, and simultaneously describes the value stances around which Jewish families are organized. With each successive generation in America, a general tendency in family lines is to move from the more traditional Orthodox denomination to the lesser traditionalist denominations (Lazerwitz and Harrison, 1979; Lazerwitz, 1978, 1995a).

Yet according to the NJPS 2000–01 (NJPS, 2004) data, Orthodox Jews made up 10 percent of the adult Jewish population (up from 6 percent in 1990 and comparable to the 1971 figure of 11 percent). They seek to carry out historic Jewish religious practices, value orientations, and social roles into modern life with as few changes as possible. Orthodox Jews rank higher than Conservative or Reform Jews in Jewish education, maintaining kosher homes, observing ritual behavior, and participating in Jewish communal and primary groups.

According to NJPS 2000–01 (NJPS, 2004) data, Conservative Jews comprise about 27 percent of American Jewish adults (down from 40 percent in 1990 and 1971). As a whole, they seek a balance between traditional ways and the demands of modern life and are more inclined than the

Orthodox toward social change in Jewish life. For example, Conservatives favor retention of kosher dietary laws and the observance of most Sabbath (Shabbat) and holy-day injunctions but permit use of electrical devices and automobiles on the Shabbat.

Those persons who regard themselves as Reform Jews constitute 35 percent of the adult Jewish population in 2000 (unchanged from 1990). As a group, they have given considerable emphasis to doing what they regard as "modernizing" Judaism. For them, traditional practices depend upon individual desires, and they have abandoned many practices and rituals.

At the furthest extreme from the Orthodox are those Jews who have no specific denominational preference, and many in this group are secular in outlook. This group, referred to in the NJPS 2000–01 (NJPS, 2004) survey as "Just Jewish," constitutes 26 percent of the Jewish population as of 2000 (up from 15 percent in 1990) and is, as a whole, marginal to the Jewish community and its religious practices.[5]

These findings emphasize the diversity among American Jews. It is likely that the denominational differences in outlook apply to additional areas of life—family patterns, sex roles, leisure activities, and basic value orientations. For example, divorce is much more prevalent among Jews brought up in homes with a low level of religious observance than among those whose parents were ritually observant. Moreover, "the lowest amount of divorce occurs among those who are most committed to the Judaic religious traditions as . . . practiced today" (Brodbar-Nemzer, 1986).

Dispersion, Kinship, and Cohesiveness

NATIONAL ORIGIN.   NJPS 2000–01 (NJPS, 2004) tells us that the overwhelming majority (85 percent) of adult Jews were born in the United States. Most of the foreign-born came from the former Soviet Union, with Ukraine (20 percent) and Russia (13 percent) accounting for the most. There were also smaller numbers of immigrants from Israel and Germany. Tobin, Tobin, and Rubin (2005) studied the American Jewish population and concluded that around 1.2 million American Jews consisted of "African-American, Asian-American, Latino, Sephardic, Middle-Eastern, and mixed-race Jews."

DISPERSION AND COHESIVENESS.   The initial concerns of immigrant Jewish families in the United States were the effects of their new environment on the integrity of their family life. W. I. Thomas's analysis of the *Bintel Brief* ("Bundle of Letters") in the Yiddish-language *Daily Forward* (Bressler, 1952) focused on the immigrant generation. Thomas regarded "the key motif expressed in Jewish family patterns [to be] . . . an effort to preserve the solidarity of the family" (Balswich, 1966:165). As time went on, the threat to family solidarity came not only because of isolation from European roots but also from the process of Americanization, which fostered mobility—both socially and spatially. Table 19-1 presents data on trends in the distribution of the American Jewish population from 1918 to 2008.

Table 19-1 indicates that there have been important shifts in the Jewish population. Although immigration during the first part of the twentieth century concentrated the bulk of the Jewish population in the Northeast, especially in the Middle Atlantic states, since World War I a

---

[5]Some of these variations in denominational change may be due to methodological error. The Brandeis meta-study argues that the NJPS 2000–01 states, "Substantial evidence indicates that the population of 35- to 55-year-olds was substantially undercounted by NJPS 2000–01. Evidence from NJPS itself suggests that this resulted in an underestimate of the non-Orthodox population (those who identify as Reform or Conservative). Our conclusion is that the estimated 800,000 to 1,300,000 additional Jewish individuals identified by the present study are disproportionately non-Orthodox and, on average, younger than the NJPS population" (Saxe et al., 2007).

TABLE 19-1   Distribution of the Jewish Population, Percentage by Regions: 1918, 1930, 1972, 1990, 2000, and 2008

Region	1918	1930	1972	1990	2000	2008
NORTHEAST	**69.9**	**68.3**	**62.6**	**50.6**	**46.4**	**43.5**
New England	8.6	8.4	6.8	7.1	6.8	6.8
Middle Atlantic	61.3	59.9	55.8	43.6	39.6	36.7
NORTH CENTRAL	**20.2**	**19.6**	**12.2**	**11.2**	**11.6**	**10.8**
East North Central	15.7	15.7	9.8	9.2	9.4	8.6
West North Central	4.5	3.9	2.4	2.0	2.2	2.1
SOUTH	**6.9**	**7.6**	**11.8**	**19.3**	**21.1**	**21.5**
South Atlantic	4.0	4.3	9.4	16.4	18.0	18.6
East South Central	1.3	1.4	0.7	0.7	0.7	0.6
West South Central	1.6	1.9	1.9	2.2	2.4	2.3
WEST	**3.1**	**4.6**	**13.3**	**18.8**	**20.9**	**24.3**
Mountain	0.7	1.0	1.1	2.6	3.7	4.4
Pacific	2.4	3.6	12.2	16.3	17.2	19.9
TOTAL (percent)	100.0	100.0	100.0	100.0	100.0	100.0

Sources: Data on distribution of Jewish population from *American Jewish Year Book,* 1919:606; 1931:14; 1973:309; 1991:204–224; 2000:248; 2008:151,222

steady redistribution of the Jewish population has taken place, with major losses in the urban centers in the Middle Atlantic and East and North Central regions.

Dramatic shifts occurred between 1930 and 2008 in the movement of the population to the South Atlantic and Pacific states—often to Florida and California—and by 2008, almost half of the Jewish population resided in the South and the West (currently 46 percent, in contrast to 10 percent in 1918).

Goldstein and Goldstein (1996:178) examined the relationship between denomination and migration for the five years prior to the 1989–1990 NJPS survey. They found that only 10 percent of the Orthodox migrated from their local community in that period as compared with the Conservatives (22 percent), Reform Jews (24 percent), and Jews without a denominational preference (26 percent). They also found that the percentages of persons ages 18 to 44 responding that they would "very likely" move within the next three years were 29 percent for the Orthodox, 34 percent for the Conservative, 37 percent for the Reform, and 44 percent for the nondenominational Jews. Goldstein and Goldstein (1996:206) conclude from their analysis of ritual practices that "those whose behavior conforms more closely to traditional practices are generally much more stable than the less observant" and that "with a shift away from extensive ritual practice among large segments of American Jewry, mobility may well increase further than its present level."

KINSHIP AND COHESIVENESS.   Numerous studies have shown connections between migration and ties with extended family (e.g., Litwak, 1985; Sklare and Greenblum, 1967:252). However, given the diversity of family lifestyles associated with denomination and ritual observance, one would expect that relationship between migration and extended family would vary depending on the family and kinship orientation.

Anthropologists have used the term *collaterality* to refer to the fact that people regard some kinds of relatives as genealogically closer than others. For example, some people are considered too closely related to marry one another—perhaps a first cousin or an uncle. In traditional Jewish law, however, such marriages are permitted. Differences in collaterality are important because they express different ways of looking at family and kinship.

These collaterality systems, or models, are the Parentela Orders model (with origins in ancient Judaism and classical Greece), the Civil Law model (whose source was the Twelve Tables of the early Roman republic), and the Canon Law model (which appeared in the twelfth-century systemization of church law). In the contemporary world, proposals have been made to apply genetic relatedness (i.e., shared chromosomes) to inheritance and marriage laws. A fifth model, the Standard American model, is a mirror image of the Parentela Orders model—focusing on an individual's ancestral line instead of the perpetuation of the family line. Its pattern suggests an emphasis on one's past family history rather than a concern with the family's destiny (Farber, 1981:45–65).

The Civil Law model emerged to balance family and civil interests at the founding of the Roman Republic. The Canon Law model, consistent with church writings, is minimally oriented toward family perpetuation, focusing instead on subordinating family continuity to church interests.

As described in the Torah and the Mishnah,[6] the Parentela Orders model places primary emphasis on the continuity of the family line. Jews tend to cluster around the Parentela Orders pattern, with persons raised in Orthodox homes showing a greater inclination toward the Parentela Orders pattern than individuals from the less traditional branches (Farber and Gordon, 1979, 1981). What does conformity to the Parentela Orders model imply about family relationships? Regardless of religious affiliation, people who hold a Parentela Orders orientation exhibit certain characteristics in their family and kinship ties. Compared with persons who conform to other kinship-collaterality perspectives, (1) their age at first marriage tends to be high; (2) they and their parents and siblings show a high degree of marital stability; (3) their fertility level tends to be above average for their particular religious group (as does that of their parents and siblings); (4) when they marry someone of another faith, both husband and wife adopt the same religious affiliation; (5) there is a somewhat greater proclivity to live near the husband's rather than the wife's parents; but (6) despite residential distance, there is still often intense involvement with relatives (Farber, 1981). A German study by Luschen (1986) suggests that conformity to the Parentela Orders model is also related to a tendency to name children, instead of spouses, as primary heirs (Luschen, 1986: tables 8 and 9).

Moreover, holding a Parentela Orders view of collaterality is related to ethnic identity. A study of the Kansas City Jewish community found that persons with a Parentela Orders orientation, more often than Jews with other kinship orientations, tend to live in areas with a high Jewish concentration and maintain Jewish communal ties. They are generally nonmigrants; their close friends tend to be Jewish; they are more active than their parents in Jewish matters; and they disapprove of intermarriage (Farber and Gordon, 1979). Research in a Chicago suburb during the 1960s indicated that familism among Jewish families was more a basis for reluctance to migrate than a result of family stability (Winch, Greer, and Blumberg, 1967).

---

[6]The Mishnah is the first major written document of the Jewish oral traditions and is often called the "Oral Torah." It was compiled c. 220 CE, when the persecution of the Jews and the passage of time raised the possibility that the details of the oral traditions would be forgotten. Rabbinic commentaries on the Mishnah over the next three centuries were compiled as the Gemara, which, coupled with the Mishnah, comprise the Talmud.

Marriage, Fertility, and Family Roles

MARRIAGE.   In 2000 more than half of Jewish adults (57 percent) were married, 9 percent were divorced, 8 percent were widowed, and 1 percent were separated. The remaining 25 percent were single or never married (NJPS, 2004).

Jewish marital trends are not dissimilar to American marital trends; during the past three decades age-at-first-marriage has been increasing for men and for women in both populations. For the general population, the age of first marriage has increased from 21 (women) and 23 (men) during the 1970s, to 26 (women) and 28 (men) in 2001 (U.S. Census Bureau, 2004). The age of first marriage for American Jews is even older. It has been suggested that this is most likely related to their higher levels of education (NJPS, 2004; Ukeles, Miller, and Beck, 2006).

Delayed marriage is further illustrated when we look at the unmarried population by age. By age 35, 52 percent of Jewish men are unmarried and 36 percent of Jewish women are unmarried. The same statistics for the general population show that only 41 percent of men and 30 percent of women are unmarried at age 35 (Ukeles et al., 2006). According to the 2000–01 NJPS (NJPS, 2004), "in every age group under 65, proportionally fewer Jews than all Americans have ever married, with the largest gap being among those ages 25–34."

FERTILITY.   Several national fertility studies (Freedman, Whelpton, and Campbell, 1959, 1961; Whelpton, Campbell, and Patterson, 1966) report that American Jews have historically been the most successful of American major ethnic groups in the areas of family planning and birth spacing. Indeed, the first birth-control clinic opened by Margaret Sanger was in Brownsville, then a Jewish immigrant neighborhood in Brooklyn, New York. Estimates are that from about 1920 to 1940, the Jewish birthrate in America fell almost 40 percent (Seligman, 1950:42). Rapid fertility reduction has permitted Jewish parents to support the educational desires of their fewer offspring and thereby give strong support to the rapid socioeconomic mobility that has been the outstanding achievement of American Jews (Lazerwitz, 1971).

Reduction in the Jewish birthrate derives not only from effective use of contraceptives but also from late marriage. Goldstein (1971:24) indicates that "later age of marriage has characterized Jewish women since at least 1920." In 1971, the average age at first marriage for Jewish women was 21.3 years. By 1990, the average marital age for Jewish women in the 25–34 age bracket was 23.1, and about one-third of the women in that age range were as yet unmarried (Goldstein, 1992:165, table 16). However, coupled with later age at marriage for career reasons, first births are sometimes delayed until women are in their thirties. In 2004, 20 percent of American women ages 40–44 had not yet had children of their own, twice the percentage that was childless by that age in 1976.

According to the NJPS 2000–01 (NJPS, 2004), "At all ages, fertility among Jewish women is lower than fertility for all U.S. women, whether gauged by the percent who are childless or the average number of children ever born." The fertility gap between Jewish and other American women by age 35 is dramatic: Approximately 50 percent of Jewish women are childless until the ages of 35–39, whereas only 20 percent of American women are childless at that age (Ukeles et al., 2006).

Sergio Della Pergola (1980) estimated that American Jewish fertility at the start of the 1970s was slightly below the level needed to replace the Jewish population and was still declining. By 1990, fertility of Jewish women was well below the replacement level—1.5 children per woman (for women ages 35–39) (Goldstein, 1992:169, table 18). More recently the average number of children born to Jewish women is somewhat less than 1.9, whereas 2.1 is the required rate for population replacement. Others have quarreled somewhat with the predictions of declining fertility. Ukeles et al. (2006) argues that "given the high intermarriage rates, these numbers do not include children born to Jewish men married to non-Jewish women. If these children are raised as Jews, then Jewish "population replacement" parameters may be achieved. Saxe et al. (2007), examining a wider assortment of survey data, "suggest that the estimates of the number of Jewish children is substantially larger than the number provided by NJPS."

Jewish religious involvement accounts for only insignificant portions of variations in fertility among younger women. There is little difference in fertility of women under age 40 for denominational Jews by birth, secular Jews, and Jews by choice. Nevertheless, frequent synagogue attenders who prefer Orthodox or Conservative denominations do have higher fertility rates than others (Goldstein, 1992:169, table 18; Lazerwitz, Winter, Dashefsky, and Tabory, 1997:chap. 7).

FAMILY ROLES.   The trimming down of the size of Jewish families implies profound changes in family roles during the twentieth century. The opening section of this chapter portrayed a traditional ethnic base for the Jewish family in America. The dual roots of the American Jewish family—in religious injunctions and European ethnicity—are both vulnerable to the competition of family norms associated with other religions and with the "Americanization" of family life. Those immersed in observance of religious ritual and traditional religious views find reinforcement of the religious aspects of family life. However, as one generation succeeds another, we would anticipate that ethnic family norms and practices would readily disintegrate.

Gordon (1959:59) asserts that among immigrant Jewish families "there was a far greater degree of equality between husband and wife than is generally assumed. . . . The mother was the homemaker, but it was she whose personal piety and example within the home was [sic] expected to influence her children, while winning their love and veneration." The maternal role was, in part, a carryover from the woman's traditional responsibility through the centuries primarily to run the household but also to contribute to its livelihood.

In the immigrant family, the proverbial Jewish mother still saw her maternal role as her primary responsibility, but her daughter in the next generation did so a bit less, and so on. In Phoenix in 1978, only 25 percent of Jewish women under 40 reported that their mothers worked during the time that they themselves were growing up—in contrast to 35 percent for non-Jewish responses. However, for the respondents themselves, differences by religion disappear; regardless of religion, approximately 60 percent were working mothers (Farber, 1981).

Traditionally, the father in the Jewish family provided a link between the family and religious community. This link was important to the family's welfare in that Jewish communities in Europe were organized as corporate bodies until the twentieth century (Elazar and Goldstein, 1972). The father's personal religious dedication was the basis for his role in promoting the piety, morality, and ethical standards of family members. In the secularized American context, his position as linking the family to community has been translated into his occupational dedication and his passing on achievement values to his children (Slater, 1969; Strodtbeck, 1958).

Consistent with the concept of family as a descending line of relationships (as suggested by the Parentela Order model of kinship collaterality), the parent–child relationship in the traditional family is "complementary rather than reciprocal. Parents are donors and should not receive from children. The children can make return by passing benefits to their [own] children" (Mandelbaum, 1958:512). Sklare (1971:87) points out that in the traditional Jewish family a child is never considered to be truly emancipated from his or her parents. He suggests that children are extensions of their parents rather than distinct entities. One of the basic forms of exchange for parent and child is for parents to provide a basis for their children's own success in family and community, whereas children have an obligation to supply *nakhus* (prideful pleasure or gratification) for the parents. In establishing the conditions for nakhus, the parents create a lifelong obligation for their children. Findings indicate that high-achievement motivation is related to parental praise and expression of parental pride (Rehberg, Sinclair, and Schafer, 1970).

With Americanization has come a dimming of the focus on the concept of *family* as encompassing a line of descent linking one generation to its past and future. Instead, as the association of less traditional Jewish denominations with kinship models other than the Parentela Orders suggests, emphasis on the independence of the nuclear family unit in one's concept of family is growing. With the decay of the lineal conception of family, the basic glue for molding the structure of roles in the traditional family is disappearing.

Traditionally, in the family's socialization of children, "each year adds new responsibilities in the child's life" (Zborowski and Herzog, 1952:350). With each responsibility, the child is seen as becoming more of a *mensch* (a reliant and moral human being, sensitive to the needs of others). Bit by bit, the growing child assumes the *olfun Yiddishkeit* (the discipline imposed by the Jewish way of life). The shift in socialization practices accompanying the changing views of family life is suggested by the findings on kinship models and school achievement in Phoenix in 1978. In that study, among Jewish respondents, 88 percent of those holding a Parentela Orders conception of kinship collaterality regarded high grades as important, as compared with 82 percent in the Standard American category, 63 percent in the Civil Law group, and only 56 percent in the Genetic and Canon Law approaches to kinship collaterality (Farber, 1981). Moreover, in an analysis of scholastic achievement of students at a large state university, students (of all religions) who conformed to the Parentela Orders model tended to have the highest cumulative grade point averages (GPAs), and those whose pattern of answers conformed to the Canon Law or Genetic kinship models had the lowest GPAs (Farber, 1977).

Intermarriage

Probably no other issue relating to the Jewish family and to Jewish ethnic identity is more challenging that the issue of intermarriage. For example, Cohen (2008) has stated that "the key challenge by which history will judge us revolves around how we will respond to the impact of intermarriage upon our individual and collective Jewish futures."

It is only in recent decades that intermarriage has affected large segments of the Jewish population in the United States. For Jewish adults who were married before 1970, the intermarriage rate was 13 percent. For those whose marriage began in 1985, the intermarriage rate had climbed to 38 percent. Most recently, for those married between 1996 and 2001, the figure is estimated to be 47 percent (NJPS, 2004).

Ukeles et al. (2006) point out that "NJPS 2000–01 data indicate that current intermarriage rates for American Jews range from 41 percent among those 35 and under, to 37 percent of those ages 35–54, to 20 percent of those over 55. Moreover, 52 percent of young Jews between the ages of 18 to 24 were born to families with one Jewish and one non-Jewish parent." The data also show that approximately three-quarters of those growing up in interfaith families ultimately marry non-Jews, as compared to 28 percent of those from in-married Jewish homes (Fishman, 2004).

The NJPS 2000–01 (NJPS, 2004) study also found that intermarriage has been more frequent among younger than older adults. They found that among those 55 and over, 20 percent were currently intermarried while among those 35–54 intermarriage stands at 37 percent and 41 percent among those younger than 35.

The nature of Jewish intermarriage has also changed. Although overall the intermarriage rate among men (33 percent) is somewhat higher than among women (29 percent), the gender composition of intermarriage varies with age. Among older Jewish adults, men above the age of 55 are more likely to be intermarried than women. However, within the 35- to-54-year-old age group, equal proportions of men and women are intermarried. But for those under the age of 35, men are more likely than women to be intermarried (NJPS, 2004).

One of the concerns with the increase in intermarriage is the loss of Jewish identity among the intermarried families. Concern about the rising intermarriage rate has been a longstanding one, and extensive debate has been waged on the consequences for the Jewish people. Cohen (2008:1) describes some responses to the increase:

> In the 1990s, following reports of exploding rates of intermarriage, American Jewry mobilized expressly to address the intermarriage challenge to Jewish continuity. We dramatically increased our investment in Jewish education—including day schools, Israel travel, Jewish studies, Hillels, and most recently Jewish summer camping. And, simultaneously, we dramatically increased our efforts at outreach, seeking to welcome the intermarried and remove both explicit and implicit barriers to engaging them in congregational life. One sign of success is that today, about half of the newly affiliated married couples in Reform temples have at least one member who was not raised Jewish.

A major fear is that although many of the non-Jewish spouses in an intermarried couple convert to Judaism, overall the Jewish population experiences a net loss. For example, Phillips (1997) reported that 98 percent of children with two Jewish parents are raised as Jews, whereas only 39 percent of children with one Jewish parent are raised as Jews. He points out noticeable differences when the mother is Jewish than when the father is Jewish.

Benjamin Phillips and Fern Chertok (2004), using the NJPS 2000–01 data, pointed out that about 42 percent of children of intermarriages are being raised exclusively as Jews (32 percent as religious Jews, 10 percent as secular Jews, plus an additional 11 percent as Jewish plus another religion) versus 50 percent as another religion. They also argue that these data represent "substantial progress from a decade ago, when Bruce Phillips (1997) found that only 18 percent of children of mixed marriages were raised exclusively as Jews (vs. 32 percent today), and Christianity was part of the child's upbringing in 58 percent of cases (vs. 46 percent today)." Though, as they mention, "even given this apparent progress, the current pattern of childrearing among intermarried families represents a net loss to the Jewish community."

Saxe, Chertok, and Phillips (2008) and Chertok, Phillips, and Saxe (2008), using NJPS 2000–01 data, found that it is the experiences in Jewish living, education, and social networks that contribute to maintaining a Jewish identity and not so much whether one's parents were intermarried or not. Of course, if the intermarried or the in-married have not been engaged in these experiences, then it is also probable that their children are less likely to self-identify as Jews.

The NJPS 2000–01 study (NJPS, 2004) compared the in-married adults with intermarried ones on a range of Jewish experiences and community connections (see Table 19-2). Two relevant conclusions are apparent: There is a large variation among in-married Jews in these experiences and connections, with less than half of them involved with nine of the experiences or activities in the list, including keeping kosher at home (26 percent), attending religious services at least monthly (37 percent), lighting Shabbat candles (39 percent), and belonging to Jewish organizations (29 percent Jewish community centers or 39 percent another organization).

The second finding is that in-married Jews maintain more Jewish connections and greater engagement with Jewish life than intermarried Jews. The largest differences between in-married

TABLE 19.2 Jewish Connections of In-married and Intermarried Jews

	In-Married	Intermarried
Light Chanukah candles	88	53
Hold/attend Passover Seder	85	41
Half or more of close friends are Jewish	76	24
Feel emotionally attached to Israel	76	45
Fast on Yom Kippur	66	26
Contribute to Jewish cause (not federation)	60	19
Belong to synagogue	59	15
Visited Israel	49	16
Contribute to federation campaign	41	9
Light Shabbat candles	39	5
Belong to other Jewish organization	39	9
Attend Jewish religious service monthly or more	37	8
Volunteer under Jewish auspices	33	8
Participate in adult Jewish education	31	7
Belong to Jewish community center	29	6
Keep kosher at home	27	5

Source: NJPS, 2004.

and intermarried Jews are associated with synagogue membership and attendance, memberships in JCCs (Jewish community centers) and other Jewish organizations, donations to federation campaigns, volunteerism under Jewish auspices, adult Jewish education, lighting Shabbat candles, and keeping kosher (NJPS, 2004).

Interestingly, although there are substantial differences between the in-married and the intermarried regarding all of the experiences and connections in the list, for a number of important Jewish forms of engagement the large segments of the intermarried are connected. As the NJPS 2000–01 (NJPS, 2004) report describes it, "Common forms of Jewish engagement among the intermarried revolve around three major Jewish holidays, with more than half of intermarried Jews lighting Chanukah candles, a significant minority attending or holding a Passover Seder, and slightly more than a quarter fasting on Yom Kippur. A substantial minority of intermarried Jews are also emotionally attached to Israel, and just under a quarter report that half or more of their close friends are Jewish."

Coming to any firm conclusions about the impact of intermarriage is very difficult. Definitions of who is Jewish and who is not differ; differing definitions have been used in the various population studies, leading to differing interpretations. Perhaps statements from several points of view can capture the confusion.

Cohen (2008:3) states rather alarmingly for Jews and perhaps others that "we are now in the midst of a non-Orthodox Jewish population meltdown. Its signs are as visible and frightening as is global warming. Among Jews in their 50s, for every 100 Orthodox adults, we have 192 Orthodox children. And for the non-Orthodox, for every 100 adults, we have merely 55 such children. In nearly two generations, in our own lifetime, the Orthodox have embarked on a path to nearly doubling their size. At the same time, the non-Orthodox are en route to nearly half their number. Rising intermarriage rates over the years past are right now engendering sharp declines in the non-Orthodox Jewish population, not in generations yet to be born, but among our own children and grandchildren, those now under 25."

On the other hand, others have contributed to a more optimistic view. Saxe et al. (2005) in a study of the Jewish community in Boston found that a majority of children from intermarried homes are being raised as Jews. They point out substantial differences in the way in which adult children of in-married and intermarried households were raised on a number of dimensions. Those with intermarried parents had fewer formative Jewish experiences. But when one takes account of critical socializing experiences such as Jewish education, Jewish friends, and exposure to home ritual, the impact of intermarriage on Jewish identity is significantly reduced (Saxe et al., 2008).

Chertok et al. (2008:8) warn that "it is engagement and not intermarriage that presents both the greatest challenge and the most promising arena for intervention for Reform Jews and Reform Judaism." They further conclude, based on an analysis of the sample of Reform Jews in the 2000–01 NJPS, that "accepted wisdom has been that the root of the problem for American Jewry is intermarriage and the dissolution of traditional, endogamous Jewish families. Our conclusion is different. Whether or not the identity of the next generation is strengthened depends on our ability to educate and transmit Judaism. It depends less on whom young Jews marry than their capacity to find meaning in Judaism and the ability of parents to be role models in this endeavor."

The Intersection of Religio-Ethnic Communities: A Fourth Melting Pot?

For a long time, sociology has referred to three American religio-ethnic communities: Protestant, Catholic, and Jewish. The basic contention has been that each of these communities constitutes a cultural caldron that unifies the diverse national, social class, and ethnic components. This unification occurs through a series of basic beliefs, moral principles, and ritual practices, and the religious community incorporates the ethnic backgrounds into its structure. A vital socializing agency in this process is the family, which in some ways symbolizes the close, unifying force in transmitting religious injunctions and practices to the next generation.

The religiously heterogeneous family by its very nature transcends the boundaries of the three "melting pots." In doing so, it has the task of developing a modus vivendi that enables it to endure effectively. This modus vivendi involves beliefs, norms, and practices that permit a religio-ethnic diversity while simultaneously embodying emotional growth and smooth functioning.

To operate effectively, the religiously heterogeneous family would likely be obliged (1) to take on a point of view that accommodates diversity, probably involving a liberal perspective—often secular—that overpowers the traditional religious backgrounds of the married couple and (2) to isolate itself from traditional religio-ethnic traditions that might divide the couple.

Liberality in political orientations generally embodies the overall weltanschauung (worldview) of the people who hold them. NJPS findings on marriage types and the political orientation of Jewish-born adult respondents in the 1989–1990 NJPS indicate that compared with about 40 percent of respondents in the in-married, 52 percent of those in the intermarried category are inclined to hold a "liberal" political orientation. These percentages support the position that a successful intermarriage requires a liberal outlook on life that would accommodate the persistence of religious diversity in the marriage and family.

The liberal accommodation of religious diversity in families where one spouse is Jewish and the other is not is suggested in findings on two religious practices: one Christian (having a

Christmas tree in the home) and the other Jewish (having a Seder to celebrate Passover). Among couples in which both spouses had been born into Jewish families, virtually no one has a Christmas tree in the home, and almost everyone celebrates with a Seder at Passover (especially among those identifying with any particular denomination). The religious symbolism of the Christmas tree and Seder is somewhat muffled in some convert-in families, in which 22 percent (33 percent for convert-in Reform families) have a Christmas tree and 87 percent have a Seder. Finally, for the religiously heterogeneous families, 62 percent report having a Christmas tree and 52 percent also report having a Seder. However, data also suggest that a significant minority of the religiously heterogeneous couples have neither Christmas tree nor Seder. Thus, the distinction in symbolism between the Christmas tree and the Seder is erased in perhaps most of the religiously heterogeneous families as part of their liberal orientation.

JEWISH–CATHOLIC–PROTESTANT MIXTURES.   As noted, a second element in sustaining a religiously heterogeneous marriage is to isolate oneself from religious services that bind one to a particular religious community. Table 19-3 presents percentages pertaining to marriage types and frequency of attendance at religious services for Catholics, Protestants, and Jews. In contrast to those in religiously homogeneous and convert-in marriages, persons in all three groups—Protestants, Catholics, and Jews—in religiously heterogeneous marriages attend services infrequently (if at all). Especially among Protestants and Jews, those in religiously heterogeneous marriages rarely attend services regularly. Thus, in its isolation from the institutional ties of church

TABLE 19-3   Percentage of Marriage Types and Frequency of Attendance at Religious Services for Protestants, Catholics, and Jews (GSS and 1989–1990 NJPS)

Frequency of Attendance	In-Married	Converted In-Marriage	Intermarried
Protestants (GSS[a])			
Less than once per month[c]	44	39	76
Once to three times per month	17	17	11
More than three times per month	39	44	13
Catholics (GSS[a])			
Less than once per month[a]	32	27	56
Once to three times per month	14	15	15
More than three times per month	54	58	29
Jews (NJPS[b])			
Less than once per month[a]	41	28	77
Once to three times per month	38	46	19
More than three times per month	21	26	4

[a]GSS data are derived from the General Social Surveys conducted by the National Opinion Research Center from 1985 to 1989.

[b]NJPS, 1989–1990.

[c]Except for the Jews, the majority of responses in this category were never or once a year. (Because many Jews attend synagogue only on Rosh Hashanah and Yom Kippur, a slim majority of responses were 2 to 11 times per year.) However, for the religiously heterogeneous marriage type for all three religions, more than two-thirds of responses in this category were 0 to 1 times per year.

(or synagogue), as well as in its relationship to a liberal orientation in the blurring of traditional religious distinctions, the religiously heterogeneous marriage type emerges as a generic kind of family life.

CHANGE AND ADAPTATION

The American Jewish family is becoming increasingly diverse. This chapter has focused on some consequences of this diversity. By and large, the major segment of the American Jewish population consists of people descended from Eastern European immigrants who arrived in America in the late nineteenth and early twentieth centuries. Further diversification has been wrought by the more recent inflow from the former Soviet Union, Israel, Africa, and various Middle Eastern countries. But this recent migration adds only a small increment to the diversity of family forms.

In the core population, profound changes have taken place in Jewish family life and, more generally, in American family life since 1960. As noted earlier, sociologists have described American society as consisting of three melting pots—Catholic, Protestant, and Jewish. However, the amount of religious intermarriage taking place in the past few decades seems to represent a departure from that characterization. The growing sector of families of religiously intermarried couples may well constitute a fourth melting pot in American society.

The small size of the American Jewish population (relative to that of Protestants and Catholics) magnifies the effects of intermarriage as a percentage of all marriages taking place. The NJPS 2000–01 data (NJPS, 2004) suggest that in the next generation intermarriages may comprise a majority of marriages among Jews (particularly among Reform Jews.) Given this potentiality, one must regard the families who are religiously intermarried as a distinct form of Jewish family life. Part of this distinctiveness derives from the fact that religiously intermarried couples ordinarily are at the margins of the Jewish community and often raise their children as non-Jews. Hence, the potential prevalence of the families evoke questions about the future character of Jewish families in American society.

Forecasts about the future of American Jewish families fall into three groups: the pessimists, the ambivalents, and the optimists. Each group has its fervent proponents, and each group establishes its case using different facts and assumptions.

The Pessimists

The pessimists view trends in Jewish family organization as mirroring those of middle-class families generally. According to this position, the same forces that are weakening traditional family bonds in the American middle class are destroying the Jewish family. This group sees the steady increase in mobility and migration within the United States, the continued growth of individualism, and the heightening of cosmopolitanism as undermining the basis for strong family ties in American society.

Focusing on the role of the family in establishing Jewish identity to children, Sklare (1971) regards the very social and economic success of American Jews as contributing to the downfall of the traditional *mishpokheh* (family), which long has acted as a bedrock of Jewish community institutions. Sklare (1971:89–100) proposes the following:

> The changing significance of the family, and particularly declines in the frequency and intensity of interaction with the kinship group means that identity can no longer be acquired through this traditional institution. . . . However significant the communal network

and the [Hebrew day] school system are as building blocks, they are a kind of superstructure resting upon the foundation of the family—for it is the family that has been the prime mechanism for transmitting Jewish identity. This system of identity-formation is currently on the decline. . . . [This decline] is traceable to . . . the high acculturation of many Jewish parents, the diminished interaction with relatives, and the presence of Gentiles in the Jewish kinship network.

As Goldstein and Goldstein (1996) indicate, the identity supports among the Orthodox stand in sharp contrast to those families to which Sklare referred. The Orthodox are characterized generally by strong communal ties and ready accessibility to ritual-based facilities and religious schools. These supports are sufficient to inhibit the disintegration of traditional religious practices and of stable relationships with kith and kin. However, the shrinking of the Orthodox community (as a percentage of the Jewish population) bodes ill for the endurance of the traditional Jewish family.

In general, the pessimists emphasize the continuing decrease in differences between Jewish and non-Jewish family life in the American middle class.

The Ambivalent Position

The ambivalent position suggests that there are upper limits to the ability of disruptive factors to interfere with the integrity of Jewish communities and families. For example, Rabinowitz, Lazerwitz, and Kim (1995:429) have found that the dispersion of Jewish families westward and southward may have reduced the concentration of the Jewish population in the large metropolitan centers of the Northeast, but it also eventually provided an opportunity for a multiplicity of new centers to develop. As communities increase in size, so does primary group participation among their inhabitants (see Blau and Booth, 1984; Fischer, 1984).

Indeed, the association between the size of the Jewish community and the extent of primary-group participation among Jews actually increased in the period from 1971 to 1990. The growth of new urban Jewish centers has made possible the spread of support institutions (such as new Jewish day schools, synagogues, availability of kosher products, and so on), as well as local Jewish singles groups, kin groups made possible by chain migration, and other primary groups. Community size is also associated with larger proportions preferring the Conservative denomination (Rabinowitz et al., 1995).

What is considered pessimistic by some observers is regarded as optimistic by others. The marginality of religiously heterogeneous couples to the Jewish community is regarded by some as their perceiving "the traditional ethnic network of kin, neighbors and synagogue as constrictive" (Toll, 1991:185). Only a minority of non-Jews who marry Jews convert to Judaism. Of those married between 1970 and 1990, 78 percent of marriages in which the wife was non-Jewish and 89 percent of marriages in which the husband was non-Jewish remained as religiously heterogeneous marriage (Lazerwitz, 1995b:461). Yet although the percentage of marriages in which one spouse converts to Judaism is small, the 1989–1990 NJPS data indicate much similarity to marriages in which both spouses were born Jewish in behavior and attitudes associated with household ritual, synagogue attendance, and activity in Jewish organizations. Probably this emphasis in convert-in families will endure into the next generation. Moreover, as the new generation of "born Jews" matures, one can expect a lessening of distinctions between marriages in which both spouses are "born Jews" and convert-in marriages. Possibly a new Americanized Jewish ethnicity may emerge—perhaps a blend between the precepts of a Jewish way of life and middle-class cosmopolitanism.

The Optimists

For the optimists, the fact that Judaism and its way of life has survived numerous threats to its integrity gives hope for a resurgence of its traditional family forms. These threats include not only the oppression by its enemies but also the threat of freedom from constraints. At this time, the optimists are concerned with the latter threat—that of freedom to live any kind of existence.

With regard to the threat of freedom, there are various parallels between Americanization and the Hellenization that took place in the aftermath of the Alexandrian conquest of the Middle East in ancient times. Politically, Hellenism gave the Jews equal status with other peoples. This entailed giving up Jewish law as a basis for governance and accepting Greek institutions—the establishment of Greek educational institutions and the introduction of Greek customs into the daily life of Jerusalem. Although the people were permitted to live their lives according to "ancestral laws," there was "perhaps also public belittlement of the Jewish religious customs existent since the days of Ezra" (Tcherikover, 1959:168–169). The Jewish Hellenists abandoned the Torah, rejecting its divine origin. Instead, they accepted Greek religious opinion that "several features of the Jewish religion (such as self-seclusion, the prohibition of certain food, etc.) were symptomatic of a late degeneration" of Judaism (Tcherikover, 1959:184). Yet with the eventual revival of Jewish nationalism and upheaval, these Hellenistic tendencies subsided.

Glazer and Moynihan (1974) regard the revitalization of ethnic identity associated by Tcherikover with political concerns and dominance pertaining to Hellenization as relevant in the modern world. They propose that (1) diverse ethnic groups occupy conflicting positions in modern social structures, (2) because of their opposing positions ethnic groups become rallying points in the identification of interest groups in the society, (3) in becoming rallying points, ethnic groups stress those features that define their uniqueness, and (4) these features thereby tend to survive. One of the features Jews have claimed as unique is their family life—concepts such as *nakhus* (parental pride), *yichus* (honorable accomplishment of one's ancestral line), peace of the household, *basherte* (one's fated spouse), and so on—hence, the optimist would see the people in society.

Jonathan Sarna (1995) chooses as the historical inspiration for his optimism the "Great Awakening" in late nineteenth-century Judaism. The Awakening included (1) a heightened sense of Jewish peoplehood as opposed to Judaism simply as another "faith," (2) a renewed emphasis on "spiritual and emotional" elements in Judaism, and (3) a focus on establishing a Jewish homeland. Sarna's (1995) position is that we use not the specific content of the Great Awakening but, rather, its "four lessons from history" as guides to reinvent American Judaism today:

1. Challenging basic assumptions about past applications of Judaism to life in American society—to be willing to change in a fundamental way so that "continuity may depend upon discontinuity."
2. What worked in revitalizing Judaism in the nineteenth century—spiritual renewal, Jewish education, Zionism, the unleashing the potential of Jewish women, and so forth—may not work in contemporary society.
3. The search for novel solutions should be sought not so much from current leadership but from those who do not have a vested interest in the established way of doing things.
4. The act of attempting to meet the challenges of the American Jewish community itself may result in strengthening community and family by increasing self-awareness and sustaining a hope for the future.

References

American Jewish Committee. 1919. "World Jewish Population, 1919." In *American Jewish Year Book* (p. 606). New York: American Jewish Committee.

———. 1931. "World Jewish Population, 1931." In *American Jewish Year Book* (p. 14). New York: American Jewish Committee.

———. 1973. "World Jewish Population, 1973." In *American Jewish Year Book* (p. 309). New York: American Jewish Committee.

———. 1991. "World Jewish Population, 1991." In *American Jewish Year Book* (pp. 204–224). New York: American Jewish Committee.

———.1997. *A Statement on the Jewish Future: Text and Responses*. New York: American Jewish Committee.

———. 2000. "World Jewish Population, 2000." In *American Jewish Year Book* (p. 248). New York: American Jewish Committee.

———. 2007. "World Jewish Population, 2007." In *American Jewish Year Book* (pp. 551–600). New York: American Jewish Committee.

———. 2008. "World Jewish Population, 2008." In *American Jewish Year Book* (p. 222). New York: American Jewish Committee.

Balswich, J. 1966. "Are American-Jewish Families Closely Knit?" *Jewish Social Studies 28,* 159–167.

Blau, P., and A. Booth. 1984. *Crosscutting Social Circles.* Orlando, FL: Academic Press.

Bressler, M. 1952. "Selected Family Patterns in W. I. Thomas's Unfinished Study of the Bintel Brief." *American Sociological Review 17,* 563–571.

Brodbar-Nemzer, J. Y. 1986. "Divorce and Group Commitment: The Case of the Jews." *Journal of Marriage and the Family 48,* 329–340.

Chertok, F., B. Phillips, and L. Saxe. 2008. "*It's Not Just Who Stands Under the Chuppah: Intermarriage and Engagement.*" Waltham, MA: Steinhardt Social Research Institute at the Maurice and Marilyn Cohen Center for Modern Jewish Studies.

Cohen, S. M. 2008. "Seeking a Third Way to Respond to the Challenge of Intermarriage." Paper delivered at CCAR Convention, Cincinnati, March 2008.

Della Pergola, S. 1980. "Patterns of American Jewish Fertility." *Demography 17*(3), 261–273.

Elazar, D. J., and S. R. Goldstein. 1972. "The Legal Status of the American Jewish Community." *American Jewish Year Book, 73,* 3–94.

Farber, B. 1977. "Social Context, Kinship Mapping, and Family Norms." *Journal of Marriage and the Family 39,* 227–240.

———. 1981. *Conceptions of Kinship.* New York: Elsevier.

Farber, B., and L. Gordon. 1979. "Kinship Mapping Among Jews in a Midwestern City." *Social Forces 57,* 1107–1123.

Fischer, C. 1984. *The Urban Experience,* 2nd ed. New York: Harcourt, Brace.

Fishman, S. B. 2004. *Double or Nothing? Jewish Families and Mixed Marriage.* Dartmouth, NH: Brandeis University Press/University Press of New England.

Freedman, R., P. Whelpton, and A. Campbell. 1959. *Family Planning Sterility, and Population Growth.* New York: McGraw-Hill.

———. 1961. "Socio-Economic Factors in Religious Differentials in Fertility." American Sociological Review *26,* 608–614.

Glazer, N. 1957. *American Judaism.* Chicago: University of Chicago Press.

Glazer, N., and D. P. Moynihan. 1974, October. "Why Ethnicity?" *Commentary 58,* 33–39.

Golden, H., and M. Rywell. 1950. *Jews in American History.* Charlotte, NC: Henry Lewis Martin.

Goldstein, S. 1971. "American Jewry, 1970." *American Jewish Year Book 72,* 3–88.

———. 1992. "Profile of American Jewry." *American Jewish Year Book 92,* 77–173.

Goldstein, S., and A. Goldstein (Eds.). 1996. *Jews on the Move: Implications for Jewish Identity.* Albany: State University of New York Press.

Gordon, A. I. 1959. *Jews in Suburbia.* Boston: Beacon Press.

Kliger, S. 2004. "Russian Jews in America: Status, Identity, and Integration." Paper presented at the International Conference, Russian Speaking Jewry in Global Perspective: Assimilation, Integration and Community-Building, June 14–16, 2004, Bar Ilan University, Israel.

Landes, R., and M. Zborowski. 1968. "The Context of Marriage: Family Life as a Field of Emotions." In H. Kent Geiger (Ed.), *Comparative Perspectives on Marriage and the Family* (pp. 77–107). Boston: Little, Brown.

Lazerwitz, B. 1971. "Fertility Trends in Israel and Its Administered Territories." *Jewish Social Studies 33,* 172–186.

———. 1978. "An Approach to the Components and Consequences of Jewish Identification." *Contemporary Jewry 4,* 3–8.

———. 1995a. "Denominational Retention and Switching Among American Jews." *Journal for the Scientific Study of Religion 34,* 499–506.

———. 1995b. "The American Jewish Community at the End of the Twentieth Century." In Andrew Greeley (Ed.), *Sociology and Religion* (pp. 452–456). New York: Harper-Collins.

Lazerwitz, B., and M. Harrison. 1979. "American Jewish Denominations: A Social and Religious Profile." *American Sociological Review 44,* 656–666.

Lazerwitz, B., J. A. Winter, A. Dashefsky, and L. Tabory. 1997. *Jewish Choices: American Jewish Denominationalism.* Albany: State University of New York Press.

Litwak, E. 1985. *Helping the Elderly: The Complementary Roles of Informal Networks and Formal Systems.* New York: Guilford Press.

Luschen, G. 1986. "Zur Kontext und Interaktions—Analyse familial—verwandtschaftlicher Netzwerke." Paper presented at symposium on Change and Continuity of the Family, Bamberg, West Germany.

Mandelbaum, D. G. 1958. "Change and Continuity in Jewish Life." In Marshall Sklare (Ed.), *The Jews, Social Patterns of an American Group* (pp. 509–519). New York: Free Press.

Manners, A. 1972. *Poor Cousins.* New York: Coward, McCann & Geoghegan.

National Jewish Population Survey (NJPS). 1989–1990. "National Jewish Population Survey 1990." New York: Council of Jewish Federations.

———. 200. "The National Jewish Population Survey 2000–01: Strength, Challenge and Diversity in the American Jewish Population. Updated January 2004. New York: United Jewish Communities.

Phillips, B. (Benjamin), and F. Chertok. 2004, December 21. "Jewish Identity Among the Adult Children of Intermarriage: Event Horizon or Navigable Horizon?" Presented at the 36th Annual Conference of the Association for Jewish Studies, Chicago, IL.

Phillips, B. (Bruce). 1997. *Re-examining Intermarriage: Trends, Textures and Strategies.* Boston, MA, Los Angeles, CA, and New York: Susan and David Wilstein Institute of Jewish Policy Studies and American Jewish Committee.

Rabinowitz, J., B. Lazerwitz, and I. Kim. 1995. "Changes in the Influence of Jewish Community Size on Primary Group, Religious, and Jewish Community Involvement—1971–1990." *Sociology of Religion 56,* 417–432.

Rehberg, R. A., J. Sinclair, and W. E. Schafer. 1970. "Adolescent Achievement Behavior, Family Authority Structure, and Parental Socialization Practices." *American Journal of Sociology 75,* 1012–1034.

Sarna, J. 1995. *A Great Awakening: The Transformation that Shaped Twentieth Century Judaism and Its Implications for Today.* New York: Council for Initiatives in Jewish Education.

Saxe, L., F. Chertok, and B. Phillips. 2008. "Intermarriage: Reframing Discourse and Action." Paper presented at the 119th Central Conference of American Rabbis (CCAR) Convention, Cincinnati, OH.

Saxe L. B. Phillips, C. Kadushin, G. Wright, and D. Parmer. 2005. "Greater Boston 2005 Community Study: Steinhardt Social Research Institute, Brandeis University." Boston: Combined Jewish Philanthropies (CJP) of Boston.

Saxe, L., E. Tighe, B. Phillips, and C. Kadushin. 2007. "Reconsidering the Size and Characteristics of the American Jewish Population: New Estimates of a Larger and More Diverse Community." Working Paper Series: Understanding Contemporary American Jewry. Waltham, MA: Steinhardt Social Research Institute, Brandeis University.

Seligman, B. B. 1950. "The American Jew: Some Demographic Features." *American Jewish Year Book 51,* 3–52.

Sklare, M. (Ed.). 1958. *The Jews, Social Patterns of an American Group.* Glencoe, IL: Free Press.

———. 1971. *America's Jews.* New York: Random House.

Sklare, M., and J. Greenblum. 1967. *Jewish Identity on the Suburban Frontier: A Study of Group Survival in the Open Society.* New York: Basic Books.

Slater, M. K. 1969. "My Son the Doctor: Aspects of Mobility Among American Jews." *American Sociological Review 34,* 359–373.

Strodtbeck, F. 1958. "Family Interaction, Values and Achievement." In Marshall Sklare (Ed.), *The Jews, Social Patterns of an American Group* (pp. 147–165). Glencoe, IL: Free Press.

Tcherikover, V. 1959. *Hellenistic Civilization and the Jews.* Philadelphia: Jewish Publication Society.

Tobin, D., G. Tobin, and S. Rubin. 2005. *In Every Tongue: Ethnic and Racial Diversity in the Jewish Community.* San Francisco: Institute for Jewish and Community Research.

Toll, W. 1991. "Intermarriage and the Urban West." In M. Rischin and J. Livingstone (Eds.), *Jews of the American West* (Jewish Civilization Series, pp. 164–189). Detroit, MI: Wayne State University Press.

Ukeles, J. B., R. Miller, and P. Beck. 2006. *Young Jewish Adults in the United States Today.* New York: American Jewish Committee.

U.S. Census Bureau. 2004. *Family Supplement to the Current Population Survey.* Washington, DC: U.S. Government Printing Office.

Weinryb, B. D. 1958. "Jewish Immigration and Accommodation to America." In M. Sklare (Ed.), *The Jews, Social Patterns of an American Group* (pp. 5–25). Glencoe, IL: Free Press.

Whelpton, P., A. Campbell, and J. Patterson. 1966. *Fertility and Family Planning in the United States.* Princeton, NJ: Princeton University Press.

Winch, R. E., S. Greer, and R. L. Blumberg. 1967. "Ethnicity and Extended Familism in an Upper-Middle-Class Suburb." *American Sociological Review* 32, 265–272.

Zborowski, M., and E. Herzog. 1952. *Life Is with People: The Culture of the Shtetl.* New York: Schocken.

20

■ ■ ■

The Amish American Family

Donald B. Kraybill
Gertrude Enders Huntington

INTRODUCTION

The Amish of North America are an ethno-religious group that has successfully preserved many of its distinctive traditions and family patterns in the face of modernization.[1] All Amish affiliations share a common religion, history, German-Swiss cultural background, and distinctive practices—using horse-drawn transportation, wearing distinctive clothing, and selectively adopting technology. They speak a German-derived dialect known as Pennsylvania German (a few settlements speak a Swiss-German dialect) in their homes, read Luther's translation of the German Bible, and terminate formal schooling at the end of the eighth grade.

Amish communities are located in rural areas of 28 U.S. states and the Canadian province of Ontario. Their population, estimated at 250,000, doubles about every twenty years, mostly through biological reproduction and a robust retention rate of 85 percent or higher.[2] Although family income varies widely, there are no extremes of poverty or affluence. The Amish social structure has four components: geographic settlement, church district, family, and affiliation.

The powerful forces of modernization in the last half of the twentieth century have brought many challenges to Amish life. Specific threats to Amish community structure and family organization have been posed by the (1) federal Social Security program, (2) consolidation of elementary and junior high schools, (3) compulsory school attendance policies, (4) conscription, (5) scarcity of farmland, (6) large-scale corporate farming, (7) tourism and suburbanization, (8) mass media, (9) capitalist consumption practices, (10) high medical costs, and (11) technological penetration into all areas of life. All these forces have posed inherent dangers to Amish society and their traditional family practices.

---

[1] Some segments of this chapter are adapted from Kraybill, Johnson-Weiner and Nolt (forthcoming).

[2] These statistics are gathered each year by the Young Center for Anabaptist and Pietist Studies at Elizabethtown College and posted on its Web site: www2.etown.edu/amishstudies. The population estimates are derived from various Amish directories, publications, and informants as well as from Raber (2010) and Luthy (2009).

The Amish selectively accept and reject modern technology based on its possible impact on the welfare of their community. Their ability to resist assimilation is grounded in their religious commitments and embedded in their social practices and family organization. They negotiate with modernity—retaining key values and practices while relinquishing and adapting others (Kraybill, 2001).

This chapter focuses on the Amish groups that use horse-and-buggy transportation and speak a German-derived dialect. It does not cover car-driving groups such as Amish Mennonites and Beachy Amish, who have Amish origins and use the Amish name but have adopted modern practices and family patterns.

HISTORICAL BACKGROUND

The Amish descend from the Swiss Anabaptists of the sixteenth century. *Anabaptist* is a historical and theological term used to designate various religious groups on the left wing of the Protestant Reformation (Williams, 1992). *Anabaptist,* meaning "rebaptizer," denotes sixteenth-century groups that refused to baptize infants—the common practice of both Catholic and Reformed churches—and insisted on voluntary adult baptism. They rebaptized adults who were previously baptized as infants. In the twenty-first century, four Anabaptist groups in North America—the Amish, Brethren, Mennonites, and Hutterites—trace their roots to the sixteenth-century Anabaptist movement. These four groups are composed of more than 150 distinct subgroups, most of which espouse pacifism, separation from mainstream culture, adult rather than infant baptism, and simple living. They vary greatly in their degree of assimilation into American society. The Amish are one of the more tradition-minded groups in the North American Anabaptist world.

The Amish developed between 1693 and 1697 as a distinctive group within Anabaptist communities in Switzerland, South Germany, and the Alsace area of present-day France (Nolt, 2003). Their leader, a convert named Jakob Ammann, introduced shunning (avoidance of certain types of social interaction with excommunicated members), foot washing in the communion service, communion twice instead of once a year, the censure of persons who attended the state church, and greater uniformity of dress and hairstyle. Ammann's followers became known as Amish and emigrated to North America in the 1700s and 1800s. The last congregation in Europe disbanded in 1937.

The Amish came to North America in two major waves (Nolt, 2003). The first immigrants arrived between 1736 and 1770 and settled in eastern Pennsylvania. The second wave (1817 to 1860) settled in a number of states, including Ohio, Illinois, Indiana, New York, Iowa, and the Canadian province of Ontario. In contrast to their experience in Europe, Amish immigrants in America found cheap land and religious toleration. They purchased farms near other Amish people in rural areas away from the influence of cities. That pattern persists in the twenty-first century with none of them living in urban areas.

Amish family practices reach back to the group's formation in Europe. Persecution was severe in some areas where Anabaptists lived in the sixteenth century. Many were harshly persecuted because of their religious beliefs and practices, especially adult baptism and other practices that challenged civil law and long-established religious beliefs. As late as the seventeenth century, some Amish were forbidden citizenship and could not own land, which made it difficult to establish permanent, stable communities. Lack of religious toleration meant that some of them remained renters and were forced to move as political situations changed. Their livelihood, place of residence, and church life were subject to the whim of rulers and neighbors. This mobility, isolation, and persecution meant that the family carried the major responsibility for teaching and instructing children.

Anabaptist theology, which emphasized adult baptism, also supported the role of the family in child development.[3] Menno Simons (1496–1561), an Anabaptist leader in Holland for whom the Mennonites are named, viewed child rearing as the primary responsibility of parents. He wrote, "For this is the chief and principal care of the saints, that their children may fear God, do right, and be saved" (Simons, 1956:950). He also taught that parents are morally responsible for the condition of their children's souls: "Watch over their souls as long as they are under your care, lest you lose also your own salvation on their account" (Simons, 1956:391).

In addition to setting a pious example for their children and teaching and disciplining them, parents were advised to protect their children from worldly influences and from wrong companions. "Keep them away from good-for-nothing children, from whom they hear and learn nothing but lying, cursing, swearing, fighting, and mischief" (Simons, 1956:959). Parents were directed to teach their children to read and write in order to learn godly principles from Scripture.

One Anabaptist, Jacob the Chandler, wrote to his wife about child training shortly before he was burned at the stake: "Furthermore, I pray you, my dear and much beloved wife, that you do the best with my children, to bring them up in the fear of God, with good instruction and chastening, while they are still young. . . . For instruction must accompany chastisement: for chastisement demands obedience, and if one is to obey he must first be instructed." The father then clarified the meaning of instruction: "[It] does not consist of hard words, or loud yelling; for this the children learn to imitate; but if one conducts himself properly towards them they have a good example, and learn propriety; for by the children the parents are known. And parents must not provoke their children to anger, lest they be discouraged; but must bring them up with admonition and good instruction" (Braght, 1998:798–799). Contemporary Amish views of childrearing still reflect the sentiments of this seventeenth-century writer.

THE SOCIO-RELIGIOUS CONTEXT

The Church-Community

It is impossible to separate religion from ethnicity in Amish society, a fact underscored by their use of one dialect word, *Gmay,* to refer to both church and community. Religious beliefs and values have crafted long-standing norms, practices, and church regulations that create a distinct Amish identity. For the Amish, religion is not a specialized activity but a pervasive influence that penetrates all sectors of life.

The Amish are organized into some 1,825 church districts, each composed of 20 to 35 households in geographic proximity. A settlement—district(s) in a specific geographic area that share a common history—may be composed of only one district or more than a hundred. The geographical area of a church district is crossed by roads and interspersed with non-Amish farms and homes. The Amish families in a district hold church services in their homes. Typically, each district has a bishop, two ministers, and a deacon who serve as ordained leaders. When the group becomes too large to meet in a home or barn for the worship service, the district divides.

The church district is a cultural, social, and religious group of families bound together by similar beliefs and a common way of life. The family, rather than the individual, is the foundational

---

[3]Hostetler (1968) compiled a collection of Anabaptist source materials used by the Amish related to child nurture and schooling.

unit of church life. Amish people always describe the size of their district by stating the number of families, not the number of individuals.

Districts with similar beliefs and practices form affiliations—networks of church districts—that cooperate and fellowship together. Church districts that are "in fellowship" share similar beliefs and practices and exchange ministers for Sunday services. There are some forty different affiliations.

A small-scale quality of life pervades all aspects of Amish society. Within the settlement, people walk, bicycle, or travel by horse and buggy. Social groups are small, and a farm or a small business can be managed by a single family. Amish schools have one or, at the most, two rooms. People know one another and the details of the physical environment in which they worship, live, and work. Upon returning home after a day visiting in a large city, an Amish farmer commented, "I know myself around here." He is the very antithesis of modern alienation.

Beliefs and Practices

Adult Amish people voluntarily accept a high degree of social obligation. This is symbolized at the ritual of baptism, when the person being baptized renounces the world, the devil, and his or her own flesh and blood, and acknowledges Christ as the Son of God and as Lord and Savior. He/she accepts a personal willingness to suffer persecution or death in order to maintain the faith. In addition, he/she promises to abide by the *Ordnung* (a set of regulations that apply biblical principles to practical issues such as dress and technology) of the church and not depart from it in life or death. No one may be married in the Amish church without first being baptized in it.

Each young man promises to accept ministerial duties should the church ever call him to that task. Applicants are warned not to make these promises if they cannot keep them, for once made there is no turning back. It is not unusual for young people to drop out during the period of instruction. Generally they join the church a year or two later.

The Amish lifestyle is distinctive and consciously maintained. In an effort to build a "church without spot or blemish" and to remain a "peculiar people," church districts develop an Ordnung. Most of these rules are unwritten, and they vary slightly from one church district to another. Ordnung expectations are taken for granted, but those pertaining to borderline issues are reviewed twice a year by all baptized members of the church district.

The Amish lifestyle is characterized by cultural separation from the world, which the Amish interpret quite literally. For example, they wear distinctive church-prescribed dress (which varies by affiliation), speak a distinctive Pennsylvania German dialect, and prefer to keep some social distance between themselves and non-Amish people, heeding the Bible verse "Be ye not unequally yoked together with unbelievers; for what fellowship hath righteousness with unrighteousness? And what communion hath light with darkness?" (II Cor. 6:14). The church prohibits membership in unions and discourages business partnerships with non-Amish because these actions would join the believer with the unbeliever. In spite of this social distance, the Amish are not self-righteous or judgmental in their relations with outsiders (Huntington, 1956).

The Amish forbid all forms of retaliation to hostility. They may not physically defend themselves or their family, even when attacked. Amish people may not defend themselves legally, even when their civil rights have been violated. They are taught to follow the New Testament teaching of Jesus to love enemies and not retaliate in the face of injustice or violence: "My kingdom is not of this world; if my kingdom were of this world, then would my servants fight" (John 18:36). Observing this teaching, the Amish may not serve in the military. If conscripted before World War II, they paid fines or served prison sentences; now, if drafted, they perform alternative service as conscientious objectors (Kraybill, 2003). They also heed the biblical example of Isaac: After the warring Philistines had stopped up all the wells of his father Abraham, Isaac moved to new lands and dug new wells (Gen. 26:15–18). The Amish accept this advice, and if they face too much conflict with local authorities, they may move to new locations.

When deemed necessary, the Amish use excommunication *(the Bann)* followed by shunning *(Meidung)* to enforce the Ordnung and to keep the church pure and separate from the world. An Amish person in good standing may not receive favors from, buy from, sell to, or eat at the same table as an excommunicated person. The Bann also applies between husband and wife, who may neither eat at the same table nor sleep in the same bed. However, members are permitted to talk with ex-members and help them if they need assistance.

The Bann and Meidung are used to protect the individual and to shield the church. Erring members are shunned to help them realize the moral gravity of their sin and encourage them to confess and return to the church. This disciplinary process is also used to encourage forgiveness and help wayward individuals deal with guilt. The Bann and Meidung serve to protect the church by removing disobedient individuals from both ceremonial and social participation in the community, thus protecting the believers from disruptive influences and temptations. Ex-members may return and be reinstated in the church any time they are willing to confess their wrongs, agree to follow church regulations, and demonstrate by their behavior that they humbly accept the Ordnung.

Occupation and Social Class

Because they have the same level of education (eighth grade) and similar occupations, the Amish have fewer social-class distinctions than people in modern society. They operate small family farms or businesses and, in some instances, work in nonunion factories or businesses owned by outsiders. Most of these occupations place them in the rural working class. Although family income ranges considerably and some families have a higher status than others, no sharp class distinctions are made because having a similar lifestyle is more important than income level.

Historically, family farming was both the typical and the ideal occupation for a head of household with growing children (Ericksen, Ericksen, and Hostetler, 1980). Since 1975, Amish-owned businesses have grown rapidly because of the escalating cost of farmland. In some settlements, farming remains the dominant occupation, but in other communities most members work in microenterprises or small factories. Because of the increasing cost and scarcity of land, a growing number of Amish are accepting employment in the small nonunion factories that have sprung up in Amish areas: aluminum plants, sawmills, recreational vehicle factories, and brickyards. Thus, in many settlements, over half of Amish heads of households are working in nonfarming occupations. This trend toward nonfarm occupations will have a profound long-term effect on Amish society (Kraybill and Nolt, 2004).

Traditional Amish culture depends on both parents working at home—where they are available to each other, to the children, and to the community any hour of the day, on any day of the week. Historic Amish patterns of childrearing were built on the concept of shared parental responsibility, an expectation that both parents working together will care for the farm and the children, and that both parents will almost always be at the homestead supporting one another in guiding and teaching their children. For example, family devotions are led by the father, a practice that is difficult when the father has to leave early each morning to travel to a construction job or a distant urban farmers market rather than being able to adjust his farm chores to the sleeping patterns of his growing family. Authority patterns within the family change when the father is absent most of the day. A sick baby or a fussy three-year-old is a minor inconvenience when both parents are available. On an Amish farm, the boys spend most of their nonschool time working with or under the direction of their father. When fathers hold nonfarm occupations, they rarely can consistently teach, instruct, admonish, and correct their children.

Moreover, the social structure of the Amish community is based on the availability of people to gather for work parties, barn raisings, daylong weddings, and funerals. The Amish share labor within the family, between families, and among church members whenever there is extra work. This combination of mutual aid and social interaction enhances communal solidarity. These rhythms are more easily achieved in farming districts with flexible schedules than those in which men work in shops, factories, or on construction crews.

LIFE CYCLE STAGES

The goal of the Amish family is the achievement of eternal life for each member. On an existential level, parents aim to teach children right from wrong, to be socially responsible as defined by the Amish community, to join the Amish church, and to remain faithful to the Ordnung until death. A person passes through six distinct age categories or stages of socialization as he/she progresses through life: infancy, childhood, scholar, youth, adulthood, and old age. Different behavior is expected at each stage, as described in detail by Hostetler and Huntington (1992).

Infancy covers the period from birth until the child walks. Children of this age are generally referred to as "babies." Preschool children are called "little children." They know how to walk but have not yet started school, which they generally enter at age six or seven. Schoolchildren, called "scholars" by the Amish, are between the ages of six and fourteen and attend Amish schools or, in a few cases, rural public schools. "Young people" are in a transitional period between school and marriage. Adults are traditionally married. An unmarried person, even middle-aged and older, is referred to as an "older girl" or an "older boy." "Old folks" are those whose children are all married or independent.

Infancy

Babies are enjoyed by the Amish. They are viewed as gentle, responsive, and secure within the home and the Amish community, but vulnerable when out in the world. Babies are not scolded or punished, and there is no such thing as a bad baby, although there may be a difficult baby. A baby may be enjoyed without fear of self-pride, for the child is a gift from God and not merely an extension of the parents. A baby who cries is in need of comfort, not discipline. Mothers believe a baby can be spoiled by wrong handling, especially by nervous, tense handling, but the resultant irritability is the fault of the environment, not the baby, who remains blameless. Amish parents give generous attention to their babies' needs, both physical and social. An Amish baby is born into a family and into a community and is welcomed as a "new woodchopper" or a "little dishwasher." Each baby is greeted happily as a contribution to the security of the family and the church. When babies turn one year old they begin the transition into childhood.

Childhood

Amish children are taught to respect authority, and respect is shown by obedience. The Amish do not strive for blind obedience but for obedience based on love and on the belief that those in authority have deep concern for the child's welfare and know what is best. Most traditional Amish parents teach obedience by being firm and consistent rather than by violent confrontations or single instances of breaking the child's will. Spanking is done freely but not harshly.[4] The prevailing attitude is matter-of-fact rather than moralistic in dealing with children. Not only are children taught to respect and obey those in authority, but they also learn to care for their younger and less able siblings. Moreover, they learn to share with others, to do what is right and avoid what is wrong, and to fulfill their work responsibilities cheerfully.

Parents create a safe environment for their children. They live separated from the world, maintaining a boundary that protects their children from malevolent influence. Parents are responsible to punish transgressions, but they also have the power to forgive. Admonishment is used primarily to ensure the safety of the child: for physical safety, "Stay away from that nervous horse"; for cultural safety, "Be respectful to older people"; for legal safety, "Don't fish without a fishing license"; and for moral safety, "Be obedient." Rewards are used to develop the proper attitudes of humility, forgiveness, admission of error, sympathy, responsibility, and appreciation of work. Children are motivated primarily by concern for other people and not by fear of punishment.

Although children are primarily the responsibility of their parents, the community also plays an important part in their socialization. Families attend church every other Sunday. The children sit through a three-hour service, learning to be considerate of others, quiet, and patient. Until they are about nine years old, the girls sit with their mothers or grandmothers, and the boys with their fathers or grandfathers. After the service, the children share in the community meal and the youngest may nap on a big bed with other babies. The rest of the time the children play freely and vigorously in the house and yard, safe in the presence of many adults who care for them and guide them. A small child who suddenly feels lost will be quickly returned to a family member. Amish children experience the community as being composed of people like their parents, all of whom know them and direct them. They are comfortable and secure within the encompassing community.

Scholars

Children are called scholars when they begin their formal education upon entering first grade. For many of them this is their first exposure to English, which is spoken and taught in school. Although a few Amish offspring attend rural public schools, the vast majority of them go to one- or two-room community schools taught by an Amish man or woman and administered by a school board of chosen community men. Amish schools support the teachings of the home.[5]

Amish private schools emphasize basic educational skills in reading, writing, and arithmetic. Just as important, schools continue socializing the scholars in Amish cultural values because the goal of these schools, unlike public ones, is to prepare young people for a successful life in Amish society rather than in a pluralistic world. With several children from each family, the twenty-five pupils in a one-room school may come from eight to ten families. Parents are actively involved in the school, and teachers typically visit in their homes. Thus, formal schooling

---

[4]For an extended discussion of the rationale and purpose of spanking, see the Amish publication *1001 Questions and Answers on the Christian Life* (2007:98–101).

[5]Johnson-Weiner (2007) and Huntington (1994) provide excellent introductions to Amish schools and education. *Blackboard Bulletin* is a monthly educational resource for Amish teachers.

promotes the same values as the home and in some ways is an extension of it. Throughout childhood, Amish children spend the greatest part of their time interacting with family members. Unlike typical suburban schoolchildren, Amish scholars are usually in a mixed-age group rather than isolated with their peers. Amish children's parents and siblings play a central role in their development. The primary and extended family, school, and church-community work closely together in the socialization process before young people step into a new stage of freedom when they turn sixteen.

Youth

This age category spans the years between sixteen and marriage and corresponds roughly to adolescence. This period of time, also known as *Rumspringa,* is described in detail in a later section. The teenage years are the most individualistic period in the life of an Amish man or Amish woman and are considered to be the most dangerous. If an individual is to become Amish, he or she must be kept within the Amish community, physically and emotionally, during the crucial adolescent years. Yet, during this time the family's control of the young person is somewhat limited, the community's control is informal, and the lure of the world is great.

During adolescence, the peer group is of supreme importance, for during these years more of the young person's socialization takes place within this group than within the family or the church. If a youth's peer group remains Amish, he or she has a reference point, a buffer, and a support. Even though some youth transgress rules and cross boundaries between the Amish community and the world, most of them eventually return to the church to become lifelong members. The community indirectly counteracts youthful rebelliousness by providing social activities and vocational training for adolescents.

Sunday evening singings are important social events in most Amish settlements, which young people begin attending when they are about sixteen years old. The singings are held in homes, and the family that hosts Sunday services typically hosts the singing for the young people that evening.

Proper vocational training is essential if the young person is to become productive in the community. Young Amish men and women work for different people, learning various vocational roles and, through their jobs, gain knowledge of other Amish families, and sometimes even a glimpse of worldly society by working for non-Amish people. The skills the Amish need are best learned by doing, and they have developed an informal community apprentice system that serves the needs of the individual and the culture.

The relative freedom to test the boundaries of the culture, to make mistakes, and to become aware of human weakness is counterbalanced by a youth's growing responsibility to be economically productive and to prepare for marriage. These changes encourage youth to think seriously about joining the church. When a young man or woman finally makes this commitment in the late teens or early twenties, the parents have fulfilled their moral duty to the child, to the church, and to God.

Adulthood

Marriage is the beginning of adulthood, but full adulthood is attained with parenthood. Adults are responsible for the maintenance of their culture. They produce the children, raise them in such a way that they want to become Amish, and teach them the skills and attitudes that will enable them to remain Amish. The adults watch over the boundaries of their culture, participating in the selective acculturation that is necessary for their survival as "a visible church of God" in twenty-first-century America. Financially they must be sufficiently successful to support a large family and to help their children eventually become economically independent. The Amish community generally does not accept Social Security, welfare, or Medicare, nor does it purchase commercial health insurance. Rather, Amish people care for the needy, ill, and elderly within the community.

Adults have no set retirement age. Retirement is voluntary, usually gradual, and related to the individual's health and the needs of the family. It usually takes place sometime after the youngest child is married and has started to raise a family.

Old Age

The elderly normally signify their retirement by moving into the *Dawdyhaus* ("grandfather house"), a small house or apartment adjacent to the main house on the family homestead ("on the home place"). This may occur while the grandparents are still young and vigorous, but the grandfather will shift to a new occupation, such as a craft or repair shop, in order to turn the farm or business over to one of his children. With retirement or semiretirement, the parents' role changes but still continues, for they remain physically and emotionally close to their children and grandchildren. Adult children discuss issues and seek advice on children, farming, and business with their parents. The old folks still engage in the process of helping their youngest children become established economically. Grandparents and grandchildren interact frequently.

Older people have an increased obligation to attend funerals and to visit the sick and bereaved. When the elderly are ill, members of the community visit them as well. As long as health permits, old folks spend a considerable amount of time visiting their children, nieces, nephews, and friends in their local community and in other settlements. They form an important link in the network of informal communication that ties together the larger Amish community. They are also reliable sources of news as well as of local history and genealogical relationships. Moreover, the elderly exert a conservative influence as they fulfill their accepted roles of admonishing the young.

As the elderly age and perhaps become senile or bedridden, they are cared for at home, sometimes by one child, sometimes rotating through the homes of their adult children, spending several weeks at a time with each. With a large number of children available, this responsibility can be easily shared.

Typically, dying takes place in the home, the person surrounded by family and friends—not in the lonely, impersonal, mechanical environment of a hospital. One member described a death in these words: "On June 19th she . . . was admitted and put under oxygen. . . . She seemed to be losing out fast, as she had to labor to breathe even with oxygen. On Fri. we pleaded to go home. So arrangements were made with an ambulance to take her home, she being under oxygen all the while. . . . At daybreak in the mornings for the last 3 mornings were her hardest and on the morning at 4:45 of the 26th of June she easily and peacefully faded away."[6]

When death occurs, neighbors and friends relieve the family of all responsibility, leaving them free for meditation and conversation with the guests who come to see the deceased and to talk to the bereaved family at home. Funerals, especially those of elderly people, are large; often 500 mourners are present. After burial in an Amish graveyard, the mourners return to the house for a meal. With this meal, normal relationships and responsibilities are restored. The family circle has been broken by death, but the strong belief in eternal life means that the break is only temporary.

---

[6] *The Budget*, August 2, 1973.

FAMILY PATTERNS AND PRACTICES

Rumspringa

Rumspringa, which means "running around" in the Pennsylvania German dialect, begins at age sixteen and continues until a young person joins the church. It is a time when the *Youngie*, as the Amish affectionately call their youth, begin going out on weekends with their peers. Prior to age sixteen, young people are typically with their parents and siblings on weekends. In many settlements, a boy receives his first buggy so he can go to youth activities alone. Courtship begins during Rumspringa as young people engage in many activities beyond the gaze of parental eyes. Indeed parents, having gone through this stage themselves, grant their offspring a remarkable degree of independence.

During this period, young people face the two most important decisions of their lives: church membership and marriage. These are individual choices, albeit helped by God, the concern of parents, and the support of the community. Such important decisions require a degree of independence from family and, to some extent, from community in order to develop one's own identity. "Running with the young folk," teens enjoy a newfound freedom before being baptized, getting married, and becoming adults. Rumspringa is thus both an exciting venture as well as a potential time of inner turmoil.

Youth may test some of the boundaries of the Amish community, sampling the world by owning a radio or video player, driving a car, attending movies, and wearing stylish clothing on weekends. As long as these forays into worldliness remain discreet, they are ignored by the parents and the community, for it is believed that young people should have some idea of the world that they may eventually reject.

The Anabaptist tradition advocates adult voluntary choices related to religious faith and church membership. Youth have been immersed in Amish culture and have worn the distinctive garb of their community since birth, but they are not formal members until they are baptized, typically between the ages of eighteen and twenty-two. Rumspringa is thus an ambiguous time, a liminal space when unbaptized youth are betwixt and between the supervision of their parents and the authority of the church.

Contrary to popular mythology, Rumspringa is not a culturally mandated period when parents encourage or urge their children to explore the outside world. It is true that socializing with peers during Rumspringa is a long-standing cultural tradition, and that parents and elders tolerate some rowdiness and rebellion as an adolescent milestone on the road to adulthood. Some parents worry that their offspring will make foolish choices that will affect them forever. Respecting the notion of voluntary church membership, elders do tolerate, however, some otherwise unacceptable behavior.

Another persistent myth is that youth who leave the community will be shunned for the rest of their lives. On the contrary, those who reject baptism and the church may freely interact with family and community because they have not broken any religious vows. Parents may be brokenhearted and feel shame for failing as parents (the response varies by family), but the church does not punish those who leave the faith before baptism.

Some media portrayals of Rumspringa show Amish youth abandoning their rural homes for wild city living. The overwhelming majority of Amish teens spend their Rumspringa years at home. The only difference is that after their sixteenth birthday, they socialize with their Amish friends and engage in new activities. Although they live at home and work at home or nearby, many of their peer-based activities become private matters.

The Rumspringa experience varies from community to community. The length of time can stretch from one or two years in more conservative communities to as long as six or eight years for other youth. The involvement of parents in youth activities and the amount of youthful experimentation with the outside world vary by locale.

Sensational media accounts imply that Amish youth get high on drugs, experiment with sex, stagger in drunken stupors, and frolic in wild parties. Some Amish youth are involved with these activities, but most are not. In some areas, parties are rare and youth sing German hymns on Sunday nights and engage in only mild forms of mischief. In other communities, some youth own cars, join the party scene, and give their parents anxious nights, while other nearby teens ride in plain buggies, play volleyball, and hit hockey pucks on local ponds. Rumspringa comes in many forms, shaped by many factors, including local tradition, community size, family reputation, and the church-community's values. The many renditions of Rumspringa make simplistic and sweeping generalizations risky.

Stevick (2007) makes the helpful distinction between peer-centered and adult-centered gangs. In smaller communities, groups tend to be more adult centered because there are fewer Youngie, and parents are more likely to know who they are and what they are doing. Moreover, most activities occur in the context of the church-community. Unlike the teens in large settlements where there are hundreds of youth, teens in smaller settlements cannot easily don a mask of anonymity. Large settlements with big groups crisscrossing many church districts enable peer-centric activities and less parental oversight.

The most notorious parties, as well as drug and alcohol abuse, occur in the larger settlements. Members of some groups buy forbidden things—cameras, radios, DVD players, televisions, or even cars—and store them at the homes of non-Amish neighbors or in a clubhouse rented by their group. Small clusters of friends may take long-distance trips to go snow or water skiing, fishing, big game hunting, or snowmobiling.

Developmental psychologists view the teenage search for identity and autonomy as a necessary development on the journey toward adulthood. Western psychological models of human development assume that identity is self-constructed and that autonomy—especially independence—is a virtue. Similarly, self-esteem and self-actualization are highly valued. The construction of self-identity and the search for autonomy are different in a collective society such as the Amish. Stevick (2007) notes that although identity and autonomy are independent and complementary psychological states in mainstream culture, in Amish society they are in tension, which produces ambivalence and uncertainty.

An Amish child's identity is both collective and personal, but the group identity supersedes self-identity, especially in interactions with the outside world. Dressed in the garb of their tribe, children grow up with a keen sense of being different from outsiders. Riding in a carriage and being subject to curious stares for sixteen years crystallizes a deep sense of group identity. The personal identity that emerges in church-community interactions is shaped by one's niche in the thick web of extended family. But personal identity is somewhat blurred because playmates dress similarly and adhere to the same behavioral norms. Moreover, cooperation, obedience, submission, and humility—not autonomy—are highlighted in hundreds of ways in the eyes of children for sixteen years.

As they step into Rumspringa, the locus of external control suddenly shifts from parents to peers. It is a psychological journey in self-understanding, a search for a self-identity that fits within the contours of Amish society or within mainstream culture for those who decide to defect. On the religious level, it brings youth face-to-face with spiritual questions. Will they embrace Amish understandings of Christian faith or seek alternatives? Are they willing to submit themselves to the authority of the church for the rest of their lives?

In seeking baptism and church membership, a person agrees to accept the roles, behaviors, and expectations of the church-community. Young Amish women, like men, must decide for themselves if they want to be baptized. Women are somewhat more likely than young men to take this step, in part because they have fewer occupational opportunities outside the Amish community. Nevertheless, some of them also struggle with the decision. Though the percentage of youth joining the church varies by affiliation—most conservative groups have higher rates—the average rate in general, for all groups exceeds 85 percent.

Courtship

The Amish are strictly monogamous. The individual's first lifelong commitment is to God; the second is to the spouse. Divorce is not permitted, and under no circumstances may an Amish person remarry while his or her spouse is living. (That is, if an Amish person's spouse leaves the Amish church, divorces him or her, and remarries someone else, the Amish person is not permitted to remarry.) Thus, mate selection and marriage are paramount decisions that have enduring consequences throughout the life cycle.

The Amish practice endogamy (marriage within their group). Marriage must be "in the Lord," meaning to a church member but usually not one in their own district. Anyone who marries outside the church forfeits membership and becomes non-Amish. In support of this practice, church leaders cite the words of Apostle Paul: "Be not unequally yoked together with unbelievers" (2 Cor. 6:14). This same verse is used to admonish youth not to date outsiders. Thus, with a few exceptions, dating partners find each other within similar church affiliations. Although the church does not arrange marriages, it does sanction them by requiring church membership. Although first-cousin marriages are forbidden, the total Amish population has such a small genetic base that marriage partners are sometimes second or third cousins.

As with other aspects of Rumspringa, courtship does not follow a standard template, but some common patterns exist.[7] The fact that marriage and having children are highly valued in all Amish communities energizes interest in courtship. It is rare for a person to elect to be single or for married couples to decline having children. (Contraception is forbidden although it is sometimes used.) Childlessness and singleness are viewed with a sense of sadness and disappointment. Apart from baptism, marriage is the most important rite of passage because it signals the step from boy to man, from girl to woman. Marriage, not baptism, is the doorway to adulthood. Unmarried baptized youth in their late twenties are still considered boys and girls and sit with the boys or girls in church services rather than with the married men or women. If it appears that they will never marry—by their mid thirties—single people, although still referred to as "older boys" and "older girls," join the ranks of the married in church services.

Dating rarely begins before age sixteen. Most youth wait until they are seventeen or eighteen or sometimes even older. A few communities only permit baptized youth to date. This tends to lower the age of baptism, gives the church more control over dating, and increases the age of marriage by a year or so.

Traditionally, secrecy surrounded courtship and even parents did not always know who their children were dating. Members of the community supposedly learned about romances when a couple was "published"—that is, when their wedding plans were announced in church

---

[7]R. A. Stevick (2007:173–197) provides a thorough description of courtship.

two weeks before the wedding. Although secrecy still protects courtship in most Amish communities, the relationship becomes unofficial knowledge when preparations for the wedding begin. Nolt and Meyers (2007) explain that the most conservative groups follow traditional dating practices with minimal interference from parents, but in other communities courting activities are known and watched by adults. Although it is often widely known when a boy and girl are dating, couples try to keep it quiet despite widespread speculation about when they will be "published." The secretive nature of courtship permits some privacy in a closely knit community and within a large extended family.

Youth do not find their partners through online dating services. They typically find them when visiting other church districts where they join in Sunday evening singings and recreational events such as volleyball games. The boy always takes the initiative. Prospects may learn to know each other at social or work gatherings, but the initial date typically happens during the fraternizing after a singing. A boy may express his interest to a girl in advance by sending her a card or letter. Or, he may ask a friend to alert her of his interest so she is not completely stunned if he asks to go walking with her or to take her home after a singing.

Courting usually proceeds at youth gatherings or at the home of the girl. When a couple begins dating, they may see each other every other week for several hours at the girl's home and otherwise communicate by letters. In settlements where some teens have cell phones, they may call or text message their dating partners throughout the week. They may also hang out with their date during the week and attend parties together on weekends. Boys travel by horse and buggy, bicycles (if permitted), inline skates, or bus to see their girlfriends. (If traveling more than twenty miles by horse and buggy, some exchange horses at a friend's home at a midway point.) In the rare cases of out-of-state dates, boys may travel with a group of youth in a hired van, bus, or train.

Some leaders stress the serious side of dating by saying its sole purpose is to find a spouse. In such communities, a boy may date very few, if any, other girls, but in other communities, a boy may date several girls in the course of a year.

Weddings

Weddings signal the passage to adulthood in Amish society, and they underscore the paramount status of marriage and its potential for procreation and community growth. The energy, excitement, and festive fanfare surrounding a wedding signal its significance. Although wedding customs vary from community to community, some typical practices span all of them.

Weddings are typically held during the week, or on Saturday in some communities to accommodate factory workers. (Occasionally a widow and widower will be married at the conclusion of a regular Sunday church service.) In some communities, weddings are held throughout much of the year, and others hold them on Tuesdays and Thursdays at the end of the fall harvest. In large settlements, a dozen or more weddings may occur on the same day during a wedding season. Thus, it is not unusual for people to receive several invitations for the same day. Friends and family from out of state may travel by train, van, or bus to participate in the joyous event. Guests to a wedding in Delaware traveled from nine settlements stretching from Texas to Ontario.[8] A central Pennsylvania woman said, "Our community had a round of weddings, ten in all, and now we are leaving for two more in Kentucky."[9]

---

[8] *The Diary* (letter), December 2008, 85.
[9] Ibid, 37.

Because the Amish do not have church buildings, the wedding ceremony is never held in a sanctuary but, rather, in a house, shop, or other building at the home of the bride or a nearby relative. In some communities, the reception occurs at the same place as the ceremony, whereas in others the festivities are hosted elsewhere. There is never a rehearsal because the ritual steps are well known to all and require no practice. Unlike the customized ceremonies crafted by modern couples, Amish weddings, like all Amish rituals, are owned and operated by the community, not the individual.

No photographers, candles, flowers, gowns, veils, rings, or tuxedos are part of the event. The music consists of slow-paced German hymns that are sung a cappella by the congregation. One observer notes that the simplicity of Amish weddings reinforces the values of relationships, community, and faith rather than calling attention to fashion, style, and lavish expenses.[10]

Two couples who accompany the bride and groom constitute the wedding party. Although they wear new clothing, it is the same style they wear to church. The bride and her two attendants wear the same color dresses, typically a shade of blue. The three women wear white capes and aprons over their dresses. The three men wear black suit coats and white shirts as they normally do for church. The bride dons a white prayer covering, worn by married women, either before or after the service. During the opening singing, the couple meets privately with the ministers for about twenty minutes for admonition before embarking on their marital journey.

The five-minute wedding ceremony comes near the end of a three-hour church service. The wedding vows vary somewhat by affiliation. Regardless of their wording, they seal an eternal and holy bond because divorce is forbidden. Typical vows include the following among other questions:

1. Do you promise that if he/she should be afflicted with bodily weakness, sickness, or some similar circumstance that you will care for him/her as is fitting a Christian husband/wife?
2. Do you solemnly promise with one another that you will love and bear and be patient with each other, and shall not separate from each other until the dear God shall part you from each other through death?[11]

After making their vows, the couple returns to their seat without a kiss or other outward display of affection. After a prayer, the bishop completes his sermon and invites words of blessing for the couple from various ministers. The service concludes with a kneeling prayer, and then the festivities begin.[12]

Despite the sober tone of the church service and the ceremony, the day is a happy one with food, fellowship, and fun for 300 to 500 hundred invited guests. In many communities, a bounteous noon meal follows the nuptials, then singing and games are followed by supper and more festivities that may drift toward midnight. A few communities have established "day weddings," without an evening meal because those sometimes turned into boisterous parties and mischief. Pranks that target the couple, such as hiding a horse's harness, placing a carriage on top of a small shed, or putting flour between the sheets of the newlyweds' bed, are not unusual in some communities. Tossing the groom over a fence or the bride over a broomstick to symbolize their new status is also a rite in some locales.[13] In other settlements it is not the custom to play tricks on the couple.

---

[10]P. Stevick, 2006:50.
[11]In *Meiner Jugend*, 2008:211.
[12]Miller (2000:243–288) lists all the songs, prayers, and Scripture readings that are used for weddings.
[13]R. A. Stevick (2007:223–224) describes numerous pranks that occur at weddings.

To orchestrate such a large gathering and prepare two meals for several hundred people without a catering service requires an enormous outpouring of free labor. Each community has its own ways of sharing the burdens of preparation. In some areas, the bride's mother and family lead the planning, but someone else coordinates the events of the day itself; in other communities, the bride's family actively works on the wedding day. Members of the local church district provide food, help to prepare the property, and assume various roles—cooks, ushers, waiters, dishwashers, table setters, and hostlers who care for the horses—throughout the day. Some communities have wedding trailers equipped with propane-powered refrigerators and stoves, as well as storage areas for food and utensils, which are towed by truck or tractor to the wedding site. Most communities have a wedding meal, but the menu varies by locale.[14]

Nevertheless, the challenge of making and serving so much food so quickly is daunting for volunteers. Cooking, peeling, slicing, and mashing enough potatoes for 500 people is not a science. One couple, explaining why they ran short on potatoes at one wedding, said, "It's hard work to make mashed potatoes for hundreds of people. It's not something you can practice!"[15]

A hot noon meal eaten in several shifts is typically followed by visiting, games, and singing in the afternoon. In most communities the bride and groom receive practical gifts at the wedding, but in others they receive them some weeks later as they visit family and friends. In some communities the wedding party opens the gifts while the guests watch. If the donor is present, he or she is thanked immediately.

An evening highlight that stirs excitement in many communities is the pairing of the unmarried youth to enter the dining area as couples after the adults have eaten. Partners are assigned by the bride at the request of the boys or by convenience before the meal. Guests scan the lineup looking for new romantic pairs who may be appearing in public for the first time. More singing and games follow the evening meal, including square dancing in some locales.

Newlyweds do not take a honeymoon. In some areas, they spend their first night at the bride's home and help to clean up the house the next day. Some move to their new home shortly after the wedding, but in one affiliation the bride and groom live with their own parents for several weeks before setting up their household.

Role Expectations

Except in the case of a widow, the head of the Amish household is always a man.[16] The rare bachelor may have a sister or other relative who lives in his household and helps out. Roles are well defined in the Amish family. The man is the head of the woman as Christ is the head of the Church (I Cor. 3). Although the wife is to be subject to her husband, her first commitment is to God, and her second is to her husband. Because she has an immortal soul, she is an individual in her own right. She is not a possession of her husband, nor is she merely an extension of him. Husband and wife become one flesh, a single unit separable only by God. She follows her husband, but only in that which is good. At the council service before each communion service, she decides, as an individual, if she is ready for communion. Should her husband transgress to the extent that he is placed under the Bann, she also will shun him, as he will her in a similar situation.

---

[14]See Scott (1988:35) for a comparison of menus in various settlements.

[15]Quoted in R. A. Stevick (2007:277).

[16]A description of gender roles in the Amish family appears in *1001 Questions* (2007:96–98) in the form of twelve questions and answers. This Amish publication covers a variety of topics related to Amish religious beliefs and daily practice, including dress and technology.

For an Amish man, the question of sacrificing his family for his job never arises. The family comes first. A job is of no intrinsic importance; it is necessary because it supplies the economic basis for the family. The work of the household should provide vocational education for the children and fulfill the biblical standard, "In the sweat of thy face shalt thou eat bread" (Gen. 3:19). The wife's relative position is illustrated by her status in church, where she has an equal vote but not an equal voice. Farms are owned in the name of both husband and wife. Important family decisions are made jointly.

An Amish wife participates actively in any decision to move to a different locality. She also makes an active contribution to the production of the household. She may help with the farm or shop work; grow and preserve fruits and vegetables for her family; make the clothing; and care for the house, lawn, and garden; in addition to giving birth to numerous children and caring for their well-being. Thus, the wife plays a paramount role in the economic survival of the family and the Amish community.

Although some Amish women may appear docile and submissive, this does not mean that they have low self-esteem. Most Amish women are happy and content in their role and find fulfillment in the valued contribution they make to the family. In response to formal interview questions about how much money they had made last year, some wives list one-half of their husbands' income from the farm and say (Abigail Mueller in Hostetler et al., 1977:107), "We're in it together. We're partners." Olshan and Schmidt (1994:220) argue that submission for Amish women does not mean exploitation or mistreatment, but rather that "areas of authority and responsibility are clearly defined and 'adhered to.'"

Parents present a united front to their children and to the community by discussing any differences privately and prayerfully. Admonitions to parents in Amish writings and sermons are directed not to fathers or to mothers alone but, rather, to parents together. Couples rarely disagree in public. The wife is expected to support her husband in all things, especially in his relationship with other people, whether it is their children, their parents, or their friends and neighbors. The husband, in turn, is expected to be considerate of his wife and respect her physical, emotional, and spiritual well-being. The ideal is to be individuals to one another, making decisions jointly, and acting in a unified way to their children and others.

The major role of Amish adults is child rearing. Parents of growing children carry the primary responsibility and obligation for the correct nurture of their children. They are to be examples to their children in all things so that the children become stalwart members of the community and eventually, through the grace of God, achieve everlasting life.

The role of children within the family is more closely related to age than to gender. The older children assume a key role in caring for and helping their younger siblings. The younger children are expected to obey the reasonable demands of the older ones. Older children do not physically punish younger children, but cajole them into obeying. Although there is a division of labor by gender, children help one another and their parents rather than strictly dividing the work by gender. On small, labor-intensive farms, children make a major economic contribution.

Typically, children are not paid for their labor until they are twenty-one and, if they work away from home, their wages are returned to their family until they reach that age. In turn, the parents try to assist each child in establishing a household and an occupation. Austerity must be practiced by the whole family in order to help the next generation become established financially.

Children do not have a low status, although they are expected to be obedient and polite to those who are older. They are highly valued as "the only possessions we can take to heaven with us," and as contributors to the family, both economically and emotionally. Children also function as socializing agents for the parents, for as parents strive to be good examples for their children, the parents become better Amish people themselves.

Parents of young married couples have an important role in the Amish community. They often help their married children get established on a farm or in a business. Parents have a great influence on where their children will settle. They help the young couple with advice, labor, materials, loans, and sometimes purchasing the property where they move. They also support them by visiting frequently. In one settlement, almost 90 percent of the parents saw all of their grown children at least once a month—in a culture in which car ownership is forbidden.

Grandparents act as a buffer between young married couples and "the world." They provide labor, teach skills, and supply information about where to obtain services and products. They teach the young family about community networks and help them interact within the community. As the young couple's children become old enough to do chores, the supportive role of the grandparents diminishes while advising and admonishing continue. At some stage, the older couple retires, passing the farm or business (if they own one) on to one of the children. Depending on his age, the grandfather may then run a small business of his own for a few years.

Kinship

Kinship ties are maintained throughout the life of the individual. Excerpts from correspondents' columns in Amish newspapers such as *The Budget, Die Botschaft,* and *The Diary* that circulate across Amish settlements illustrate the importance of kinship ties both to the families and the community. "The children, grandchildren and great-grandchildren of Levi L. Slabach of Berlin were together for Sunday dinner at Bish. Roy I. Slabach's. All were present but three grandchildren. This was in honor of Levi's birthday which is August 6," said one writer. Another noted, "Mother and us sisters were together at Benuel Stoltzfous, Jr. (sis. Mary). Mother Fisher is having quiltings this week and next to finish the quilts grandmother Fisher had started."[17]

Extended families gather to celebrate birthdays and Christmas; brothers and sisters meet to work together, to help one another harvest vegetables, clean for church, sew rags for woven rugs, or construct an addition to a house. And in the case of an illness or other stressor, the extended family, the members of the church district, and other Amish neighbors rally around to help. A typical thirty-five-year-old married woman is ensconced in an extended family network of 250 adults—parents, siblings, in-laws, first cousins, aunts, and uncles (assuming an average of seven children per family).

Members of an Amish settlement are always identified by kinship groups. The names of the husband and wife are used together: Joe-Annie to signify Annie, the wife of Joe, or Annie-Joe, meaning Joe, the husband of Annie. Or the father's name may be used: Menno's Annie to identify Annie, the daughter of Menno. Traditionally, children in some communities were given their father's first name as their middle initial to help identify them. In some settlements, the initial of the mother's first name or maiden name is used for an identifying middle initial. In change-minded groups, parents may use any middle name, such as Darlene Rose or James Lamar.

Last names are so few in most settlements that first names are used more frequently than last names; families are identified as "the Raymonds" or "the Aden Js" instead of "the Millers" or "the Detweilers." Even in large settlements, ten to twelve surnames account for 85 percent of the families. Only about 125 different Amish surnames are found in a population of about 250,000. Therefore, it is not surprising that nicknames are widely used to distinguish individuals:

---

[17] *The Budget* (letter), August 7, 1973.

"Barefoot Sam," "Turkey John," "Cookie Ike." Individuals are always identified by their family lineage, their *Fruendschaft* ("extended family").

Children in Amish schools introduce themselves by giving their father's first name so the other children know which extended family they come from. The signers of Amish guest books are sometimes asked to indicate their date of birth and, if they are unmarried, to add their father's name.

Kinship networks function to tie distant settlements together. Families visit married sons and daughters; brothers and sisters visit one another to "help out" or for family get-togethers. Marriages, when outside the settlement, tend to take place between settlements that are closely related by kinship ties. The Amish both publish and purchase genealogies, and family reunions are widely attended.

It is impossible to overestimate the importance of the extended family's influence in Amish society. Although each nuclear family will eventually achieve economic independence, this is not expected of the newly married family. The kinship network, especially that involving parents of married children and siblings, plays a crucial role in establishing young Amish families on farms and businesses. In one settlement, 76 percent of the young Amish men who were farming had obtained their farm from relatives and the same percentage had obtained loans from family members. Among the renters, 74 percent were renting land owned by relatives, and only 10 percent were renting from non-Amish (Ericksen et al., 1980).

In spite of a strong community, Amish norms stress dependency on the family, especially on the extended family, for normal economic support. However, when catastrophic events, such as fire or unanticipated hospital expenses occur, the community supplements the kinship aid.

Birthing

Birthing practices vary in different Amish communities and also by family tradition. In some communities, most of the children are born in hospitals, and in others almost all children are born at home under the supervision of a midwife. In the most tradition-minded groups, children are more likely to be born at home. In those groups, the midwives may lack formal training and certification. Some midwives are members of related Anabaptist groups, and others are outsiders who provide services to Plain communities. Certified midwives who deliver babies in many settlements often provide the most direct link to outside medical care. In one community, mothers typically have their first baby in the hospital and then deliver the rest at home. Some settlements have birthing clinics tailored to Amish culture where the mother can come to deliver the baby and spend several nights, if needed, before returning home. In general, Amish women prefer the assistance of midwives who provide personal care and understanding in a home-based context rather than the technology, bureaucracy, and expense of a hospital setting. Most midwives and birthing clinics maintain professional connections with obstetricians in case of difficult deliveries or emergencies.

Fertility and Growth

Some people think that the Amish are a shrinking remnant whose days are numbered, but the group is in fact growing rapidly. Because the Amish do not proselytize, their growth depends primarily on biological increment and their ability to keep their children in the faith. (Although outsiders may join the Amish, only several dozen have become permanent members because of the cultural hurdles.) The Amish have increased from a population of about 7,000 in 1905 to 250,000 in 2010. Church districts in this time period have increased from 43 to 1,825.

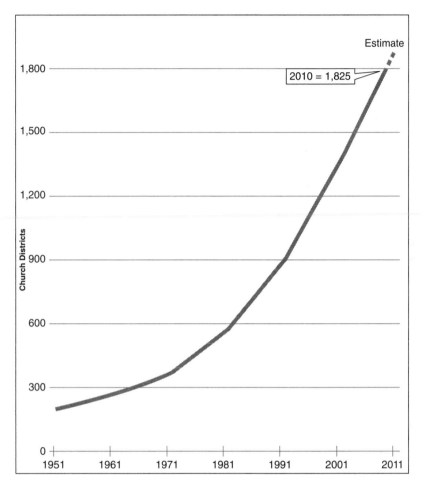

FIGURE 20-1   Growth of Church Districts, 1951–2010

Sources: Raber (2010), settlement directories, and informants.

Household size ranges from married couples unable to have children to some with upward of fifteen. The average number of living children in an Amish family is about seven. This greatly exceeds the national average for White rural households. The number of children varies somewhat by settlement, affiliation, and occupation. The most traditional and agricultural households have the largest families with eight or more children, and the change-minded non-farm families are more likely to have four to six. Although the Amish discourage artificial birth control, couples in some change-minded groups do use contraceptives such as condoms and IUDs (Miller et al., 2007).

Not only do the Amish continue to maintain a high birthrate, but they successfully retain their children within their community. Detailed interviews with Amish women in one settlement indicated that over 90 percent of their grown children remained Amish. The 61 women interviewed had already produced a total of 385 grown children, of whom 347 were Amish (Hostetler et al., 1977:39–40). Although the retention rate varies by affiliation, settlement, and family, the national rate on average likely exceeds 85 percent. The robust birthrate and high retention combine to produce a growing population that doubles about every twenty years.

The Amish birthrate resembles the profile of nonindustrialized countries, and their death rate parallels that of industrialized countries. When plotted by age, the Amish population forms a wide-based pyramid, with over half the population under eighteen years of age. The shape of the Amish population pyramid contrasts with that of the U.S. rural population, which has a relatively narrow base. Within the typical American farm population, there is a small proportion of youth to old people. The age structure in Amish society makes it easy for the large proportion of youth to care for the relatively few old people.

Sexuality

SEXUAL TRANSGRESSIONS.   The Amish strongly oppose premarital and extramarital coitus, although it does occur with greater frequency in some communities than in others, and any transgression must be confessed to the total membership of the church whether or not pregnancy results. Males and females have equal responsibility to confess. As one housewife put it, "If you commit adultery or fornication, you go tell the ministers. That's how they find out. Usually people are so ashamed that they request their membership be put aside [that they be excommunicated]." However, after a period of punishment, during which the transgressor is under the Bann, repentant individuals are welcomed back into full church membership and completely forgiven.

After noting how rigorously some communities punish those who engage in premarital sex, a woman added, "In our church, they're in the Bann just over one church Sunday. If a girl gets pregnant, we say that's too bad, and then we move on." Weakness of the flesh is less of a crime than breaking a baptismal vow or serious disobedience to the Ordnung.

In addition to a public confession in church, couples who have conceived before marriage may receive a temporary, two- to six-week excommunication. In addition, wedding festivities, should they be planned, may be shortened, with fewer guests, fewer gifts, or by holding the ceremony on a different day of the week than is customary. Or the day of matrimony may be moved ahead of the regular wedding season to accommodate the impending birth. All these public changes bring shame to the couple and help to discourage premarital intercourse. However, understanding can be shown, as in the case of a well-respected, well-behaved couple who were joining church and became pregnant. The community speeded up the period of instruction for everyone so the couple could be baptized into the church and married before the baby was born.

Although pregnancy is not always considered sufficient reason to marry, if the couple decides to get married, an effort is made to have the wedding before the birth of the baby. The amount of community pressure for the marriage of a couple who has fornicated or conceived varies from one settlement to another. If the parents do not marry, the mother may keep the baby or it may be adopted by an Amish couple.

Abortions are universally considered sin in the Amish world. With rare exception, a pregnant woman delivers the baby and marries the father if he is Amish. If he is not, she may leave and marry him outside the church or remain in the community and raise the child as a single parent, or she may eventually marry an Amish man and incorporate her child into that nuclear family.

SEXUAL ORIENTATION.   The Amish consider homosexual practice a sin. Because they are not exposed to television or other forms of mass media, some Amish are not familiar with terms such as *gay* and *lesbian* or the public discussion about these issues. Many, however, do read local newspapers and sometimes learn about same-sex issues in news stories. In the settlement in Lancaster,

Pennsylvania, some Amish people were motivated to vote for George Bush in the 2004 presidential election because they thought he would prevent the country from accepting abortions and endorsing gay marriages (Kraybill and Kopko, 2007).

No surveys have measured the prevalence of homosexuality in the Amish community. Nevertheless anecdotal evidence shows that some Amish people do have same-sex feelings and inclinations. Because church leaders view homosexual relations as sin, people with these feelings and orientations tend to keep them under cover. Some who are married may feel dissatisfied and unhappy, but nevertheless they continue in the marriage. In other cases, individuals who recognize and claim a homosexual identity may seek out like-minded others in the community or find counselors who try to help them claim a heterosexual identity. In other cases, individuals leave the community because they realize it is impossible to openly live and practice as a homosexual in Amish society.

SEXUAL ABUSE.   No systematic or evidence-based studies have documented the extent of sexual abuse in Amish families. Nevertheless anecdotal evidence and legal charges against some individuals indicate that Amish communities, like other human societies, include members who sexually abuse others. Sexual violations may take place inside the nuclear family, within the extended family, or within the neighborhood. Typical cases involve teenage boys or adult men preying on young women before they are baptized or married. The size of extended families and the high density of Amish communities provide a large pool of accessible subjects for predators. Thus, compared with societies with small families, male predators have relatively easy access to a sizable number of potential victims (sisters, nieces, granddaughters, and neighbors) in Amish society.

The Amish church forbids sexual abuse and considers it a sin. If a case of sexual abuse becomes public knowledge in the Amish community, the offender is typically called before the church, makes a public confession, and then is placed in the Bann for several weeks. In some instances, this shaming ritual is adequate punishment to terminate the abuse. In cases of a predator with a serious psychological disorder and addictive patterns, the abuse may continue with the same or other victims.

In general, the Amish prefer to deal with offenders inside their own church-based system of justice rather than to report abusers to outside authorities. The church-based system of forgiveness and pardon coupled with social shaming, however, does not provide therapy for sexual addicts or adequate protection for potential victims in the Amish community. Despite their aversion to reporting their internal problems to public authorities, some church leaders have reported cases of abuse to outside authorities and cooperated with law enforcement officials.

Several cultural factors make it challenging to report sexual abuse to outside authorities. Because of the cultural barriers between the Amish community and the outside world, some victims as well as concerned adults are not aware of how to report abuse. Sexual education is not included in the school curriculum, and some youth do not understand inappropriate sexual advances nor know what to do if violations occur. Because Amish people in general have less exposure and interaction with public social services, counseling, and health care professionals, outside experts are less likely to learn of or detect abuse in Amish clients.

Problems of abuse are typically reported to church leaders, who are male. Because the church, family, and community are closely knit together and the authority structure is patriarchal, male leaders may not be sensitive to the realities and needs of female victims. Males may minimize the acts of a male perpetrator or place responsibility for violations on female victims. Furthermore, church leaders, who do not have a high school education or knowledge of addictions and treatment therapies, may not understand that their church-based justice system is inadequate to address serious psychological disorders.

Despite some of the complications of identifying, reporting, and responding to abuse, some Amish people have actively sought to raise awareness about it and support victims and their families. In one settlement, an outside social agency prepared a booklet about sexual abuse that has been reprinted by the Amish and widely distributed in Amish communities by church leaders (Mayes, 2002). *Walk in the Light* (n.d.), a pamphlet written and distributed within Amish communities, offers an explicit discussion of the psychological damage related to sexual abuse and ways to prevent it. It includes a list of seven "guardrails" to help prevent abuse and also offers instructions on what to do when it occurs. One woman who experienced sexual abuse wrote a book about her story that was sold within and outside the Amish community (Ingham, 2005). An Amish periodical, *Family Life,* published numerous articles on abuse in an effort to inform families and assist victims.[18] In some cases, ex-Amish people point to sexual abuse as one reason for leaving the community.

In the last decade, numerous outside counselors and Amish people have proactively worked to alert other members to the problem of abuse and provided information on how to receive help and treatment.

DOMESTIC VIOLENCE.   Although Amish religion emphasizes peaceful, nonviolent living, the Amish community is not entirely immune to domestic abuse, which typically comes from domineering and abusive husbands. Anecdotal evidence, reports of counselors, and concerns of church leaders indicate the presence of some domestic violence in Amish communities. The same issues that obstruct the reporting of sexual abuse to outside authorities also obstruct the reporting of domestic violence.

Family Life published three articles on the topic in the mid-1990s.[19] In one settlement, a group of Amish women, calling themselves the Sewing Circle, collected and printed stories of domestic violence to raise awareness of the problem. Their purpose, in their own words, is "to encourage Plain People who are victims of domestic violence to know that there is hope and healing for their pain. . . . We reached out from our own abuse and found people who responded; and in their response was hope. In turn . . . we are offering the same hope that was offered to us" (Sewing Circle, 2009:2). Occasionally the Bann is imposed on the husband to protect his wife from domestic abuse.

In a study in which 288 Amish women ranging in age from eighteen to forty-five were interviewed, only two (0.7%) reported that "a spouse or boyfriend had pushed, grabbed, shoved or slapped them," in the past twelve months. None of the women in this sample reported that they were kicked, beaten, threatened with a gun, or forced to have sex in the previous year. In comparison, 7 percent of the non-Amish women of the same age in the study reported that they had suffered violence at the hands of a spouse or boyfriend (Miller et al., 2007).

CONCLUSION

During their sojourn in America, the Amish have successfully protected their family system by anchoring it in a rural way of life. Although many of them are no longer farming, they have retained a distinctive rural culture that continues to support strong kinship and community ties and some insulation from the surrounding culture. They have successfully resisted the lures of

---

[18]Five articles focusing on sexual abuse appeared in December 1999, February 2000, May 2002, November 2002, and March 2003.

[19]These essays appeared in the February 1994, January 1995, and November 1996 issues.

mass consumption and mass communication, emphasizing limited gratification and consumption, frugality, and a plain way of life. Life is too short, the Amish argue, to risk losing one's eternal soul for some fleeting comfort or pleasure.

For the most part, Amish communities have successfully resisted many of the forces of assimilation that threatened to destroy their culture. Although relatively immune to changes in their worldview, they are more open to adaptations in commerce and technology. They know they must survive economically in order to survive culturally, but they also believe that it is better to suffer economic hardship than to lose their religious faith. Although more and more are involved in business, they have retained a small-scale way of life that remains centered on community, family, and church.

Their distinctive dress practices, modes of transportation, and selective use of technology have helped the Amish to ward off some of the more pernicious effects of modernization. Nevertheless as they have negotiated with modernity, they have incorporated some aspects of contemporary culture into their society. External practices that enhance family life, reinforce community ties, or promote economic productivity are cautiously accepted. Although their identity and practices have undergone many changes, they have successfully preserved a distinctive Amish way of life in the face of a high-tech, fast-paced modern culture.

Their religious commitments to God and other community members and their dedication to follow the teachings of the Bible and the Ordnung of the church have enabled Amish society to survive. Their family system will change as it adjusts to economic, technological, and social conditions in the surrounding culture that impact Amish life. Amish society will persist, despite changes in its identity and practices, as long as it maintains a distinctive cultural configuration, unique worldview, and control of its social structure.

References

Blackboard Bulletin. [A monthly published "in the interests of Amish Parochial schools."] Aylmer, ON: Pathway Publishing Corporation.

The Budget. ["A Weekly Newspaper Serving the Sugarcreek Area and Amish-Mennonite Communities Throughout the Americas."] Sugarcreek, OH.

Braght, T. J. van. 1998. *The Bloody Theatre or Martyrs Mirror of the Defenseless Christians,* rev. ed. Scottdale, PA: Herald Press.

The Diary. [A monthly that is "a Contribution of the Church for the Church by the Church in the Interest of Collecting and Preserving Its Historical Virtues."] Bart, PA: Privately published.

Die Botschaft. ["A Weekly Newspaper Serving Old Order Amish Communities Everywhere."] Millersburg, PA.

Ericksen, E. P., J. Ericksen, and J. A. Hostetler. 1980. "The Cultivation of the Soil as a Moral Directive: Population Growth, Family Ties, and the Maintenance of Community Among the Old Order Amish," *Rural Sociology* 44 (Spring), 49–68.

Family Life. [A monthly "dedicated to the promotion of Christian living among the plain people, with spe-cial emphasis on the appreciation of our heritage."] Aylmer, ON: Pathway Publishing Corporation.

Hostetler, J. A. 1968. *Anabaptist Conceptions of Child Nurture and Schooling: A Collection of Source Materials Used by the Old Order Amish.* Philadelphia: Temple University.

Hostetler, J. A., E. Ericksen, J. Ericksen, and G. Huntington. 1977. "Fertility Patterns in an American Isolate Subculture." Final report. NICHD Grant No. HD-08137-01A1.

Hostetler, J. A., and G. Enders Huntington. 1992. *Amish Children: Education in the Family, School, and Community,* 2nd ed. Fort Worth, TX: Harcourt Brace Jovanovich.

Huntington, G. Enders. 1956. "Dove at the Window: A Study of an Old Order Amish Community in Ohio." Ph.D. dissertation, Yale University.

_____. 1994. "Persistence and Change in Amish Education." In D. B. Kraybill and M. A. Olshan (Eds.), *The Amish Struggle with Modernity* (pp. 77–95). Hanover, NH: University Press of New England.

Ingham, L. S. 2005. *God Moves Mountains One Pebble at a Time: The Healing Journey of Naomi Stoltzfus.* Morgantown, PA: Masthof Press.

In Meiner Jugend: A Devotional Reader in German and English. 2008. Aylmer, ON: Pathway Publishers.

Johnson-Weiner, K. M. 2007. *Train Up a Child: Old Order Amish and Mennonite Schools.* Baltimore: Johns Hopkins University Press.

Kraybill, D.B, K.M. Johnson-Weiner, and S. M. Nolt. Forthcoming. *The Amish in America.* Baltimore: Johns Hopkins University Press.

Kraybill, D. B. 2001. *The Riddle of Amish Culture,* rev. ed. Baltimore: Johns Hopkins University Press.

_____ (Ed.). 2003. *The Amish and the State,* 2nd ed. Baltimore: Johns Hopkins University Press.

Kraybill, D. B., and K. C. Kopko. 2007. "Bush Fever: Amish and Old Order Mennonites in the 2004 Presidential Campaign." *Mennonite Quarterly Review* 81(2), 165–205.

Kraybill, D. B., and S. M. Nolt. 2004. *Amish Enterprise: From Plows to Profits,* 2nd ed. Baltimore: Johns Hopkins University Press.

Luthy, D. 2009. *Amish Settlements Across America: 2008.* Aylmer, Ontario: Pathway Publishers.

Mayes, M. 2002. *Strong Families, Safe Children: An Amish Family Resource Book.* LaGrange, IN: Pathway Press.

Miller, K., B. Yost, S. Flaherty, M. M. Hillemeier, G. A. Chase, C. S. Weisman, and A. Dyer. 2007. "Health Status, Health Conditions, and Health Behaviors Among Amish Women: Results from the Central Pennsylvania Women's Health Study (CePAWHS)," *Women's Health Issues 17,* 162–171.

Miller, M. M. 2000. *Our Heritage, Hope, and Faith.* Shipshewana, IN: Author.

Nolt, S. M. 2003. *A History of the Amish,* rev. ed. Intercourse, PA: Good Books.

Nolt, S. M., and T. J. Meyers. 2007. *Plain Diversity: Amish Cultures and Identities.* Baltimore: Johns Hopkins University Press.

Olshan, M. A., and K. D. Schmidt, 1994. "Amish Women and the Feminist Conundrum." In D. B. Kraybill and M. A. Olshan (Eds.), *The Amish Struggle with Modernity* (pp. 215–230). Hanover, NH: University Press of New England.

1001 Questions and Answers on the Christian Life. 2007. Aylmer, ON: Pathway Publishers.

Raber, B. J. (Ed.). 2010. *The New American Almanac.* Baltic, OH: Author.

Scott, S. E. 1988. *The Amish Wedding and Other Special Occasions of the Old Order Communities.* Intercourse, PA: Good Books.

Sewing Circle. 2009. *The Doorway to Hope for the Hurting, Struggling and Discouraged. Unlocking the Door to Hope, You Can Be The Key.* Fort Wayne, IN: Sewing Circle.

Simons, M. 1956. *The Complete Writings of Menno Simons.* Scottdale, PA: Herald Press.

Stevick, P. 2006. *Beyond the Plain and Simple: A Patchwork of Amish Lives.* Kent, OH: Kent State University Press.

Stevick, R. A. 2007. *Growing Up Amish: The Teenage Years.* Baltimore: Johns Hopkins University Press.

Walk in the Light. [no date]. Millersburg, PA.

Williams, G. H. 1992. *The Radical Reformation,* 3rd ed. Kirksville, MO: Sixteenth Century Journal Publishers.

RECOMMENDED FILMS

The Amish: How They Survive. 2005. Produced by Burton Buller. Massanutten, VA: Buller Films LLC. Focuses on Ohio.

The Amish: Backroads to Heaven. 2007. Produced by Burton Buller. Massanutten, VA: Buller Films LLC. Focuses on Pennsylvania.

The Amish: A People of Preservation. 2006. Produced by John L. Ruth. Harleysville, PA: Heritage Productions. Focuses on Pennsylvania.

21

■ ■ ■

The Mormon American Family[1]

David C. Dollahite
Loren D. Marks[2]

INTRODUCTION

To best understand a culture, particularly a religiously based one, it is vital to be aware of that culture's *axis mundi* or sacred center of meaning (Eliade, 1959). In other words, to really understand a religiously based culture, it is important to understand the core religious doctrines and practices of that faith. The Church of Jesus Christ of Latter-day Saints (LDS or Mormon) includes members who are disaffected, nominal, or less engaged. Although there are things to learn from those who are unsatisfied or disaffected with a faith community, we believe it is more helpful to focus on (1) the core ideals of the community and (2) the way of life of those who are committed to and involved in the community.

Thus, in this chapter we focus on selected beliefs, practices, and cultural characteristics of American Mormon Families who are religiously *active*—the term Mormons use to refer to a believing, devout, orthodox, or involved member. We will discuss ideals that Mormon families

[1]The authors are grateful to Wes Burr, Mary Dollahite, Kathryn Dollahite, Tom Draper, Jeff Hill, and Noel Reynolds for helpful feedback on a previous version of this chapter.

[2]We believe readers deserve to know something about the perspective that authors have on their subject. Both authors are active Latter-day Saints (LDS) and provide a believing insider's perspective on Mormonism. The first author is a Professor of Family Life, Brigham Young University (which is sponsored by the LDS Church). He converted to the faith at age nineteen, served as a full-time missionary for two years, and married a fifth-generation LDS woman in the Salt Lake Temple, and they are raising their seven children in the faith. The second author also served an LDS mission. He married an LDS convert in the Temple in Portland, Oregon, and they are raising their five children in the LDS faith. In sum, we strongly believe in and happily practice Mormonism. However, we are also social scientists and honor the scholarly values of evidence, academic honesty, scientific method, reasoned criticism, and effort at objective treatment of the subject of one's scholarship. Although we are certainly *not* objective about Mormonism, we believe we can accurately report the basic beliefs and practices of LDS families. Of course, the thoughts expressed are our own and do not necessarily reflect the views of The Church of Jesus Christ of Latter-day Saints. As part of our research projects, both authors have interviewed hundreds of practicing members of various Christian, Jewish, and Muslim faiths; have attended many services; and have developed great respect and admiration for our friends of other faiths and for the beliefs and practices of those faiths.

strive for, as well as what social science research has shown that active Mormon families do (Hawkins, Dollahite, and Draper, in press; Loser, Hill, Klein, and Dollahite, 2009; Loser, Klein, Hill, and Dollahite, 2008). We draw on research done by LDS scholars as well as by those who are not LDS. Mormons have a distinctive lingo, so we will either define LDS terms or put distinctly LDS words and phrases in italics when we feel the meaning is evident from the context of a sentence. We also capitalize certain terms that Mormons emphasize. Before we discuss the core doctrines and practices of Mormon family life, we provide brief historical and statistical profiles.

HISTORICAL AND STATISTICAL PROFILES

America has been and remains a haven for believers from other lands seeking refuge from religious persecution, and it has been a place where distinctive versions of Judaism, Christianity, and Islam have arisen (Bloom, 1992). America also has been a cradle of indigenous faiths, including the Jehovah's Witnesses, the Shakers, and the Mormons. About Mormonism, Bickmore (1999) stated:

> The Church of Jesus Christ of Latter-day Saints (Mormon) is a radical religion by the standards of most modern religions—and it was considered even more strange in the time and place it originated. Perhaps no other major religious movement in American history has given rise to so much controversy, curiosity, admiration, and animosity. (p. 21)

This opposition was present from the beginning of Mormonism, and much of it derives from the astounding claims made by the founder of the faith, Joseph Smith, Jr.

Historical Profile of Mormonism

The Church of Jesus Christ of Latter-day Saints was established in 1830 by Joseph Smith, Jr., in Palmyra, New York. Like many nineteenth-century Americans, he was very religiously inclined. Smith sought to know which Christian church was true and attended many religious meetings, held religious discussions with pastors and believers, and studied the Bible. After reading a New Testament passage that stated "If any of you lack wisdom, let him ask of God, that giveth to all men liberally, and upbraideth not; and it shall be given him" (James 1:5), Smith reported, "Never did any passage of scripture come with more power to the heart of man than this did at this time to mine" (Joseph Smith History,[3] 1:12). He decided to ask God for wisdom and direction. In his personal history, he recorded what occurred when he prayed:

> I saw a pillar of light exactly over my head, above the brightness of the sun, which descended gradually until it fell upon me. . . . When the light rested upon me I saw two Personages, whose brightness and glory defy all description, standing above me in the air. One of them spake unto me, calling me by name and said, pointing to the other—*This is My Beloved Son. Hear Him!* My object in going to inquire of the Lord was to know which of all the sects was right, that I might know which to join. No sooner, therefore, did I get possession of myself, so as to be able to speak, than I asked the Personages who stood above me in the light, which of all the sects was right (for at this time it had never entered into my heart that all were wrong)—and which I should join. (JSH 1:17-18)

---

[3]LDS Scripture includes four "standard works" in its canon: The Holy Bible, The Book of Mormon: Another Testament of Jesus Christ, The Doctrine and Covenants (D&C), and the Pearl of Great Price, which includes the Joseph Smith History (JSH).

Joseph Smith reported that he was told that he must join none of the existing churches and that he would be given further direction later. About three years later, he said that while praying he was visited by an angel named Moroni who told him about a record of the ancient inhabitants of America that contained the words of ancient prophets and gave an account of a brief visit by Jesus Christ to the Americas shortly after his crucifixion and resurrection. He was later permitted to obtain the record and, by divine means, translated it into English. In 1830, he published it as The Book of Mormon (JSH 1:27-75).

Early missionaries were sent to portions of America, Canada, and Europe, and the Church grew rapidly. Many early converts left their homes and "gathered with the Saints" in Mormon settlements that were frequently forced to uproot. Sociologist John Jarvis (2000) notes:

> The entire [Mormon] community pulled up stakes and relocated farther west *seven* times in its first fourteen years . . . [due to] the high tensions that the close-knit Mormon community developed with its [non-Mormon] neighbors in New York, Ohio, Missouri, and Illinois. (p. 246)

For the individuals and families who embraced Mormonism, it was viewed as the Kingdom of Christ restored to Earth in purity and power (Bushman, 1985). For many who opposed it, however, Mormonism was viewed as "a danger that seemed to arouse not only profound hatred but violent action; including mob violence, arson, pillaging, and eventually a state-sanctioned Extermination Order by Governor Lilburn Boggs of Missouri" (Marks and Beal, 2008:258; see also Roberts, [1930] 1976; Young, 1994). The early LDS history prompted no less a figure than Sir Thomas Huxley (1889) to compare the U.S. treatment of Mormons with the Roman Empire's dealings with the early Christians (Davies, 2003).

Joseph Smith and his brother Hyrum worked together to build up the Church, establish settlements with homes and meeting houses, and build temples for special worship in Kirtland, Ohio, and Nauvoo, Illinois. The brothers were devoted to the Saints and made many sacrifices for them. Both taught the central importance of marriage and family and, based on the reports of their own families and those closest to them, were devoted husbands and fathers (Dollahite and Hill, 2010).

JOSEPH SMITH AS RESTORER OF ANCIENT TRUTHS. Mormons believe there is much truth and good in other faiths, but a main distinctive claim of Mormonism is that there was a "falling away" of ancient Christianity (2 Thessalonians 2:3) that was predicted by the ancient apostles (Acts 20: 29-30; 2 Timothy 4:3-5) and that the Lord restored ancient truths, covenants, and ordinances (Sacraments) through Joseph Smith. This restoration of "all things" (Matthew 17:11; Acts 3:21; Ephesians 1:10) included ancient biblical doctrines and practices from the Old and New Testaments including (1) baptism by full immersion in water (John 3:5); (2) the possibility of becoming perfect (Matthew 5:48; John 17:23; Colossians 1:28); (3) God the Father and Jesus as separate and distinct persons (Acts 7:56; Philippians 2:6); (4) regular fasting (Isaiah 58:3; Matthew 6:18); (5) the "gifts of the spirit," including the gift of tongues (speaking and interpreting foreign languages), prophecy, revelation, and healing (1 Corinthians 12: 4-10); (6) worshiping in temples (Isaiah 2:3; Acts 2:46); (7) the second coming of Christ; (8) the Aaronic Priesthood (Exodus 19:6) and the Melchizedek Priesthood (Hebrews 7:1); (9) the premortal existence of human beings (Jeremiah 1:5; Romans 8:29); (10) eternal marriage (Matthew 16:19; 1 Corinthians 11:11; Mark 10:9); (11) three degrees of glory in heaven (1 Corinthians 15:40-42), (12) tithing (Malachi 3:8-10); (13) baptism for the dead (1 Corinthians 15:29); (14) Christian believers called "saints" (Romans 1:7; Ephesians 1:1); (15) the need for apostles and prophets (Ephesians

2:20; 4:11-14; 1 Corinthians 12:28); and many others. Latter-day Saint scholar Barry Bickmore (1999) did a thorough and rigorous comparison of Smith's teachings to those of the early "Christian Fathers" (the patristic literature) and summarized:

> Since he claimed to restore ancient Christian truths at a time when not much was known about that era, we have tested his claims by showing that these restored doctrines were for the most part indeed present in early Christianity. If Joseph Smith taught a number of esoteric doctrines that were unknown to have existed in the early church during his time but which research and uncovered documents now show were part of early Christianity, one has to conclude that he was either inspired or impossibly lucky. . . . Had Joseph Smith created a church which differed from other churches of his day and which had no relation to what we now know of the primitive church, his claim to be a restorer would be blatantly fraudulent, but since support for his teachings and ideas is so abundant from early documents, not in a general way, but in numerous specifics, one has to conclude that there was some source other than his own imagination for these striking parallels. (pp. 353–354)

RESTORATION OF PLURAL MARRIAGE.   Certainly the most surprising, difficult, and controversial ancient biblical practice that was restored was plural marriage (a man being married to more than one woman when commanded by God) as practiced by Abraham, Isaac, Jacob, and others (Genesis 16:1-11; 25:1, 29:28; 30:4; Exodus 21:10; 1 Samuel 30:5). Joseph Smith was commanded by God to practice this principle (Doctrine & Covenants [D&C] 132) and introduced it to a relatively small group of other early Mormons. Many men and women had an extremely difficult time accepting and living this principle, and it was the source of much opposition—from both inside and outside the Church (Bushman, 2005). Ultimately, partly because of this practice but for several other alleged reasons as well, a mob comprised of both non-Mormons and Mormon dissidents murdered Joseph and Hyrum Smith on June 27, 1844, in Carthage, Illinois (D&C 135).

JOSEPH SMITH'S PLACE IN AMERICAN RELIGIOUS HISTORY.   Smith's own history records that, in 1823, he was told by an angelic messenger that his name "should be had for good and evil among all nations, kindreds, and tongues, or that it should be both good and evil spoken of among all people" (Joseph Smith History 1:33). At that time, Smith was an obscure 17-year-old farm boy living in rural upstate New York. In the nearly 190 years since this statement was made, much has been written about Joseph Smith by his friends, followers, historians, enemies, and detractors. Few Americans have been more revered and lauded on one hand *and* more vehemently castigated as the worst brand of charlatan and deceiver on the other (Bushman, 1985). Not long before he was martyred, while speaking at the funeral of Church member King Follett, it is reported that Joseph Smith said:

> You don't know me; you never knew my heart. No man knows my history. I cannot tell it: I shall never undertake it. I don't blame any one for not believing my history. If I had not experienced what I have, I could not have believed it myself. (Roberts, [1930] 1976)

Richard Bushman (2005), Gouverneur Morris Professor of History Emeritus at Columbia University, summarized Smith's contributions to religious life in America:

> Joseph Smith is one of those large Americans who like Abraham Lincoln came from nowhere. Reared in a poor Yankee farm family, he had less than two years of formal schooling and began life without social standing or institutional backing. His family rarely attended church. Yet in the fourteen years he headed The Church of Jesus Christ of Latter-day Saints, Smith created a

religious culture that survived his death, flourished in the most desolate regions of the United States, and continues to grow worldwide after more than a century and a half. In 1830 at the age of twenty-four, he published The Book of Mormon, the only person in American history to produce a second Bible—an entirely new revealed work to stand beside the traditional scriptures. He built cities and temples and gathered thousands of followers before he was killed at age thirty-eight. (p. xx)

A comprehensive study of Mormonism and Smith's history (which are inseparable) led the late Harold Bloom (1992), a Jewish literary critic and Sterling Professor of the Humanities at Yale University to write:

[Joseph Smith was] the most gifted and authentic of all American prophets. . . . There have been many other religion-making imaginations in America before, contemporary with, and since Joseph Smith's, but not one of them came near his courage, vitality, or comprehensiveness, or in so honest a realization of the consequences of a charismatic endowment. (pp. 109–110)

MORMONISM AFTER JOSEPH SMITH'S MARTYRDOM.   After the death of Joseph Smith, Brigham Young led the Saints to the Rocky Mountains, where they flourished as a people despite sustained opposition to the Church from the federal government because of the practice of plural marriage. Eventually, the financial assets of what historian Leonard Arrington (1966) called the "Great Basin Kingdom" were seized by the federal government. Plural marriage was practiced until a revelation was received by the fourth LDS Church president, Wilford Woodruff, which formally discontinued the practice in 1890.

Under Brigham Young's leadership the Mormons established colonies throughout the intermountain west from Canada to Mexico and from California to Wyoming. Until the middle of the twentieth century, most Mormons gathered in the intermountain region to be close to other Latter-day Saints. From the middle of the twentieth century to the present, however, Church leaders have urged those who have joined the Church to build up the Church in their native lands, and gradually the Church has grown throughout the world. There likely are now about as many Mormons who speak a language other than English as their first language—and there are more Mormons who live outside the United States than inside it (Dollahite and Marks, 2006; The Church of Jesus Christ of Latter-day Saints, 2010).

Statistical Profile of Mormonism

According to official LDS Church membership records (The Church of Jesus Christ of Latter-day Saints, 2009), about 14 million Mormons reside worldwide. About 6 million Mormons are in the United States, making, by some counts (Wikipedia, 2010), The Church of Jesus Christ of Latter-day Saints the fourth largest denomination of Christians (and comparable in number to the American Jewish community). In addition to being the dominant faith in Utah (70 percent), Latter-day Saints constitute a significant minority of religious adherents in parts of several states in the intermountain West. Mormons constitute the majority (more than 50 percent) of religious adherents in southern Idaho and make up a substantial minority (5 to 25 percent) of religious adherents in northeastern Nevada, northern Arizona, southwestern Wyoming, southwestern Washington, northwestern New Mexico, eastern Colorado, and southwestern Montana—and they have a strong presence in certain parts of southern California (Jones et al., 2002). After the Roman Catholic Church, the LDS Church is the largest religion by population in ten U.S. states (Mormon Wiki, 2010).

MORMON FAMILY CULTURE

As we discuss what we call "Mormon family culture," we respond to ideas about LDS culture, beliefs, and practice suggested by Douglas J. Davies (a British scholar who is not LDS) in his book *The Mormon Culture of Salvation* (2000). As LDS Americans writing from an insider perspective, we are indebted to Davies's enriching "friendly outsider" perspective that generates several novel and insightful perspectives on Mormons and Mormonism, and we recommend his work to those (LDS and non-LDS) who desire an additional look into the heart of Mormon culture that goes well beyond what we are able to cover in a chapter-length discussion.

In his discussion of Mormon culture, Davies integrates analyses of LDS scripture, policies, and observational worship at home and in church and holds up a mirror that reflects perceptions and realities that warrant our attention here. Elsewhere, Marks (2006) argued:

> Perhaps the core issue at hand in connection with religion . . . is whether religion satisfactorily responds to "the terrifying question" that has troubled philosophers and humankind from the outset: "Is this life all there is?" . . . [The social and medical] knowledge base seems to indicate that how individuals respond to the terrifying question vis-à-vis religion may impact a number of health domains, mental and physical. . . . If our disciplines are to best understand the healthy and unhealthy human mind—complete with its most profound troubles and triumphs—we cannot ignore the influence of religious belief on our universal, yet ultimately personal wrestle with the terrifying question [of whether we continue to exist after this life or not]. (pp. 5–6)

On a closely related note, a number of social scientists, including Davies, have argued that what religions really do is confront this profound existential question by helping believers "conquer death." More specifically, many religions, including Mormonism, strive to provide believers with a meaningful set of beliefs, rituals, and sacred relationships that allow them to transcend the hardships, tragedies, and inevitable end of mortal life. Davies (2000) acknowledges that Latter-day Saints have "generated a practical culture of salvation [with] . . . an extensive folk art, architecture, literature and music . . . [as well as] a characteristic style of life that expresses and reinforces a distinctive identity" (p. 107). Yet he rightfully contends that the pinnacle issue is that Mormonism provides a distinct, unique, and potent set of beliefs and practices that help Latter-day Saints face life and death. Indeed, the animating center of Mormon culture involves what psychologist Robert Emmons (1999) has generally labeled "the psychology of ultimate concerns"—the struggle to respond to the terrifying question. The Mormon answers regarding the meaning, nature, and eternal destiny of human life are conveyed, taught, and enacted in LDS homes, chapels, and, most profoundly, in temples.

THE ETERNAL FAMILY IN RELATION TO OTHER DOCTRINES

For Latter-day Saints, the idea and ideal of eternal marriage and family life are part of a constellation of revealed religious doctrines. The most fundamental doctrines of the restored gospel of Jesus Christ pertain to (1) the nature of God, (2) the purpose of life, (3) the atonement of Jesus Christ, and (4) the potential for marriage and family life to be eternal.

THE NATURE OF GOD.   Mormons believe that the *Godhead* consists of God the Eternal Father; His Son, the Lord Jesus Christ; and the Holy Ghost. Unlike the traditional Christian concept of the Trinity, Mormons believe that members of the Godhead are distinct personages who are one in purpose but not in essence. Mormons believe that God the Father is an actual person with "a body of flesh and bones as tangible as man's" (D&C 130:22). The apostles who lead the Church proclaimed in 1995 that "[a]ll human beings—male and female—are created in the image of God. Each is a beloved spirit son or daughter of heavenly parents" (First Presidency and Council of the Twelve Apostles of The Church of Jesus Christ of Latter-day Saints, 1995). Mormons believe that Jesus Christ is the firstborn of the Father in the Spirit and "the only begotten Son of God" (John 3:18) in the flesh who also now has a glorified resurrected body as tangible as man's (Luke 24:30; John 20:27; D&C 130:22). They believe that the Holy Ghost is a "personage of spirit" (D&C 130:22) and that, after baptism, a person receives "the laying on of hands for the gift of the Holy Ghost" (The Church of Jesus Christ of Latter-day Saints, 2006, 4th Article of Faith, *Pearl of Great Price*), which entitles the person to the constant companionship of the Holy Spirit if they live worthy of that divine gift.

THE PURPOSE OF LIFE. An all-embracing doctrine called "Heavenly Father's Plan of Redemption" (also called the "Plan of Salvation" or "Plan of Happiness") outlines the eternal progress of all human beings as God's children. Mormons believe that men and women are equally endowed with the power to become like their heavenly parents as they progress from the premortal realm to becoming the spirit children of heavenly parents to birth into mortal life to death (the separation of their eternal spirit and mortal body) to the eternal union of their spirit with a resurrected body in one of three kingdoms "of glory" (D&C 76). They believe that the third and highest degree of glory in heaven (2 Corinthians 12:2) is the Celestial Kingdom and that the highest degree of the Celestial Kingdom consists of married couples who have been sealed "for time and all eternity" in LDS temples (D&C 131:1-4).

THE ATONEMENT OF JESUS CHRIST. Soon after his resurrection, Jesus taught his gospel to a group of people living in the Americas whose ancestors were led away from Jerusalem in about 600 BCE:

> Behold, I have given unto you my gospel, and this is the gospel which I have given unto you—that I came into the world to do the will of my Father, because my Father sent me. And my Father sent me that I might be lifted up upon the cross; and after that I had been lifted up upon the cross, that I might draw all men unto me, that as I have been lifted up by men even so should men be lifted up by the Father, to stand before me, to be judged of their works, whether they be good or whether they be evil. . . . And it shall come to pass, that whoso repenteth and is baptized in my name shall be filled; and if he endureth to the end, behold him will I hold guiltless before my Father. (Book of Mormon: 3 Nephi 27:13-16)

Mormons believe that without the redeeming sacrifice of Jesus Christ (which began in the Garden of Gethsemane and was completed on the cross at Calvary) no one would be able to return to the presence of our heavenly parents. This is the basic doctrine of Christ that Mormons teach their children.

THE POTENTIAL FOR MARRIAGE AND FAMILY LIFE TO BE ETERNAL. In "The Family: A Proclamation to the World" (First Presidency and Council of the Twelve Apostles of The Church of Jesus Christ of Latter-day Saints, 1995), it is stated that "marriage between a man and a woman is ordained of God and that the family is central to the Creator's plan for the eternal destiny of His children." Thus, Mormons believe that, through obedience to the laws and ordinances of the gospel of Jesus Christ, men and women may be eternally *sealed* as husband and wife and together become like their heavenly parents and work together throughout the eternities doing what God does, which God the Eternal Father stated in LDS scripture (Moses 1:39): "For behold, this is my work and my glory—to bring to pass the immortality and eternal life of man." Mormons are unique among Christians in believing that all human beings are the spiritual off-spring of heavenly parents (not just God the Father). The concept of a Heavenly Mother was taught by Joseph Smith and is one of the most inspiring and comforting doctrines for LDS men and women.[4]

SUMMARY OF CORE DOCTRINES.   A concise summary of these four core doctrines was stated by an LDS Apostle, Elder Dallin H. Oaks (2011) in an address to faculty and students at Harvard Law School:

> Our theology begins with the assurance that we lived as spirits before we came to this earth. It affirms that this mortal life has a purpose. And it teaches that our highest aspiration is to become like our heavenly parents, which will empower us to perpetuate our family relation-ships throughout eternity. We were placed on earth to acquire a physical body and—through the Atonement of Jesus Christ and by obedience to the laws and ordinances of His gospel—to qualify for the glorified celestial condition and relationships that are called exaltation or eter-nal life. (p. 25)

To Mormons, worship of God the Eternal Father and his son, the Lord Jesus Christ, is fun-damental, and marriage and family life is a primary objective in the present mortal life and in the anticipated eternity to come. Thus, for most active Mormons, the power of family, as an ideal, cannot be overstated.

The Mormon Doctrine of Eternal Marriage and Family

We now turn to a closer look at LDS doctrine and belief surrounding family. Latter-day Saints who have made the "new and everlasting covenant" of eternal marriage in a temple (D&C 132) believe they will be married not only until death but throughout eternity. The Apostle Paul taught that "neither is the man without the woman, neither the woman without the man, in the Lord" (1 Corinthians 11:11), and Jesus taught that "what therefore God hath joined together, let not man put asunder" (Mark 10:9). Some critics of LDS teachings about eternal marriage cite the words of Jesus in Mark 12:25: "For when they shall rise from the dead, they neither marry, nor are given in marriage; but are as the angels which are in heaven." Mormons interpret this to mean that all eternal marriages must be entered into before the resurrection since Jesus said that "when [after] they rise from the dead," they will not marry.

THE CENTRALITY OF THE TEMPLE TO MORMON FAMILY CULTURE

In Mormonism, the capstone of both faith and family life is found in LDS temples (Packer, 1995; Talmage, [1912] 1962). Underlying LDS temple worship and rites are distinct doctrines that have been called "a veritable theology of the family" (Jarvis, 2000:245). In this theology, "exaltation is the ultimate word" (Davies, 2003:195), and exaltation includes, at its core, a belief in eternal

---

[4]The beloved LDS hymn "Oh My Father," written by Eliza R. Snow, includes the verse, "In the heavens are parents single? No the thought makes reason stare! Truth is reason; truth eternal, tells me I've a mother there. . . . When I leave this frail existence, when I leave this mortal by, Father, Mother, may I meet you in your royal courts on high? Then, at length, when I've completed all you sent me forth to do, with your mutual approbation, let me come and dwell with you." (Hymns #292)

marriage and family ties. This aspect of LDS theology is succinctly expressed in "The Family: A Proclamation to the World," a formal Church statement (First Presidency and Council of the Twelve Apostles of The Church of Jesus Christ of Latter-day Saints, 1995), a portion of which reads:

> [T]he family is central to the Creator's plan for the eternal destiny of His children. . . . In the premortal realm, spirit sons and daughters knew and worshipped God as their Eternal father and accepted His plan by which His children could obtain a physical body and gain earthly experiences to progress toward perfection. . . . The divine plan of happiness enables family relationships to be perpetuated beyond the grave. Sacred ordinances and covenants available in holy temples make it possible for individuals to return to the presence of God and for families to be united eternally.

This belief that a man and woman may be married to one another forever, and have their children eternally "sealed" to them as well, lies at the very heart of Mormonism. Being part of an eternal, marriage-based family is central to life.

No element of Mormon culture draws more attention, insight, and discussion from Davies than the anomalous LDS temple. Davies sees "temples as markers of Mormon identity and destiny" (2000:40) and goes so far as to suggest that "without temples, there would be no Mormon culture of salvation" (2000:67) because "only the temple walls insure an essentially distinctive Mormon culture of salvation" (2000:68). In none of these claims and observations does Davies overstate the salience of the temple in the LDS faith. It is indeed, the "house at the center of the world" for Mormon families (Eliade, 1976:24), the place where heaven and earth intersect.

As "The House of the Lord," the temple is the holy place where Mormons go to commune with God and receive the saving and exalting ordinances that prepare them to return to the presence of God united in eternal marriage. An outsider may well wonder how a building can mean so much to a people. The short answer is that it is not the building itself but the message taught, the sacred covenants made, and the eternally binding *sealing powers* available within its walls that make "the temple [the] power-generating centre" of Mormonism (Davies, 2000:155). Emile Durkheim (1915), stated:

> The believer who has communicated with his god is not merely a man who sees new truths of which the unbeliever is ignorant; he is a man who is *stronger*. He feels within him more force, either to ensure the trials of existence, or to conquer them. It is as though he were raised above the miseries of the world, because he is raised above his condition as a mere man. (p. 416)

For active Mormons, the temple is a place where "the believer . . . communicate[s] with his god . . . and sees new truths." Temples are where active members participate in sacred ordinances intended to *endow* members with *power from on high* and to seal married couples and children *for time and all eternity,* thus preparing them for the "highest degree of the Celestial Kingdom" as an eternal family (see D&C 76). Davies (2000:198) refers to this aspired-for and ultimate blessing (*Exaltation*) as Mormon "super-salvation." He further argues that because LDS theology does not have a traditional heaven or hell but rather envisions three degrees of glory (see 1 Corinthians 15; 2 Corinthians 12:2; D&C 76) that "the afterlife becomes the vehicle for achievement, not primarily of the individual as a lone soul but of the family as a collective unit" (Davies, 2000:67). As a result, both in this life and the next, "the family is nothing less than the framework for salvation" (Davies, 2000:155).

Correspondingly, although few faiths place more emphasis on personal religious study than the Mormons, home-based faith fundamentally lies in LDS family religious rituals and activities including family prayer, family scripture study, and family home evening (Marks and

Dollahite, 2005). These emphasized practices have been collectively referred to by Davies as "domestic Mormonism" (2000:6). The message and the covenants that inspire hope for an eternal family are housed and conveyed in the temple, but the enactment, fulfillment, and realization of those covenants must be *lived* within the walls of the home (Klein and Hill, 2005).

TEMPLE GARMENT.   In many religious communities special clothing is worn to symbolize commitment to God and/or the faith community. Examples include the robes or vestments worn by priests, monks, nuns, and pastors. Many committed rank-and-file (nonclerical) members of various faiths wear religious clothing or jewelry. For example, Orthodox Jewish men wear the *tallit* (prayer shawl) and the *tefillin* (phylacteries) for daily prayers and the *kippah* (skullcap) and the *tzitzit* (undergarment with ritual fringes) at all times. For purposes of modesty, many Muslim women wear the *hijab* (veil), and Orthodox Jewish women also cover their hair for the sake of modesty.

Latter-day Saints also have sacred clothing they wear as a reminder of their sacred temple covenants. While in the temple they wear ceremonial robes and, at all times where physically practical, those who have received their "temple endowments" wear a sacred undergarment. Under the entry "Garments," *The Encyclopedia of Mormonism* (Ludlow, 1992) states:

> The word "garment" has distinctive meanings to Latter-day Saints. The white undergarment worn by those members who have received the ordinance of the temple Endowment is a ceremonial one. All adults who enter the temple are required to wear it. . . . Having made covenants of righteousness, the members wear the garment under their regular clothing for the rest of their lives, day and night, partially to remind them of the sacred covenants they have made with God.
>
> The white garment symbolizes purity and helps assure modesty, respect for the attributes of God. . . . It is an outward expression of an inward covenant, and symbolizes Christlike attributes in one's mission in life. Garments bear several simple marks of orientation toward the gospel principles of obedience, truth, life, and discipleship in Christ.

Mormons sometimes face misunderstanding or ridicule for wearing garments in the same way Jews or Muslims sometimes do for their religious clothing. However, for most Latter-day Saints that wear the temple garment, the blessings obtained from the constant reminder of the sacred covenants they have made more than compensate for any intended or unintended disparagement.

Having briefly outlined a part of the Mormon ideals regarding the importance of family, we now turn to the culture Mormons have created as they strive to live out their ideals. The blending of ideals and beliefs with actual practice and the challenges of contemporary life in America are, arguably, a complex mixture of culture and subculture. In this vein, Gottlieb and Wiley have referred to Mormons as a "curious combination of typicality and peculiarity" (1986:253). The rest of this chapter illuminates why, with respect to Mormon families, both portions of this statement are true. If the Mormons have indeed become a "people," what truly differentiates them from others—and just as significantly—what unites them? Our responses to these critical questions comprise the balance of this chapter.

MORMONS: NOT AN ETHNICITY, BUT A "PEOPLE"

Although historically considered a "Utah Church" or an "American Church," we restate that more than half of the LDS Church's members live outside the United States, and English likely is the first language for only half the members of the worldwide Church. Within the United States, a very high percentage of "Utah Mormons" are of western European ancestry, but an increasing proportion of American Mormons live outside of Utah and come from other cultural backgrounds.

Both authors of this chapter have lived in multiple regions of the United States where we were active participants in LDS congregations and Mormon subculture. With respect to foods, local customs, speech, and other readily observable elements of culture, the diversity of local and regional culture seems to vary greatly for Mormon families by region—as it does regionally for most families (Roof and Silk, 2005). Further, as social scientists, we have interviewed Mormon families (and many other religious families) in all eight major geographic regions of the United States (Dollahite and Marks, 2009; Marks, Dollahite, and Baumgartner, 2010). These LDS families have been from a variety of racial and ethnic backgrounds, including Latino, Asian, African, and Polynesian. The families we have interviewed, particularly those who are first-generation immigrants, tend to maintain strong ties to their native ethnicity—while simultaneously being actively LDS.

When interviewed by American talk show host Larry King, former LDS Church President Gordon B. Hinckley extended the invitation he had frequently issued to those of various faiths and cultures to "Bring all the good that you have, and see if we can add to it" (CNN, 1998). Beneath this idyllic hope lies an unresolved challenge. With respect to culture, Davies (2000) has observed:

> Indeed, there is little doubt that Mormonism did come to comprise a distinctive way of life in its geographical heartland. . . . The real issue concerns just what it seeks to bring to other parts of the world. To what extent is the LDS message separable from a particular form of organizational life and values that are, themselves, a development of a particular North American way of life? (p. 242)

The LDS Church, as an organization, and its increasingly pluralistic membership, are still wrestling to find pragmatic answers to this question. What elements of Church culture, structure, and organization are fundamental—and what elements are replaceable with local cultural and subcultural elements? Although LDS missionaries are instructed to teach only doctrine and not cultural practices, this complex question presents challenges both inside and outside the U.S. borders of Mormonism.

Although the preceding section outlines the reality of racial/ethnic and regional cultural differences among American LDS families, American Mormon families *do* have a distinctive culture based in shared religious belief, practice, and community. In the words of Harold Bloom (1992):

> [The] Mormons, like the Jews before them, are a religion that became a people. That . . . always was [founder] Joseph Smith's pragmatic goal, for he had the genius to see that only by becoming a people could the Mormons survive. (p. 83)

A People of Religious Principles

Bloom is correct that the Mormons became "a people," but they are a people based on shared belief in and adherence to divinely revealed doctrines, covenants, and principles rather than a people based in shared geography, ethnicity, or politics. Latter-day Saints use the term *principles* to refer to ideas based in doctrines that often have behavioral implications. An oft-repeated axiom among Mormons is that when asked how he governed his people so well, Joseph Smith said, "I teach them correct principles and they govern themselves" (Taylor, 1851). In many ways Mormons are a "people of principles" in that they believe in certain doctrinal principles that unite them with others who believe and live these same principles.

Some of these principles have been formulated into oft-repeated phrases that frequently derive from scripture or hymns, such as "Follow the prophet," "Sacrifice brings divine blessings," "Families are forever," "I am a child of God," "If ye are not one, ye are not mine," and "Keep the commandments." Other principles are more involved and involve if/then premises, such as "If you keep the commandments you will be blessed," "If you are married (sealed) in the temple, your marriage will last for time and all eternity," "If you pay a full tithe you will be blessed materially and spiritually," "If you keep your covenants you will have the Holy Spirit to guide you," and "If you hold regular family home evenings, your family will be blessed and protected." It is shared belief in core doctrines and principles that binds Mormons.

SEEKING AND FOLLOWING SPIRITUAL GUIDANCE.   One of the most important of all the principles that LDS individuals, couples, and families believe is to seek and follow inspiration from the Holy Ghost—what Mormons refer to as "following the Spirit." In LDS scripture the Lord said, "I will tell you in your mind and in your heart, by the Holy Ghost, which shall come upon you and which shall dwell in your heart" (D&C 8:2). In personal, couple, and family prayer, specific inspiration from God will be sought to provide guidance, correction, comfort, and confirmation of personal choice. Mormons believe God delights to answer the prayers of His children and is willing to provide guidance for questions big and small. Guidance may be sought for a range of issues including whether to marry a particular person, whether to have a child, whether and where to seek additional education, whether to accept a certain job, whether to move, how to resolve difficult couple/family challenges, and who the family might serve. In LDS doctrine, human agency (moral choice) is paramount, and it is believed that the Lord does not seek to command His children so much as bless and guide them and help them to learn to make righteous choices.

COUPLE RELIGIOUS PRACTICES.   In addition to practices that couples of many faiths share such as attending church, saying grace at meals, and reading the scriptures together, LDS couples also are encouraged to participate in other activities of a religious character (Dollahite, 2005). LDS couples are exhorted to participate in shared couple prayer, particularly at the end of each day. Also, in addition to attending church each Sunday, LDS couples are encouraged to attend the temple together regularly to serve the Lord and their deceased ancestors for whom they perform vicarious ordinances such as "baptism for the dead" (see I Corinthians 15:29), endowments, and the sealing together of couples and families who were not able to be sealed in this life. Couples are also encouraged to hold regular/periodic "couple council" sessions where they plan, discuss, set goals, and strengthen the couple relationship.

Because LDS men are ordained to the priesthood, some may assume that males are privileged above females. Eternal equality between a husband and wife is enshrined in LDS doctrine even if not always practiced in reality (Hudson and Miller, in press). The priesthood that an LDS husband and father holds is intended to endow him with a sacred responsibility to serve his wife and children (as well as others). Only active adult Mormons are allowed to participate fully in temple ordinances, and Latter-day Saints are enjoined not to discuss outside of temple walls the specifics of some of what takes place in the temples. Thus, the extent to which women and men in the temple work side by side in administering the sacred priesthood ordinances (sacraments) is not widely known. Male and female "temple workers" are both privileged to administer the most sacred priesthood ordinances on Earth in the most holy places on Earth. Likewise, LDS leaders have repeatedly taught the doctrine of "equal partnership" between a husband and a wife and that there is no hierarchy whatsoever in LDS marriage. For example, Gordon B. Hinckley (2002), a former president of the LDS Church, stated that:

> In the marriage companionship there is neither inferiority nor superiority. The woman does not walk ahead of the man; neither does the man walk ahead of the woman. They walk side by side as a son and daughter of God on an eternal journey. (p. 52)

Valerie Hudson Cassler (2010), Professor and George H.W. Bush Chair at the Bush School of Government and Public Service at Texas A & M University stated that:

> LDS doctrine teaches that men and women are equals before the Lord and before each other. "Equal" does not mean "identical"—for example, there are no two men who are identical, and yet they stand as equals before each other and before the Lord. Can we imagine an understanding of equality that means that a man and woman, though different, can be equals before the Lord and before each other? That is the vision of equality that the Restored Gospel teaches.

THE CULTURE OF ETERNAL FAMILY.   Active LDS families strive to create and maintain an "eternal perspective" toward their daily family life by participating together in a variety of religious activities intended to build a relationship with "God the Eternal Father" (Heavenly Father) and His son Jesus Christ. These religious activities include (1) daily personal, couple, and family prayer, including offering blessings (grace) at meals, (2) daily personal and family scripture study, (3) weekly attendance at Sunday worship services (Sacrament Meeting) in which family sits together for worship, and (4) weekly Family Home Evening (FHE), typically held on Monday evening in the home.

The purpose of all of these activities is to more closely unite the family to each other and to their Heavenly Father, through the sealing power of Jesus Christ. The entry for "Sealing of Families" in the *Encyclopedia of Mormonism* (Ludlow, 1992) states:

> Marriage and sealing covenants are performed in temple sealing rooms convenient to the celestial room. Officiators and close family and friends often attend the couple. Kneeling opposite each other at the altar, the bride and groom are placed under mutual covenants to each other, and are married through the sealing power of Jesus Christ; their children will thus be born in the covenant, and the family kingdom will become a nucleus of heaven. . . . By apostolic authority, the blessings of Abraham, Isaac, and Jacob are explicitly invoked upon all marriages and sealings. It is envisioned that eventually further sealings will link all the couple's progenitors and all of their descendants in an unbroken chain. Thus, divine parenthood is imaged on earth. The saintly life is not in renunciation but in glorification of the family. The quest for happiness and completeness within the marital state is transformed from the banal and temporary toward the divine and eternal.

FAMILY SERVICE.   LDS families are encouraged to engage in service of various types such as (1) serving each other—including siblings serving each other (Mosiah 4:14-15), (2) serving others in the community, neighborhood, and faith community, and (3) serving deceased persons through family history and temple work (as discussed below).

FAMILY HISTORY AND TEMPLE WORK.   Revelations and visions given to Church presidents Joseph Smith, Jr. (in 1842) and Joseph F. Smith (in 1918) have provided what the prophet Joseph Smith called "the great and grand secret" (D&C 128:11) and "a whole and complete and perfect union" (D&C 128:18) and "a voice of gladness for the living and the dead" (D&C 128:20) whereby living Latter-day Saints can provide great blessings for their deceased ancestors (and all others who wish to receive them). Mormons believe that the spirit (soul) of a person goes to the "spirit world" (see D&C 138) after death. They believe that all God's children will have the opportunity to hear and accept the gospel of Jesus Christ at some point before the Judgment (either on Earth or in the spirit world). If a person chooses to accept the gospel they may enter heaven when a living LDS person (age twelve or older) goes to the temple and performs a vicarious baptism for the deceased person known as "baptism for the dead" (see 1 Corinthians 15:29; D&C 138). Families search out deceased ancestors who were not LDS in life, then go to the temple together, where the father may baptize his wife and/or children for their deceased ancestors. This "temple work" is considered a sacred, bonding experience that unites families throughout eternity. Contemplating this eternal union of family members, the prophet Joseph Smith declared:

> Let your hearts rejoice, and be exceedingly glad. Let the earth break forth into singing. Let the dead speak forth anthems of eternal praise to the King Immanuel. . . . And again I say, how glorious is the voice we hear from heaven, proclaiming in our ears, glory, and salvation, and honor, and immortality, and eternal life. (D&C 128:22-23)

EARLY MARRIAGE AND BIG FAMILIES.   McClendon and Chadwick (2005) indicate that LDS young adults tend to marry about three years earlier than the national average. They also desire (and ultimately have) more children than the national average (Carroll, Linford, Holman, and Busby, 2000). Until fairly recently it was not uncommon to see LDS families with six or more children. Family size has decreased in the last couple of decades but, according to McClendon and Chadwick (2005), the average LDS family is still about twice the national average (more than three children in LDS families). Thus, the average LDS person spends a significantly greater proportion of his or her life directly engaged in marriage and family life as opposed to single life. It can be argued that because the family size is larger this also means that family likely has a larger place in the consciousness and daily experience of LDS children and adults.

EXTENDED FAMILY AND INTERGENERATIONAL TIES.   Because LDS families tend to be larger, they also tend to include more aunts, uncles, cousins, nieces, and nephews. In addition, many LDS children and youth experience unusually strong ties among extended families. Many LDS families have annual family reunions, maintain family Web pages or newsletters, and in other ways stay connected. Mormon families tend to have strong and frequent ties across generations. This is due in part to the fact that LDS theology emphasizes parental and grandparental responsibility and that children should honor parents and grandparents. In practical terms, this means that grandparents are likely to be involved in the life of their grandchildren including attending grandchildren's religious, academic, musical, and other activities; attending family home evenings occasionally; and participating in annual family reunions and family service projects. Working together on family history is also common, as many LDS grandparents devote substantial time to family history and temple work.

LOW DIVORCE RATE.   Mormon emphasis on marriage as an eternal relationship, combined with substantial support from the Church to support marriage, translates into a relatively low divorce rate. The best estimates are that for marriages sealed in an LDS temple the divorce rate is between 0 and 20 percent (and probably closer to 10 percent), which is much lower than the divorce rate of the nation as a whole (McClendon and Chadwick, 2005). In addition, Lehrer and Chiswick (1993) found that Mormon interfaith marriages were more than three times as likely to end in divorce as Mormon–Mormon marriages. Mormon intrafaith marriages were considered "remarkably stable" (13 percent dissolution rate) by the researchers, and the divorce rate for Mormons married to non-Mormons was labeled "extremely high" (40 percent) during the five-year time frame of the study.[5]

FAMILY PRAYER AND BLESSINGS.   Regular family prayer is part of the pattern of many LDS families—*regular* meaning one to several times a day (morning prayer; prayer at mealtimes, and family prayer before bedtime). Because the Church has a lay priesthood, the LDS father typically holds the Melchizedek (or higher) priesthood (D&C 84) and is able to give priesthood blessings, acting as a voice for divine inspiration to his wife and children when they are ill, discouraged, or desire spiritual guidance (Dollahite, 2003). Those blessings often facilitate greater closeness between fathers and children and husband and wife. Blessings are one of the things LDS fathers report as doing the most to help and guide children in need (Dollahite, 2003). A related part of the culture of an LDS family is to seek spiritual blessings from God and to express gratitude to God for blessings received.

FAMILY HOME EVENING.   Another distinctive religious practice that LDS families participate in on a regular basis is family home evening. This weekly religious devotional activity involves setting aside time each week (typically Monday evening) for the family to interact together meaningfully (Marks, 2004). Commonly it involves the family opening with prayer and singing hymns/songs, having some kind of lesson on gospel topics (often taught by parents and older children), engaging in some type of game or fun activity (e.g., a board game, charades, etc.), and ending with "refreshments" (homemade or store-bought treats).

Research on LDS families indicates that religious rituals such as family home evening and family prayer have been associated with several attributed benefits, including greater spiritual growth, happiness, focus and direction for individuals and stronger relationships, more unity, and better communication for families (Loser et al., 2009).

In addition to the doctrines of eternal marriages and families sealed together in LDS temples and the home-based, family practices of "domestic Mormonism" (Davies, 2000:6), some other vital distinctive LDS beliefs and practices make up the Mormon family culture. The following are some of the most salient of those.

THE WORD OF WISDOM: "A BADGE OF ZION."   "Temples are a central feature of Mormon culture" (Davies, 2000:39), but they are not the only important feature, nor the most apparent. Like members of many other faiths (e.g., Jews, Muslims, Seventh-Day Adventists), Mormons have several religious proscriptions and prescriptions pertaining to food and drink. The "Word of Wisdom" (D&C 89) was revealed to Joseph Smith in 1833 and proscribes the use of alcohol, tobacco, coffee, and certain teas and other harmful and/or addictive substances. The Word of Wisdom also prescribes the use of grains, wholesome herbs, fruits, and meat (meat is to be eaten "sparingly"). Although most Mormons likely eat about the same amount of grains, fruits, and meat as the average American, the *proscriptions* (alcohol, tobacco, illegal drugs, etc.) are actively enforced, and an LDS member must be living these standards to worship in an LDS temple (although any Mormon or non-Mormon may worship in an LDS chapel). Due to the Word of Wisdom, actively practicing Mormons have been

---

[5]Additional interesting statistical data on Mormons, Mormonism, Mormon culture, and Utah are available at a Web site, "Sampling of Latter-day Saint/Utah Demographics and Social Statistics from National Sources," www.adherents.com/largecom/lds_dem.html.

examined in several medical and social research studies on cancer, longevity, and other issues. One recent review (Marks and Beal, 2008) summarizes:

> There are several studies that shed light on potential health benefits of the Word of Wisdom. These include Simmerman's [1993] and Enstrom's [1998a] findings of substantially (up to 50 percent) lower cancer rates among practicing Mormons, and Enstrom's [1998b] finding that highly involved Mormons live an average of eight to eleven years longer than the general [U.S.] population. (p. 261)

In addition to health and longevity benefits stemming from the Word of Wisdom, significantly lower rates of alcohol and drug use mean that active Mormon families are less likely to be affected by the negative consequences of alcohol/drug *abuse*. Indeed, an estimated 65 to 80 percent of domestic violence is alcohol and drug related, as is a large percentage of other family dysfunction (Burger and Youkeles, 2000).

On another note, observance of the Word of Wisdom—which sociologist Thomas O'Dea (1957) called "the [Mormon] badge of Zion" (p. 146)—means that like Jewish families that "keep kosher" and Muslim families that "keep halal," active Mormon families have a distinct dietary identity that is part of their family culture.

FINANCIAL MATTERS: TITHING AND OTHER GIVING.   Every enduring religious community must address financial issues in some way. Mormonism teaches the principle or law of tithing. Active Latter-day Saints contribute one-tenth of their income to the Church; this (like observance of the Word of Wisdom) is mandatory to receive a *temple recommend,* which allows admittance to LDS temples (Marks and Beal, 2008). For most active LDS families, tithing represents a significant sacrifice, albeit one that is done in faith and expectation of heavenly blessings that will be "poured out" on those persons and families that tithe (Malachi 3:10-12; D&C 119:4). Thus, like adherents of many other religious communities, Latter-day Saints are expected to contribute financially to the Church and, like those of other faiths that make such sacrifices, many report that they do so willingly and from a sense of faith (Marks et al., 2010).

In LDS church services, there is no weekly collection or offering where a plate or basket is passed among congregants who put in money or checks. Rather, the member who wishes to pay tithing will fill out a donation slip and put it in an envelope with the check, cash, or coin and privately give it to the bishop (the local lay pastor of the ward or congregation) or one of his two counselors. Then, at the end of each year, a family will meet with the bishop for "tithing settlement" to declare to him, as individuals, whether they are *full, partial,* or *non*-tithe payers. This declaration is made in private and kept confidential. Those who are not full tithe payers may participate in most ways in the life of the congregation, but only full tithe payers are entitled to enter the temple and participate in full-time missionary service.

In addition to tithing, an active Latter-day Saint will fast for twenty-four hours (or two meals) on the first Sunday of the month and contribute a "fast offering," representing the cost of the meals foregone (and often many times that amount), to the Church to help care for the poor in the community and throughout the world. Fast offerings are used by bishops to "relieve the needs" of the poor by helping them purchase food, clothing, pay rent, or other necessities. Church members also may make contributions to support missionaries serving from their own ward (congregation) or to those serving from other places around the world who need assistance. Contributions may also be made to Church Humanitarian Services to support technological improvements and relief efforts in less developed nations. Through this fund, the Church donates millions of dollars in cash and in-kind gifts each year. Member donations to the Perpetual

Education Fund help those in developing nations to obtain better education and employment. Members may also donate funds to help build temples in locales where communities are not likely to be able to afford such construction. Members also donate to provide copies of The Book of Mormon. in over a hundred different languages for those who cannot afford them or who simply desire to read more about the Church.[6] Thus, members of active LDS families (including children) are likely to have a pattern of regular donations for the benefit of others.

BISHOP'S STOREHOUSE, CHURCH WELFARE PROJECTS, AND RELIEF SOCIETY. In addition to the emphasis on financial contribution in LDS congregations and families, there is an expectation that an active Mormon family will donate time and service to care for the poor among them. The Church operates scores of bishop's storehouses, canneries, and other food and goods processing centers in the United States, where members help based on rotating assignments.

In some areas, LDS members work on Church farms or other welfare projects where they will work to produce commodities used in the Church's humanitarian aid projects intended to help the needy (both locally and throughout the world). In recent years, as hurricanes have increasingly visited the Gulf Coast region of the United States, the LDS Church has been extensively involved in volunteer-based cleanup and recovery efforts (often wearing yellow T-shirts with "Mormon Helping Hands" on them).

The LDS Relief Society, often purported to be the world's largest and oldest continuous women's organization (with over 6 million women in 170 nations and territories), meets about six times a month and engages in service to help those in temporary or permanent need in their local community through provision of meals and/or care. The Relief Society also participates in literacy education in the communities they serve and engages in a variety of other projects (e.g., making quilts, baby blankets, emergency aid kits, etc.) to send to those suffering as a result of natural disasters around the world. At the local and regional levels, the Relief Society (like the male Priesthood organization) has no paid officers and offers extensive volunteer service and leadership to many inside and outside the Church. Indeed, when LDS families experience difficulties or challenges (e.g., illness, unemployment, childbirth) they will very likely be visited by women from the Relief Society who will provide hot meals and other practical assistance as well as emotional and spiritual aid. This theme leads us to a discussion of another defining feature of Mormon culture: church callings.

CHURCH CALLINGS. Researchers have observed, "Mormons virtually equate being a Latter-day Saint in good standing with being 'active' in *church callings* . . . the term *inactive* [denotes] deviance or defection from the faith" (Shepherd and Shepherd, 1994:162). A church calling is a formal invitation (and expectation) to serve in at least one voluntary position relating to LDS Church programs. After prayers for inspiration, bishops and other leaders "extend" church callings to women and men in their local congregations. Like most responsibilities in the LDS Church, callings usually are extended for an unspecified duration that may last anywhere from a few months to several years (Bushman and Bushman, 2001; Mauss, 1994). Although unpaid LDS priesthood and clergy are male, the typical LDS congregation has many—often more than half—of its necessary operating positions staffed by women (Cornwall, 1994), and even teens and preteens have callings in the LDS youth programs.

---

[6]For more information on missionaries, see mormon.org/missionaries.

The word *Work* carries a sacred and specialized meaning in Mormon culture and extends to business, home, and church callings. LDS doctrine from 1832 states:

> Verily I say unto you, that every man . . . is obliged to provide for his own family . . . and let him labor in the church. Let every man be diligent in all things. And *the idler shall not have place in the church*, except he repent and mend his ways. (D&C 75:28-29, emphasis added)

In a recent related review, Marks and Beal (2008) emphasize the salience of Mormon work and church callings from several scholars' perspectives:

> Max Weber (1976) once described the lay-operated, activist Mormonism as "half-way between monastery and factory" (p. 264). Indeed, sociologist James Duke (1997) estimates that the average LDS ward (congregation) receives between 400 and 600 hours of volunteer service per week from those serving in "callings"; a remarkable pool of human resources at no direct cost to the Church. This figure adds context to Shepherd and Shepherd's (1994) statement that "To understand Mormonism, one must understand the lay character of the Mormon religion" (p. 162). Indeed, the unpaid LDS bishops [lay clergy] are not the only laborers who are promoting and preserving lived Mormon values, [all those who hold callings contribute]. (p. 272)

Davies (2003) has added the observation that the various demands of the LDS faith and culture "make calls upon individual [and family] commitment which, when all works well, provides the LDS Church" with resources to be a great success. He goes on to explain, however, that this perennial activity through serving in church callings and other assignments "can also demoralize some Saints through sheer volume of activity and high level of expectation" (p. 170).

Most LDS Church callings require at least a couple of hours devoted to the calling each week, with others requiring many times that, in addition to attendance at a three-hour series of meetings each Sunday. In connection with significant temporal and financial costs related to religious involvement, sociologists Stark and Finke (2000) have asked: "*Why do they do it?* Why are people willing to make the very high levels of sacrifice required . . .?" (p. 145; emphasis in original).

WHY DO THEY DO IT?   Why is it worth it? This answer, too, is built into Mormon doctrine and culture. LDS Church founder, Joseph Smith, declared that "a religion that does not require the sacrifice of all things never has power sufficient to produce the faith necessary unto life and salvation" (Smith, [1835] 1985:69). From the Church's origins "besides being a faith and an ethic, Mormonism [has been] a work" (Bushman, 1985:153). According to God's words, in LDS scripture, "This is my work and my glory—to bring to pass the immortality and eternal life of man" (Moses 1:39). *Eternal life* or *exaltation* involves returning to God the Eternal Father as an Eternal family. The temple is, in a very real sense, a symbol of a great family home—a celestial one—to which Mormons long to eventually return. For many active Mormons, it is this celestial and eternal hope that drives their willing sacrifice of time and money.

ACHIEVEMENT ORIENTATION.   About Mormon religious life, Davies (2000) has stated, "Holiness results from activity and not from passivity, as reflected in the widely used LDS term that speaks of someone as 'active in the church'" (p. 33). He also stated, "In Mormonism, however, wisdom is achieved rather than merely ascribed, and this is because of the foundational tenet of achievement and the striving for progressive development that lies at the heart of Latter-day Saint culture" (p. 37). LDS families often tend to be oriented toward personal achievement in their children, including excellence in academics, music, boy scouting, and athletics. This means that parents expect children to "develop their talents and spiritual gifts," which are believed to be a divine endowment given to individuals in their premortal existence when all of God's children lived, in spirit form, with God, the Eternal Father.

Mormon parents have some clear and widely shared goals for their children. Dyer and Kunz (1994) found that active LDS parents are nearly universal in wanting their kids to (1) be active in the Church, (2) serve a full time mission (male children), (3) marry in the LDS temple for "time and all eternity" (males and females), and (4) get a good education, preferably a college degree (males and females). Socializing toward accomplishing these religious goals may take place in various family activities, such as family home evening and family conversations, including conversations at mealtime.

MISSIONARY WORK AND MORMON YOUTH.   Many LDS families are involved in "sharing the gospel" with others who are not LDS. This may lead to an individual, couple, or family being mentored by the family, and that may entail hosting the person or family in the home for the *missionary discussions* (a set of lessons that teach LDS doctrines and practices to persons investigating the Church). This may also entail having the person or family sit with the LDS family at church services and in other ways serving this person or family. Another way LDS family culture is influenced by missionary work is that parents will devote substantial attention to preparing their sons to serve full-time missions for the Church. These efforts involve helping all of their children learn LDS doctrine; having them teach gospel lessons during family home evenings; and helping them learn about other cultures, nations, languages, and people. There is often practical preparation that occurs as well, such as teaching children to do basic cooking, cleaning, repairing, sewing, ironing, laundry, financial management, and planning and developing their language skills and physical fitness. These skills are also useful in helping children achieve independence as they emerge into adulthood as missionaries, college students, or employees. Some parents who learned a language on their missions teach that language to their children to help prepare them for both missions and life in an increasingly cosmopolitan world.

As full-time missionaries send home letters and e-mails that describe the places they are laboring in and the people they are teaching, these letters are often read in family gatherings (e.g., dinner and family home evening) and shared with the extended family via e-mail or blogs. This influences younger siblings who read and hear about the exciting, challenging, and spiritual experiences their older sibling is having on his or her mission as they see the support, affection, and importance the wider family places on voluntary missionary service.

Full-time missionary service often involves significant financial sacrifice to the missionary and/or their family due to the current cost of approximately $10,000 for a two-year mission (Marks and Beal, 2008). As a result, many LDS boys begin saving for their missions at relatively early ages. Many retired LDS couples also choose to serve missions (sometimes multiple missions), making similar financial and familial sacrifices and likewise sending letters and e-mails home to children and grandchildren.

Recent research by Smith and Denton (2005) has shown that LDS youth are among the most devout and committed of American religious teenagers. They studied a national sample of 3,700 teens in America that included teens from various faiths as well as nonreligious youth. They found that religious youth did better on a variety of measures of health and well-being. They also found that Mormon teens are the most likely among all U.S. teens to (1) hold religious beliefs similar to those of their parents, (2) say their faith is important in shaping daily life and major life decisions, (3) have a very moving or powerful spiritual experience, (4) report they had "ever experienced a definite answer to prayer or specific guidance from God," (5) report that they denied themselves something as a "spiritual discipline," (6) pray often, (7) be involved in religious youth groups and be leaders in their youth groups, (8) talk with parents about religious and spiritual matters, (9) frequently express their faith at school, (10) report a high number of nonparent adults who played a meaningful role in a teenager's life, and (11) report that they anticipated attending the same faith community when they were twenty-five years old.

Research has shown that LDS youth are fairly similar to religious youth of other faiths in how they converse with parents about religious issues (Dollahite and Thatcher, 2008), and in the kinds of sacrifices they make for religious reasons (Dollahite, Layton, Bahr, Walker, and Thatcher, 2009). However, LDS youth reportedly tend to make more sacrifices, and their religious sacrifices and commitments are more likely to be attributed to an anchoring in their families and faith communities (Layton, Dollahite, and Hardy, 2011).

HOW MORMON FAMILY BELIEF AND CULTURE COMPARE TO OTHER FAITHS

In a recent book-length study, Robert Putnam and David Campbell (2010) reported that (1) Mormons are among the most devout religious groups in the country, (2) Mormons are among those most likely to keep their childhood faith as adults, (3) in terms of giving money and time Mormons are among the most charitable of Americans in both religious and nonreligious causes, (4) Mormons are among those most friendly toward those of other faiths (even though Mormons themselves are among those viewed least positively by many American religious groups), and (5) although Mormons are the most likely Americans to believe that one true religion exists, they also believe that those outside their faith can attain salvation or reach "heaven." This latter statement includes those who did not have the opportunity to "know Christ" during their mortal life because of the LDS belief that the gospel is preached in the "spirit world" after death and can be embraced there by those who desire it (see John 5:28-29; 1 Corinthians 15:29).

Other similarities and differences between Mormons and other faiths including the following (Dollahite, 2007):

> Like Catholicism, Mormonism is hierarchical in structure and culture; the authority to declare doctrine and policy clearly resides in church leaders. Thus, for the word of the Lord on [some] matters of marriage and family life, the Saints look to the prophets and apostles in Salt Lake City, just as their more traditional Catholic friends look to the pope in Rome.
>
> Like evangelical Christians and Jehovah's Witnesses, Latter-day Saints believe strongly in the written word of God and in the importance of expending significant effort studying and sharing the word with others near and far. Thus Latter-day Saints are likely to search the scriptures for personal answers to family challenges and are likely to invite their friends and neighbors to find answers to their family struggles in Mormonism.
>
> Like Catholics, Orthodox Christians (i.e., Eastern Orthodox), and Anglicans, Latter-day Saints believe they are the possessors of an essential and unbroken line of ecclesiastical authority and power (in the case of Latter-day Saints, priesthood authority restored by angelic visitations of the resurrected ancient apostles Peter, James, and John to the Prophet Joseph Smith). Thus Latter-day Saints grant those who hold this priesthood and lead their congregation unique spiritual authority to assist them in dealing with the challenges of contemporary marriage and family life.
>
> Like Orthodox Jews and Seventh-day Adventists, Latter-day Saints believe strongly in the sanctity of the Sabbath day, and generally choose not to work, make purchases, or seek entertainment on Sunday. Thus active Latter-day Saints typically spend the entire Sabbath day involved in personal and family activities of a religious character.
>
> Like Muslims, Latter-day Saints believe God revealed many great and important things to a prophet hundreds of years after Christ and believe that the scripture revealed to that

prophet joins the canon of holy writ. Thus, as Muslims look to the Qur'an and the Hadith (sayings) of the Prophet Mohammed, Latter-day Saints look to revelations received by Joseph Smith and to his successors for teachings on marriage and family. (pp. 144–145)

Although some LDS beliefs and practices pertaining to marriage are distinctive, research we have conducted has shown that Mormons are fairly similar to many other religious couples in the other Abrahamic faiths (other forms of Christianity, Judaism, Islam) when it comes to things such as making God part of the marriage (Goodman and Dollahite, 2006), making marriage and family life sacred (Marks, 2004), and drawing on religious belief, practice, and community to (1) strengthen commitment in marriage (Lambert and Dollahite, 2008), (2) avoid or resolve conflict in marriage (Lambert and Dollahite, 2006), and (3) support fidelity in marriage (Dollahite and Lambert, 2007).

Mormons are not the only ones who believe family relations can exist in heaven. Orthodox Christians believe that marriage endures beyond the grave because God performs the marriage and Jesus said, "What therefore God hath joined together, let not man put asunder" (Mark 10:9), and Ecclesiastes 3:14 states "whatsoever God doeth, it shall be forever." Jehovah's Witnesses believe that if a couple is married when Jesus returns, they will stay in that state in the new order of things. Muslims also believe that they will enjoy family relations in the next world. What sets LDS doctrine apart is that the new and everlasting covenant of marriage promises that couples who keep the covenant will together inherit all that God has, become literally like God, and have eternal offspring, or what LDS scripture calls a "continuation of the seeds forever" (D&C 132:19). Indeed, the idea that the kind of love that motivates the desire for marriage lasts "forever" seems to be deeply imbedded in human beings (as evidenced by many love poems and songs).

Social science research conducted by LDS scholars Carroll et al. (2000) found that highly religious LDS young adult couples are similar to other highly religious Christians (Catholics and Protestants) with whom they share a number of beliefs and behaviors about marriage and family life including (1) a strong commitment to marriage, (2) low acceptance of extramarital sex, (3) high levels of relationship satisfaction, and (4) good relationship stability. Carroll et al. (2000) also found that, even compared to other highly religious Christians, highly religious LDS young adults were (1) less likely to engage in premarital sex, (2) more likely to support a more traditional division of labor in marriage, (3) more likely to desire a large family, and (4) confident that they were more ready for marriage. Although it is beneficial to be aware of general similarities and differences between Mormon and other families, readers should always remember that there is usually *significant variation within* each cultural group as well—a point that holds true for Mormon families, and probably for all other family types.

ADDRESSING CHANGES AND CHALLENGES

Contemporary American family life is undergoing significant changes and challenges. We have argued elsewhere (Dollahite, Marks, and Goodman, 2004) that:

A key challenge for most American churches in the 21st century will be to find a balance between supporting the standard of marriage-based families that are idealized in most American churches, while addressing the pluralistic family realities that confront them. (p. 414).

This is as true for Mormonism as for any faith. Mormonism has high standards and expectations for its members in relation to chastity before marriage; complete fidelity in marriage; and avoiding divorce, abuse, substance abuse, pornography, extreme materialism, and any other behavior that harms marital and family well-being.

Of course, many LDS individuals, couples, and families struggle to uphold these high standards. Accordingly, local leaders such as bishops as well as General Authorities (leaders of the worldwide Church headquartered in Salt Lake City, such as the Quorum of the Twelve Apostles) work to find ways to both hold high ideals of personal and relational conduct and also help those who find themselves in less than ideal circumstances to move forward in faith, including the LDS Addiction Recovery Program, LDS Social Services, and extensive counseling from local Church leaders.

Because of the relatively low LDS divorce rate and the emphasis on family life, many LDS children and youth benefit from a secure home life. Of course, some children and youth from strong families struggle; and some kids from families that do not meet the ideals of LDS family life thrive.

WHEN CULTURE CLASHES WITH MORMON IDEALS.   LDS leaders have occasionally spoken to Church members about leaving behind certain cultural practices when converts come into the Church—for example a culture that encourages or tolerates inequality between men and women or abusive behavior in parenting or substance use. Elder Richard G. Scott, a member of the Quorum of Twelve Apostles, stated in a General Conference of the Church that it is dangerous to place cultural heritage above membership in the Church of Jesus Christ in one's priorities and as an example of this asked this question:

> Is yours a culture where the husband exerts a domineering, authoritarian role, making all of the important decisions for the family? That pattern needs to be tempered so that both husband and wife act as equal partners, making decisions in unity for themselves and their family. No family can long endure under fear and force; that leads to contention and rebellion. (Scott, 1998:85)

THE LAW OF CHASTITY.   LDS leaders and parents teach children and youth to remain sexually chaste (no sexual relations) before marriage. Church leaders and educational materials actively teach the importance of maintaining "complete fidelity" in marriage. The standard for sexual purity is the same for men and women and is a requirement of full Church participation. Of course, not all LDS youth or adults are chaste before marriage or faithful in marriage, and Church leaders teach preventative measures but also counsel with those who have not lived up to these standards. An even more pronounced challenge has arisen in recent years because of changing American standards concerning what is considered moral and permissible for youth and adults in the area of sexual behavior. In many ways, LDS youth are attempting to live in a way that is at odds with the norms depicted in much youth-directed media.

American society has been changing and evolving in a number of important ways, and some of the changes are harmonious with LDS beliefs and practices while others are inconsistent. The aspects that are consistent have been incorporated readily while struggling to remain unique with regard to the aspects that are not consistent. For example, technological innovations in medicine; innovations in communication such as the Internet, broadcast, and telephone technologies; increases in the emphasis on equality; and decreasing discrimination based on race and ethnicity are all harmonious with LDS ideology, and they have been incorporated into the culture easily. However, changes in some other areas, such as high levels of individualism, public sensuality in entertainment and dance, permissiveness in sexuality, materialism, and alternative family forms present challenges for the LDS community in finding ways to remain unique in areas that have traditionally been important. More in-depth discussion of these issues may be found in Dollahite (2007).

CONCLUSION

Although some aspects of American Mormon culture vary widely by race and region (e.g., foods, local customs, and speech), research demonstrates that American Mormons share much in common culturally with other Americans, particularly those who are religiously involved. Even so, actively practicing Mormon families have unique elements of religious community, religious practice, and religious belief that make these families a "curious combination of typicality and peculiarity" (Gottlieb and Wiley, 1986:253). This peculiarity is quintessentially familial—rooted in a belief that God is literally our Eternal Father, that all persons are His children, and that our greatest joy and meaning in this life and in the life to come flow from uniting as a family in the worship and service of God.

The most important relationships are those with God the Father and His Son Jesus Christ. Beyond the worship of God and Jesus, the most profound and binding principles in Mormonism concern marriage and family. Doctrines about marriage and family life revealed to Joseph Smith and his successors as president of The Church of Jesus Christ of Latter-day Saints constitute the deep foundation on which the observed behaviors in LDS couples and families is built. Practices such as couple and family prayer, family scripture study, serving others as a family, family home evening, family history and genealogy, and sending children on missions are all predicated on belief in the core doctrines of Mormonism and a commitment to keep the covenants made at baptism and in holy temples. All is done to build marriage and family relationships and bonds that transcend earthly ties and last for time and all eternity.

References

Arrington, L. 1966. *Great Basin Kingdom: An Economic History of the Latter-day Saints, 1830–1900*. Lincoln: University of Nebraska Press.

Bickmore, B. R. 1999. *Restoring the Ancient Church: Joseph Smith and Early Christianity*. Ben Lomond, CA: Foundation for Apologetic Information and Research.

Bloom, H. 1992. *The American Religion: The Emergence of the Post-Christian Nation*. New York: Simon & Schuster.

Burger, W. R., and M. Youkeles. 2000. *Human Services in Contemporary America*. Pacific Grove, CA: Brooks/Cole.

Bushman, C. L., and R. L. Bushman. 2001. *Building the Kingdom: A History of Mormons in America*. New York: Oxford University Press.

Bushman, R. L. 1985. *Joseph Smith and the Beginnings of Mormonism*. Urbana: University of Illinois Press.

———. 2005. *Joseph Smith: Rough Stone Rolling*. New York: Knopf.

Carroll, J. S., S. T. Linford, T. B. Holman, and D. M. Busby. 2000. "Marital and Family Orientations Among Highly Religious Young Adults: Comparing Latter-Day Saints with Traditional Christians." *Review of Religious Research 42*, 193–205.

Cassler, V. H. 2010. "I Am a Mormon Because I Am a Feminist." mormonscholarstestify.org/1718/valerie-hudson-cassler (accessed April 10, 2011).

CNN. 1998, September 8. "Gordon Hinckley: Distinguished Religious Leader of the Mormons," *Larry King Live* (transcript). www.lds-mormon.com/lkl_00.shtml (accessed April 10, 2011).

Cornwall, M. 1994. "The Institutional Role of Mormon Women." In M. Cornwall, T. B. Heaton, and L. A. Young (Eds.), *Contemporary Mormonism: Social Science Perspectives* (pp. 239–264). Chicago: University of Illinois Press.

Davies, D. J. 2000. *The Mormon Culture of Salvation*. Burlington, VT: Ashgate.

———. 2003. *An Introduction to Mormonism*. New York: Cambridge University Press.

Dollahite, D. C. 2003. "Fathering for Eternity: Generative Spirituality in Latter-day Saint Fathers of Children with Special Needs." *Review of Religious Research 44*, 237–251.

———. 2005. "Family Worship at Home." In S. R. Klein and E. J. Hill (Eds.), *Creating Home as a Sacred Center: Principles for Everyday Living* (pp. 191–202). Provo, UT: Brigham Young University Press.

———. 2007. "Latter-day Saint Marriage and Family Life in Modern America." In D. S. Browning and D. A. Clairmont (Eds.), *American Religions and the Family: How Faith Traditions Cope with Modernization* (pp. 124–150). New York: Columbia University Press.

Dollahite, D. C., and E. J. Hill. 2010. "A House of God: Joseph and Hyrum as Husbands and Fathers." In M. E. Mendenhall, H. B. Gregersen, J. S. O'Driscoll, H. S. Swinton, and B. England (Eds.), *Joseph and Hyrum: Leading As One* (pp. 145–163). Provo, UT: BYU Religious Studies Center.

Dollahite, D. C., and N. M. Lambert. 2007. "Forsaking All Others: How Religious Involvement Promotes Marital Fidelity in Christian, Jewish, and Muslim Couples." *Review of Religious Research 48,* 290–307.

Dollahite, D. C., E. Layton, H. M. Bahr, A. B. Walker, and J. Y. Thatcher. 2009. "Giving Up Something Good for Something Better: Sacred Sacrifices Made by Religious Youth." *Journal of Adolescent Research 24,* 691–725.

Dollahite, D. C., and L. D. Marks. 2009. "A Conceptual Model of Family and Religious Processes in Highly Religious Families." *Review of Religious Research 50*(4), 373–391.

———. 2006. Teaching correct principles: Promoting spiritual strength in Latter-day Saint young people. Chapter in K. M. Yust, A. N. Johnson, S. Eisenberg Sasso, and E. C. Roehlkepartain (Eds.), *Nurturing childhood and adolescent spirituality: Perspectives from the world's religious Traditions* (pp. 394–408). Lanham, MD: Rowman & Littlefield.

Dollahite, D. C., L. D. Marks, and M. Goodman. 2004. "Families and Religious Beliefs, Practices, and Communities: Linkages in a Diverse and Dynamic Cultural Context." In M. J. Coleman and L. H. Ganong (Eds.), *The Handbook of Contemporary Families: Considering the Past, Contemplating the Future* (pp. 411–431). Thousand Oaks, CA: Sage.

Dollahite, D. C., and J. Y. Thatcher. 2008. "Talking About Religion: How Religious Youth and Parents Discuss Their Faith." *Journal of Adolescent Research 23,* 611–641.

Duke, J. T. 1997. "Church Callings as an Organizational Device in the LDS Church." Paper presented at the annual meeting of the Association for the Sociology of Religion.

Durkheim, E. 1915. *The Elementary Forms of the Religious Life,* J. W. Swain (Trans.). London, UK: Allen & Unwin.

Dyer, W. G., and P. R. Kunz. 1994. *10 Critical Keys for Highly Effective Mormon Families.* Springville, UT: Cedar Fort.

Eliade, M. 1959. *The Sacred and the Profane: The Nature of Religion.* New York: Harcourt Brace Jovanovich.

———. 1976. *Occultism, Witchcraft, and Cultural Fashions.* Chicago: University of Chicago.

Emmons, R. A. 1999. *The Psychology of Ultimate Concerns.* New York: Guilford.

Enstrom, J. E. 1998a. "Health Practices and Cancer Mortality Among Active California Mormons." In J. T. Duke (Ed.), *Latter-day Saint Social Life: Social Research on the LDS Church and Its Members* (pp. 441–460). Provo, UT: Brigham Young University Press.

———. 1998b. "Health Practices and Mortality Among Active California Mormons, 1980–1993." In J. T. Duke (Ed.), *Latter-day Saint Social Life: Social Research on the LDS Church and its Members* (pp. 461–472). Provo, UT: Brigham Young University Press.

First Presidency and Council of the Twelve Apostles of The Church of Jesus Christ of Latter-day Saints. 1995, November. "The Family: A Proclamation to the World." *Ensign, 25*(11), 102.

Goodman, M. A., and D. C. Dollahite. 2006. "How Religious Couples Perceive the Influence of God in Their Marriage." *Review of Religious Research 48,* 141–155.

Gottlieb, R., and P. Wiley. 1986. *America's Saints: The Rise of Mormon Power.* San Diego, CA: Harcourt Brace Jovanovich.

Hawkins, A. J., Dollahite, D. C., & Draper T. W. (in press). *Successful marriages and families: Proclamation principles and scholarly perspectives.* Provo, UT: BYU Studies Press.

Hinckley, G. B. 2002, May [first broadcast April 2002]. "Personal Worthiness to Exercise the Priesthood." *Ensign,* 52. lds.org/conference/talk/display/0,5232,49-1-266-21,00.html (accessed April 10, 2011).

Hudson, V. M., & Miller, R. B. (in press). Equal partnership between men and women in families. In Hawkins, A. J., Dollahite, D. C., & Draper T. W. (in press). *Successful marriages and families: Proclamation principles and scholarly perspectives.* Provo, UT: BYU Studies Press.

Huxley, T. H. 1889, February. "Agnosticism." *The Nineteenth Century* CXLIV.

Jarvis, J. 2000. "Mormonism in France." In S. K. Houseknecht and J. G. Pankhurst (Eds.), *Family, Religion, and Social Change in Diverse Societies* (pp. 237–266). New York: Oxford University.

Jones, D. E., S. Doty, C. Grammich, J. E. Horsch, R. Houseal, M. Lynn, et al. 2002. *Religious Congregations and Membership in the United States, 2000.* Nashville,

TN: Glenmary Research Center. [See especially maps on pp. 547 and 562.]

Klein, S. R., and E. J. Hill (Eds.). 2005. *Creating Home as a Sacred Center: Principles for Everyday Living*. Provo, UT: Brigham Young University Press.

Lambert N. M., and D. C. Dollahite. 2006. "How Religiosity Helps Couples Prevent, Resolve, and Overcome Marital Conflict." *Family Relations 55*, 439–449.

———. 2008. "The Threefold Cord: Marital Commitment in Religious Couples." *Journal of Family Issues 29*, 592 – 614.

Layton, E., D. C. Dollahite, and S. A. Hardy. 2011. "Anchors of Religious Commitment in Adolescents." *Journal of Adolescent Research 26*, 381–413.

Lehrer, E. L., and C. U. Chiswick. 1993. "Religion as a Determinant of Marital Stability." *Demography 30*, 385–403.

Loser, R. W., Hill, E. J., Klein, S. R., & Dollahite, D. C. (2009). "Perceived Benefits of Religious Rituals in the Latter-day Saint Home." *Review of Religious Research 50*(3), 345–362.

Loser, R. W., S. R. Klein, E. J. Hill, and D. C. Dollahite. 2008. "Religion and the Daily Lives of LDS Families: An Ecological Perspective." *Family and Consumer Sciences Research Journal 37*, 52–70.

Ludlow, D. H. (Ed.). 1992. *Encyclopedia of Mormonism*. New York: Macmillan. eom.byu.edu/index.php/Encyclopedia_of_Mormonism (accessed April 10, 2011).

Marks, L. D. 2004. "Sacred Practices in Highly Religious Families: Christian, Jewish, Mormon, and Muslim Perspectives." *Family Process 43*, 217–231.

———. 2006. Mental Health, Religious Belief, and "The Terrifying Question." *Journal of Child and Family Studies 15*(2), 135–141.

Marks, L. D., and B. Beal. 2008. "Preserving Peculiarity as a People: Mormon Distinctness in Values and Internal Structure." In C. K. Jacobson, J. P. Hoffmann, and T. B. Heaton (Eds.), *Revisiting "The Mormons": Persistent Themes and Contemporary Perspectives* (pp. 258–285). Salt Lake City: University of Utah.

Marks, L. D., and D. C. Dollahite. 2005. "Family Worship in Christian, Jewish, and Muslim Homes." In C. H. Hart, L. D. Newell, E. Walton, and D. C. Dollahite (Eds.), *Helping and Healing Our Families* (pp. 259–263). Salt Lake City, UT: Deseret Book.

Marks, L. D., D. C. Dollahite, and J. B. Baumgartner. 2010. "In God We Trust: Qualitative Findings on Finances, Family, and Faith from a Diverse Sample of U.S. Families." *Family Relations 59*, 439–452.

Mauss, A. L. 1994. *The Angel and the Beehive: The Mormon Struggle with Assimilation*. Urbana: University of Illinois Press.

McClendon, R. J., and B. A. Chadwick. 2005. "Latter-day Saint Families at the Dawn of the Twenty-First Century." In C. H. Hart, L. D. Newell, E. Walton, and D. C. Dollahite (Eds.), *Helping and Healing our Families* (pp. 32–43). Salt Lake City, UT: Deseret Book.

Mormon Wiki. 2010. "Demographics." www.mormonwiki.com/Demographics (accessed April 10, 2011).

Oaks, D. H. 2011, November. "Fundamental to Our Faith." *Ensign*, 22–29. www.lds.org/fundamental-premises-of-our-faith (accessed April 10, 2011).

O'Dea, T. F. 1957. *The Mormons*. Chicago: University of Chicago Press.

Packer, B. K. 1995, February. "The Holy Temple." *Ensign*, 32–36.

Putnam, R. D., and D. E. Campbell. 2010. *American Grace: How Religion Divides Us and Unites Us*. New York: Simon & Schuster.

Roberts, B. H. [1930] 1976. *A Comprehensive History of The Church of Jesus Christ of Latter-day Saints* (6 vols.). Provo, UT: Brigham Young University.

Roof, W. C., and M. Silk. 2005. *Religion and Public Life in the Pacific Region*. Lanham, MD: Altamira.

Scott, R. G. 1998, May. "Removing Barriers to Happiness." *Ensign*, 85.

Shepherd, G., and G. Shepherd. 1994. "Sustaining a Lay Religion in a Modern Society: The Mormon Missionary Experience." In M. Cornwall, T. B. Heaton, and L. A. Young (Eds.), *Contemporary Mormonism: Social Science Perspectives* (pp. 161–181). Chicago: University of Illinois Press.

Simmerman, S. R. 1993. "The Mormon Health Traditions: An Evolving View of Modern Medicine. *Journal of Religion and Health 32*, 189–196.

Smith, C., and M. L. Denton. 2005. *Soul Searching: The Religious and Spiritual Lives of American Teenagers*. New York: Oxford University Press.

Smith, J. [1835] 1985. *Lectures on Faith*. Salt Lake City, UT: Deseret Book.

Stark, R., and R. Finke. 2000. *Acts of Faith*. Berkeley: University of California Press.

Talmage, James E. [1912] 1962. *The House of the Lord*. Salt Lake City, UT: Bookcraft.

Taylor, J. 1851, November. *Millennial Star 13*(22), 339.

The Church of Jesus Christ of Latter-day Saints. 2006. "The Articles of Faith of The Church of Jesus Christ of Latter-day Saints." *The Pearl of Great Price*. scriptures.lds.org/en/a_of_f/1 (accessed April 10, 2011).

————. 2009. "Statistics of the Church." lds.org/church/statistics?lang=eng (accessed April 10, 2011).

————. 2010. "Mormon Population." www.mormon-wiki.com/Mormon_Population (accessed April 10, 2011).

Wikipedia. 2010. "Religion in the United States. secure.wikimedia.org/wikipedia/en/wiki/Religion_in_the_United_States (accessed April 10, 2011).

Young, L. A. 1994. "Confronting Turbulent Environments: Issues in the Organizational Growth and Globalization of Mormonism." In M. Cornwall, T. B. Heaton, and L. A. Young (Eds.), *Contemporary Mormonism: Social Science Perspectives* (pp. 43–63). Chicago: University of Illinois Press.

Weber, M. 1976. *The Protestant Ethic and the Spirit of Capitalism*. Talcott Parsons (Trans.). London: Allen & Unwin.

22

■ ■ ■

The Muslim American Family[1]

Bahira Sherif-Trask

INTRODUCTION

Recent social and political events have triggered a growing curiosity in the United States about the lives and beliefs of Muslim American families. This interest can be attributed to several factors: world events that have brought issues occurring in the Islamic world to the foreground, the rapid growth of Islam among African Americans, and a recent large influx of Muslim immigrants from the Middle East, North Africa, Sub-Saharan Africa, Pakistan, India, and Southeast Asia. Despite this interest and concern about the global role of Islam, there is relatively little research or public knowledge about Muslims and their families in the United States. In the Western context, Islam and Muslims are often viewed from a monolithic perspective. In fact, although Islam is characterized by a common underlying belief system, there is a great deal of variation in its actualization. This diversity is also reflected in the beliefs and traditions of adherents to Islam in the United States. This chapter seeks to elucidate some of the basic tenets of Islam with respect to family life and to highlight aspects of contemporary research that illustrate the diversity that is characteristic of Muslim families in the United States.

DEMOGRAPHICS

Although Islam is one of the youngest religions in the world (its inception dates to 622 A.D.), it is, globally, the fastest growing religion, with currently approximately 1.3 billion adherents worldwide. Estimating an exact figure for the number of Muslims in the United States is complicated by the fact that the U.S. Census does not require religious information as part of its surveys. Thus, estimates for the number of Muslims in the United States range from approximately 3 million (Smith, 2002) to 4 to 6 million (Stone, 1991; *World Almanac,* 1998). The question about ancestry in the 2000 census shows that 0.7 percent of the population claimed to have origins in countries with a majority Muslim population (Smith, 2002: 413). Crude estimates from census and Immigration and Naturalization Service figures indicate that the Muslim population ranges between 1,456,000 and 3,397,000, or 0.5 percent to 1.2 percent of the total population when the American-born Muslim population is included (Smith, 2002:414). Most of these statistics rely on percentages derived from data on national origin, language use, and mosque association and how these are linked to religious affiliation. These are, however, such tenuous linkages that it is uncertain which estimates of the Muslim population are reliable (Smith, 2002).

American Muslims can be roughly divided into several groups: immigrants who came from Asia, Africa, Iran and the Middle East; African Americans; and converts from other groups found in the United States (Cooper, 1993). From 1924 to 1975, Muslim immigrants from the Middle East and North Africa outnumbered all those from other parts of the world. More recently, Muslim immigrants have come primarily from western Asia, specifically Iran, Pakistan, and India (Walbridge, 1999). In the last several years, there has also been a very small increase in the number of immigrant Muslims from eastern Europe (Smith, 2002). Recent immigrants tend to be highly educated professionals, independent businesspeople, or factory workers.

According to estimates, nearly half of all Muslim Americans are African Americans who have converted to Islam. The other half are almost entirely immigrants, except for a few converts to Islam from various other cultural groups (Cooper, 1993; Stone, 1991). Immigrant Muslims live primarily in major metropolitan areas that have historically drawn new arrivals. These include some of the largest cities in the United States (e.g., New York, Los Angeles, Chicago). The largest numbers of mosques and prayer halls are found in California, New York, Michigan, Illinois, and Pennsylvania (Nimer, 2002). The fewest Muslim immigrants are located in the U.S. Southeast and Northwest regions, with the exceptions of southern Florida and the Seattle area. The largest concentration of African American Muslims is in Illinois (Stone, 1991).

The majority of immigrant Arab, African, and Asian Muslims subscribe primarily to Sunni (or orthodox) Islam, while those from Iran, Bahrain, and Oman tend to be Shi'ites. Some immigrant Muslims are also adherents of less familiar, sects such as the Alawis or Zaidis. African American Muslims include Sunnis, members of the Nation of Islam, and members of other smaller denominations.

Historically, interaction between immigrant Muslims and African American Muslims has been limited. Language skills, historical factors, racial issues, and vastly different cultural traditions form major barriers between these groups. Furthermore, unlike immigrants, many African Americans are converts. To observe their new religion, the converts tend to alter every aspect of their lives. They usually adopt Muslim names, styles of dress (particularly, among women, veiling), and a consciously projected Islamic image. For many converts, their new religious identity may take precedence over their former ethnic/racial identity. In contrast, many Muslim immigrants work harder to maintain their ethnic than their religious identities, while trying to assimilate into American culture (Kolars, 1994).

American Muslims are distinguished by different levels of education, types of occupations, arrival time in the United States, adherence to religious beliefs, and desire to assimilate in society. The diversity among Muslim Americans has contributed to the lack of a feeling of solidarity or group identity. This also makes it difficult to generalize about American Muslim families, for this is equivalent to trying to find commonalities among all Christian families in the United States. It is possible, however, to explicate some of the basic beliefs in Islam with respect to family issues and to examine the current state of scholarship on Muslim Americans in the United States. Religious principles constitute only one arena from which individuals actively and selectively draw their beliefs. These beliefs are negotiated within sociohistorical contexts and may vary over time, not just among specific groups, but also among individuals themselves.

ISLAMIC PRINCIPLES

Islam provides a foundation for understanding the religious beliefs and practices of Muslim families (Al-Hali and Khan, 1993). Islam is a monotheistic religion based on the belief that there is one God and that this is the same God that Christians and Jews believe in. *Islam* is an Arabic word meaning "submission to the will of God." A Muslim is anyone who follows the religion of Islam.

Muslims regard the Old and New Testaments as revelations that came from God (Allah). With respect to morals and human behavior, Islam, Judaism, and Christianity are virtually identical. A primary difference is that Islam does not accept the Christian concept of the Trinity or Jesus Christ as the Son of God. Instead, Jesus is regarded as a prophet who was then followed by Muhammad, the last prophet. Furthermore, the two major strands of Islam—Sunni Islam and Shi'a Islam—are distinct due to a crisis of succession after the death of Muhammad.

Islam has a somewhat less formal structure than the other monotheistic religions (Cooper, 1993). The imam of a mosque is perceived as a teacher rather than a leader or mediator, and every individual is thought to have a direct relationship to God. Another distinctive feature of Islam is the five pillars of faith. In addition to worshipping Allah, a practicing Muslim must pray five times a day, practice the yearly fast from sunrise to sunset during the month of Ramadan, contribute to the poor, and make a pilgrimage to Mecca at least once in his or her lifetime. Furthermore, every Muslim is expected to be moderate, and he or she may not drink alcohol, eat pork, or gamble. Due to the visible, daily nature of these practices, Islam is often perceived as more ritualized than other religions (El-Amin, 1991).

ISLAMIC TEACHINGS ON FAMILY

Both the Qur'an and the *hadiths* (the collection of sayings and teaching of the Prophet Muhammad) deal with issues relating the regulation of mate selection, marriage, children, divorce, authority, inheritance, and family rights and responsibilities. Of the legal injunctions in the Qur'an, about a third relate to marriage and the family (Nasir, 1990). To understand some of the principles underlying Islamic beliefs with respect to family, it is instructive to look at some Islamic teachings on gender, marriage, parent–child relationships, and divorce.

Gender Roles

Many Islamic religious injunctions deal specifically with the relationship between men and women in families. These are often regarded by Muslims as the basis for *legitimizing* gender roles. Islamic teachings stress the equality of all people before God. Nonetheless, interpretations vary considerably, particularly with respect to women's roles.

A fundamental Islamic belief is the distinct difference between male and female in terms of their personalities, social roles, and functions. References to women and their appropriate behavior are scattered throughout the Qur'an and the hadiths, and their meanings and interpretation have been a source of controversy since the earliest days of Islam. Various Qur'anic passages focus specifically on women's unique nature, place in society, and role within the general congregation of believers. Innate differences between the sexes are not perceived in terms of a dichotomy of superior and inferior but as complementary (Macleod, 1991). However, underlying Islamic ideological formulations with respect to gender is the belief that women must remain in their place for political and social harmony to prevail. Practices such as veiling and distinct male and female activities, both inside and outside the family, often reinforce this gender dichotomy. If women do not adhere to this moral order, then society runs the risk of degenerating into *fitna* (temptation or, more important, rebellion, social dissension, or disorder). A saying of the Prophet Muhammad is that there is no fitna more harmful to men than women. Women are potentially so powerful that they are required to submit to their husbands, segregate themselves from men to whom they are not immediately related, and restrain themselves lest the pattern of gender relations at the core of a properly ordered society be overturned.

Even though the Qur'an is the central source of Islamic beliefs with respect to gender roles, there is considerable controversy about the meaning of passages and their implications for the status of women (Fernea and Bezirgan, 1977). Contemporary scholarship illustrates that, rather than determining attitudes about women, parts of the Qur'an are used at certain times to legitimate particular acts or sets of conditions with respect to women (Marcus, 1992; Mernissi, 1987). This selective use is partly how gender hierarchies and sexuality are negotiated and enforced. It does not explain gender roles; instead, it is part of a constant process of gender role negotiation. Muslim feminist writers have gone to great lengths to illustrate that gender asymmetry and the status of women cannot be attributed to Islam. Instead, beliefs and practices with respect to the roles of women and men are part of a complicated interwoven set of social traditions, religions, and ever-changing political and economic conditions (Chatty and Rabo, 1997). Recent research has highlighted that the teachings of the Prophet Muhammad specified protections and rights for women that were radical departures from the existing culture. These included limitations on polygyny, inheritance and property rights for women, and marriage contracts and maintenance in cases of divorce and child custody (Baron, 1994). These studies highlight that gender constructions are always embedded in sociohistorical contexts. What it means to be a Muslim male or female is shaped not only by Islamic traditions and beliefs but also by the social environment in which these concepts are negotiated and the personal characteristics of the individual.

Significance of Marriage

Marriage is a central aspect of the lives of all Muslim men and women. Every Muslim is expected to marry, and marriage is governed by a complex set of legal rules. A Muslim family is established on the concept of a contractual exchange that legally commences with a marriage contract and its consummation. Every school of Islamic law perceives marriage as a contract, the main function of which is to make sexual relations between a man and a woman licit (Nasir, 1990). Several conditions make a Muslim marriage valid: consent of the bride and her legal guardian; two witnesses; and payment of a dower, or *mahr*. The mahr, depending on custom, can range from gifts of a coin to large sums of money or valuables. The signing of the contract entitles the bride to the mahr, a suitable home, maintenance (i.e., food, clothes, gifts), and a partial inheritance from the husband. According to Islamic law, women are not required to share in the costs and expenditures of their spouses or their male relatives. They are not expected or required to work outside the home. In return for financial investment, husbands acquire authority as the head of the family and access to the sexual and reproductive abilities of their wives (Mir-Hosseini, 1993).

Once an Islamic marriage becomes valid through the signing of the marital contract, it is the duty of the husband to provide for his wife under three conditions: She also signs the contract; she puts herself under her husband's authority and allows him free access to her; and she obeys him for the duration of the marriage. This division of gender roles in the family is often legitimated by the following quote from the Qur'an:

> Men are in charge of women, because Allah hath made the one of them to excel the other, and because they spend of their property [for support of women]. So good women are the obedient, guarding in secret that which Allah hath guarded. As for those from whom ye fear rebellion, admonish them and banish them to beds apart, and scourge them. Lo! Allah is ever High Exalted, Great. (4:34; Pickthall, 1994:80)

Beyond its legal components, marriage also has a religious dimension and is invested with many ethical injunctions. Any sexual contact outside marriage is considered adultery and is subject to punishment. Islam also condemns and discourages celibacy. Muslim jurists have gone so far as to elevate marriage to the level of a religious duty. The Qur'an supports this notion with the phrase "And marry such of you as are solitary and the pious of your slaves and maid servants" (24:32), which is commonly interpreted as advocating marriage to fulfill religious requirements. An often-quoted hadith states that the prayer of a married man is equal to seventy prayers of a single man.

The significance of the Islamic ideals of marriage inherent in the Qur'an and the *shari'a* (legal interpretations) is that they provide a primary frame of reference for legitimizing the actions of individuals and validating certain power relations within the family. Ideologies are, however, not static. They are forged, negotiated, and re-expressed in connection with other social, economic, and historical factors. These ideals provide one *potential* area from which individuals draw their beliefs, which they negotiate within their social and cultural environment.

Parent–Child Relationships

The Qur'an and the *sunna* (practices) are extremely concerned with motherhood, fatherhood, and the protection of children from the moment of conception until the age of maturity. In addition to the Qur'an, many significant Islamic texts indicate the primary importance of children and their well-being in the family unit. This emphasis can be attributed to several factors: Children are believed to strengthen the marital tie, they continue the family line by carrying their father's name, they provide for their parents in old age, and they are partial inheritors of their parents' estate.

The legal aspects of Islam deal with the socioeconomic conditions of children, both within the family and in the event of divorce or death of the parents (Schacht, 1964). Islamic law states that every Muslim infant is entitled to *hadana,* which loosely translates as the fulfillment of physical and emotional needs. This includes, besides care and protection, socialization and education. The child is entitled to love, attention, and devotion to all his or her needs.

According to religious law, the responsibilities of parents to children and of children to parents parallel rights and obligations established through marriage, notwithstanding specific social contexts. An examination of the Islamic religious and legal ideals regarding the relationship between children and parents reveals a strong emphasis on the guardianship of the individual throughout the various stages of his or her life. The shari'a reflects the highly protective attitude of the Qur'an toward minors and aged parents. Specifically, the primary legal relationship centers around adequate maintenance of dependents and parents. Islamic tenets stress parental responsibility, which begins at conception, for the economic and social welfare of children. This parental responsibility is enforceable under Islamic law (Fluehr-Lobban, 1987). Reciprocally, it is the responsibility of children to take care of their aged parents, both financially and socially: "And that ye show kindness to parents. If one of them or both of them attain old age with thee, say not 'fie' unto them nor repulse them, but speak unto them a gracious word" (Qur'an, 17:23). It is important to note the reciprocal rights and obligations of *both* parents and children.

Divorce

Divorce is treated as a serious matter in the Qur'an and hadiths and Islamic law. Several *suras* (passages) (2:225–232; 65:1–7) deal in detail with divorce, and an often recited hadith states that "[n]o permissible thing is more detested by Allah than divorce." Divorce implicates men and women differently in the legal domain. According to Islamic law, a Muslim husband has the unilateral right to divorce his wife without having to justify his actions before any legal body or any witnesses. A wife, however, to initiate a divorce, must place her claim before a shari'a court and argue her case on the basis of certain legal precepts. Legally, the most concrete factor that prevents divorce is the portion of the mahr that becomes owed to the wife upon the dissolution of the marriage (Nasir, 1990). Women who stipulate a mahr in their marriage contracts will use it primarily as a bargaining tool should their husband threaten to divorce them. Thus, the mahr acts as a deterrent to divorce and may give a woman some financial security and bargaining power.

Besides the mahr, the *idda* also acts as a restraint to divorce. The idda is the period between separation of the couple and the final termination of marriage, and it carries with it certain obligations and rights for both spouses. These include a temporary legal restraint from remarrying, sexual abstinence for a woman, the mutual entitlement to inheritance, and the maintenance and lodging of the wife, who must wait three menstrual cycles before the divorce is final (Qur'an, 2:228). According to Islamic law, a divorce cannot be finalized until the idda requirement is completed. In the case of a pregnant woman, the idda continues until her child is born (Qur'an, 65:6). The reasons for observing the idda are threefold: (a) to ascertain the possibility of a pregnancy and, if necessary, to establish the paternity of the child; (b) to provide the husband with an opportunity to return to his wife if the divorce is revocable; and (c) to enable a widow to mourn her deceased husband (Nasir, 1990). The stress in the Qur'an and Islamic law on the idda illustrates the Islamic emphasis on ensuring the well-being of the unborn child. Again, this points to the religious emphasis on creating a family and ensuring that the woman and her children have a form of social protection.

Islamic Family Structure

An examination of the specific Islamic rulings that deal with marriage and the maintenance of the wife, the child, and elderly parents reveals a concern with a social group that can be characterized as a nuclear family. Throughout the Qur'an, even though the Arabic terminology is inconsistent, the relations within the nuclear family are primary, and the concept of the extended family (three generations or more within the same household) is only secondary (Lecerf, 1956). This is further emphasized by the Qur'anic conception that believers should enjoy the pleasures of paradise as a family—that is, as the conjugal couple together with their children and parents (Qur'an, 3:23; 40:8; 52:21). Furthermore, all of the religious provisions concerning wifely maintenance, divorce, and the economic and social well-being of children and parents indicate the supreme importance in Islam of the sustenance and stabilization of the family unit. These provisions also point to the importance attributed to the protection of the individual and the necessity of ensuring this protection through the stability of the family.

RESEARCH ON MUSLIM AMERICAN FAMILIES

Trends in Contemporary Research

Researchers have focused on several distinct areas with respect to Muslim American families, but many aspects of these families have not been explored. Muslim American families, therefore, provide a venue for the further development of theories, frameworks, and empirical studies that can assist family scholars in developing a greater understanding of culturally diverse families.

THE "MUSLIM FAMILY" DEFINED AS A RELIGIOUS INSTITUTION. Some studies on Muslim families focus specifically on the Islamic family as a religious institution. These works have become almost exclusively the focus of Muslim researchers bent on defending their faith against perceived Western imperialistic threats to their social order. These works do not acknowledge religious variation or interpretation. Instead, they deal with Islam as a unified body of dogma that is not linked with popular practice (Abd al Ati, 1977; Barakat, 1985; Disuqi, 1996). These religiously oriented works have fallen prey to the orientalist truism that Islam is about texts rather than people (Said, 1978). More recently, they tended to ignore the relationship between individuals, social classes, and ideologies. Even so, there is evidence in these studies that far from uniform, Muslim families vary in size, composition, and according to historical social circumstances.

OVERVIEWS OF MUSLIM AMERICAN FAMILIES. Several recent compilations on family ethnicity and diversity (McAdoo, 1999; McGoldrick, Giordano, and Pearce, 1996) included overviews of the current state of understanding about Muslim families. These works, whose purpose was to provide general information, focused either on the Arab Family (Abudabbeh, 1996) or on aspects of Muslim families (Carolan, 1999; Sherif, 1999). For the most part, they were not based on ethnographic or other social scientific data; instead, they outlined basic principles that can be applied to contemporary understandings of Muslim families. Although these types of works may provide insight into Muslim families, they run the risk of promoting stereotypes by not adequately addressing the diversity that belies categorical designations. The few other overview studies on Muslim American families (Aswad and Bilge, 1996; Haddad, 1991; Waugh, Mclrvin, Abu-Laban, and Qureshi, 1991) are rarely used or cited in family studies research. Although these particular works focus specifically on Muslim families in the United States, their interdisciplinary orientation (anthropology and religion) has aroused only marginal interest in the field.

MUSLIM AMERICAN FAMILIES AS MENTAL HEALTH AND SOCIAL SERVICES CLIENTS. Recently, the greatest proliferation of research on and about Muslim American families has taken place in the mental health domain. Several articles have sought to address the needs of Muslims and to provide specific recommendations for providing culturally relevant service delivery. The authors have focused on these primarily qualitative studies in an attempt to understand mental health issues and appropriate forms of care for American Muslims (Abudabbeh and Nydell, 1993; Carolan, Bagherinia, Juhari, Himelright, and Mouton-Sanders, 2000; Erickson and al-Timimi, 2001; Faragallah, Schumm, and Webb, 1997; Jackson, 1997; Lawrence and Rozmus, 2001; Nobles and Sciarra, 2000). These works, which focus primarily on Arab Muslims, highlight the importance of understanding family issues in providing services. They attempt to negate stereotypes that Muslim families are more patriarchal than other types of families by providing multiple examples of how women's roles can vary both before and after marriage (Carolan et al., 2000; Erickson and al-Timimi, 2001). Issues such as veiling as a symbolic statement and not as a symbol of subjugation are also highlighted (Erickson and al-Timimi, 2001). These studies indicate that, as with many other groups in the United States, the importance of extended family for providing social and emotional support remains at least a sought-after ideal, even if not actualized in practice.

GENDER ISSUES IN MUSLIM AMERICAN FAMILIES.   Several recent works have highlighted issues specifically facing Muslim women in the United States. They deal with topics such as domestic violence (Ayyub, 2000), religiosity and veiling (Bartkowski and Read, 2003), wife abuse and polygamy (Hassouneh-Phillips, 2001), gender roles and egalitarianism (Juhari, 1998), female role identity (Abu-Ali and Reisen, 1999), and discrimination against African American Muslim women (Byng, 1998). These studies indicate that religion is only one aspect of identity formation among young Muslim women. Varying constructions of appropriate gender roles, as they are defined not only in the home but also in the wider society, play a crucial role in the lives of both unmarried and married women. These works indicate that among American Muslims the strict gender hierarchy commonly portrayed in the media and scholarly literature is often not followed. It is common for women to work outside the home and contribute to the family income. This phenomenon is congruent with changes in the Middle East and Asia, where it is increasingly common for women to secure and maintain external employment. Such economic involvement does not support the traditional Islamic model of distinct marital spheres. Instead, among many American Muslims a more egalitarian model of shared economic responsibilities and household obligations is becoming the norm. Furthermore, as Carolan et al. (2000) pointed out, for many individuals gender equity may be defined as respect rather than complete equality in the Western sense. Other issues faced by some Muslim American families are young women's rebelliousness regarding issues of modest dress and veiling. Although the return to veiling in many parts of the Islamic world has taken the form of a culturally symbolic statement for young women, some young Muslim American women fear that it will target them for harassment and discrimination. This creates unique problems for Muslim families trying to maintain their religious identity in the United States.

Many research trends with respect to Muslim American families are comparable to those regarding other culturally diverse groups in the United States. A distinguishing feature of Muslim Americans, however, is their extreme heterogeneity, which creates unique research obstacles as well as opportunities.

Theoretical and Methodological Issues

In the field of family studies, research on Muslim families in the United States has been sporadic at best. This paucity of research on Muslim American families can be attributed to a myriad of issues. One contributing factor pertains to the lack of culturally sensitive frameworks for studying ethnically diverse families in general (Dilworth-Anderson, Burton, and Johnson, 1993). This problem is compounded because Muslim American families elude research categories that often classify individuals along racial or ethnic lines. Their voices are thus not represented when family diversity issues are addressed. In addition, designating individuals purely by religion can be deceptive. Labels such as *Christian, Muslim,* or *Jewish* do not address degree of belief, measures of religiosity, or the relationship between belief and practice (Waugh et al., 1991). Further, determining whether a family is Muslim, or for that matter Christian, Jewish, or any other religious category, can be ambiguous if family members are not part of a formal community such as a mosque, neighborhood, or association. And with respect to Muslim Americans, national origin cannot be equated with religious affiliation, beliefs, race, or ethnicity. For example, many immigrants from the Middle East, particularly before 1975, were Christians and not Muslims. More recently, a large group of Middle Eastern immigrants to the United States has been from Iran. Many of these Iranian immigrants, though designated as Muslim, are highly secular and identify themselves by their cultural and not their religious backgrounds (Walbridge, 1999).

DEFINITIONAL ISSUES WITH RESPECT TO FAMILY. The paucity of studies on American Muslim families is part of a larger problem that is reflected in the overall field of research on Islamic marriage and family formation. Until very recently, definitional issues hampered studies of all Muslim families, both in the United States and abroad. Although recognition of family diversity is now an integral aspect of research on more mainstream families, many studies of Muslim families have assumed that the terms *Arab family,* and *Middle Eastern family* were interchangeable (Barakat, 1985; McGoldrick et al., 1996). This family was primarily described in opposition to its Western counterpart: It was purported that the institution of the Muslim family had not undergone the significant structural transformations that are associated with the rise of capitalism in the West and that it had not been the object of modernization that promoted individualism at the expense of family control (Tucker, 1993). These static conceptualizations of Islamic families abroad were applied to understandings of Muslim families in the United States. This has led to a certain degree of stereotyping, particularly with respect to gender issues in Muslim families. In one sense, Muslim families, both in the United States and abroad, are now understood to face the same globalizing challenges, constraints, and opportunities as other families with respect to issues of gender roles, marital stability, and parenting. In another sense, Muslim families must deal with the unique dilemma of being characterized and frequently stereotyped as adherents of a religion that is falsely thought to be, in the popular consciousness, particularly prescriptive with respect to women's and men's roles, both in the family and in the larger society.

DEFINING MUSLIM COMMUNITIES. The complexity of Muslim American communities is another barrier to studies on Muslim American families. There exists a wealth of diversity between and within Muslim communities. For example, there are older Muslim communities in the United States that are composed of Arab immigrants; and there are Muslim neighborhoods that are composed of African Americans who have converted to Islam (Haddad and Smith, 1994). Clearly delineating specific Muslim communities is complicated by the fact that until the mid-1970s, immigrant Muslims and African American practitioners had very little contact with each other. As part of its policy, the Nation of Islam (NOI) excluded non-Blacks, and for their part, immigrants perceived NOI followers as un-Islamic (Kelley, 1994). In the 1970s, as more African Americans converted to orthodox Islam, some joined largely immigrant religious communities. Nevertheless, the relationship between these groups has not improved due to widely varying experiences and concerns.

DEMOGRAPHICS. Another complicating factor with respect to researching American Muslim families is demographics. Only a relatively small number of American Muslims live in recognized Muslim communities. Most Muslims are spread out over metropolitan areas and tend to congregate more by ethnicity or national origin than by religious affiliation. Lack of common experiences also divides communities. Third- and fourth-generation Muslim families may know little of the immigrant experience and may practice a version of Islam that is dissimilar to that of their parents or their country/community of origin. These factors do not allow researchers to easily identify where and how to identify Muslim American families.

The study of Muslim families shares a problem with other culturally diverse families that are not easily accessible to researchers. Linguistic, religious, and cultural barriers make social scientific studies of Muslim Americans by non-Muslims particularly difficult. Minority populations in the United States have long been suspicious of outside researchers, and Muslim Americans are no exception. In the contemporary context, where some Muslim Americans feel stereotyped and discriminated against, these suspicions may, in some communities, become even more heightened (Walbridge, 1999).

Future Theoretical Research

DIRECTIONS.   Currently, understandings about the dynamics of culturally diverse families, in general, are limited at best (Allen, 2000; Andersen and Collins, 1995; Bacca-Zinn, 2000; Dilworth-Anderson et al., 1993; Thompson, 1995; Thorne, 1997). This problem is exacerbated in research on amorphous groups such as Muslim Americans. A common approach is to portray culturally diverse groups by a series of descriptive characteristics. This is neither an accurate nor a fruitful approach to explaining intragroup or intergroup variability, and it can lead to stereotyping or worse. By choosing to designate families by a label, be it religious, racial, or ethnic, we run the risk of implying that this is the main determinant of identification for these individuals and their families.

ECOLOGICAL/SYSTEMS APPROACHES.   Although Muslim American families are among the most diverse groups today in the United States, the study of their experiences is constrained due to the inadequacy of frameworks that are unable to capture their heterogeneity. Muslim American families, like all culturally diverse families, need to be studied as the product of complex interactions among various social subsystems operating outside the ethnic cultures. These interrelated systems include not only the individual and environment but also a myriad of situational, temporal, cultural, and societal influences. Class, family composition, regional differences, and gender relations all affect Muslim American families. By applying an ecological/systems approach to the study of issues relevant to these families, we may be able to better determine the extent to which religious beliefs, cultural traditions, and external and internal familial factors play a role in their lives.

FEMINIST PERSPECTIVES.   Feminist perspectives also offer potential frameworks for the deconstructive analysis of Muslim American families. In-depth qualitative studies of specific issues such as marital relationships or the role of working Muslim immigrant women could provide further insight into specific group dynamics with respect to power and privilege.

Although it is now understood that gender roles and expectations differ significantly between families of varied traditions and cultures, we do not know to what extent there may be variables that bind groups together. We do not know, for example, the extent to which regional variations, class, and education play a role in the types of interpretations of appropriate gender roles among Muslim women. Developing a well-articulated analysis of gender among different groups of Muslim American women would allow for a clearer insight into family relationships, power relations, and family dynamics.

SYMBOLIC INTERACTIONISM.   A symbolic interactionist framework allows researchers to understand the experiences of Muslim American families from their vantage point. By incorporating a perspective that group experiences are always the product of social constructs, researchers move away from a static perspective on the role of Islam in individuals' lives. From this perspective, it is possible to debate "when and under what circumstances does Islam direct [individuals' lives], and when under what conditions does it reflect [individuals' actions]?" (Mir-Hosseini, 1993:1).

LIFE COURSE ANALYSIS.   Life course analysis provides an important venue for understanding the experiences of both immigrant and African American Muslims. By focusing on the intertwined nature of individual trajectories within kinship networks in the context of time, culture, and social change, this framework offers the conceptual flexibility to address a variety of family forms in diverse environments (Dilworth-Anderson et al., 1993). Given the particularly diverse nature of Muslim Americans, this perspective has the potential for the development of culturally relevant constructs of family and family experiences.

These theoretical frameworks provide a foundation for capturing the intertwined, complex nature of Muslim American families. These families do not live in a vacuum but are instead part of the larger American and world landscape. Theoretical approaches that incorporate concepts of agency and systemic change are best used to assist in interpreting the relationship between religious values and ideals and people's actual lives in a constantly shifting environment.

Future Empirical Research Directions

The study of Muslim American families provides a useful venue for theoretical and empirical contributions not only about these families but also about the study of group complexity and family experiences in general. As globalizing influences are felt in all parts of the world, taken-for-granted assumptions about families and approaches to studying them are increasingly being questioned. Thus, researchers need to employ new paradigms in their studies and formulate new types of questions about the subject matter. As a discipline, [the discipline of] family studies also needs to reinvestigate its multidisciplinary roots in an effort to build on what we know that we still need to learn. This may be accomplished by reconceptualizing the focus of study in less traditional terms and innovative collaborative approaches.

INTERDISCIPLINARY COLLABORATIONS.   Interdisciplinary comparative studies between religious groups could provide one potential area for exploration. *Muslim* is a religious designation, and Muslim families' experiences should thus be compared to those of other such groups, such as Christian, Jewish, or Mormon families. Comparisons between Muslim and American, White, or ethnic families are misleading because the latter designate geographic and/or racial affiliations instead of religious connections. Cross-disciplinary research, specifically in conjunction with anthropology, history, and religious studies, could lend insight into the complexity of understanding the dynamic relationship between religion and social groups.

THE IMMIGRATION EXPERIENCE.   Comparisons of aspects of the immigration experience are another crucial area of study. All immigrants share the experience of uprooting themselves from one culture and trying to establish themselves in a new one. The extent to which religious beliefs play a role in those experiences has not been widely pursued. Do strong religious beliefs and identification perhaps facilitate this transition? With respect to Muslim Americans, the literature takes a negative slant on this topic, adhering to the view that Muslims face prejudice due to their religion (Abudabbeh and Nydell, 1993; Erickson and al-Timimi, 2001; Jackson, 1997). But given the heterogeneity of Muslims and their patterns of regional settlement, this may not always be the case. Furthermore, immigration research draws attention to the international aspect of these families. Many different ethnic groups maintain strong ties with friends, relatives, and colleagues from their country of origin. This creates a flow of movement of people, information, and ideological orientations. Studies of Muslim immigrant families' experiences could provide insight into global influences on family structures and relations by highlighting the different experiences within families associated with the adaptation to new environments.

SOCIALIZATION OF CHILDREN.   The socialization of children with respect to their religious, gender, and linguistic identities provides another venue for better understanding Muslim families. Although currently some studies are looking at the acculturation of young Muslim women (Byng, 1998; Abu-Ali and Reisen, 1999), the discussion of gender with respect to the development of boys has been completely ignored. Also, the many issues raised with respect to immigrant parent–child relations provide multiple opportunities for research.

MUSLIM FATHERHOOD.   The lack of research on Muslim men also extends to the issue of fatherhood and Islam. Although there is acknowledgment that parenthood is an important aspect of religious ideals, there are no empirical studies on the relationship between Islamic values of parenting and men. Particularly given the recent emphasis on fatherhood initiatives, examining the relationship between men, Islam, and fatherhood in African American Muslims may provide valuable insights.

INTERFAITH MARRIAGES.   Another long-neglected area of study is interfaith marriages with respect to Muslims. According to religious law, Muslim women must marry within the faith, whereas Muslim men may marry outside the faith. Research that examines the extent of influence of varying religious ideals in the broader context of civil marriage in the United States may give us more insight into the dynamics of religiously heterogeneous marriages.

CONCLUSION

Muslim American families provide a rich new area of exploration for family scholars interested in issues of diversity, gender, religion, and group identity. The heterogeneity of Muslim Americans provides an opportunity for the testing and application of new theoretical and empirical research approaches. On the one hand, this group is characterized by its adherence to Islam. On the other, Muslim Americans include devout believers and practitioners as well as secular individuals with no visible ties to the religion. This provides both a barrier and an opportunity for researchers grappling with capturing the social complexity of families. Research on Muslim American families illustrates that with respect to family life, most are dealing with issues that are in many ways similar to those faced by others in the United States. Families struggle with issues concerning gender roles and the division of labor, the raising of children, caretaking of the elderly, immigration-related concerns, and many other topics. A specific difference is that one area of definition for many Muslim American families is their negotiation of religious concepts derived from the teachings of the Qur'an. The significance of the Islamic ideals with respect to family lies not in the extent to which they reflect actual practice but in the frame of reference they provide for legitimizing individual actions. These ideals validate certain power relations in the family but are not unchanging. They are forged, negotiated, and re-expressed in connection with other social, economic, and historical factors. This dynamic relationship between religion and families needs to be explored through the conscious application of frameworks such as ecological systems theory or symbolic interactionism and may in fact lead to new theoretical designs that more concisely capture complex phenomena. In an increasingly global world, static theoretical frameworks do not allow us to fully understand how families perceive themselves and their issues or how they are adapting to the stresses and challenges around them.

Currently, the study of culturally diverse families needs to be invigorated through the application of more explicit theoretical approaches, the development of culturally sensitive frameworks, and a wider, more imaginative range of topics to be studied. The study of Muslim American families provides family scholars with the chance to pursue truly innovative research that will further the field of family diversity as well as family studies as a whole.

References

Abd al Ati, H. 1977. *The Family Structure in Islam.* Indianapolis, IN: American Trusts.

Abu-Ali, A., and C. Reisen. 1999. "Gender Role Identity Among Adolescent Muslim Girls Living in the U.S." *Current Psychology 18,* 185–192.

Abudabbeh, N. 1996. "Arab Families." In M. McGoldrick, J. Giordano, and J. K. Pearce (Eds.), *Ethnicity and Family Therapy* (2nd ed., pp. 333–346). New York: Guilford.

Abudabbeh, N., and M. K. Nydell. 1993. "Transcultural Counseling and Arab Americans." In J. McFadden (Ed.), *Transcultural Counseling* (pp. 261–284). Alexandria, VA: American Counseling Association.

Al-Hali, T., and M. Khan. 1993. *Interpretation of the Meanings of the Noble Qur'an in the English Language.* Riyadh, Saudi Arabia: Maktaba Dar-us-Salam.

Allen, K. 2000. "A Conscious and Inclusive Family Studies." *Journal of Marriage and the Family 62,* 4–5.

Andersen, M., and P. Collins. 1995. *Race, Class, and Gender.* New York: Wadsworth.

Aswad, B., and B. Bilge. 1996. *Family and Gender Among American Muslims.* Philadelphia: Temple University Press.

Ayyub, R. 2000. "Domestic Violence in the South Asian Muslim Immigrant Population in the United States." *Journal of Social Distress and the Homeless 9,* 327–248.

Bacca-Zinn, M. 2000. "Feminism and Family Studies for a New Century." *Annals of the American Academy of Political and Social Science 571,* 42–57.

Barakat, H. 1985. "The Arab Family and the Challenge of Social Transformation." In E. Fernea (Ed.), *Women and the Family in the Middle East* (pp. 27–48). Austin: University of Texas Press.

Baron, B. 1994. *The Women's Awakening.* New Haven, CT: Yale University Press.

Bartkowski, J., and J. Read. 2003. "Veiled Submission: Gender, Power and Identity Among Evangelical and Muslim Women in the United States. *Qualitative Sociology 26,* 71–92.

Byng, M. 1998. "Mediating Discrimination: Resisting Oppression Among African-American Muslim Women." *Social Problems 45,* 473–489.

Carolan, M. 1999. "Contemporary Muslim Women and the Family." In H. McAdoo (Ed.), *Family Ethnicity* (pp. 213–221). Thousand Oaks, CA: Sage.

Carolan, M., G. Bagherinia, R. Juhari, R., J. Himelright, and M. Mouton-Sanders. 2000. "Contemporary Muslim Families: Research and Practice." *Contemporary Family Therapy 22,* 67–79.

Chatty, D., and A. Rabo. 1997. *Organizing Women.* New York: Berg.

Cooper, M. H. 1993. "Muslims in America." *National Law Journal 17,* 363–367.

Dilworth-Anderson, P., L. Burton, and L. Johnson. 1993. "Reframing Theories for Understanding Race, Ethnicity and Families." In P. Boss, W. Dougherty, R. La Rossa, W. Schumm, and S. Steinmetz (Eds.), *Sourcebook of Family Theories and Methods* (pp. 627–665). New York: Plenum.

Disuqi, R. 1996. "Family values in Islam." In S. Roylance (Ed.), *The Traditional Family in Peril* (pp. 33–42). South Jordan, UT: United Families International.

El-Amin, M. M. 1991. *Family Roots.* Chicago: International Ummah Foundation.

Erickson, C. D., and N. R. al-Timimi. 2001. "Providing Mental Health Services to Arab Americans: Recommendations and Considerations." *Cultural Diversity and Ethnic Minority Psychology 7,* 308–327.

Faragallah, M., Schumm, W., and Webb, F. 1997. "Acculturation of Arab-American Immigrants: An Exploratory Study." *Journal of Contemporary Family Studies 28,* 182–203.

Fernea, E., and B. Bezirgan. 1977. *Middle Eastern Muslim Women Speak.* Austin: University of Texas Press.

Fluehr-Lobban, C. 1987. *Islamic Law and Society in the Sudan*. London: Frank Cass.

Haddad, Y. 1991. *The Muslims of America*. New York: Oxford University Press.

Haddad, Y., and J. Smith. 1994. *Muslim Communities in North America*. Albany: SUNY Press.

Hassouneh-Phillips, D. 2001. "Polygamy and Wife Abuse: A Qualitative Study of Muslim Women in America." *Health Care for Women International 22*, 735–748.

Jackson, M. 1997. "Counseling Arab Americans." In C. Lee (Ed.), *Multicultural Issues in Counseling* (2nd ed., pp. 333–349). Alexandria, VA: American Counseling Association.

Juhari, R. 1998. "Marital Quality as a Function of Gender-Role Egalitarianism Among the Malay-Muslim Student Couples in the Midwest Region of the United States." *Dissertation Abstracts International, 58*, 4754B.

Kelley, R. 1994. "Muslims in Los Angeles." In Y. Haddad and J. Smith (Eds.), *Muslim Communities in North America* (pp. 135–167). Albany: SUNY Press.

Kolars, C. 1994. "Masjid ul-Mutkabir: The Portrait of an African American Orthodox Muslim Community." In Y. Haddad (Ed.), *The Muslims of America* (pp. 475–499). New York: Oxford University Press.

Lawrence, P., and C. Rozmus. 2001. "Culturally Sensitive Care of the Muslim Patient." *Journal of Transcultural Nursing 12*, 228–233.

Lecerf, J. (1956). "Note sur la Famille dans le Monde Arabe et Islamique." *Arabica 3*, 31–60.

Macleod, A. 1991. *Accommodating Protest*. New York: Columbia University Press.

Marcus, J. 1992. *A World of Difference*. London: Zed.

McAdoo, H. 1999. *Family Ethnicity*. Thousand Oaks, CA: Sage.

McGoldrick, M., J. Giordano, and J. Pearce. 1996. *Ethnicity and Family therapy*. New York: Guilford.

Mernissi, F. 1987. *Beyond the Veil: Male-Female Dynamics in Modern Muslim Society*. Bloomington: Indiana University Press.

Mir-Hosseini, Z. 1993. *Marriage on Trial: A Study of Islamic Family Law*. London: I. B. Tauris.

Nasir, J. 1990. *The Islamic Law of Personal Status*. London: Graham & Trotman.

Nimer, M. 2002. "Muslims in American Public Life." In Y. Haddad (Ed.), *Muslims in the West: From Sojourners to Citizens* (pp. 169–186). New York: Oxford University Press.

Nobles, A., and D. Sciarra. 2000. "Cultural Determinants in the Treatment of Arab Americans: A Primer for Mainstream Therapists." *American Journal of Orthopsychiatry 70*, 182–191.

Pickthall, M. (Trans.). 1994. *The Glorious Qur'an*. Des Plaines, IL: Library of Islam.

Said, E. 1978. *Orientalism*. New York: Pantheon.

Schacht, J. 1964. *An Introduction to Islamic Law*. Oxford, UK: Clarendon.

Sherif, B. 1999. "Islamic Family Ideals." In H. McAdoo (Ed.), *Family Ethnicity* (pp. 203–212). Thousand Oaks, CA: Sage.

Smith, T. 2002. "The Polls-Review. The Muslim Population of the United States: The Methodology of Estimates." *Public Opinion Quarterly 66*, 404–414.

Stone, C. 1991. "Estimate of Muslims in America." In Y. Haddad (Ed.), *The Muslims of America* (pp. 25–36). New York: Oxford University Press.

Thompson, L. 1995. "Teaching About Ethnic Minority Families Using a Pedagogy of Care." *Family Relations 44*, 129–135.

Thorne, B. 1997. *Feminist Sociology*. New Brunswick, NJ: Rutgers University Press.

Tucker, J. 1993. "An Introduction." In J. Tucker (Ed.), *Arab Women* (pp. vii–xvii). Bloomington: Indiana University Press.

Walbridge, L. 1999. "Middle Easterners and North Africans." In E. Barkan (Ed.), *A Nation of Peoples* (pp. 391–410). Westport, CT: Greenwood.

Waugh, E., S. McIrvin, B. Abu-Laban, and R. Qureshi. (Eds.). 1991. *Muslim Families in North America*. Edmonton, Canada: University of Alberta Press.

World Almanac and Book of Facts. 1998. Mahwah, NJ: World Almanac Books.

INDEX